D1726311

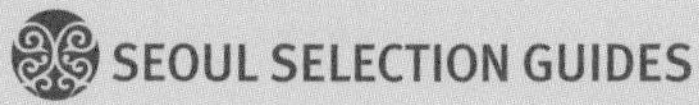

BAEKDU DAEGAN TRAIL

Written by
Roger Shepherd & Andrew Douch
with David A. Mason

Baekdu-daegan Trail

Hiking Korea's Mountain Spine

Written by Roger Shepherd & Andrew Douch with David A. Mason
Photographed by Roger Shepherd & Andrew Douch

First edition published on Jul. 2010. Updated on Feb. 2011.

Published by Seoul Selection
B1 Korean Publishers Association Bldg., 105-2 Sagan-dong,
Jongno-gu, Seoul 110-190, Korea
Tel: 82-2-734-9567
Fax: 82-2-734-9562
E-mail: publisher@seoulselection.com
Website: www.seoulselection.com

ISBN: 978-89-91913-67-7 13980

Printed in the Republic of Korea

Printed by Leeffect Prepress & Print
Effect Bldg., 459-13 Seogyo-dong
Mapo-gu, Seoul 121-841, Korea
Tel: 82-2-332-3584

Photo credits
Liz Riggs : 10, 19, 25, 33, 71, 148, 166, 203, 243

Limit of Liability: The authors and the publisher assume no liability for accidents happening to, or injuries sustained by, readers who engage in the activities described in this book.

Table of Contents

Foreword

The Baekdu-daegan trail starts at Mt. Baekdu-san and stretches down through the Geumgang, Seorak, Taebaek, Sobaek, Songni, Deogyu, and Jiri Mountains, making up an unbroken mountain range and repository of ecology coursing throughout the Korean Peninsula. To the Korean people, who value the harmony of nature and humans, the Baekdu-daegan represents the core of cultural heritage that is deeply intertwined within the very lives of the people.

Numerous Koreans traverse the ridges of Baekdu-daegan that is so symbolically significant to the country, and the Korea Forest Service (KFS) has recognized the importance of the Baekdu-daegan by establishing legislation for the protection of Baekdu-daegan. Mandating conservation, the KFS is striving to systematically preserve and manage the Baekdu-daegan mountain range, including within its legislation clauses that prohibit development and protect flora and fauna.

The critical importance of this is supported by the efforts of three writers, who provide from a foreigner's perspective their observations of our country's Baekdu-daegan in their soon-to-be-released book, *Baekdu-daegan Trail*. Compared to existing translated Baekdu-daegan literature, which covers only the very basics of Baekdu-daegan trekking, these authors compile vivid details about the forests, history and cultural heritage that surround the Baekdu-daegan, deriving from their own journey along the trail. Moreover, the book divides the Republic of Korea portion of the Baekdu-daegan into 17 sections, providing comprehensive information about each hiking course including travel time, distance, cultural resources, traffic and accommodations.

As such, I am confident this book will act as a guide that allows those foreigners who hope to visit the Baekdu-daegan trail nothing but an efficient, informative and above all rewarding hike. I hope that as much as possible, foreigners will regard this book as their go-to for advice and facts when hiking the Baekdu-daegan trail, and moreover anticipate that the book will help them to perceive and fully understand the beauty of Korea's Baekdu-daegan.

Last but not least, I wish to extend high regards and acknowledgement to Roger Shepherd, Andrew Douch and David A. Mason, who endlessly devoted their efforts and energies into creating this book.

Chung Kwang-soo, Ph.D.

Minister, Korea Forest Service

Baekdu-daegan in Korean Peninsula

Duman-gang River
Najin
Baekdu-san
China
Hamgyeongbuk-do
Yanggang-do
Jagang-do
Amnok-gang River
North Korea
Sinuiju
Pyeonganbuk-do
Hamgyeongnam-do
Pyeongannam-do
DMZ
Pyeongyang
EAST SEA
Geumgang-san
Hwanghaebuk-do
Hwanghaenam-do
Gaeseong
Seorak-san
Hyangno-bong
Sokcho
Yangyang
Taebaek mountain range
South Korea
Odae-san
Gangneung
Hongcheon
Donghae
Samcheok
Ulleungdo
Seoul
Ansan
Gangwon-do
Suwon
Gyeonggi-do
Taebaek
Dokdo
Taebaek-san
Danyang
Anseong
Chungju
Chungcheongbuk-do
Sobaek-san
Worak-san
Yeongju
Sobaek mountain range
Yecheon
Chungcheongnam-do
Mungyeong
Songni-san
Sangju
Daejeon
Gyeongsangbuk-do
YELLOW SEA
Yeongdong
Gimcheon
Muju
Deokyu-san
Daegu
Jeollabuk-do
Geochang
Hamyang
Namwon
Jiri-san
Gyeongsangnam-do
Cheonwang-bong
Jinju
Busan
Gwangju
Korea Strait
N
Jeollanam-do
Jejudo

INTRODUCTION

What Is the Baekdu-daegan?

The Baekdu-daegan, or "white head great ridge," is a 1,400 km mountain system that forms the backbone of the Korean Peninsula. Fittingly, it starts on the peninsula's highest feature, Mt. Baekdu-san (2,744m), a dormant volcano with a gigantic crater lake that sits on the current border between China and North Korea. To its east, Mt. Baekdu-san forms the natural river frontier of the Duman-gang (Tumen) River all the way to the East Sea, and to its west the other water frontier of the Amnok-gang (Yalu) River, which empties into the Yellow Sea. From the mythological hideouts of Baekdu-san, a ridgeline runs south down the east coast of North Korea, mutating into the Taebaek ("grand white") Mountain Range, piercing the barbed wire frontier of the DMZ, entering South Korea, and then veering west toward central South Korea, where it subsequently becomes the Sobaek ("small white") Mountain Range. There, it turns south and abruptly ends at South Korea's highest mainland peak of Cheonwang-bong (1,915m) in Jiri-san National Park.

This ridgeline is genuine in that it never crosses water, and it is therefore the disperser of all water all along the peninsula. Assisting the Baekdu-daegan with water management are fourteen subsidiary ridges known as *jeongmaek*, which channel all of Korea's major rivers into its flanking seas. The Baekdu-daegan's

geographical territory therefore includes most of Korea's highest peaks, many of which have been regarded as holy places since ancient times. The sacred virtues of the mountains of Korea were historically recorded by early Korean scholars and Buddhists more than a thousand years ago, and the topography of this nation is recognized as a living entity consisting of mountains and water that sustain life.

Topography of South Korea

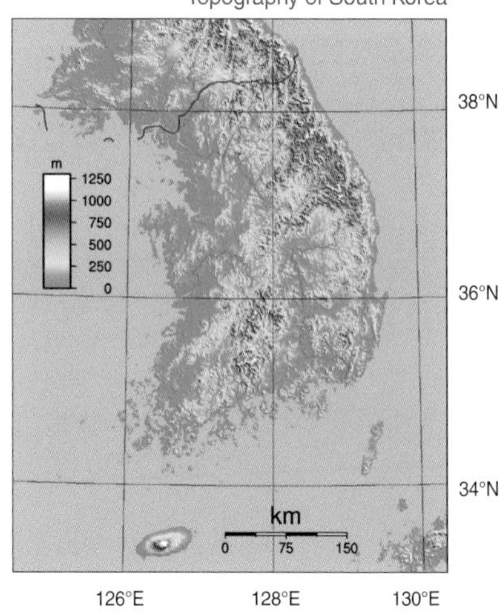

Despite the hard-frowned concerns of modernism, the spirit of the Baekdu-daegan still emanates, and efforts to maintain its existence as an ecological zone, a religious philosophy, a nationalistic icon, a mythological beginning, or more recently, as a long-distance hiking trail that encapsulates all of those concepts have been the subject of academic studies and conservation projects. In South Korea, its spirit still rumbles in the background as the nation continues to reenergize and direct itself away from a period of pre-World War II Japanese colonization, a tragic civil war and economic recovery toward a renewed, modern, prosperous identity that stands successfully amongst "first world" countries.

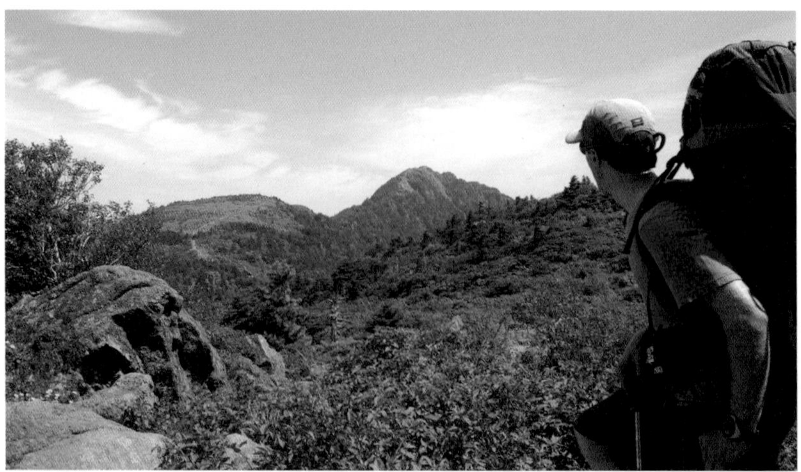

© Liz Riggs

The Baekdu-daegan, in its essence, is a geographical feature. The idea of hiking it probably developed in the 1980s as a result of South Korea's development in personal wealth, recreational freedom, cultural globalization, and a genetically ingrained predilection for mountain-roaming. Over the next three decades, subsequent academic and empirical research has seen the Baekdu-daegan slowly become dotted with certain pieces of memorabilia and monuments that mark a newly blazed trail reflecting an ancient course that covers the history of Korea.

The Baekdu-daegan as a Hiking Trail

At this stage in time, the Baekdu-daegan can only be hiked in South Korea. Within South Korea, it reportedly extends for 735 km from Hyangno-bong in the DMZ to Cheonwang-bong (1,915m) in the central south. In some sections of the seven national parks it passes through, the trail is closed for as much as 80 to 100 km of the entire 735 km distance. The ridgeline of the Baekdu-daegan is tough and by no means an easy task to hike. It continuously undulates steeply up and down over features ranging from 200 to 1,915 m ABSL, all of it evenly distributed. However, these attainable heights make the Baekdu-daegan accessible for anyone with the determination and will to complete it, either in short sections each weekend or vacation, or as a grand two-month trek.

Weather and Conditions

The Korean Peninsula hosts four seasons, and the best times of the year to visit and complete the walk are in the spring months between April (average daytime temp 11°C) and early June (22°C), or in the autumn months of September (21°C) to early November (7°C). The Baekdu-daegan can also be completed in the harsh semi-

Climate Chart of Korea, 2008 (Korea Meteorological Administration)

	JAN	FEB	MAR	APR	MAY	JUN	JUL	AUG	SEP	OCT	NOV	DEC
Mean Temperature (°C)	-5	-2	4	11	17	22	25	26.5	21	14	7	-1
Precipitation (mm)	17	21	56	68	86	169	358	224	142	49	36	32
Relative Humidity (%)	64	64	64	63	66	73	81	78	73	63	68	66

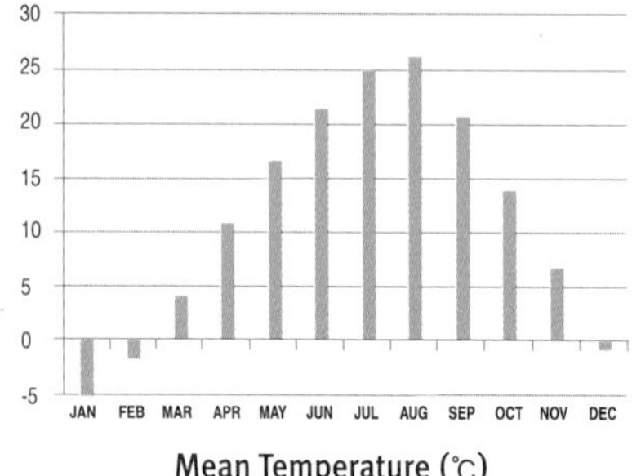

Mean Temperature (℃)

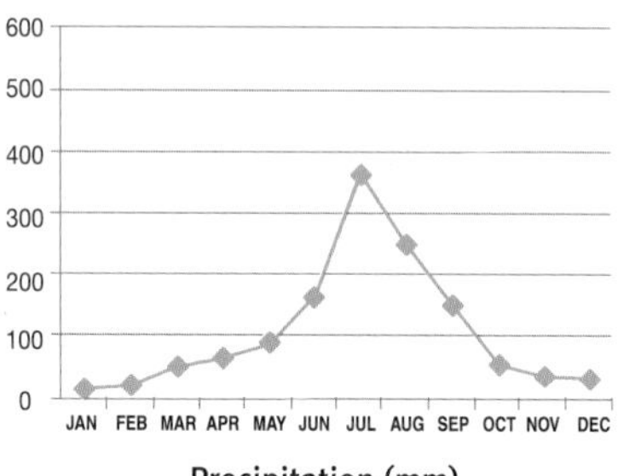

Precipitation (mm)

Siberian Korean winter, with temperatures ranging from 5 to –20°C, provided one has adequate alpine cold weather gear such as axes and crampons. The oppressively hot and humid months between late June and late August suffer from extreme temperatures above 30°C, with up to 100% humidity (although mountain areas above 500 m are cooler and nicer). From July through early September, monsoon fronts and occasional typhoons can bring very heavy winds and rain that force all

hikers off the trails and flood the gorges. Despite it all, the Baekdu-daegan's moderate heights make it survivable even for the amateur walker willing to be challenged.

An Unexplored Journey

The scenery along the trail includes low-lying green hills studded with deciduous forests that fringe the backyards of small rural farming communities, transforming hikers into traveling pilgrims and allowing them to explore the social traits of rural Korean society. At its max, in contrast, the trail presents a mixture of high, hard, gnarly, smooth, rocky mountain peaks that range in color and shape, offering the hiker mind-blowing and wondrous vistas that can only be found in northeast Asian art and cinema, with reflections of the ancient presence of mountain spirits and magical powers. The valleys that form beneath the ridge offer a plethora of colorful foliage that cradles romantic boulders basking in crystal clear mountain streams.

Unlike some of the other long-distance hikes around the world, the Baekdu-daegan also supports these spectacular vistas with a slowly developing infrastructure of historical monuments, steles, and signboards that narrate for the hiker a social study and scientific account of the history and geography of the Baekdu-daegan, including the various toils, love stories, and folk tales it hosts. Augmenting that is the religious history that the trail strongly represents for its pilgrim users. With that, the Baekdu-daegan becomes a powerful discovery of Buddhist energy and shamanistic beliefs that emanate their reverence from the hundreds of temples, shrines, *doltap* (cairns) and altars that decorate the Baekdu-daegan's ridgeline, its contours, and its valleys.

In conclusion, the Baekdu-daegan becomes more than a panoramic montage of natural beauty and powerful imagery; it is also a social and religious journey that provides the hiker with ample opportunity to meet and greet the rural people of Korea who live their agricultural and religious lifestyles along the spiritually and nationalistically significant (and sometimes spookily haunting) zones of the Baekdu-daegan mountain system.

Landscape

Finally, the Baekdu-daegan long distance trail is a great opportunity for outdoor enthusiasts living in Korea or abroad to hike their way through a 735 km geographical folder of culture and history that continuously reveals new finds and experiences in what is a still largely unexplored part of a busy peninsula. There is so much more information out there waiting to be found and discovered by the international hiker. These particles of discovery lie on the trail, at its peaks, on its side tracks, in its valleys, around its villages, inside its temples and in the broad, beaming smiles of its people. Treat it with care and respect and leave good impressions on the folk and the land. Be humble, appreciative and cheerful—and the peaks, ridges, gorges, residents, travelers and ghosts of the Baekdu-daegan will take care of you.

The Baekdu-daegan, Home of Historical & Cultural Treasures

by David A. Mason

The Baekdu-daegan is the spine of the Korean nation and has always had a very special place in Korean hearts. More than just a series of rocky ranges, it is the source of their lives and their dynamic energy, and a refuge home for many of their cultural and historical treasures. By hiking along it, you can not only appreciate its splendorous physical beauty and remarkable religious treasures, but also share in the monumental relevance, deep consequence and life-root blessings that the Koreans have long believed it conveys.

This gigantic continuous mountain system begins at the height of the sacred peaks of Baekdu-san ("white head mountain"), where the Korean Peninsula begins to emanate from Manchuria. It runs for about 1,400 km southward, its ridgeline never crossed by any body of water, which then is its essential definition. All of Korea's rivers and streams begin from it and are channeled by more than a dozen of its "*jeongmaek*" branches to the sea, carrying their fresh, clean waters past all the sites where Korean civilization has flourished. It ends at the mighty Jiri-san cluster of mountains near the south coast, home to much of the nation's most profound religious heritage.

Along the way, it includes some of the other most sacred mountains, each embodying powerful spirits and decorated with treasured shrines. Sites of important historical events, including great battles, achievements and tragedies of ancient kingdoms, are found all along the great ridge.

The line passes through seven of South Korea's twenty national parks, and four of the major provincial and county parks. Each has its own remarkable history and cultural assets that are easy and pleasant to tour. In addition, each area has its own

healthy and delicious offerings of mountain foods within a rich countryside cuisine–and even local specialties of wines and liquors to be enjoyably explored. Hosting by the locals is usually gregarious and generous in the family-run restaurants and inns along the trailways.

Three Kingdoms Period (5th Century)

The Baekdu-daegan divides Korea into its distinct regions and has thus always been a cultural and political separator, the definer and defender of tribal groups, kingdoms and provincial cultures. At the same time, it has hosted sites where the differing Koreans could meet and exchange. Its southern third in particular divides the provinces of Gyeongsang-do–which long ago made up the seminal Silla kingdom in Korea's southeast, and which have subsequently been called the Yeongnam region–from the provinces of Jeolla-do and Chungcheong-do (once the Baekje kingdom, then known as the Honam region) to the west. It further divides that distinct Gyeongsang-do from the Han-gang River basin that forms scenic Gangwon-do to the north, an area once symbolized by the Goguryeo kingdom and then contested over with the other two for centuries. During the many invasions of Korea by other nations, the key passes of the great ridge have been primary points for attempted defenses of the homeland.

Mountains of Spirits

This guidebook is specifically about the long-distance trekking trail that runs right on the crest of the entire Baekdu-daegan within South Korea, which has been in a process of grassroots creation during just the past couple of decades, and which is now becoming increasingly popular with the many Koreans who love alpine hiking. But there is much more to this mountain system when it is considered as a geocultural region of its own. When people talk about the Baekdu-daegan, they may be referring to just that crest trail, or to the line of peaks, ridges and passes itself, or to the entire region of mountains, parks, valleys, gorges, villages, towns, temples and shrines–

Sansin painting

everything that falls within about 10 km or so from the crest. The richness of physical and cultural assets of this last definition of the entire Baekdu-daegan region is simply astounding in its value, depth and variety; one could spend a lifetime exploring it all.

Ever since the tribal times up to 3,000 years ago, Korea's shamanic leaders held certain prominent mountains of this super-range to be highly sacred, especially those at which the great rivers of the peninsula were found to originate. They believed in *sansin* ("mountain spirits"), which were venerated in rituals in order to secure peace, prosperity and fecundity for their people. These mountain spirits became the central hubs of Korea's traditional religious culture, closely related to all the advanced traditions that have been imported to this land, and are still omnipresent today. Hikers along the ridgeline trails and its associated areas can find hundreds of surviving shrines to them, ranging from simple stone altars and rock towers to elaborate paintings and statues housed in temple buildings. Active veneration of these powerful spirits, by professional shamans, Buddhist monks, passionate mountain hikers and common folk, can often be witnessed by travelers passing by. They may wish to join in this ritual respect for the great mountains, or simply watch in fascination.

The *feng shui* theoretical sciences of geomancy from Chinese Daoism were imported more than 1,100 years ago by the great Buddhist master Doseon-guksa, who refined them into Korea's own such geomantic system, *Pungsujiri*. Thinking within that system during his exploratory travels, he may have been the first to declare the Baekdu-daegan as the national backbone. These ideas of how the energies of landforms and the flows of wind and water influence the courses and fortunes of human lives were nearly forgotten during Korea's rapid 20th century modernization, but they have been recently revived as potentially useful for ecological thinking and as a part of traditional culture for contemporary citizens to be proud of.

The philosophical successors of Doseon envisioned mighty Baekdu-san on the northern border as the source of the nation's telluric "energy" (*gi*, *ch'i* or *ki*), thought to flow southward along the Baekdu-daegan super-range and then distribute through its many branches and sub-branches. Communicating through the food and water, it provides the dynamism that has always been a notable Korean cultural characteristic. In this way, the entire mountain system is held sacred as the source of national vitality. The peninsula is

A roaring tiger shaped into a map of Korea

sometimes envisioned as a tiger, the national symbolic animal, and this set of ranges is truly the tiger's energetic "spine."

Some hikers who cherish this idea choose to trek the Baekdu-daegan from north to south, following the flow of this theoretical spirit-energy. A majority, however, seem to determine that it's better to hike the line from south to north, walking into the current and letting the vitalizing forces flow head on into them. Some of them regard this trek as a symbolic pilgrimage toward holy Baekdu-san itself. This direction has the added advantage of keeping the sun mostly behind the hikers all day long, permitting them fantastic clear views and avoiding having the sunlight constantly glaring into their face.

Temples and Shrines

A half dozen of Korea's greatest Buddhist monasteries are found within the wider Baekdu-daegan region, along with several dozen medium-sized or small Buddhist temples—with a few small ones located very close to the crest line trail itself. Many of these have interesting ancient histories and profound religious significance and are connected to some of Korea's most fascinating historic figures. Almost all of them can be visited and enjoyed; hikers may be invited in for tea, meals, snacks and even meditation sessions or chanting services, if they desire to partake. Some of the monasteries along the way offer Korea's unique temple-stay program, where travelers can spend 24 hours experiencing and learning about the Korean Zen lifestyle for a very reasonable fee. Spiritually minded trekkers can approach the Baekdu-daegan as a gigantic and adventurous pilgrimage trail, hiking from one great temple to another over anything between one to five days for each section. See page 45 regarding temples for much more information.

Beopju-sa Temple

There are also Neo-Confucian shrines and schools all along this region, along with other evocative relics of the Joseon Dynasty, Korea's last traditional era. Travelers cannot stay or be educated in these institutions, but they are great places to understand the historical development of this nation's spiritual culture. There are also sites related to Korea's version of Daoism, evidence of which will be found during your journeys, with deep veneration for the cycles and symbolism of nature and humanity's path for living in harmony with it. Even some Christian churches of

various denominations are found nearby the various trails that hikers of this range may follow.

Altogether, the strong presence of many distinct sects of shamanism, Buddhism, Neo-Confucianism, Daoism and Christianity all along the Baekdu-daegan region and its trails make it a vast conglomeration of multi-religious travel/pilgrimage opportunities—all in addition to the magnificent natural scenery, crags and forests to be enjoyed. This makes the Baekdu-daegan unique among adventure-travel offerings in the entire world; nowhere else can this variety and concentration of profound spiritual cultures be found among such beautiful geographical features. Not even Peru's Inca Trail can compare.

There is even more significance to the Baekdu-daegan for Koreans and those who have come to love and respect their culture. Baekdu-san, the super-range's distant and powerful beginning site, is strongly associated with the myths of national origin and a pervasive symbol of national character and anciently based unity. The many historic and sacred sites along the way combine with this idea to make the entire mountain system symbolize all that is treasured about Korea by its residents. Especially these days, it is widely invoked as a paragon of national strengths, beauties and other qualities, and it is broadly venerated as a symbol of the national reunification that most Koreans desire in their hearts. For them, visiting parts of the Baekdu-daegan and hiking along it have become pilgrimages to the national spirit.

International visitors can partake of any or all of these factors as they choose; however, they may wish to travel in the Baekdu-daegan region. Hiking its trails, admiring its scenery and visiting its cultural wealth will be endlessly rewarding for all those who make themselves aware of what it has to offer. This relatively new travel opportunity offers a grand new dimension to Korean tourism, one that I believe will deservedly become world-famous over time.

How to Use This Book

This book is a hiking guide that introduces the Baekdu-daegan ridge in a series of courses. After dividing the ridge into 17 large zones, starting from the southern end of South Korea and continuing north to the peak of Hyangno-bong, it then divides each zone into day-long hiking courses, giving detailed explanations accompanied by maps. The Baekdu-daegan ridge actually continues up into North Korea and up to Mt. Baekdu-san, on the Chinese border. But because of the current division of Korea into southern and northern states, this book only introduces the ridge as far north as Hyangno-bong.

- **Maps:** The maps in this book are sketch maps, based on observations and charts made by the authors as they hiked the trail. We therefore recommend that hikers also acquire surveyed maps before commencing a hike. There are currently no surveyed maps of the Baekdu-daegan ridge in English on sale in Korea, but since the sketch maps in our book are labeled in both English and Korean, they should be helpful when used in coordination with Korean surveyed maps.

- **Courses:** Each day's course has been divided between several points. The book gives the distance and time required to hike from each point to the next, as well as the points' position on the relevant map grid (e.g. C1, D4), places to drink water, spots of interest and so on. (Note: The times for the distances in the hiking sections can be considered the maximum times for those carrying large packs. Section-hikers or fitter, stronger individuals may be expected to knock a couple of hours off some of the longer legs.)

- **Vantage Points:** These are detailed explanations focusing on certain places requiring further information.

- **Lodgings:** These sections give information on places to sleep near the beginning and end of each daily course. Emphasis is placed on proximity and ease of access, while types of accommodation range from motels with showers to dormitory-style national park shelters and camping grounds.

The following Information for Hikers section is centered on tips for planning traveling the Baekdu-daegan ridge. It gives wide-ranging and detailed explanations of hiking equipment, direction finding, mountaineering etiquette, health and transport. The appendix consists of a list of essential Korean language.

Trail Jargon

M & Meters

When referring to the height of a peak or the altitude of a certain feature using the acronym "ABSL" (meaning "above sea level"), the letter *m* will precede or follow the written height. This figure simply means "meters" indicating the amount of meters it stands above sea level, e.g. "Cheonwang-bong, 1,915m ABSL."

When we use the word "meters" in the guidebook, we are referring to the distance over ground covered or remaining, e.g. "800 more meters to the peak of Cheonwang-bong."

A combined example might be as follows: "From here, the trail steeply ascends for the next 300 meters, gaining about 80 m in altitude, until it reaches the bald summit of Cheonwang-bong located at 1,915 m ABSL." Another example may be when we write, "You continue climbing northward on the trail for another 900 meters." By this, we simply mean distance and not altitude.

Baekdu-daegan Trail

For the simplicity of the exercise, the Baekdu-daegan is always referred to in this book as the "trail," the "Baekdu-daegan," or sometimes "the ridge" or other such dramatic descriptors. All pathways or routes *off* the Baekdu-daegan trail are referred to as "tracks" unless otherwise described.

Roads

In this book, certain descriptors are used for roads. "NE" means "National Expressway" and is followed by a number. These expressways act as the major movers of goods and services around the peninsula, with varying speed limits of between 100 and 110 km/h. Care must be taken in the few places where the Baekdu-daegan crosses these. "NH" means "National Highway" and is normally followed by a two-digit number. It is the older but more widely located national highway network, which still traverses the Baekdu-daegan in places. The "PR" network, which means "Provincial Road" and is normally followed by a three-digit number, is probably the oldest sealed

road network built after the Korean War, retracing the older routes that migrate along the river valleys up the windy contours of Korea's mountains, and into the foothills of Korea. They are still excellent roads in good sealed condition.

Normally, in this book, a sealed road with no number or letter representing it is just that...an old road cemented with concrete or bitumen that is probably an extension of one of the three aforementioned road networks. A "mountain road" means a vehicle track over which a sedan motor vehicle could probably still pass. A "4WD track" is quite simply one only a four-wheel-drive vehicle could manage; these are also sometimes found following the ridge as a result of military intervention or pylon or forestry maintenance.

Steles

Steles are normally found on the most prominent peaks or passes of the Baekdu-daegan. They are mounds or slabs of rock that are normally rectangular or horn-shaped in appearance. They range anywhere from 30 cm to 8 m in height and are always engraved with a combination of the peak's name and height and the name "Baekdu-daegan," as well as the occasion message, story, or map on the back of it.

Cairns

Cairns *(Doltap)* are mounds and piles of loose rock and stone that have been erected by human beings as symbols of heavenly worship or as trail markers. It is also believed that *doltap* brings good fortune to travelers.

Altars

Altars (open areas) are more rock- or stone-like features that have exposed platforms with a purpose and design as venues of reverence or worship to the local mountain spirits.

INFORMATION FOR HIKERS

PLANNING

Deciding what to take and bring for the Baekdu-daegan presents scenarios that hold a huge amount of variation. It all depends on what the individual wants to do. What to take into consideration when doing your planning could depend on whether you want to thru-hike the Baekdu-daegan (two months) or hike it in sections. Compounding those two scenarios will be the influential ingredients of time, money, fitness, confidence, your social network in Korea, and the season in which you wish to walk it. Most of the information in this section is catered to the wants and needs of the thru-hiker, as a lot of their demands are also the demands of the section-hiker.

Either way, whatever it is you decide to take with you, you will more than likely end up having to carry it as well. Although long-distance hikes are arduous, physically demanding exercises, they should not be performed at a level where you struggle to enjoy it. This normally comes as a result of carrying too much equipment or being ill-prepared. What you can take into account is that walking is not racing, and that regardless of your physical condition, it literally is one step at a time, one day at a time. Take the time to appreciate the scenery and people of the Baekdu-daegan mountain system.

Section-hiker

For those living in Korea, section-hiking the Baekdu-daegan on your weekends can become an enjoyable and educating way to discover and see the ridgeline during your contractual work period on the peninsula. One of the benefits of this is that after each weekend, you have a full week to recover and carry out further study on your next weekend's route from the comfort of a home computer or book. You are also obligated to carry less, with the option of basing yourself in nearby accommodations giving the conditions of the walk more ease and luxury. It's also a great opportunity for people living in Korea to get off the beaten track and discover some of the trail's small and inconspicuous starting and ending points, which lie hidden in valleys at the end of provincial road systems. This offers a complete contrast from the hustle and bustle of mainstream Korea and even removes one from the manic congestion of Korea's national parks on weekends. Eventually, the section-hiker on sojourns in the countryside will fall in love with its charm and antiquity. Most public transportation networks will also get the hiker to the starting and ending points. For more details, refer to the transportation sections in the daily hiking Sections.

Thru-hiker

For those who want to complete the Baekdu-daegan in one long, swift movement, there are a few things that need to be recognized, but none of them detracts in any way from achieving this walk. If you are a resident of Korea and you already have some familiarity with the language and culture, you will be at an advantage. For first-time visitors to Korea, with absolutely no language skills or cultural awareness at all, this walk is going to be an even more exciting and challenging prospect. What we can assure the foreign hiker is that Korea is a safe country to travel in, with practically no crime, no dangerous wildlife except snakes, and

© Liz Riggs

people who are famously hospitable and curious toward foreigners. Because the hiker will be residing mainly in rural, unvisited areas on the Baekdu-daegan, the aforementioned traits are magnified even more. A thru-hiker can be expected to complete his or her walk comfortably in 50 days (excluding rest days). A lot of Korean thru-hikers complete the walk in 35 days; they are perhaps forced to do this because of time constraints, or out of competitiveness. A good procedure is to walk at the beat of five days in a row, followed by a two-day break. One should be looking at an average of about 14.5 km a day over what will for the most part be steeply undulating country.

EQUIPMENT LIST FOR THE THRU-HIKER (excluding winter attempts)

Containers

- [x] Pack (50 to 70 liters)
- [ ] Waterproof bags for cameras, etc.
- [ ] Sewing awn and thread
- [ ] Water bottle (250 ml)
- [ ] Waterproof pack liner (inner and outer)
- [ ] Foldable day pack (grab bag)
- [ ] Water bladder (3 liters)

Hardware

- [ ] Gas oven and lighter
- [ ] Cooking utensils
- [ ] Good knife or multi-tool
- [ ] Small scouring pad
- [ ] Personal hygiene kit
- [ ] First aid kit—emphasizing foot care
- [ ] Sunscreen and insect repellent
- [ ] Maps/compass and writing utensils
- [ ] The Baekdu-daegan guidebook
- [ ] Camera equipment and necessary cables, etc.
- [ ] Power point adapter for Korea
- [ ] Head lamp and batteries
- [ ] Ear plugs—great when sharing national park sleeping shelters
- [ ] Toilet paper or wipes
- [ ] Small plastic e-trenching tool for disposing of excretion

Clothing

- [ ] Socks x 2
- [ ] Hiking trousers (convertible into shorts) x 2
- [ ] Long johns, top and bottom x 1 pair
- [ ] Outdoor Gortex weatherproof jacket
- [ ] Wet weather trousers (optional)
- [ ] Hiking shirts x 2
- [ ] Sun hat
- [ ] Balaclava and gloves
- [ ] Sunglasses
- [ ] Hiking boots and spare pair of boot laces
- [ ] Sandals
- [ ] Camp towel

Sleeping Gear

- [ ] Tent and/or flysheet—refer to sleeping section
- [ ] Thermal mat
- [ ] Sleeping bag, bivvy bag or mosquito net (depending on weather and season)
- [ ] Groundsheet (optional but useful)

Hiking Equipment

Probably the best way to plan for a thru-hike of the Baekdu-daegan is to imagine that you are planning for an unaided one-week hike, since you are probably unlikely to fit much more into your pack anyway. Of course, there are other things to factor in as well, like laptops, cameras, and all the cables, batteries, and chargers that come with paraphernalia, along with the maintenance and care of such expensive and sensitive equipment. Another factor will be the experience and confidence of the hiker, although we urge even those with little experience to tackle this safe and hospitable long-distance hike, as it is the only way to get experience. Have a look at the list below and combine it with your own personal extras. Once you've gotten what you think you need, lay it all out on a large floor and have a go at packing it neatly, compartmentalizing it as you go. By the time you've packed and repacked, you should be able to know where everything is inside your bag even in pitch-black darkness.

Food

The longest period one can normally expect to carry food without restocking is a mere three days and nights. Most of the time, hikers will only be expected to carry two days' worth of food with them, and once they get the hang of it, they will be able to find places to purchase food almost daily. Hopefully, a good study of this guidebook prior to their excursions will strengthen that likelihood.

What you as a hiker decide to take in the way of food is once again entirely up to your individual needs and wants. However, a small gas cooker and eating vessel are just some of the basic items you will require in most places on the trail to prepare food, should you end up camping. As fires are generally forbidden in Korean forests, gas is cheap and readily available throughout Korea in the form of canisters or bottles. In the larger centers, most outdoor camping stores will also sell dehydrated foods if that's your wish. Otherwise, all small Korean shops that you locate at the foothills or the passes along the Baekdu-daegan will sell various food items, including pre-cooked rice, foiled or canned tuna, Korean condiments and sauces, chocolates, sweets, hard steamed eggs, processed meats, noodles, fruit, bread, small sachets of instant coffee mixes, and many other local items you may be interested in trying out.

Water

Throughout this guidebook, three different indicators are used for water. The first one is an index in the back of the book, with the entire water log formatted into latitude-longitude coordinates. Secondly, at the start of each day in each hiking section, water stops are numbered sequentially in the order one can expect to find them. These water stops also contain the lat-long coords, followed by a bracketed number. The bracketed numbers run sequentially from the very first water stop to the very last, a total of 83 found and used by us. Thirdly, the bracketed number for each water stop can be found highlighted in blue brackets within the particular leg of the course description in which it is located on the trail, bringing an animated description of its location to the hiker.

Availability

On the Baekdu-daegan, water will be the biggest challenge you face. As the trail's terrain is quite tough and physically demanding, your body will constantly crave rehydration. The only source of information you have prior to walking the great ridge will be what's mentioned in this book and its maps. What you have to remember is that you should never, ever take water for granted and expect it to be there on your arrival. The springs marked in this book, although consistently flowing, will not always be working. This is because each season and each year normally differs from the previous. If you arrive at a marked spring and cannot locate its source, the most obvious solution is to search further down its watershed for its next source. You will become good at this technique and eventually be able to choose quite correctly which side of the ridge you believe will hold the highest water source.

Planning

As a hiker, you must plan your days around the availability of water. In fact, your survival and comfort depend purely on this basic element. How far you plan to walk in one day will be controlled by the supposed location and availability of water at the end of that day. When the day comes to an end, your objective should always be to try to set up camp at a spring or near one. During the course of your day, you may come across more than one spring from which to replenish. Take the time to sit down and drink as much of it as you can. It's also a good idea to stop and cook food without contaminating the spring. After eating and drinking, fill up your water carriers and take note of how far you may have to travel until you find your next unconfirmed water stop! Never, ever expend your water until you have confirmed and found more! Save even the last 100 ml.

How Much Water Can I Expect to Use?

As a good average, a hiker on this trail may be expected to carry 20 kg of pack. An experienced and disciplined hiker will be expected to have on him or her as little as three liters of water at any given moment. This is not a large amount of fluid in what will be a very demanding hike, which at certain stages will be performed in temperatures over 28°C. If your water supply runs out for whatever reason, and you are still many kilometers away from the next unconfirmed source on the map, consider leaving the ridge on the next side track and walking to the nearest village or temple. Before you do that, take time to try and spot a temple or village from the ridge. In Korea, your search for such civilization could be anywhere from 2 to 15 km away...a long haul with a heavy pack and a dehydrated body.

Water Quality

You can rest assured that whatever water you do find high up on the ridges of the Baekdu-daegan will always be of great quality and excellent to drink, as it is mainly filtered through hard granite rock. On the other hand, other than temples or controlled wells or taps, if you are sourcing water near stream heads located near villages, 4WD tracks, or other forms of human habitation, be sure to take your water well above the first human source, and decant it from a fast-moving section of the stream. Water-purifying tablets are not essential items for the Baekdu-daegan, but if hikers wish to use them, that's entirely up to them.

Sleeping and Tents

Sleep is as important as food and water. A good night's sleep on a long-distance hike is one way of allowing the body to recover. How you decide to sleep is once again a point of personal preference. However, if you opt to do as much tenting as possible, you must decide on what type of tent you wish to use and the number of people sleeping in it. For the solo hiker or a group of individuals, this may just be a small cocoon-style tent that offers shelter from the wind, rain, and mosquitoes at night (during the summer). These individuals may also simply wish to sleep in a bivvy bag under a fly-sheet (bivouac), which means they will carry less. On a warm or hot and clear summer night on the Baekdu-daegan, the hiker can get away with just a thermal mat and a sleeping bag liner.

Make sure your thermal mat is a rugged one, as there is a strong likelihood of it being punctured at some stage if you are not sleeping inside a tent. As far as sleeping bags go, the cooler spring and autumn months may require that you sleep in a bag with a 0 to –10 grading. In later spring and midsummer, you will only need a thin summer bag rated 1 to 10°C. Winter explorations of the Baekdu-daegan should be treated as polar, as the temperatures can plummet well below the zeros, with strong and bitter trans-Siberian winds to contend with as well. Tenting is advised, along with polar-style sleeping bags and arrangements.

Fitness Levels

If you decide to thru-hike the Baekdu-daegan, you should at least have a good basic fitness prior to starting. However, we urge all people of all shapes, sizes, and ages to enjoy walking the Baekdu-daegan. Everything must be done in moderation according to each individual's own ability. This includes how much weight you wish to carry, how much food you will need to eat to maintain your energy levels, and how much time you think you need to complete the Baekdu-daegan in a thru-walk. Over the entire 735 km, you should be trying to average around 14 km a day. That would give you 52 hiking days to complete it. What you have to remember is that 14 mountain kilometers is a lot more demanding than 14 km on a flat road. Later on in your journey, there will be occasions on the trail where you may be able to achieve as much as 20 or more kilometers in one day. There may be other times when you quite simply don't feel like doing big legs and wish instead to rest and take in the scenery at a healthier pace. There will even be many moments when the outstanding scenery doesn't allow the hiker to push forward too hard, as it is too distracting and demands appreciation. The figure of 14 km a day is a good pace to walk at, as it is achievable for most people and it also allows you plenty of time in your day to stop and take in the sights. Ideally, the fitter you are, the better shape you will be in to start this walk. However, as long as you don't have any health alerts that may affect your passage along this route, you can literally start this walk in just about any condition if you want to, and continue for as long as you have the determination to keep going. Regardless of how good or poor your condition is, it will still take about three weeks to get mountain-fit, especially if you are carrying anything over 15 kg each day. Some hikers will carry as much as 25 kg or more.

Maintaining Health

In the case of a thru-hike, it is your responsibility to maintain your fitness through regular sustenance. Otherwise, you will begin to lose condition and possibly struggle near the later stages of this long journey. Remember, although none of these mountains are deadly high, they are all very steep, and there are many of them. If you are in a position to carry liniment or muscle relief lotions, then do so. Stretching before walking or in the evening is also beneficial to your long-term health and fitness. On certain parts of the trail, you will also get opportunities to find and visit sauna houses or *jjimjilbang*. These are great places to go to and wind down in. Soaking the body in hot, steaming baths or saunas bring great relief to the skin, muscles, tendons, and ligaments. These places often have a sports masseuse working on their premises, providing another great option to remove some of those unwanted knots from your now hardwood legs.

Walking Techniques

When you are walking, focus on technique rather than speed. Keep using those thigh muscles when descending hills; don't let your knee and ankle joints bear the brunt of all that exertion on those steep descents, and maintain your form and technique. If hiking poles aid your ability and technique, then use them.

When packing your pack, make sure you have it balanced nicely. One way of determining whether this is the case is to see how it stands by itself. If it keeps rolling over or falling forward or backward, it isn't set right. Whether you keep your heavy objects at the top or the bottom of your pack depends on how often you wish to access them during your hiking day. Personally, you may feel more comfortable with the majority of your equipment weight balanced out at the bottom of your pack. Others may wish to have most of the weight up at the top between their shoulders. Sometimes, the only way to find out if your pack is properly balanced is during your first week of continuous hiking, adjusting and testing as you move along. More than overly heavy packs, badly packed ones can wind up causing temporary, if not permanent, damage to the body on long-distance hikes of this nature. Also, take care of your pack—if you damage or lose a strap or buckle, it can be a long and painful walk carrying it on one shoulder or on your head to the nearest road to get it fixed. Don't drag it around by its shoulder straps; pick it up and carry it by the top loops on top of the frame, thereby removing any unnecessary burden on clips and buckles.

Money and Cash

If you are not residing in Korea, the issue of currency is also another minor obstacle that needs to be considered. Carrying cash along the trail will be necessary, as it is unlikely that you will find any ATM machines along the ridge. The easiest way to obtain cash from banks in Korea is probably by way of traveler's checks, US dollars, or travel cards. If you are using a credit card, most banks' ATMs will be able to give you local currency. However, some of these machines have daily limits on the amounts they can give out. On the trail, it will always make sense to carry an amount of cash that might see you through the next month. You will normally have to travel a long way from the trail to get to a bank. Currently the biggest denomination of South Korea currency is a 50,000 won bill, which at time of print equated to about U$ 42.

Computers and Internet Cafés

South Korea is well connected when it comes to its broadband network. It boasts some of the fastest connection speeds in the world, and the Korean people have a close relationship with computer usage. For this reason, it should come as no surprise to find *PC bang* (internet cafés) even in some of the smaller towns that you end up in during your days of rest from the ridge. This allows you the opportunity to keep in touch with the outside world and carry out other functions like photo downloading, internet banking, blog updating, Ipod downloading, and global news catch-up. These PC rooms normally run 24 hours a day, 7 days a week and cost anywhere from 1,000 to 2,500 won per hour of usage.

Navigation

For the thru-hiker and foreign visitor, the task of navigating through a long-distance hike in a remote and culturally diverse nation like South Korea is understandably a daunting one. The thought of getting lost and stranded is enough to make one question even the motives of a hardy hiker. A poor understanding or lack of experience in more advanced methods of navigation beyond using street atlases to get around town can add to that anxiety. Although the Baekdu-daegan is not an official long-distance hiking trail, its usage has created various celebrations, blazers and signposts along its route that keep the hiker informed of his or her course. This, in turn, combines with the favorable geographical conditions and hospitable people to make navigating the Baekdu-daegan completely achievable for any person regardless of experience in navigation.

Viewing the Landscape

Perhaps if you view the Baekdu-daegan as the continuous backbone of the peninsula and as a feature that never crosses water, in that sense, it is, for most of your journey, the highest ridgeline feature that you walk along. In a nation that is inundated with mountains, hills, and valleys, the Baekdu-daegan trail is the one that very rarely breaks off the main ridge or goes down a spur and onto another ridge—although you need to be aware that it does do this in places. Adding to

© Liz Riggs

this big picture description, if you were to arrive at an unmarked trail junction, the Baekdu-daegan trail is more than likely the trail going straight up the nearest highest hill in the same direction that you came from. Before we break into the finer points of navigating the Baekdu-daegan, we can gladly report that navigating it is not a difficult task, and that the trail is for the most part well marked and prominent.

Transliterating Trail Markers

Your biggest obstacle and waster of time in those moments of uncertainty about your direction or placement will be trying to read and transliterate most of the information boards and signposts on the trail to the map series that you are using. As the trail is often marked as the Baekdu-daegan trail, it will pay for you to memorize and become familiar with identifying the *hangeul* script for Baekdu-daegan: 백두대간. This art, for first-time visitors to Korea, involves matching the *hangeul* text on your map with the *hangeul* text on the signpost or marker, a tedious code-cracking exercise that needs to be carried out when you are unsure of your direction or location. In this guidebook, most of the prominent mountain peaks and passes along the trail have been transliterated back into *hangeul* from English to help you with this chore. At the beginning of your walk, you may well find yourself transliterating signposts with your maps quite often; there is nothing wrong with this procedure, as it is better to get familiar with this art when you are safe.

Hiking Ribbons

One of the better navigational aids, although not completely reliable, is the striking and colorful hiking ribbons that hang from the branches of trees like prayer flags. They have been installed there by local hikers. However, there are disadvantages to this sometimes nonchalant manner of trailblazing. One must be aware that some of these ribbons do not represent the path of the Baekdu-daegan and instead belong to local hiking clubs who have marked routes from nearby villages to the ridge crest of the Baekdu-daegan. There is also the other scenario in which hikers brazenly marked the Baekdu-daegan trail with ribbons before realizing they were going the wrong way...leading you astray at the same time.

Remember to combine the usage of Baekdu-daegan hiking ribbons with the common sense factor of what you understand the biggest ridgeline in Korea should be doing, and avoid being led astray down some foggy track into the backyard of someone's village or temple. It is good to be able to identify in the words "Baekdu-daegan" in *hangeul* and follow the ribbons of that ilk. As you progress along the trail, you will begin to identify closely with one or two certain ribbons that keep popping up; these often become your most reliable guides among the many others that flutter in the wind.

Maps

A good set of 1:50,000 topo maps is the ideal scenario for the Baekdu-daegan. Apart from the useful set in the book, there is no harm in carrying an extra set of larger sheet maps that provide you with a wider scope of the landscape and surrounding environs. In Seoul, the most notable map shop is Jung-ang Atlas 중앙지도문화사 (sometimes spelled "Chungang Chido Munhwasa" in Korean), located at 125-1 Gongpyeong-dong in the Jongno-gu District; it's on Gongpyeong-ro Street (running eastward from the US Embassy through Insa-dong and Nagwon Arcade), right at its intersection with Ujeongguk-ro Avenue (running from the Jonggak subway station north past Jogye-sa Temple). That intersection is named Jogyesa-ap. To get there, use Exit 2 from Jonggak Station and walk one big block north, ignoring tiny alleyways; turn left and it's right there (T. 02-730-9191~4). In that shop, you will be able to find a couple of mapmakers that specialize in the manufacture of good 1:50,000 topographical hiking maps for the trail.

Map Reading and Compasses

South Korea is a great place to practice the art of map reading. When you are standing on a peak or ridgeline in Korea and looking out over the horizon, the landscape is almost unidentifiable, due to the similar appearance of the mountains' heights and shapes. When reading a map, if you cannot point out a prominent feature by using your eye, then a compass will most definitely be

needed to shoot bearings with which to perform re-sections. For those who do not know how to use a compass to its max, it is still a handy and easy thing to use. Left simply hanging around your neck on a good piece of cord, it is a useful and timely gadget to have when reconfirming your direction of travel. The best type of compass to use is any Zone 3 model. What this means is that the magnetic needle inside the compass has been balanced so that it doesn't drag or stick to the face or housing of the compass, allowing for quicker and more accurate compass bearings. Zone 3 represents one of the five zones on the globe that have been identified by all compass manufacturers as areas of magnetic variance. All maps are oriented north. There are three norths represented on most good maps: true north, grid north and magnetic north. The magnetic variation in South Korea is 7° west of grid north. For those who don't know what that means, never mind, as this variation is quite small—it is highly unlikely to affect you.

GPS Devices

Global Positioning Satellite devices are useful gadgets to have in the event that you need to know exactly where you are. That said, you will also need to have the ability to pinpoint where you are on a map from the coords you receive. Otherwise, a GPS is useful for way-pointing your future destinations or water stops in the event that you need to find them due to bad weather or disorientation.

Getting Lost

In the unfortunate scenario that you become misplaced, don't panic—it's not such a drama in the condensed peninsula of Korea. Although for the thru-hiker on the Baekdu-daegan, there will be many days where you feel quite isolated and do not meet another hiker for the whole day, there will nonetheless be a small mountain village, temple, town, or even a large thriving city no more than two to 20 kilometers away; most of the time, you will be able to see these places from the ridgeline. If you think you don't know where you are, and you are reluctant to turn back and retrace your steps, then stay on the trail or track you are lost on, as it will eventually take you to a temple, village, 4WD track or road. Once you get a feel for the ridge and an understanding of how the Baekdu-daegan navigates itself northward with its hiking ribbons, signposts, steles, altars, information boards, and users, a lot of your navigational decisions will become second nature and instinctive.

Transportation

Through South Korea, the Baekdu-daegan is crossed by a total of 82 roads, both paved and unpaved. This is an average of one road crossing every nine kilometers or so, ranging from rarely used mountain tracks to National Highways connecting the main cities. This high frequency of road crossings makes the Baekdu-daegan trail very accessible, enabling hikers to enjoy short sections of the trek on holidays, weekends, or even single days before seeking the comforts of a small town or heading back to their homes.

Whether you intend to thru-hike the Baekdu-daegan or walk the trail in sections, the roads crossing the ridge will be your access points to supplies and accommodation from the small towns and villages below. Most sealed roads crossing the ridge are served by local buses running to the nearest villages on both sides, and large roads are often crossed by intercity buses that will pick you up or drop you off at the pass. The frequency of buses leaving the Baekdu-daegan varies depending on the population of the area, and the buses are not always practical options for the hiker, so you can also make use of the rural call taxis that most small towns have, or else rely on the kindness of strangers and hitch a ride—an experience that will provide you with many great memories from your hike.

Local Buses

Korea has a very good bus service connecting most mountain villages with their nearest town, and running to or near most major road crossings of the Baekdu-daegan. In most cases, these buses do not climb to the high passes of the ridge but will turn around at the nearest main village, usually no further than a few kilometers from the ridge, before heading back into town. Buses run to villages with varying frequency, with many small areas only seeing a couple of buses per day, while others will see a couple every hour. When possible, we have included bus schedules in the guide; these are listed in all Sections. Depending on how far you wish to travel, the local bus fare will cost between 1,000 and 2,000 won.

Intercity Buses

Along main roads or in isolated country where tunnels don't pass through the ridge, intercity buses will cross the Baekdu-daegan on their route between main centers. If you're on the pass at the right time, it is usually possible to get on board and join the ride for the rest of the trip. It is also possible to catch these buses from their origin and get off at or near the ridge if you state your intention before departure. Throughout the guide we have included, when possible, the schedules for buses running over or near the Baekdu-daegan.

Taxis

Most small Korean towns have a call taxi service specializing in rural pickups and drop-offs; these are usually located near the local bus station.

Local taxi drivers will be familiar with the road passes in their area and should

be used to delivering hikers to and from the ridge. The meter is usually turned off for these trips, and you will be expected to pay a fixed fare, as the driver will most likely have to travel one way without a passenger. Generally speaking, rural taxi drivers are a fairly honest bunch, and you are unlikely to be ripped off. If, however, you feel you've had a raw deal, the driver can probably show you a printout of fares to different points back at the depot.

If you have trouble communicating your wishes to a taxi driver, it is possible to use the tourist information number 1330 as a translation service—see Useful Services in page 54 for details. When possible and applicable, we have provided contact information for local taxi companies alongside bus schedules.

Hitchhiking

Although not commonplace, hitchhiking is by no means frowned upon in rural Korea, and it will become your number one means of footless transport throughout your hike. In isolated areas, buses running to villages do so only a couple of times a day, and the nearest bus stop is often kilometers from the ridge, so hitchhiking is an essential and often fun way to get around.

Foreigners are not a common sight in rural Korea, so you'll be sure to get a ride before too long, and you are likely to meet some classic characters. You may even receive some trail magic—a hot coffee, free meal, bed for the night, or tour of the local area.

"Thumb out, big smile" is the accepted hitchhiking signal in Korea. We also found that removing sunglasses and hats, keeping on shirts and looking exhausted but happy also helped.

Hitchhiking in Korea is as safe as anywhere, and you have little need to fear robbery or criminal activity. Drinking and driving is a problem in rural areas, however, with a large percentage of accidents attributed to alcohol—never get into a car with someone who appears intoxicated.

Accommodations

Along the course of the Baekdu-daegan, you will have the chance to experience the full range of accommodation options available in rural South Korea. The trail does not have a system of shelters that stretches along its length, although shelters are available in a number of national parks. Between these areas, you can camp freely in the highlands or search out accommodation from an ever-growing number of lodges, inns and campsites along the flanks of the ridge. In a number of areas, you will also have the unique opportunity to participate in a temple-stay at one of the many Buddhist temples that dot the mountains of the Baekdu-daegan.

Throughout this guide, we have provided, when possible, accommodation options and contact details for each day of your journey along the Baekdu-daegan. What with the ever-changing nature of the Korean landscape, these are bound to change, with new options emerging and others disappearing. If you cannot locate accommodation, you can always call the Tourist Information Hotline page 54 or find assistance in nearby towns.

National Parks

Most major national park entrances are set in valleys and offer a large number of accommodation options for visitors, ranging from campgrounds to hotels. As you make your way along the Baekdu-daegan, you will, with the exception of Jiri-san, be entering parks by the "back door," high on the ridge away from the main gates. Through the parks, you will have the opportunity to stay in back country shelters, push through to road passes, or leave the ridge to seek out campgrounds and accommodation as you explore the features of the parks.

Camping

Within national park boundaries, camping is only permitted on designated campgrounds. These are predominantly located at park entrances and in valleys, with a few high in the mountains and none on the direct course of the Baekdu-daegan. Camping fees range from 3,000 to 6,000 won per person per night, depending on the size of your tent.

Inquire at the ticket booth or information center, or just go ahead and set up and someone will come and find you. Booking a campsite in advance is not essential, but it is recommended during the peak summer season of mid-July to mid-August and weekends, and this can be done by calling the area National Park Office.

Shelters

Back country shelters are available in Jiri-san, Deogyu-san, Odae-san and Seorak-san National Parks.

Jiri-san National Park has eight shelters located in its vast expanse, five of them on the ridge of the Baekdu-daegan and two on tracks leading to Cheonwang-bong, the beginning of the trail. Deogyu-san has two shelters, the first perfectly located for the hiker coming from the south and the second 2 km off the ridge below the largest peak in the park. Odae-san has one shelter at the peak of Noin-bong, on the border of its closed section, and Seorak-san has six shelters, two of them on the Baekdu-daegan trail, with only an hour of walking separating them.

The presence of these shelters gives you the opportunity to travel through the parks without a heavy pack laden with camping equipment and associated paraphernalia, allowing more time and energy to enjoy the attractions for which the parks are famous.

The shelters are for the most part modern, well-built, log cabin-style structures. They are equipped with generators that provide light until 9 pm and heating throughout the night, which is effective in keeping the rooms cozy and warm on the bleakest of winter nights and stiflingly hot in the middle of summer.

Smaller shelters consist of a large split-level communal sleeping area with men and women sleeping separately, usually with women on the top level and men on the bottom, while larger shelters have different rooms for men and women.

Each guest is allocated a numbered sleeping space, which is big enough for a bed roll and no more, so during the peak holiday periods, public holidays and weekends, shoulder-to-shoulder sleeping can be expected.

Shelters are manned by National Park Authority officials at all times; their office near the front entrance of each shelter also serves as a small store providing trekkers with small luxuries such as cans of coffee and cola, chocolate bars and biscuits, basic meal ingredients such as pre-cooked rice, cans of tuna, and occasionally instant noodles. They also sell supplies such as gas bottles and tissue paper. Blankets can be rented for 1,000 won apiece. Manned shelters have weather-recording devices that offer digital readouts of the temperature and conditions.

All shelters have a kitchen area with large benches for preparing food. This area becomes a hive of activity at the end of the day as Korean hikers prepare their often extravagant evening meals while sharing stories of the mountain and leg pain over a bottle of *soju*. The kitchen areas have no cooking facilities, so you should bring your own stoves and utensils.

Rats and mice are a problem in and around the kitchens of many of the shelters; cleaning the cooking area after use and disposing of all food waste thoughtfully is advised in order to help reduce this problem. Clean drinking water can be found at all of the shelters, often from fresh mountain springs near the building.

Smoking is only permitted in designated areas outside the shelters.

The cost is 5,000-8,000 won per person per night, with the price depending on the size and popularity of the shelter and on the season. Reservations can be made online for six shelters in Jiri-san, one in Deogyu-san and one in Seorak-san at http://english.knps.or.kr, and it is also possible to make a phone booking by calling the park office. Reservations are not essential, but they are recommended for those available online and for all shelters on weekends and public holidays. Specific details for all shelters are provided in the trail guide.

Note: Pack earplugs if you plan to sleep in the shelters! Otherwise, expect to be kept awake by a chorus of snoring and the desperate whinnying of cramp victims.

National Park Office Contact Info http://english.knps.or.kr/

• **Jiri-san National Park HQ**	055-972-7771	jiri@knps.or.kr
• **Jiri-san Southern Office**	061-783-9100	
• **Jiri-san Northern Office**	063-625-8911	
• **Deogyu-san National Park**	063-322-3174	togyu@knps.or.kr
• **Songni-san National Park**	043-542-5276	songni@knps.or.kr
• **Worak-san National Park**	043-653-3250	worak@knps.or.kr
• **Sobaek-san National Park**	054-638-6196	sobaek@knps.or.kr
• **Odae-san National Park**	033-332-6417	odae@knps.or.kr
• **Seorak-san National Park**	033-636-7700	sorak@knps.or.kr

Outside National Parks

Between National Parks, you will have the opportunity to camp on majestic peaks, under a canopy of trees or in well-maintained *jeongja* in roadside parks. The large number of roads that cross the ridge also gives you the option of enjoying the full range of accommodations available throughout rural Korea, from staying in a farmhouse to the invigorating experience of a temple-stay.

Camping

Outside of national parks, camping is permitted in Korea Forest Service-managed forests and mountains. You will find many great places to pitch a tent along the trail on high mountain peaks and in sheltered passes. Access to water will often be an issue when camping, so if you plan to camp high on the ridge, you should be aware that there will likely be no water available for the night.

If you are camping in the forest, it is recommended that you pitch your tent in an already cleared area and not over unspoiled forest undergrowth. Never start a fire, and be careful with any open flames, as the Korean mountains can be very dry, particularly in the autumn and winter months.

A large number of the roads that cross the ridge have cleared rest areas on the passes that are suitable for pitching a tent and often have a raised, roofed pavilion, or *jeongja*.

Jeongja

Raised above the ground to keep away moisture and with roofs tall enough to stand under, these often extravagant structures offer fine shelter, and if your preference is for camping along the trail, it will likely be a boon to find one at day's end.

In rural Korea, *jeongja* are traditionally found in village centers and fields, providing a communal resting and gathering spot for hard-working farmers, as well as a place for *yangban* (aristocrats) to gather on to enjoy the views of nature while drinking, picnicking, making music, writing poetry and discussing philosophy together. *Jeongja* still serve both purposes in city and country alike

and are as popular as ever in Korea, cropping up all over the place in modern city parks, on beaches, in backyards, at bus stops, on school grounds, on roadsides and on riversides—anywhere where people can be found who might want to lay out in the shade.

Jeongja are present in many places along the trail, often at scenic viewing points where roads cross the ridge. Sleeping in a *jeongja* is permitted, but it is good practice to wait until sightseers have left for the day before setting up camp. If you wish to stay in a *jeongja* located in a village, it is important that you first seek the permission of local elders, as the building of these structures has often been funded by the community; the structures are their communal property, and in many cases the pride of the village.

Note: Although located outside, a jeongja is still considered a room, and footwear must be removed before entering.

Minbak

Minbak guest lodges are the most common and cheapest form of accommodation in rural Korea. Although the word *minbak* translates as a "home-stay," your room will in most cases be detached from the main residence of the proprietor, and you can expect a certain level of privacy.

Your room will be clean and bare. In a corner or cupboard, there will be a large pile of blankets from which you build your own bed. Most *minbak* rooms have TVs and their own bathrooms and showers, but this is not universal, particularly in smaller areas.

In tourist areas, many *minbak* also operate as restaurants, which is usually their primary business. *Minbak* that don't have restaurants will usually cook your meals upon request; you can expect to pay about 5,000 won per meal and be filled with delicious Korean *jeongsik*. *Minbak* hosts are for the most part friendly and inquisitive people, as is the case with most people who take strangers into their home, and in small *minbak* you can expect a sociable evening.

You can expect to pay 20,000–30,000 won per night for a room in a *minbak*.

Sanjang

A *sanjang*, or mountain villa, is essentially a mountain-themed *minbak*, usually with a rustic feel and run by people who have an affiliation with the mountains and hiking. As you might expect, *sanjang* are often found in remote areas of the Baekdu-daegan. In most cases, the owners of the *sanjang* will be well used to Baekdu-daegan trekkers and can give you information on the trail conditions, as well as drive you to the trailhead if they are not busy.

Yeogwan / Motel

Yeogwan inns and motels can be found in most reasonably sized towns and throughout the countryside in scenic areas. They are usually multi-storied box-shaped buildings and can be identified by the Korean symbols given above or by a sideways crescent with squiggly lines rising from it, representing a sauna—some have saunas in their basement, although most that display the symbol do not. You can expect a clean room with a double bed, a bathroom, and often a cable TV. *Ondol-bang* rooms are usually available if you prefer sleeping on the floor.

Most modern *yeogwan* are now simply called "motels." You can expect to pay 20,000-40,000 won for a room, depending on its age and features. At the upper end, you can expect a few luxuries such as a computer, plasma TV, spa bath or even a vibrating bed! We have provided contact details when possible throughout the guide. These will help you locate the nearest accommodation, especially if you are hitchhiking or seeking to be picked up. However, there is usually no need to book a minbak, sanjang or motel room in advance.

Temple-Stay

The Korean Temple-Stay Program began in April 2002, and there are currently about 25 temples of the Jogye Order of Buddhism around the country where foreigners can stay and experience a day in the life of a monk.

If you participate in the program, you will be provided with appropriate garb (in our case, bright orange robes), receive a guided tour of the temple buildings and attend the evening ceremonial service, as well as the pre-dawn Buddhist ceremonial service beginning at 3:30 am. You will be given a room in the temple

Major Temples along the Baekdu-daegan

Daewon-sa	Located at the trail entrance to Jiri-san T. 055-972-8068 (office) or 055-974-1112 (temple-stay number) daewonsa@daewonsa.net / www.daewon-sa.net
Hwaeom-sa	Located at the end of the track running southwest from Ko-jae in western Jiri-san National Park T. 061-783-7600 / www.hwaeom-sa.org
Songgye-sa	Located in northeastern Deogyu-san T. 055-942-5184
Jikji-sa	Located east of Hwangak-san in the Gimcheon area T. 054-436-6174 / www.jikjisa.com (Korean site)
Beopju-sa	Located in Naesongni-san, above the main entrance to the park T. 043-543-3615 / www.beopjusa.or.kr
Biro-sa	Located in the southeast of Sobaek-san National Park T. 054-746-1832
Buseok-sa	Located in the far northeastern corner of Sobaek-san National Park T. 054-633-3464 / www.pusoksa.org
Manggyeong-sa	Located just below Cheonje-dan in Taebaek-san Provincial Park. No contact details; lodging is available for pilgrims.
Samhwa-sa	Located at the road end to the Mureung-gyegok scenic gorge T. 033- 534-7661 (office) or 534-7676 (temple-stay number) www.samhwasa.or.kr
Woljeong-sa	Located at the main entrance to Odae-san National Park T. 033-339-6800 / www.woljeongsa.org
Baekdam-sa	Located in western Seorak-san National Park in Yongdae-ri T. 033-462-5565 / www.baekdamsa.org
Sinheung-sa	Located in Seorak-dong at the main eastern entrance to the park T. 033-636-7044 / www.sinhungsa.or.kr

quarters, with men and woman sleeping in different rooms, and fed spare but delicious and nutritious vegetarian meals. Some of the larger and busier temples will provide additional activities such as tea ceremonies, craft workshops and English guidance. Staying in a temple is great opportunity not only to experience a monk's life but to reflect on your walk in a peaceful environment, and it is highly recommended for all trekkers of the Baekdu-daegan.

Four temples near the Baekdu-daegan have been included in the temple-stay program: Hwaeom-sa in southwestern Jiri-san (Section 1), Jikji-sa in the Gimcheon area (Section 4), Woljeong-sa in Odae-san National Park (Section 14) and Baekdam-sa in western Seorak-san National Park (Section 16). Information on the temple-stay program can be found at http://eng.templestay.com. Bookings can easily be made at the website or by contacting the temples directly from the list below.

The temple-stay list changes seasonally, with new temples added and occasionally removed; check the website for the latest information.

Although not included in the official temple-stay list, most major temples have lodging available for guests and often offer their own temple-stay program for Korean visitors on their own websites. There is no reason why foreigners can't participate in these temple-stays, but don't expect any English guidance or translation. If you wish to contact these temples about your trip, you may get an offer to stay. If you are not confident in speaking Korean on the phone, you can always call the Tourist Information Hotline or the BBB translation service for assistance (see Useful Services in page 54). Alternatively, you can just turn up and ask politely at any temple and you may be offered the chance to stay.

Pensions

Pensions represent the higher end of rural Korean accommodation and have become increasingly popular throughout the country over the past few years.

Usually well-built homes with grassy lawns and white picket fences, pensions offer the discerning traveler a taste of the "ideal country lifestyle." Their architecture and interior design is often themed with motifs ranging from "Swiss chalet" (very popular) to mushroom-shaped "Smurf villages" and recreated Joseon

era Korean homesteads.

Pensions are quite expensive but very nice, with modern amenities and a comfortable atmosphere. Prices range from about 60,000 won per night to 200,000 won per night, but this price is often split among a large group sharing a room. If you need somewhere to stay, don't immediately dismiss pensions on the basis of price, as a lot of pensions also offer *minbak* accommodation, and if you're passing through on a quiet night, you may just get a deal.

Korea Forest Service Recreational Forests

Recreational forests offer a peaceful environment, with cabins and campsites dotted along mountain streams leading to hiking trails.

The first recreational forest was established in 1988 at Daegwan-ryeong as forest management policy switched from forestry to recreation, which coincided with the Korean people having more free time and money to spend on recreation, and with the forests of Korea reaching maturity following the great afforestation projects that were carried out after the Japanese occupation and the Korean War.

There are now about 120 recreational forests located throughout Korea, and 36 of these are managed by the Korean Forest Service, which aims to provide a peaceful environment for city dwellers to unwind while educating them about the ecology of the Korean forests. The recreational forests are located near the line of the Baekdu-daegan like the following: in northern Deogyu-san (Section 4), at Jo-ryeong (Section 8) and at Daegwan-ryeong (Section 13).

The entry fee to a recreational forest is 1,000 won. Campsites cost 2,000 won per night, and wooden "camping decks" cost 4,000 won per night.

Cabin prices vary depending on the season. During the "low season" (Sunday to Thursday), basic 13 m^2 cabins that can sleep 1-3 people will cost 21,000 won. During the "high season" (July 1 to August 31 and all weekends), a basic cabin will cost 39,000 won.

Cabins range in size from 13 m^2 to 70 m^2, with prices rising according to size.

There is currently no English website for accommodation bookings, but general information on recreational forests can be found at http://english.forest.go.kr. Bookings can be made by visiting the Korean site www.foreston.go.kr or by calling the phone numbers provided in the appropriate Section.

Health & Safety

Traveling in the mountains excites a sense of adventure. The rugged countenance of these landscapes, with their looming peaks and sinuous ridges, stirs in us thrilling visions of exploration and escape. However, in that roughhewn beauty, one constant element remains: potential danger. Mountains are hard places, and although their slopes may be inviting, they are also to be respected. Mountains are temperamental; they can change their attitudes on a whim, and like all adventures, highland journeys contain inherent risk and uncertainty. Being unprepared for these risks will invite danger. Therefore, it is extremely important to be knowledgeable about the risks and how to deal with them. Mountains can affect us in many ways, from the natural elements to sickness, slips and falls, and it's vital that we know what to do if we face such situations. A heightened level of preparedness may not only limit dangers, but also increase one's enjoyment of the trek. Remember, safety comes first.

Before Leaving Home

Fortunately, there are no serious threats of disease in South Korea, and so there are no regulations stipulating vaccinations before entering the country. For in-depth information about health for general travel, read the World Health Organization's annually updated free online book *International Travel & Health* at www.who.int/ith. If you require medication, be sure to bring enough with you, as what you require may not be readily available in South Korea. Note that a doctor's prescription is needed in order to receive medications in South Korea. Look into travel insurance as well. Potential injuries incurred on the trail may be severe, and a "better safe than sorry" attitude toward travel insurance may make all the difference in hefty medical costs. Consider getting a medical check up before heading out for the trek.

Medical Care in South Korea

Quality of medical care in South Korea can vary. In Seoul, the system is advanced and at modern Western standards. In rural areas, however, the care may be less standardized and of poorer quality. In Seoul, the Samsung Medical Centre & International Health Service in Gangnam (T. 02-3410-0200), the International Health Services Department at Seoul National University Hospital in Hyehwa (T. 02-760-2890), and the International Clinic at the Yonsei

Severance Hospital in Sinchon (T. 02-361-6540) are all recommended for any medical needs you may have while in the capital.

Potential Diseases

This is a brief list of diseases in South Korea that may affect travelers, particularly while trekking through the montane, afforested, and rural regions of the country.

- **Diarrhea**, specifically "traveler's diarrhea," is a bacterial ailment common to those who first arrive in South Korea. Often no more than an annoyance, traveler's diarrhea can inhibit progress on the trek, but it can be treated easily.
- **Filariasis** (a.k.a. Philariasis) is a parasitic disease commonly found in rural areas, especially in rice-growing regions. It is spread by mosquito bites.
- **Hepatitis A** is an infectious disease that targets the liver. It is a food- and waterborne virus that commonly enters the body via the fecal-oral route (fecal particles of one host entering the body of another via the mouth through food or water). Vaccines are available for hepatitis.
- **Japanese encephalitis** is a mosquito-borne virus that is commonly found in birds and domestic pigs and in rural regions. Affecting the central nervous system, the disease can be severe. There have been recent epidemics of the disease in Korea, but it is currently controlled via vaccination.
- **Leptospirosis** is a bacterial disease and one of the most common zoonoses. It is usually transmitted through the urine of an infected host, and it is most commonly found along moist, muddy areas frequented by wild and domestic animals. Humans become infected via contact with food, water, or soil containing traces of infected urine.
- **Lyme disease** (a.k.a. borreliosis) is caused by species of the bacteria Borrelia, the vectors of which are ticks. Borreliosis is currently listed as an "emerging infectious disease," meaning that incidences of it in the past two decades have increased and are threatening to grow further. Be cautious of ticks when trekking through afforested areas.
- **Malaria** is no longer very common in South Korea, but cases still occur from time to time. Cases of malaria are generally limited to the northern provinces of Gangwon and Gyeonggi, as well as around the demilitarized zone.

• **Rabies** is a neuroinvasive disease that causes potentially fatal swelling of the brain. The risks are perhaps low, but there are many mammals along the Baekdu-daegan route, particularly dogs and cattle in the villages. See a doctor immediately if you are bitten by any animal.

• **Typhoid** is a bacterial infection transmitted by the ingestion of fecal particles of an infected host in the food or water of another potential host. Typhoid causes inflammation and ulceration of the intestine. It is most common in summer. A vaccine is available.

• **Giardia** is a waterborne protozoan infection causing diarrhea and "rotten egg burps." It is treatable with tinidazole.

Potential Physical Conditions

Blisters, fractures, frostbite, heat stroke, hypothermia, lacerations, and snakebites. This is a brief list of the most common conditions one may expect to face on the Baekdu-daegan trek. They are common ailments throughout the world, and treatment of them is covered in most pocket-sized first aid manuals. For the sake of the guidebook, we have mentioned in more detail ailments that are unique to Korea. It would be beneficial to have first aid training to increase safety on the trek. Contact your local Red Cross or any other medical service that offers first aid courses, and consider taking classes. If you're interested in first aid courses in Korea, contact the Korean branch of the Red Cross via their website (www.redcross.or.kr/www/eng/index.jsp). They offer first aid courses in English. Note that there's no danger of acute mountain sickness while trekking along the Baekdu-daegan. The highest point you'll reach will be Cheonwang-bong, the summit of Jiri-san, at 1,915 m ABSL.

Snakebites

There are various species of snake found in South Korea. Not all of them are venomous, but all can bite. Unless you are an ophiologist, it is best to treat all snakes as potentially dangerous. Snakes are remarkable

Red-tongue viper

Short-tailed mamushi

reptiles and must be treated with the utmost respect and care. The following is a list of the most common species of terrestrial snake found in South Korea, along with their common Korean names:

NON-LETHAL

- **Amur rat snake (*Elaphe schrenckii*)** – *gureongi* 구렁이
- **Asian keelback (*Amphiesma vibakari*)** – *daeryuk yuhyeol mogi* 대륙유혈목이
- **Black-headed snake (*Sibynophis collaris*)** – *bibari baem* 비바리뱀
- **Cat snake (*Elaphe dione*)** – *nuruk baem* 누룩뱀
- **Red-banded odd-tooth snake (*Dinodon rufozonatus*)** – *neung-gureongi* 능구렁이
- **Slender racer (*Coluber spinalis*)** – *sil baem* 실뱀
- **Tape snake (*Zamenis spinalis*)** – *bisa* 비사

POTENTIALLY LETHAL

- **Red-tongue viper (*Gloydius ussuriensis*)** – *soe salmosa* 쇠살모사
- **Short-tailed mamushi (*Gloydius blomhoffii brevicaudus*)** – *salmosa* 살모사
- **Short-tailed viper (*Gloydius saxatilis*)** – *kkachi salmosa* 까치살모사
- **Tiger keelback (*Rhabdophis tigrinus*)** – *yuhyeol mogi* 유혈목이

Prevention

Snakes will not actively attack humans and usually only attack when provoked. A snake will prefer to flee rather than fight something bigger than itself, such as a burly trekker. Snakes can accidently be stepped on, though, especially in tall grasses, so watch your step. Be aware when you are moving up rocks or a steep part of the trail where you cannot see what's just beyond the rise. If you are lucky enough to come across a snake, keep your distance and do not disturb it. Let the snake go along on its way. If you are sleeping outdoors, a thorough check of your sleeping bag before you sleep may be a good idea.

Treatment

Since you will not likely know if the snake that has inflicted a bite is venomous or not, it is important to follow the necessary first aid procedures against venomous bites for all snakes. Act quickly. Have the bitten individual lie down and get as comfortable as possible. Some first aid procedures suggest not washing the bite wound, because physicians may require samples of the venom left on the skin to determine what kind of snake inflicted the bite. Other institutions do suggest washing the wound with soap and water. Do not irritate the wound by rubbing or touching it. Do not incise the wound, and do not try to suck out the venom. If the bite is on a limb, bandage the entire limb from the top joint to the bottom. If possible, before bandaging the wound with clean dressings, draw a circle around the area of the bite with a pen (a marker pen would be good), write down the date and time of the bite either on the skin or on a piece of paper, and stick it in the patient's pocket for future reference. It is not uncommon for bite marks to completely disappear from the affected area; the bite mark indicated by the pen will assist the doctor in locating the area of impact. Immobilize the wounded area; use a splint if possible. Begin evacuation procedures and get to the nearest medical center as soon as possible.

Rescue Services

Emergency services in South Korea have been steadily evolving since the 1988 Olympic Games were held in Seoul. By dialing 119 (not 911, as is common in most Western countries), the caller activates the Emergency Medical Service and automatically obtains access to the National 119 Rescue Service. The National 119 Rescue Service and its regional 119 Rescue Service sub-organizations are responsible for all emergency rescue services in South Korea, including mountain rescue. In an emergency situation, get access to a telephone as quickly as possible. Luckily, most local hikers carry cell phones, and villages, towns, and temples dot most of the Baekdu-daegan, thus making it relatively easy to contact rescue services. They also get quite good, consistent coverage in the mountains of Korea. Note that cell phones are also available for rent upon arrival at Incheon International Airport. If you must leave an injured individual on the trail to find help, be certain to make sharp note of his or her location so he or she can be administered to quickly.

First Aid Kit

A first aid kit is your primary tool in administering help to an injured individual. All Baekdu-daegan trekkers should have a well-stocked kit. It is also a good idea to consider carrying more than one kit, depending on the size of your trekking group. A first aid kit is useless unless you know how to use the items contained within it. Read the manual, and know exactly where all the items are located in the kit. Keep the kit in an easy-to-reach place in your backpack; don't store it at the bottom. Talk with your doctor or pharmacist for more tips on how to stock a first aid kit.

Useful Services

Traveling through rural Korea, you will not meet a lot of English-speaking locals, and if you can't speak Korean, communication can be quite the challenge. There is also not a lot of English tourist information available in rural areas. Two excellent services, the Tourist Information Hotline and Before Babel Brigade, offer free tourist information and translation services over the phone in a number of languages. At a local level, you can also expect ready assistance from the police force and the use of free internet in post offices.

Tourist Information Hotline—1330

The Tourist Information Hotline is a great service and has operators available 24 hours a day to answer general inquiries in English, Japanese, Chinese or Korean. Dial the area code of the province you wish to inquire about, followed by 1330 (or 02-1330 for the HQ in Seoul, which will redirect you), and you will be connected to a guide who is there to answer your questions, no matter how specific. The operators should be able to answer all of your queries, and they will call you back if your question is a tricky one.

Before Babel Brigade (BBB)

Whether you're trying to direct a taxi or get your point across over a drink, the BBB translation service is the place to call. BBB offers free translation in 16 languages. Simply dial 1588-5644 and choose your language and you'll be connected to a volunteer who will help you out.

Police Stations

Most small Korean towns have a police station. These are very useful places for information and help along the Baekdu-daegan. Small town police are generally very friendly, not very busy, and always willing to help with your queries. Throughout our expedition, we often used the police to help find accommodation in the area, information about transportation to larger centers, and weather information–they even watched our gear on occasion while we were exploring the area. It is worth noting that all police stations have a coffee machine and will serve you a hot brew if you stop by.

Post Offices

All small town post offices provide a computer with free internet access, and they are very happy for you to use it at your leisure—free coffee is also often provided by the inquisitive and friendly postal workers.

Etiquette

The thin line of the Baekdu-daegan is very sensitive ecologically and cannot sustain irresponsible hiking practices. It is therefore important that all hikers tread carefully and respectfully along the trail, following a code of minimal impact to ensure the future health of this region and its biodiversity.

The Baekdu-daegan is a social journey of cultural and historical significance, and as you pass through the ever-changing beauty of the landscape, you will also pass through some of Korea's most isolated mountain villages and visit a number of temples and shrines. Many of these areas see few tourists, and you should be aware and respectful of their customs and traditions when visiting.

Along the Trail

Although it is protected at the governmental level, the true responsibility for the well-being of the Baekdu-daegan lies with the hikers, who should ensure their impact on the trail is minimal. The following ten-point Minimal Impact Code was authored by the Korean Mountain Preservation League and is specific and relevant to hiking throughout the peninsula.

1. Stay on established trails and do not enter preservation areas.
2. If you are in a group, travel in single file to avoid making existing trails wider. Widening trails spreads erosion.
3. Stay away from delicate ecological regions such as meadows, marshes, and wetlands.
4. Tread lightly and be careful not to destroy endemic plants, animals and insects as you hike.
5. Properly dispose of bodily waste by burying it in a shallow hole. Fill the hole with the soil that was removed and cover it with nearby leaves or rocks. Be sure to relieve yourself a far distance from natural water sources, trails, and campsites (at least 50 meters). Don't leave toilet paper behind! Pack it out! Don't dig up the ground for any other reason.

6. If you are lucky enough to observe wildlife, be quiet and do not disturb the animal. Let it pass freely. Do not feed it and do not call out to it. Remember, you are a guest in its home.

7. Take out everything that you bring in. Don't burn or bury trash in the mountains.

8. Avoid changing the natural surroundings of the trail. Don't move rocks or fallen trees even if they cross the trail. Leave the trail as you found it.

9. Avoid the common Korean practice of yelling "Yaho!" while in the mountains. It has been proven to harm bird populations by scaring birds into not procreating. It is also not courteous to your fellow hikers.

10. Be courteous to others who wish to use the trails. The mountains are places of solitude. Noise has no home in the highlands.

The minimal impact code is a good general guide for walking in the Korean highlands, but if you are walking the entire length of the ridge, there are a few other factors that you need to take into account.

Within the boundaries of national parks, human-based activities outside of hiking are kept to a minimum. For this reason, camping is not permitted anywhere in the parks outside of designated campgrounds, and walking off the trail is highly discouraged, and in many cases prohibited. Smoking is also banned in the parks as a consideration to fellow hikers and also to help cut the risk of forest fires, which are a large problem in Korea during the dry autumn and winter months. There is no such smoking ban outside of the national parks, but if you do smoke, it is advised that you refrain from doing so in all wooded areas, particularly in the dry months. The lighting of camp fires is also prohibited in all Korean mountain forests at all times of the year. If you must light a fire for emergency reasons, only use dead wood and ensure you are in an area clear of dry undergrowth.

Mountain Villages and Farms

Between the high peaks the trail crosses, you will pass through a number of highland farming areas and the small villages that support them. Mountain villages in Korea have largely middle-aged and elderly populations, as the majority of young people move to larger centers for educational and employment opportunities, returning for holidays and weekends to help on the family farm.

The villages are therefore quiet and conservative, with a feel of strong tradition and pride.

Many of these areas see very few, if any, foreign visitors and your arrival will attract a fair deal of curiosity, ranging from long, suspicious stares to open excitement. A friendly smile and polite introduction and you will soon feel very welcome in all villages and carry away great memories of your many classic encounters. If you are walking through the harvest season, you will often be offered fresh fruit from the village orchards, including apples, pears, grapes, nectarines and peaches. For these occasions, it is useful to have some small memento to give in return, such as mini-flags or stickers from your home country; rural Koreans really do enjoy receiving such tokens. Carrying name cards to distribute is also a good idea, especially those with a national flag or some meaningful symbol of your identity.

The majority of all farms in the highlands are unfenced, but they are privately owned, and this needs to be considered when passing by on the trail or getting off the ridge. Stay on the paths running through the farms, and don't cut through fields and orchards in search of a shortcut or take produce from the fields–the sight and smell of fresh fruit is tempting for any tired hiker, but you should never take any fruit from the trees unless offered, which, as mentioned above, you likely will be.

If you need to camp in a rural area, check first with the locals and you will be shown an area where it is suitable, often the village *jeongja* or communal area.

Temples and Shrines

There are literally thousands of Buddhist temples in Korea, and walking the Baekdu-daegan is a great opportunity to visit temples of all styles, from small mountain hermitages to major centers of Buddhist practice. Korean temples are relaxed places, and visitors are largely free to explore the buildings and surroundings as long as respect is shown to customs and appropriate etiquette is followed.

When entering a temple, don't announce your arrival with loud or boisterous behavior; keep noise to a minimum and remember that these are places of meditation and quiet reflection. When meeting monks, you should refer to them as *seunim*, and it is good practice to bow with your palms together and say hello in the formal manner.

There will often be certain areas of the temple that are closed to visitors, including the monk's quarters and other areas, when meditation is in progress; these areas will be indicated by a closed gate or sign.

Do not picnic or camp on the grounds of a temple. If you arrive at meal time, find a quiet spot outside the gates or make your way to the communal dining area to eat at the tables, where you will often be asked to join the monks for a meal if you arrive at the right time. If you are eating your own food, avoid meat, including fish and eggs, and never smoke on any part of the temple grounds. If you are invited inside for a meal or drink but you don't have time, just smile and say that you have to get going, offering warm thanks.

Before entering any temple building, you must first remove your shoes. In the main hall, never enter through the central door, which is traditionally reserved for the Buddha and the spirits; instead, use either of the side doors. Inside, it is good practice to bow with palms together to the deities.

There is no official religious policy regarding photography within temple buildings; some have signs banning all photos, while others don't allow flash photography, and still others encourage visitors to take as many pictures as they like. If you wish to take photos inside, ask a monk or attendant and respect their wishes. If you are granted permission, try to be unobtrusive by not interfering with ceremonies or meditation, and never move any objects.

Many Buddhist monks consider it a requirement to be generous hosts, and you will often be offered food, drinks, snacks, and sometimes more significant gifts as you explore the temple grounds. It is considered rude to refuse anything you are offered; accept with a smile and warm thanks, and if you don't want it, pass it on to someone else later. You should only refuse gifts if you simply don't have space in your hiking pack. For these situations, it is once again useful to have a small something to give in return, but this is not essential.

If you feel some obligation to give compensation to monks at a temple for all the great free things they've given you, don't try to just hand them cash. They won't take it, and it's insulting. It's a very good idea to go to the main hall (a *sansin-gak* is even better for hikers!), light the candles and incense, and place a little cash in the donation box before making three bows. If you are seen doing this, the monks will really love you, and if they don't see it, you will have clean karma anyway!

Who Looks After the Baekdu-daegan?

by Shawn Morrisey

As an entity that encompasses the ecological integrity of the Korean landscape, the Baekdu-daegan and all her sub-ranges serve as the fundamental bio-regions of the peninsula, providing the land with water, effects on climate, habitat, and ultimately nourishment. In recent years, in light of the severe damage sustained by these great ecosystems due to Korea's nearly unstoppable rapid development, measures have been researched and implemented to provide greater restoration, management, and protection.

These management issues took seed on December 29, 1967 when the National Parks Act was enacted and Jiri-san was designated as Korea's first national park. For the next twenty years, nineteen more regions were designated as national parks, ending with the designations of Wolchul-san and Byeonsan-bando on June 11, 1988. In total, Korea's twenty national parks constitute 6,580 square kilometers of land and sea. Fifteen of the twenty parks are categorized as mountain parks, meaning they were designated solely for the purpose of enclosing a mountain ecosystem, clearly indicating just how dominant highlands are upon the landscape. The remaining parks consist of two seashore parks, two marine parks, and one historical park. All of the parks, except Gyeongju and Halla-san, fall under the jurisdiction of the Korea National Parks Service (KNPS).

Korea National Parks Services

The KNPS was established in July 1987 under the control of the Ministry of Construction. The service was commissioned as the sole authority over the national parks; previous authority had been given to local governments, resulting in fragmented policies, non-cooperation, and inappropriate management. By 1991, the KNPS was transferred to the Ministry of Interior, and finally to the Ministry of Environment in 1998.

The primary goal of the KNPS involves management of the parks to suit ecological necessities and recreational demands. Like most national park services around the world, however, the KNPS is direly understaffed, with fewer than 1,000 permanent employees, leaving approximately 6.5 km2 per employee to manage, research, and protect.

A major part of the KNPS management program involves the reintroduction of endangered species into the wild. Paramount among them is the Asiatic black bear (Ursus thibetanus). The International Union for Conservation of Nature & Natural Resources (IUCN), the chief authority on the conservation status of species, lists Asiatic black bears as globally vulnerable; however, in South Korea, they are critically endangered. The black bears, also called moon bears, are traditionally the target of medicine hunters, as the bears' bladder bile is considered a prized remedy. Currently, fewer than twenty are present in the Korean wild, all in Jiri-san, and many of them were introduced from either Russia or North Korea. The KNPS has therefore implemented a black bear restoration project that aims to enhance the biodiversity and ecological stability of the mountains, particularly Jiri-san, by reintroducing the bears into the wilderness, monitoring their progress, and maintaining protection of both the species and their habitat. Along with the restoration program, the KNPS has set up the Species Restoration Centre, as well as a shelter for orphaned or injured bears, where they are nursed back into the wild, and an education facility, where the public, and children in particular, can learn about the bears, their biology and their importance in the ecosystem.

The KNPS also carries out the Temporary Closure Program, which is designed for the purposes of restoring ailing ecosystems and habitats and preserving regions rich in biodiversity. First implemented in 1991 and currently in its sixth incarnation, the program oversees the closure of regions for periods up to ten years or more. Some closed areas don't include the trails that run through them, but rather the buffer zones on either side of a trail. It is important to note the closed areas that may affect your trek along the Baekdu-daegan, even though most of them do not actually run the course of the Great Ridge itself. If you decide to take a side trip down a valley or up a peak, or if you are compelled to explore an intriguing region, it is important to know whether the area is closed or not. The hiking Sections in this guidebook have quite clearly labeled the closed sections that were encountered at the time of the expedition. They are more than likely still in place.

Korea Forest Service

The KNPS is not the only functional body that manages Korea's wildernesses, and in fact the KNPS does not have jurisdiction over the Baekdu-daegan. That power lies in the hands of the Korea Forest Service (KFS). The KFS, which was originally called the Forest Bureau and is under the control of the Ministry of Agriculture & Forestry, was established in 1967. The service's initial major projects included their successful Forest Rehabilitation Programs, which aimed to restore Korea's forests, some 80% of which had been devastated in the Korean War, with further degradation coming from deforestation. Eventually, and perhaps much to the chagrin of the KNPS, the KFS was given jurisdiction over the Baekdu-daegan. This jurisdiction runs in conjunction with the Act on the Protection of the Baekdu-daegan Mountain System, legislated in 2004 by the federal government. The Act has designated 263,427 hectares of the Baekdu-daegan as protected land. This is not an immense figure, unfortunately, as it represents only 4% of South Korea's total forest area and 2.6% of its total landmass. Furthermore, despite this designation, much of the Baekdu-daegan remains threatened by overuse, mining, ill-respecting mountaineers, and even certain government programs.

Much of the biodiversity of the Baekdu-daegan has declined, as most of its top-level predators like wolves, leopards, and tigers are now extinct in South Korea. It is the aim of the Act and the KFS to restore biodiversity as much as possible. Unfortunately, wolves will likely never roam here again, as their need for vast swaths of land can no longer be met due to the urban sprawl predominant in South Korea. Amur leopards, the rarest feline on Earth, number fewer than 40 in the entirety of Earth's wildernesses. And tigers, the classic symbol of the integrity and spirit of the Korean nation, could no longer have the ecological means to survive here in sustainable numbers. Nonetheless, the vision of the KFS to harmonize nature, humanity, and culture via the protection of the Baekdu Daegan carries forth.

Currently, the KFS is carrying out its Ten Year Plan for the Protection of the Baekdu-daegan. The main points of this management plan, which will end in 2015, emphasize enhancing the ecological health and biodiversity of the Great Ridge. Furthermore, environmental restoration of degraded land is considered paramount in strengthening the connection between the ecology, culture, and history of the Baekdu-daegan. As mountain recreation becomes more and more popular in South Korea, and as more Koreans are beginning to recall their natural and cultural roots in the ridge, the KFS says it will boost infrastructure and education to foster eco-friendly mountaineering practices. The KFS also aims to restore historically significant aspects of the Baekdu-daegan through eco-friendly conservation and restoration. As many people make a living in the regions surrounding the Baekdu-daegan, and many of these residents are opposed to the protection plan, the government intends to initiate welfare projects that will stimulate income via green economics, therefore encouraging voluntary initiatives in the locals to protect the Baekdu-daegan. Hopefully, these welfare projects will make a healthy ecosystem more valuable to the locals than one that is exploited. Whether this plan will be successful remains to be seen; however, with Korea's access to modern technology and economy, going green, educating the public, and seeing the Ten Year Plan through to fruition are certainly obtainable goals. Ultimately, the goal of the KFS's protection plan is to conserve the Baekdu-daegan and the cultural spirit that flows out from within it—a three-tiered plan that the KFS says considers ecology, culture, and economy.

Management of the Baekdu-daegan Mountain System is of great importance. The foundations of everything that the Baekdu-daegan encompasses—culture, recreation, life—are products of ecological processes fundamental to the well-being of each. The culture of Korea, like all cultures, was born out of its landscape, the landscape out of the environment, and the environment out of a vast web of natural relationships ebbing and flowing to create the necessities of life. The mountains are there not for our sake, but for the sake of the whole. As we use these mountains for our recreational desires, we must not only be responsible mountaineers, but also caring custodians. As we tread upon them, mountains give us joy, but they'll continue to provide us with the elements of survival long after we've packed up and headed home.

The management of the Baekdu-daegan cannot be left only to the powers that be, but ultimately and more so to us, the mountaineers who take to those hills with passion in our blood and adventure in our bones. Be responsible and make the management of the Baekdu-daegan your duty as you trek along her sinuous lines and remarkable beauty.

Shawn Morrissey is founder of the Korean Mountain Preservation League (www.kmpl.org). He is the author of *In the Land of the Morning Calm and Reverence: A Personal View on Korean Environmentalism*. Shawn can be contacted at: highland-peace@hotmail.com.

Baekdu-daegan Course Outline

Section 1 Cheonwang-bong → Gogi-ri (4 days over 39.2km)
Section 2 Gogi-ri → Yuksip-ryeong (4 days over 58.2km)
Section 3 Yuksip-ryeong → Bbae-jae (2~3 days over 32km)
Section 4 Bbae-jae → Gwaebang-ryeong (3~4 days over 50km)
Section 5 Gwaebang-ryeong → Hwaryeong-jae (4 days over 62.8km)
Section 6 Hwaryeong-jae → Neul-jae (2 days over 28km)
Section 7 Neul-jae → Ihwa-ryeong (3 days over 44.5km)
Section 8 Ihwa-ryeong → Haneul-jae (2 days over 17.5km)
Section 9 Haneul-jae → Jeosu-ryeong (3 days over 32.2km)
Section 10 Jeosu-ryeong → Doraegi-jae (3 days over 71km)
Section 11 Doraegi-jae → Pi-jae (2 days over 45km)
Section 12 Pi-jae → Baekbok-ryeong (3 days over 54.2km)
Section 13 Baekbok-ryeong → Daegwan-ryeong (3 days over 43km)
Section 14 Daegwan-ryeong → Guryong-ryeong (2 days over 46.6km)
Section 15 Guryong-ryeong → Hangye-ryeong and the Osaek Gorge (2 days over 46.5km)
Section 16 Hangye-ryeong → Jinbu-ryeong (4 days over 43km)
Section 17 Jinbu-ryeong → Hyangno-bong near the DMZ (over 18km)

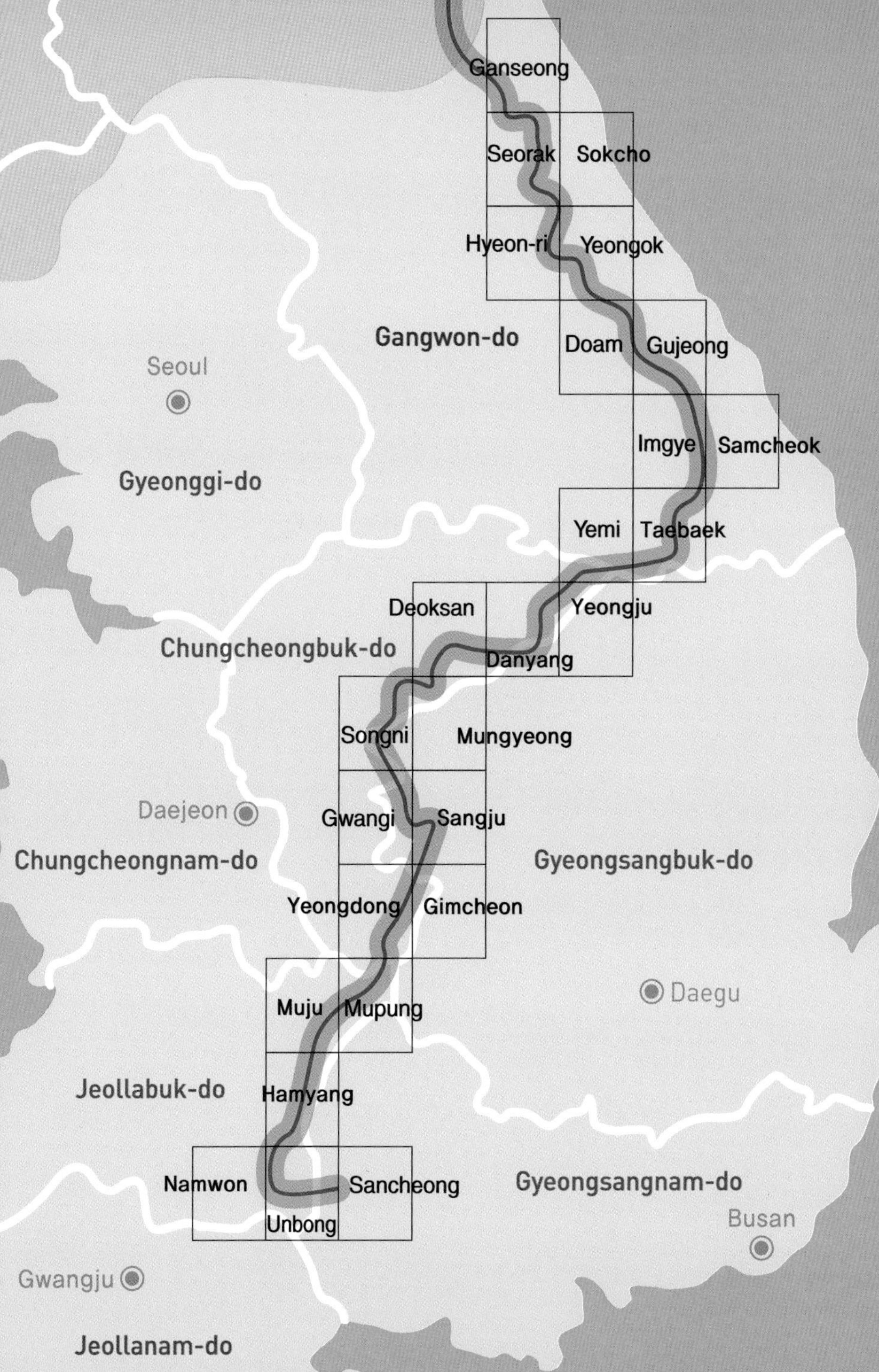

Ganseong
Seorak
Sokcho
Hyeon-ri
Yeongok
Gangwon-do
Doam
Gujeong
Seoul
Imgye
Samcheok
Gyeonggi-do
Yemi
Taebaek
Deoksan
Yeongju
Chungcheongbuk-do
Danyang
Songni
Mungyeong
Daejeon
Gwangi
Sangju
Chungcheongnam-do
Gyeongsangbuk-do
Yeongdong
Gimcheon
Daegu
Muju
Mupung
Jeollabuk-do
Hamyang
Namwon
Sancheong
Gyeongsangnam-do
Unbong
Busan
Gwangju
Jeollanam-do

FOUR DAYS

39.2 km

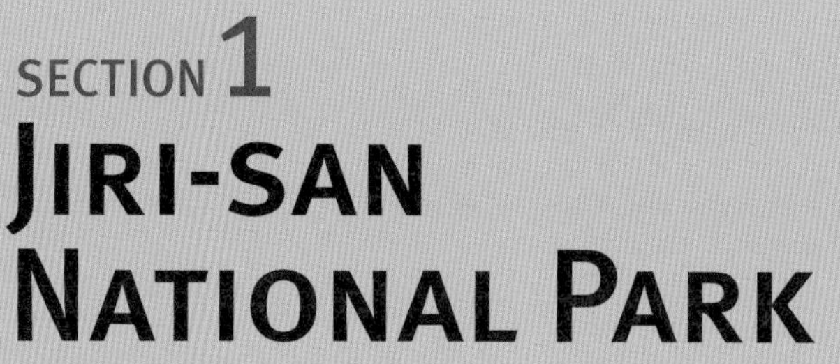

SECTION 1

JIRI-SAN NATIONAL PARK

Cheonwang-bong → Gogi-ri

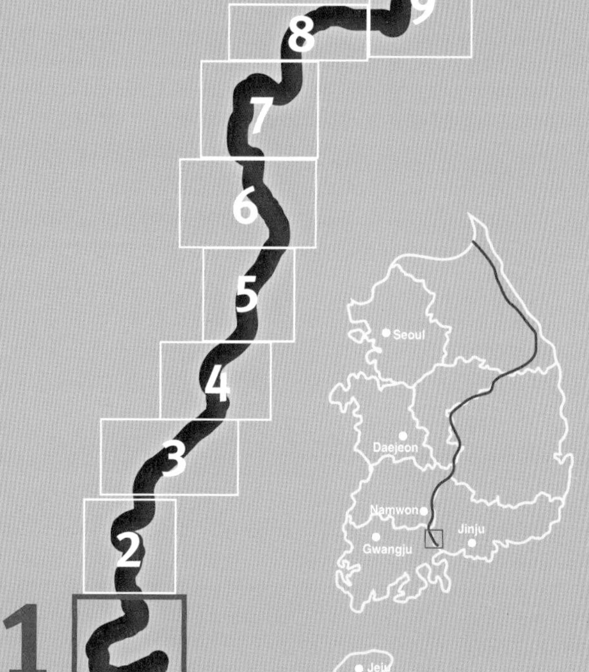

A
B
C
D
1
2
3
4
SECTION 1
11.2km in 5hr 40min
DAY 1 & 2
From Cheonwang-bong to Byeokso-ryeong
N
Chilseon Hyugeso
칠선휴게소
칠선계곡
Hamyang-gun
함양군
Macheon-myeon
마 천 면
Jan
Byeokso-ryeong Shelter
벽소령대피소
(5)
Day-2
FINISH
Byeokso-ryeong
벽소령
1,522m
Deokpyeong-bong
덕평봉
(4)
Seonbi-saem
선비샘
1,558m
Chilseon-bong
칠선봉
Soji-bong
소지봉
1,622m
Yeon
영신봉
Seseok Shelter
세석대피소
Jiri-san National Park
지 리 산 국 립 공 원
Daeseong-gol
대성골

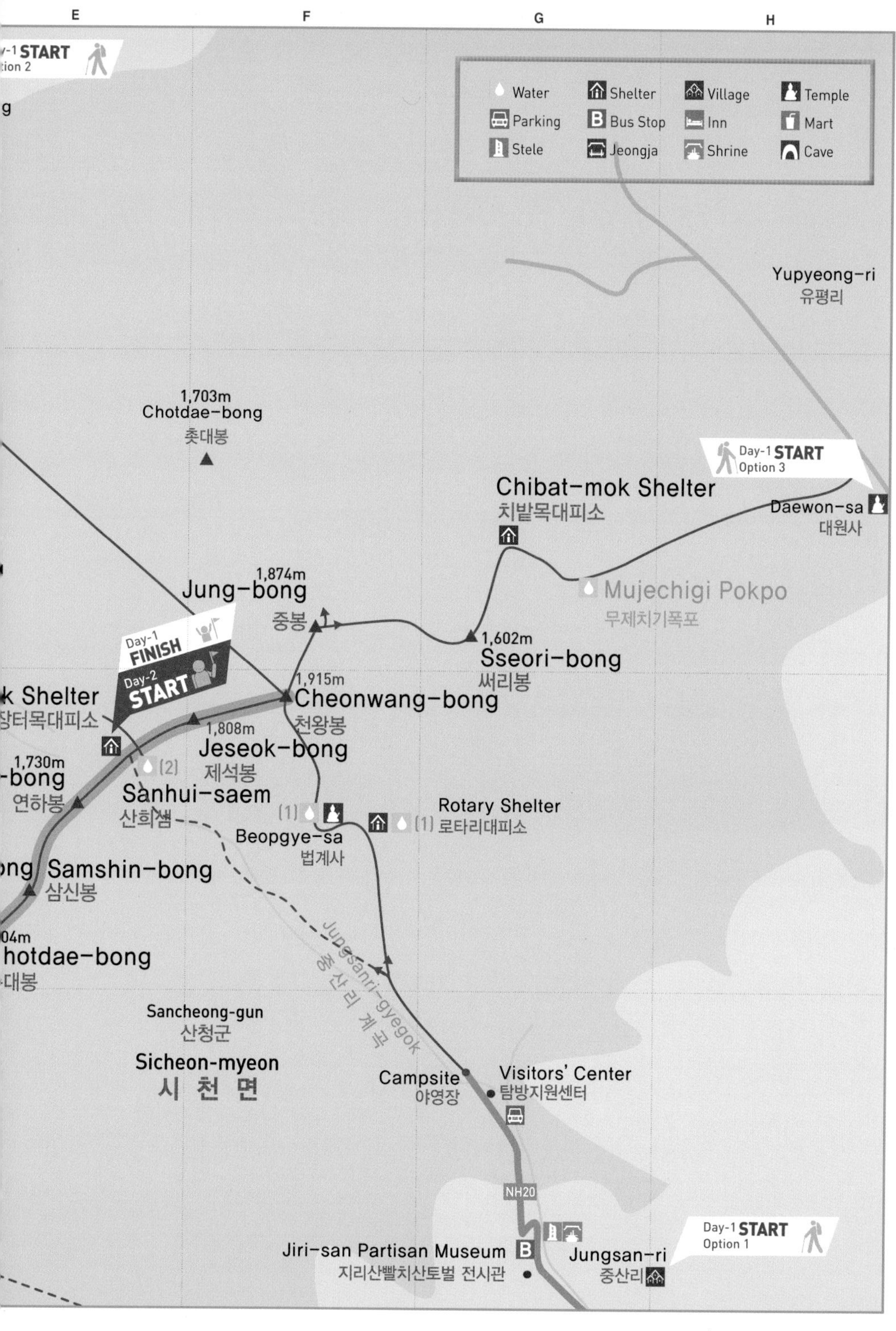

E
F
G
H
-1 START
tion 2
Water
Shelter
Village
Temple
Parking
Bus Stop
Inn
Mart
Stele
Jeongja
Shrine
Cave
Yupyeong-ri
유평리
1,703m
Chotdae-bong
촛대봉
Day-1 START
Option 3
Chibat-mok Shelter
치밭목대피소
Daewon-sa
대원사
1,874m
Jung-bong
중봉
Mujechigi Pokpo
무제치기폭포
1,602m
Sseori-bong
써리봉
Day-1
FINISH
Day-2
START
k Shelter
장터목대피소
1,915m
Cheonwang-bong
천왕봉
1,808m
Jeseok-bong
제석봉
1,730m
-bong
연하봉
(2)
Sanhui-saem
산희샘
(1)
Beopgye-sa
법계사
Rotary Shelter
(1) 로타리대피소
ong
Samshin-bong
삼신봉
04m
hotdae-bong
대봉
Jungsanri-gyegok
중산리 계곡
Sancheong-gun
산청군
Sicheon-myeon
시 천 면
Campsite
야영장
Visitors' Center
탐방지원센터
NH20
Jiri-san Partisan Museum
지리산빨치산토벌 전시관
Jungsan-ri
중산리
Day-1 START
Option 1

DAY 1

From Cheonwang-bong to Jangteomok Shelter

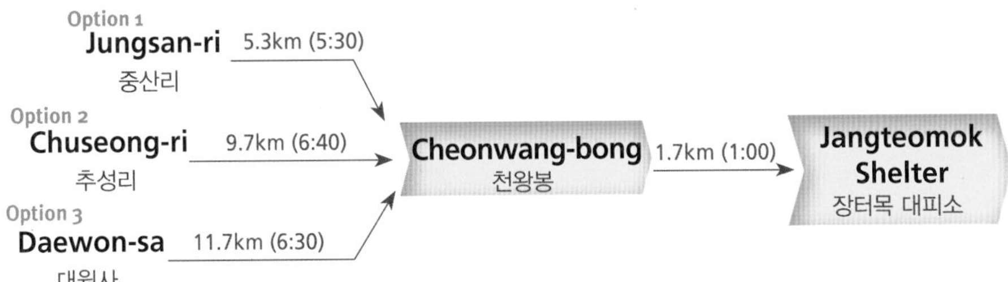

The Baekdu-daegan trail itself starts at the summit of Cheonwang-bong, at 1,915 m ABSL, on the eastern arm of Jiri-san National Park in South Korea. You can choose one of three routes to get to Cheonwang-bong. The Day 1 course in this Section includes those options, concluding at the Jangteomok Shelter, 1 km west along the trail from Cheonwang-bong. All three routes to the summit are spectacular and tough, and they are uncompromising indicators of what this long-distance hike is all about. Once on Cheonwang-bong, you will see the turbulent shape of this land, as ridges stretch endlessly in all directions like an astronomical explosion.

Getting to Cheonwang-bong 천왕봉 F3

There are three possible starting points from which you can begin the climb to Cheonwang-bong. Trails run to the summit from Option 1. the Jungsan-ri ticket booth in the southeast, Option 2. the Chuseong ticket booth in the north and Option 3. Daewon-sa temple, above the Yupyeong ticket booth in the northeast.

Option 1. From Jungsan-ri 중산리 G4 5.3km (5:30)

Located at the western end of a high road from National Highway 20 (hereinafter NH), Jungsan-ri is the most practical way to get to the starting point of the Baekdu-daegan at the summit of Cheonwang-bong. The high mountain village has an interesting museum telling the story of North Korean guerrillas who survived, hidden in Jiri-san, for up to ten years after the Korean War. On the hillside just across the small, strong waterfall-stream from Jungsan-ri is a modern statue of the holy mother-spirit of Jiri-san. This is a popular place for devotees of Korea's traditional shamanic religion to worship, and you too might want to go over and ask for safe guidance across her great ridge. Along with its accommodations, Jungsan-ri, also has a number of restaurants and stores from which to purchase last-minute meals or wares .

Following the road northwest through the village takes you to the trail entrance and parking lot. In this area, the modern Jiri-san National Park Visitors' Center, is located behind the ticket booth, offering information on flora and fauna and focusing in particular on the population of Asiatic black bears. The trail follows the mountain road past the visitors center for about 500 meters before heading northwest at the campsite while the road continues north high into the hills. From here, you walk for 1 km on an easy gradient along the eastern bank of the

Transport Info

Joining the trail at Jungsan-ri: Buses run 18 times a day from the Jinju local bus terminal 진주 시외버스터미널 to Jungsan-ri, between 6:40 am and 8:35 pm daily. The trip takes 1 hr 10 min.

West from Cheonwang-bong

Cheonwang-bong

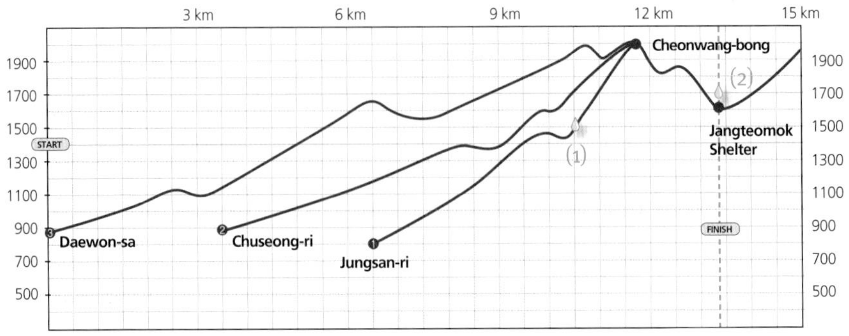

WATER STOPS
(1) Daepiso (shelter) near Beopgye-sa Temple: **N35°19'33" E127°44'14"**
(2) Jangteomok Shelter: **N35°19'56" E127°42'59"**

Junsan-ri Gyegok, a scenic gorge that runs between the peaks of Cheonwang-bong and its southwestern neighbor Yeonha-bong 연하봉, until you arrive at a track junction. Take the north-side or right-hand trail toward the summit of Cheonwang-bong, the starting point of the Baekdu-daegan. The climb will cover more than 500m in altitude over the next 1.8 km of trail to Beopgye-sa Temple*. From Beopgye-sa begins the final, difficult slog up to Cheonwang-bong summit. The rocky terrain becomes very steep over the final 1.8 km to the peak, over which the trail climbs almost 600 m in altitude. The short climb from Beopgye-sa may take up to two hours to complete, depending on your load and fitness.

* Beopgye-sa Temple 법계사 F3

Beopgye-sa was built in AD 544 by the Indian missionary-monk Yeongi-josa, who, according to legend, enshrined some of the Buddha's cremated remains (sarira) here. Lying in the southern shadow of Cheonwang-bong, it is one of Korea's highest temples and offers fine sweeping views southeast along spurs of the ridge. An information board at the temple tells of a famous legend: stating that if Beopgye-sa prospered, it would destroy the spirit of Japan. This belief led to a number of attacks, first by Ajibaldo pirates from Japan who destroyed the temple near the end of the Goryeo Dynasty (918-1392). It was rebuilt in 1405 and destroyed again by the Japanese during the Imjin invasion of 1592-1598, and again later when Korea became a colony of Japan in 1910. Following a divided Korean independence in

LODGING

A hundred meters before Beopgye-sa is the Rotary Shelter 로타리 대피소, a shelter that sleeps about 40 people and sells hot and cold drinks as well as basic trail food. There is also a large toilet block here, and water(1) can be found from a nearby spring.

Beopgye-sa © Liz Riggs

1948, the temple was again rebuilt before being partially destroyed during the Korean War (1950-1953), and the main hall and shrine weren't restored again until 1981. On display outside the administration building at Beopgye-sa are two large iron spikes. These were driven into the ground on the ridgeline above the temple during the Japanese occupation in an effort to cut the spirit of Beopgye-sa. The spikes were removed recently, one in 2005 and one in 2006. An information board says that the small shrine to the spikes is lucky and that you can wish for the happiness of your family and the prosperity of the nation here. Climbing to the top of the temple compound, you reach the "Pavilion of the Guardian Deity of the Mountain" (National Treasure No.473) which has an impressive three-story pagoda. This is the only remaining original artifact of Beopgye-sa.

Option 2. **From Chuseong-ri** 추성리 D1 9.7km (6:40)

Located at the end of a road two kilometers south of the junction of Provincial Road 1023 (hereinafter PR) and PR60 is the Chuseong ticket booth in Chuseong Village, on the northeastern side of the park. Chuseong-ri is located between the temples of Byeoksong-sa* and Seo-am 서암, 2.6 km northeast of Macheon-myeon

Transport Info

Joining the trail at Chuseong-ri: Buses run 20 times a day from the Hamyang local bus terminal 함양 시외버스터미널 to Chuseong-ri, the small village at the trailhead of the Chilseon Valley, between 7 am and 7:40 pm. The bus from Hamyang-gun will take you to a parking area between the temples of and the Chilseon Hyugeso, a convenience store and restaurant located near the ticket booth.

마천면. Chuseong-ri also has the Chilseon Hyugeso 칠선 휴게소, (*hyugeso* means "rest area") and other shopping amenities suitable for hiking.

The track from Chuseong-ri begins at the ticket booth, from which it initially runs southwest for 1 km before turning southeast and following a very steep and deep ravine known as the Chilseon Gyegok 칠선 계곡 ("seven immortals gorge") to the summit of Cheonwang-bong. Chilseon Gyegok is widely considered one of the most beautiful scenic gorges in Korea, with full, mature forest and a number of impressive waterfalls along a mountain stream that starts less than 1 km below Cheonwang-bong. The trail climbs more than 1,400 m in the 9.7 km hike.

* Byeoksong-sa 벽송사

Byeoksong-sa ("wall of pines temple") is a beautiful, small temple dating back to the Unified Silla Dynasty and boasting a three-story granite pagoda. Due to a lack of room for expanding the Byeoksong-sa site, nearby Seo-am ("west hermitage") was later constructed. Seo-am is an amazing palace of rock, with stupendous large stone carvings of all the principal Buddhist and folk-Buddhist deities.

Option 3. From Daewon-sa 대원사 H2 11.7km (6:30)

This trailhead starts at the temple of Daewon-sa, located about 11 km northeast of Cheonwang-bong. The temple itself is near the Yupyeong ticket booth 유평 매표소, at the end of a scenic 10 km valley road that travels west from Sancheong 산청 on NH59. Said to have been established in AD 583 by the missionary-monk Yeongi-josa, Daewon-sa is set amid beautiful forest and offers great views of the peaks running west to Cheonwang-bong. Its best known treasure is the pagoda built by great master Jajang-yulsa, which originally had nine stories; one was knocked down by Japanese invaders in 1592 and never replaced. Ancient legend has it that as a warning, the pagoda glows with a strange bluish light when Korea is in danger. On the other hand, when Korea is in good fortune, the temple compound is filled with a sweet hopeful fragrance, and the image of the holy sarira enshrined within the pagoda can be seen in a nearby pond. The catch is that all of these blessings can only be perceived by people with a very "clean" personal energy.

From Daewon-sa, the trail follows the mountain road, heading northwest for 1 km before turning southwest, away from the Daewon-sa valley and into the forest. From here, you climb about 500 m over the next 2 km of trail, crossing a ridgeline into a high gorge running between Sseori-bong Peak 써리봉 (1,602m) and a 1,470 m

Transport Info

Joining the trail at Daewon-sa: Buses leave the Jinju local bus terminal 진주시외버스터미널 for Daewon-sa temple 15 times daily, between 6:40 am and 8:30 pm.

peak to its north. Reaching the top of this gorge, you pass the Mujechigi-pokpo waterfall 무제치기폭포, 1 km from the Chibatmok Shelter 치밭목 대피소, one of the largest and most impressive waterfalls in Korea, well worth the two-minute marked walk. The shelter is small and sleeps 40 people. From there, a three-hour walk to Cheonwang-bong takes you south for 1 km to the summit area of Sseori-bong before turning west to Jung-bong 중봉 (1,874m), and then south for the final 1 km climb to Cheonwang-bong (1,915m), the "official" start of the actual Baekdu-daegan trail.

Cheonwang-bong 천왕봉 F3 → Jangteomok Shelter 장터목 대피소 E3

1.7km (1:00)

From Cheonwang-bong*, the trail heads off the southwestern side of the summit toward the neighboring peak of Jeseok-bong 제석봉. The 1 km walk between these two peaks is a welcome contrast from the grind up Cheonwang-bong, as it passes along a rocky trail that descends quite steeply in places. The walk can be completed at a leisurely pace in 40 minutes, as staircases and railings have been built to negotiate the terrain, enabling you to admire the view northwest over the expanding spurs of the ridge arching down into Hamyang-gun and south into Hadong-gun. The ridge is largely open, due to the high altitude, and dotted with large stands of the Korean yew tree (*jumok-namu*), an extremely tough hardwood species that can live for over 1,000 years and remain rooted to the ground long after it has died, creating a highland drama of skeletal landscapes—particularly in

Cheonwang-bong center from Nogo-dan

winter, when snow cloaks its emaciated limbs. The morose yew grows only in the highest reaches of the peninsula and is a feature you will encounter on occasions when the trail passes through the harsher climate this tree prefers, above 1,200 m. After reaching Jeseok-bong, the trail continues southwest across rocky terrain for 700 meters, dropping 100 m to the Jangteomok Shelter.

* Cheonwang-bong ("Heavenly King Peak") 천왕봉 F3

At 1,915 m, Cheonwang-bong stands higher than any other peak on the South Korean mainland. It is a mighty summit, dominated by a prehistoric mound of high, gnarly rock, atop which stands a thumb-shaped tablet bearing its name. In favorable conditions, the view from the peak is spectacular, offering panoramic views of blue ridges that give the foreign hiker a scary and wondrous illustration of the mountainous nature of the peninsula into which they are about to venture! Guarding Cheonwang-bong are mainland Korea's second and third highest peaks: Jung-bong (1,874m), 800 meters to the northeast, and Jeseok-bong (1,808m), 1 km to the southwest.

* Navigation from Cheonwang-bong

From Cheonwang-bong, you can see the first large chunk of the Baekdu-daegan as it winds its way southwest to Jeseok-bong, then another 3 km to Chotdae-bong 촛대봉 (1,703m), before heading west for 10 km to Myeongseon-bong 명선봉 (1,586m) at 275°W, where it then turns southwest. The lofty peak of Banya-bong 반야봉, at 1,732 m ABSL, lies about 4 km directly behind Myeongseon-bong. If you can see as far as Banya-bong, then you should be able to see at 275°W the 1,507 m peak of Nogo-dan 노고단 a good 21 km away from your current location on Cheonwang-bong. Inspiring stuff!

LODGING

Jangteomok Shelter (T. 016-852-1426) sleeps 150 people and is located at a four-way junction in a saddle between Jeseok-bong and Yeonha-bong. The name "Jangteomok" originates from its past as a high country market area where the people of Sicheon-myeon 시천면, in Sancheong-gun to the southeast, traded on foot with those of Macheon-myeon 마천면, in Hamyang-gun to the north. A notice board near the shelter shows an illustration of the old market. Jangteomok is a nice spot to rest at and a good location to end the first day. Outside the main building is a decked area with a number of picnic tables to accommodate day trippers who use Jangteomok as a lunch spot. The sleeping quarters are located up the stairs on the first floor, as is the office, which serves as a kiosk. A large cooking area is located on the ground floor, and toilets are at the rear of the building. Fresh water(2) is available from the Sanhui-saem spring 산희샘, which begins its flow 10 meters down the southeast track.

JIRI-SAN NATIONAL PARK 지리산 국립공원

Jiri-san was designated Korea's first national park on December 29, 1967, and it remains the country's largest national park in land area, , covering 471.758 km². Its summit, Cheonwang-bong, soars to 1,915 m ABSL and is the highest on mainland South Korea, second only to Halla-san (1,950m) on the southern island of Jeju-do. Cheonwang-bong is flanked by the peaks of Jung-bong (1,874m) to the northeast and Jeseok-bong (1,808m) to the west, which are respectively the second and third highest peaks on the mainland. These high peaks are by no means alone, as Jiri-san is home to scores of peaks over 1,000 m ABSL, of which the Baekdu-daegan trail crosses more than 21. The name "Jiri" is a Buddhist-based term meaning "exquisite wisdom," a spiritual wisdom that is above the ordinary, refined, precious and rare, and nowhere in Korea is there a greater concentration of religious sites than within the boundaries of the Jiri-san area, where there may be more than a hundred Buddhist, shamanic, Neo-Confucian and even Christian temples, shrines and prayer camps dotting the myriad ridges and valleys.

The park is also South Korea's largest area of refuge for wild animals. Buoyed by the photographing of a surviving native "half-moon" Asiatic black bear in 2000, the Korea National Parks Authority has released some captive-bred bears into the park. The bear reintroduction program has been underway since 2001, with the released population currently standing at 11. The hope is that this very low gene pool will be boosted by an Asiatic black bear restoration camp and sanctuary located at Deoggunnae in Gurye-gun, in the southwest of the park. Plenty of Korea's other native species of fauna and flora flourish on these vast slopes.

More to the point, Jiri-san National Park is the starting point for the Baekdu-daegan trail and for all hikers walking north toward the end of the ridge in South Korea at Jinbu-ryeong Pass, 735 km later.

 Lodgings in Jiri-san on the Baekdu-daegan

Camping is forbidden throughout Jiri-san National Park, except at Jungsan-ri (see below). Hikers must stay in one of the shelters that dot the ridge. Along the Baekdu-daegan Trail, there are five shelters:

1. Jangteomok Shelter 장터목 대피소 (T. 055-972-7772), sleeping 135
2. Seseok Shelter 세석 대피소 (T. 055-972-7772), sleeping 190
3. Byeokso-ryeong Shelter 벽소령 대피소 (T. 055-972-7772), sleeping 120
4. Yeonha-cheon Shelter 연하천 대피소 (T. 063-625-1586), sleeping 35
5. Nogo-dan Shelter 노고단 대피소 (T. 061-783-1507), sleeping 108

Sleeping at these shelters costs 8,000 won per person during the busy months of April, May, July, August, October and November, and 7,000 won in other months. The Yeonha-cheon Shelter is an exception, costing 5,000 won a night year-round. Bookings can be made online at http://english.knps.or.kr.

DAY 2

From Jangteomok Shelter to Byeokso-ryeong Shelter

• **Distance:** 9.5km
• **Time:** 4hr 40min

For those who have endured the steep climb to Cheonwang-bong, the next section of walking to Byeokso-ryeong Shelter is a welcome relief to tired legs and a good chance to admire panoramic views from rare vantage points. The 9.5 km walk between these two shelters sees the trail cross the summits of six peaks, all of which are over 1,500 m in height. The popular and distinctive ridge-top path is impossible to stray from accidentally. Heading over Yeonha-bong, you walk southwest to Chotdae-bong before descending west to Seseok Shelter, which is set among a field of royal azaleas that bloom pink in the early summer and, according to legend, mourn the childless woman who tended them before turning to stone on nearby Chotdae-bong (Candlestick Peak). From the shelter, the trail continues west, crossing Deokpyeong-bong, before descending onto an old mountain road to the Byeokso-ryeong Shelter.

Jangteomok Shelter 장터목 대피소 E3 → Seseok Shelter 세석 대피소 D3 — 3.4km (1:50)

From Jangteomok, the trail leads southwest, ascending gently for 800 meters to the summit of Yeonha-bong 연하봉 at 1,730 m ABSL. From there, the trail continues southwest again for 500 meters before turning south on a gentle climb toward the eastern side of Samsin-bong 삼신봉 another 500 meters away. After that, it's good walking for the next 800 meters, providing occasional views down the southeastern gorge to your left before reaching a signpost located near the summit of Chotdae-bong* at 1,703 m ABSL. Projecting from the southern face of the peak is a large rocky outcrop, providing good views down to Seseok Shelter and the Seseok-pyeongjeon field 세석 평전 of royal azaleas.

* Chotdae-bong 촛대봉 E3

Chotdae-bong means "Candlestick Peak," and a translation found at its summit describes how, once upon a time, a childless couple lived in the nearby Daeseong Valley. One day, a bear visited the woman and told her of a secret spring that could make women fertile. This excited her greatly, and she ran to the spring and drank thirstily. A tiger, seeing that the bear had given away the secret, rushed to the Mountain Spirit, informing her of the bear's disloyalty. Enraged by the news, the Mountain Spirit locked the bear in a cave and forced the woman to work by herself in the stony azalea fields at Seseok. From that day on, the woman cried as she worked and cursed her miserable existence alone among the flowers. The red-specked royal azaleas of Seseok, having being sprinkled with the blood of the woman's fingers, are said to be mournful, filled with the woman's pain, opening and closing sadly. The woman turned to stone and can now be seen at night, sitting atop Chotdae-bong, holding a lit candle and yearning for forgiveness.

Mountain Spirit and a tiger

Seseok Shelter 세석 대피소 D3 → Deokpyeong-bong 덕평봉 C3

3.7km (1:50)

The trail continues west from Seseok Shelter, climbing 500 meters to Yeongsin-bong 영신봉 (1,651m). The area on both sides of the trail leading to the peak is clear of tall forest, with alpine bamboo sprouting as the primary growth between

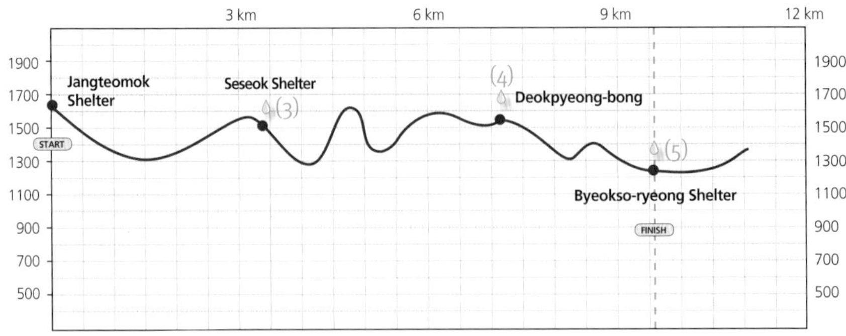

WATER STOPS

(3) Seseok Shelter: **N35°19'04" E127°41'35"**
(4) Seonbi-saem (Deokpyeong-bong): **N35°19'15" E127°39'42"**
(5) Byeokso-ryeong Shelter: **N35°19'34" E127°38'33"**

azalea trees. From the peak, the trail turns northwest, descending steeply along an impressive staircase that winds its way through and above the high alpine forest line, clutching onto the northern flank of the ridge, where it then turns west, dispersing and becoming a trail that gently ascends for the next kilometer to Chilseon-bong 칠선봉 (1,576m). The summit area of Chilseon-bong is marked by a signpost jutting out from a peak consisting of large rocky outcrops that point to the sky, providing you with expansive southern views. After descending west for 500 meters, you begin walking on an easy gradient for the next kilometer before turning north to the peak of Deokpyeong-bong at 1,522 m ABSL. Water(4) is available from the Seonbi-saem spring 선비샘, which is easily visible below Deokpyeong-bong.

LODGING

Located in a large saddle between Yeongsin-bong to the west and Chotdae-bong to the east, Seseok Shelter (T. 016-346-1601) is the largest in Jiri-san National Park, sleeping 220 people. For weekend stays, internet or phone bookings are advised. The outside area, much of it covered, consists of large tables that offer excellent views to the southeast. Water(3) is available from a spring near the shelter.

Deokpyeong-bong 덕평봉 C3 → Byeokso-ryeong Shelter 벽소령 대피소 B3

2.4km (1:00)

From Deokpyeong-bong, you descend north and then veer northwest as the ridge sweeps for 500 meters around a deep gorge to the southwest. The gorge leads down to the village of Daeseong-ri 대성리, the home of the unfortunate woman immortalized in stone on Chotdae-bong. At the head of the gorge, the trail then turns southwest, joining an old mountain road and following it for 1 km to the Byeokso-ryeong Shelter. Looking down the southern face of the ridge, you can see this old road snaking high up the steep valley on what looks like impassable land.

LODGING

Byeokso-ryeong is located in a saddle between Deokpyeong-bong (1,522m) and Hyeongje-bong 형제봉 (1,452m), at the top of an old route between the counties of Hadong-gun to the south and Hamyang-gun to the north. Byeokso-ryeong Shelter (T. 016-852-1426), facing southeast, sleeps 190 persons and is equipped with a kitchen area and water supply(5), both of which are located at the rear of the shelter. The toilets are connected to the west side of the main building by a platform of decking. The location offers stunning views of the early morning sunrise, and National Parks also claim that watching the moonrise over Byeokso-ryeong is one of the "ten most beautiful landscapes" that you will see in Jiri-san. The famous Korean poet Ko Un (Go Eun) reinforces this claim:

"When a full moon sits above from the dusky mountain-top,
The moonlight silently scatters far and wide.
The scenery is so breathtaking,
You cannot see it in any other place in this world."

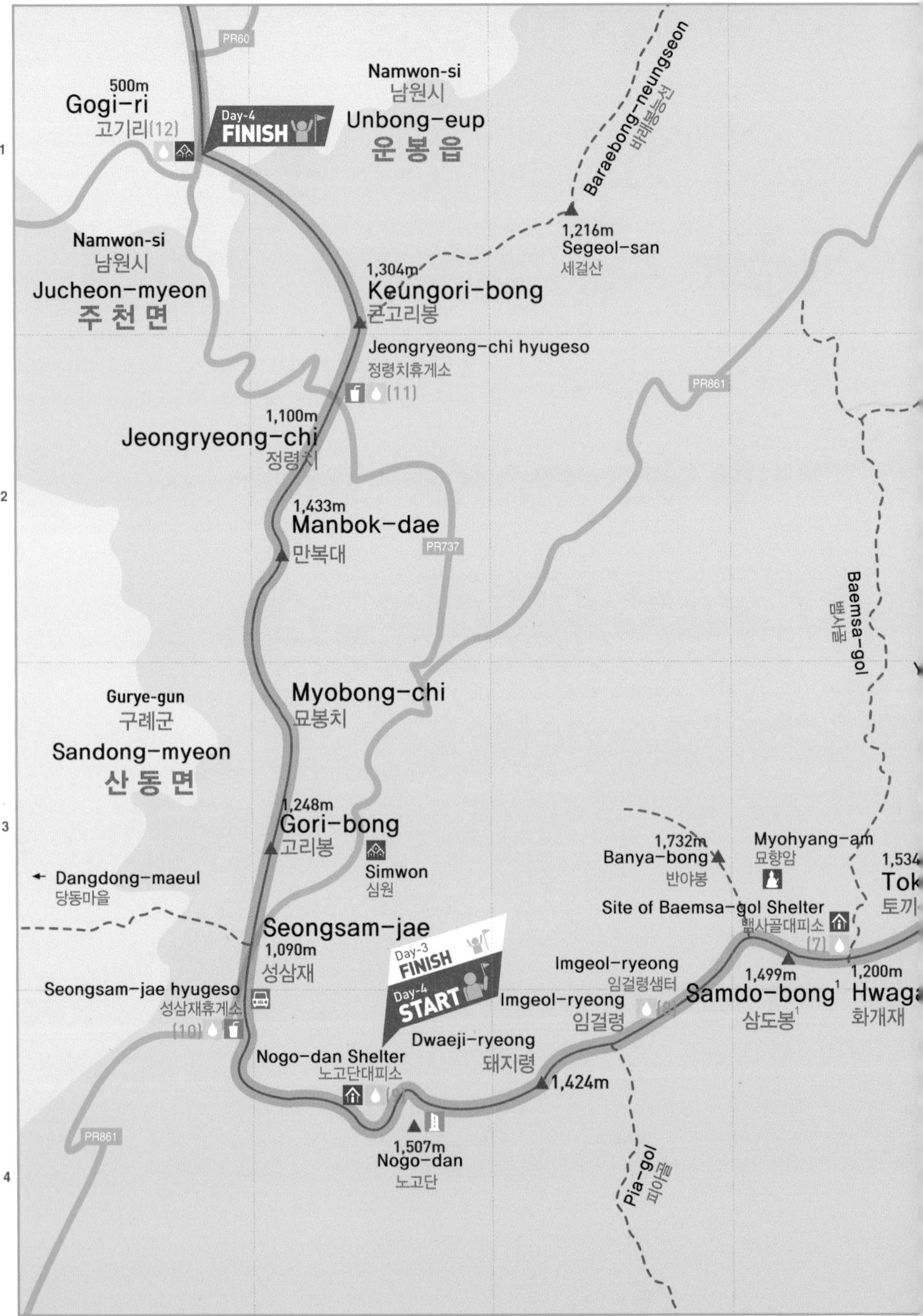

A
B
C
D
1
2
3
4
PR60
500m
Gogi-ri
고기리(12)
Day-4
FINISH
Namwon-si
남원시
Unbong-eup
운봉읍
Baraebong-neungseon
바래봉능선
1,216m
Segeol-san
세걸산
Namwon-si
남원시
Jucheon-myeon
주천면
1,304m
Keungori-bong
큰고리봉
Jeongryeong-chi hyugeso
정령치휴게소
(11)
PR861
1,100m
Jeongryeong-chi
정령치
1,433m
Manbok-dae
만복대
PR737
Baemsa-gol
뱀사골
Gurye-gun
구례군
Sandong-myeon
산동면
Myobong-chi
묘봉치
1,248m
Gori-bong
고리봉
Simwon
심원
1,732m
Banya-bong
반야봉
Myohyang-am
묘향암
Dangdong-maeul
당동마을
Site of Baemsa-gol Shelter
뱀사골대피소
(7)
Seongsam-jae
1,090m
성삼재
Day-3
FINISH
Day-4
START
Imgeol-ryeong
임걸령샘터
1,499m
Samdo-bong[1]
삼도봉[1]
1,200m
Seongsam-jae hyugeso
성삼재휴게소
(10)
Imgeol-ryeong
임걸령
Dwaeji-ryeong
돼지령
Nogo-dan Shelter
노고단대피소
1,424m
PR861
1,507m
Nogo-dan
노고단
Pia-gol
피아골

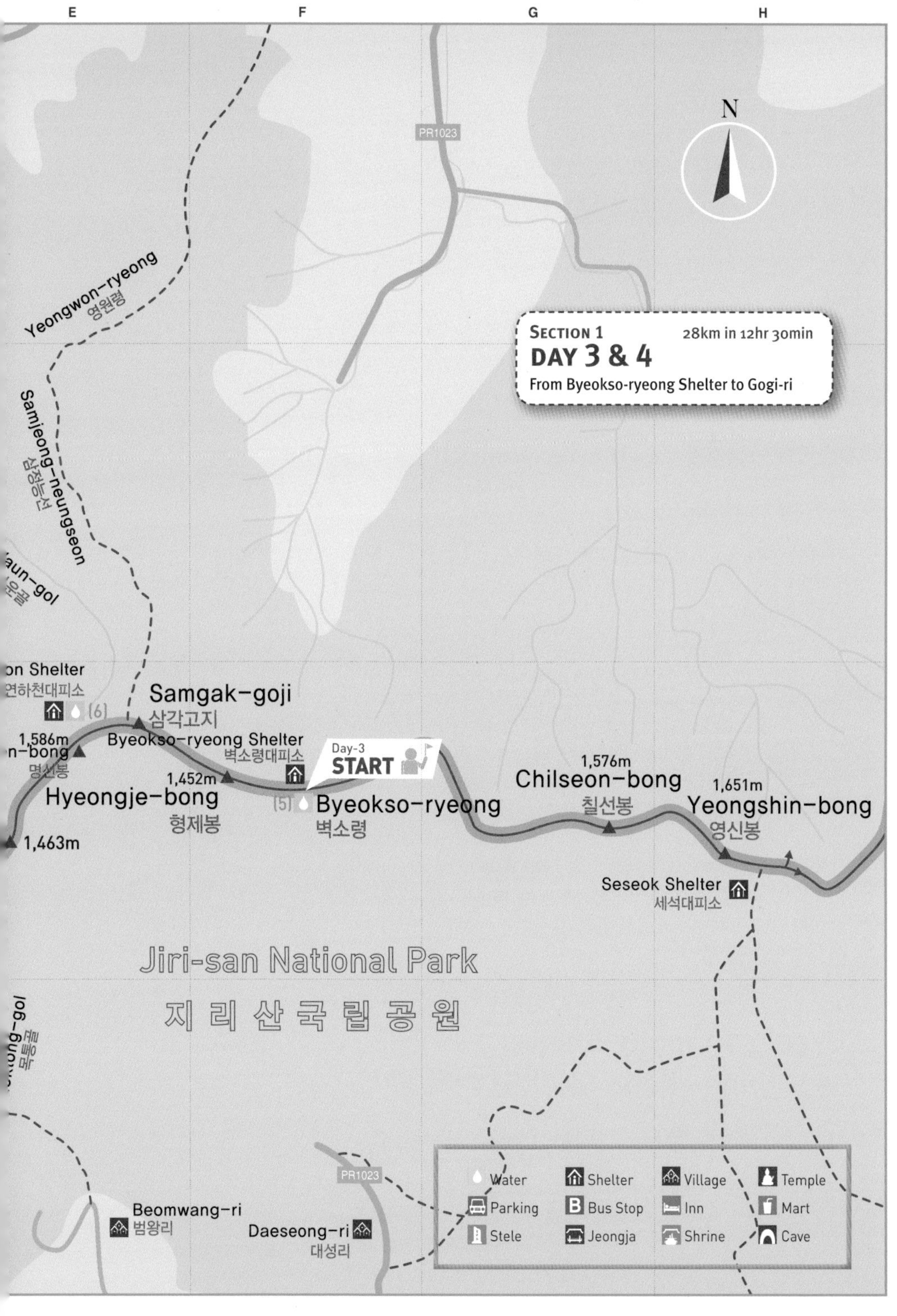

E
F
G
H
N
PR1023
Yeongwon-ryeong
영원령
Samjeong-neungseon
삼정능선
SECTION 1
28km in 12hr 30min
DAY 3 & 4
From Byeokso-ryeong Shelter to Gogi-ri
on Shelter
연하천대피소
(6)
Samgak-goji
삼각고지
1,586m
n-bong
명선봉
Byeokso-ryeong Shelter
벽소령대피소
Day-3
START
1,452m
Hyeongje-bong
형제봉
(5)
Byeokso-ryeong
벽소령
1,463m
1,576m
Chilseon-bong
칠선봉
1,651m
Yeongshin-bong
영신봉
Seseok Shelter
세석대피소
Jiri-san National Park
지 리 산 국 립 공 원
Beomwang-ri
범왕리
Daeseong-ri
대성리
PR1023
Water
Shelter
Village
Temple
Parking
Bus Stop
Inn
Mart
Stele
Jeongja
Shrine
Cave

DAY 3

From Byeokso-ryeong Shelter to Nogo-dan Shelter

- **Distance:** 13.9km
- **Time:** 5hr 55min

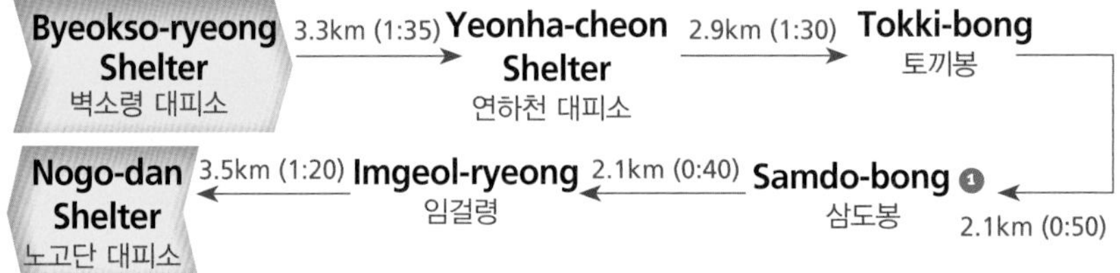

Leaving Byeokso-ryeong, and the jaffa glow of the early morning sunrise, you walk west on what will be the last day of the high east-west ridgeline. Crossing the next peak of Hyeongje-bong, you enter the thick green forest that cultivates its way to the charming rest area of Yeonha-cheon Shelter. From there, the trail turns southwest, crossing Tokki-bong and descending into Hwagae-jae above Baemsa-gol (the Valley of Snakes). Take a few deep breaths here before climbing a true marvel of mountain engineering, a grueling staircase that drags you to Samdo-bong (Three-Province Peak). Bypassing the mighty Banya-bong, you'll descend into the wide pass of Imgeol-ryeong, above the scenic Pia-gol gorge, then amble along a wide, popular trail to Nogo-dan Shelter in the shadow of Crone Altar Peak.

Byeokso-ryeong Shelter 벽소령 대피소 F3 → Yeonha-cheon Shelter 연하천 대피소 E3

3.5km (1:35)

From Byeokso-ryeong, you head west for 600 meters before climbing over a rocky knob and then turning northwest on a very rocky trail for 700 meters to the summit of Hyeongje-bong 형제봉 at 1,452 m ABSL. Progress can be very slow as you hike along this section, particularly over the final 400 meters before

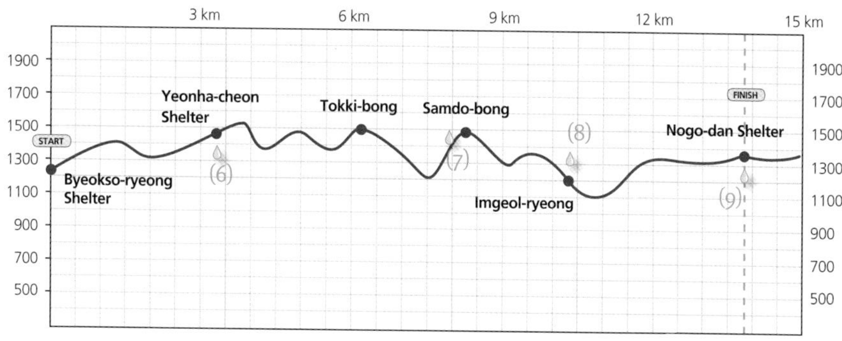

WATER STOPS

(6) Yeonha-cheon Shelter: **N35°19'42" E127°36'51"**
(7) Baemsa-gol Shelter: **N35°18'29" E127°35'09"**
(8) Imgeol-ryeong Pass: **N35°18'00" E127°33'46"**
(9) Nogo-dan Shelter: **N35°17'45" E127°31'35"**

reaching the peak, where basic scrambling over Hyeongje-bong's rocky southeastern face is occasionally required. Hyeongje-bong is a pretty peak, housing impressive rocky outcrops that support crags of pines, and it is one of the best vantage points along the Jiri-san trail for taking in northern views. From the peak, you look northwest down a long spur of the ridge called the Samjeong-neungseon 삼정능선, above Macheon-myeon 마천면. To the immediate northeast and east, your eyes can follow a large chunk of the ridge back to Cheonwang-bong looming in the distance. From Hyeongje-bong, the trail descends west for 500 meters into a saddle before joining a staircase and climbing northwest for a further 500 meters to a point called Samgak-goji 삼각고지 ("triangle highland"), where the Baekdu-daegan and Samjeong-neungseon ridges meet. From the southwestern vertex of the triangle, the trail descends into thick, rich forest for 700 meters before reaching Yeonha-cheon Shelter 연하천 대피소, which is located at the head of the Waun-gol stream 와운골. This section of the trail is known to be inhabited by a population of eleven Asiatic black bears, and the trail is barricaded on both sides and marked with signs showing what to do if a bear is sighted.

Nestled among dense forest on a northern bend of the Jiri-san ridge, the recently renovated Yeonha-cheon Shelter (T. 063-625-1586) is a quaint rest area for 40 people. The stone hostel is privately run by a friendly old mountain man, and the area's ambience is laid back compared to that of other, manically overcrowded National Park shelters. Clear water(6) flows from the spring in front of the shelter.

Yeonha-cheon Shelter 연하천 대피소 E3 → Tokki-bong 토끼봉 D3 2.9km (1:30)

From Yeonha-cheon Shelter, the trail turns south for 500 meters, joining a staircase that bypasses the peak of Myeongseon-bong 명선봉 (1,586m) east of the trail. As it passes Myeongseon-bong, the trail turns southwest for 500 meters before descending south on another staircase for 200 meters into a saddle, where it then ascends a similar distance in the same direction to an unnamed peak located at 1,463 m ABSL. From this peak, the trail turns southwest, providing great walking along a ridgeline dotted with azalea trees to the summit of Tokki-bong at 1,534 m ABSL. Tokki-bong mandates good views to the west, especially of the eastern face of Banya-bong.

Tokki-bong 토끼봉 → Samdo-bong ❶ 삼도봉 D3 2.1km (0:50)

From Tokki-bong, it's all downhill for the next 1.3 km as the trail descends southwest into the pass of Hwagae-jae, located at 1,200 m ABSL. The descent is fairly steep, but the trail is good and connects onto a boardwalk near the bottom. Located on the boardwalk is a viewing platform offering panoramas of the southern landscape over the Moktong-gol Gorge 목통골, which runs down into the village of Beomwang-ri 범왕리. To the north, a track becomes a steep descending staircase to the site of the now closed **Baemsa-gol*** Shelter 뱀사골 대피소. Water(7) can still be found at the spring by this old shelter.

* Baemsa-gol 뱀사골 D3

The legend of Baemsa-gol, meaning "valley where the snake died," tells how an ancient, but now non-existent, temple named Songnim-sa would hold an annual ritual every July where one selected monk would pray on the rocky platform used for mountain-spirit worship, subsequently disappearing and ascending into the heavens to become a spirit-immortal. One July, a skeptical but great priest named Seosan visited the temple to investigate this ritual. He smeared poison over the selected monk and waited keenly with other monks and townsfolk for the next morning to arrive. During the night, a large snake, nearly a dragon, leapt from the waters below the mountain-spirit rock and attacked the praying monk, disappearing with him back into the dark waters of the stream. At sunrise, Seosan, along with the townsfolk, headed smartly up the valley, eager to see what had become of the poison-coated monk. They found the dragon snake dead with half the monk's body protruding from its mouth. Seosan had discovered how to kill a dragon snake: by sacrificing monks! The valley has been called "Baemsa-gol" ever since. The small village at the end of the valley is called "Banseon," which, interestingly enough, means "half immortal".

From Hwagae-jae, the trail climbs steeply northwest, more than 250 m in altitude over a 600 meter section, to the next peak of Samdo-bong at 1,499 m ABSL. Through dense forest, the climb to Samdo-bong ❶ is done almost entirely on a modern, and quite impressive, elevated staircase that seems never to end as it snakes toward the peak. The name Samdo-bong means "three provinces peak," and it is the meeting point of Jeollabuk-do to the northwest, Jeollanam-do to the southwest and Gyeongsangnam-do to the southeast. A small cardinal marker at the summit explains the name, with illustrations. The Baekdu-daegan trail passes over another two "Samdo-bong" peaks on its route through the peninsula.

Samdo-bong ❶ 삼도봉 D3 → Imgeol-ryeong 임걸령 C4

2.1km (0:40)

Heading northwest, you dip briefly off the peak for 200 meters, reaching a tomb marking a hidden and closed track that heads north around the eastern face of Banya-bong 반야봉 for 1 km to the small and little-known temple of Myohyang-am 묘향암. From the tomb, the trail continues northwest for 400 meters to the Banya-bong junction, where it meets a junction where a track heads northwest

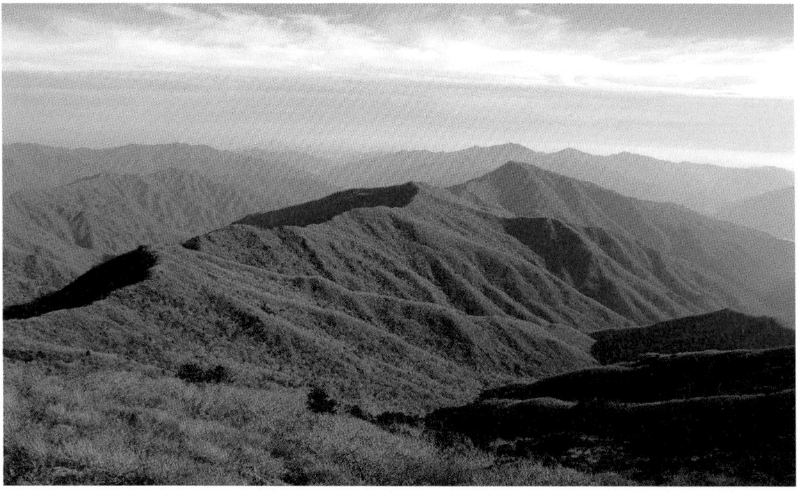

North from Nogo-dan

700 meters to the peak of Banya-bong ("prana wisdom peak"). Banya-bong (1,732m) is famous for stunning views to the northeast, and the return trip from the ridge takes about an hour to complete. Back at the junction, the Baekdu-daegan turns southwest on a path strewn with small rocks, descending gently for about 1.5 km into the wide pass of Imgeol-ryeong. At the pass is a large cleared area containing a south-facing viewing platform that looks over the scenic gorge of Pia-gol 피아골. Also at the area is a boardwalk that runs north to a steady-flowing(8) spring. The water from this spring is considered by many to be the purest in all of Jiri-san.

Imgeol-ryeong 임걸령 C4 → Nogo-dan Shelter 노고단 대피소 B4

3.5km (1:20)

From Imgeol-ryeong, you continue southwest on a well-walked path that heads through idyllic, thick highland forest, climbing gently for 1.5 km to an unnamed peak located at 1,424 m ABSL. From there, the trail starts to turn west, maintaining good height for the next 800 meters and traversing a helipad before arriving at the pass of Dwaeji-ryeong 돼지령. The pass is marked by an open area of low scrub, where it straightens to head west for the final 1.5 km to Nogo-dan Shelter. The trail itself zooms beneath the northern side of Nogo-dan* peak before arriving at a distinctive highpoint saddle called Nogodan-gogae 노고단 고개, marked by a *doltap* (cairn). To get to the well-visited altar of Nogo-dan from here, simply turn left and walk 500 meters southeast up the path. The track to Nogo-dan altar has restricted entry and is currently open only four times a day, at 10:30 am, 1 pm, 2:30 pm and 4 pm.

* Nogo-dan 노고단 B4

Nogo-dan (1,507m) is famous for its huge stone towers and commanding view over most of Jiri-san. The name translates as "crone altar" and refers to a female mountain-spirit regarded as the mythical mother of the founder-king of the Silla Dynasty. She was revered as a guardian deity of the nation, and memorial rites to her were traditionally held every spring and autumn at Nogo-dan. Near the shelter, below the peak, are ruins of stone-walled buildings built by American Protestant missionaries in the early 20th century as a summer retreat. These were later used as a base for communist partisan guerrillas during the Korean War, and they were destroyed in fighting. Remains of the buildings can be seen from Nogodan-gogae as you walk down to the shelter.

Top of Nogo-dan

Lodging

The newly renovated Nogo-dan Shelter (T. 061-783-1507) sleeps 180 people and marks the endpoint of the east-west ridge of Jiri-san. Hot coffee and basic amenities can be bought from the kiosk attached to the administration office. It has a large, detached cooking area with water[9], seating and a modern toilet block with flushables. The shelter also houses a small museum illustrating the earlier hunting of tigers and bears in the area, which is now trying to reintroduce the Asiatic black bear. Nogo-dan Shelter is also a common trailhead or endpoint for hikers walking the east-west Jiri-san ridge.

DAY 4

From Nogo-dan Shelter to Gogi-ri

• **Distance:** 14.1km
• **Time:** 6hr 10min

Whether you're taking the road or walking the ridge, your first stop after leaving Nogo-dan Shelter is the Seongsam-jae Hyugeso, a hugely popular rest area on a high mountain road. It serves hot meals and cold drinks and provides a rewarding conclusion to a few days in the hills. With ice cream still on your lips, you cross the road and go back onto a ridgeline that is isolated and arid on its 5 km route to the great peak of Manbok-dae. From there, you descend into another serviced rest area at Jeongryeong-chi pass before ascending to your last peak of Jiri-san and breaking left, tumbling down to the snoozy charms of rural Korea at the mountain stream village of Gogi-ri.

Seongsam-jae Hyugeso 성삼재 휴게소 A3 → Manbok-dae 만복대 B2 4.9km (2:10)

The trail passes through the Seongsam-jae(10) service area, crosses PR861, and reenters the forest approximately 100 meters north of the parking lot. Once you're back on the trail, the conditions are markedly different from those encountered so far through Jiri-san. This area sees fewer hikers than the main east-west ridge, and the trail is much narrower, less defined, and enclosed in thick vegetation. From the road, the trail climbs steadily along a thin ridge for about

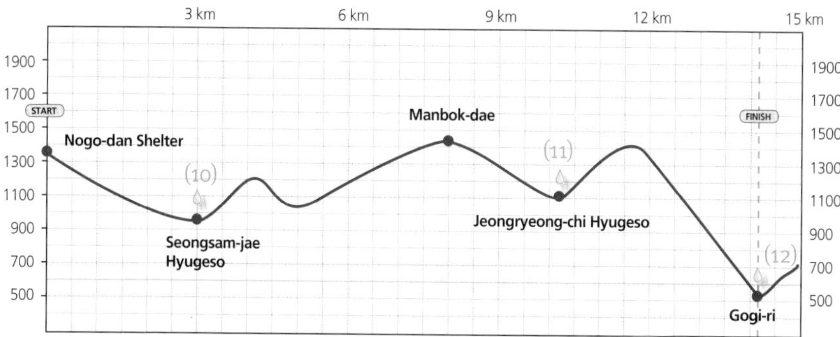

WATER STOPS

(10) Seongsam-jae: **N35°18'08" E127°30'50"**
(11) Jeongryeong-chi: **N35°21'35" E127°31'26"**
(12) Gogi-ri: **N35°23'00" E127°30'30"**

600 meters before reaching a junction marked by a signpost that indicates a westerly track to Dangdong-maeul Village 당동마을.

From the junction, the trail continues north on a steady 900 meter climb to the summit of Gori-bong 고리봉, at 1,248 m ABSL. From this peak, you enjoy good ridge-walking for about 1 km before dropping into a saddle named Myobong-chi 묘봉치, marked by a helipad. The trail ascends 300 m in altitude north out of Myobong-chi over 2 km, passing through young bamboo and weather-beaten deciduous forest before leaving the tree line and traversing open country to the rocky peak of Manbok-dae at 1,433 m ABSL. The summit area is marked by a large cairn and offers sweeping panoramic views. Manbok-dae also marks the last peak on the ridge over 1,400 m ABSL until you reach Deogyu-san National Park.

Manbok-dae from Nogo-dan

* Seongsam-jae 성삼재 B3

Located at 1,090 m ABSL, Seongsam-jae is connected to PR861, which runs 6 km southwest to the fields of Sandong-myeon 산동면, home to the Jiri-san Oncheon Hot Springs Resort 지리산 온천, and 20 km northeast into the stunning Simwon Valley 심원계곡. At Seongsam-jae, there is a small gift shop, a larger convenience store, and a good restaurant selling hot Korean meals such as *pajeon* (a seafood and vegetable omelet), *mandu* (steamed dumplings) and *udong* (thick white noodles), all to be doused with hot coffee, green tea, soda, or beer. The restaurant also has computers with free access to the internet. Outside and across the busy highway, the view from the pass is deep and spectacular. This area was once a strategic point for the chief of the prehistoric Mahan tribal federation (100 BC-AD 300), who had been chased by warriors of the rival Jinhan tribes. He built a residence below the pass in the Simwon Valley to the northeast and posted men on all surrounding ridges to look out for invading forces. He sent General Jeong to protect the west ridge, the pass now named Jeongryeong-chi (the pass that Jeong governs), and General Hwang to the East Ridge, now called Hwangryeong-jae. The south ridge, which begins at Seongsam-jae, was considered the most strategic point for defense of this area by those rival proto-states and the kingdoms that developed from them.

TRANSPORT INFO

Leaving the trail at Seongsam-jae: If you wish to leave the ridge from Seongsam-jae, buses run from the *hyugeso* to the town of Gurye-gun 구례군 15 km to the south. Buses leave the pass six times a day, at 7, 9, 11 am, 1, 3 and 6 pm, and the trip takes about 40 minutes. Returning to Seongsam-jae, buses leave Gurye terminal at 6, 8, 10 am, noon, 2 pm and 5 daily.

From Gurye, buses run to Seoul four times a day, at 9:10, 11:10 am, 2:40 and 5:10 pm. To Busan, they depart every 30 minutes from 7 am to 6:40 pm, and to Gwangju, every 20 minutes from 6:30 to 8:30 am. From Seongsam-jae city, buses run to Gurye, a fairly large town to the southwest.

Manbok-dae 만복대 → Jeongryeong-chi Hyugeso 정령치 휴게소 B2

2.2km (0:50)

From Manbok-dae, the trail descends northwest for about 500 meters before descending 2 km northeast to the pass of Jeongryeong-chi, at 1,100 m ABSL, passing one signpost and a fire tower on its way.

Jeongryeong-chi is named after General Jeong, defender of the Mahan warriors' western ridge. The Jeongryeong-chi pass is connected to PR737, which descends northwest for 12 km to the village of Gogi-ri, where today's walk ends, and southwest for 5 km, where it joins the PR861 in Simwon Valley below Seongsam-jae pass.

Jeongryeong-chi is a popular spot for Sunday drivers, with panoramic views off the ridge in both directions, and thus it has a large service area offering hot food, snacks and refreshments as well as a clean toilet block. The *hyugeso* does not offer accommodation, and it closes in the early evening. Above the *hyugeso* is a park containing some *jangseung* (Korean spirit-guardian poles) and a *jeongja* (a resting place with a roof). There is also enough space in this area to pitch a tent. Clean water(11) for washing and cooking can be obtained from the toilet block.

Jangseung

Buses do not run to the high pass of Jeongryeong-chi, so you will need to hitchhike or walk northwest down PR737 to Gogi-ri if you wish to leave the ridge and catch a bus.

Jeongryeong-chi Hyugeso 정령치 휴게소 B2 → Gogi-ri 고기리 A1

4km (1:50)

The trail continues northeast from the rest area above the restaurant, ascending 100 m over 1 km to the peak of Keungori-bong 큰고리봉, at 1,304 m ABSL. About 600 meters into your ascent, you pass the rocky remains of fortress walls that once lined this ridge. At the summit of Keungori-bong is a junction where a track continues northeast on what is the main ridge of Jiri-san, called Baraebong-neungseon 바래봉 능선, for 7 km to the famous peak of Barae-bong 바래봉 (1,165m), after which the ridge is named. Barae-bong is a beautiful peak, famous for its large fields of royal azaleas that bloom in early summer. However, from the junction at Keungori-bong at 1,300 m ABSL, the Baekdu-daegan trail becomes a spur and descends northwest off the peak for three steep kilometers to the pleasant village area of Gogi-ri at 500 m ABSL. From the junction, you descend very steeply and drop about 200 m in altitude over a 500 meter section of trail until it is obtruded upon by a rocky area. From here, the trail continues its descent northeast for the next kilometer, dropping to a height of 840 m ABSL, before dropping again north for 200 meters and then snapping sharply left and falling west for 500 meters, passing one tomb. After that, the trail turns northwest for the final 600 meters, passing two tombs, and then on to PR60 in Gogi-ri Village.

Gogi-ri is an idyllic village that sits on the junction of PR60 and PR737, nestled along the banks of a fast-flowing mountain stream(12) that sources its water from Manbok-dae, Jeongryeong-chi and Keungori-bong. PR60 connects the small town of Jucheon-myeon 주천면 8 km to the west (6 km southeast of Namwon), and the small town of Unbong-eup 운봉읍 7 km to the northeast. The trail exit at the bottom of the Jiri-san spur sees you stepping out of the forest and onto PR60 under a canopy of trees adorned with hiking ribbons. These colorful markers will become landmarks for the remainder of your Baekdu-daegan journey in South Korea. They are the spoor of previous hikers, and if you use and read them properly, they will become useful navigational tools outside the boundaries of National Parks, where their display is now understandably prohibited. On the south side of the trailhead is a modern toilet block in a small park marked by a row of stone memorial tablets, along with a raised, covered platform suitable for camping.

TRANSPORT INFO

Leaving the trail at Gogi-ri: Buses run west along PR60 from Gogi-ri to the city of Namwon eight times daily between 6:45 am and 7:55 pm. Buses heading north along PR60 run to the town of Unbong-eup.

LODGING

Gogi-ri is a popular rest spot for travelers coming in and out of Jiri-san National Park, and there are a number of restaurants dotted around the village, specializing in freshwater fish and mountain vegetable dishes. There are several *minbak* (homestay style accomodation) and restaurants along the main road running through this small village, including some directly opposite the trailhead. The Jeongryeong-chi Motel (T. 063-626-1011) is located 30 meters north along PR60, and another motel can be found about 1 km further north toward Unbong-eup, with an excellent restaurant in its basement.

FOUR DAYS

58.2km

SECTION 2

RURAL KOREA

Gogi-ri → Yuksip-ryeong

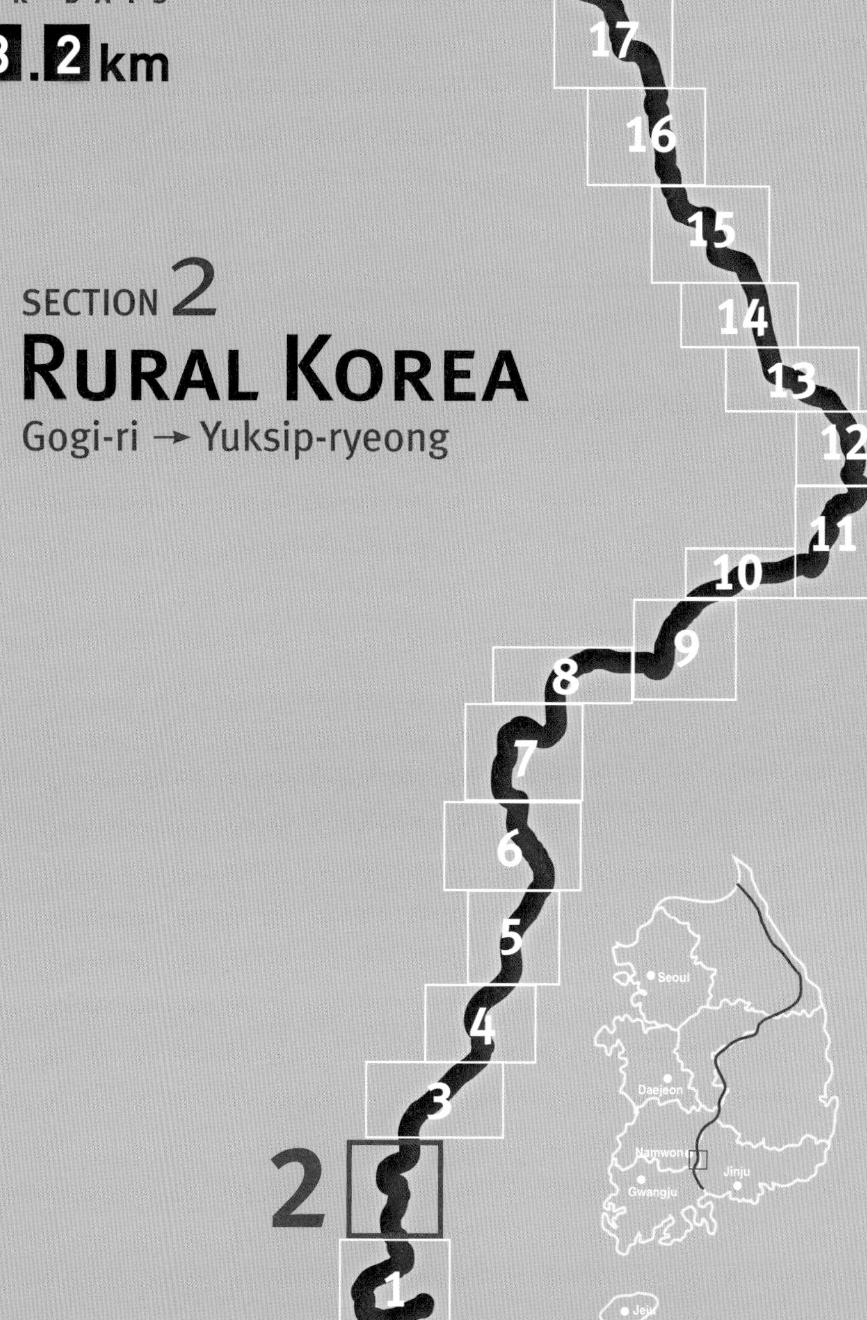

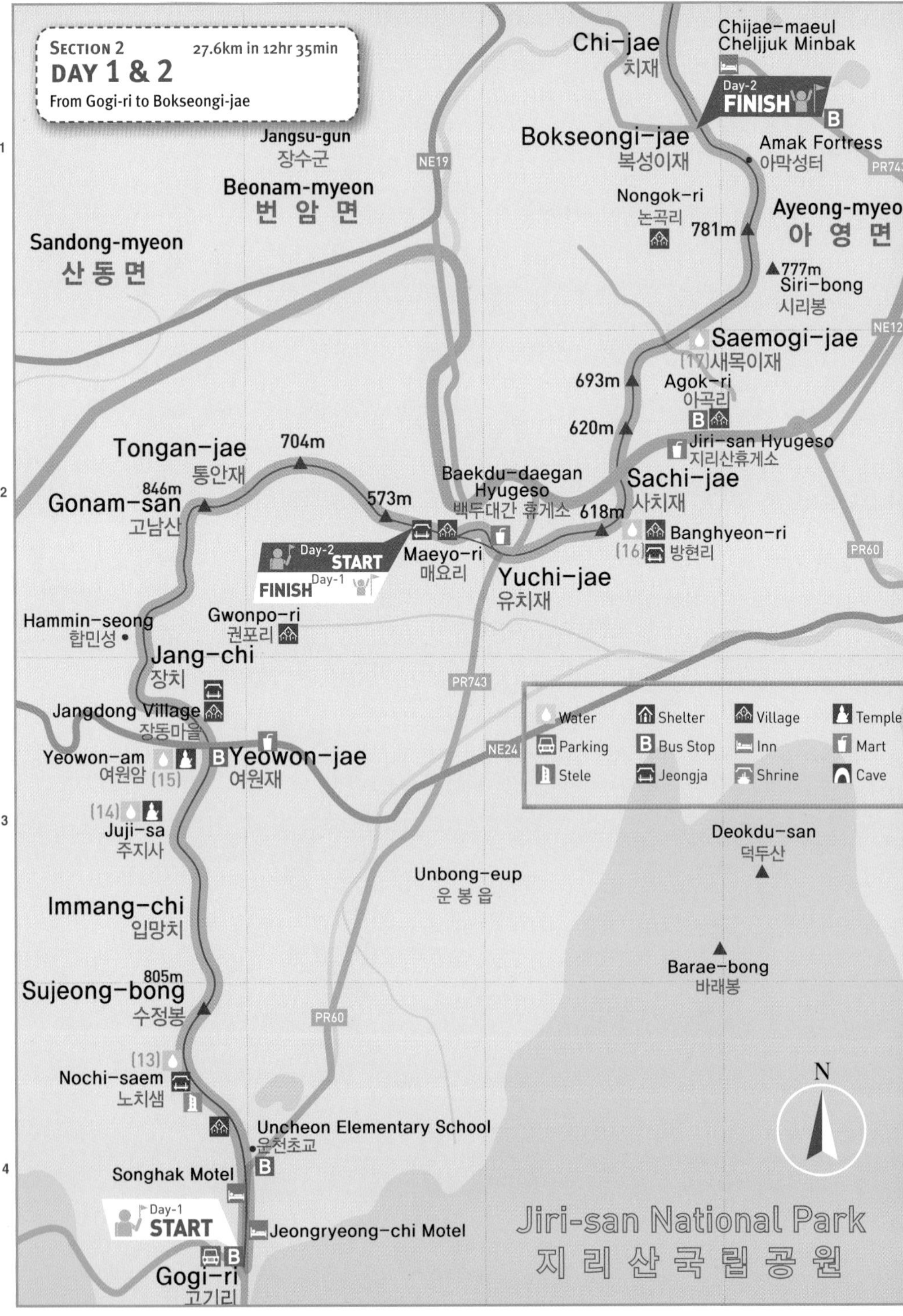
A
B
C
D
1
2
3
4
SECTION 2 27.6km in 12hr 35min
DAY 1 & 2
From Gogi-ri to Bokseongi-jae
Chi-jae
치재
Chijae-maeul Cheljjuk Minbak
Day-2 FINISH
B
Bokseongi-jae
복성이재
Amak Fortress
아막성터
PR743
NE19
Jangsu-gun
장수군
Beonam-myeon
번 암 면
Nongok-ri
논곡리
781m
Ayeong-myeon
아 영 면
777m
Siri-bong
시리봉
Sandong-myeon
산 동 면
Saemogi-jae
(17)새목이재
NE12
693m
Agok-ri
아곡리
B
620m
Jiri-san Hyugeso
지리산휴게소
Tongan-jae
통안재
704m
846m
Gonam-san
고남산
573m
Baekdu-daegan Hyugeso
백두대간 휴게소
618m
Sachi-jae
사치재
Banghyeon-ri
(16)방현리
PR60
Day-2 START
FINISH Day-1
Maeyo-ri
매요리
Yuchi-jae
유치재
Hammin-seong
합민성
Gwonpo-ri
권포리
Jang-chi
장치
PR743
Jangdong Village
장동마을
Yeowon-am
여원암 (15)
B Yeowon-jae
여원재
NE24
Water
Shelter
Village
Temple
Parking
B Bus Stop
Inn
Mart
Stele
Jeongja
Shrine
Cave
(14)
Juji-sa
주지사
Deokdu-san
덕두산
Unbong-eup
운 봉 읍
Immang-chi
입망치
Barae-bong
바래봉
805m
Sujeong-bong
수정봉
PR60
(13)
Nochi-saem
노치샘
N
Uncheon Elementary School
운천초교
B
Songhak Motel
Day-1 START
Jeongryeong-chi Motel
B
Gogi-ri
고기리
Jiri-san National Park
지 리 산 국 립 공 원

DAY 1

From Gogi-ri to Maeyo-ri

• **Distance:** 17.7km
• **Time:** 7hr 40min

As you leave Gogi-ri, the trail becomes the road before entering the charming village of Nochi-maeul, where you will see your first striking and impressive monument to Baekdu-daegan. After freshening up at the spring in the village, you cross the wooded peak of Sujeong-bong, with the option of visiting Juji-sa, near the ridge, before crossing NH24 at the ancient pass of Yeowon-jae. Skirting around the edge of a small farming village, you climb the brutally steep peak of Gonam-san, descending by its eastern spur and ending the day in the quirky little village of Maeyo-ri.

Gogi-ri 고기리 → Nochi-maeul 노치마을 A4 2km (0:40)

From Gogi-ri, the trail joins PR60 and heads north toward Nochi-maeul. The road is flat and provides a good chance to stretch your legs after spending a few days on hiking trails. Farmland, predominantly rice fields, dominates the landscape on both sides of the road, and after about 700 meters, you pass the Songhak Motel, which is on the western side of the road and has a restaurant attached. Continuing past the motel, the road reaches a sharp bend about 300

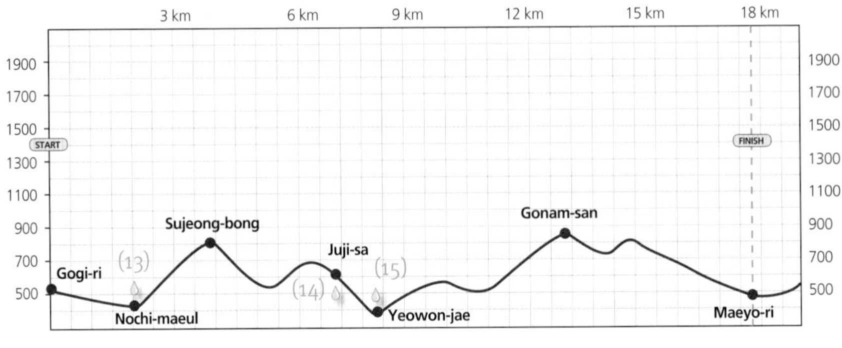

WATER STOPS

(13) Nochi-saem: **N35°24'00" E127°30'09**
(14) Juji-sa: **N35°26'22" E127°29'41"**
(15) Yeowon-jae and Jangdong village 장동마을: **N35°26'42" E127°30'10"**

meters later where PR60 turns northeast past a small bus stop and supermarket and heads on a further 5 km to the town of Unbong 운봉. At this distinctive bend, the trail joins the country road that continues north into Nochi-maeul*. After about 200 meters, the route passes a small health clinic located on the western side of the road and Uncheon Elementary School 운천초등학교 located on the opposite side, to the east, shortly after the road splits into streets that head to all of the houses in the small village. The route appears to veer mainly to the eastern side of the village, before turning northwest towards the center. The best way to find the right direction is to follow the trail of hiking ribbons left by past Baekdu-daegan trekkers.

Nochi-maeul 노치마을 → Sujeong-bong 수정봉 A4 1.8km (1:00)

Ribbons mark your way from the spring of Nochi-saem(13) 노치샘 into the pine forest, passing tombs overlooking the village. You climb steadily to the northwest on a thin trail that cuts through the pine forest, gaining about 200 m in altitude over a 700 meter section of trail before reaching the main ridge to Sujeong-bong. A small workman's hut stands near the trail, which at this point turns north toward the peak of Sujeong-bong (804m) on a gradual ascent through pleasant pine forest and passes a tomb moments before the summit.

* Nochi-maeul 노치마을 A4

In Nochi-ri, the Baekdu-daegan trail approaches an impressive spring with a regular flow, known as Nochi-saem. The spring was constructed with pride from concrete and granite by the locals. Just before that spring, there is a small four-way intersection, also marked by ribbons. The western arm of this intersection goes left to an impressive Baekdu-daegan monument located about 100 meters away. This was erected by the Namwon city government in November 2005, in recognition of the importance of the Juchon pass as the first pass of the Baekdu-daegan outside Jiri-san National Park, and thus practically the first on the 735 km trail. The large granite monument includes an engraving of the full Korean Peninsula, which highlights thc coursc of the Baekdu-daegan ridge and the ridges that which stem from it, known as *jeongmaek*. Around the central monument are three tablets engraved with information about Nochi-maeul and the Baekdu-daegan. Facing the monument, the tablet to the left tells the length of the Baekdu-daegan (1,470 km) and lists the names of the fourteen *jeongmaek* ridges stemming from it, as well as the ten great rivers it generates. The tablet to the right gives some history about of Nochi-maeul, describing it firstly as the one and only village through whose center the Baekdu-daegan passes. It then goes on to state that in the early period of the Joseon Dynasty, two clans, called the Gyeongju Jeong and Gyeongju Yi clans, moved here and founded the village. The village

BDDG monument at Nochi-maeul

was first named Galle because of the pampas grasses that grew on nearby Manbok-dae and Gori-bong, the gateway peaks to Jiri-san from here. After the Korean War, the village was completely burnt down as part of military operations to eliminate communist guerrillas hiding in Jiri-san. Behind the village, there is supposedly a mountain fortress that was built during the Later Three Kingdoms Period (AD 892-936). During this time, the village was on the border between Silla and Baekje; now it is a peaceful resting spot for the tired walker of the Baekdu-daegan.

Sujeong-bong 수정봉 A4 → Juji-sa 주지사 A3 3km (1:20)

From Sujeong-bong, the trail descends steeply northwest for 1 km, passing a helipad, before reaching the pass of Immang-chi 입망치, which is located at 580 m ABSL and marked by a small mountain road. The trail from there continues north, passing another tomb before arriving at an unnamed 700 m peak some 600 meters later. From there, it heads northwest for 500 meters before turning northeast and then passing another tomb. After another kilometer it meets a mountain road running over the ridge. The trail follows the road northeast, while the road to the west heads down toward the mysterious temple of Juji-sa. To get there, follow the western road, which soon becomes a path running for 250 meters down to the temple grounds, hidden in bamboo and thick forest. Like all temples, Juji-sa has an abundance of fresh water(14) available to all visitors.

Sanshingak at Juji-sa

Juji-sa 주지사 → Yeowon-jae 여원재 A3 1km (0:30)

Back on the ridge, the trail follows the mountain road for 25 meters before heading back into the forest on the right-hand side at a point blazoned with ribbons. From there, the trail flanks the road as you descend toward Yeowon-jae* Pass. Before that, the forest gives way to farmland, reaching a junction near some tombs overlooking rice fields. The trail continues north through the junction, following hiking ribbons to Yeowon-jae on NH24. About 50 meters before the pass is a small cement road heading west down to the hermitage of Yeowon-am*.

* Yeowon-jae 여원재 E3

Yeowon-jae is connected to NH24 and marked by a large totem pole, eyes bulging, that keeps watch over the Yeowon-jae pass. To the west lies the large city of Namwon, about 12 km away, and to the east the small town of Unbong 운봉, only 4 km away. On the northern side of the pass is the delightful communal village of Jangdong-ri 장동리.

There are no formal accommodations at Yeowon-jae. If you are looking for accommodations, it is advisable to head west to Namwon or east to Unbong. About 500 meters east of the pass is a *hyugeso* that sells hot food and cold beverages. On the northern side of the road is the village of Jangdong-ri, which has a proud wooden *jeongja,* or pavilion, located under a large tree at its center. This is a great place to relax and take in the sleepy rhythms of rural Korea. You may be able to sleep in this pavilion, with the permission of the locals.

* Yeowon-am 여원암 E3

Yeowon-am is an interesting little temple that appears to be privately-run. Its garden is lavishly adorned with all manner of Buddhist statues and figurines around a concrete lily pond. The main features are two shrines built into a large natural rock near the pond, one for the Sanshin ("mountain spirit") and another for the *Yongwang* ("dragon king").

TRANSPORT INFO

Joining the trail at Yeowon-jae: Buses leaving every 15 to 20 minutes during the day from Namwon to the west and Unbong-eup 운봉읍 to the east cross Yeowon-jae on their route and will stop at the bus stop in Yeowon-jae.

Yeowon-jae 여원재 A3 → Gonam-san 고남산 A2 5.1km (2:00)

About 100 meters to the west, the trail reenters the forest on the northern side of NH24 at a point marked by a large stainless steel plaque. Heading northwest into the tree line, the trail skirts around the western side of Jangdong-ri. In front of the *jeongja*, located in the center of the village, is a tablet describing the origins of the village's name. It states that the area is traditionally known to be tranquil, resembling a roe (female) deer taking a nap. For that reason, it was named *Norugol* ("roe town"), which is pronounced Jangdong when written in Chinese characters. Resembling the gentle traits of a roe, the people of this village are good-natured and polite, keeping the place peaceful. And on the rear of the plaque, a poem entitled "Jangdong-maeul People's Spirit" reads as follows:

We were born receiving jeonggi *(vital energy) from Gonam-san.*
We will strive to do good things.
We will cooperate, trusting each other with true hearts.
Someday we will say that we have made Jangdong a good place to live
With our wisdom and persistence.

Leaving Jangdong, the trail turns west and takes you to your first unnamed peak, 700 meters later, marked by a couple of tombs on its summit. From there, the trail turns northeast as it joins the southern arm of the ridge to the dominance of Gonam-san, which stands over the village of Gwonpo-ri 권포리 to its east. Gwonpo-ri has been a traditional center for the playing of the *geomungo* (Korean lute) since the time the Silla Dynasty unified the peninsula (668-935). It has been said that when the legendary *geomungo* genius Ok Bogo played the instrument, it touched even the emotions of animals, making horses and cows laugh in swinging melodies and dogs cry in sentimental tones. The tradition has been passed down through the generations, and the large modern building Unsangwon Sori-teo 운상원 소리터, which you may occasionally see through the trees to the east of the trail, has been built in Gwonpo-ri to keep the tradition alive.

From this area, you descend gently northeast for 500 meters to Jang-chi Pass 장치, where you continue northeast, passing a number of tombs and a steel pylon before the trail turns northwest to a point located above the ruins of the Hammin-seong fortress 합민성 to the west. There is no trail to these ruins. The trail then turns north for 500 meters before heading northeast along a relatively flat ridge for 1 km, providing occasional views over the fields of Gwonpo-ri to the east. After that, the trail straightens north as it approaches the summit of Gonam-san, assisted by fixed ropes and staircases on the final few hundred meters to the summit at 846 m ABSL. The peak area is marked by a fire tower and a small monument celebrating the mountain. Views from here are very good to the northwest over the Sandong-myeon area and southeast over Unbong-eup to the peaks of Jiri-san National Park.

Gonam-san 고남산 E3 → Maeyo-ri 매요리 B2 4.8km (2:10)

From Gonam-san, you walk northeast for 600 meters to a large, fortified building that appears to be a military communications base. From there, the trail initially follows a road that services the facility on the summit. The trail joins the road at least three times on its descent to the pass of Tongan-jae 통안재 about 1 km later. From the pass, the trail continues northeast for 500 meters before turning east for 1 km and passing another set of tombs. After that, it turns southeast towards a 573 m peak, from which it then descends east gradually for the next 1.5 km to the village of Maeyo-ri. Near Maeyo-ri, the ridge is crossed by a narrow country road, acting as an extension of PR743. You turn left onto that road in a northerly direction, which takes you on a loop around the back of Maeyo-ri before coming out at the village center and passing a modern town hall that serves as a central meeting place for the residents of the village. In front of the hall is a large wooden *jeongja*, fitted with enclosed glass windows, screen doors and electricity.

LODGING

The large enclosed *jeongja* in the center of Maeyo-ri is the only accommodation in this big village, and the area outside it is suitable for pitching a tent. Permission must be obtained from locals to sleep in the *jeongja*. Following the ribbons to the southern end of the village, the road turns east and passes a small store, known as the Baekdu-daegan Hyugeso, and marked by a small tree weighed down with a spectrum of hiking ribbons. The store sells snack foods, cold drinks (including beer) and basic camping supplies such as gas bottles and canned tuna. The store is run by an elderly woman who is known affectionately as the "Baekdu-daegan grandmother."

Gonam-san

DAY 2

From Maeyo-ri to Bokseongi-jae

- **Distance:** 9.9km
- **Time:** 4hr 35min

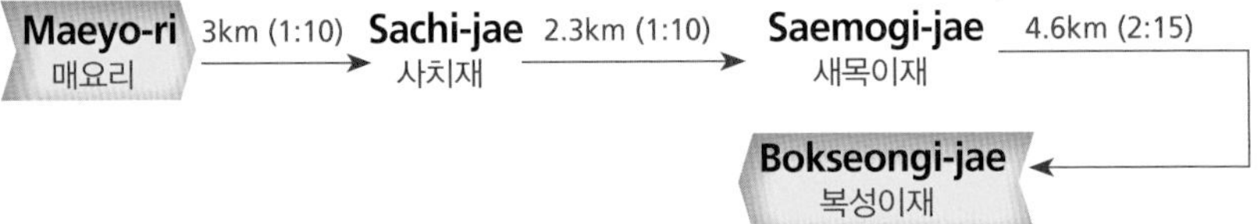

After a night in the small, quiet village of Maeyo-ri, you might stock up at the Baekdu-daegan Hyugeso and then head east out of town, and crossing the 88 Olympic Expressway above the Jiri-san service area. Gaining height north of the road, you walk through the mottled mountains of Korea on what feels like a back-country block. Near the end of your day, you reach your last high point and notice on the trail beneath you the broken rims of the Amak Mountain Fortress. The Baekdu-daegan escorts you right along the broken ramparts of its fortress walls before descending into Bokseongi-jae on PR751.

The village of Maeyo-ri

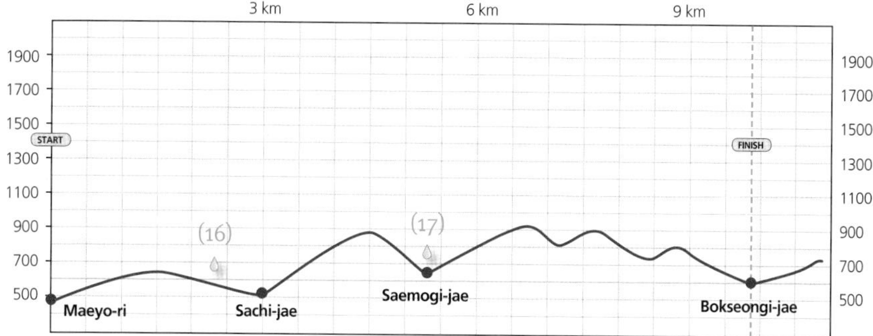

WATER STOPS

(16) Banghyeon-ri: **N35°28'16" E127°33'40"**
(17) Saemogi-jae: **N35°28'22" E127°43'14"**

Maeyo-ri 매요리 B2 → Sachi-jae 사치재 C2 3km (1:10)

From the Baekdu-daegan Hyugeso, the trail follows the cement road east for a short distance to where it meets PR743. On the northern edge of the road is a trailhead, marked heavily by hiking ribbons, that takes you for 300 meters into the forest before arriving at the pass of Yuchi-jae 유치재, also on PR743. From there, the trail splits, giving the option of turning left and heading north on PR743 or going straight on past a set of sheds, following the trail into the hills in an easterly direction.

Turning left at Yuchi-jae, the trail descends north along the road for 1 km before crossing under National Expressway 12 (hereinafter NE) and turning east for 800 meters through the small farming village of Sachi-maeul 사치마을 as it flanks the expressway. It then meets up with the main trail at the base of a hill, located on the northern side of the expressway. Sachi-maeul is a small place with no indication of services, except for a small *jeongja* where rest may be taken.

The *jeongja* of Banghyeon-ri

Heading straight at the Yuchi-jae junction, the forested trail heads northeast for 1 km, passing a number of tombs toward an unnamed peak of 618 m marked by a *doltap* (cairn). From there, the ridge begins turning to the north, where, about 400 meters later, the trail passes along the western flanks of a small village called Banghyeon-ri 방현리. A small detour to this village takes you to fresh water(16) and a great-looking *jeongja*, located on a piece of high ground between the village and the small country road running parallel to it.

* 88 Olympic Expressway at Sachi-jae

Shortly thereafter, you arrive at the pass of Sachi-jae, which is crossed by NE12, also known as the 88 Olympic Expressway. This road connects the cities of Gwangju in Jeollanam-do with Daegu in Gyeongsangbuk-do. It was built to commemorate the 1988 Olympic Games held in Seoul. The Olympic Expressway should not be confused with NH88 in Seoul, also known as the Olympic Expressway, or small PR88 in rural Yeongyang-gun, Gyeongsangbuk-do. The Olympic Expressway is a busy highway, and crossing it should be done with care, as pedestrians are not normally seen on Korean expressways—especially foreign ones lugging large packs.

About 500 meters east of where the trail crosses the expressway is the Jiri-san Hyugeso 지리산 휴게소, which serves motorists traveling on the expressway. This busy rest area is a worthy detour if you have a craving, as all manner of fast food, meals and drinks can be bought there. It's also a strange trip into the manic world of Korean expressway service areas, where loud trot music—the preferred musical accompaniment of Korean travelers—pumps from the speakers as visitors stretch their legs and eat ice cream.

Sachi-jae 사치재 → Saemogi-jae 새목이재 C2 2.3km (1:10)

After whisking you over the expressway, the trail climbs steeply north to a 620 m peak marked by a helipad on its flat surface. The summit area offers good views of Gonam-san 고남산, 6 km to the west and 6-7 km southeast to the large peaks of Northern Jiri-san National Park: Deokdu-san (1,149m) at 160° and Barae-bong (1,186m) at 165°. The trail drops northeast, heading through waist-high grasses, and then climbs over largely open ground for about 800 meters to a rocky 693 m peak. About 400 meters later, you reach a couple of old tombs, from which the ridge turns east and descends 300 meters down the trail to the pass of Saemogi-jae, marked by a junction. Water(17) can be located toward the southeastern side of the ridge by following the grassy road. Be sure to ignore the first right-hand fork and continue following the road down to your left for about 100 meters, or possibly further in dry weather. The streams intersect with the road.

Saemogi-jae 새목이재 C2 → Bokseongi-jae 복성이재 C1

4.6km (2:15)

Back at the pass, the trail climbs to the northeast for 1 km until it arrives at a helipad. From the helipad, the trail heads north for another kilometer to the highest peak of the Amak-san area, at 781 m ABSL, which offers good views to the west over the village of Nongok-ri 노곡리. From this peak, you can also see below you the Amak Fortress, located 500 meters north along a thin rocky ridgeline. From Amak Fortress*, the trail descends northwest for 1 km toward the pass of Bokseongi-jae.

Bokseongi-jae is connected to PR751, which descends northwest about 5 km to the town of Beonam-myeon 번암면 in Jangsu-gun and southeast 7 km to the small town of Ayeong-myeon 아영면. The eastern region below Bokseongi-jae claims to be the home of the younger brother in the famous "Nolbu and Heungbu*" Korean folktale.

* Amak Fortress 아막성 D1

According to information we found at the site, the fortress is 633 meters in diameter. However, this would appear unlikely on a ridge, and it may well be that the complex was once 633 meters in circumference, with walls 1.5 meter

Transport Info

Leaving the trail at Agok-ri: Buses leave from Agok-ri 아곡리, which is the small village located under the highway below the Jiri-san Hyugeso. You can get to Agok-ri by taking the small service road that runs to the *hyugeso*. From there, buses leave for Namwon four times day at 7:50 am, 11 am, 2:40 pm and 4:45 pm. From Namwon, buses leave for Agok-ri at 8:10 am, 11:40 am, 2:50 pm, 4:05 pm and 8:40 pm. Express buses running between Daegu and Gwangju often stop at the Jiri-san Hyugeso. It is also possible to take one of these buses and get off at the *hyugeso* if you inform the driver before departure, as not all buses stop at this rest area. It may also be possible to leave the ridge on one of these buses if you catch a friendly driver and the bus is not full.

Lodging

The Chijae-maeul Cheol-jjuk Minbak 치재마을철쭉민박 (T. 063-626-1307) is located about 800 meters northeast of the pass on PR751. This *minbak* has a small supermarket attached, as well as a restaurant that also acts as a local tavern. A further 5km down the road is the small town of Ayeong, which has a number of restaurants, as well as a supermarket, police station and medical center. On the western side of the ridge, about five road kilometers later, is Beonam-myeon, which lies below the artificial Donghwa Lake 동화호. Beonam is home to the Jangsu Hot Springs 장수온천, which have a tourist hotel attached as well as *minbak* accommodations. Beonam has an impressive new temple and memorial shrine to the celebrated patriot-monk Baek Yong-sung (1864-1940), who was born in the town.

thick, much like the ones the trail passes along. The fortress was built by the Silla Kingdom, which ruled the peninsula's southeast during the early Three Kingdoms Period, (50 BC-AD 668), to guard against invasion from the Baekje Kingdom, which controlled the southwest. The Baekdu-daegan formed the boundary between the two kingdoms. The fortress was the scene of battles between the Silla and Baekje armies before victorious Silla unified the peninsula in AD 668. One of the great stories associated with the Amak Fortress is the tale of Gwisang and Chuhang, two *hwarang* (flower-youth warriors) who died here, as first told in the book *Samguksagi Yeoljeon*. Gwisan and Chuhang, from Saryang District, visited the great master-monk Wongwang, seeking his advice on purifying their minds and regulating their conduct. The monk told them the five commandments of the Bodhisattva ordination for laymen: serve your king with loyalty, tend to your parents with filial piety, treat your friends with sincerity, do not retreat in battle, and be discriminating about the taking of life. The two vowed to always be true to these commandments. In 602, Baekje forces invaded Amak Fortress, with Gwisan and Chuhang fighting under Gwisan's father, General Muun. During the battle, the general ran into an ambush, falling from his horse. Gwisan ran to his rescue, killing a number of Baekje troops in the process. He returned the horse to his father and cried to the troops, "Now is the time to follow the commandment never to retreat in battle!" Chuhang fought alongside Gwisan, both of them dying on the battlefield, "bleeding from a thousand wounds." Because of their courage, King Jinpyeong posthumously granted them religious titles.

Tale of Nolbu & Heungbu

This is the tale of two brothers, Nolbu and Heungbu. Nolbu is older and wealthy, but has a wicked heart. After inheriting his father's riches, Nolbu sends his younger brother Heungbu out of the household, broke, to fend for himself. Heungbu, although poor, is a kind soul and finds a lovely wife with whom he shares a modest mountain home and a number of children. Heungbu later comes into fortune by helping a broken-legged swallow, which in turn gifts him with a seed that produces giant melons full of jewels. Upon hearing of his brother's wealth, the envious Nolbu purposely breaks the leg of a swallow and fixes it before setting it free in the hopes that he will be likewise rewarded. The swallow does indeed give Nolbu a seed, and it does grow melons; however, they're not full of jewels but rather bandits, who then steal all his belongings, burning his house down at the same time. This leaves Nolbu broke and remorseful...he goes to Heungbu's home to beg forgiveness and ask for help, and both requests are of course granted.

DAY 3

From Bokseongi-jae to Baegun-san

• **Distance:** 15.8km
• **Time:** 6hr 40min

From the peak of Bonghwa-san, you walk on an undulating open ridge that cuts through high grasses and then enters charming woodland before falling into the pass of Jung-jae. There you take a rest, collect water, and embark on a punishing climb through an emerald forest to the tops of the White Cloud Mountain—Baegun-san. Sleep out on its flat peak and enjoy the moon-lit night, alive and excited on this walk back in time.

Bokseongi-jae 복성이재 A4 → Bonghwa-san 봉화산 A3

4km (1:50)

From Bokseongi-jae, the trail crosses PR751, ascending north for 1 km through long grass and small bushes to a peak marked by a helipad. The area around this helipad is clear of trees, offering an expansive view to the west over Beonam-myeon 번암면, where the southern half of Donghwa-ho Lake 동화호 can also be seen. The trail briefly descends north from the helipad through a colony of azaleas to Chi-jae Pass 치재. From Chi-jae, the trail remains north on open ridge for 1.3 km, cutting through mountain grasses and azaleas to the next pass of Kkoburang-jae 꼬부랑재. Continuing north, the trail ascends 1.7 km up the open ridge towards Bonghwa-san at 919 m ABSL. At its open summit, great views can be seen in all directions above the grasses and small bushes. A large white stone

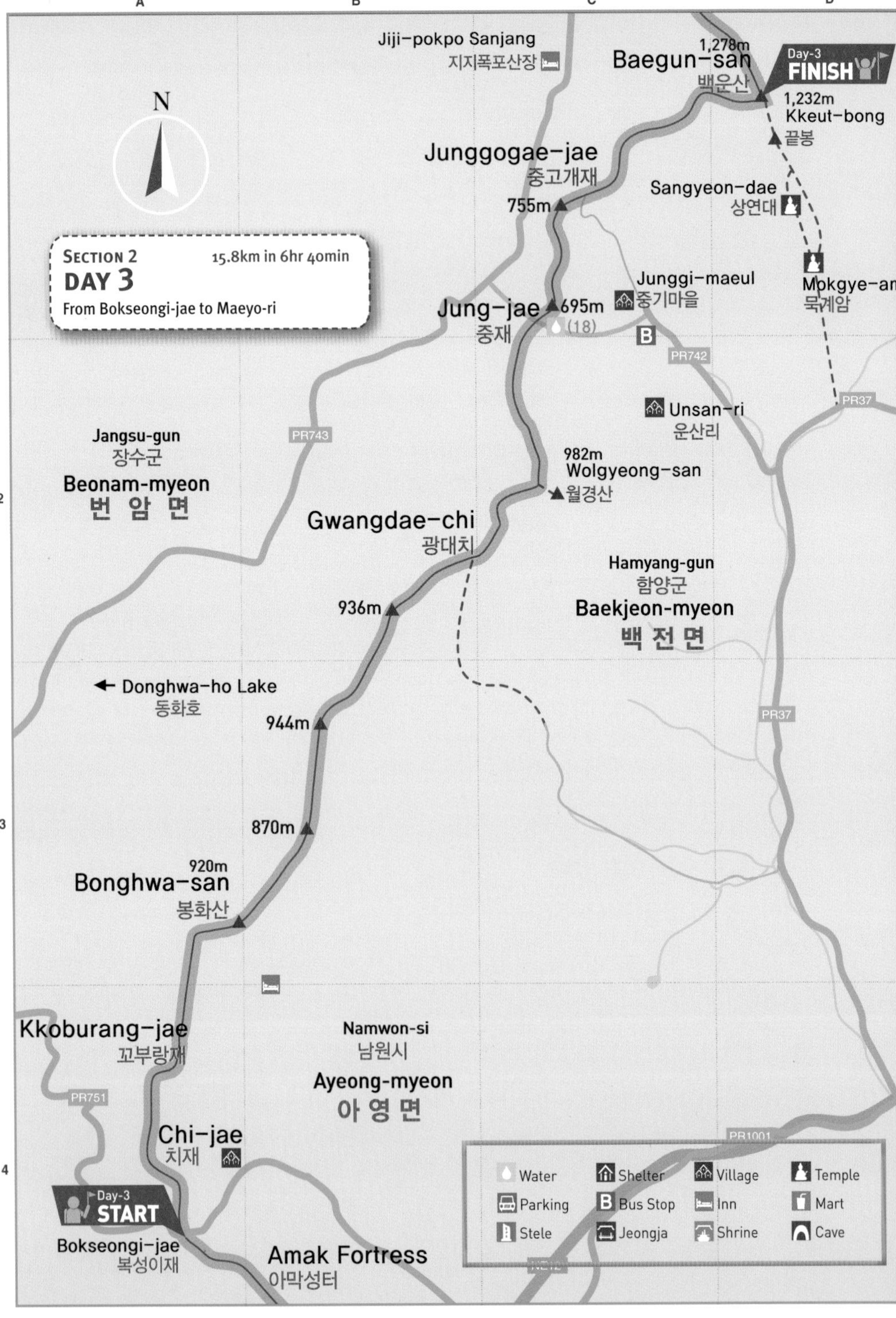
A
B
C
D
1
2
3
4
N
SECTION 2
15.8km in 6hr 40min
DAY 3
From Bokseongi-jae to Maeyo-ri
Jiji-pokpo Sanjang
지지폭포산장
1,278m
Baegun-san
백운산
Day-3
FINISH
1,232m
Kkeut-bong
끝봉
Junggogae-jae
중고개재
755m
Sangyeon-dae
상연대
Junggi-maeul
중기마을
Mokgye-am
묵계암
Jung-jae
중재
695m
(18)
B
PR742
PR37
Unsan-ri
운산리
PR743
Jangsu-gun
장수군
Beonam-myeon
번 암 면
982m
Wolgyeong-san
월경산
Gwangdae-chi
광대치
Hamyang-gun
함양군
Baekjeon-myeon
백 전 면
936m
Donghwa-ho Lake
동화호
944m
PR37
870m
920m
Bonghwa-san
봉화산
Kkoburang-jae
꼬부랑재
Namwon-si
남원시
Ayeong-myeon
아 영 면
PR751
Chi-jae
치재
PR1001
Day-3
START
Bokseongi-jae
복성이재
Amak Fortress
아막성터
Water
Shelter
Village
Temple
Parking
Bus Stop
Inn
Mart
Stele
Jeongja
Shrine
Cave

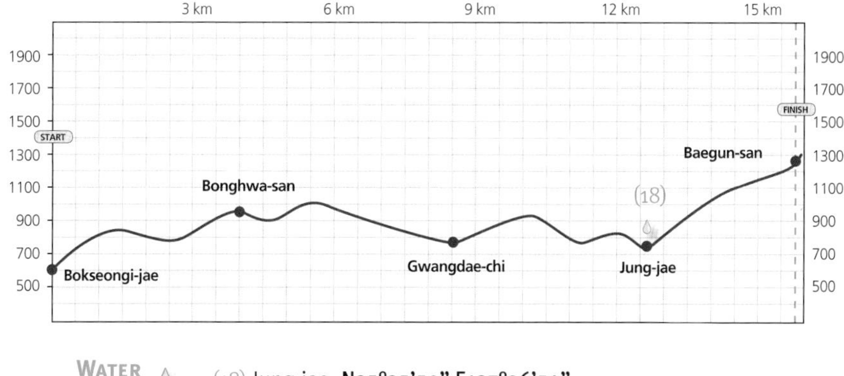

WATER STOPS (18) Jung-jae: **N35°35'50" E127°36'54"**

stele celebrating the trail also crowns the peak. Carved on its face is a map of the Korean peninsula, including the course of the Baekdu-daegan, indicting your paltry effort so far. On a clear day, it is also possible to see the high peaks of Jiri-san, including Cheonwang-bong, miles away to the southeast. The large peak 40° to the northeast, about 10 km away, is Baegun-san, the end-point of today's hike.

Bonghwa-san 봉화산 A3 → Gwangdae-chi 광대치 B2

4.5km (1:30)

From Bonghwa-san, the trail descends northeast, reaching a pass about 800 meters later that is crossed by the same mountain road that has followed the ridge from Chi-jae. At this pass is a Baekdu-daegan information board showing the course of the ridge through the peninsula. The trail continues northeast for 400 meters to an 870 m peak, then straightens to the north for 1 km along a good ridge to a 944 m peak. From there, the trail turns slightly northeast, where, about 1.2 km later, it reaches a peak standing at 936 m ABSL. From there, the trail becomes more densely forested, featuring occasional clumps of large rock and allowing stunted views to the west through the latticed tree line. The descent from the 936 m peak is initially very steep, with a sheer two-meter rope in place for the leap off it. Once off the rock, the trail stays northeast, descending gently for 1 km onto Gwangdae-chi Pass.

Morning views from Baegun-san

Gwangdae-chi 광대치 B2 → Jung-jae 중재 C1 3km (1 : 20)

The trail ascends northeast out of Gwangdae-chi, and 500 meters later reaches a well-maintained barbed wire security fence that, for no reason known to us, encloses a valley on the southern side of nearby Wolgyeong-san 월경산. You follow the ribboned fence north for about 50 meters before it marches away to the southeast, allowing the trail to continue northeast straight up the ridge towards Wolgyeong-san at 982 m ABSL. The trail doesn't cross the peak itself, but instead reaches a fork where the Baekdu-daegan takes the left path and heads north, beginning a 1.5 km descent into Jung-jae Pass.

Jung-jae is marked by a signpost and a set of benches put there by the Korea Forest Service. The pass is connected to a small mountain road that descends east 1 km to meet the end of PR742, where there is a bus stop. Water(18) can be found in a stream a short distance down this road. On the western side of the pass, water

Transport Info

Leaving the trail at Jung-jae: From Jung-jae, follow the mountain road 1.5 km east and you will reach the village of Junggi-maeul. Buses run from Junggi-maeul to Hamyang three times daily, at 7 am, 2:20 pm and 7:10 pm. A further 1.5 km down the road southeast of Junggi-maeul is Unsan-ri 운산리, located at the junction of PR742 and PR37. Buses run more regularly from here, leaving for Hamyang every 30 minutes between 7:05 am and 8:20 pm. Returning to the pass, buses to Junggi-maeul leave Hamyang daily at 6:20 am, 1:30 pm and 6:20 pm. To Unsang-ri, buses leave Hamyang at 30-minute intervals between 6:20 am and 7:40 pm.

can also be found down the mountain road where it eventually meets PR743 at a small village. Fueling up is recommended at Jung-jae, as the next section begins with a long, steep climb to Baegun-san with no water available along the way or at the summit.

If you are looking for accommodation, follow the mountain road west about 800 meters to PR743. The Jiji-pokpo Sanjang is located about 3 km north along PR743.

Jung-jae 중재 C1 → Baegun-san 백운산 D1 4.3km (2:00)

From Jung-jae, the trail begins climbing to the east, and after about 300 meters it reaches a peak of 695 m ABSL. From there, it turns north through beautiful green deciduous forest for 1 km to its next peak at 755 m ABSL, where it then descends east into Junggogae-jae Pass 중고개재. Tighten your boot laces, because now the real climb to Baegun-san begins. Heading northeast from the pass, the ascent is steady and unrelenting as the trail climbs 520 m in a 2.5 km stretch of walking. However tiresome it may be, the walk is beautiful, with occasional vantage points looking to the south and a full felt of verdant forest. Along its route, you will notice that the Korea Forest Service has done some work to aid the walker by cutting steps into steep areas and building benches for resting at some vantage points.

About 800 meters before reaching the peak, the trail turns to the east and onto a rocky surface for about 500 meters before reaching a flat, cleared area that houses two tombs—whose occupants must have had very good friends to carry them up to this majestic resting place! Near the tombs is a junction in the trail. To the right, a trail heads south about 700 meters to Kkeut-bong peak 끝봉 (1,232m)

The peaks of Jung-bong and Kkeut-bong

and continues a further 800 meters to the temple of Sangyeon-dae*, at a road end that runs a further 800 meters down to the Buddhist Nnunnery of Mukgye-am*.

* Sangyeon-dae 상연대 D1

Sangyeon-dae, meaning "sitting on the lotus" temple, was established in 924, near the end of the Silla Dynasty, as people believed that the mother of the great Confucian/Daoist sage "Go-un" Choe Chi-won prayed here before conceiving him. Later on, it became a stronghold of Silsang-seonmun ("true reality Zen Buddhism"), home to many great monks practicing spiritual discipline and religious purification. It was tragically destroyed by fire during the Korean War, but it was rebuilt immediately afterwards in 1953.

* Mukgye-am 묵계암 D1

Lying in a deep ravine, 800 meters down the road from Sangyeon-dae is Mukgye-am, a beautiful little temple with a large modern main hall set on an expansive grassy lawn. Mukgye-am is a tranquil place to rest and appears to be attended by female monks.

LODGING

Back on the trail, you head north from the junction with the tombs to the summit of Baegun-san (1,278m), which is less than 100 meters away. As you break from the tree cover, you walk out onto a grassy area where the grass is in some parts slashed down to ground level. If this is the case, then the large summit area will provide you with a great place to camp on what is a 360°-view mountain top. No water is found near the summit, so you should carry your own if you wish to camp. A large stone stele stands in the cleared area, celebrating the peak and the Baekdu-daegan. It states that Baegun-san means "white cloud mountain," and that there are over 30 peaks with that name in Korea, but this is the highest of them all. There are always snow and clouds on this mountain, where feeder streams of the Nakdong-gang and Seomjin-gang rivers originate. At the peak proper is a rocky mound marked by a signpost, standing next to a ribboned tree. Views from Baegun-san allow you to see south to the high range of Jiri-san and along the highest peaks of the ridge running to Bonghwa-san, now 10 km to the southwest. The view to the north gives you your first view of Deogyu-san National Park, where you may be able to see the two prominent peaks of Seo-bong ("west peak") and Namdeogyu-san ("south deogyu mountain"), forming the park's southern gate 15 km to the north. To the northwest lies the remaining ridgeline, protruding from the earth like the sharp edge of a dark piece of ocean jade. If you sleep on Baegun-san, get up early, and catch the sunrise, and see how the mountain lives up to its name as low fog and clouds seep through the valleys below like an incoming tide.

DAY 4 From Baegun-san to Yuksip-ryeong

• **Distance:** 14.8km
• **Time:** 6hr 40min

After admiring the spectacular morning view from Baegun-san, you head along the ridge to Yeongchwi-san above the groovy pass of Muryeong-gogae, where you can step off the ridge and drink some rice wine to the soulful tunes of an electric guitar plugged into a karaoke machine. Buzzing on local hospitality, you might want to pitch your tent and spend the night at the haunted pass. Heading on from Yeongchwi-san, you walk on a quiet section of the ridge that pops in and out of tree cover to Gitdae-bong. This last prominent peak allows you to study the sharp edges of Deogyu-san, the next national park area ahead of you. After that, wind your way down to Yuksip-ryeong Pass and enjoy the luxuries of the *hyugeso* there.

Baegun-san 백운산 B4 → Yeongchwi-san 영취산 A4

3.4km (1:30)

From Baegun-san, the trail descends northwest through ribbon-laden trees for the walk to Yeongchwi-san. For 3.4 km, the section of trail between these two peaks is covered with beautiful, mature forest and a dense blanket of mountain bamboo. The trail is quite steep for the first 500 meters, before leveling out and climbing over a rocky area. Staircases and guide rails have been installed to help you negotiate the terrain in places, as the trail continues northwest for 1 km before

A
B
C
D
1
2
3
4
SECTION 2
14.8km in 6hr 40min
DAY 4
From Baegun-san to Yuksip-ryeong
Yuksip-ryeong Hyugeso
육십령휴게소
Day-4
FINISH
(22)
Yuksip-ryeong
육십령
Odong-ri
오동리
Jangsu-gun
장수군
Gyenam-myeon
장 계 면
NH26
Jangsu-gun
장수군
Gyenam-myeon
계 남 면
1.014m
Gitdae-bong
깃대봉
(21)
PR3
Hamyang-gun
함양군
Seosang-myeon
서 상 면
Daegok-ho
대곡호
Min-ryeong
민령
Yuksip-ryeong Tunnel
육 십 령 터 널
Daegok-ri
대곡리
PR743
Bok-bawi
복바위
Birthplace of Ju Non-gae
논개생가지
977m
NE35
(20)
983m
Deogun-bong
덕운봉
Oksan-ri
옥산리
Water
Shelter
Village
Temple
Parking
Bus Stop
Inn
Mart
Stele
Jeongja
Shrine
Cave
Muryeong-gogae
무령고개
1,075m
Yeongchwi-san
영취산
(19)
Seonbawi-gogae
선바위고개
Campsite
야영터
Bujeon Valley
부 전 계 곡
1,066m
N
Jiji-pokpo Sanjang
지지폭포산장
Day-4
START
1,278m
Baekun-san
백운산

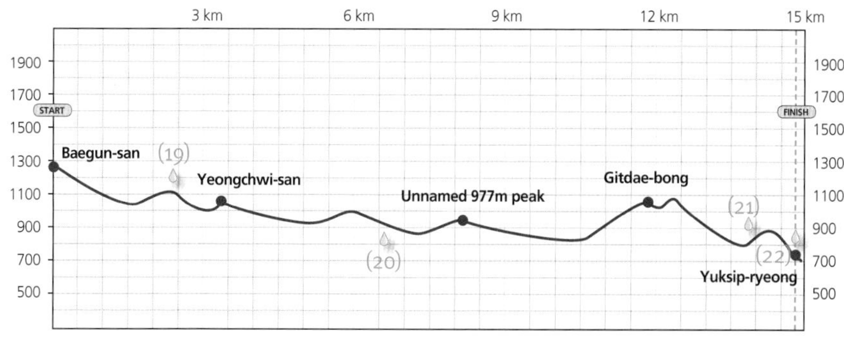

WATER STOPS

(19) Muryeong-gogae: **N35°38'37" E127°36'59"**
(20) Junction north of Deogun-bong: **N35°39'52" E127°37'49"**
(21) Between Gitdae-bong and Yuksip-ryeong: **N35°42'09" E127°39'33"**
(22) Yuksip-ryeong: **N35°43'08" E127°39'36"**

straightening north, climbing to a 1,066 m grassy peak with picnic benches and views to the northeast down the Bujeon Valley 부전계곡. Here, the ridge turns west, dropping into the shallow pass of Seonbawi-gogae 선바위고개, marked by a junction and a signpost. The trail continues northwest toward Yeongchwi-san, but shortly afterwards there is a track that heads west from the ridge to the pass of the Muryeong-gogae 무령고개 camp ground. Otherwise, the trail continues northwest 500 meters up to the summit of Yeongchwi-san. The unusual name Yeongchwi-san comes from Magadha, India, and means "a mountain with sacred and beautiful features." The small area on the peak has two *doltap* (cairns), welcoming hikers coming from the south, and a large new stele erected by the Korea Forest Service to celebrate the peak and its place on the Baekdu-daegan. A trail-head to the west

North to Deogyu-san from Muryeong-gogae

follows a modern staircase 500 meters to Muryeong-gogae, a pass located on PR743, while the original trail continues north.

Muryeong-gogae is connected by PR743, running 10 km north to Odong-ri 오동리 and 15 km south to Beonam-myeon 번암면. At the pass, there is an excellent camp ground picnic area, public toilets, fresh water(19) and a small shack which operates as a casual restaurant, selling basic Korean *anju* style food such as *pajeon*,

Birthplace of Ju Non-gae A2

About 5 km north from Muryeong-gogae along PR743, in the village of Daegok-ri 대곡리 at the head of Daegok-ho Lake 대곡호, is Uiam Ju Non-gae Saenggaji, the birthplace of Ju Non-gae. In 1593, Non-gae's husband was killed in the battle for the Jinju fortress during the seven-year Japanese Invasion (1592-1598). Seeking revenge for her husband and her beloved country, Ju Non-gae disguised herself as a *gisaeng* (an entertainer and hostess similar to a geisha in Japan) and joined other *gisaeng*s to entertain General Keyamura Rokusuke and other victorious Japanese at the Chokseong-nu pavilion on the banks of the Nam-gang River. She led the General to the edge of a cliff, embraced him, and threw herself off the rock, killing them both. The rock in Jinju she leapt from is now known as Uiam ("rock of righteousness") and is famous throughout Korea. The large, modern, plush park in nearby Daegok-ri is a grand tribute to Non-gae and is built below the tomb of her parents. The park has a large statue of Non-gae and restored traditional houses. The bushes growing on the hillside have been planted to read (*nara sarang* 나라사랑, "love of country"). A poem to Non-gae at the park, penned by Beon Yeong-rho, reads:

Great resentment goes deeper than religion
Flaming passion is stronger than love
On the water, bluer than a haricot bean
Flows her spirit, redder than flowers

Gorgeous eyebrows shaking
Her lips, like pomegranate, kissed death
On the flowing blue river, your beautiful spirit stands out all the more
On the water, bluer than a haricot bean
Flows her spirit, redder than flowers

If you travel 10 more kilometers west of Uiam Ju Non-gae Saenggaji, you will arrive in the town of Jangsu, where the Uiam-sa temple and the Nongae-sadang, a shrine to Non-gae, are located.

the Korean vegetable pancake to accompany thick *dongdong-ju* rice wine, which is the specialty. The host of this place has a karaoke machine, along to which he plays his electric guitar. Muryeong-gogae is a peaceful spot on a quiet road, and it is a recommended camping area. Alternative accommodation, in the form of the Jiji-pokpo Sanjang, is located about 4 km south of the Muryeong-gogae pass on PR743.

Yeongchwi-san 영취산 A4 → Unnamed 977m peak 977m봉 B3

4.7km (2:20)

From Yeongchwi-san, the trail descends 150 m in altitude over the next 600 meters before arcing to the northeast toward Deogun-bong 덕운봉, marked by a track junction. From there, the trail continues northwest for the next 900 meters following a thin rocky ridge, which then curves to the northeast and drops steeply into a pass marked by an obscure junction. From here, a thin, overgrown track heads southeast and meets the previous track running to Oksan-ri 옥산리. Water(20) can be found from the head of a stream about 200 meters down this track, or maybe further in dry weather. Back on the ridge, the trail continues northeast through high grasses, pine and shrubs, climbing gently for 1.7 km toward an unnamed peak standing at 977 m ABSL.

Unnamed 977m peak 977m봉 B3 → Gitdae-bong 깃대봉 C1

3.7km (1:45)

From this peak you will continue north, maintaining good height, for about 1 km before reaching Bok-bawi 복바위, an unusual rocky formation protruding off the western side of the ridge like a crooked tooth. The view from this rock is spectacular, with the side of the ridge dropping steeply to Daegok Village near the park dedicated to Non-gae. From Bok-bawi, you drop 150 m in altitude over the next 1.3 km to Min-ryeong Pass 민령. This area is a wide pass, with a track running northwest for 2.5 km down the side of the ridge to the edge of Daegok Lake while the main trail heads north. After another 500 meters, you arrive at the foot of a large pylon above the Yuksip-ryeong Tunnel 육십령 터널, where NE35 drills through the ridge. From the pylon, the trail ascends north, then northeast, as it climbs to the summit of Gitdae-bong about 1 km further on. On Gitdae-bong (1,014m) is a signboard with a large photo displaying the peaks of Deogyu-san National Park, which you can see to the north. The end point of Yuksip-ryeong can be seen from here, 30° to the northeast, marked by a large *jeongja* 3 km away.

Gitdae-bong 깃대봉 → Yuksip-ryeong 육십령 C1 3km (1:05)

From Gitdae-bong, the trail drops north off the peak, continuing for about 100 meters before reaching a helipad. In this region, the trail starts to veer northeast for 1 km, arriving at a well-built spring with a steady flow of fresh water(21). The trail now becomes wider, and for 300 meters it follows a pebble path designed for barefoot reflexology to soothe sore feet after hiking. About 200 meters short of Yuksip-ryeong*, the trail forks, with both branches ultimately heading to the pass. The left trail, heading northwest, emerges on the Jeollabuk-do side of the pass, while the right trail heads northeast, leading to the Gyeongsangnam-do side of the pass. Both are on NH26 and are separated by about 100 meters of road.

* Yuksip-ryeong 육십령 C1

Yuksip-ryeong (696m) is connected by NH26, which runs west off the ridge into Jangsu-gun in Jeollabuk-do, and east into Hamyang-gun in Gyeongsangnam-do. On both sides of the pass are war memorials: one dedicated to soldiers and policemen who served during the Korean and Vietnam Wars; and another that pays respect to soldiers who died while conducting an operation after the Korean War to exterminate North Korean guerrillas and sympathizers holding out in the nooks and crannies of Deogyu-san.

Joining the trail at Yuksip-ryeong: Buses head to Yuksip-ryeong along NH26 from Janggye-myeon to the west and Seosang-myeon to the southeast. The Janggye-myeon···›Yuksip-ryeong bus runs hourly from 7:40 am to 6:40 pm. The Seosang-myeon···›Yuksip-ryeong bus runs 12 times daily from 8:30 am to 7:55 pm. Buses leave hourly in both directions from the pass.

Minbak accommodation is available on both the western and eastern sides of the pass. On the western side is the large Yuksip-ryeong Hyugeso 육십령 휴게소, which has *minbak* rooms, toilets, a good restaurant and a well stocked supermarket. Also in front of the *hyugeso* is a large two-story concrete *jeongja,* which is suitable for sleeping in after sightseers have left. On the eastern side of the pass are a small supermarket and restaurant; *minbak* rooms are available to the rear of the restaurant. Water(22) can really only be found at the pass from local tap sources and public toilets, or as bottled water purchased from the *hyugeso*.

THREE DAYS

32.0km

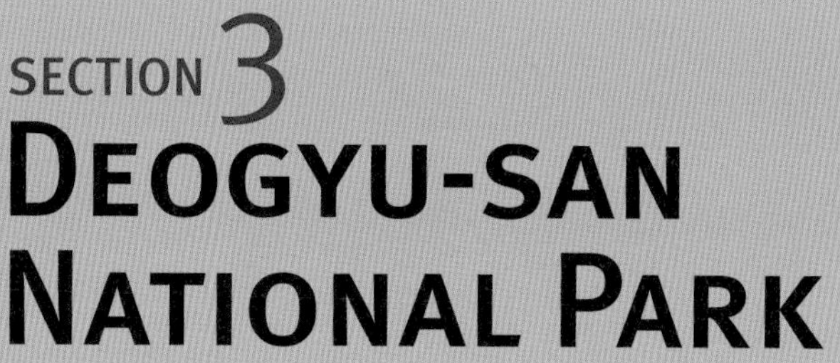

SECTION 3

DEOGYU-SAN NATIONAL PARK

Yuksip-ryeong → Bbae-jae

17
16
15
14
13
12
11
10
9
8
7
6
5
4
3
2
1

Seoul
Daejeon
Namwon
Jinju
Gwangju
Jeju

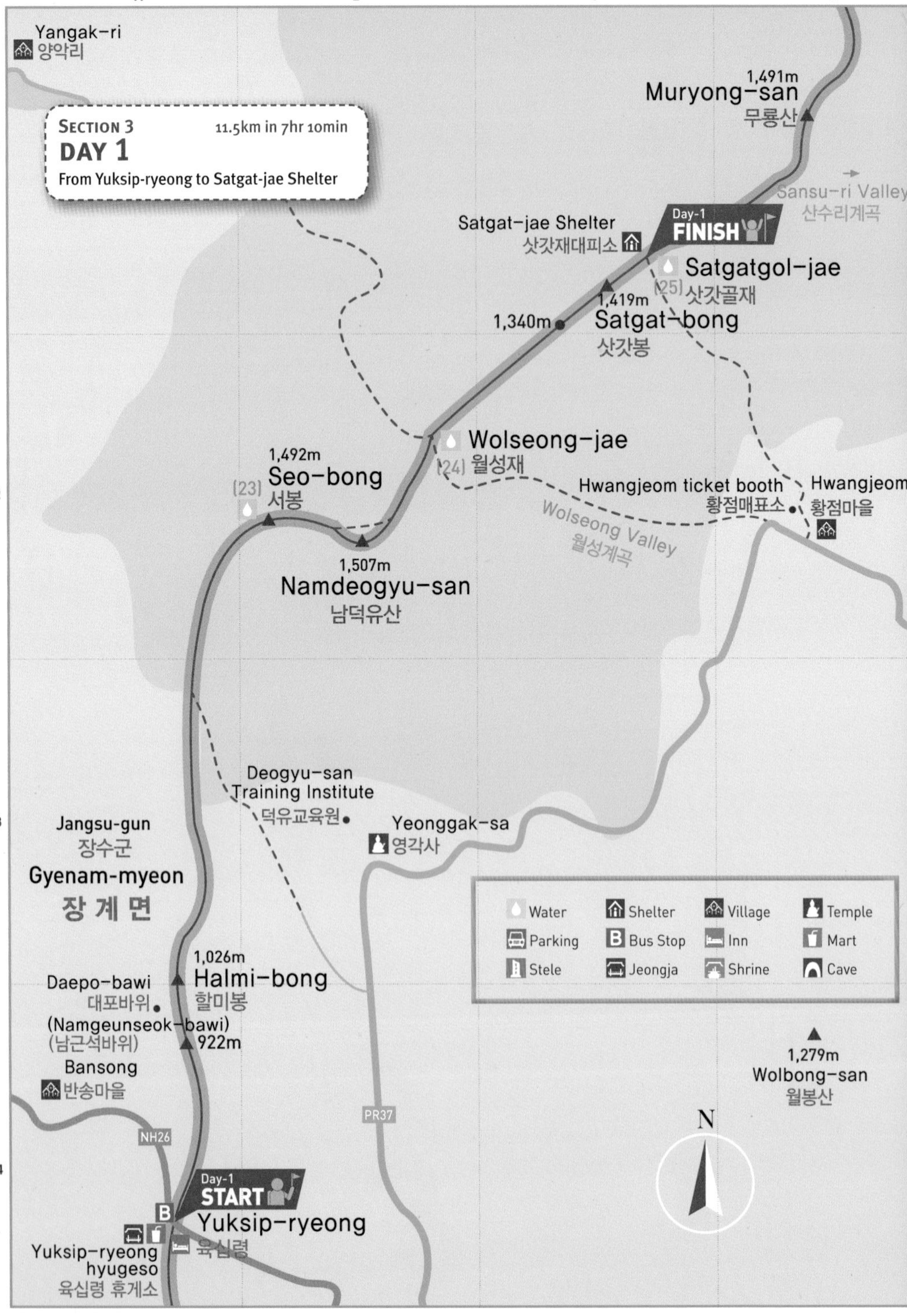

A
B
C
D
1
2
3
4
Yangak-ri
양악리
SECTION 3
11.5km in 7hr 10min
DAY 1
From Yuksip-ryeong to Satgat-jae Shelter
1,491m
Muryong-san
무룡산
Sansu-ri Valley
산수리계곡
Day-1
FINISH
Satgat-jae Shelter
삿갓재대피소
Satgatgol-jae
(25) 삿갓골재
1,419m
1,340m
Satgat-bong
삿갓봉
Wolseong-jae
(24) 월성재
1,492m
Seo-bong
(23)
서봉
Hwangjeom ticket booth
황점매표소
Hwangjeom
황점마을
Wolseong Valley
월성계곡
1,507m
Namdeogyu-san
남덕유산
Deogyu-san
Training Institute
덕유교육원
Yeonggak-sa
영각사
Jangsu-gun
장수군
Gyenam-myeon
장 계 면
Water
Shelter
Village
Temple
Parking
Bus Stop
Inn
Mart
Stele
Jeongja
Shrine
Cave
1,026m
Halmi-bong
할미봉
Daepo-bawi
대포바위
(Namgeunseok-bawi)
(남근석바위)
922m
Bansong
반송마을
1,279m
Wolbong-san
월봉산
PR37
NH26
N
Day-1
START
Yuksip-ryeong
육십령
Yuksip-ryeong
hyugeso
육십령 휴게소

DAY 1 From Yuksip-ryeong to Satgat-jae Shelter

• **Distance:** 11.5km
• **Time:** 7hr 10min

From the soldiers' tablets at Yuksip-ryeong, make your way straight up the southern face of Deogyu-san to arrive at Halmi-bong, noting the finger of ridge that takes you up the hind of the dog like a flea. Four hundred more meters of altitude later, stop at the top of Deogyu-san and marvel at the impressive parade of peaks that forms a rank of sparkling brilliance. Tuck down into the crown between the two horns of Seo-bong and Namdeogyu-san and look north along the fevered back of the dog that is the Baekdu-daegan. Cast your eye back south, feel the impunity of your effort, and wonder when the mountains will cease. Adjust your pack, turn and look north, feel the sun on your neck, and march onwards, slowly but surely, like a man pushing his car up a hill.

Yuksip-ryeong 육십령 A4 → Halmi-bong 할미봉 A3

2km (1:20)

Crossing to the northern side of NH26, you see the entrance to the trail, clearly indicated by a tree adorned with ribbons. Heading north, you ascend through tall, thin trees that flank the eastern fringe of the trail down to a road leading to the quarry. About 600 meters later, you pass a solitary tomb as the trail steepens dramatically toward an unnamed peak located at 922 m ABSL, just beneath Halmi-bong. The trail climbs more than 100 m over a 300 meter section of

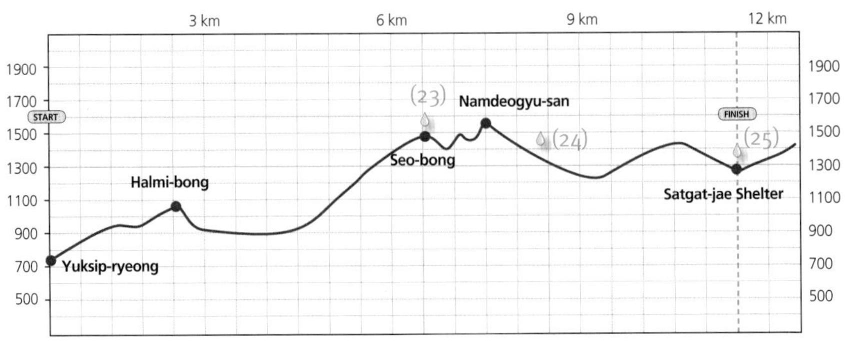

Water Stops

(23) Seo-bong: N35°46'04" E127°40'12"
(24) Wolseong-jae (west track) 월성재: N35°46'29" E127°41'09"
(25) Satgatgol-jae 삿갓골재: N35°47'12" E127°40'27"

hardened earth to the 922 m peak. Near the top of your first ascent, the trail breaks into a rocky surface departing the forest, forcing you to scramble up, over, and around large mounds of rock. Once at 922 m, the views are predominantly to the south and southeast, where you can see Gitdae-bong 깃대봉 (1,014m) 5 km to the south, and to the east the deep valley carved by the head of the Nam-gang River. On the other side of that valley is Wolbong-san 월봉산 (1,279m), 6 km due east. If you move east a little from the trail, you may be able to see a symmetrical, manmade hole that has been drilled into one of the rocks on this unnamed peak, which could very well be from an iron spike driven into the peak during the years of Japanese occupation as a symbolic gesture of Japanese dominance over the sacred mountains of the Baekdu-daegan. Then again, it could be anything. The hole is well weathered.

Leaving the unnamed peak, the trail heads north for 200 meters, crossing an undulating rocky surface before climbing again, steeply north, toward Halmi-bong. The ridge rises dramatically to this peak, gaining 105 m in altitude over another 300 meter section of trail. More basic scrambling is required, but it's very manageable and doesn't require technical ability. Once on the summit of Halmi-bong, located at 1,026 m ABSL, you have a great 360° view. The peak area provides numerous ledges for you to sit on and bask in the sweat of your effort, make a brew and enjoy the moment, or look to your north and heed the ridge climbing to Seo-bong (1,492m), then falling east into a prominent saddle toward the summit of Namdeogyu-san (1,507m), casting the image of two horns.

Halmi-bong 할미봉 A3 →Seo-bong 서봉 B2 4.5km (2:50)

From Halmi-bong, you descend northeast for 70 meters before reaching a junction. The western track from the junction will take you 400 meters to the rock of Daepo-bawi*, also known as Namgeunseok-bawi 남근석바위.

Halmi-bong from PR37 near Yeonggak-sa

From the junction continuing north, you begin descending steeply off Halmi-bong. At times, the drop is near vertical over boulders, and a series of fixed ropes are in place to aid the descent. The series of steep descents lasts for about 200 meters, dropping around 80 m in altitude. Following the rappel from Halmi-bong, the trail turns slightly to the northeast for 500 meters before straightening again to the north. From there, the ridge levels out for the next 2.5 km, and you can expect good walking conditions, maintaining good height without any dramatic climbs or drops. The first 1.3 km sees you descending gradually before reaching a cleared area from which you climb gently north for 1.2 km, reaching a junction marked by a signpost that has a track heading southeast from the ridge for 1.6 km down to the Deogyu-san Training Institute. From the junction, the Baekdu-daegan trail heads northeast, climbing steeply toward a helipad 400 meters away, which offers good views south along the completed ridge. From the helipad, you begin the steep climb north to the summit of Seo-bong. The trail climbs 150 m in altitude over a 500 meter section toward a rocky outcrop. This feature offers good views to the west over the Jangsu-gun area. The next kilometer sees you gaining 200 m in altitude as the trail becomes very rocky, punching into high altitude open country before arriving at Seo-bong at 1,492 m ABSL.

* Daepo-bawi 대포바위 A4

Daepo-bawi is a large, phallic rock protruding rigidly from a spur on the ridge. This is a popular side trail for ridge-walkers and an interesting place to have your picture taken. A signboard at the intersection shows a photo of the rock and gives a brief description of the history of its name. It states that during the Imjin Invasion (1592-1598), Japanese forces, after capturing Jinju Castle, were on an advancing campaign north when they spied what appeared to be a large cannon and fortifications on Halmi-bong peak in Deogyu-san. This illusory sight forced them to halt their progress. Further study and reconnaissance of the large cannon revealed that it was indeed only a rock. As a result, the locals affectionately called it Daepo-bawi, meaning "cannon rock." Later on, due to its new fame, phallic shape and strong appearance, the rock became a popular place for women to come and pray for the birth of a son, and it gained a strong reputation for making this miracle come true. A note on the sign reads that although this rock is recognized as Daepo-bawi, we should call it Namgeunseok-bawi ("phallic rock"), as the idea that it looks like a cannon was a Japanese one. The track from there continues for 2 km down to Bansong village, located on NH26.

Seo-bong 서봉 → Namdeogyu-san 남덕유산 B2 1km (1:00)

Seo-bong, meaning "west peak," has a large rocky summit offering multiple areas to stop and rest, taking in the grand vista of where you are. It also marks the beginning of the high ridge of Deogyu-san National Park (see p127). From the large peak area, you can follow a long section of the ridge with your eye, running east from Seo-bong to Namdeogyu-san at 1,507 m. The extra height at Seo-bong also offers you lofty views to the south of Gitdae-bong at 1,014 m ABSL, and the great white-clouded peak of Baegun-san at 1,278 m ABSL, a good 16 km away. Also at the summit area is a sign that marks the direction toward a spring(23) supposedly located 100 meters southwest down a rocky path. Although well known, this spring can be difficult to find, and in dry weather, it may be necessary to walk as much as 500 meters down the steep track to find the water source. From Seo-bong, the trail heads to the east, dropping 100 m into the deep, prominent saddle separating the two peaks. Your descent is aided by two sets of impressive green steel staircases, which make easy work of crossing the boulder-ridden eastern face of Seo-bong. At the saddle, the trail enters low, verdant forest and continues east

Climbing to Seobong

for 500 meters along a mixture of tree line and rocky terrain before beginning an ascent toward Namdeogyu-san. Just as the trail starts heading southeast, there is a track junction offering you the opportunity to detour from Namdeogyu-san and contour east around its northern face, joining the ridgeline north of its summit. It is a good detour. Otherwise, you can follow the trail southeast as it begins a tough 150 m climb up to Namdeogyu-san.

Roger walking east down the staircase from Seo-bong

Namdeogyu-san, located at 1,507 m ABSL, is the third highest peak of Deogyu-san National Park and the highest in its southern area. The peak is rocky and open with great views, particularly to the south and east. On a clear day, way over in the distant east, you might be able to see the massif of Gaya-san National Park (1,430m). To the south, the high peaks of Jiri-san, including Cheonwang-bong (1,915m), the beginning of the Baekdu-daegan ridge, can still be seen, now almost 60 km away. To the immediate northeast is the continuation of the Baekdu-daegan ridge, looking like the back of an angry dog.

Namdeogyu-san 남덕유산 B2 → Satgat-jae Shelter 삿갓재 대피소 C1

4km (2:00)

Following the trail north off Namdeogyu-san, you drop about 100 m in altitude over the next 250 meters before reaching the junction of the bypass track, marked by a signpost. From here, you continue northeast, dropping 200 m in altitude over the next 1 km as the well-worn path meanders its way through lush tree line, aided by staircases in its steeper sections. At Wolseong-jae 월성재, there is a four-way junction with tracks meeting the Baekdu-daegan from the east and the west. To the west, a manmade spring(24) can be found about 200 meters down, with a good flow of water. From the pass, you have a climb up a small knoll before the trail begins a gradual 1 km ascent to a signpost located at the base of a 1,340 m unnamed peak. At this stage, the trail steepens for the 200 meter walk to the 1,340 m peak, which has views to the west over the Yangak-ri 양악리 area. From here, the next 400 meters see you arriving at a fork in the trail about 50 meters after a signpost. The right arm heads east 100 meters to the summit of Satgat-bong peak 삿갓봉 (1,419m), while the left arm maintains the same altitude and contours northeast along the eastern face of Satgat-bong. Both trails meet up 100 meters north of the peak. Satgat is a popular mountain name in Korea, and it refers to the conical bamboo hat traditionally worn in the rain by Korean men. Satgat-bong has an open area on its summit and a small stele bearing its name. From the peak of Satgat-bong, you head north and meet up with the bypass trail, whereupon the reunited trail begins a steep northeast descent over its final 700 meters into the saddle of Satgatgol-jae 삿갓골재, identified by the quaint, quiet wooden National Park shelter facing southeast toward Wolseong Valley 월성계곡.

The Satgat-jae Shelter sleeps 70 and costs 5,000 won per night. Blankets can be rented for 1,000 won each. Bookings can be made by calling the main Deogyu-san National Park office (T. 063-322-3174) or by visiting http://english.knps.or.kr. The office inside the front door serves as a kiosk where you can buy cans of soda, bottled water, biscuits, tinned sardines and tuna. Sleeping quarters are on this main floor, while the kitchen is detached at a lower level, accessible down some stairs and through a drying room at the rear of the main building. The kitchen has large benches and running water for cooking. Fresh drinking water(25) is available from a spring located 50 meters down a stairwell at the top of the southeast track to Hwangjeom ticket booth. Toilets are located outside the front of the main building, 20 meters to the south.

The ridge from Satgat-bong to Muryeong-san from PR37

Deogyu-san National Park 덕유산 국립공원

Deogyu-san was designated a national park on February 1, 1975, and covers an area of 231.65 km^2. The main ridge of Deogyu-san spans more than 30 km from south to north and represents the southern reaches of the Sobaek-sanmaek Range, which extends north through Songni-san, Worak-san and Sobaek-san National Parks to form the southern section of the Baekdu-daegan mountain system. The ridge of Deogyu-san rises dramatically along the Baekdu-daegan trail with impressive sharp, steep peaks averaging over 1,300 m ABSL along its route. Hyangjeok-bong 향적봉, the park's highest peak and the fourth highest summit in South Korea, stands at 1,610.6 m ABSL (some maps say 1,614 m) in the center of the park. This peak is not part of the Baekdu-daegan ridge, soaring about 2 km to its north, but the trail leading toward it will delight you with the traverse of seventeen distinctive peaks, all over 1,000 m ABSL and seven of which are higher than 1,400 m ABSL. With the high altitude comes a change in vegetation from the previous section of the walk, with low subalpine species thriving on the high ridge. In late spring and early summer, large colonies of royal azalea and magnolia trees come into full bloom; in summer, wildflowers, including day lilies and edelweiss, can be found in great numbers in the shade of the low forest cover; and during winter, the Korean yew and Korean fir create dramatic landscapes in the deep snow, standing frozen like abstract statues glazed in ice, victims of a mountain Medusa. Many professional photographers brave the climb to the high slopes of Deogyu-san in the colder seasons to capture these twisted features and the blankets of thick cloud that sweep over the saddles like a mysterious potion.

 Lodgings in Deogyu-san on the Baekdu-daegan

Camping on the ridge is not allowed anywhere throughout Deogyu-san, as with all national parks. However, there are two shelters well located for Baekdu-daegan hikers inside the park. The first one you will come across is the Satgat-jae Shelter. It is located 12 km north along the trail from Yuksip-ryeong; the second is located in the southern shadow of Hyangjeok-bong peak, 10 km further north and 2 km off the trail of the Baekdu-daegan.

Muju Resort 무주 리조트, the largest single ski slope complex in Korea and holder of Winter Olympics-hosting ambitions, is located in the center of the park running off Seolcheon-bong 설천봉, 500 meters north of Hyangjeok-bong peak. There is a restaurant on the peak and a cable car running year-round, which is a good option for getting off the ridge and enjoying the attractions of wider Deogyu-san National Park.

Aside from the high ridge, Deogyu-san is home to eleven scenic valleys, the most famous being the Gucheon-dong valley. This valley runs 30 km north from Hyangjeok-bong peak to Najetong-mun gate 나제통문, a rock tunnel which once served as a border entrance between the Baekje and Silla Kingdoms. The gate serves as the most popular entrance to the park, and near its entrance are numerous restaurants, bars and accommodations, including a huge campground that can sleep 10,000 people.

Temples in Deogyu-san

There are four major Buddhist temples within Deogyu-san National Park: Anguk-sa 안국사, in the northwestern corner of the park within the remains of the Jeok-san mountain fortress; Baekryeon-sa 백련사, below Hyangjeok-bong at the head of the Gucheon-dong valley; Songgye-sa 송계사, in the east of the park below Mot-bong on the Baekdu-daegan; and Wontong-sa 원통사, in Anseong-myeon in the west of the park. In addition, historic Yeonggak-sa 영각사 lies just outside the National Park boundary below Namdeogyu-san in the south of the park and is located 6km up PR37 from its intersection with NH26, 5 km southeast of Yuksip-ryeong.

Yeonggak-sa was founded in AD 877 by Master Shimgwang-daesa during the Unified Silla Dynasty. It was renovated again under King Sejong of the Joseon Dynasty in 1449 and has been remodeled several times since then. In 1834, all of the buildings on the site were destroyed by fire. The temple wasn't reconstructed until 1886, by Gangyongwol-daesa, and since then, numerous other famous monks have also resided there. It was at Yeonggak-sa that 81 famous wooden printing blocks of the Hwaeom-gyeong (or "flower garden sutra") were made. However, the temple was again destroyed during the Korean War, with only the sansin-gak surviving. The wooden plates were destroyed in the fire, but they were later restored by the monk Haeun-seunim and are now housed in the Geungnak Hall, restoring the temple's pride and honor. It is now a branch temple of the famous Haein-sa 해인사 Monastery in Gaya-san 가야산.

Yeonggak-sa beneath the southern face of Namdeogyu-san

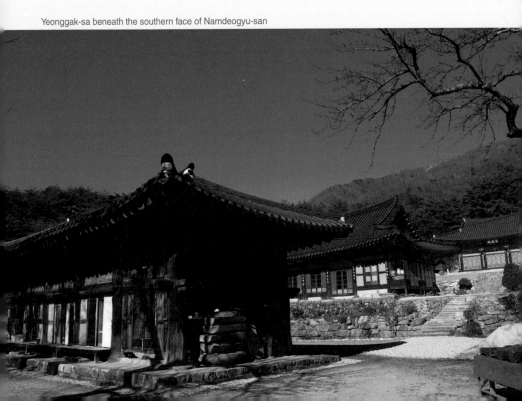

DAY 2 From Satgat-jae Shelter to Hyangjeok -bong Shelter

• **Distance:** 9.7km
• **Time:** 4hr

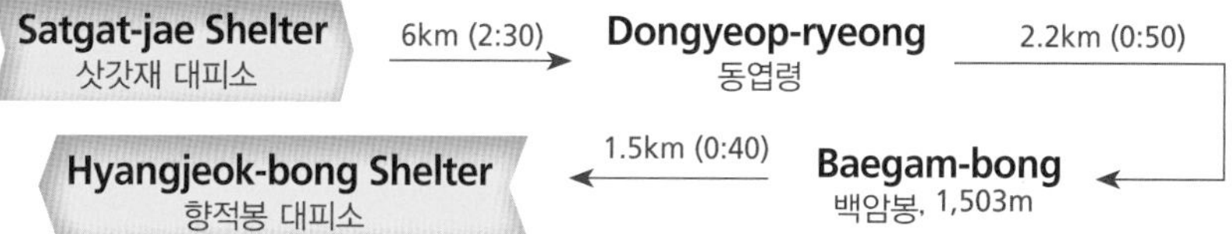

You are now effectively walking a high ridgeline that connects Deogyu-san's highest southern peak with the highest peak to its north. A view from the top gives the appearance that this ridge's vertex is thin with high empty sides, like a tightrope. It traverses seven peaks, all of which are over 1,300 m ABSL. From the first peak of Muryong-san, the ridge becomes open, and you walk through low alpine forest that includes fields of royal azaleas, mountain flowers and stands of yew trees. Meanwhile, the Baekdu-daegan wobbles and balances his way along the tightrope toward the perfumed clutch of Hyangjeok-san, tragically falling short of her elegant reach and tumbling down east to the pass of Bbae-jae.

Satgat-jae Shelter 삿갓재 대피소 A4 → Dongyeop-ryeong 동엽령 C3 6km (2:30)

The trail leaves Satgat-jae Shelter, climbing to the northeast and then turning east, arriving at a helipad about 200 meters later. The trail stays flattish for the next 300 meters before arriving at a signpost. The next kilometer to Muryong-san 무룡산 sees you rising about 250 m in altitude over a well-maintained trail. About 500 meters into that leg, you come across a case of well-built stairs, which act as a boardwalk crossing a helipad, before continuing for another 200 meters toward

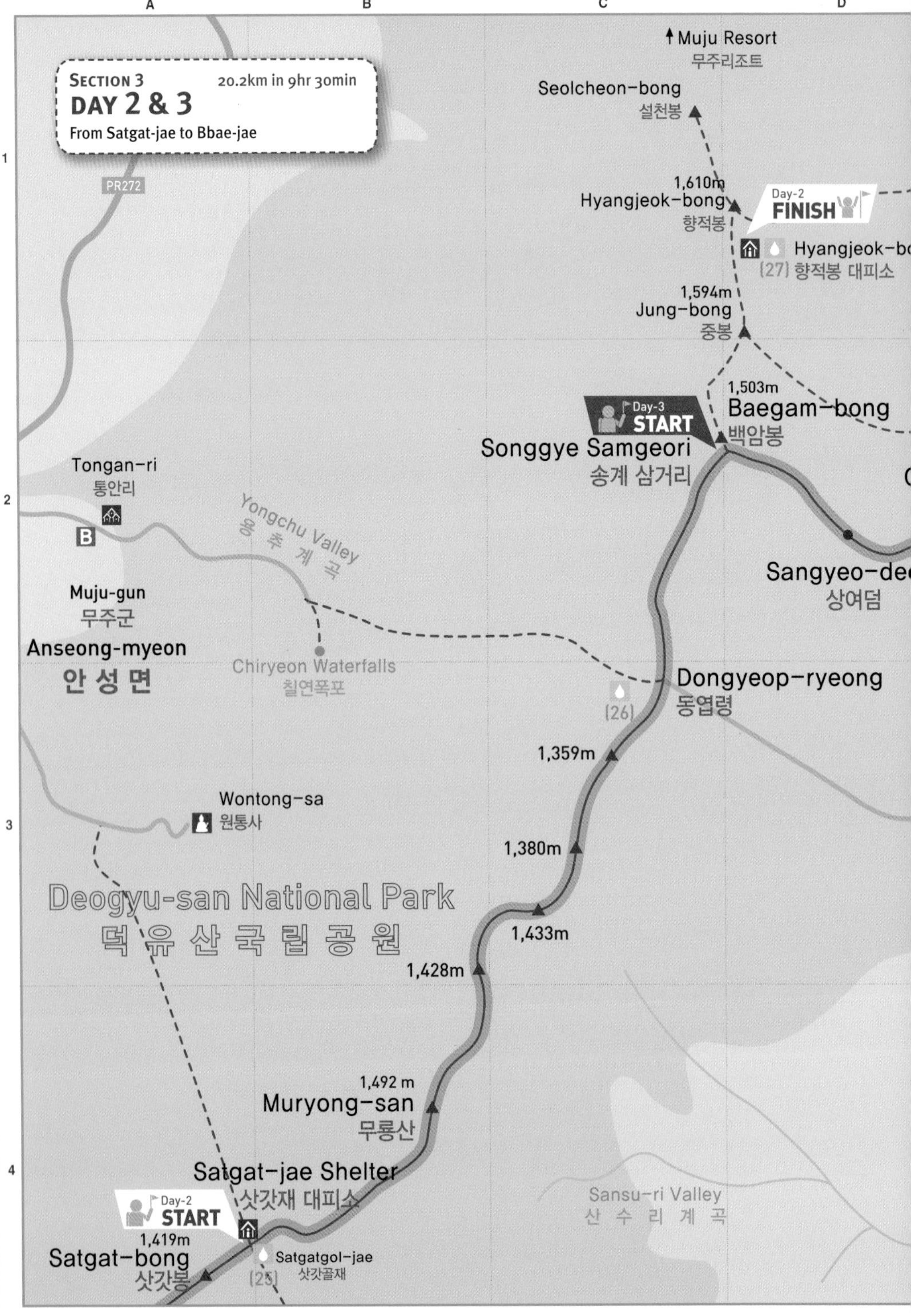

A
B
C
D
1
2
3
4
SECTION 3
20.2km in 9hr 30min
DAY 2 & 3
From Satgat-jae to Bbae-jae
PR272
Muju Resort
무주리조트
Seolcheon-bong
설천봉
1,610m
Hyangjeok-bong
향적봉
Day-2
FINISH
(27) 향적봉 대피소
1,594m
Jung-bong
중봉
1,503m
Baegam-bong
백암봉
Day-3
START
Songgye Samgeori
송계 삼거리
Tongan-ri
통안리
B
Yongchu Valley
용 추 계 곡
Sangyeo-de
상여덤
Muju-gun
무주군
Anseong-myeon
안 성 면
Chiryeon Waterfalls
칠연폭포
Dongyeop-ryeong
동엽령
(26)
1,359m
Wontong-sa
원통사
1,380m
Deogyu-san National Park
덕 유 산 국 립 공 원
1,433m
1,428m
1,492 m
Muryong-san
무룡산
Satgat-jae Shelter
삿갓재 대피소
Sansu-ri Valley
산 수 리 계 곡
Day-2
START
1,419m
Satgat-bong
삿갓봉
Satgatgol-jae
삿갓골재
(25)

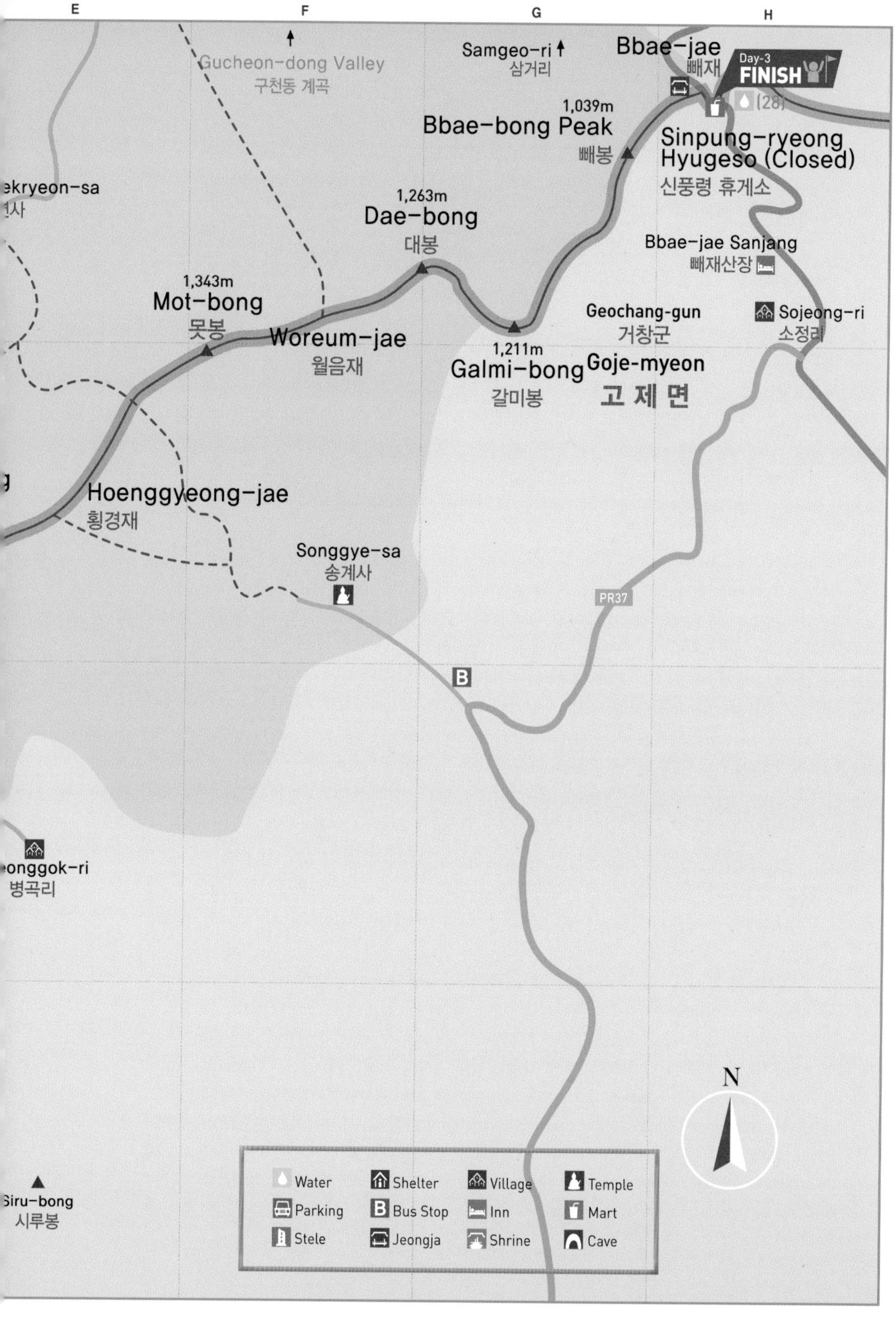

E
F
G
H
Gucheon-dong Valley
구천동 계곡
Samgeo-ri
삼거리
Bbae-jae
빼재
Day-3
FINISH
(28)
1,039m
Bbae-bong Peak
빼봉
Sinpung-ryeong
Hyugeso (Closed)
신풍령 휴게소
ekryeon-sa
1,263m
Dae-bong
대봉
Bbae-jae Sanjang
빼재산장
1,343m
Mot-bong
못봉
Woreum-jae
월음재
1,211m
Galmi-bong
갈미봉
Geochang-gun
거창군
Goje-myeon
고 제 면
Sojeong-ri
소정리
Hoenggyeong-jae
횡경재
Songgye-sa
송계사
PR37
B
onggok-ri
병곡리
N
Siru-bong
시루봉
Water
Shelter
Village
Temple
Parking
Bus Stop
Inn
Mart
Stele
Jeongja
Shrine
Cave

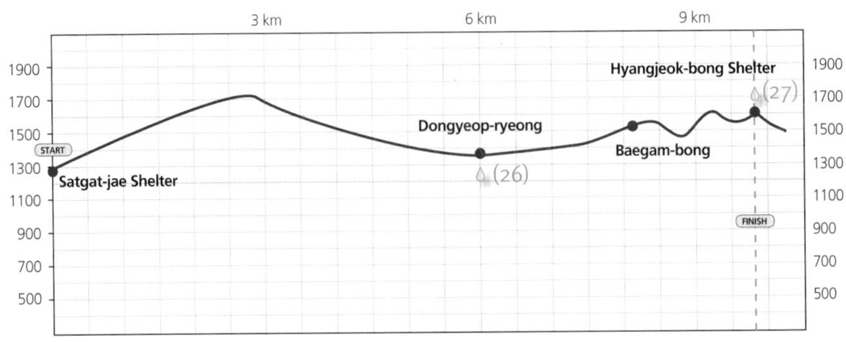

WATER STOPS

(26) Dongyeop-ryeong: **N35°49'41" E127°44'13"**
(27) Hyangjeok-bong Shelter: **N35°51'19" E127°45'00"**

the foot of Muryong-san. The boardwalk runs through an area of grasses and wildflowers that has been built to keep hikers in one zone, limiting the erosion in this open area—an effective idea! Near the top of the boardwalk, the views back along the tightrope are exceptional toward Satgat-bong, Namdeogyu-san and Seo-bong. At the end of the boardwalk, the trail turns north, where you continue your ascent on an open trail among knee- to waist-high grasses and wildflowers for the final 400 meters to Muryong-san, located at 1,491 m ABSL. The summit area offers 360° views over some low-lying shrubs. In the far distant east, you might be able to see the sharp peak of Gaya-san 가야산, cutting its way through the oceans of blue thermal ridges like a dorsal fin.

From Muryong-san, you descend gently north for 500 meters. The trail then levels out for the next 400 meters before climbing briefly to an unnamed peak located at 1,428 m ABSL. From this peak, you descend sharply to the northeast and, after 200 meters, meet a fork in the trail. To the northwest, a thin track heads down a steep ravine about 3 km to the source of the Chiryeon waterfalls 칠연 폭포. There is an easier way to see the waterfalls, by using the main trail down the Yongchu Valley 용추 계곡 from your next stop at Dongyeop-ryeong, 2.3 km further along the trail. From that junction, you continue northeast, then east, flanking the Sansu-ri Valley 산수리 계곡 to your southeast, where, 500 meters later, you arrive at another unnamed peak located at 1,433 m ABSL and marked by a large doltap. From there, the trail turns north for the 2 km walk to Dongyeop-ryeong Pass. About 500 meters after leaving the peak, the trail levels out to an unnamed 1,380 m peak marked by a signpost, where it begins a descent into a saddle. The drop into the saddle is about 400 meters long, taking you down another 100m in altitude. Rising again from the lowest point of the saddle, you summit out at another unnamed feature located at 1,359 m ABSL. From this peak, it's a 500 meter walk and a gentle descent into Dongyeop-ryeong.

Dongyeop-ryeong 동엽령 C3 → Baegam-bong 백암봉 C2

2.2km (0:50)

Dongyeop-ryeong is a large, open pass and popular resting area. A large wooden viewing platform has been constructed facing east. About 100 meters north of the pass, a track to the west heads for 3.3 km down the Yongchu Valley to the Chiryeon Waterfall 칠연 폭포, where it joins a road that heads into the Anseong area. You can find water(26) on this track, 500 meters down the staircase and located 20 meters to the left in a rocky area.

Tongan-ri 통안리 is located at the end of the Yongchu valley trail, down the western track from Dongyeop-ryeong. This popular park entrance has a number of restaurants and *minbak*, including Pureun Minbak 푸른 민박 (T. 063-323-0596), the Sanjang Minbak 산장 민박 (T. 063-323-1136) and the Chiryeon Sikdang Minbak 칠연식당 민박 (T. 063-323-1881).

From Dongyeop-ryeong you continue walking north on an impressive rocky landscape that continues to offer great, uninterrupted views. About 1 km later, you arrive at the base of the clearly visible ascent to your next peak, marked by a western track junction. The next 1.2 km sees you climbing 175 m in altitude to the large summit area of Baegam-bong, located at 1,503 m ABSL. The trail to its peak is wide and open as it continues to pass through a high alpine area. Baegam-bong is a large, flat open area and the site of the Songgye Samgeori 송계 삼거리 (three-way junction). The auxiliary arm of this junction is the Baekdu-daegan trail, which departs the main ridge of Deogyu-san National Park, heading east toward the pass of Bbae-jae 빼재. Heading north from Baegam-bong takes you to the most popular areas of Deogyu-san. Quite distinctively, about 800 meters north of Baegam-bong, you can see the lofty peak of Jung-bong 중봉 at 1,594 m

Transport Info

Joining the trail at Tongan-ri: Buses run to Tongan-ri from the nearby town of Anseong-myeon seven times a day, at 6:50 am, 8:40 am, 11:20 am, 12:40 pm, 2:10 pm, 4:40 pm and 6:20 pm. Four of these buses start their journey from the larger center of Muju at 8 am, noon, 1:30 pm and 5:40 pm. Express buses run from Anseong to Seoul four times daily, at 9:10 am, 10:30 am, 3:10 pm and 5:10 pm, and from Anseong to Daejeon eight times daily, from 7:30 am to 6:10 pm.

ABSL. A further 800 meters north of Jung-bong, on a flat path that sneaks between the jagged taunts of deceased, ghostlike yew trees, is the Hyangjeok-bong Shelter 향적봉 대피소, lying in the southeastern shadow of Hyangjeok-bong.

* Hyangjeok-bong 향적봉 D1

A 400 meter climb up from the shelter is the summit of Hyangjeok-bong (1,610m), which offers unimpeded 360° views of the park. From Hyangjeok-bong, trails run east and north. The northern trail heads 500 meters to Seolcheon-bong 설천봉, the top of the ski runs of Muju Resort 무주 리조트. This peak has a large, food court-style restaurant area and a cable car that runs down to the Muju Resort accommodation area, from which a free shuttle bus runs to Samgong-ri 삼공리. A round trip on the cable car costs 11,000 won; a one-way trip is 7,000 won. The eastern trail takes you 2 km down to Baekryeon-sa Temple 백련사 at the head of the Gucheon-dong Valley 구천동 계곡 and on to the Samgong accommodation and restaurant area, which we can recommend for a couple of days off.

Hyangjeok-bong Shelter (T. 063-322-1614) is located under the highest peak in the park and charges 5,000 won per night, with blankets for rent at 1,000 won apiece. Bookings can be made by calling the main Deogyu-san National Park office (T. 063-322-3174). The shelter sits on the southeastern face of Hyangjeok-bong, on a contour from the south saddle. It is a small shelter,

sleeping 67 people inside a clean, well-groomed domain that is decorated with some brilliant photographs of the area, taken by some rather rugged-looking rangers. It also has a small store and a clean separate kitchen area, with picnic benches outside. Water(27) can be fetched from a fast-flowing spring near the benches, whose source is claimed to be 150 m below the surface. The toilets are located south of the shelter, with good early morning views east over the ridges. The saddle in which the shelter is located is well positioned for capturing images of the horizontal fingers of white cloud that roll ghoulishly over the Baekdudaegan ridge to the southeast like a silent tsunami. Many a photographer gets up early in the morning to try and catch this natural phenomenon, as its opaque skin shines in the piercing rays of the brilliant early morning sun.

Transport Info

Leaving the trail at Hyangjeok-bong: From the small terminal at Samgong-ri 삼공리, buses run regularly throughout the day to Muju. Long distance buses also leave the terminal heading to Yeongdong and on to the city of Daejeon 15 times a day, from 6:55 am to 7:30 pm. Once a day, a bus heads to Gimcheon and on to Daegu, leaving at 4:30 pm.

Lodging

The main entrance to the park at Samgong-ri has a huge amount of accommodation, both *minbak* and motels, as well as scores of restaurants. There is also a large campsite near the park entrance. The camping fee is 3,000–6,000 won, depending on tent size.

The spiny ridge of Deogyu-san from PR37

DAY 3 From Baegam-bong to Bbae-jae

- **Distance:** 10.5km
- **Time:** 5hr 30min

Falling with the Baekdu-daegan, you cascade east down its heartbroken ridge as it leaves the verdant vertex of Deogyu-san. Stagger from the woods and assemble your tired, aching bones into the soft bosom of the pass. Feel the fresh wind push through your sticky clothing as it blows away at your thinning frame. Study your map and heed how the trail plunges and undulates heavily into the big unexplored space between here and your next National Park. Ahead, rural Korea celebrates with the masked heathen tones of *pansori*—anticipating your return, its people bang their drums and charge their vessels—gleeful.

Baegam-bong 백암봉 C2 → Mot-bong 못봉 F2

4.5km (2:30)

Leaving Baegam-bong, the trail descends east through subalpine forest for 400 meters before changing its path southeast. About 600 meters later, you should arrive at a signpost. This is the start of a rocky area known as Sangyeo-deom 상여덤. From there, the trail continues descending for a further 200 meters, after which you should have reached the bottom. From there, the trail ascends northeast for 300 meters, climbing to the wooded summit of Gwi-bong 귀봉 at 1,390 m ABSL. You drop steeply southeast off Gwi-bong for 200 meters before the trail flattens out a little and turns to the northeast, where it rises again before

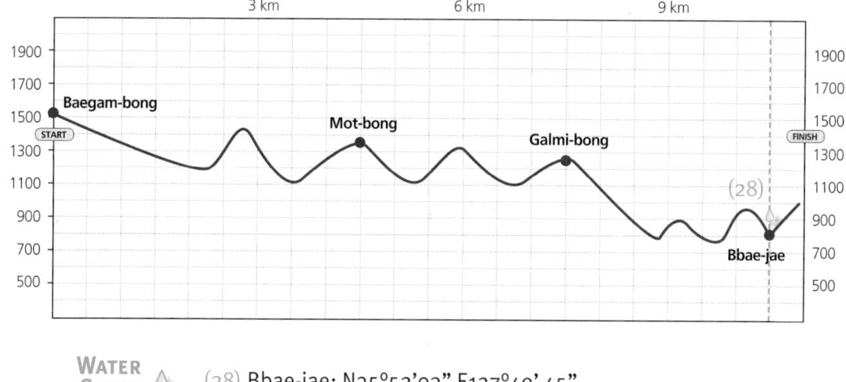

WATER STOPS (28) Bbae-jae: N35°52'03" E127°49' 45"

undulating for the next 500 meters to the pass of Hoenggyeong-jae 횡경재. From the pass, the trail dips into a long saddle area running for almost a kilometer in length. At the end of the saddle, you come across a signpost on the trail, marking a track junction named after the peak under which it lies, Mot-bong. From the junction, you continue northeast and climb a hard 100 m in altitude to a helipad, then turn east, continuing with your ascent to the summit of Mot-bong, also known as Ji-bong. At 1,343 m ABSL, Mot-bong sits high above the ridge and offers good views in all directions. From the summit, you can see the next 3 km of your walk northeast to Dae-bong 대봉, and the peak of Galmi-bong 1 km to its southeast. To the west, you can look back on Baegam-bong, now 5 km away, and Hyangjeok-bong 285° to the west, north of Baegam-bong.

Mot-bong 못봉 F2 → Galmi-bong 갈미봉 G1 3km (1:50)

From Mot-bong, the trail begins a 300 meter northeastern descent through deciduous forest over the next kilometer of ground before arriving at the pass of Woreum-jae 월음재. From the pass, the trail ascends a good 200 m in altitude for another kilometer to Dae-bong Peak, located at 1,263 m ABSL. From Dae-bong, the Baekdu-daegan takes a southern turn as it makes a dip into a saddle, arriving at the bottom about 400 meters later. The trail then ascends another 400 meters to the summit of Galmi-bong, located at 1,211 m ABSL. The summit of Galmi-bong is covered in grasses and low shrubs, offering good views along the ridge.

Bbae-jae

Galmi-bong 갈미봉 G1 → Bbae-jae 빼재 H1 3km (1:10)

From Galmi-bong, the ridge turns to the north, then to the northeast, dropping 250 m in altitude over the next kilometer of this very steep descent. The bottom of the descent is marked by a helipad, after which the trail makes an undulating 400 meters of ground to Bbae-bong Peak 빼봉, located at 1,039 m ABSL and marked by a signpost. The next kilometer of trail descends and winds its way down through wooded forest to the road pass of Bbae-jae, of which you will be able to catch occasional glimpses along the way. The exit onto Bbae-jae passes a communications facility before spilling out onto a road located right at the crux of the western side of the pass. In front of you, there should be a beautiful wooden jeongja perched on the southern lip of the pass, overlooking the valley beneath it.

* Bbae-jae 빼재 H1

Bbae-jae is located on NH37 between the Deogyu-san Samgong-jigu area 삼공지구 8.5 km to the northwest, and Goje-myeon 고제면 12.5 km to the southeast. The pass has a large *jeongja* pavilion with views south to the peaks of Siru-bong and Hoeum-bong and southeast to Gaya-san in the far distance.

The history of the *jeongja* is an interesting one. It was erected here as a resting place in memory of persons who died in the area as a result of the many bloody struggles throughout Korea's history. This *jeongja* was named Sinpung-jeong, meaning "fresh wind pavilion." According to the information board next to it, this pass has for many years been called Bbae-jae, meaning "bone pass." It acquired this name during the volatile Three Kingdoms period (57 BC-AD 668), and the name was made official in AD 936 by the subsequent Goryeo Dynasty. Local history states that during those turbulent times, many different battles were fought at this highly important strategic pass. Later, during more peaceful times, it was not uncommon for peddlers and travelers to find the skeletal remains of victims from previous conflicts, at or near the pass. The pass colloquially became known as Bbae-jae—"bone pass." More notably, later on in time during the Imjin War initiated by the Japanese invasion of the peninsula in 1592, many local people from this region fled to the pass and trained as insurgents in the Baekdu-daegan mountain system in an effort to launch deadly raids on the Japanese occupiers. These hardy folk lived and survived off the land, prowling for local wildlife, and it was said that they became so emaciated during their rebel existence that their bones protruded distinctively from their starved torsos, lending animation and distinctiveness to the pass's name.

In reflection, it is perhaps possible to imagine that the *jeongja* was put there and given its present name as a way of hurling these horrible memories into the mountain thermals forever. It is accepted practice to sleep at night in the fresh winds of this *jeongja* at Bone Pass, but don't be surprised if your dreams are haunted!

Sinpung-ryeong *jeong-ja*

TRANSPORT INFO

Leaving the trail at Bbae-jae: From the northern side of Bbae-jae, the closest bus stop is located 3.8 km away on NH37 at Sangojeong 상오정. Buses run from here to Seolcheon-myeon 설천면 five times daily, between 9:15 am and 7 pm. Seolcheon-myeon is located near the main entrance to Deogyu-san National Park, and buses run on to larger centers from here. On the southeastern side of the pass, the closest bus stop is located about 4 km away at Sojeong-ri 소정리. Buses leave here for Geochang-gun three times a day, at 12:10 pm, 3:50 pm and 5:30 pm. About 12 km southeast of Bbae-jae on NH37 is the small town of Goje-myeon 고제면. Call taxis will run to the pass from here; you can reach the Goje taxi service at 055-942-7277.

LODGING

About 100 meters down the eastern side of the road is the old Sinpung-ryeong Hyugeso 신풍령 휴게소. This large brick facility was once a restaurant and supermarket, but it unfortunately closed down in 2006, leaving behind the building and huge parking lot. The toilet facilities are still working and may be open. There is no controlled fresh water source at the pass, apart from a stream(28) flowing from the hills on the opposite side of the road and resurfacing at the hyugeso, near the vehicle entrance from the main road. Camping in this area should be okay; otherwise, the nearest accommodations are at the Bbae-jae Sanjang 빼재 산장 (T. 055-943-2957), located about 2 km southeast on NH37. Northwest of the pass, a number of motels and pensions can be found along NH37 in the direction of Samgong-ri, including the Geoseong Motel 거성모텔 (T. 063-322-9511), located about 3 km northwest in Samgeo-ri 삼거리. About 2 km after that is the Deogyu-san Recreational Forest 덕유산 자연휴양림, located about 1 km up a mountain road that leads off NH37. It is run by the Korea Forest Service and offers "forestel" accommodation, cabins and a large camping area. For bookings, call 063-322-1097 or visit www.huyang.go.kr.

DEOGYU-SAN NATURAL RECREATION FOREST 덕유산 자연휴양림

- Location: Samgeo-ri, Mupung-myeon, Muju-gun, Jeonbuk-do
- Total Area: 744 ha
- Year of Establishment: 1993
- Accommodation Capacity: 730 persons
- Management Office: National Natural Recreation Forest Office
- Telephone Number: 063-322-1097

Features

Deogyusan Natural Recreation Forest, 85 km from Daejeon via Muju and 34 km from Geochang, is easily accessible. Adjoining Deogyusan National Park, it is approximately 4 km from the entrance of the valley in Gucheon-dong, Muju. It has an abundance of Japanese Larch and Korean Pine trees, and the roads in the forest enable tourists to enjoy cycling. Such tourist attractions as Muju Resort, Deogyusan National Park, Muju water pumping power plant, and Jeoksangsanseong (Mountain Fortress) are located nearby.

THREE DAYS

50.5 km

SECTION 4

THE STELE TRAIL

Bbae-jae → Gwaebang-ryeong

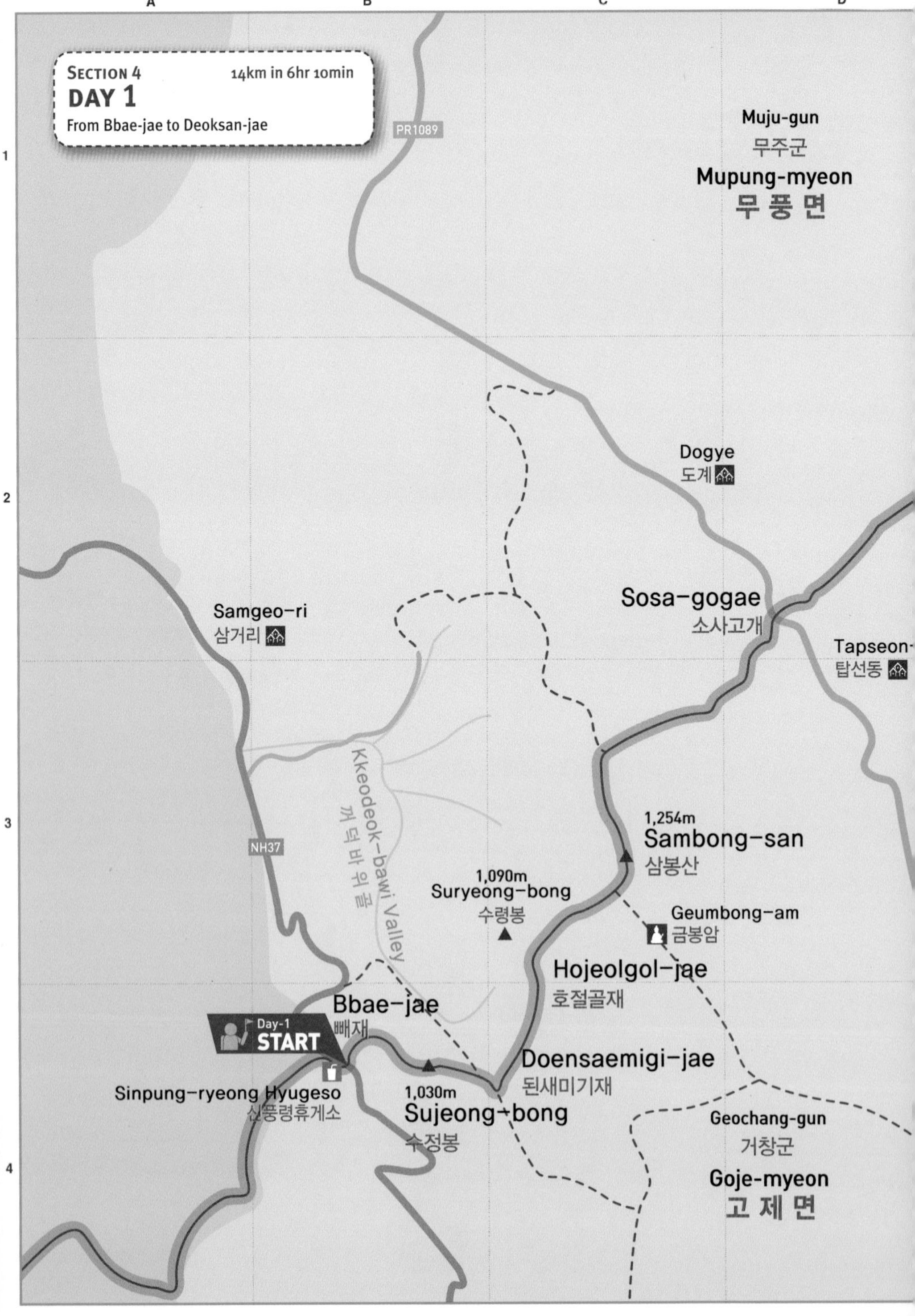

A
B
C
D
1
2
3
4
SECTION 4
14km in 6hr 10min
DAY 1
From Bbae-jae to Deoksan-jae
PR1089
Muju-gun
무주군
Mupung-myeon
무 풍 면
Dogye
도계
Samgeo-ri
삼거리
Sosa-gogae
소사고개
Tapseon-
탑선동
Kkeodeok-bawi Valley
꺼 덕 바 위 골
NH37
1,254m
Sambong-san
삼봉산
1,090m
Suryeong-bong
수령봉
Geumbong-am
금봉암
Hojeolgol-jae
호절골재
Bbae-jae
빼재
Day-1
START
Doensaemigi-jae
된새미기재
Sinpung-ryeong Hyugeso
신풍령휴게소
1,030m
Sujeong-bong
수정봉
Geochang-gun
거창군
Goje-myeon
고 제 면

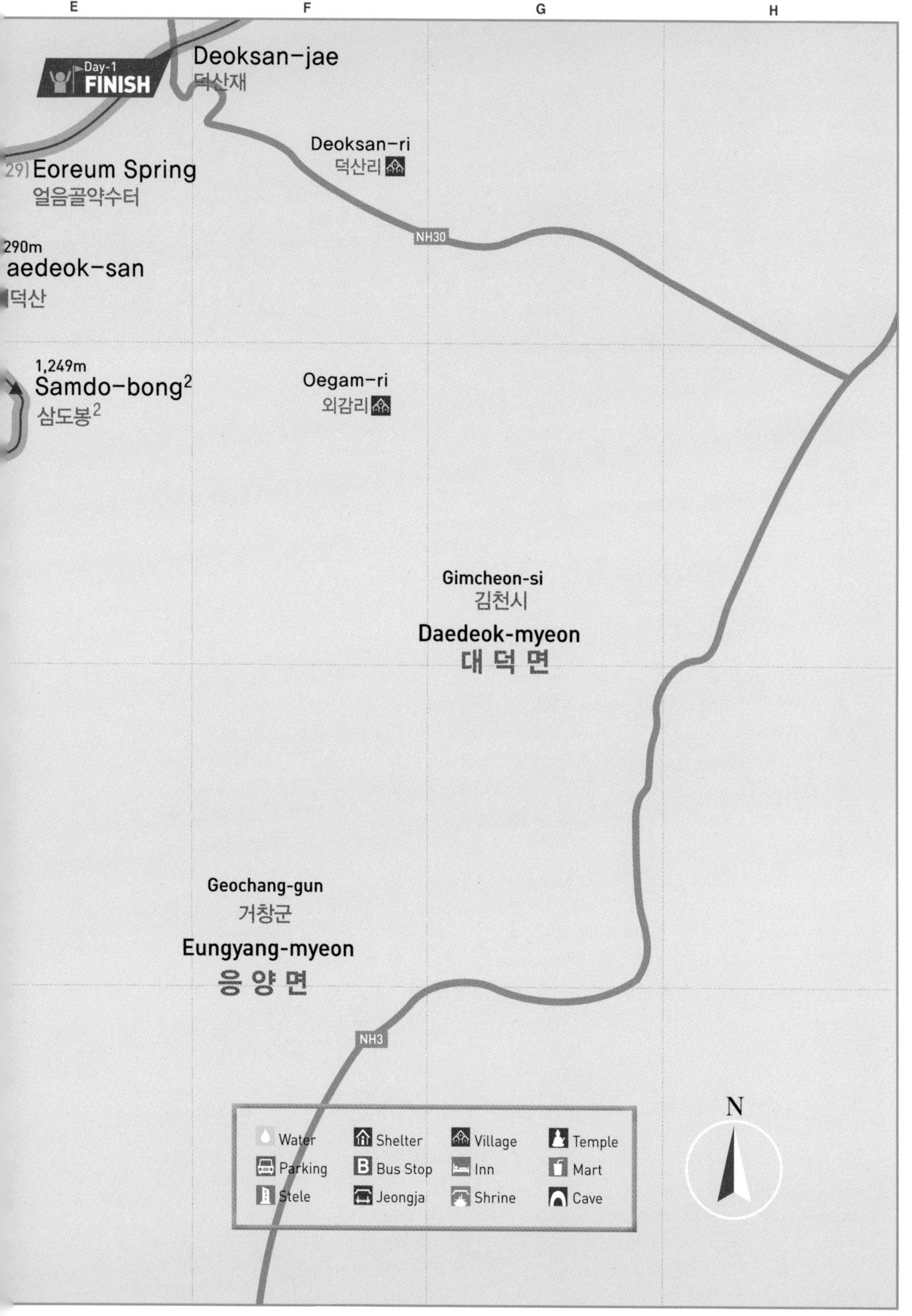
E
F
G
H
Day-1
FINISH
Deoksan-jae
덕산재
Deoksan-ri
덕산리
29) Eoreum Spring
얼음골약수터
NH30
290m
aedeok-san
덕산
1,249m
Samdo-bong²
삼도봉²
Oegam-ri
외감리
Gimcheon-si
김천시
Daedeok-myeon
대 덕 면
Geochang-gun
거창군
Eungyang-myeon
응 양 면
NH3
Water
Shelter
Village
Temple
Parking
Bus Stop
Inn
Mart
Stele
Jeongja
Shrine
Cave
N

DAY 1

From Bbae-jae to Deoksan-jae

- **Distance:** 14km
- **Time:** 6hr 10min

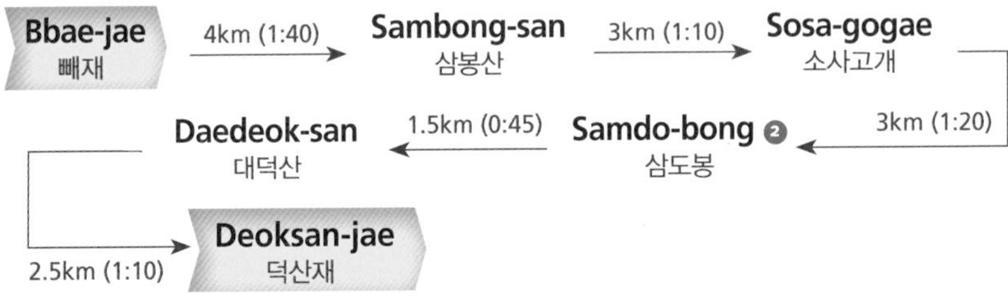

After spending a fresh, windy night sleeping on the bony remnants of the hallowed ground at Bbae-jae, awaken to the new dawn and make your way back to the ridge. Walk up over the lofty heights of Sambong-san, recede down into the pleasant pastures of rural Korea, and be delighted by the fragrances of fresh apples. Stop and have a cold drink at the local supa and see if any of the locals attempt to engage in idle chatter with you. Head back up the ridge again and belt your way to the sacred mysterious peak of Daedeok-san. Feel the pride it emits as a past bastion of national defense. Walk down its ridge and taste the effervescent blood the peak donates back to its followers. Walk out onto the pass at Deoksan-jae and admire the hermitage of the local herbalist and artist. Stand back and pose for the camera next to the giant stele, a USB stick plugged into the earth.

Bbae-jae 빼재 B4 → Sambong-san 삼봉산 C3 4km (1:45)

The trail entrance for this leg is located approximately 50 meters down the road from the top of the pass in the direction of the former Sinpung-ryeong 신풍령 rest area. From there, you climb north on an impressive, modern staircase that

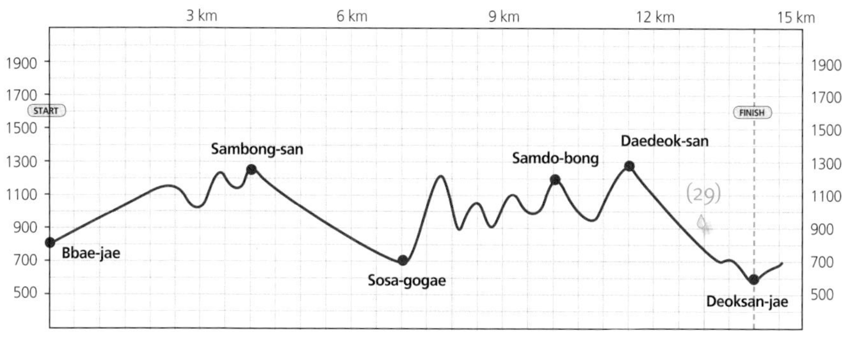

WATER STOPS (29) Eoreum Yaksuteo (spring): **N35°55'50" E127°53'06"**

scaffolds itself up the hillside before meeting the crest of the main ridge. Leaving the staircase, the trail turns northeast, climbing gradually through a thick cover of trees for 400 meters before it turns southeast, ascending gently for 600 meters to the wooded summit of Sujeong-bong 수정봉 (1,030m). From that peak, the trail descends southeast through pink-flowered bush clover and zebra grasses for 700 meters until it reaches a distinctive track junction that almost represents an old 4WD track. From this junction, the Baekdu-daegan turns north to a pass known as Doensaemigi-jae 된새미기재. From there, the trail climbs northeast, and after 400 meters, it goes over the brow of two large rocks. From this place at 60° NE, you can see the temple of Geumbong-am 금봉암 tucked 2 km away in a valley, just south of Sambong-san (1,254m). From the rocks, the trail straightens north, allowing you to walk on a good ridge climbing 80 m in altitude over the next 600 meter section, with the peak of Suryeong-bong 수령봉 (1,090m) lingering away to the east, before dropping into the pass of Hojeolgol-jae 호절골재, marked by a helipad, 300 meters later. The trail continues northeast, ascending 150 m in altitude over the next 600 meters, turning north just before the summit of Sambong-san. The 1,254 m peak is ringed by low trees and is celebrated by a relatively modern-looking stone tablet that stands atop an old cairn of large stones held together by dirt. The tablet names this peak as Deogyusam-bong 덕유삼봉. From this summit, the highest point on this leg, there are good views to the west over the farmland of Samgeo-ri 삼거리 and the Kkeodeok-bawi Valley 꺼덕바위골.

Sambong-san 삼봉산 C3 → Sosa-gogae 소사고개 D2

3km (1:10)

From Sambong-san, you continue north 200 meters before veering northwest onto a very thin and tree-covered trail that occasionally crosses over and below large boulders. On a grand day, it is a spectacular part of the walk and gives you fantastic views to the west, north, and east. In particular, you can quite clearly see that there is no distinctive ridgeline connecting you with Samdo-bong ❷, 40° to the northeast on the other side of the valley. The trail will in turn leave the current ridgeline you are on and descend down into the farming community of Sosa-gogae, crossing the road there, not crossing water, before gutsing it up the western face of Samdo-bong to continue on the Baekdu-daegan.

About 1 km after leaving Sambong-san, you reach a junction in the trail. At this junction, you should notice a trail marked by ribbons, running northeast off the ridge. This is the Baekdu-daegan, and it heads that way for approximately 2 km toward the road pass at Sosa-gogae. The descent is steep, dropping 200 m in altitude over 500 meters of trail before reaching a cluster of large boulders. The trail starts to free up, and over the next kilometer it will drop a further 250 m in altitude and come out of the forest into the large cabbage patches above Sosa-gogae. From there, the trail strays along the edges of the main patches, following the strategically placed ribbons, as you continue to descend through acacia trees and grasses. Shortly later, while on your rural jaunt, you come across apple orchards emanating delectable aromas, tempting you to do as Eve did and take one... just one. The rural pleasantries brighten your spirit as you admire the charms of this lifestyle before walking down a farm track onto the pass at Sosa-gogae. The quiet sleepy pass of Sosa-gogae is connected by PR1089, which runs north to Mupung-myeon 무풍면, approximately 10 km away, and south to the village of Goje-myeon 고제면, also 10 km away.

About 100 meters to the northwest of the pass is the Tapseon Supa 탑선수퍼, a small but well-stocked supermarket that also offers *minbak* accommodation in the ground-level rear part of the building. Depending on how many of you there are, the three rooms should cost you 30,000 won for the lot. The front entrance to the *minbak* rather bizarrely backs onto a small farmyard containing chickens, ducks, rabbits and two beehives...located on both sides of your front door like small guardian pillars. The rooms are comfortable but modest. The bathrooms have hot running water that needs to be turned on by the owners, but no showers. The long-drop toilets are located outside in the farmyard.

Tapseon Supa at Sosa-gogae with Sambong-san in the background.

TRANSPORT INFO

Leaving the trail at Sosa-gogae: From Tapseon-dong on the southeastern side of Sosa-gogae, buses leave to Geochang eight times daily from 6:50 am to 7:10 pm. Buses for Geochang leave eight times daily from 7 am to 7:40 pm. From Dogye, on the northwestern side of Sosa-gogae, buses head for Muju five times daily at 7:30 am, 11:30 am, 3:20pm, 5:40 pm and 7:25 pm.

Sosa-gogae 소사고개 D2 → Samdo-bong ❷ 삼도봉 E2

3km (1:20)

Leaving Sosa-gogae, the trailhead is located on the small rise on the road and is well marked with ribbons hanging next to a signboard for the Tapseon Supa. From there, you head northeast up an old farm track, passing a set of stunning tombs on the southeastern side of the trail. The trail passes through farmland located on both sides of a chiseled spur that takes you back to the ridge. Following the ribbons, you eventually meet a sealed farm road that maintains a northeast direction for the next 500 meters before reaching a large greenhouse and lean-to overlooking the farmland. The large greenhouse serves as a communal kitchen and social area for the workers of the Busan-nongjang Farm 부산 농장, and coffee and light food may be available if you arrive at the right time. From there, the trail leaves the road, and ribbons mark the way as you walk onto the top of a wooded bank that flanks the farmer's fields. Continue northeast, following the ribbons for about 500 meters, after which you should cross a vehicle track that eventually continues on in the same direction. The trail becomes a 4WD track in places.

In this area, the Baekdu-daegan trail will break east up to your next peak, called Samdo-bong ❷. This entrance is well marked by ribbons. The climb to the high ridge of Samdo-bong ❷ is quite steep and messy as you push through large bundles of overgrowth just before the summit. The ascent will see you climb more than 250 m in altitude over the last 800 meters, passing a well-placed tomb short of the ridgeline. This is a great spot to rest after the grueling climb, with great views west back to Sosa-gogae and the peaks north of Sambong-san. The Baekdu-daegan joins a north-south ridgeline, turning north onto it, through low trees and high grasses for 500 meters on its way to the peak of Samdo-bong ❷. The slopes to the west of the trail appear to have been used as highland farming grazing areas, and it is not uncommon to see domestic goats walking freely on the trail. The summit of Samdo-bong ❷ at 1,249 m ABSL is also known as Chojeom-san 초점산. It has a small tablet bearing its name located in a cleared grassy area with great views on all sides. This is the second Samdo-bong of the walk, the first being in Jiri-san National Park, and the trail will pass a third peak of the same name 17 km further north. The name, as mentioned, means "three provinces peak"; in this case, it is the intersection of Gyeongsangbuk-do to the northeast, Gyeongsangnam-do to the southeast and Jeollabuk-do to the west.

Looking at Samdo-bong after crossing Sosa-gogae © Liz Riggs

Samdo-bong ❷ 삼도봉 E2 → Daedeok-san 대덕산 E1 1.5km (0:45)

From Samdo-bong ❷, the trail heads northwest, descending 100 m in altitude for the next 400 meters down a wide path into the bottom of a saddle. On your descent, you should easily be able to see ahead of you the grassy knoll of Daedeok-san. From the saddle, you climb north for 50 m in altitude before coming out onto a bit of a ledge that pans out toward the foot of Daedeok-san. From there, it is another short ascent to the summit, located at 1,290 m ABSL. The summit of Daedeok-san, also known as Tugu-bong 투구봉, is a large, open, cleared area marked by a cobblestoned helipad edged with tall grasses to the west and open views to the east off the steep ridge over the fields of Oegam-ri 외감리 below.

The peak is celebrated by a small stele and an information board, offering some good history on the mountain and surrounding areas, translates to say: "Daedeok-san (1,290m) is a sacred and mysterious mountain standing high at the hip of the Baekdu-daegan, which begins at Baekdu-san and constitutes the backbone of the Korean peninsula. We can feel not only magnificence, but also tenderness from this mountain. In 1598, during the second wave of Japanese aggression, Yi Gwang-ak, commanding officer of Jeolla-do, drove the Japanese army away from this peak. Again in 1728, the army drove rebel soldiers from this peak. The water from Daedeok-san that streams down the western valley is the upper source of the Geum-gang River. Water formed from ice melting off Banga-gol 방아골 (980m), the eastern rock wall of this mountain, is the source of the Nakdong-gang River. A mineral spring to the north of the peak has tasty carbonic acidic water with a touch of brimstone. The taste of this ice cold water cannot be compared with any other spring, and it never runs dry even in the longest droughts. It is indeed a mysterious spring."

Daedeok-san 대덕산 E1 → Deoksan-jae 덕산재 F1 2.5km (1:10)

From the summit of Daedeok-san, the trail continues northeast, maintaining good height for the next 600 meters before reaching the end of the high ridge. From there, the trail descends northeast, dropping steeply 140 m over the next 400 meters before reaching the mineral spring(29) of Eoreum-gol 얼음골, which lies just to the right of the trail. As mentioned on the information board at Daedeok-san, this spring water has a distinctive taste and is identified by the colorful plastic ladles hanging above it. From the spring, the descent continues steadily, dropping more than 250 m in height over the next 800 meters of trail, but in places, the trail provides manmade switchbacks as it zigzags through the thick forest, making your descent a little less arduous. Reaching a height of 800 m

ABSL, the path straightens to the northeast, and the descent becomes gentle and undulating over the final 1.5 km to the road pass of Deoksan-jae. The path is well walked and quite scenic, passing through a mature stand of pine and deciduous trees before reaching the pass.

* Deoksan-jae 덕산재 F1

Deoksan-jae is connected by NH30, which runs between the town of Mupung-myeon 무풍면, about 8 km to the west, and Daedeok-myeon 대덕면, a similar distance to the southeast at the junction of NH3. It is home to an impressive, well-shaped, four meter high stele machined from granite. This monument was erected in October 2006 by the trail's guardians, the Korea Forest Service. The stele is carved with general information and statistics on the ridge. It is a symbol of the national spirit. As an indication that the Korea Forest Service wishes to internationalize the Baekdu-daegan, the inscription concludes that "We value the importance of the Baekdu-daegan and will make it known to the world. Preserving this indispensable place, we set up this milestone on Deoksan-jae Pass, which is on the borderline between the Yeongnam (Gyeongsang-do) and Honam (Jeolla-do) regions."

Transport Info

Leaving the trail at Deoksan-jae: Buses running between the cities of Muju and Gimcheon via Deoksan-jae will stop here if you wish to get off. Buses leave Muju seven times a day from 6:50 am to 6:37 pm and travel from Gimcheon eight times a day from 6:30 am to 5:55 pm. Leaving the ridge, you have to hike about 3 km southeast on NH30 to Deoksan-ri to the nearest bus stop, from which local buses run into Daedeok-myeon and on to Gimcheon. Local buses don't run to the pass, but they do run from Daedeok to Deoksan-ri, about 2 km southeast of the pass.

Lodging

The Deoksan-jae stele stands in front of the grounds of an artist's hermitage. There is no accommodation or store at the pass, but it may be possible to camp on the grounds of the building. Water is available within this building and will be gladly provided by the friendly artist. Seven kilometers to the east, Daedeok-myeon is a fair-sized town with a number of good restaurants and supermarkets. The most independent way you can camp at this pass is to walk about 400 meters down the south side of NH30 until you arrive at a sharp elbow in the road that provides a large grassy area with park benches and a partial shelter suitable for camping. There is no water here, but it can be found flowing in a stream 100 meters further down the road. Accommodations can be found in Mupung-myeon, located about 7 km northwest, and Daedeok-myeon, a similar distance southeast on NH30.

DAY 2

From Deoksan-jae to Udu-ryeong

• **Distance:** 23.5km
• **Time:** 10hr 5min

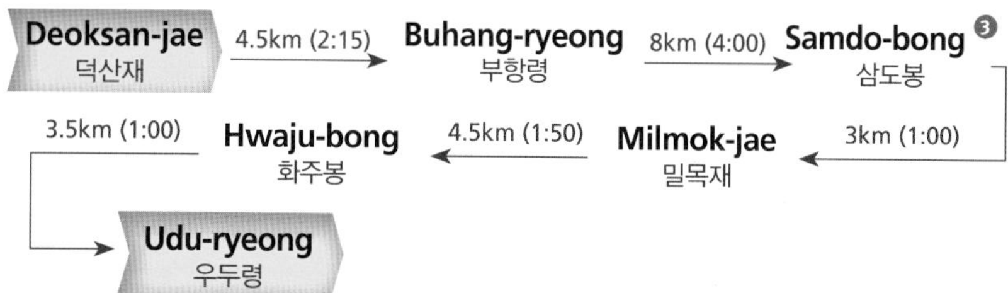

Climb your way back to the ridge and gait north through dense bush line, edging your way resolutely up the crest toward the high country of Samdo-bong ❸. Break from the forest and bask in the majestic views from the ridge. Observe from a distance the strange winged creature leering atop Samdo-bong ❸. Treat yourself to some mountain hospitality and rest your tempered body in papered rooms, sleeping to the gleeful sounds of mountain water as it crushes its way to the city like a mad rush of kids escaping from class. The next day, crash and burn your way to the isolated "cow's head pass."

Deoksan-jae 덕산재 B4 → Buhang-ryeong 부항령 B3

4.5km (2:15)

Leaving Deoksan-jae, the trail is clearly marked by ribbons to the north of the artist's hermitage behind an old shed. You enter the bush and walk in a northeastern direction, climbing sharply 150 m in altitude over the next 900 meters to an unnamed 833 m peak. From there you turn north, following the ridge for 400 meters before meeting a tomb where the trail turns to the northeast

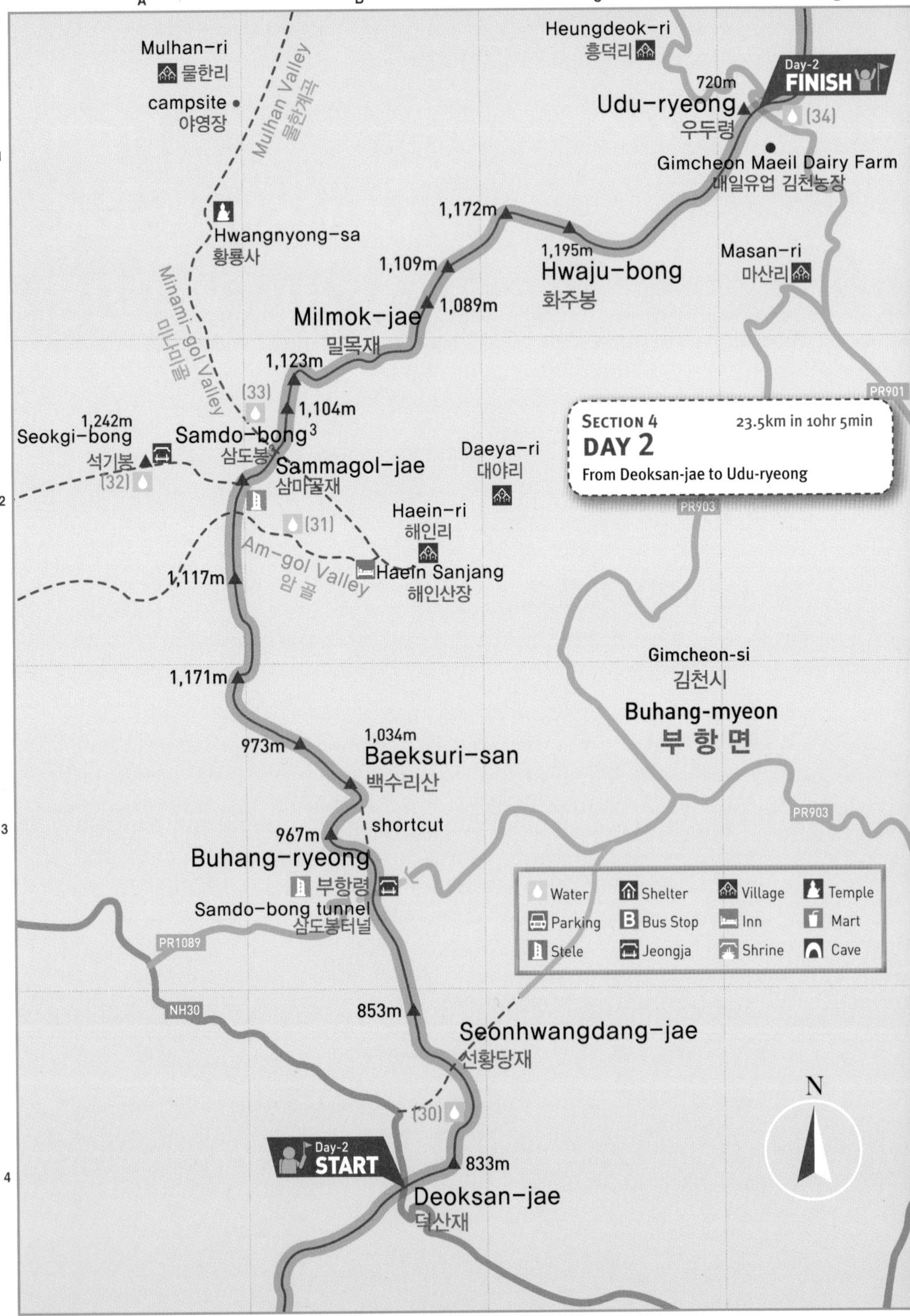
A
B
C
D
1
2
3
4
Mulhan-ri
물한리
campsite
야영장
Mulhan Valley
물한계곡
Hwangnyong-sa
황룡사
Minami-gol Valley
미나미골
Heungdeok-ri
흥덕리
Day-2
FINISH
720m
Udu-ryeong
우두령
(34)
Gimcheon Maeil Dairy Farm
매일유업 김천농장
1,172m
1,195m
Hwaju-bong
화주봉
Masan-ri
마산리
1,109m
1,089m
Milmok-jae
밀목재
1,123m
(33)
1,104m
PR901
1,242m
Seokgi-bong
석기봉
(32)
Samdo-bong[3]
삼도봉[3]
Sammagol-jae
삼마골재
Daeya-ri
대야리
(31)
Haein-ri
해인리
Am-gol Valley
암 골
Haein Sanjang
해인산장
1,117m
SECTION 4
23.5km in 10hr 5min
DAY 2
From Deoksan-jae to Udu-ryeong
PR903
1,171m
Gimcheon-si
김천시
Buhang-myeon
부 항 면
973m
1,034m
Baeksuri-san
백수리산
shortcut
967m
Buhang-ryeong
부항령
Samdo-bong tunnel
삼도봉터널
PR903
PR1089
NH30
Water
Shelter
Village
Temple
Parking
Bus Stop
Inn
Mart
Stele
Jeongja
Shrine
Cave
853m
Seonhwangdang-jae
선황당재
(30)
Day-2
START
833m
Deoksan-jae
덕산재
N

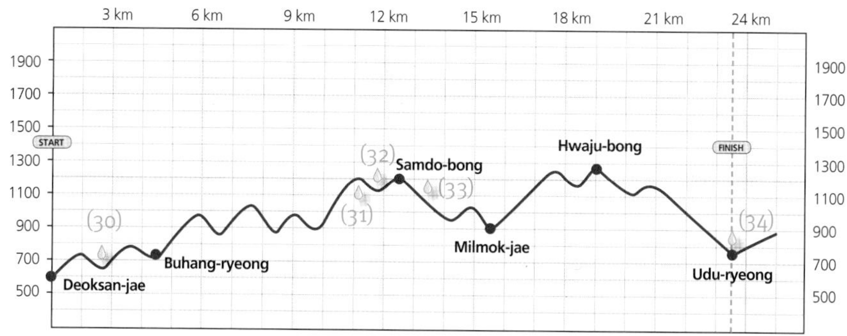

WATER STOPS

(30) Off old mining track: **N35°56'35" E127°54'44"**
(31) Track to Haein Shelter: **N36°00'51" E127°53'07"**
(32) Seokgi-bong near Samdo-bong: **N36°01'16" E127°52'00"**
(33) Sammagol-jae: **N36°01'39" E127°52'54"**
(34) Udu-ryeong: **N36°04'03" E127°57'17"**

and, after a couple hundred meters, meets up with an old mining track. Stream water(30) can be found 50 meters down the southern/western side of the track behind a thick layer of bush. From the track junction, the trail continues north for 500 meters before turning northwest and descending into the pass of Seonhwangdang-jae 선황당재, marking a four-way junction. Continuing northwest from the pass, you climb gently for 1.2 km before reaching a helipad located below an unnamed peak standing at 853 m ABSL. From there, you continue northwest through good forest, descending nicely for 1.6 km before reaching a helipad marking the pass of **Buhang-ryeong*** just ahead of it.

* Buhang-ryeong 부항령 B3

The trail passes right over the top of a tunnel that threads PR1089 through the ridge 6 km to the east from Buhang-myeon 부항면 and 5 km to the west to NH30. Tracks lead from the pass both east and west down to the road on either side of the tunnel. The eastern side of the pass celebrates the Baekdu-daegan with a three-meter engraved stele located in front of the tunnel. A further 50 meters down the road is a small park with a large, elegant blue-tiled *jeongja* passing as a very good camping spot.

Buhang-ryeong 부항령 B3 → Samdo-bong ❸ 삼도봉 A2

8km(4:00)

Back above the tunnel, the trail heads north, climbing gradually for about 700 meters and gaining 150 m in altitude as it passes through high stands of forest, where you should come across a series of tombs near the trail. At this point, the trail begins to steepen in a westerly direction, and a short moment later, you should see a track heading northwest from the main trail. The track bypasses and contours for about 350 meters along the eastern face of your next peak (located at 967 m ABSL), cutting about 600 meters off your walk. The western fork is the continuation of the true Baekdu-daegan trail, and following this sees you climbing steeply for the next 300 meters to the top of 967 m. You have now effectively reached the base of the high ridge, with a couple more bounds left to get consistently above the 1,000 m ABSL mark. At 967 m, the trail turns northeast, descending into a saddle where it meets the end of the previous shortcut. The next 400 meters sees the trail rise steeply to Baeksuri-san 백수리산, located at 1,034 m ABSL.

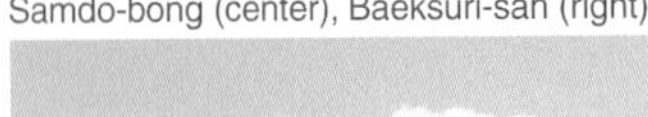

Samdo-bong (center), Baeksuri-san (right)

The summit of Baeksuri-san is a cleared area with a small stone tablet nestled proudly in the center. Views are great in all directions. Looking back south, you can see Daedeok-san 대덕산 (1,290m), now 10 km away. Rising from the ridge directly to the northwest and stretching to the north is the main ridge of Samdo-bong, the next large peak of the Baekdu-daegan. Leaving Baeksuri-san, you cross a rocky area and drop steeply 100 m in altitude northwest down the ridge into a saddle. From there, you continue northwest through a colony of thick bush clover as you climb back to an unnamed 973 m peak. From here, you only have 1 km of distance to cover before you plane out on the highest features of the ridge in this area, over 1,000 m ABSL.

From this area, the trail becomes the main ridge and maintains this height for the next 2.5 km north to Samdo-bong ❸*, dipping occasionally for the sake of topography. The forest gives way to subalpine grassland, and you join a modern boardwalk called a "namu (tree) deck." The impressive structure stretches for more than 100 meters and serves to keep hikers from wandering through and damaging the sensitive ecosystem of wildflowers and grasses that lies exposed on this high ridge. Leaving the boardwalk, the trail continues north, maintaining

good height on the ridge for about a kilometer before rising over an unnamed 1,117 m peak. Approximately 500 meters north of that peak, you reach a junction in the trail, marked by a signpost.

To the east of the track junction is a staircase heading 3 km down the Am-gol Valley 암골. About 700 meters into this descent, the track meets a road where you can also find spring water(31). The road continues for 2 km to the impressive mountain village of Haein 해인리, home of the Haein Sanjang* mountain shelter. This detour provides you with your first form of comfort accommodation should you decide to break this leg into two days. If you choose to rough it out on the ridge, your best option is probably on the peak of Samdo-bong just in front of you.

* Haein Sanjang 해인산장 B2

Built on the banks of a fast-flowing stream, the Haein Sanjang mountain shelter is a well-built log cabin with a *minbak* and casual restaurant serving home-style Korean meals. Home of Mr. Kim Yong-won, an experienced international mountaineer, the main building is decorated with photographs and memorabilia from his career in the mountains. The treed grounds are large, with tables and benches located alongside the river. The family-style hospitality is warm and laid-back at the Haein Sanjang, and the accommodations are very clean and comfortable—definitely worth the walk down the valley. The Haein Sanjang is advertised from the junction, and phone numbers are provided (T. 054-437-1991 or 011-555-2419). If your Korean is sufficient, it is possible to arrange a pickup from the top of the road down to the shelter.

* Samdo-bong ❸ 삼도봉 A2

From the junction, you can see the highest feature of this leg, Samdo-bong ❸ (1,176m), standing right in front of you. The trail to the summit is via a 100 m climb up its face. This Samdo-bong ("three provinces peak") divides Chungcheongbuk-do to the northeast, Jeollabuk-do to the southeast and Gyeongsangbuk-do to the east. The summit of Samdo-bong is also the meeting place of three trails. A trail to the west heads along a spur for 1.3 km to the summit of Seokgi-bong 석기봉. Just short of Seokgi-bong is an elaborate *jeongja*, offering shelter for the hiker. Water(32) can also be found at this peak, marked by a *doltap*.

The 1,176 m peak of Samdo-bong is celebrated by a huge monument called Hwahap-tap 화합탑 ("harmony monument"). This large stone statue features three turtles, with three dragons standing on top of them and a large stele atop the dragons. The structure is encircled by a hexagonal white stone fence. The turtles represent the earth, while the dragons represent the powers of heaven and hold the pearl of wisdom in their mouths. The stele represents humanity and records what we have done while standing between heaven and earth. This is the grandest monument to any peak on the Baekdu-daegan ridge, and its theme is harmony among the three bordering provinces, which have not had the most peaceful relationship over history.

There is enough space on Samdo-bong ❸ to pitch a tent. On the western side, there is a flat area of land that looks like it has purposely been put there for tents (but is probably a drop-zone for helicopters). It has been cut out of the peak, protecting it from the easterly winds.

TRANSPORT INFO

Leaving the trail at Samdo-bong: Buses run from Mulhan-ri in the Mulhan Valley to Yeongdong five times daily at 7:10 am, 9:30 am, 2:20 pm, 5 pm and 7 pm.

Samdo-bong ❸ 삼도봉 A2 → Hwaju-bong 화주봉 C1

7.5km (2:50)

From Samdo-bong ❸, the trail heads northeast, descending 150 m before arriving at the pass of Sammagol-jae 삼마골재 900 meters later. The pass is marked by a large open area with a concrete helipad situated in the middle; it is also the site of a four-way junction. The northwest track runs 3.5 km down the scenic gorge of Minami-gol 미나미골 and into the Mulhan Valley 물한계곡 to the temple of Hwangnyong-sa 황룡사. Mulhan-ri 물한리 is a popular trail entrance and has a number of minbak and restaurants, as well as a campsite 2 km further north along the road from the temple. From the ridge, water(33) can be found about 500 meters down this trail in a stream on the southern side of the track.

From the helipad on Samdo-bong ❸ , the Baekdu-daegan heads northeast, climbing steadily over the next 600 meters to an unnamed peak located at 1,104 m ABSL. From there, the trail levels out, and views are expansive on both sides as you walk a further 500 meters north to your next unnamed peak at 1,123 m ABSL. From 1,123 m, the trail descends about 200 m in height in a northeasterly direction for 1 km to the pass of Milmok-jae 밀목재, which is marked by numerous ribbons. After Milmok-jae, the trail continues northeast, climbing gently through lush forest on a good trail for just over 1 km before turning to the north. From there, the trail levels out, and the next 2 km is very good, covering consistently high ridge that offers you frequent views through the low forest. The next 800 meters after that see you briefly climbing to an unnamed peak located at 1,089 m ABSL, which is marked by a helipad and provides views to the southeast down the valley into the village of Daeya-ri 대야리.

From this peak, the trail dips northeast into a shallow saddle, where it then ascends northeast for 700 meters to an unnamed peak located at 1,109 m ABSL. Here, the trail turns east into a saddle before climbing northeast for 800 meters to another unnamed peak located at 1,172 m ABSL. This peak is a rocky outcrop rising above the low trees and bushes of the high ridge and offering fantastic 360° views from its summit. To the east, you can see the summit of Hwaju-bong (a.k.a. Seokgyo-san 석교산) at 1,195 m ABSL, the next peak of the Baekdu-daegan. Following the trail to the southeast, you drop steeply off the peak onto a series of fixed ropes that take you vertically down its face into the deep saddle beneath. Once in the abyss of the sharp saddle, the trail meanders its way back up the ridge through more deciduous forest to the open summit of Hwaju-bong.

Hwaju-bong 화주봉 C1 → Udu-ryeong 우두령 D1

3.5km (1:00)

The summit of Hwaju-bong (1,195m) has a small stone tablet bearing its name and height set at the edge of a small clearing that is open to the east, offering great views for a good 20 km back along the eastern face of the Baekdu-daegan. The low trees at the southeastern edge of the peak are heavy with colorful ribbons that indicate the continuation of the trail. The 3.5 km stretch from Hwaju-bong to Udu-ryeong is downhill the whole way, and you can expect to complete the walk in about an hour, descending 470 m in altitude before meeting PR901. Before you arrive at Udu-ryeong, you see a lime-green wire fence that acts as a crush for the nature bridge traversing the road at Udu-ryeong. Keep to the left of the fence, and you will soon walk under a tall steel pylon into a small loose metalled rest area known as Udu-ryeong on PR901.

Hwaju-bong

* Udu-ryeong 우두령 D1

The cow stele of Udu-ryeong

Connected by the PR901, Udu-ryeong, or "cow's head pass," is also known as Jilmae-jae 질매재, meaning "pack saddle pass." It is celebrated by a large stone statue of a cow in a small pebbled rest area. The statue was erected by the Korea Forest Service in October 2006. The cow is a strange removal from the powerful stone steles erected on many of the other peaks and passes of the Baekdu-daegan, and it is a caricatured tribute to the meaning of "Udu-ryeong." It may also have some relationship to the large Maeil dairy company and farm that dominates the southern side of the ridge below the pass. If you stay overnight at this pass, you will get well chorused by the beasts at night. The inscription on the statue gives general information on the Baekdu-daegan and points out the importance of the ridge as the core axis of Korea's ecosystem and a treasure trove of biodiversity. The inscription concludes with this message: Mountains are the basis, the source, of life. We erect this monument here with the heart to love and protect the Baekdu-daegan.

Above the rest area, on the crest of the ridge, the road is crossed by an "eco bridge." This grand structure is designed as a crossing for animals on the Baekdu-daegan as an alternative to the road, with fences extending below the ridge on each side in an effort to herd the animals toward the bridge.

TRANSPORT INFO

Leaving the trail at Udu-ryeong: To the northwest from Udu-ryeong, the nearest bus stop is located 3.7 km from the pass in Heungdeok-ri 흥덕리. From here, buses run into Yeongdong-gun four times a day at 8 am, 10:50 am, 3:40 pm and 6:30 pm, returning to Heungdeok at 6:40 am, 9:20 am, 2 pm and 5:10 pm.

To the southeast, the closest bus stop is located 3 km from Udu-ryeong in Masan-ri 마산리, at the junction of PR901 and PR903. Buses leave for Gimcheon four times a day at 7:35 am, 9:55 am, 3 pm and 6:10 pm, returning to Masan-ri at 6:50 am, 8:30 am, 1:50 pm and 5:10 pm.

LODGING

Udu-ryeong has no facilities, but the area around the monument is a good place to camp. Water(34) can be found about 300 meters on the eastern side of the pass from runoff coming out of the forest. On the other side of the pass, there is a large concrete helipad located about 100 meters into the trail, which could also act as a safe and peaceful alternative away from the roadside. From the pass, PR901 runs northwest for 12.5 km to the small, well-stocked and pleasant town of Sangchon-myeon 상촌면, which has one small *minbak* with hostel-style accommodations, run by an elderly couple. Ask at the main supa for directions.

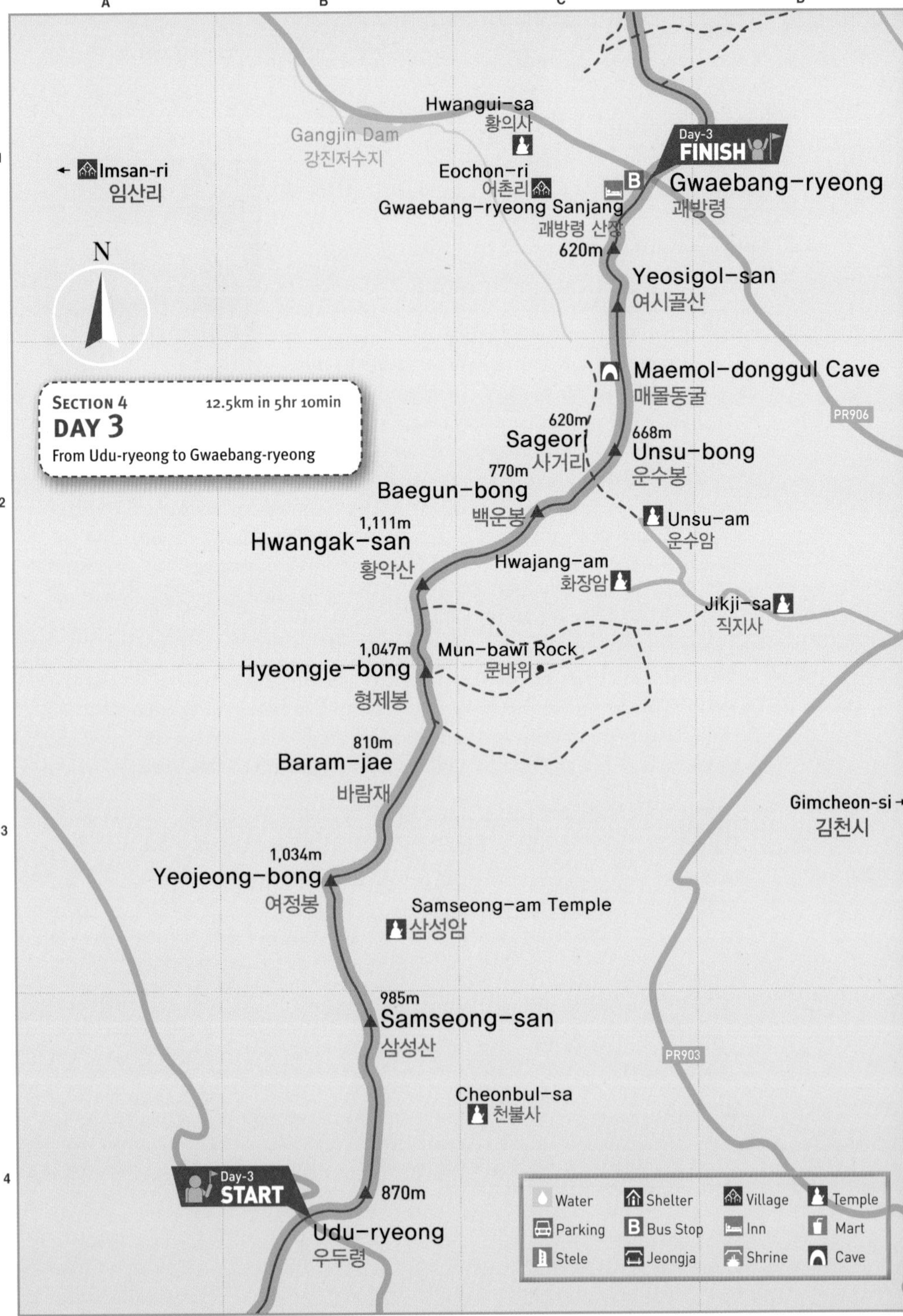

A
B
C
D
1
2
3
4
Imsan-ri
임산리
Gangjin Dam
강진저수지
Hwangui-sa
황의사
Eochon-ri
어촌리
Gwaebang-ryeong Sanjang
괘방령 산장
Day-3
FINISH
Gwaebang-ryeong
괘방령
620m
Yeosigol-san
여시골산
Maemol-donggul Cave
매몰동굴
PR906
620m
Sageori
사거리
668m
Unsu-bong
운수봉
770m
Baegun-bong
백운봉
Unsu-am
운수암
1,111m
Hwangak-san
황악산
Hwajang-am
화장암
Jikji-sa
직지사
1,047m
Hyeongje-bong
형제봉
Mun-bawi Rock
문바위
810m
Baram-jae
바람재
Gimcheon-si
김천시
1,034m
Yeojeong-bong
여정봉
Samseong-am Temple
삼성암
985m
Samseong-san
삼성산
PR903
Cheonbul-sa
천불사
Day-3
START
870m
Udu-ryeong
우두령
SECTION 4
12.5km in 5hr 10min
DAY 3
From Udu-ryeong to Gwaebang-ryeong
N
Water
Shelter
Village
Temple
Parking
Bus Stop
Inn
Mart
Stele
Jeongja
Shrine
Cave

DAY 3

• **Distance:** 12.5km
• **Time:** 5hr

From Udu-ryeong to Gwaebang-ryeong

Reveille from your sleepless plight...and wonder how many beasts the lions ate that night. Head back to the ridge. Don't complain—walking is now your job. Good or bad, you do it! As the body warms up, it starts to enjoy its punishment, and your head swims in drowned pleasure. Walking along the ridge, you see the small temples wedged into its sides, and you slowly start to understand why they are there. Pass the oblique military structure and admire the zircon green blades of Hwangak-san. Force your way up its back and stop to point out the holy grounds of Jikji-sa, the mother of all temples. Be drawn to its grounds and marvel at its magic. Stay the night and pray in the dark early morning winds with the monks. Return to the ridge, refreshed, rejuvenated and enlightened, and continue your pilgrimage. Walk from the tree line onto the pass of Gwaebang-ryeong and check out the funkiest venue you will find on this walk...a live music café. Have a beer with the crooners, and ask yourself again: "Where am I? Is this really Korea?"

Udu-ryeong 우두령 B4 → Baram-jae 바람재 B3 5km (2:10)

The trail enters the forest on the northern side of the road. As usual, a large number of ribbons hang from the trees at the trail entrance, which is next to a blue road sign indicating the height of the pass. About 100 meters later, you walk

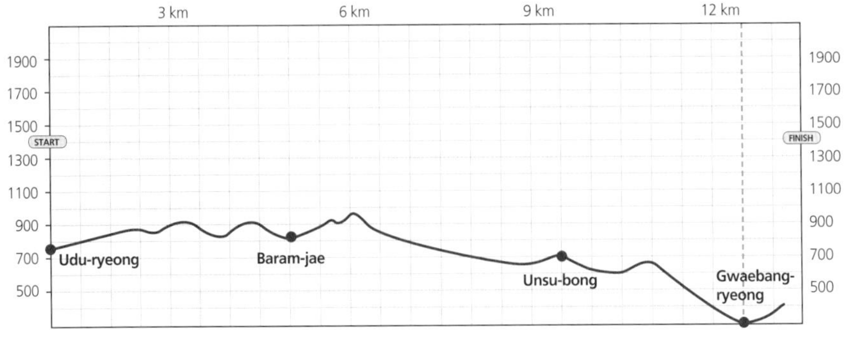

WATER STOPS No water stops for this course

across a large concrete helipad as the trail heads east, climbing through a tall forest of deciduous trees with vibrant undergrowth, for about 500 meters before reaching the edge of the high ridge at an 870 m peak marked by a tomb. From there, the Baekdu-daegan turns north, allowing you to walk on a relatively flat ridge for more than a kilometer through a thinning forest before veering northwest slightly into an open area of silver grasses and low shrubs, enabling views back south to the 870 m peak and east down a steep valley at the temple of

Cheonbul-sa 천불사. Reentering the forest, you have a brief but steep climb to the rounded summit of Samseong-san 삼성산, located at 985 m ABSL. From the summit, the trail continues north, descending gently over the next 500 meters into a saddle before regaining its height for the next 500 meters to Yeojeong-bong 여정봉, located at 1,034 m ABSL. The ridge is open at times, with good views to the east. About 600 meters before reaching Yeojeong-bong, you can see Samseong-am 삼성암 jammed into the corner of a valley about 700 meters east down the steep valley from the ridge. There is no known track to this temple from the ridge trail.

The summit of Yeojeong-bong is thick with low shrubs and is marked by a small wooden signpost bearing its name. From the peak, the trail turns east, dropping to a military facility dug into the peak. The mountain road built to make this structure traverses the ridge from the east. Oddly enough, there is an abandoned mid-green porta-loo perched on the edge of the road. The east, facing amenity provides outstanding sojourns back over the valleys. The northern side of Yeojeong-bong gives you stunning views forward to the sacred Hwangak-san 황악산, with its long, sweeping ridgeline standing with great prominence on the Baekdu-daegan. From the barren, militarized summit, the trail joins the mountain road, descending off the peak to the northeast where, shortly thereafter, you have the option of leaving the road and joining the hiking trail to the left, which tries

Looking at the sacred peak of Hwangak-san from Gimcheon city

to stay on the ridge heading down to Baram-jae. Otherwise, the other, easier option is to simply stay on the mountain road for the 800 meter walk down to Baram-jae pass, which you should also be able to see from the road. The pass, located at 810 m ABSL, is marked by a large helipad in an open area, with a small stone stele bearing its name and position on the Baekdu-daegan. It also serves as a four-way track junction.

Baram-jae 바람재 B3 → Unsu-bong 운수봉 C2 4.5km (1:50)

The Baekdu-daegan continues to the northeast, entering the forest and climbing steadily but surely on a well-maintained trail, pocketed with occasional stairwells, for 700 meters before reaching the edge of the high north-facing ridge of Hwangak-san, which is marked by a signpost. To the north is the continuation of the Baekdu-daegan, and you walk on a good ridge trail for 500 meters to your next ledge of Hyeongje-bong 형제봉, located at 1,047 m ABSL. At this location between the gaps in the trees, you can see the massive grounds of **Jikji-sa*** 75° to the east, with the large metropolis of Gimcheon 김천시 filling the landscape behind it. A steep trail heads east off the peak about 1.2 km down to Mun-bawi Rock 문바위, also known as Birotong-mun 비로통문, which can also be seen from the ridge and then down the Mun-bawi stream to Jikji-sa.

From this vantage point, you continue north off the peak, descending briefly before ascending gently for 900 meters on a good ridge trail to the sacred summit Hwangak-san, which protects Jikji-sa. About 100 meters before reaching the peak, there is another track heading east from the ridge, facilitating itself as the main artery to the temple. Jikji-sa is well worth a visit, and although this is the main route to it from the guardian mountain, it is a better idea to continue onwards to the summit of Hwangak-san and then exit the ridge about 2 km later on a shorter passage to the temple, thereby gifting yourself with a more forgiving climb back to the great ridge upon your return.

Back on the ridge, it is a short 200 meter walk from the Jikji-sa track junction to the summit of Hwangak-san, which means "yellow crag mountain." The summit, located at 1,111 m ABSL, features a simple plain *doltap* with two small stone steles standing loyally to its side. This particular area offers excellent views

TRANSPORT INFO

Leaving the trail at Jikji-sa Temple: Buses run with great frequency from Gimcheon to Jikji-sa Temple. They leave Gimcheon Terminal every 5–10 min from 6:10 am to 10:40 pm.

The grounds of Jikji-sa from Hwangak-san

for the deprived hiker, directed east toward the alluring attractions of Gimcheon. There is also a large information board at the peak depicting the Baekdu-daegan and its sibling *jeongmaek*. The trail heads off the peak in a northeast direction, dropping immediately to a helipad located in a grass clearing and then terracing again down one more level to another helipad about 100 meters later. On your descent, you stay briefly above the bush line covering a thin rocky ridge before entering the forest. From here, you begin a steady descent, dropping more than 400 m over the next 2 km. The popular trail is well maintained, with modern stairs and fixed ropes at the steepest points. About 1.5 km after leaving Hwangak-san, the trail levels out to Baegun-bong 백운봉 (770m) before continuing northeast for another 600 meters to the saddle of Sageori, meaning "four-way junction," located at about 620 m ABSL. The saddle is situated in a large, picturesque open area, containing tall trees that stand over sets of welcoming park benches. From this place, a track heads southeast down a staircase for 600 meters to Unsu-am Hermitage 운수암, located about a kilometer above Jikji-sa. This is the shortest route to Jikji-sa. The Baekdu-daegan continues northeast, climbing immediately for the next 400 meters up to the summit of Unsu-bong at 668 m ABSL. This summit is ringed with tall trees and has a small stone stele at the center of a large clearing.

* Jikji-sa 직지사 D2

Jikji-sa Temple may be one of the oldest temples in Korea. Believed to have been built in AD 418 by Master Ado, a legendary missionary of the more northern Goryeo Kingdom, it has a construction date reputed to be more than 100 years prior to the mandated acceptance of Buddhism in Korea by the more shamanistically inclined Silla Kingdom. Its site was inspired by the broad and high ridge of Hwangak-san, and it is said that Master Ado simply pointed to this valley below the peak, saying, "This is a good place to build a temple." The temple has been rebuilt and renovated many times since. The road leading to the temple is dotted with motels and restaurants serving delicious mountain vegetable meals. There is also a rose of Sharon botanical garden and a culture park with a number of interesting sculptures.

Jikiji-sa is part of the Temple Stay Program of the Jogye order of Buddhism. If you wish to experience a day in the life of a monk, visit http://eng.templestay.com for bookings, or contact Jikji-sa directly by phone at 054-436-6084 or on the net at www.jikjisa.or.kr.

Unsu-bong 운수봉 C2 → Gwaebang-ryeong 괘방령 C1

3km (1:10)

Dropping off Unsu-bong, you descend gently north on a good trail before reaching a shallow saddle 800 meters later. From here, the trail continues north, and after about 200 meters, you pass the Maemol-donggul Cave 매몰동굴, which waits like a giant snake pit for you on the western side of the trail. From here, it's a 400 meter undulating walk to the summit of Yeosigol-san 여시골산, located at 668 m ABSL at the lower end of the high Hwangak-san ridge. It should also be noted that beneath the summit of Yeoshigol-san is a 10 km train tunnel for the new super-express KTX train that runs between Seoul and Busan. From there, it's all downhill for the final 1.5 km or so to the pass of Gwaebang-ryeong, over which you drop about 300 m in altitude. About 800 meters after Yeoshigol-san, you meet a mountain road that runs northwest through a dairy farm and onto PR906. From there, the trail crosses the road and reenters the tree line before turning to the northeast, passing through vegetable farms and following more trees marked with ribbons before disappearing back into the tree line, passing a water duct, and then falling out onto the pass of Gwaebang-ryeong at PR906. Right in front of you sits the new and modern Live Music Café of this pass, built by the young semi-retired musician Baek Gi-su.

* Gwaebang-ryeong 괘방령 C1

Gwaebang-ryeong, located at 300 m ABSL, is connected by PR906 and acts as a border between Chungcheongbuk-do to the west and Gyeongsangbuk-do to the east. Located on the roadside on the southern side of the pass is a bus stop that also acts as a well-constructed information board. Gwaebang-ryeong was once the main route that Gyeongsang-do scholars took when travelling to Seoul to partake in the *gwageo* (national civil service examinations) during the Joseon Dynasty (1392-1910). Quite separately, Gwaebang-ryeong was also the location of fierce fighting during the Imjin Invasion of 1592-1598, in which General Park E-ryong defeated the Japanese. A shrine to General Park is located at Hwangui-sa 황의사, about 1.5 km west along the road near Eochon-ri 어촌리. The notice concludes in a rather holistic manner that although the pass is low, it is also a part of the Baekdu-daegan, the symbol of the Korean spirit. Here, the Baekdu-daegan takes its breath and stretches powerfully toward Hwangak-san, and it is a source of waters for the Nakdong-gang River to the east and Geum-gang River to the west.

Leaving the trail at Gwaebang-ryeong: Buses running between Imsan-ri to the west and Gimcheon to the east cross Gwaebang-ryeong. Buses leave from Gimcheon for Imsan at 6:35 am, 8:35 am, 2:35 pm, 5:05 pm and 7:05 pm and from Imsan for Gimcheon at 7:05 am, 10 am, 4 pm, 6:20 pm and 7:45 pm. Leaving the pass, these buses will stop if you wave them down or wait at a bus stop.

The Gwaebang-ryeong Sanjang 괘방령 산장 (T. 011-281-8008) is a modern, rustic building. Opened in 2007, it is the home of Mr. Baek Gi-su and his wife. The Gwaebang-ryeong Sanjang offers accommodation and meals in a friendly environment, with atmosphere provided by Mr. Baek, who plays a mean guitar. The grounds resemble a shrine to the Baekdu-daegan, with large *doltap* that stand throughout the garden, carved with the names and heights of major peaks on the ridge. Another cairn and a number of totem poles also stand around a barbecue area where a cord has been erected for hikers to place their ribbons. Located outside the front of the building is a wash bay for cleaning your gear and selves with. Camping in this area should be fine, upon consent from the owner. To the west of the pass is the small village of Eochon-ri, 1.5 km away, with its charming lakeside mannerisms and restaurants that prepare fish caught locally from the nearby Gangjin Dam 강진 저수지. Also located on its main road is a small, rough-looking supa that sells just about every amenity you could need.

FOUR DAYS

62.8 km

SECTION 5

CENTRAL KOREA

Gwaebang-ryeong → Hwaryeong-jae

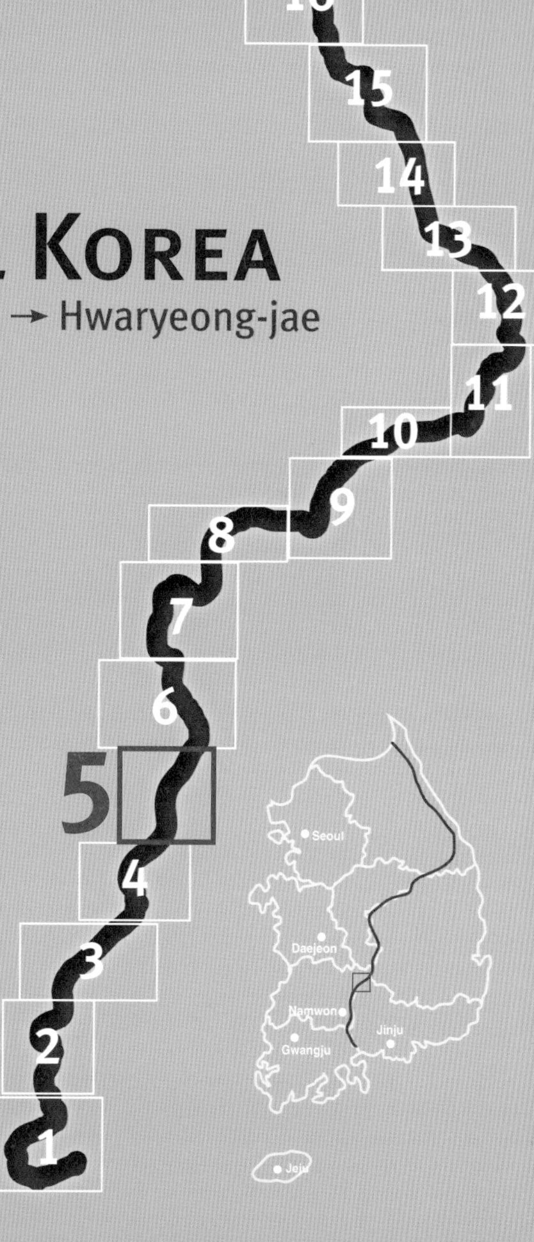

SECTION 5
28.5km in 12hr 40min
DAY 1 & 2
From Gwaebang-ryeong to Keun-jae
Keun-jae
(36)큰재
Day-2 FINISH
Oksan
옥산
Ewha-jang Motel
이화장모텔
Sangpan-ri
상판리
Sangpan Reservoir
상판저수지
NH3
PR997
683m
795m
Guksu-bong
국수봉
Sangju-si
상주시
Gongseong-myeon
공 성 면
Yeongdong-gun
영동군
Chupungryeong-myeon
추 풍 령 면
708m
Yongmun-san
용문산
Cheonseong Christian prayer camp
천성기도원
573m
Dongmugol-san
동무골산
687m
Gido-bawi
기도바위
Galhyeon
갈현
Neungchi-ri
능치리
Gimcheon-si
김천시
Jukjeon-ri
죽전리
474m
Mujwagol-san
무좌골산
Eomo-myeon
어 모 면
Chupungryeong
추풍령
Chupung-ryeong Reservoir
추풍령저수지
230m
Chupung-ryeong
추풍령
Jakjeom-jae
작점재
(35)
Day-2 START
Day-1 FINISH
Karib Motel
카리브모텔
360m
Geum-san
금산
Maebong-jae
매봉재
744m
Nurui-san
눌의산
498m
Mae-bong
매봉
Sagijeom-gogae
사기점고개
NE1
690m
733m
Nanham-san
난함산
625m
Janggun-bong
장군봉
730m
Gaseong-san
가성산
Gimcheon-si
김천시
Bongsan-myeon
봉 산 면
NH4
N
Day-1 START
418m
Gwaebang-ryeong
괘방령
Gwaebang-ryeong Sanjang
괘방령 산장
Water
Shelter
Village
Temple
Parking
Bus Stop
Inn
Mart
Stele
Jeongja
Shrine
Cave

DAY 1

From Gwaebang-ryeong to Jakjeom-jae

- **Distance:** 19km
- **Time:** 8hr 15min

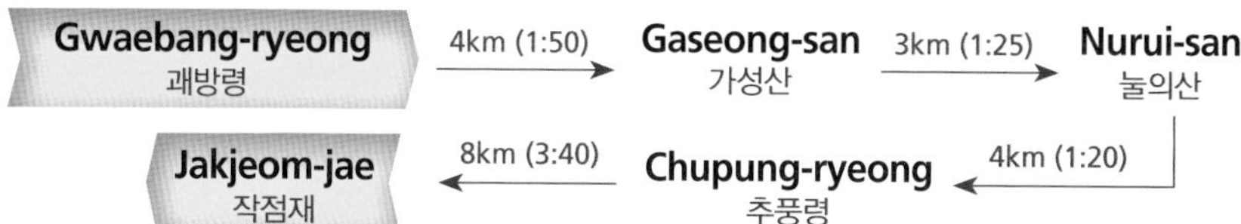

After a night of funk and groove at the live music café, you ascend above the farmland of Gwaebang-ryeong, trudging through the green prism of light on a testing ridge to the peak of Nurui-san, and sight the railside town of Chupung-ryeong. Scurry down to its forgotten charm, passing through orchards. Inject yourself into the national artery of Korea and quench your thirst. Head west from the southern end of town, reaching the 200 km marker of the trail at the crest of an old quarry above the Chupung-ryeong Reservoir 추풍령 저수지, before arriving at a great camping spot at the bough of Jakjeom-jae.

Gwaebang-ryeong 괘방령 → Gaseong-san 가성산 A4

4km (1:50)

From Gwaebang-ryeong, the trail crosses the road and ascends northeast into thick forest for 800 meters before reaching an unnamed peak located at 418 m ABSL. At this point, the trail turns northwest, and you walk above farmland in a valley to the south as you slowly descend for the next 600 meters into a saddle, the site of a four-way trail junction. From the junction, the trail continues northwest, climbing steeply before reaching the edge of a north-facing ridge 300

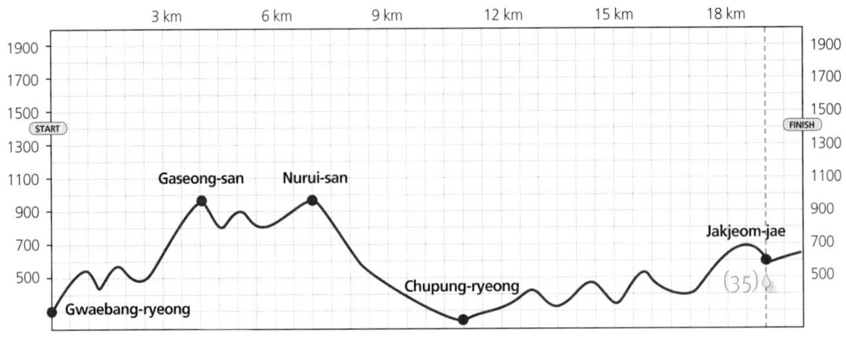

WATER STOPS (35) Jakjeom-jae: **N35°12'38" E128°03'10"**

meters later. From there, the trail turns north, descending gently for about 500 meters into a wide saddle where tracks run west and east off the ridge. From the saddle, the trail heads north for 600 meters on a good trail before dropping into another trail junction. Around the small farming communities on this section of the Baekdu-daegan, there are always numerous tracks running to and from the ridge. From the junction, the trail turns northwest as you begin the ascent of Gaseong-san, climbing about 300 m in altitude over the next two kilometers towards its summit. The summit of Gaseong-san is thick with trees surrounding what is supposed to be a helipad, offering no views. On one edge of the helipad is a small stele set amidst a stone pile.

Gaseong-san 가성산 A4 → Nurui-san 눌의산 A3 3km (1:25)

Leaving Gaseong-san, you head northwest, dropping steeply through thick forest for about 700 meters into a saddle located at 530 m ABSL. The trail continues northwest from the saddle, climbing 600 meters to the summit of Janggun-bong 장군봉 (625m), a peak surrounded by trees. From Janggun-bong, you descend northeast for 200 meters, meeting another track in the trail that loops east 500 meters back to a valley road southwest of Chupung-ryeong. From the junction, the trail continues to a shallow saddle for 500 meters before turning north, where it then ascends 100 m over the next 700 meters to an unnamed peak located at 690 m ABSL. The tip of this summit indicates the edge of the northeast ridge to the highest feature of your day at Nurui-san. But before you reach it, you drop into another saddle on this rollercoaster leg, marked by a helipad, before ascending one more bound of 50 m in altitude over 300 meters of trail and finally breaking out onto the summit of Nurui-san, located at 744 m ABSL.

Have a well-deserved break at this peak. You've broken the camel's back, as it's all downhill from here. On the summit of Nurui-san, there's a helipad and a small stele celebrating the peak and the Baekdu-daegan. Take a look north and east from the well-fringed summit at the landscape ahead of you. Instantly, you can see South Korea's busiest highway, NE1, running parallel with NH4 and a central railway system; all three of these arteries cut straight through the center mass of South Korea at what is the lowest pass over the Baekdu-daegan. Despite this amalgamation of networks, the small dwelling that they cut through is just that: a livid, dusty township that was once the most viable way to get from east to west. Its name is Chupung-ryeong, and to its northwest are the major cities of Daejeon and Seoul, while to its southeast are the metropolises of Daegu and Busan. About 30° to the northeast, you can see straight up a valley road located behind the township of Chupung-ryeong. The Baekdu-daegan mountain system more or less runs along the eastern side of that valley. On its eastern flank at 40°, you should be able to see the peak of Yongmun-san 용문산 (708m) about 6.5 km away, standing about a kilometer behind the smaller peak of Dongmugol-san 동무골산 at 573 m. Yongmun-san is part of the Baekdu-daegan trail. Also to your northeast, you can easily see a dam known as the Chupung-ryeong Reservoir. The road on its northern bank passes east over the Baekdu-daegan at the Jakjeom-jae pass some 9 km later at 65° northeast from your current position. While you're admiring the navigational opportunities of this stop, it is also a good opportunity to get some

Looking NE from Nurui-san to the central town of Chupung-ryeong

idea of where your next leg at Chupung-ryeong will begin. If you shoot a compass-bearing of 60°, you will notice the low ridge on the southern side of the dam. At the foot of that ridge, right where it meets NH4 next to a stack of about 10 greenhouses, is the trailhead.

Nurui-san 눌의산 A3→ Chupung-ryeong 추풍령 B3 4km (1:20)

From Nurui-san, the Baekdu-daegan descends northwest for about 400 meters to another helipad before entering the forest and turning northeast toward Chupung-ryeong. At that stage, you begin a sharp descent, passing through tall, thin stands of larch forest and dropping roughly 400 m in height over the next kilometer before coming out of the forest into farmland and orchards south of Chupung-ryeong*. The trail basically meets a vehicle track that passes alongside orchards in a northeast direction. Keep an eye out for ribbons if things get confusing. You should soon arrive at a flat, grassy area containing some well-manicured tombs. Continue walking past the edge of these tombs and you will drop onto a dirt farm road. Turn right here and follow it all the way down to NE1. The farm road will take you through a small vehicular tunnel under NE1 and out into a greenhouse area. You should be able to see some more hiking ribbons hanging from the intersection at this point, making you turn left toward the railway tracks and the pillars that support and elevate NH4. Pass by an oddball-looking communications facility on your right (which probably powers rail signals for kilometers) and literally walk right under NH4. Just as you get to the other side of the underside of the flyover, you come to a level railway crossing!! Yep, and a high speed crossing at that so pay heed to the signals, because the trains move quick in Korea, and it would look pretty bad for long-distance hiking if you became the first foreign fatality on the Baekdu-daegan—one hit by an express train!

Cross this bizarre part of your walk and straight into the shanty-style back blocks of Chupung-ryeong. Follow what is now a small, narrow road for about 100 meters until it reaches the main north-south drag of Chupung-ryeong. At this point, if you look to your right or south, you may see the five- or six-story white building of the Karib Motel standing on the opposite side of the road from a large, scripted stone menhir located next to a large park area that could double as a campsite. The trailhead begins on a small cement road that runs east up a small rise between the Karib Motel and NH4. Depending on the time of day you arrive at this stage of your walk, you may have enough time to knock off the remaining 8 km, or four hours of walking, left to complete the leg to Jakjeom-jae. If you decide to do this, it is only a short 6 km lift from there back down to Chupung-ryeong. Or you may decide to stay in that town for a couple of nights and base yourself from there. Back on the roadside, if you look left or north, you see that this simple two-lane road runs up into the achromatic structures of Chupung-ryeong. There is another accommodation option up there for you as well. Follow it up there and take a look.

* Chupung-ryeong 추풍령 B2

The low pass of Chupung-ryeong is understandably threaded with three major transportation routes. Fast-moving NE1 runs all the way from Seoul in the northwest to its diagonal opposite Busan in the southeast. The other but older NH4 runs 15 km southeast to Gimcheon and 25 km northwest to Yeongdong-gun. The third network is the old Gyeongbu railway line, which hems the main rail line between Seoul and Busan. Chupung-ryeong has long been an important crossing of the Baekdu-daegan, connecting southeastern Korea with Seoul since the Joseon era, and probably millennia before that, because of its low unobtrusive passage. In this small town, one gets the feeling that it was a bit of a rough diamond in all eras of Korea's history. Its geographical location has placed it right smack bang in the middle of Korea's cultural developments. Chupung-ryeong is the largest town the Baekdu-daegan passes directly through, and arriving here is a good opportunity to experience small-town Korean life. The town center is located 500 meters to the north of the railway crossing and has a number of restaurants with menus ranging from traditional Korean to fried chicken, a couple of bars, a large Nonghyeop supermarket and a Family Mart convenience store. There is also a post office with free internet service further west from the bus terminal, as well as some small marketplaces in the back streets west of the main drag.

Chupung-ryeong has a few motels, the best of which is the Karib Motel 카리브 모텔 (T. 043-742-9938), located at the southern edge of town near the continuation of the trail. An older *yeogwan* is located near the bus terminal in the west of town. The new park located opposite the Karib Motel, and under the expressway, is an acceptable place to set up a tent.

Leaving the trail at Chupung-ryeong: The Chupung-ryeong bus terminal is located on the western edge of town, with buses that run regularly into Gimcheon and Yeongdong-gun. Buses run to Gimcheon every 10-20 minute from 8 am to 9 pm daily and to Daejeon 12 times daily from 7:40 am to 7:50 pm.

Chupung-ryeong 추풍령 B3 → Jakjeom-jae 작점재 C3

8km (3:40)

The trail leaves Chupung-ryeong from a small cemented driveway that heads east between NH4 and the Karib Motel. The driveway runs past a farmhouse that doubles as an implement shed. Greenhouses line the road to the trailhead at the end of the driveway. Once there, you notice a new staircase that elevates its way through low shrubs and trees for about 600 meters northeast to the peak of Geum-san 금산, located at 360 m ABSL. Once on the summit of Geum-san, you get good views back over the town. The northern edge of Geum-san has been eaten almost to the summit by an expired mine, and you stand right on the lip of a sheer drop that is being held together by green expanded mesh. Although an ugly scar, this does open up the view to the northeast, and you can look down to the Chupung-ryeong Reservoir in the valley leading to Jakjeom-jae. From Geum-san, the trail starts to head southeast and elevates slightly for the next 1.5 km to the pass of Maebong-jae 매봉재. The trail to this pass rises about 100 m in altitude quite steeply for the next 500 meters until you reach the summit of Mae-bong 매봉

The Neungchi swimteo at Jakjeom-gogae

itself, located at 498 m ABSL. At this wooded point, a short wooden stake has been driven into the ground, labeled with a small yellow blazer stating that you have completed 200 km of the Baekdu-daegan trail. Congratulations!

Dropping off the peak in a southeastern direction, you walk on a good but rather featureless trail for the next 1 km before dropping into a shallow saddle that acts as a junction, with tracks heading northeast and southwest off the ridge. The trail continues southeast from the junction, rising back to the crest of the low ridge, where it continues in that direction for another 400 meters before reaching the northern end of what appears to be another ridgeline. By now, you should be at a wooded summit area located at about 500 m ABSL. From here, the trail will turn northeast, gradually descending for the next kilometer into the pass of Sagijeom-gogae 사기점 고개, which is crossed by a mountain road.

The trail from there continues northeast, climbing steadily for 1 km before reaching a sealed road that climbs south, servicing a KBS-TV antenna on the summit of Nanham-san 난함산 (733m). The other side of the road winds down 2 km north alongside the Baekdu-daegan trail, meeting the main road east of Jakjeom-jae. The Baekdu-daegan trail crosses the road and heads east for another 200 meters before changing direction north and meeting the same sealed road again moments later. Once you have started heading north, the trail crosses the road a number of times on its 1 km voyage to the pass, each trail entrance indicated by a large number of ribbons. About 500 meters before the pass, the trail stays west whilst the road embarks east of the ridge. Shortly thereafter, the trail descends out onto the sealed road at the pass of Jakjeom-jae. Jakjeom-jae, located at 340 m ABSL, is connected by a sealed road 6 km east of Chupung-ryeong and 8 km west of NH3.

TRANSPORT INFO

Leaving the trail at Jakjeom-jae: There is no bus service over the pass. You will have to hitch from the pass to get to Chupung-ryeong. If you're trying to get to the pass from Chupung-ryeong, the taxi rank is located outside the bus terminal.

LODGING

The pleasant Jakjeom-jae pass consists of a large, grassy rest area containing a well-built jeongja called the Neungchi Swimteo 능치쉼터. There is ample space for camping in the grass area, and water(35) is available on the eastern side of the road from a river that flows from Nanham-san. There are no toilet facilities at the pass.

DAY 2 From Jakjeom-jae to Keun-jae

• **Distance:** 9.5km
• **Time:** 4hr 25min

Arise from the wooded cradle of Neungchi and stop yourself from staying one more night. Walk up through the quirky grounds of central Korea and stumble upon a renegade church. Question the mentality of its creators and wonder why they seek seclusion. Continue to the bigger heights of Yongmun-san and Guksu-bong. Rediscover the true meaning of the Baekdu-daegan on these peaks and thank Heaven that primal rituals and superstitious fantasies still exist. Walk peacefully from its summit and abandon yourself in the days of the old schoolyard.

Jakjeom-jae 작점재 C3 → Yongmun-san 용문산 B2

4.5km (2:10)

From Jakjeom-jae, you climb north up a set of stone stairs to a couple of well-maintained tombs that look over the pass before continuing into the forest for about 200 meters, where the trail turns west. The next 800 meters after that see you climbing about 100 m in altitude to a summit in the forest called Mujwagol-san 무좌골산, located at 474 m ABSL. From there, the trail heads northwest and stays relatively flat for 700 meters before passing a fork in the trail where it turns northeast and starts heading downhill, dropping about 100 m for the next 300 meters into the pass of Galhyeon 갈현, marking a track

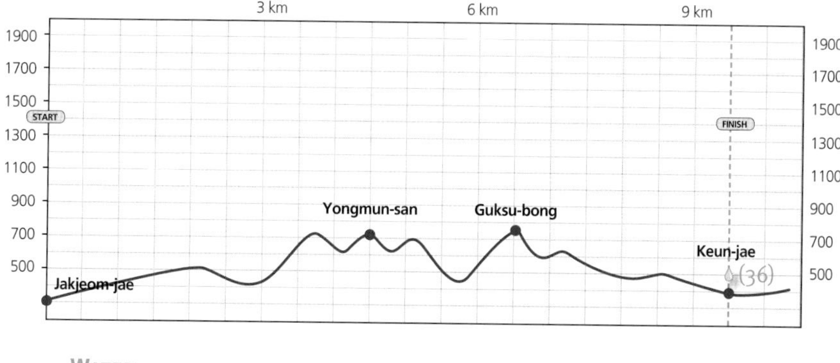

WATER STOPS (36) Keun-jae: **N35°16'35" E128°02'48"**

junction. The trail continues north from Galhyeon and starts its ascent back to the main ridge. About 300 meters later, you come across a series of rocks located in a wooded forest. These are called Gido-bawi 기도바위, which translates as "prayer rocks." Oddly enough, there is an old shack here, and located inside of it are a hymn book and polystyrene crucifix nailed to its wall...another quirky find on the trail. Down in the valley to the northwest, there is the Cheonseong Christian prayer camp; it is unknown whether this shack is related to that institution, but that'd be a good guess. From the rocks, you start to ascend northwest, and 200 meters later you meet a wide mountain road crossing the ridge. The road heads southwest into Jukjeon-ri 죽전리 and northeast about a kilometer to a country road above Neungchi-ri 능치리. Crossing the road, you head northwest, passing through more rocky outcrops, and continue climbing to the top of the ridge. The trail remains delightful to be in, with pretty stands of deciduous forest, and the next 1.5 km should see you gain about 250 m in altitude until you reach an unnamed peak located at 687 m ABSL. The trail from there makes a distinctive turn northeast as it begins its final ascent to the summit of Yongmun-san about 400 meters away. Yongmun-san, at 708 m ABSL, is also known as Maetdol-bong 맷돌봉. It has a large, open grassy area that provides enough space for camping and is also marked by a helipad. A small stone stele celebrates the peak and the Baekdu-daegan. The peak could also be considered the halfway mark to your endpoint of Keun-jae, and its most predominant views are to the east over the southern Sangju area.

Yongmun-san 용문산 B2 → Guksu-bong 국수봉 C1 2km (1:00)

From Yongmun-san, the trail descends north briefly, where it soon starts to level out, turning northeast for 500 meters as it does so. The ground then starts to ascend, and you bound over one more peak before the trail turns east, descending into a saddle about 150 meters later. This saddle is located at 600 m ABSL and has park benches marking the site of a four-way track junction. The Baekdu-daegan heads east and climbs sharply for 100 m in altitude to a height of 700 m ABSL. You have just rejoined the main ridge again and are only 600 meters away from your highest feature on this leg, Guksu-bong, at 795 m ABSL.

Guksu-bong 국수봉 → Keun-jae 큰재 C1 3km (1:15)

From **Guksu-bong***, you drop north more than 100 m over the next 500 meters of trail before it levels out at a 683 m peak. Here, the trail turns northeast slightly and then continues on its descent northwest through a rocky area before reaching a ledge located at 475 m ABSL. From there, the trail straightens north, and 400 meters later, you meet a tomb and come out onto a country road running through an apple and rice farm. From here, you can follow the road north for 500 meters to **Keun-jae*** on PR68 or stay on the Baekdu-daegan proper and walk north for the same distance through more deciduous forest before coming out behind some old farmhouses onto the roadside at Keun-jae.

* Guksu-bong 국수봉 C1

Guksu-bong is a rocky peak with open views predominantly to the east, north and south. On a clear day, Hwangak-san to the south can be seen, and to the north as far as Mungyeong, northeast of Songni-san National Park. This celebrated summit has a large signboard providing general information on the Baekdu-daegan as well as Guksu-bong, and it appears to hold relative importance to its locals. One of the signboards asks the question, "What is the Baekdu-daegan?" and it responds by saying that, upon hearing its name, we (Koreans) are immediately reminded of the magnificent scenery of Baekdu-san (in North Korea) and the energy it emits. It also explains how those Koreans who may not be familiar with the term "Baekdu-daegan" still manage to feel strong sentiments when hearing the name of the famous Baekdu-san. It then goes on to explain scientifically how the Baekdu-daegan is a mountain system connected all the way from Baekdu-san on the Chinese border to Jiri-san in the south, and that it's also the divider of all waterways on the peninsula and the foundation of Korean culture and history.

Another board tells that Guksu-bong is known by many names, including Gom-san ("bear mountain") and Ungi-san. Local legend states that the peak was once well used as an altar when praying for rain, and its slopes yield a medicinal herb similar to ones found on a mountain in China with a similar name. The small altar for the rain ritual can still be found on the peak.

One can't quite get a geographical appreciation of the hard outlines of this peak until one is off of it, standing back and looking at its sharp distinctive edges from the eastern side.

* Keun-jae 큰재 C1

Keun-jae Pass is only about 375 m ABSL and is connected by PR68, which heads northwest 5 km to a service area containing a restaurant, supermarket and motel on the banks of the Sangpan Reservoir 상판 저수지. To the east, PR68 runs 7 km into the small town of Oksan, where it meets NH3. The township has a number of restaurants and bars. Just off the countryside Keun-jae, there is an abandoned school. Outside the front gates of its flat, grassy grounds is a new spring ejecting water(36) from a concrete drinking fountain. Opposite the school is a very old traditional Korean home, made from clay, that may still be occupied by a much older, partially deaf and almost blind spinster. Inside her front courtyard exists what used to be the old water source for hikers, a pump-generated bore hole activated by a switch on one of the pillars outside the front of her house. Years of annoyance by hikers probably made the locals dig deep to tap into the same water source that she uses, and now we have the new fountain. Keun-jae is a very pleasant and quiet farming area and has no supermarket or accommodation.

Ewha-jang Motel with the sacred peak of Guksu-bong in the background

TRANSPORT INFO

Leaving the trail at Keun-jae: Buses that run between Sangju to the east and Sangpan-ri 상판리 about 8 km to the west cross Keun-jae. They leave Sangju for Sangpan-ri at 9:15 am, 12:50 pm and 5:50 pm. Going the other way, they leave Sangpan-ri for Sangju at 10:30 am, 2 pm and 7 pm.

※ The small town of Gongseong-ri 공성리, located about 6 km east of Keun-jae, has a taxi service that will run to the pass. Gongseong Taxi can be reached at 054-532-4414.

LODGING

The town of Gongseong 공성, about 4 km east at the junction of PR68 and NH3, has a motel, the Ewha-jang Motel 이화장 모텔 (T. 054-534-3301~3) located 800 meters southwest of town on NH3. About 8km to the northwest of Keun-jae is a service area containing a restaurant, supermarket and motel on the banks of the Sangpan Reservoir.

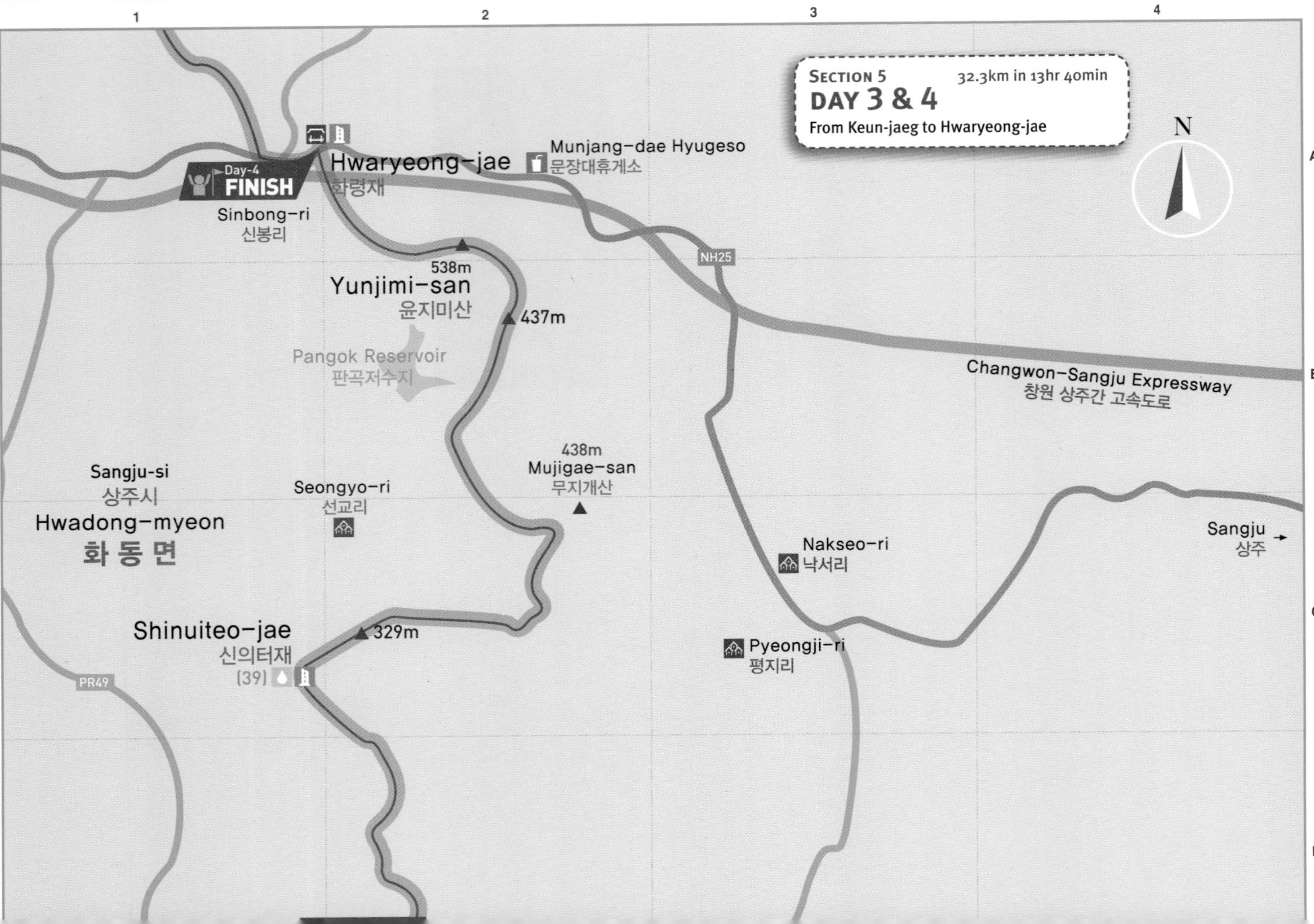

Section 5
DAY 3 & 4
32.3km in 13hr 40min
From Keun-jaeg to Hwaryeong-jae
N
Day-4
FINISH
Hwaryeong-jae
화령재
Munjang-dae Hyugeso
문장대휴게소
Sinbong-ri
신봉리
538m
Yunjimi-san
윤지미산
437m
NH25
Pangok Reservoir
판곡저수지
Changwon-Sangju Expressway
창원 상주간 고속도로
438m
Mujigae-san
무지개산
Sangju-si
상주시
Hwadong-myeon
화 동 면
Seongyo-ri
선교리
Nakseo-ri
낙서리
Sangju
상주
Shinuiteo-jae
신의터재
(39)
329m
Pyeongji-ri
평지리
PR49
1
2
3
4
A
B
C
D

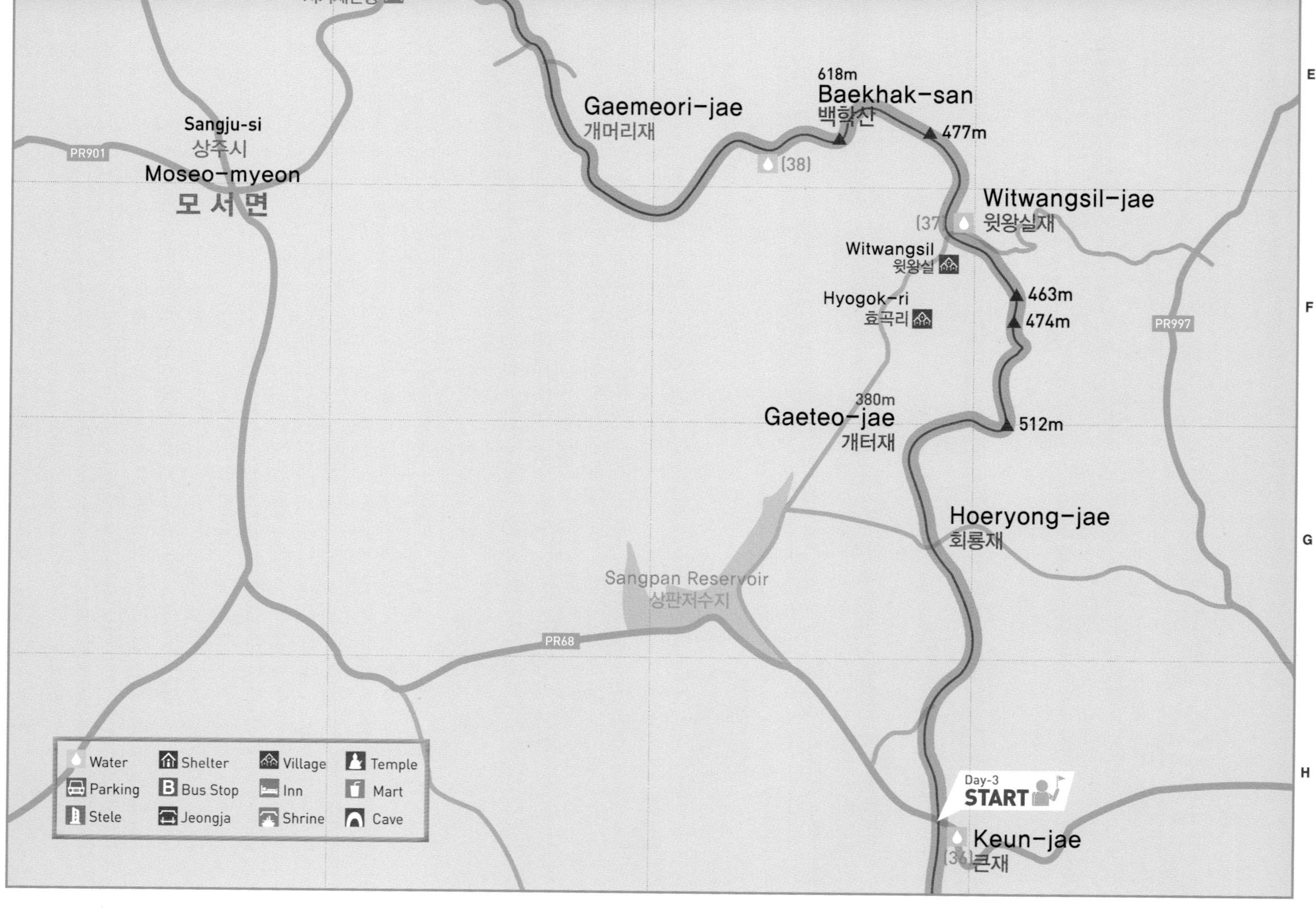
E
F
G
H
Sangju-si
상주시
Moseo-myeon
모 서 면
PR901
Gaemeori-jae
개머리재
618m
Baekhak-san
백학산
477m
(38)
Witwangsil-jae
윗왕실재
(37)
Witwangsil
윗왕실
Hyogok-ri
효곡리
463m
474m
PR997
380m
Gaeteo-jae
개터재
512m
Hoeryong-jae
회룡재
Sangpan Reservoir
상판저수지
PR68
Day-3
START
Keun-jae
(36)
큰재
Water
Shelter
Village
Temple
Parking
Bus Stop
Inn
Mart
Stele
Jeongja
Shrine
Cave

DAY 3

From Keun-jae to Jigi-jae

- **Distance:** 19km
- **Time:** 7hr 40min

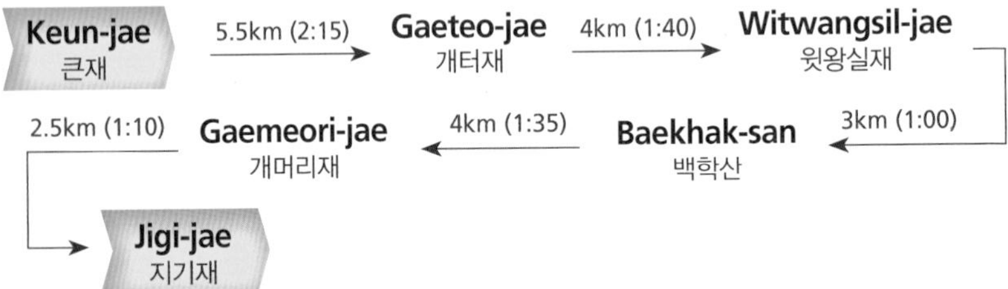

Expelled from life, leave the strict confines of the old schoolyard and become truant in the hills of Korea. Continue north, seeking fun and adventure. Stride to the top of Baekhak-san, arriving at its boutique summit and smiling at the distant wedges of Songi-san. Leave the high ground and calculate how many more days of travel are left to go. On your descent, return to the narrow lanes and pastures of rural Korea and harvest yourself in the vineyards and orchards.

Keun-jae 큰재 H3 → Gaeteo-jae 개터재 F3 5.5km (2:15)

The trail heads north along a concrete driveway next to the school before entering the forest behind an abandoned house. It continues north for 1.5 km before meeting a mountain road that runs southwest for a kilometer to PR68. You join this road, heading northeast on it for about 150 meters, where you soon come across a closed gate. On the eastern side of the gate, the trail reenters the forest and heads northeast, flanking a cattle farm. About a kilometer later, it crosses a mountain road and continues north. About 1.5 km after that, the trail arrives at the pass of Hoeryong-jae 회룡재, marked by a signpost. At Hoeryong-jae, a mountain road meets the ridge from both sides. Heading north over the road, you begin a gentle climb over the crest, descending west into the pass of Gaeteo-jae about a kilometer later.

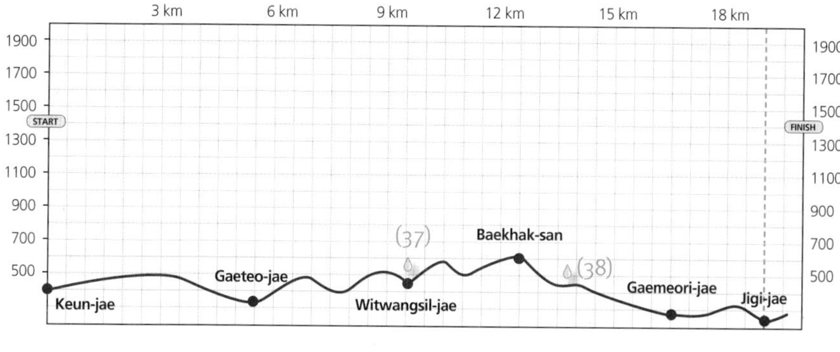

WATER STOPS

(37) Witwangsil-jae: **N36°20'04" E128°02'40"**
(38) 500 meters west of Baekhak-san: **N36°20'32" E128°01'33"**

Gaeteo-jae 개터재 F3 → Witwangsil-jae 윗왕실재 F4

4km (1:40)

Gaeteo-jae, at 380 m ABSL, is crossed by another mountain road. The Baekdu-daegan trail heads east from the pass for about 700 meters, climbing back up to the main ridgeline located at a treed peak at 512 m ABSL. From there, you may be able to see the Baekdu-daegan as it fringes north and then west around what appears to be a basin containing the village and farming area of Hyogok-ri 효곡리. From 512 m, the trail changes north, walking on a good wooded ridge for about a kilometer and passing spot heights of 474 m and 463 m before the trail turns northwest, passing a tomb and falling out onto the pass of Witwangsil-jae about 1 km later. At this pass, the Baekdu-daegan has been replaced by a small, narrow nature bridge as it crosses a mountain road that runs south, passing the small farming village of Witwangsil on its way to Hyokgok-ri and east for about 4 km to PR997. Water(37) can be found down the northeastern side of the road in a mountain stream below what appears to be a vehicle bay.

Witwangsil-jae 윗왕실재 F4 → Baekhak-san 백학산 E3

3km (1:00)

From the nature bridge, you get a good sense that there's a bit of climbing ahead of you to be done. The trail whacks its way up northwest for a short distance

Looking NE from Baekhak-san

before turning northeast and regaining some altitude when it meets up 1 km later with a tomb at about 480 m ABSL. From there, the trail turns northwest, and the next 500 meters of trail take you to the base of Baekhak-san. Now begins a grudging climb up to its summit. As you climb, the trail moves further away from the farming areas and the forest becomes vibrant with more established undergrowth. About 400 meters later, the trail turns south, and you walk 600 meters, pushing to the summit of Baekhak-san.

Baekhak-san, at 618 m ABSL, is marked by a small stele, and its delightfully shaded peak offers you your first views northwest of the ridge. On a good day, you can see the brazed crags of Songni-san National Park at 325° to the northwest, rising dramatically from the lowlands. Even farther beyond that in the distance are the lunar-shaped rocky peaks of northern Songni-san and the Mungyeong areas of the Baekdu-daegan. This is a good place to stop, rest, and have some lunch.

Baekhak-san 백학산 E3 → Gaemeori-jae 개머리재 E2

4km (1:35)

From the peak, the trail descends west off the ridge, and the next 500 meters see you dropping about 200 m in altitude to a mountain road that crosses a saddle area located at about 400 m ABSL. Water(38) is available here from a stream flowing by the road, right near the crest of the ridge. From there, you are beginning your descent to your next pass of Gaemeori-jae. You climb briefly up the ridge before descending through native pine forest in a southwest direction for 1.5 km, after which you turn northwest for 1 km, passing through some vineyards and orchards before arriving at a sealed country road connecting the pass of Gaemeori-jae, also known as Sojeong-jae 소정재. The area has no facilities for hikers, but there will be tap water available at the farms.

Gaemeori-jae 개머리재 → Jigi-jae 지기재 E2 2.5km (1:10)

From the rural pass of Gaemeori-jae, the trail continues from the crest of the pass up a grassy driveway. The trail continues through grape-growing areas before cutting back into a small stand of pine trees. From there, the trail climbs its way up toward the brow of a small hill, passing a family of tombs. A few hundred meters after you come over the crest of the brow, you come across another mountain road, which the trail follows for a couple of hundred meters before the road turns west and the trail stays north. The trail from there doesn't stay on this higher ground for long; it descends off its face in a westerly direction for about 200 meters into the farms above Jigi-jae. It then turns back to the northwest, continuing to descend gently through orchards of apple and vines of grape before meeting PR901 at the pass of Jigi-jae about 500 meters later. Jigi-jae is connected by PR901, which runs southwest 4 km into the junction town of Moseo-myeon 모서면, and northeast about 7 km to the village of Pyeongji-ri 평지리, where it meets NH25.

Transport Info

Joining the trail at Jigi-jae: Buses don't cross Jigi-jae Pass. The nearest town to the pass is Hwadong-myeon 화동면, which is about 7 km to the northwest. Hwadong Taxi can be reached at 054-534-4828 or 054-533-9793.

Lodging

Located west of the ridge is the Jigi-jae Sanjang 지기재 산장 mountain shelter; a white, blue-roofed building offering *minbak*-style accommodation. The *sanjang* is advertised at the pass and can be contacted by phone at 054-533 2579 / 011-9950-2599. There is not really any space for camping at this pass, and if you have enough time left in your day, it may well be worth it to make one more bound to the pass of Sinuiteo-jae 신의터재, 4.5 km away, which has better off-road camping space at the pass.

DAY 4

From Jigi-jae to Hwaryeong-jae

• **Distance:** 15.3km
• **Time:** 6hr

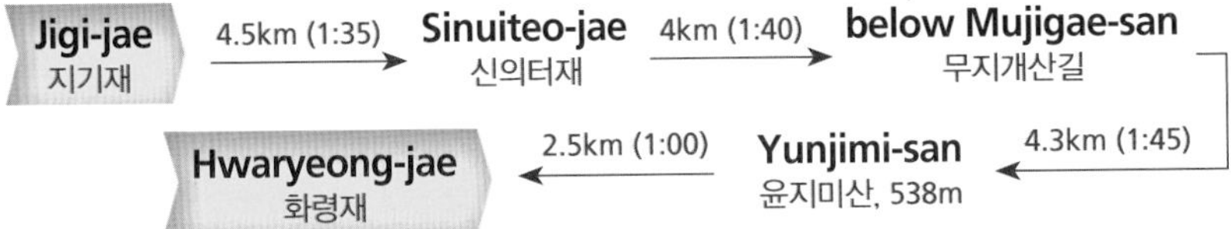

Amble from one aging farming community to the next. Return their cheerful, bony-handed waves. Pass through the ridges and hills of the rural ilk and lope quietly past their grassy tombs. Enter the taller stands of greener forest and whisper your way around even more golden-grassed tombs. Stop and rest at Yunjimi-san. Feel wealthy about your freedom, feel warm in these hills, feel nourished in this light, and admire the hiking ribbons as they flutter in the wind like hundred-dollar bills. Wonder what the next road brings and, on your way there, note the concrete wall standing behind the lattice of leaf and twig. Burst from the woodwork and look up at the guardian of the trail, a granite gatekeeper. Sleep in the *jeongja* of Hwaryeong and watch the bionic eye of the giant stele come to life under the light of the moon.

Jigi-jae 지기재 E3 → Sinuiteo-jae 신의터재 C1 4.5km (1:35)

Crossing PR901 at Jigi-jae, the trail joins a small concrete road located next to a local monument, which you follow north for about 300 meters, passing beside grapevines. The road turns west, while the trail continues north through a stand of bamboo before turning west as well and rejoining the same road 200 meters later. This road is a loop linking old farmhouses with PR901. You follow the road north

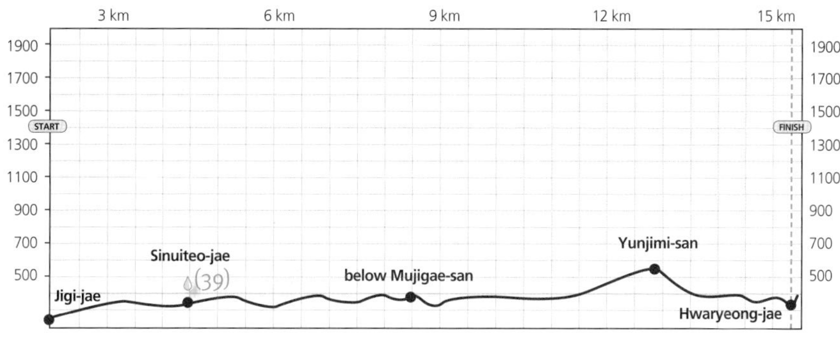

Water Stops (39) 500 meters west of Sinuiteo-jae: **N35°23'17" E127°58'24"**

for about 200 meters. At the point where it begins to turn left (west), the Baekdudaegan continues north, leaving the road at the back of a farmhouse—you will need to look out for ribbons on the southern side of the house. From behind the house, you enter the forest and climb gently north up a dirt track for about 400 meters before turning northwest and climbing toward a bald, rocky feature that grants good views back over the rice fields to the south. The trail literally goes up the face of this bald, rocky escarpment and onto the native pine-covered crest at its top. From there, it scoots northwest along its ridge and tucks away north behind a larger and more prominent peak to the nearby west. The trail stays on this low, undulating forested ridgeline, taking you through the lushly fertile farming areas of central Korea. It heads north for about 500 meters before turning northeast, flanking the eastern perimeter of rice paddies and greenhouses for the next 600 meters and then meeting a tomb located near a chestnut tree where it reenters the forest. The trail from there soon passes another tomb and then turns sharply southwest for a moment before turning northwest again, passing one more tomb and descending gently for the next 500 meters down to the pass of Sinuiteo-jae, passing under a large steel pylon on its way.

* Sinuiteo-jae 신의터재 C1

Sinuiteo-jae is located at 280 m ABSL and is connected by a quiet country road, running 5 km east to Nakseo-ri 낙서리, where it meets NH25. To the southwest of the pass, the country road runs for 1.5 km down to the village district of Hwadong-myeon 화동면, where it meets PR49.

Sinuiteo-jae has a large, grassy rest area and park benches located beneath a shaded wooden structure that makes it suitable for camping. The rest area has a large statue of a dragon-turtle, as well as an impressive stone stele commemorating the Baekdu-daegan; water(39) can be obtained from a grape farm 500 meters down the western side of the road. The small town of Hwadong-myeon has a post office and a couple of restaurants; otherwise, there is no accommodation at the pass.

Sinuiteo-jae is located less than 2 km northeast of Hwadong-myeon. Hwadong Taxi can be reached at 054-534-4828 or 054-533-9793.

Sinuiteo-jae 신의터재 C1 → Below Mujigae-san 무지개산길 C2

4km (1:40)

Crossing the road at Sinuiteo-jae, the trail joins a driveway heading northeast beside a grape farm. You follow the driveway for a couple of hundred meters before meeting the trail, which continues onward in the same direction for 600 meters, passing by a number of well-manicured tombs before crossing a 329 m peak and dropping into a saddle that marks a four-way intersection. From the junction, the trail continues to undulate northeast through deciduous and coniferous stands of forest, and after 400 meters it turns east, passing a series of tombs set amongst a small grove of chestnut trees. At certain points on the trail, you may be able to see to the northeast, the Baekdu-daegan ridgeline running north toward its most prominent peak on this leg, Yunjimi-san. You continue east, descending gently for 1 km into an area containing farms on both sides of the ridge. Here, you join a farm track and walk southeast for 300 meters before turning north, climbing gently for about another kilometer to a distinctive point in the trail located at about 400 m ABSL. This shaded spot located under heavy, verdant foliage is well marked by a number of colorful ribbons hanging from the branches and a small sign marking the direction to a peak known as Mujigae-san 무지개산 (438m) 500 meters northwest of here.

Mujigae-san 무지개산길 C2 → Yunjimi-san 윤지미산 A2

4.3km (1:45)

Below Mujigae-san, the trail heads northwest, descending gently for about 600 meters into a saddle where a mountain road heads southwest to the farms of Seongyo-ri 선교리. Continuing northwest for another kilometer, the Baekdu-daegan trail arrives at yet another tomb, where it then turns northeast for 1.5 km, climbing slowly uphill toward an unnamed peak located at 437 m ABSL. The peak offers you views back out over the Pangok Reservoir 판곡 저수지 to the southwest. From this area, the trail heads northwest, climbing a good but tough trail for the next kilometer to the summit of Yunjimi-san, located at 538 m ABSL. This peak has a flattish summit area shrouded in thick forest, offering thin views of NH25 to the north. In the center of its peak stands a cairn with a stone tablet on top naming the peak. Despite its limited vices, it is a nice peak to stop and rest at.

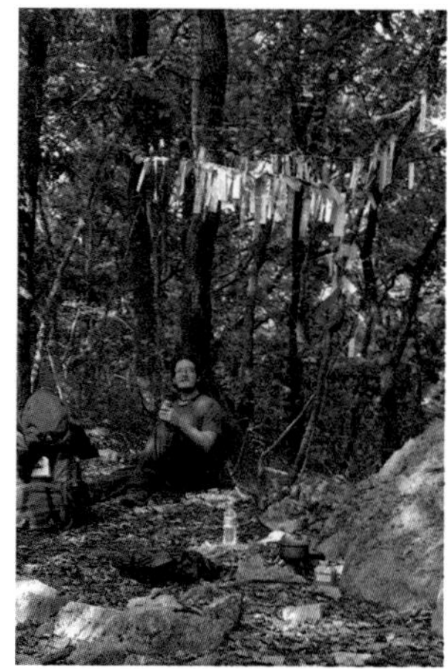

Andrew captivated by the ribbon of Yunjimi-san

Yunjimi-san 윤지미산 → Hwaryeong-jae 화령재 A2

2.5km (1:00)

From Yunjimi-san, the trail heads west, descending initially for 100 m over the next 300 meters of trail before it eases up, passing two more tombs, and after 600 more meters, the trail sees you burst from the forest onto the side of a mountain road that runs south to the Pangok Reservoir and northwest to the village of Sinbong-ri 신봉리 on NH25. The trail hugs the mountain road for a moment and heads back into the forest, following the ridge for about 500 meters before the road and the trail meet again. At this stage, you turn right, or north, and follow it for about 150 meters before heading back into the forest on the right hand (eastern) side of the road, which is marked by some hiking ribbons. The trail from there heads northwest, and after 500 meters, you see a concrete highway located only a hundred meters below the western side of the ridge. This is the newly completed Changwon–Sangju Expressway, which runs adjacent to NH25. Instead of chiseling out this piece of low-lying Baekdu-daegan, the engineers have followed the Baekdu-daegan Act and pierced a tunnel through the mighty ridge's flanks in an attempt to maintain its energy line. From above the tunnel, you are only about 400 meters from Hwaryeong-jae. As you walk across the grassy crest of the tunnel and back into the tree line, the trail straightens to the north and makes one more bound over a wooded peak, followed by a steep, slippery descent down to the southern edges of NH25.

* Hwaryeong-jae 화령재 A2

Hwaryeong was the name of the region that controlled a large area below the ridge on both sides of this pass during the Goryeo Dynasty, and the pass is named for that region. The pass is connected by NH25, which runs east about 20 km to the small city of Sangju and west 3 km into the small township of Hwaseo-myeon 화서면. At the pass, Hwaryeong-jae is celebrated by a gigantic Baekdu-daegan stele erected on September 9, 2007. The seven meter high rock stands proudly in a parking area on the northern side of the pass and is maybe the tallest on the Baekdu-daegan. The area around the stele is undergoing landscaping and will more than likely be developed into a larger resting area.

The mighty stele of Hwaryeong-jae on NH25

TRANSPORT INFO

Leaving the trail at Hwaryeong-jae: Buses cross the pass, running east to Sangju 46 times a day from 7:30 am to 9:30 pm. From Sangju, buses run to Hwaseo-myeon every 20min from 6:55 am to 7:30 pm. Hwaseo-myeon has a taxi service, and the drivers are familiar with picking up hikers from the pass. Hwaryeong Taxi can be reached at 054-533-0633 or 054-533-0063.

LODGING

About 50 meters east of the stele, a set of stairs rises up to a large wooden *jeongja*, which looks northeast to the high peaks of eastern Songni-san. This pavilion is well constructed, consisting of a concrete floor and benches attached to its inner circumference, making it a good place to camp. Hwaryeong-jae currently has no water or toilet facilities. Despite its stature, Hwaseo-myeon, 3 km to the west, is a good-sized town with motel accommodation, including the Hwaryeong-jang Yeogwan 화령장여관 (T. 043-533-3883), a hot spring, PC rooms, a major bus station, and a number of restaurants and supermarkets. It also has an interesting old produce market area in the back streets behind the supermarkets.

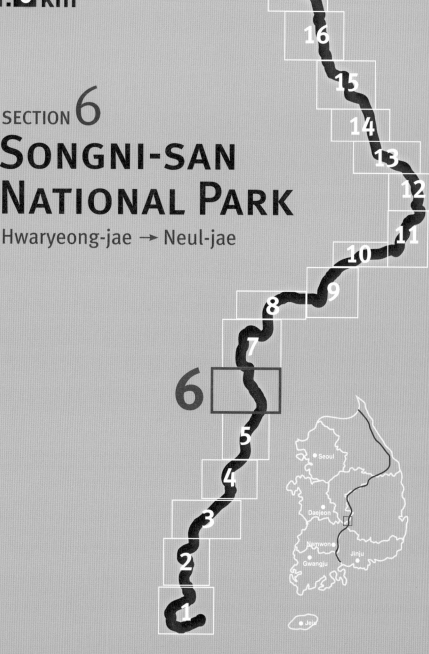

TWO DAYS

28.0 km

SECTION 6

SONGNI-SAN NATIONAL PARK

Hwaryeong-jae → Neul-jae

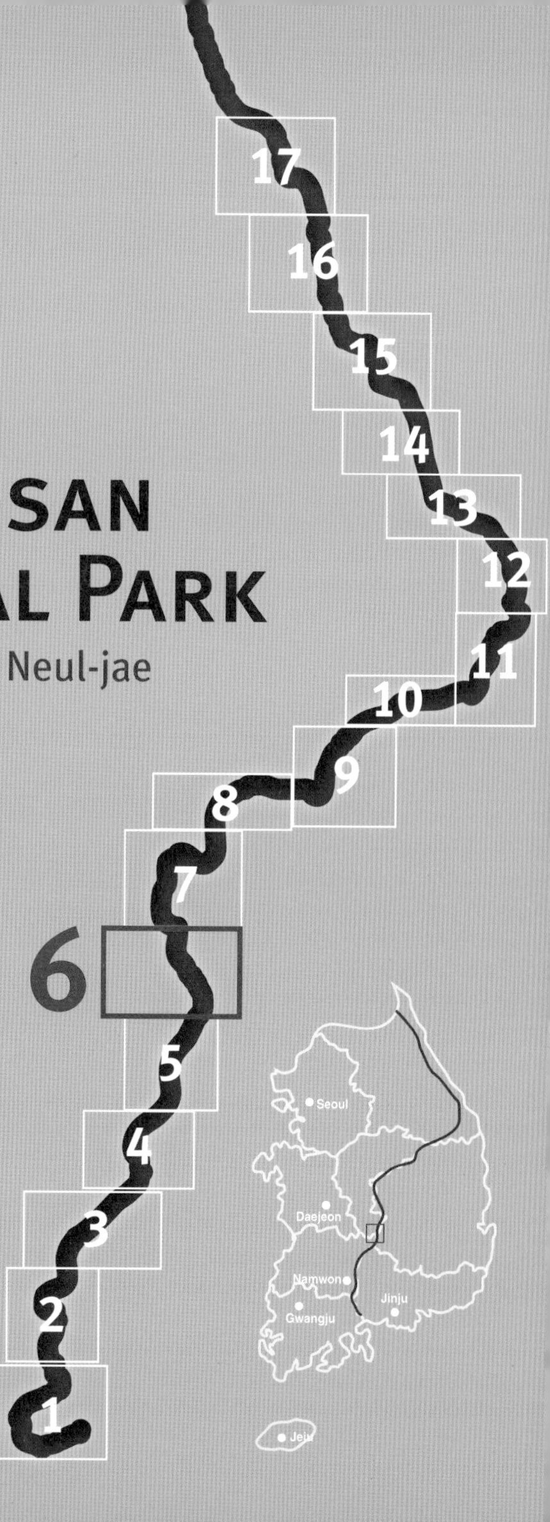

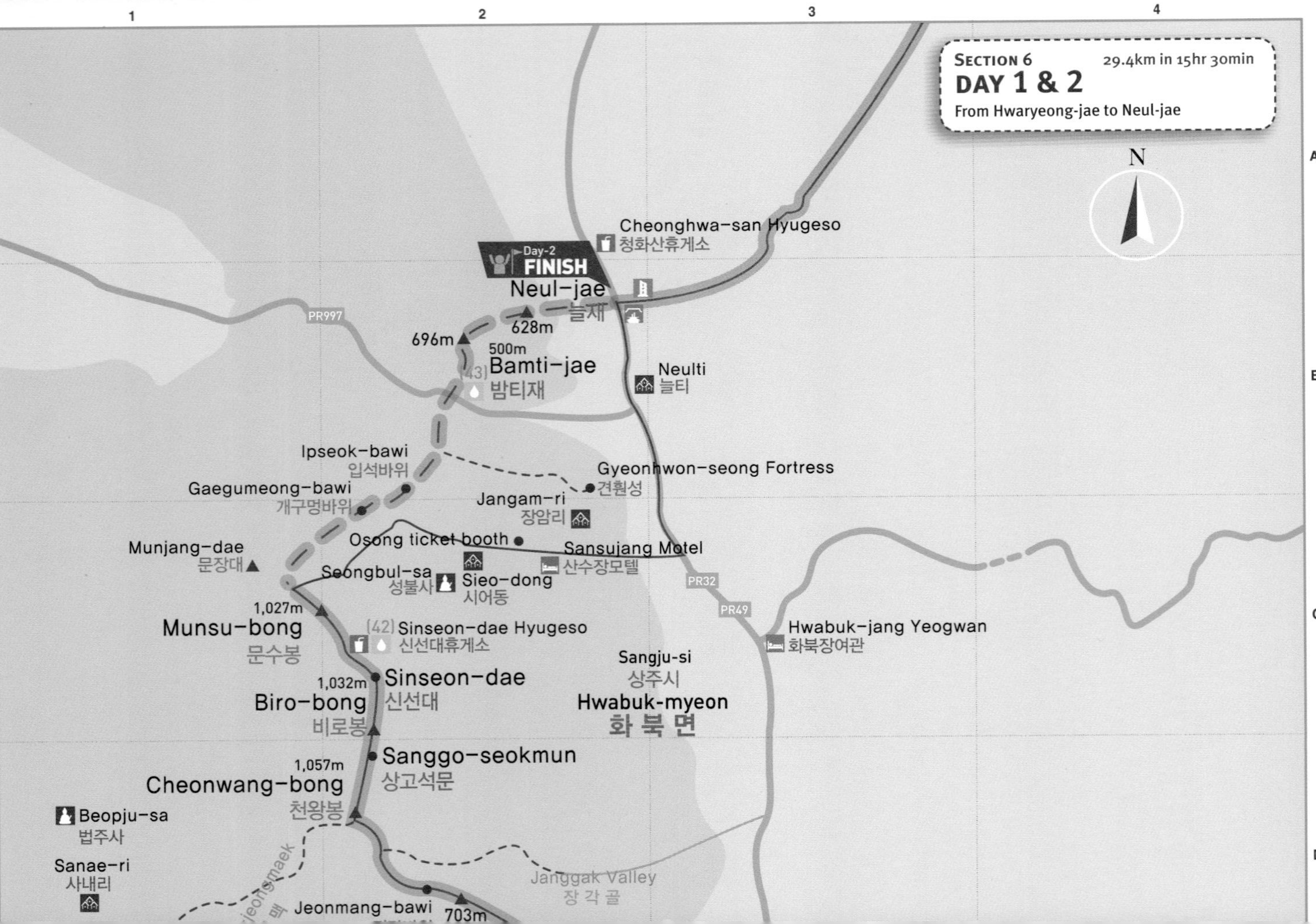

Section 6
DAY 1 & 2
29.4km in 15hr 30min
From Hwaryeong-jae to Neul-jae
N
1
2
3
4
A
B
C
D
Day-2
FINISH
Neul-jae
늘재
Cheonghwa-san Hyugeso
청화산휴게소
PR997
696m
628m
500m
Bamti-jae
밤티재
(43)
Neulti
늘티
Ipseok-bawi
입석바위
Gyeonhwon-seong Fortress
견훤성
Gaegumeong-bawi
개구멍바위
Jangam-ri
장암리
Osong ticket booth
Munjang-dae
문장대
Sansujang Motel
산수장모텔
Seongbul-sa
성불사
Sieo-dong
시어동
PR32
PR49
1,027m
Munsu-bong
문수봉
(42)
Sinseon-dae Hyugeso
신선대휴게소
Hwabuk-jang Yeogwan
화북장여관
Sangju-si
상주시
1,032m
Sinseon-dae
신선대
Biro-bong
비로봉
Hwabuk-myeon
화 북 면
1,057m
Sanggo-seokmun
상고석문
Cheonwang-bong
천왕봉
Beopju-sa
법주사
Sanae-ri
사내리
Janggak Valley
장 각 골
Jeonmang-bawi
703m

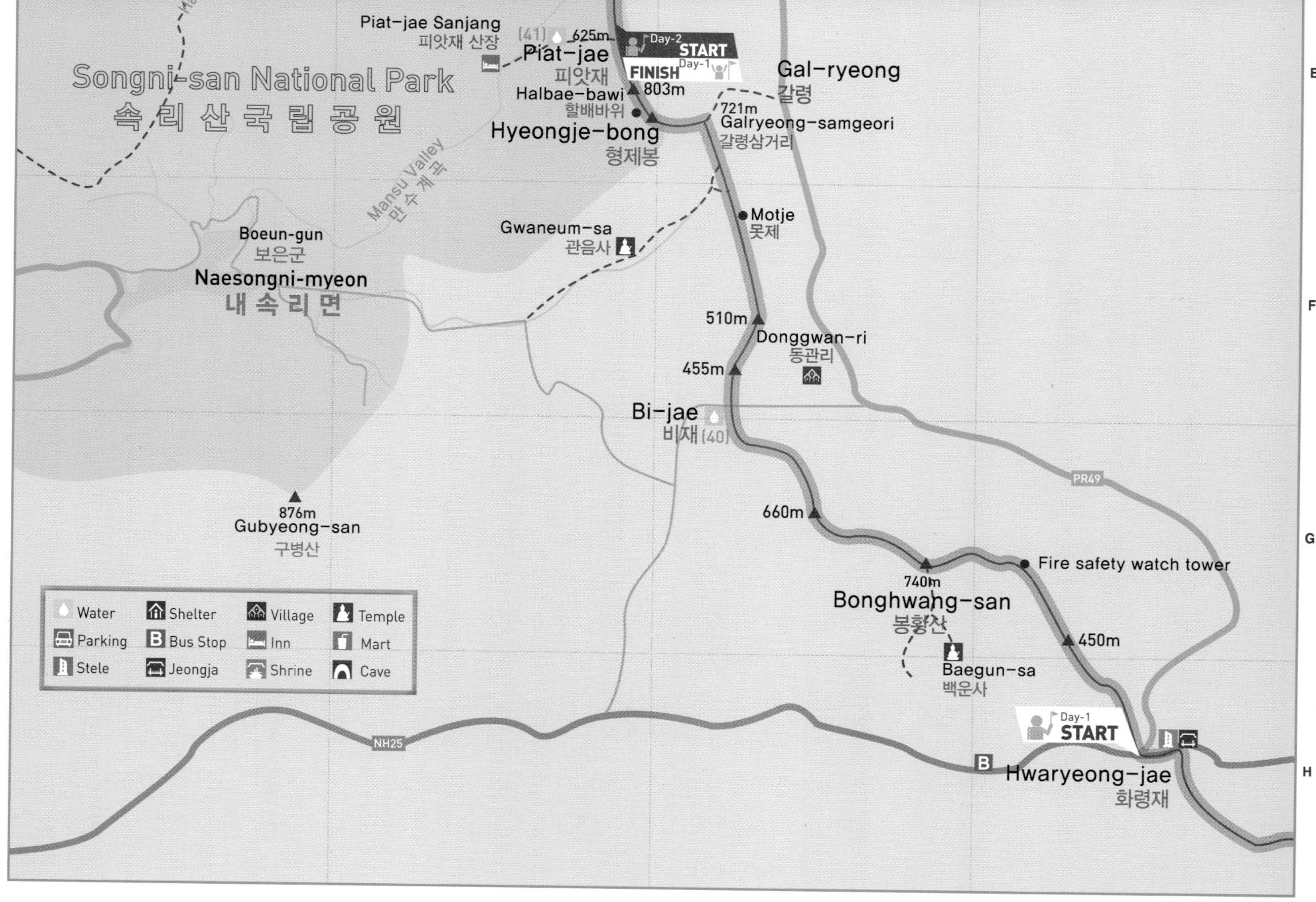
Piat-jae Sanjang
피앗재 산장
(41)
625m
Piat-jae
피앗재
Day-2 START
Day-1 FINISH
803m
Halbae-bawi
할배바위
Hyeongje-bong
형제봉
Gal-ryeong
갈령
721m
Galryeong-samgeori
갈령삼거리
Songni-san National Park
속 리 산 국 립 공 원
Mansu Valley
만 수 계 곡
Motje
못제
Gwaneum-sa
관음사
Boeun-gun
보은군
Naesongni-myeon
내 속 리 면
510m
Donggwan-ri
동관리
455m
Bi-jae
비재 (40)
PR49
660m
876m
Gubyeong-san
구병산
740m
Fire safety watch tower
Bonghwang-san
봉황산
450m
Baegun-sa
백운사
Day-1 START
NH25
B
Hwaryeong-jae
화령재
E
F
G
H
Water
Shelter
Village
Temple
Parking
Bus Stop
Inn
Mart
Stele
Jeongja
Shrine
Cave

DAY 1

From Hwaryeong-jae to Piat-jae

• **Distance:** 13.9km
• **Time:** 7hr 30min

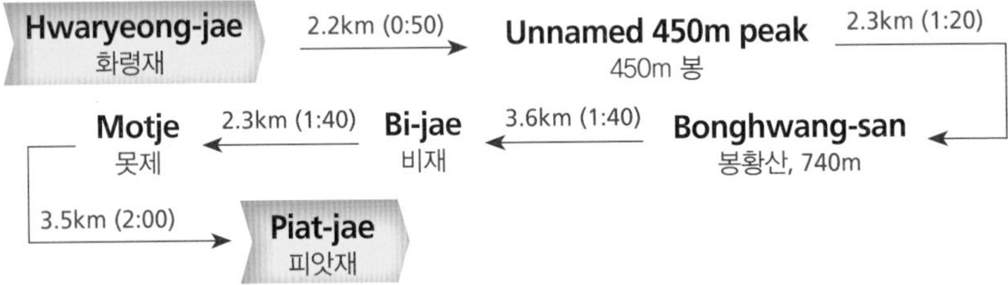

Begin the start of your next journey as you leave behind the charms of rural Korea and push forward toward the attractions of your next National Park. As you leave "Flying Pass," you look up at the steep ridge and push through into its green cover. Further on, as the day gets longer, you wonder where you might sleep. Are these woods safe? At Hyeongje-bong, you clamber up the hard summit and look out over the horizon. You shake your head and wonder if you have the energy to get through this landscape. Light pierces its way through the sulking clouds as the wind stiffens your frame. Satisfied, you return to the trail and seek solace in the woods.

Hwaryeong-jae 화령재 H4 → Unnamed 450m peak 450m 봉 G4

2.2km (0:50)

From Hwaryeong-jae, the trail joins NH25, heading west toward Hwaseo-myeon 화서면 for 500 meters to an intersection with PR49. The trail leaves the road about 20 meters west of the junction, next to an old farmhouse and small chili plantation, and is clearly marked by ribbons and a signpost. About a kilometer

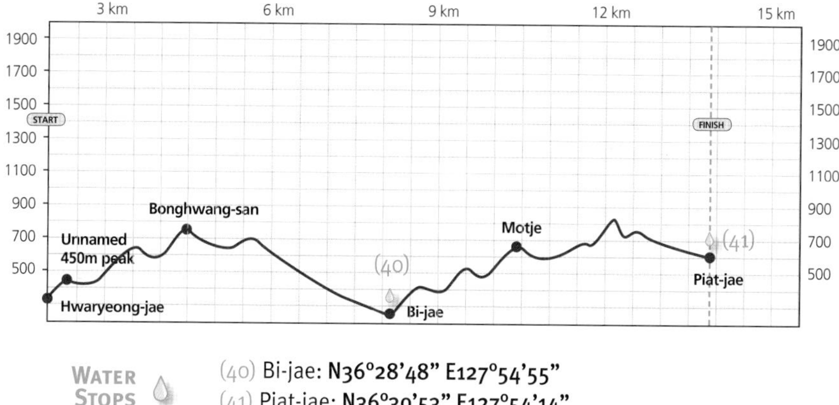

WATER STOPS

(40) Bi-jae: **N36°28'48" E127°54'55"**
(41) Piat-jae: **N36°30'53" E127°54'14"**

west past the trailhead on NH25, there is also a shrine on the roadside containing a 230 cm sitting Buddha statue. The statue's design estimates that it dates to some time around the early Goryeo period (918-1392). It is sculpted from a single piece of granite, wearing a three-sided crown with a belt and three smaller Buddhas inscribed on the crown. It's not a spectacular find, but for enthusiasts it's worth a one-kilometer detour to see it. Back at the trailhead, you walk past the farmhouse and enter the forest, heading northwest up a wide trail that passes a set of two tombs located in a forest of pines. About 900 meters later, you start to catch views southwest through the trees to the township and fields of Hwaseo-myeon. The trail steers west briefly for about 300 meters before turning northwest again, climbing gently for the next 700 meters to an unnamed peak located at 450 m ABSL and marked by a tomb and hiking ribbons.

Unnamed 450m peak 450m 봉 G4 → Bonghwang-san 봉황산 G3

2.3km (1:20)

The trail continues northwest from 450 m, dropping briefly before joining a good ridge trail on fairly flat ground for the next 500 meters as the forest begins to mature. The trail starts climbing gradually, becoming quite steep for the next 500 meters until you come to a fire safety watch tower located at 570 m ABSL. From the tower, you continue northwest on a rocky trail for about 100 meters, where it then turns west, continuing on good ground for a further 400 meters before meeting a track junction. From there, the trail keeps heading west for 1 km, climbing a rocky trail toward your next prominent feature of Bonghwang-san.

The summit of Bonghwang-san, located at 740 m ABSL, consists of a small, cleared rocky area containing a small stone stele marking the peak and a round park bench. The predominant views are to the north and west. Looking northwest at 325°, you can see Hyeongje-bong 형제봉 (829m), the next major peak of the Baekdu-daegan, rising above the ridgeline a further 8 km along the trail. Beyond Hyeongje-bong, the highest feature of Songni-san National Park, Cheonwang-bong (1,057m), can also be seen on a clear day.

Bonghwang-san 봉황산 → Bi-jae 비재 G3 3.6km (1:40)

From Bonghwang-san, the trail descends northwest along a rocky section for the next 500 meters before it turns to the west, passing a track junction 200 meters later. From there, the trail turns southwest briefly whilst continuing on its descent, before stopping in a saddle where it meets another track junction. From the junction, the Baekdu-daegan trail heads west, climbing out of the saddle, and 300 meters later you reach an unnamed peak located at 660 m ABSL. From 660 m, the trail descends north, where, about 900 meters later, it starts to turn west, continuing its descent on a good trail for another kilometer before turning north again. The next 400 meters see you walking north through pine forest and onto the road at Bi-jae*.

The ridge from Bonghwang-san to Hyeongje-bong

* Bi-jae 비재 G3

Bi-jae, meaning "flying pass" is connected by a quiet, sealed country road linking PR49 to the east 2 km away at Donggwan-ri 동관리, and to the west, the road weaves its way down off the ridge. Bi-jae is a typically quiet road pass on the Baekdu-daegan that probably won't see many, if any, vehicles come over it while you are there. It's a good time to stop and take a quick break before lunging into the unexplored southern confines of Songnisan National Park. Your nearest water(40) source from the road is probably on the eastern side of the pass alongside a stream that runs from the ridge. Your next water source on the ridge is 6 km away.

Bi-jae 비재 G3 → Motje 못제 F3 2.3km (1:40)

Crossing the road at Bi-jae, you join a blue steel staircase that climbs north straight up the very steep beginning to this leg, where it becomes a trail again at a ledge located at about 455 m ABSL, passing a tomb 300 meters later. After that, the trail reenters the tree line and arrives at your first noticeable peak, located at 510 m ABSL. From there, you drop into a steep saddle, down through tall, thin trees, and the scene and atmosphere of the area suddenly gives you the feeling that you may be entering another National Park Zone. Reaching the bottom of that saddle area, you start to ascend north out of its bowel and reach your way up the ridgeline, passing through large, chalky-colored, rounded boulder formations hidden in the tree line like disheveled polar bears. At one stage, the trail passes beneath the eastern flank of one of these fossilized creatures and comes out at the top of its northern beginning in a clearing in the trail. It's well worth tiptoeing south along its back and perching on its nose, which provides you with fantastic views south along the ridge. About 200 meters after this location, you should come across another rocky platform located next to a small native pine adorned with ribbons, which provides you with more great views to the east.

From this area, you now start climbing north, chewing 140 m in altitude over the next 800 meters of trail and passing another tomb, to another rocky section of the trail from which it turns west briefly. In this area, there is a marsh. This strange and unique area is known as Motje, and it is the only marsh on the Baekdu-daegan. There is supposedly water available at the marsh, but it is largely stagnant and should be boiled thoroughly before drinking. The area around the marsh, particularly on the western side of it, also houses some tombs.

Motje 못제 F3 → Piat-jae 피앗재 E2 3.5km (2:00)

Heading north out of Motje, you walk on a good wooded ridge trail for the next 600 meters, descending gently into a saddle where, at its bottom, it meets a track heading west down to the temple of Gwaneum-sa 관음사. From the saddle, the Baekdu-daegan trail continues north for the next kilometer, climbing up past some rocky outcrops and then turning northwest for about 100 meters before reaching a track junction located at the top of a wooded summit area, which offers through its hedge line some views northwest to Hyeongje-bong, your next prominent feature. This point is marked by a signpost and is known as Galryeong Samgeori 갈령 삼거리, a three-way intersection located at 721 m ABSL. From the wooded peak, the Baekdu-daegan trail heads west from the junction, and it's a 30 minute walk on a rocky trail to the base of Hyeongje-bong peak, which stands like a large animated gatekeeper in a green poncho, marking the western border of Songni-san National Park.

Hyeongje-bong protrudes from the tree line like the bald, shiny crown of a man's head from his receding hairline. It is a rocky feature that juts dramatically out above the ridgeline. The actual trail passes below the bald peak of Hyeongje-bong, but it is well worth the scramble up to the creased summit area for the sweeping, awe-inspiring 360° views. Standing on the blustery peak of Hyeongje-bong, you look west, north and east at a landscape that is both incredible and daunting. Here you get a frightening indication of just how hilly and undulating this walk...no, this nation...is! If the sun is making its way west at this moment, the vista is biblical, as its iconic rays stream through the billowing cloud cover like a scene from Moses and his forty years in the desert. At about 315° to the northwest, you may be able to make out the features of Cheonwang-bong (1,057m), Songni-san's highest peak, located 6 km away. About 6 km directly to the west-northwest, you may be able to see a distinctive dark ridgeline that forms the peaks of the Hannamgeumbuk-jeongmaek 한남금북정맥 (another long, distant hike), where it joins the Baekdu-daegan at Cheonwang-bong. Atop the thin, rocky highpoint of Hyeongje-bong is a new, reddish-colored stele, replacing the snapped old white wooden stake that used to exist there. From the splendor of Hyeongje-bong, the trail descends northwest, passing by a large rock feature called Halbae-bawi 할배바위 (meaning "grandpa rock") before reentering a good, verdant forest

LODGING

Located 1.5 km away at the bottom of the western track is an accommodation option called the Piat-jae Sanjang 피앗재 산장 (T. 043-543-1058 or 016-761-7761).

and arriving 600 meters later at a peak located at 803 m ABSL. From there, the descent becomes steeper, taking you north for the next 800 meters as you drop about 150 m in altitude down to the thick, wooded pass of Piat-jae*, located at about 625 m ABSL.

* Piat-jae 피앗재 E2

Marked by a signpost, Piat-jae is a wide, bare clearing surrounded by thick forest, a suitable spot for setting up camp at the end of a long day's walk from Hwaryeong-jae. The pass is the site of a four-way junction where useful tracks meet the ridge from the west and east. The track to the west runs 1.2 km down the Mansu Valley 만수계곡. Water(41) is available down this track alongside the trail at the head of the stream, about 500 meters away.

Andrew looking north from Hyeongje-bong

Songni-san National Park 속리산 국립공원

Songni-san ("renouncing the world mountain") was designated a National Park in March 1970 and covers an area of 274,541 km^2. The Baekdu-daegan enters the park at Hyeongje-bong, 13.5 km along the trail from Hwaryeong, and continues through the southern half of the park to Neul-jae 늘재, later rejoining the park at Mil-jae 밀재, near Daeya-san 대야산. This southern section is the most popular area of the park, and the 3.5 km of ridge between the peaks of Cheonwang-bong (1,057.7m), Biro-bong 비로봉 (1,008m) and Munjang-dae 문장대 (1,028m) sees the vast majority of all hikers in Songni-san. This small section is an impressive ridgeline with stunning rocky features, including the famous Ipseok-dae 입석대, Sinseon-dae 신선대, Cheongbeop-dae 청법대 and Munjang-dae boulders. The high ridge creates steep, picturesque valleys to the east and west.

To the west, three popular trails run down to a spectacular and historic valley that leads to the major Buddhist temple Beopju-sa 법주사. Dating back to the year 553, Beopju-sa is a beautiful temple and home to a number of treasures, including the tallest bronze Buddha statue in the world (*Cheongdongmireuk-bul*), built in 1990 and standing 33 m tall. Below Beopju-sa is the tourist village of Sanae-ri 사내리, the main entrance to the park. Sanae-ri is a very busy gateway with all the amenities typical of popular Korean tourist zones, including scores of restaurants specializing in fresh mountain vegetable meals, dozens of motels and *minbak*, and even a large tourist hotel.

There is also a very large National Park campground set amongst mature trees near the tourist area. Sanae-ri is located on NH37, which branches off NH25 about 20 km northwest of Hwaryeong. The eastern side of the ridge is paralleled by PR49 and is a quieter and humbler entrance to the park. From Munjang-dae, a trail runs down a steep valley, equal in beauty to its western cousin, to the Osong ticket booth 오송 매표소 in sleepy Hwabuk-myeon 화북면. This area has a few excellent restaurants and accommodation options in the nearby country town of Hwabuk-myeon.

Lodging

Sieo-dong 시어동: The quieter eastern entrance to the park has less accommodation than Sanae-ri in the west. The Sansujang Motel 산수장 모텔 is located 1 km east of the Sieo-dong park entrance, on the road heading to PR49.

Hwabuk-myeon: The small town of Hwabuk-myeon is located about 1.5 km southeast of the junction with the road heading to Songni-san and PR49. *Minbak* and motel accommodation is available here.

Naesongni-myeon 내속리면 / **Sanae-ri:** The main entrance to Songni-san National Park below Beopju-sa has a large number of *minbak* and motels, as well as a large tourist hotel. This very popular entrance also has a large camping area, the Sanae-ri campground.

Palsang-jeon at Beopju-sa in Songni-san © Liz Riggs

DAY 2

From Piat-jae to Neul-jae

- Distance: 15.5km
- Time: 8hr

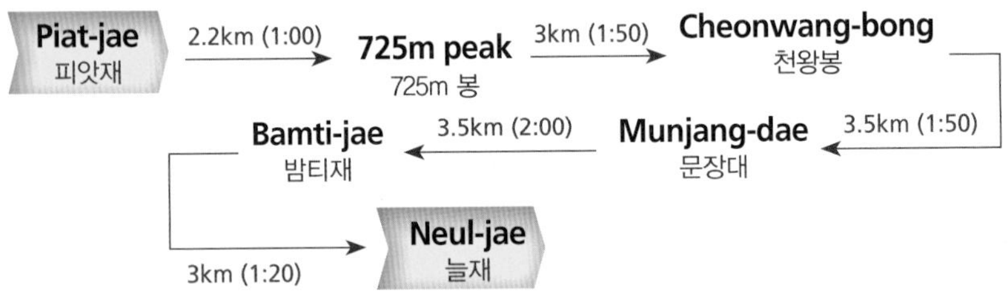

Intact, you push onward to the mighty boulders of Songni-san, racing the adjacent western ridge to the highest summit of Cheonwang-bong. Stuck at its base, you tighten your straps and bound up its face, appearing from the wooded edges out onto the white, smooth crowns of Songni-san. You are now king: you can walk north at this high altitude with the sun at your back and the wind in your face. You navigate through the mirrored maze of Songni-san rock, stopping to meet and greet fellow hikers. You see your endpoint for the high ridge, Munjang-dae, dropped from the heavens onto the edge of the Baekdu-daegan like a lost prayer bead.

Piat-jae 피앗재 E2 → Unnamed 725m peak 725m 봉 D2

2.2km (1:00)

From your sleepy hollow of Piat-jae, the trail ascends north straight up the guts of your first hill, fledged with thin oak trees, before reaching the crest of the high ridge at a point 639 m ABSL some 100 meters later. Once at that altitude, you continue north for 1.3km on a very good, well-vegetated and wide trail that fishtails its way up to your next feature, located at 667 m ABSL. From there, the trail turns northwest, remaining scenic as it slowly creeps up to its next spot height located at 725 m ABSL, some 600 meters later. From there, you see good views of Cheonwang-bong looming in the immediate northwest.

Unnamed 725m peak 725m 봉 → Cheonwang-bong 천왕봉 D2

3km (1:50)

From 725 m, the trail stays northwest, dropping slightly as it crosses a thin ridge for 1 km to its next peak, located at 703 m ABSL. After this peak, you drop again into a rocky hollow, heading northwest for about 200 meters before turning west. Then, slowly but surely, you creep your way along the back of the ridge for another 400 meters toward an open rocky outcrop called Jeonmang-bawi 전망바위. This rock feature is quite significant and easy to recognize, as it is encircled by craggy Korean pine trees covered with hiking ribbons. But most of all, it offers rubbernecking views south down the steep Mansu Valley 만수 계곡, and along the ridge back to Hyeongje-bong. It's a good place to stop and get recharged before your climb up to Cheonwang-bong, some 1 km and 250 m in altitude away.

From Jeonmang-bawi begins the climb to Cheonwang-bong, which should take an hour to complete. The trail heads off to the northwest, staying in good tree line for about 600 meters before turning to the north and meeting a distinctive clearing, harboring a pleasantly located tomb that basks in the sun like a coiled puff adder. From the tomb with the strong friends, the trail heads northwest, staying at approximately the same altitude before meeting a signpost about 200 meters later. From here on in, the trail literally scales its way up the last 160 m in altitude over the final 400 meters of trail to the summit of Cheonwang-bong, a grueling but rewarding task. Cheonwang-bong, located at 1,057 m ABSL, is a rugged peak made up of large boulders, and as it is the highest in the park, it is often referred to as Songni-san. Although the highest, its summit area is not as well frequented as those of its northern brothers, which are more accessible. It has excellent views to the north, east and south. To the north, you can see the continuation of the Baekdu-daegan along the puffy, rocky ridge to Biro-bong 비로봉. About 8 km south is Gubyeong-san 구병산 (876m), and 6 km southeast, Hyeongje-bong can be seen. To the east, the view is expansive, looking over seemingly endless ridges that rise like waves to the horizon.

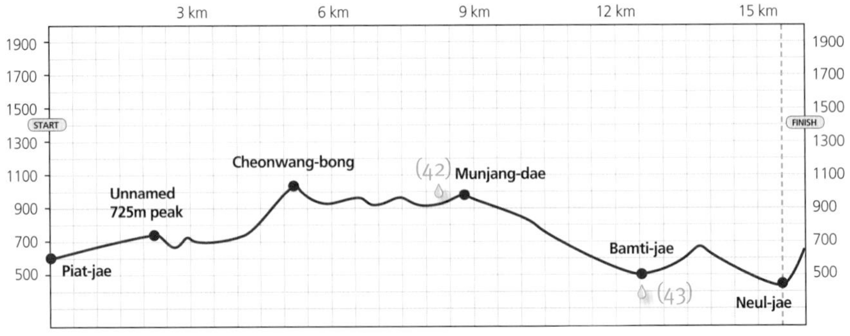

WATER STOPS
(42) Sinseon-dae Hyugeso: **N36°33'19" E127°52'26'**
(43) Bamti-jae: **N36°34'56" E127°53'06"**

* Hannamgeumbuk-jeongmaek 한남금북정맥

Also at the peak is another long-distance trail that sutures itself to the ridge from the southwest. This trail is known as the Hannamgeumbuk-jeongmaek, which heads west and then northwest for 150 km, passing through Cheongju 청주 before webbing with the nodes of two other *jeongmaek* also utilized as long-distance hikes, forming a core nucleus for these three great ridges. At this axis, the Hannamgeumbuk-jeongmaek becomes the Hannam-jeongmaek 한남정맥 and continues northwest, directing the eastern banks of the Han River through Seoul and out into the famous battle-sea coastal areas of Incheon some 200 km later. Do you want to swap ridges now?

Cheonwang-bong 천왕봉 D2 → Munjang-dae 문장대 C1

3.5km (1:50)

From Cheonwang-bong, the trail continues north for the next four kilometers, staying at about 1,000 m ABSL. Now that you are in the well-marked and well-used confines of a popular national park, you can enjoy the buzz and go with the flow. Water should also be readily available at certain parts of the trail in cool mountain runoffs. The trail stays on an open ridge for the next 400 meters before reaching a cobblestoned helipad marked by a signpost. The ridge stays north for 500 meters, meeting another junction where a track heads west from the ridge. From the junction, the trail continues north for the climb to

Biro-bong as it ducks and weaves its way from the ridge and into the beautiful high alpine forest and bush of Songni-san. Along its way, you pass through the cooled walls of a natural archway formed by large fallen boulders, called Sanggo-seokmun 상고석문. About 200 meters after that, you climb a staircase that takes you to the southwest side of the summit of Biro-bong, where it is then a short walk to the peak. Biro-bong, located at 1,032 m ABSL, has a small, rocky peak area with views east overlooking the Janggak Valley 장각골 to the southeast. From Biro-bong, the trail drops into low forest, and you stay on a very good trail as it passes through a lush undergrowth of alpine bamboo. About 500 meters later, the trail becomes rocky, with large boulders on both sides of the ridge, as it veers slightly northwest, passing by an impressive tall, phallic rock called Ipseok-dae. The trail continues northwest, ascending gradually for the next 400 meters up onto the moonscape features of a huge lunar-like boulder, which is the peak of Sinseon-dae. Back on Earth, the trail now heads west from Sinseon-dae, descending for the next 250 meters toward an intersection marked by a signpost.

From the marked junction, the trail turns north, and after a couple of minutes, you reach the high-altitude stop at the Sinseon-dae Hyugeso 신선대 휴게소. The *hyugeso* consists of public toilets and an outside area hosting tables and chairs, serviced by a small restaurant that is guarded by a grumpy mountain dog. The restaurant sells expensive refreshments such as soft drinks and coffee, as well as simple meals, including *pajeon* (vegetable pancake), *gamjajeon* (potato pancake) and soups. Water(42) can be located at the restaurant. Heading northwest from the rest area, you walk 700 meters on a very good section of trail, rising to the summit of Munsu-bong 문수봉 at 1,027 m ABSL. The smooth, rocky surface of its peak area looks northwest to the famous **Munjang-dae*** rock located at the end of the main ridge of Songni-san like a giant golf ball stuck on the lip of a sand trap.

Munjang-dae

* Munjang-dae 문장대 C1

Descending off the summit, you reach the large cleared area that is the arrival point of Songni-san's two most popular paths, coming from Beopju-sa and Sanae-ri to the southwest and Osong ticket booth in the northeast. Once you reach the top of the Munjang-dae, the boulder opens out into a flat, pocketed surface that has a steel fence erected around its circumference. It offers some of the best views in the park, scoping the horizon to the north, east and west, and then south back along the ridge.

Alternative Route

The tricky and sometimes treacherous ridge from Munjang-dae to Bamti-jae then to Neul-jae 늘재 is currently closed. The alternative is to walk east from Munjang-dae, down 3 km to the Osong ticket booth 오송 매표소 near Hwabuk-myeon 화북면, where you should be able to pick up a hiking map of the Songni-san area. From Hawbuk, you can meet the open trail again at Neul-jae on PR49 some 3 km north of Hwabuk-myeon. It is probably better to stay overnight at a *minbak* in Hwabuk-myeon and then walk, taxi, hitch or bus it the 3 km to Neul-jae the next day. Refer map on page 194.

CLOSED SECTION Munjang-dae 문장대 E3 → Bamti-jae 밤티재 D3

3.8km (2:00)

The closed section from Munjang-dae to Bamti-jae can be seen from the top of Munjang-dae at 40° to the northeast. The trailhead is hidden on the northeastern side of a nearby helipad located at Munjang-dae. The Baekdu-daegan would normally continue northeast for 300 meters, descending steeply into a plethora of large boulders called Gaegumeong-bawi 개구멍바위, which provides huge physical and navigational obstacles for the hiker. This section of rock continues downwards for about 300 more meters. There are probably ways around it to the northwest, but unless they are clearly marked (which they won't be, as it is closed), one of the best ways to tackle this obstacle is to clamber through the middle of it, therefore assuring that the hiker won't fall off the huge dropoffs to the east. In the middle of this mass of large, house-sized boulders is a pit. Falling inside the pit are some old fixed ropes and rickety branches acting as snakes and ladders that drop into its abyss, and another set of ropes on the other side that allow escape.

Despite its awkwardness, this area is fantastically spectacular, and the eastern side of this section has some awe-inspiring views over some very steep bluffs and cliffs that are folliculate with trunks of twisted native Korean pine jutting out from between the scars and crinkles of the elephant-sized boulders. Only a day pack is recommended, but an able hiker can still do it with a fully laden pack if need be. If weather conditions allow it, it is possible to see quite clearly the remainder of the ridge descending 40° northeast. The rocky maze of Gaegumeong-bawi leopard-crawls its way back to the main trail after about a kilometer, where it then returns back into the spectacular spooky tree line.

From that point, the trail turns east and begins to descend steeply off the high ridge, assisted by a fixed rope over the steepest section. After the initial descent, the trail then turns back northeast before arriving at another rocky area known as Ipseok-bawi 입석바위. From Ipseok-bawi, the Baekdu-daegan continues northeast, descending through the forest on a noticeable trail for about 900 meters before reaching a tomb. From there, another track meets the ridge, running east along a good-looking spur for 1.5 km to the remains of the Gyeonhwon-seong Fortress 견훤성. There is supposedly no other track to this castle, adding to it more intrigue. From the tomb, the Baekdu-daegan heads directly north, descending for 600 meters before turning northeast again for the last 100 meters to **Bamti-jae***. The trail spills out onto the road below an eco-bridge that crosses Bamti-jae, allowing animals to avoid the quiet road. Where the trail breaks out, there exists a small resting area with a stone monument. Water(43) is available from a stream on the northwestern side of the road.

Songni-san from 1 km north of Bamti-jae

* Bamti-jae 밤티재 B2

Located at about 500 m ABSL, Bamti-jae is connected by PR997, which runs 2 km east to a road intersection with PR49/32. This intersection is located about 3 km north of Hwabuk-myeon.

Hwabuk-myeon is a quaint, small settlement with a good number of small, tasty restaurants and a couple of motel options. The small town can also be reached from the eastern track off Munjang-dae.

CLOSED SECTION Bamti-jae 밤티재 D3 → Neul-jae 늘재 B2 3km (1:20)

Crossing the road from Bamti-jae, the trail heads northeast, climbing steadily for about 700 meters before the trail straightens north, where it meets a large set of boulders near the unnamed peak located at 696 m ABSL. This rocky point has a great view south toward the tidal wave wall of Songni-san's high peaks, stretching along the eastern side of the Baekdu-daegan mountain system from Munjang-dae to Cheonwang-bong. From the unnamed peak, the trail turns east, dropping through the forest on a good trail for about 500 meters before panning out at about 628 m ABSL. From there, you turn northeast and enjoy a good descent on a winding path for about 1.5 km before reaching the PR32/49 at the Neul-jae* road pass, home to a mountain spirit shrine, an old sacred tree and a huge new granite stele.

* Neul-jae 늘재 B2

Neul-jae is connected by the PR32/49, which runs northwest 12 km to the small town of Songmyeon-ri 송면리 in northwestern Songni-san, and about 3.5 km southeast to the township of Hwabuk-myeon. Since 2008, the pass of Neul-jae has had some landscaping improvements done to its area, and it is now the home of a huge stele commemorating the Baekdu-daegan. The large, pistol grip-shaped stele has been inscribed with Chinese characters and is set in a cleared area suitable for camping, which is also home to an old sacred tree and a *sansin-dang* (mountain spirit shrine).

The sacred tree sits on the eastern edge of the road above its shrine. The tree is a *Kalopanax septemlobus* (pictus), more commonly known as the prickly castor oil tree...a deciduous species native to China, Korea, and Japan that can grow up to 18 m in height. The small stone plaque near it was placed there in 1982 by the people of Jangam-ri, near Hwabuk-myeon. The tree is supposedly 320 years old, meaning it had a rather fortunate existence, surviving numerous conflicts and fiery battles. Beneath the sacred tree is the old shrine for the tree that almost resembles a rural fruit stand. Inside it is incense burning alongside some urns.

Further in from the road, on the eastern side of the pass near the stele, is another stone monument near what looks like the mountain spirit shrine. The monument describes the history of the pass and shrine. If you're wondering what the strange, alien-type script is on the base of the monument, they are "seal-script" Chinese characters, a very primitive alphabet modeled after the very earliest Chinese writing. The back of the monument states expansively that the shrine is a sacred precinct and that it contains the energy and spirit of the Baekdu-daegan. Its historic origins, according to the monument, explain in great detail how its early form was that of a tutelary mountain god deity style in the shape of totemism faith and worship from the Shilla (57 BC-AD 935) and Goguryeo periods (37 BC-AD 688) of the early Three Kingdoms period. The local villagers would come here to pray for the prevention of unexpected disaster, disease and infection, and for safe passage for travelers. Later on, in the Joseon period (1392-1910), the site was developed for the purposes of religious services.

As the area underwent frequent national crisis, the local officials and population sublimated the traditional faith of the shrine even more. The mountain, or it seems village, God in this case, became the most recognized and ordained subject of worship for the pass, providing national prosperity and welfare for the people. From that period on, the shrine became a registered site attached to a geographical location. As a battle zone, Neul-jae has had its fair share of military ware stampede over its brow. Neul-jae, like most other passes on the Baekdu-daegan, was a border area between the old Silla and Baekje kingdoms during the Later Three Kingdoms period in Korea (892-935). During that period, the nearby Gyeonhwon mountain fortress near Hwabuk-myeon was constructed as a garrison for soldiers of the Silla regime. The fortress was named after its creator, Gyeonhwon, who was a general of the Silla period as well as the constructor of numerous other fortifications in Korea. Later on, during the Imjin Invasion of Korea in 1592-1598, General Jeong Gi-ryong fought the Japanese

Sanshin-dang at Neul-jae

in nearby Yonghwa-dong, using the pass as a means of transporting heavy equipment. More recently, after the Japan-Korea Annexation Treaty of 1910, righteous locals raised an army in the cause of justice and used the pass as a means of passage. The current shrine was rebuilt in the early 20th century by a retired scholar named Jeon Sang-seok, and later rebuilt again, 100 years later, by his great-grandson Chung-hwan in cooperation with local Sangju officials as a measure to set an example of remembrance for the patriotism of the ancestors of this region. After all that history, it concludes remarkably that this area is a place of education, harboring the energies and spirit of the Baekdu-daegan.

TRANSPORT INFO

Leaving the trail at Neul-jae: Buses run from Neulti 늘티, the small village about 1 km south of Neul-jae, into Hwabuk-myeon seven times a day from 7:10 am to 6:50 pm. Neul-jae is only 4 km north of Hwabuk-myeon, and a taxi can be at the pass in less than 10 min. Hwabuk Taxi can be reached at 054-534-7447. Hwabuk-myeon is also the portal for the Osong ticket booth and the Seongbul-sa temple 성불사, both of which are located up a sealed road that runs west from the town back to the base and start of a track up to Munjang-dae. Buses leave Hwabuk-myeon for Sangju 17 times daily between 7 am and 6 pm. From Sangju, they leave for Hwabuk-myeon seven times a day from 7:50 am to 6:05 pm. From Hwabuk-myeon, two buses run to Seoul each day at 8:20 am and 12:30 pm.

LODGING

Camping is permitted at the pass, as long as it's done in a non-invasive manner. Approximately 600 meters north along the PR32/49 is the Cheonghwa-san Hyugeso 청화산 휴게소 restaurant and small supermarket; otherwise, the nearest accommodation can be found in the Hwabuk-jang Yeogwan 화북장 여관 (054-534-3800) 5 km to the south in Hwabuk-myeon.

Hwabuk-jang Yeogwan

THREE DAYS

44.5km

SECTION 7

THE RAMPARTS OF KOREA

Neul-jae → Ihwa-ryeon

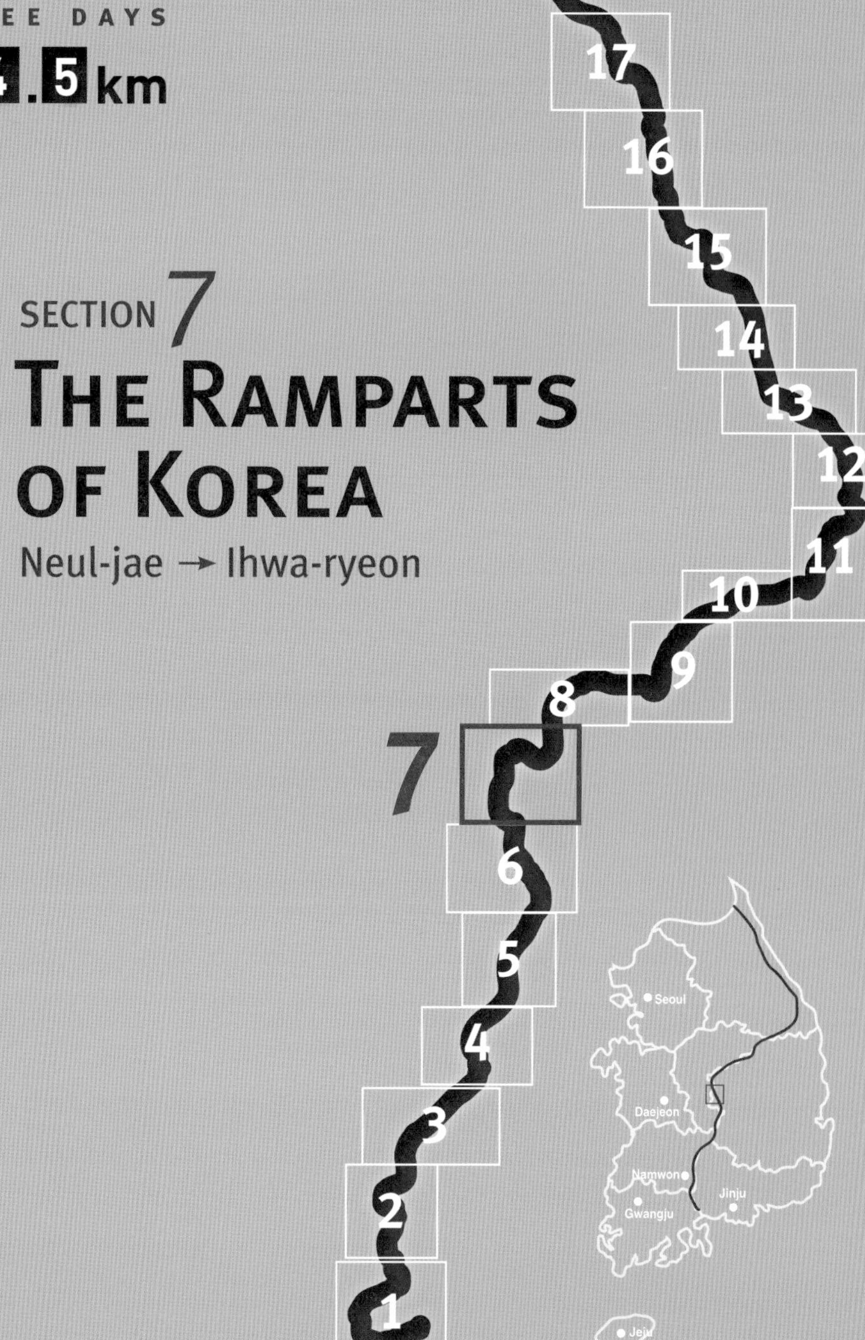

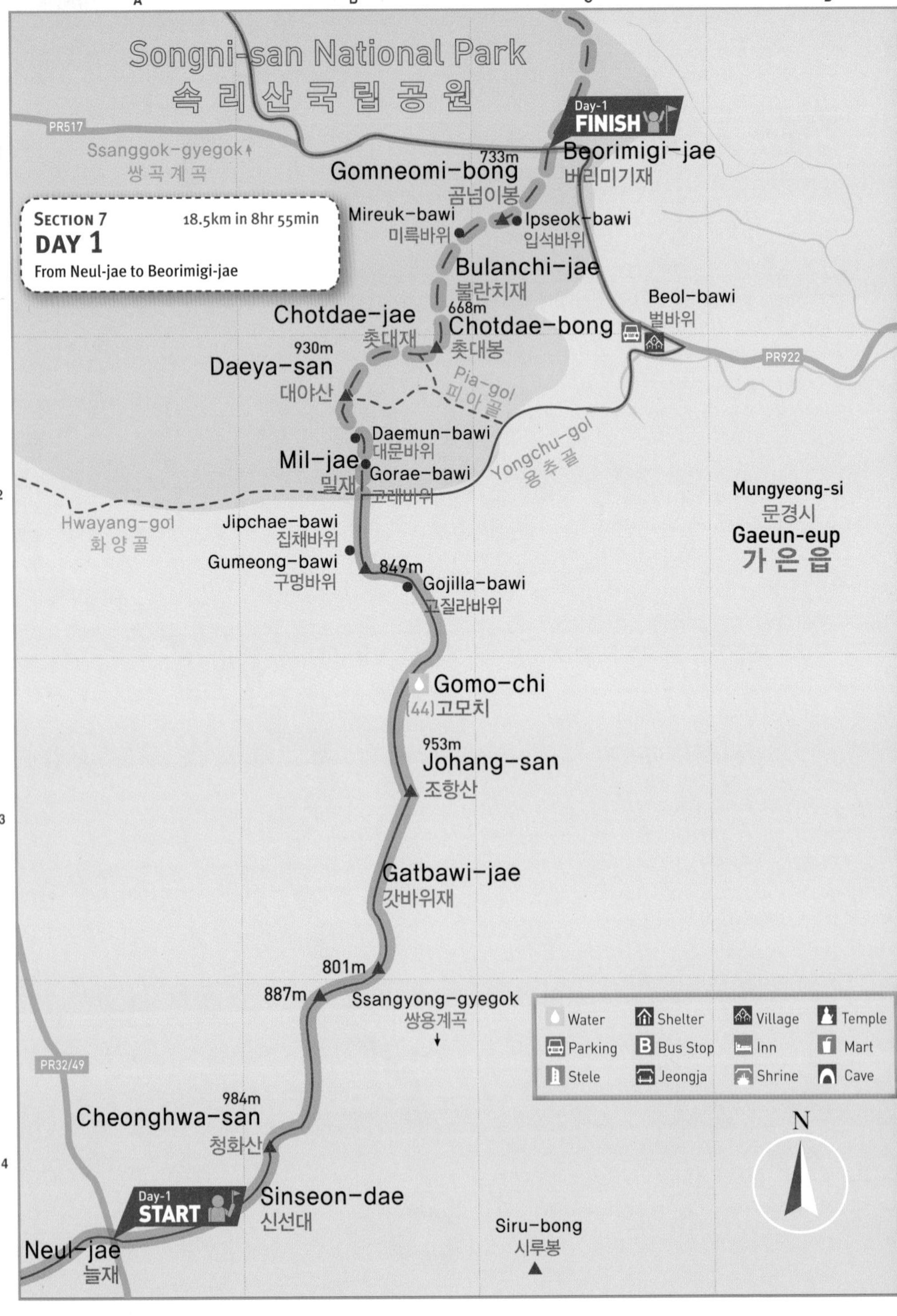

A
B
C
D
1
2
3
4
Songni-san National Park
속리산국립공원
PR517
Ssanggok-gyegok
쌍곡계곡
SECTION 7
18.5km in 8hr 55min
DAY 1
From Neul-jae to Beorimigi-jae
Day-1
FINISH
Beorimigi-jae
버리미기재
733m
Gomneomi-bong
곰넘이봉
Mireuk-bawi
미륵바위
Ipseok-bawi
입석바위
Bulanchi-jae
불란치재
Beol-bawi
벌바위
668m
Chotdae-bong
촛대봉
Chotdae-jae
촛대재
930m
Daeya-san
대야산
Pia-gol
피아골
PR922
Daemun-bawi
대문바위
Mil-jae
밀재
Gorae-bawi
고래바위
Yongchu-gol
용추골
Mungyeong-si
문경시
Gaeun-eup
가은읍
Hwayang-gol
화양골
Jipchae-bawi
집채바위
Gumeong-bawi
구멍바위
849m
Gojilla-bawi
고질라바위
Gomo-chi
(44)고모치
953m
Johang-san
조항산
Gatbawi-jae
갓바위재
801m
887m
Ssangyong-gyegok
쌍용계곡
Water
Shelter
Village
Temple
Parking
Bus Stop
Inn
Mart
Stele
Jeongja
Shrine
Cave
PR32/49
984m
Cheonghwa-san
청화산
N
Day-1
START
Sinseon-dae
신선대
Siru-bong
시루봉
Neul-jae
늘재

DAY 1

From Neul-jae to Beorimigi-jae

- **Distance:** 16.1km
- **Time:** 7hr 50min

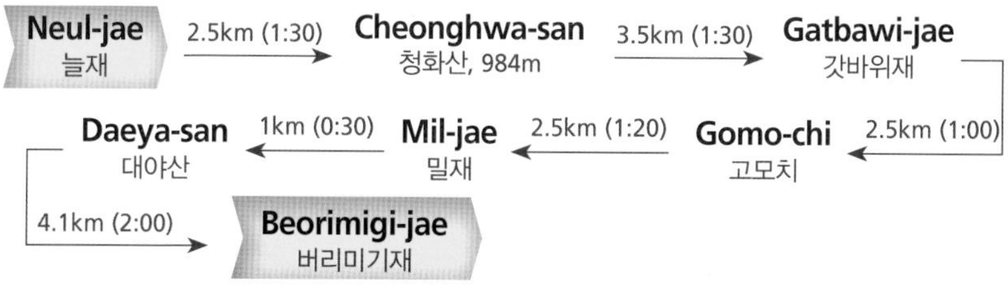

When you slept at Neul-jae, were you awoken by the clink of armor, the stampede of feet? Never mind. Push up the ridge again and stop and have tea with the sansin. Aspire to the top of Cheonghwa-san and bounce north into the grandeur of Korea. Calculate the narrow ridges and stroke the beached whales that dot the rocky landscape. Press your temple against their cooled white torsos and absorb their telepathic energy. Walk to the magic of Daeya-san and watch inscriptions appear before you in its grainy ledges. Straddle its lunar orbs and punctuate yourself at its summit. Rappel down its back and saunter through its forgotten zone, shoulders pinned back...proud as muck!

Neul-jae 늘재 A4 → Cheonghwa-san 청화산 B4 2.5km (1:30)

From Neul-jae, you head east into pine forest and begin your walk on a good trail for about 300 meters before meeting a bend in a mountain road. From there, the trail continues east for the next kilometer, zigzagging over the rocky ridgeline of Cheonghwa-san's southern face. The trail then starts to bend northeast as it meets a series of fixed ropes ascending 700 m in altitude over the next kilometer to

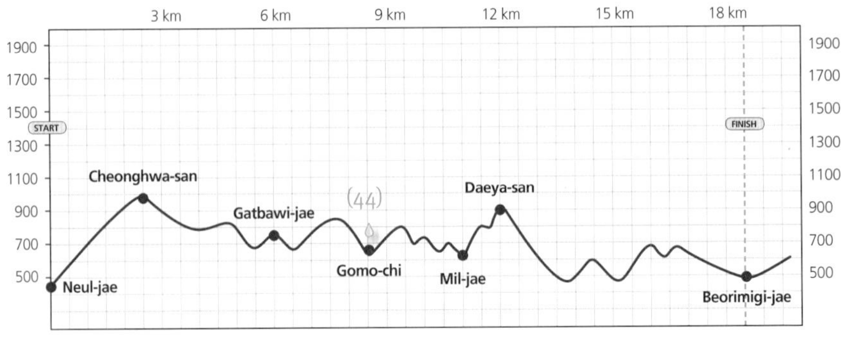

WATER STOPS (44) Gomo-chi: **N36°38'27" E127°56'21"**

Cheonghwa-san, passing a sinseon-dae ("spirit immortal platform") view point 600 meters south of the summit. The site consists of a black tablet inscribed with Chinese characters, parked in between two granite incense holders, and it offers fantastic views back toward the high ridge of Songni-san. The altar is set amongst craggy Korean pines that frame the view south, a very idyllic setting for a rest and a brew with the local *sansin* (mountain spirit). Cheonghwa-san, located at 984 m ABSL, is marked by a signpost and celebrated by a small stone stele placed in the center of a small clearing.

Sinseon-dae below Cheonghwa-san

Cheonghwa-san 청화산 B4 → Gatbawi-jae 갓바위재 B3

3.5km (1:30)

The trail heads east from the peak, maintaining good height, and meets a junction 500 meters later. The junction is marked by a signpost, and the tendency would be to continue east past the signpost, staying on a ridgeline. The actual Baekdu-daegan turns left, dropping north down a trail into the woods toward its next peak, enjoying 1.2 km of good ridge-walking where it arrives at an unnamed peak located at 877 m ABSL. From there, the trail rather dubiously turns northeast and crumbles into a thin, dicey ridgeline that crags its way down onto the lip of a steep ravine. It is a two-handed, sure-footed event in this dynamic part of the walk, offering great views south toward the Ssangyong-gyegok Valley 쌍용계곡 and Siru-bong 시루봉. Once at the bottom of the traverse, you can head back up the rocky, open-aired trail toward a spot height located at 801m ABSL on the western side of an east-pointing peak. Once again, you are enchanted by more stunning scenery and views at this vista. The mountainside is now starting to take on its own unique Korean charm, with gnarly, menacing stands of rock and mountain that in places support majestic flat ledges that only a leopard, tiger or *sansin* could get up to. To the north, you can see the dark, brooding twin-peaked feature of Johang-san 조항산, which stands at 953 m ABSL. The great part about this section of the walk is that a lot of it will be done on an open but rickety ridgeline. From here, the trail straightens up to the north again before descending northwest into the saddle and pass area of Gatbawi-jae.

Gatbawi-jae 갓바위재 → Gomo-chi 고모치 B3

2.5km (1:00)

Just north of Gatbawi-jae, the trail passes over a helipad as it begins its 200m ascent toward Johang-san, located a kilometer away. About 500 meters from the pass, the ridge again becomes thin and rocky, with steep edges on both sides. The trail follows the eastern side of the boulders that form the ridgeline, and ropes are fixed in place along the rock face. It's a challenging but rewarding scramble along the rocks to the summit of Johang-san (953m), which is celebrated by a small stele in a rocky clearing on the summit, put there by the Daehan Hiking Association. The inscription on the old stele is a poem. It says; "Vigorously hiking the Baekdu-daegan, All hopes and expectations are so sweet; Ah, ah, our mountains"

The views are understandably great, and you may be able to see the distinctive white peaks of Daeya-san a good 5 km away in the distant north. The trail heads slightly northwest off the peak and drops mildly down onto a ledge for the next 500 meters before reaching a junction marked by a signpost. From the junction, you start to leave the edges of Johang-san and descend for 200+ meters over the next kilometer into the pass of Gomo-chi. The trail to the pass is very steep, passing one signpost, and should take about 30 minutes to complete. Gomo-chi is a tightly enclosed pass marked by a signpost and signboard. The signboard states that this area was used to stage a KBS drama about Korea's famous 9th century Zen Buddhist and Daoist master monk Doseon-guksa. This remarkable man roamed the hills and mountains of Korea and created the geomantic theory of *Pungsu-jiri* (feng shui), or divination through topography. He is probably the first person to officially recognize the Baekdu-daegan as the central axis of all ecology and civilization on the Korean Peninsula, and he realized that its *jeongmaek* (subsidiary ranges) are the meridian lines of energy that flow through, charging the peninsula. The pass also contains a freshwater spring(44) that can be located about ten meters off the eastern side of the ridge. It is identified by a bamboo frame formed around the rocky spring, which is a permanent and reliable source of water.

Gomo-chi 고모치 B3 → Mil-jae 밀재 B2 2.5km (1:20)

From Gomo-chi, the trail ascends northeast for the next 350 meters, after which it straightens to the north and continues onward for another 350 meters before reaching an unmarked track junction located about 100 m higher in altitude than Gomo-chi. From the track junction, the Baekdu-daegan descends northwest, and after 500 meters, you meet a huge rock called Gojilla-bawi 고질라바위. This marks the beginning of a beautiful rocky section fringed with native pine that meanders its way through to Daeya-san, passing a number of huge and mysterious whale-like boulder formations. The top of Gojilla-bawi, near its blowhole, offers some great views north along the Baekdu-daegan. From this area, located at about 850 m ABSL, the trail dips into a shallow saddle, passing through more stunning native bush and freaky rock formations, before rolling up again to a spot height located at 849 m ABSL. Shortly before reaching 849 m, the trail forks to the right, giving you the option of heading northwest and contouring below the peak. From 849 m, the main trail turns north from the peak and meets the bypass track about 100 meters later near two more huge boulders called Gumeong-bawi 구멍바위 and Jipchae-bawi 집채바위. At this point, you begin to descend toward Mil-jae*, located some 700 meters away, causing you to drop approximately 100m in altitude before reaching the pass. If the day is getting long and you are considering sleeping out, the area you are in right now offers many small but great rocky plateaus that allow you on a fine, warm night to roll out your bivvy bag and sleep under the stars. Your next best sleeping spot is probably at the tall, wooded pass called Mil-jae.

* Mil-jae 밀재 B2

Mil-jae has a large clearing walled in by a tall, thin forest. It is the site of a four-way junction with tracks running east and west off the ridge. The western track heads 5 km down the Hwayang-gol Gorge 화양골, following a stream to PR32/49 in Song-myeon 송면. The eastern track heads down the beautiful Yongchu-gol Scenic Gorge 용추골 about 3 km to the small Yongchu trail entrance, which has a number of restaurants and a motel on the banks of an idyllic stream that churns out clear, deep jade pools of mountain water that flow through the valley. Mil-jae also marks the reentrance of the Baekdu-daegan into the northeastern section of Songni-san National Park. The trail is CLOSED from here on in, all the way north to its exit at the Akhui-bong 악희봉 junction some 12 km later.

Alternative Route

Apart from continuing, your only legal option is to head east from Mil-jae down to the Yongchu-gol, where you can explore this spectacular region along some of the open trails that blaze through the Valleys (Maps p214) There are also accommodations and camping sites in the area for you to base yourself from. After that, it is possible to travel west on PR922 for 4 km to the intersection with PR517. From there, you can turn north onto PR517 and continue for another 4 km to the Ssangok-gyegok Hyugeso. From there, you can walk east up the spectacular river valley to the Ssangok waterfalls and find the marked trail towards the peak of Chilbu-san 778 m, where further on another trail breaks east on a spellbinding leg to Akhui-bong (845m) joining the Baekdu-daegan moments later. Refer map on p224.

CLOSED SECTION Mil-jae 밀재 → Daeya-san 대야산 B2 1km (0:30)

Mil-jae is more or less the base of Daeya-san. The trail heads north toward its summit, ascending 230 m in altitude for the next kilometer. After 600 meters of walking, the trail begins to cross a large boulder known as both Gorae-bawi 고래바위 ("whale rock") and Kokkiri-bawi 코끼리바위 ("elephant rock"). As either name suggests, they are very large rocks, from which the trail climbs over, aided by fixed ropes. From here, a series of interesting rock formations begins rising out of the forest as the trail turns northwest, passing a gigantic, singular round boulder propped up by fickle twigs and surrounded by white gravel on a flat surface. This spectacular natural phenomenon is called Daemun-bawi 대문바위 ("great gate rock"). This area strongly represents the mystifying energy and spirituality of the Baekdu-daegan, and Korea in general. Walking through the "great gate" created by the rock, the trail then crosses another cluster of huge boulders before arriving at the base of Daeya-san, which stands proudly and steeply above the thin open ridge. The last remaining sections to the summit are severed by short, sharp ravines that have grated their way over the ridge, causing the hiker to stop and descend down into them by fixed rope. Just before reaching the boulder peak of Daeya-san, a track leaves the ridge, heading steeply southeast down to the Pia-gol ravine, which flows into the Yongchu-gol scenic gorge at its trail entrance on PR922. A beautiful stream flows down Yongchu-gol, strewn with deep, clear pools fed by attractive waterfalls, making for a very popular place in the summer. The trail from Daeya-san to the trail entrance is about 3.5 km.

There are a couple of false crests before Daeya-san. The only real indication that the hikers are definitely at its summit is that if they walked any further north, they would literally fall off its sheer northern face. Daeya-san, at 930 m ABSL, is a very steep mountain, and its summit has great views on all sides, particularly to the northeast across to the large peaks above the Gaeun-eup 가은읍 area. The summit surface is smooth rock and is celebrated by a small stele and some hiking ribbons fluttering nervously away, marking the continuation of the Baekdu-daegan which continues vertically straight down the northeastern face of this unforgettable peak.

CLOSED SECTION Daeya-san 대야산 → Chotdae-bong 촛대봉 B2 1.3km (0:50)

Hikers will stick their nose out over the northeastern rim of the peak and see a series of fixed ropes descending down the grey, wooded face of Daeya-san. This is the first of a series of seriously steep drops known locally as the 100 m rope. Parts of this descent are a near abseil, and serious caution is advised. However, the task is not as daunting as it sounds. The other alternative is to leave the peak and head back down to Yongchu Scenic Gorge, rejoining the open section at Akhui-bong, as explained in the alternative section. After making the 100 m descent, the hiker can take a breather and descend another 130m. A kilometer later, the hiker has consumed 500 m in altitude before standing in the beautiful wooded area of Chotdae-jae 촛대재, a pass marked by a signpost and track junction located at just under 550 m ABSL. From the pass, the hiker begins the steep climb to the next peak, Chotdae-bong, located about 300 meters to the northeast. A track heads north from just out of the pass, offering the option of bypassing the peak and meeting the main trail on the northern side of Chotdae-bong. Otherwise, the Baekdu-daegan continues steeply up the northeast face to its summit at 668 m ABSL.

Chotdae-bong 촛대봉 B2 → Beorimigi-jae 버리미기재 C1

2.8km (1:10)

From Chotdae-bong, the trail heads north for 600 meters, descending 100 m into the pass of Bulanchi-jae 불란치재. From there, the trail ascends north for 400 meters before reaching a helipad, which has a track heading southeast down to the Yongchu-gol parking lot. Continuing north from the helipad, the trail becomes steeper, entering a rocky area where hikers are assisted by the occasional fixed rope. On the climb up, the trail turns northeast, passing by a huge boulder called Mireuk-bawi 미륵바위, meaning "Maitreya rock." After that, the trail lunges into a shallow saddle continuing northeast, where about 300 meters later it arrives at the summit of its neighbor peak, Gomneomi-bong 곰넘이봉, rising 733 m ABSL from Mother Earth. The summit area is adorned with freakish and wonderful rock formations and boulders, one of which is named Ipseok-bawi 입석바위 ("standing boulder"). Once again, the hiker can revel in peaceful harmony at the amazing treasures of this region, which offer granite lounge suites broadcasting live pods of pure nature.

You descend northeast from the peak with the help of a fixed rope, which takes you off the steep boulder of the peak, and onto another fixed rope 200 meters later.

Daeya-san

At the base of this rope, the trail continues northeast for another 400 meters before meeting the final steep section of fixed rope. From there, the trail heads north, passing through marvelous stands of deciduous forest. The green felt of the canopy is broken occasionally in color by the snookered hues of a single ribbon or rainbow of hiking ribbons. Just before the pass of Beorimigi-jae, you can witness first hand the thinnest piece of watershed you will walk on. At one stage, the trail literally darns its way through two separate streams, one on either side of the trail, that spill respectively east and west away from each other—at that moment separated only by the four foot width of the trail! The Baekdu-daegan does not cross water; it is a continuous feature representing the purest definition of a ridge.

* Beorimigi-jae 버리미기재 C1

Beorimigi-jae is connected by PR922, which runs 9 km southeast to Gaeun-eup and a similar distance west to Song-myeon. About 3 km southeast of the pass on PR922 is the entrance to the Yongchu scenic gorge.

* Ssanggok-gyegok 쌍곡계곡 A1

3 km west of Beorimigi-jae is PR514, which runs north into the Ssanggok-gyegok, the number one attraction in northern Songni-san National Park, consisting of a system of scenic gorges that stretches for 13.5 km beneath the peaks of Gunja-san, Bihak-san and Chilbo-san. PR514 follows the rocky stream beneath craggy cliffs dotted with hardy Korean pines. The area is understandably popular during the summer months, and there are a number of accommodation options through the valley. It is also the alternative route for the hiker to obtain permissible access back to the Baekdu-daegan via Akhui-bong, where the trail will elbow its way east toward Mungyeong Saejae.

Leaving the trail at Beorimigi-jae: About 2.5 km southeast of Beorimigi-jae is Beol-bawi 벌바위, at the entrance to the popular Yongchu scenic gorge trails. From there, buses run to the nearby town of Gaeun-eup four times a day at 9:10 am, 9:55 am, 1:20 pm and 5:20 pm. Buses also run from Gaeun-eup to Mungyeong every 40 minutes from 6:45 am to 8:30 pm. Gaeun Taxi will run to the pass if called and can be reached at 054-571-5789. Returning to the pass, it is possible to get a bus directly from Mungyeong to Beol-bawi. They leave five times a day at 8:20 am, 9 am, 12:10 pm, 4:10 pm and 5 pm. Roughly 2.5 km to the west, buses run into Song-myeon from the junction of PR922 and PR517, which heads north about 6 km to the head of the Ssangok-gyegok.

The Yongchu scenic gorge area has restaurants with small stores and motel/ *minbak* accommodation.

DAY 2

From Beorimigi-jae to Eunti-gogae

- **Distance:** 9km
- **Time:** 3hr 55min

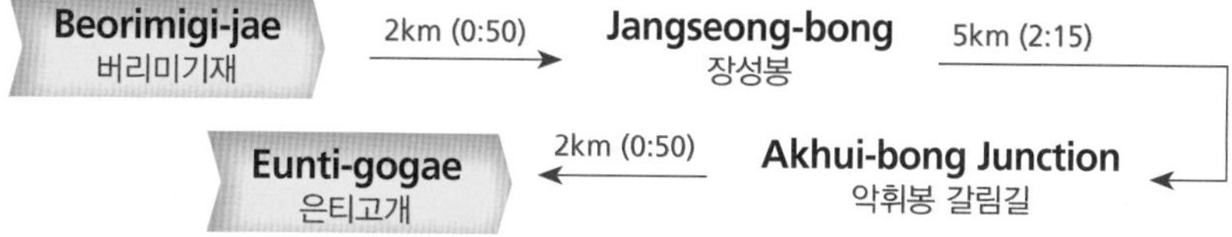

From Beorimigi-jae, you climb to Jangseong-bong and walk on the eastern border of Songni-san National Park above steep gorges that form the tributaries of the Ssanggok-gyegok. Leaving the park below the summit of Akhui-bong, you walk toward the white peaks of Huiyeong-san and Siru-bong, which form a gateway for the Baekdu-daegan, as you descend into the pass above the quaint mountain village of Eunti.

Alternative Route

The trail is CLOSED for 7 km from Beorimigi-jae to Akhui-bong. Alternative route is west 2.5 km to the intersection of PR517, north 4 km to Ssanggok-gyegok, then walk the hiking-trail east 5 km to Akhui-bong, re-joining the Baekdu-daegan there.

CLOSED SECTION Beorimigi-jae 버리미기재 → Jangseong-bong 장성봉 C3

2km (0:50)

From the northern side of PR922, the trail heads back into the forest, climbing steeply north up the southern spur of Jangseong-bong, located at 916 m ABSL, and gaining more than 400 m in altitude over the 2 km trek to the peak. About 600 meters into the ascent, the trail passes through some rocky outcrops, which

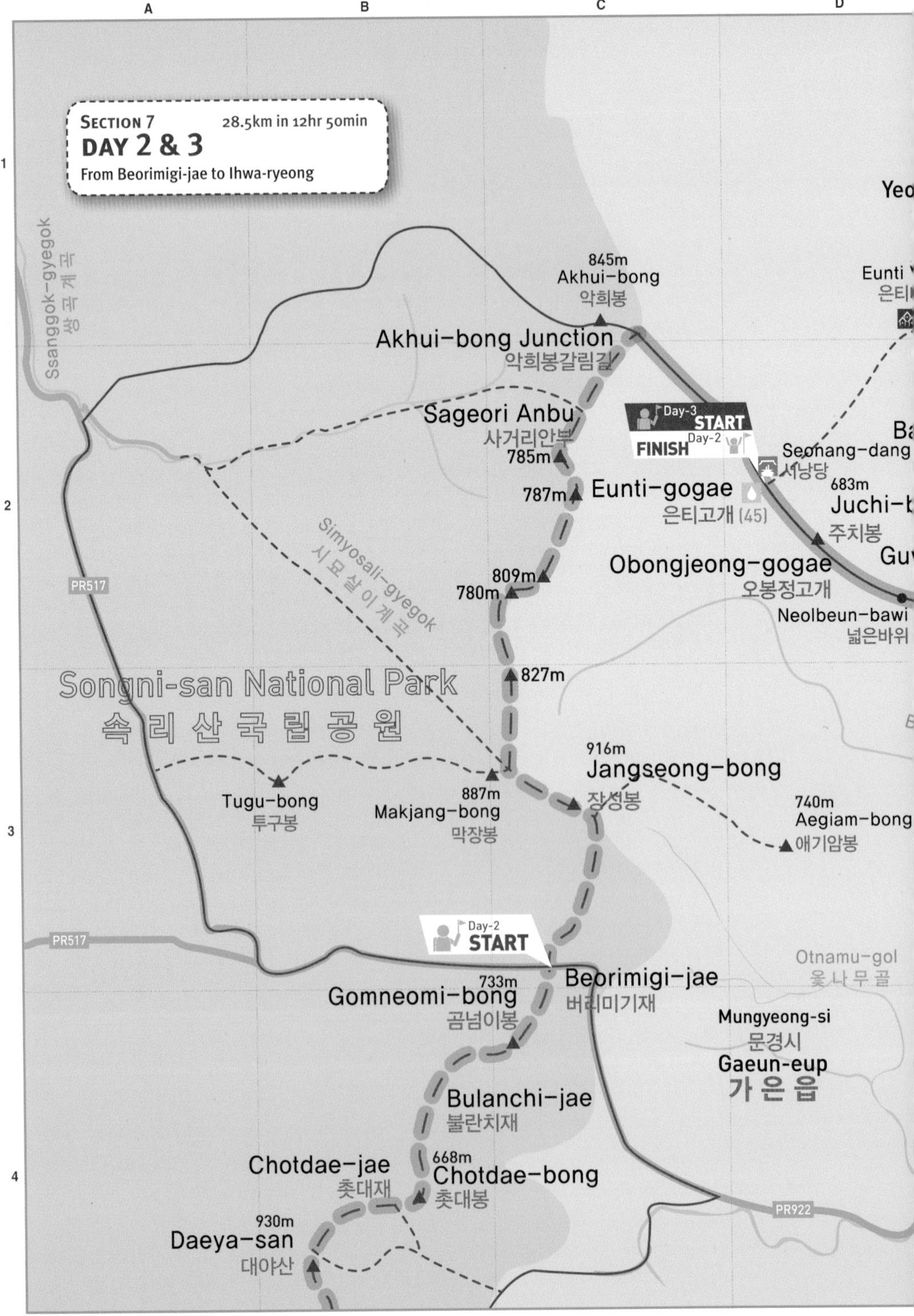

A
B
C
D
1
2
3
4
SECTION 7
28.5km in 12hr 50min
DAY 2 & 3
From Beorimigi-jae to Ihwa-ryeong
Ssanggok-gyegok
쌍곡계곡
845m
Akhui-bong
악희봉
Akhui-bong Junction
악희봉갈림길
Sageori Anbu
사거리안부
785m
787m
Eunti-gogae
은티고개 (45)
Day-3 START
Day-2 FINISH
Seonang-dang
서낭당
683m
Juchi-b
주치봉
Obongjeong-gogae
오봉정고개
Neolbeun-bawi
넓은바위
809m
780m
827m
Simyosali-gyegok
시묘살이계곡
PR517
Songni-san National Park
속리산국립공원
916m
Jangseong-bong
장성봉
740m
Aegiam-bong
애기암봉
Tugu-bong
투구봉
887m
Makjang-bong
막장봉
Day-2 START
Otnamu-gol
옻나무골
733m
Gomneomi-bong
곰넘이봉
Beorimigi-jae
버리미기재
Mungyeong-si
문경시
Gaeun-eup
가은읍
Bulanchi-jae
불란치재
Chotdae-jae
촛대재
668m
Chotdae-bong
촛대봉
930m
Daeya-san
대야산
PR922
Eunti
은티
Yeo
Ba
Gu

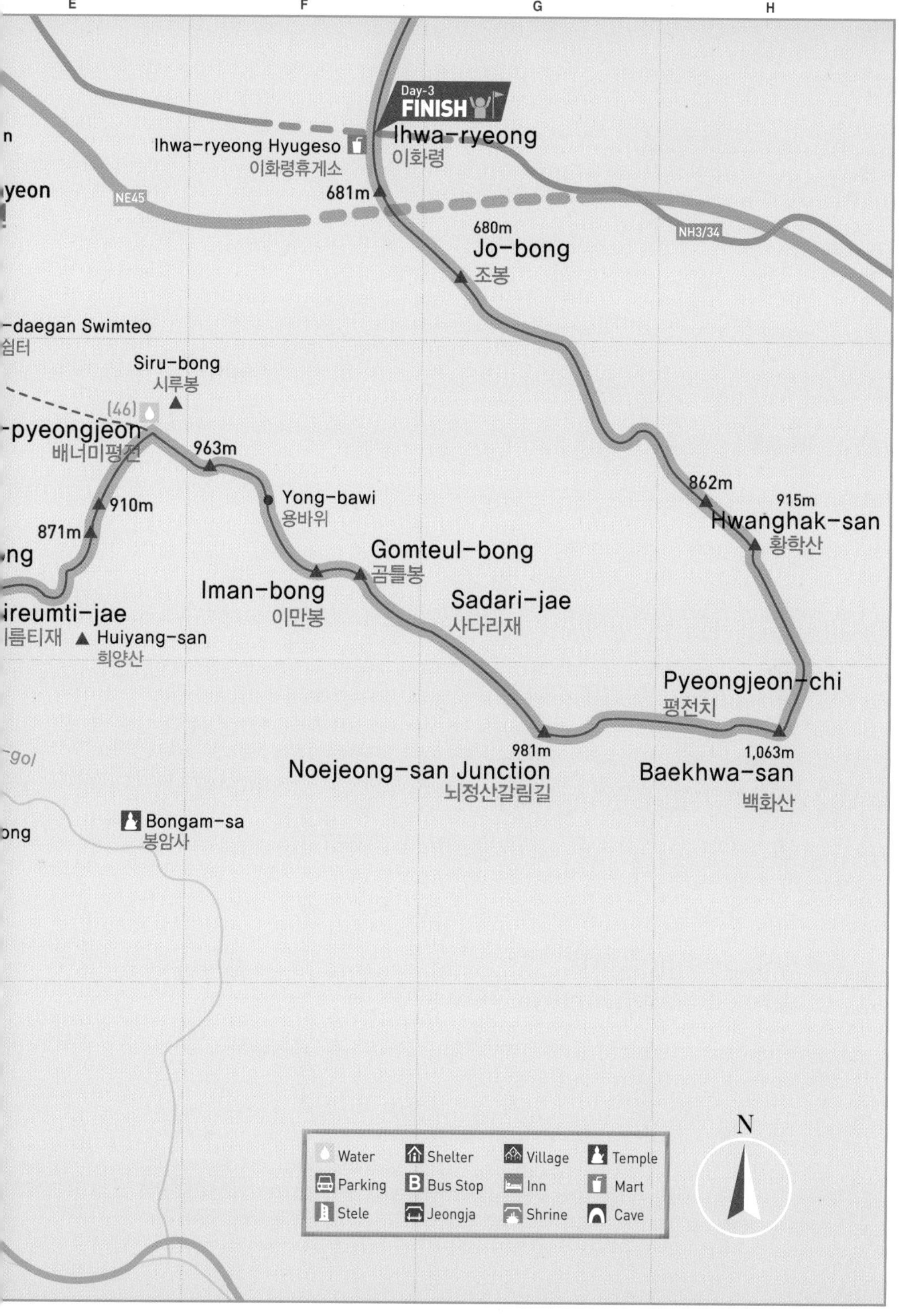
E
F
G
H
Day-3
FINISH
Ihwa-ryeong
이화령
Ihwa-ryeong Hyugeso
이화령휴게소
NE45
681m
680m
Jo-bong
조봉
NH3/34
-daegan Swimteo
쉼터
Siru-bong
시루봉
(46)
-pyeongjeon
배너미평전
963m
910m
871m
Yong-bawi
용바위
Gomteul-bong
곰틀봉
Iman-bong
이만봉
Sadari-jae
사다리재
ireumti-jae
름티재
Huiyang-san
희양산
862m
915m
Hwanghak-san
황학산
Pyeongjeon-chi
평전치
981m
Noejeong-san Junction
뇌정산갈림길
1,063m
Baekhwa-san
백화산
-gol
Bongam-sa
봉암사
Water
Shelter
Village
Temple
Parking
Bus Stop
Inn
Mart
Stele
Jeongja
Shrine
Cave
N

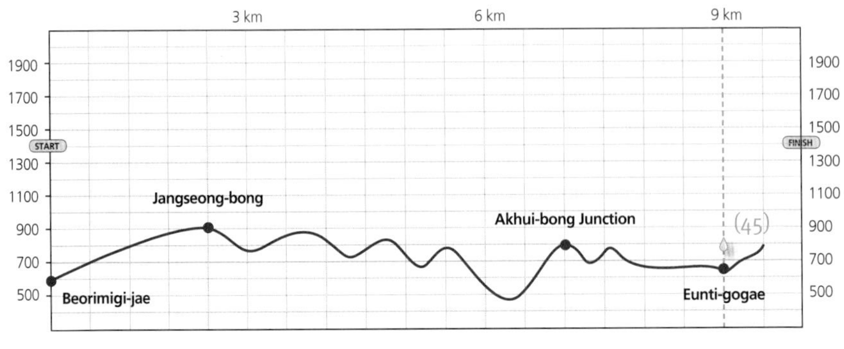

WATER STOPS (45) Eunti-gogae: **N36°43'22" E127°58'30"**

continue onward for another 300 meters. The trail tends to squeeze around the eastern side of the larger obstacles. Heading north, it becomes a thin ridge dotted with craggy Korean pine trees, hosting the occasional view east down into Otnamu-gol Gorge 옻나무골 and toward the prominent peaks of Aegiam-bong 애기암봉 (740m) and Wontong-bong 원통봉 (668m), located on an eastern spur from Jangseong-bong. Just before the summit area of Jangseong-bong, there is a break in the trail. This summit area is celebrated by a small stone stele set in a clearing, large enough to pitch a tent. The western side of the peak is open, offering views of the neighboring peaks of Makjang-bong 막장봉 (887m) at 285° 1km to the NW, and Tugu-bong 투구봉 to its immediate west, located on the same spur. None of these peaks is on the Baekdu-daegan, the trail sweeping about 200 meters east of Makjang-bong.

CLOSED SECTION Jangseong-bong 장성봉 C3 → Akhui-bong Junction 악휘봉 갈림길 C1

5km (2:15)

From the hedged summit of Jangseong-bong, the trail heads northwest off the peak, descending slightly through head-high thicket, where it continues on good ridge for the next 700 meters, passing one signpost before reaching the Makjang-bong Gallim-gil 막장봉 갈림길 track junction. From there, the Baekdu-daegan right-wheels north and begins a deep descent for the next kilometer, ending up in a saddle at the foot of an unnamed peak located at 827 m ABSL. After reaching 827 m, the trail becomes an especially enlightening experience as it passes through healthy forest that provides impressive views west into the Ssanggok-gyegok 쌍곡계곡 and the Simyosali-gyegok 시묘살이계곡. The ridgeline is predominantly north, occasionally weaving its way west or east around craggy pines emitting themselves from small blemishes of white rock. About 600 meters later, the trail arrives at another spot height located at 780 m ABSL. Once again, the trail serves you more fantastic views from these natural viewing platforms. At about this stage, the trail turns northeast, undulating its way over mounds of rock as it constricts its way for the next 400 meters to your next peak, located at 809 m ABSL. Here, the ridge returns north, full steam ahead for 700 meters to another high point located at 787 m ABSL. From there, it daunts its way northwest for 300 meters to its twin peak at 785 m ABSL. The walking so far has been easy and enjoyable, on a shady trail with no major grinds or upheavals afflicting it. From 785 m, the trail descends steeply north, dropping about 100m in altitude for the next 500 meters to the wide saddle area of Sageori Anbu. Its base is marked by a tomb and a four-way junction. From the saddle, the trail zigzags northeast for 800 meters up the southern face of Akhui-bong 악희봉 (845m), where it meets a signposted junction just east of the summit. From there, the track to Akhui-bong is northwest, reaching the summit 500 meters later. It also continues along its own ridge above the Ssanggok-gyegok, where it will come out at the National Park entrance. Akhui-bong is a rocky peak with good views in all directions, and a worthwhile detour.

CLOSED SECTION Akhui-bong Junction 악희봉 갈림길 C1 → Eunti-gogae 은티고개 D2

2km (0:50)

From the junction beneath Akhui-bong, the Baekdu-daegan reopens, does an about-face, and follows the directions of the signpost southeast to Ipseok-ri 입석리 ("standing stone village"). The trail stays at its current height for the next 400 meters and then suddenly decides it has had enough, pulling the ground out from beneath you and dropping 100 m in altitude for the next 500 meters, passing a *doltap*, until it meets its abandon and is subsequently halted at the bowel of a saddle. The saddle is known as Eunti-gogae and represents a track junction and pass area. Just before reaching the pass, you may have noticed a very old square stone *seonang-dang* (a shrine for a local tutelary spirit, in this case the pass), which appears to still be in use, as it is ringed with fresh rope. Eunti-gogae has a wide clearing walled by thick forest. Tracks run off the ridge heading northeast and southwest. Following the southwest trail for 300-500 meters will take you to drinking water(45) at the confluence of a series of streams. The northeast track heads 2 km down to Eunti Village. If you wish to see stylish cabin-style accommodation for the night, then Eunti is the place to go.

Transport Info

Leaving the trail at Eunti-gogae: Eunti Village is located 3.9 km south of Yeonpung-myeon, and no bus services the village. The Yeonpung taxi service 연풍면 is available and can be reached at 043-833-5131. Buses running to Jeomcheon from Dong Seoul Bus Terminal stop at Yeonpung-myeon and leave every 30 minutes from 6:20 am to 6:30 pm.

Lodging

Set amongst idyllic farmland and fruit orchards encircled by large peaks, Eunti is a great little village to visit. The locals have embraced the opportunity to live under the mountains of the Baekdu-daegan, and accommodation is available at a couple of modern home-stays. In the center of the village is the Baekdu-daegan Swimteo 백두대간 쉼터, a bustling watering hole and *minbak* adorned with ribbons from past trekkers...a real iconic representation for Baekdu-daegan hikers. Eunti is located at the end of a dead-end road that runs 4 km northeast into Yeonpung-myeon, a decent-sized town with a number of restaurants, motels, a post office and a police station.

DAY 3

From Eunti-gogae to Ihwa-ryeong

- **Distance:** 19.5km
- **Time:** 8hr 55min

From Eunti-gogae, you walk a thin ridge to the summit of Guwang-bong before beginning the ascent of the mighty and sacred peak of Huiyang-san, turning away just before the peak and walking into a saddle lined with fortress walls. You bypass Siru-bong, another impressive peak, and set off on a beautiful section of the ridge that sees few visitors through to Baekhwa-san. At this point, you begin a leisurely downhill cruise through a mature oak forest that casts film set-quality scenery and on to a delightful *hyugeso* at the road pass of Ihwa-ryeong, which marks the southern entrance to the dramatic ridge above Mungyeong Saejae Provincial Park.

Eunti-gogae 은티고개 D2 → Guwang-bong 구왕봉 E2

2km (1:00)

From Eunti-gogae, the trail continues heading southeast and is blocked by a crudely erected fence, although there is no indication or sign that the trail is closed, and hikers have instead forged a path through a tight opening. Breaking through the fence, you assail 170 m in altitude straight up the 500 meter

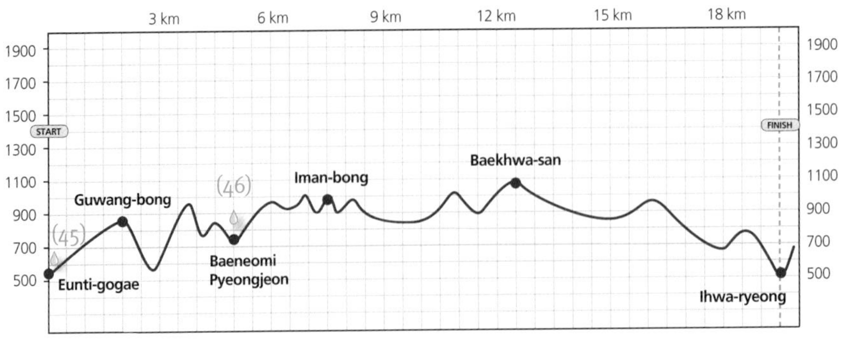

WATER STOPS

(45) Eunti-gogae: **N36°43'22" E127°58'30"**
(46) Baeneomi Pyeongjeon 배너미평전: **N36°43'37" E128°00'50"**

deciduous forest-covered face of Juchi-bong 주치봉, located at 683 m ABSL. From this peak, the trail roller-coasters back down the ridgeline, robbing you of most of the altitude you just gained, before the siege stops at Obongjeong-gogae Pass 오봉정 고개, which is marked by a tomb. From Obongjeong-gogae, the trail climbs steadily southeast, reaching a rocky ledge 600 meters later at an area known as Neolbeun-bawi 넓은바위, meaning "wide rock." From there, the trail cranks its way east one notch and, 300 meters later, arrives at another ledge displaying a quarry of large boulders where the trail levels out. It passes through a tall stand of forest for the next 500 meters before arriving at the top of Guwang-bong ("nine kings peak") at 879 m ABSL. That summit is enclosed by trees, but there are some views through the branches eastward into the white face of Huiyang-san 희양산 and north over Eunti Village.

Guwang-bong 구왕봉 → Baeneomi Pyeongjeon 배너미 평전 E2

3km (1:50)

The trail heads east off Guwang-bong, dropping about 200 m in altitude over only 500 meters of ground. If you can keep your eyes off your wrenching knees, you may notice some views through the wooded trail, southeast toward the large grounds of Bongam-sa Temple 봉암사 located in the Bongamyong-gol Valley 봉암용골. This stretch of trail is frequented by fixed ropes at its more hair-raising moments as it slides down the rocky ridge. After descending from Guwang-bong, you arrive at Jireumti-jae 지름티재, where a track runs north down a valley for about 2.5 km to Eunti Village. From Jireumti-jae, the trail jettisons almost vertically up the eastern face of Huiyang-san where about 300 meters, the climb becomes even more intensive, with the final 200 meters being particularly steep, requiring a series of ropes to guide your way over the rocky surface. The trail actually bypasses the summit of Huiyang-san, reaching a track junction located at about 960 m ABSL. To get to the summit, you can use a track that elevates itself slowly up the spur for 400 meters in a southeast direction to the peak. On a tree near this junction is a message from Daejung *seunim*, the Abbot of Bongam-sa:

> Huiyang-san is not only an ecologically protected area but also a place where monks practice meditation. Please allow it to stay clean by not dumping trash or damaging the environment, so we can pass this wonderful mountain on to the next generation. I am asking for this completely earnestly. Maya Banya Baramil (a saying in the Heart Sutra)

His monastery is one of Korea's most important, held in very high esteem for historical reasons and designated as a "special meditation center" by the Jogye Order of Korean Buddhism (the nation's dominant sect). It is not normally open to tourists or other visitors—the monks there practice their Zen disciplines without interruption or distraction. For this reason, all hikers are expected to follow the simple rules listed above. There will also be times when access to the peak is prohibited for laymen, and so another nearby sign asks that you not be offended should a monk deny you access to the area. Huiyang-san obviously holds high sacredness for this great temple at its feet.

From the junction, the trail descends steeply to the north. About 300 meters later, it reaches the site of an ancient mountain fortress 산성터 and follows along its spectacular stone walls into a saddle. This fortification stretches across the small pass and is impressively built, probably first constructed by Silla during the 6th century Three Kingdoms Period, as a bastion against the northern Goguryeo kingdom. The exact age of the various sections of this wall you now see is unknown to us, as they must have been repaired and reconstructed many times over the following 1,400 years.

Ancient fortress walls

The trail heads north out of the pass, following the antique fortress walls for about 100 meters before climbing another 300 meters to an unnamed 871 m peak. It's about a 300 meter walk from there to the next sibling peak of 910 m ABSL. The terrain between these two peaks is very rocky, and fixed ropes are in place to help your progress. Once you're at the 910 m peak, the going becomes much easier as you descend steadily north through verdured forest for the next 700 meters, after which you arrive at the high-altitude junction known as Baeneomi Pyeongjeon, located below the southern side of Siru-bong Peak.

Baeneomi Pyeongjeon 배너미 평전 E2 → Iman-bong 이만봉 F2 2.5km (0:50)

The Baeneomi Pyeongjeon junction is located in nice, clear area surrounded by tall deciduous trees and would make a pretty decent campsite. Water(46) flows between the two northerly tracks from a stream 30 meters below the ridge. This is a good source of water during the summer months, but you may have to walk further down the streambed during dry periods to find water. From the junction, the trail ascends southeast, climbing steadily for 700 meters through tall forest containing lush undergrowth to an unnamed peak located at 963 m ABSL. From there, the trail turns east for 400 meters, maintaining its height, before meeting a track junction that contours northwest back to Siru-bong. The trail continues southeast, and the ridgeline becomes thinner and the trail rockier. As the trail continues to ascend, it arrives 300 meters later at an outcropping called Yong-bawi 용바위 ("dragon rock"). The trail continues southeast from this junction on a thin, rocky ridgeline for 800 meters before rising to meet the summit of Iman-bong (a.k.a. Eman-bong), located at 990 m ABSL. The summit of Iman-bong is marked by a signpost in a very small area enclosed by a low forest, and it is celebrated by a modern tablet resembling a headstone, which is placed awkwardly between some rocks.

Iman-bong 이만봉 F2 → Baekhwa-san 백화산 H3 5km (2:30)

From Iman-bong, it's a short 500 meter hop east to the next peak on the trail, Gomteul-bong 곰틀봉. This crag is not announced by a monument, but it does have good views southeast along the ridge and north across a steep valley where the Baekdu-daegan can be seen horseshoeing northwest from the summit of Baekhwa-san, 4 km southeast of Gomteul-bong. From Gomteul-bong, the trail heads southeast off the summit, descending 100 m over 600 meters of rocky trail through thick, low forest into the pass of Sadari-jae 사다리재. From the pass, the

Roger peering at Siru-bong

trail continues southeast for 1 km through forest stretching on relatively flat ground before climbing for 600 meters to the Noejeong-san Junction 뇌정산 갈림길 at 981 m ABSL. It then heads east from the junction, descending gently for 850 meters into the pass of Pyeongjeon-chi 평전치.

About 800 meters after leaving the pass, you reach an area of particularly large boulders marking a track junction. The trail heads northeast from this junction for about 200 meters before turning southeast and climbing for a further 500 meters to the summit of Baekhwa-san ("white flower mountain") at 1,063 m ABSL. This peak is celebrated by a small stone stele in a flat clearing, which is ringed by forest on all sides.

Baekhwa-san 백화산 F2 → Ihwa-ryeong 이화령 F1 7km (2:45)

The 7 km walk from Baekhwa-san for the final stretch to Ihwa-ryeong is a good one, as it passes steadily downhill on an excellent trail. The trail leaves Baekhwa-san descending off its northern face, aided by two fixed ropes. After that, you head northwest, crossing a helipad before meeting another track junction 200 meters later (a.k.a. Ehwa-ryeong). This junction marks where the trail now swings northwest all the way down to Ihwa-ryeong. From there, it enjoys good walking for the next 800 meters, passing yet another track junction before gently climbing for 200 meters to the summit of Hwanghak-san ("yellow crane mountain"), 915 m ABSL, marked by a small stone stele. The trail heads northwest off Hwanghak-san, descending 100 m over the next 500 meters of trail into a saddle marking a track junction. From the saddle, you continue northwest, climbing for 300 meters to an unnamed 862 m peak before descending gently for about 800 meters, after which the trail meets a vista with views northeast to Juheul-san. It then turns southwest for 400 meters before veering northwest again. The trail passes through stands of larch and oak, reaching a small tarn with a mature tree growing from a root ball-sized island in its center. Passing the pond, the trail continues northwest past a signpost and two helipads before undulating gently for 2 km to the summit of Jo-bong 조봉 (680m), which is marked by a small stele. The trail continues northwest on fairly flat ground for about 700 meters to a helipad that lies below an unnamed 681 m peak. It then meets a fork, with both options meeting again 200 meters north of that peak, after which it then descends down a concrete staircase onto NH34 at Ihwa-ryeong for a well-earned beer at the *hyugeso* located on the western side of the crest.

* Ihwa-ryeong Pass 이화령 F1

Ihwa-ryeong is crossed by a quiet extension of NH34 that heads east 7 km to Mungyeong-eup 문경읍 and west 6 km to Yeonpung-myeon in Goesan-gun. This was once the main passage over the Baekdu-daegan for people of the area, but now two roads, NE45 and NH3/34, run through tunnels below the pass. However, the pass still supports the Ihwa-ryeong Hyugeso 이화령 휴게소, which is located on a large rest area on the western side of the pass, selling hot meals, snacks and basic supplies. A clean set of public toilets is attached to the complex. This was obviously once a thriving business, as the parking lot area is huge, with great views to the west over Yeonpung-myeon. In the parking lot is an interesting statue of a large, boggle-eyed, bearded bushman-farmer holding a huge chili pepper (*gochu*); this fine-looking gentleman is the mascot of Goesan-gun, where *gochu* is the number one product.

TRANSPORT INFO

Leaving the trail at Ihwa-ryeong: Buses no longer run up the quiet extension of NH3/34 to Ihwa-ryeong. You'll have to call a taxi if you can't hitch a ride. Taxis from Mungyeong-eup 7 km to the east will pick you up for about 15,000 won; the restaurant owner should be willing to assist with your phone call.

LODGING

Through an arrangement with the owner of the *hyugeso*, it is possible to sleep in the small shed located in the parking lot. The shelter has a heated floor and an electric outlet.

TWO DAYS

17.5km

SECTION 8

MUNGYEONG SAEJAE

Ihwa-ryeong → Haneul-jae

SECTION 8
DAY 1 & 2
17.5km in 8hr 40min
From Ihwa-ryeong to Haneul-jae
Worak-san National Park
월악산국립공원
PR597
NH3
Saejae Hyugeso
새재휴게소
Sinseon-bong
신선봉
Leports Park
레포츠공원
Geumran Seowon
금란서원
Hotel San Green
Heungcheon-sa
흥천사
Joryeong-san
Jayeon Hyuyangrim
조령산자연휴양림
Suok waterfall
수 옥 폭 포
Suokjeong Hyugeso
수옥정휴게소
922m
Mapae-bong
마패봉
642m
Joryeong
조령
Seon-bawi
선바위
Bugam-mun
북암문
Joryeong, Third Gate
조령제3관문
(48)
Day-2
START
Day-1
FINISH
730m
Gitdae-bong
깃대봉
Madae-bawi
마대바위
Dongam-mun
동암문
934m
Bu-bong
부봉
908m
Joryeong, Second Gate
Doyoji
도요지
Mireuk-ri
미륵리
Buddha statue
미륵불
Mireuk-sa Temple site
미륵사지
Day-2
FINISH
550m
Haneul-jae
하늘재
Poam-san
포암산
Haneul-jae Sanjang
하늘재산장
Poham
포함
(49)
856m
Tanhang-san
탄항산
766m
Gul-bawi
굴바위
Pyeongcheon-jae
평천재
Juheul-san Junction
주흘산갈림길
Juheul-san
1
2
3
4
A
B
C
D

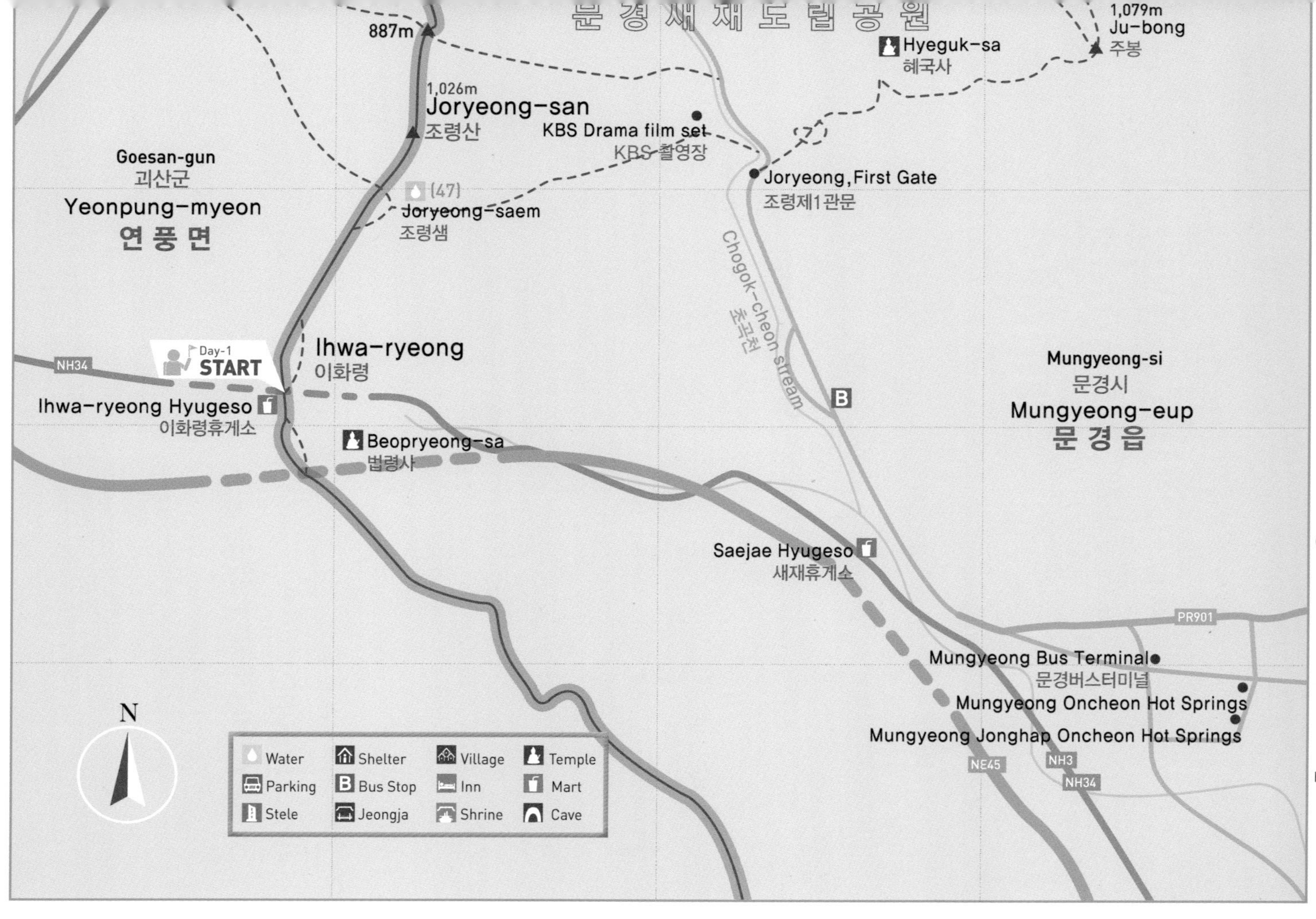

문경새재도립공원
887m
1,079m
Ju-bong
주봉
Hyeguk-sa
혜국사
1,026m
Joryeong-san
조령산
KBS Drama film set
KBS 촬영장
Joryeong, First Gate
조령제1관문
Goesan-gun
괴산군
Yeonpung-myeon
연풍면
(47)
Joryeong-saem
조령샘
Chogok-cheon stream
초곡천
Ihwa-ryeong
이화령
Day-1
START
NH34
Ihwa-ryeong Hyugeso
이화령휴게소
Beopryeong-sa
법령사
B
Mungyeong-si
문경시
Mungyeong-eup
문경읍
Saejae Hyugeso
새재휴게소
PR901
Mungyeong Bus Terminal
문경버스터미널
Mungyeong Oncheon Hot Springs
Mungyeong Jonghap Oncheon Hot Springs
NE45
NH3
NH34
N
Water
Shelter
Village
Temple
Parking
Bus Stop
Inn
Mart
Stele
Jeongja
Shrine
Cave
E
F
G
H

DAY 1

From Ihwa-ryeong to Jo-ryeong, Third Gate

- **Distance:** 8.5km
- **Time:** 4hr 25min

Climbing to Joryeong-san, the first peak of this leg, you begin a spectacular ridge walk, enjoying some of the most dramatic scenery of the journey. The ridge is razor thin and extremely rocky, and as you negotiate a number of fixed rope obstacles between four jagged peaks, you soon understand why these ridges were chosen as natural fortress walls to line the Great Yeongnam Road. The rewards for your toil are fantastic vista views from rocky outcrops down to the historic Yeongnam roadway and across to the imposing eastern ridge. You end the day at the most attractive road crossing of the Baekdu-daegan at Jo-ryeong Third Gate, where you can explore the attractions of Mungyeong Saejae Provincial Park.

Ihwa-ryeong 이화령 F1 → Joryeong-san 조령산 E2

2.7km (1:25)

The trail resumes on the northern side of NH34 from a small garden, east of the ridge, that houses a large stele welcoming travelers to Gyeongsangbuk-do. Passing a small fire safety hut at the edge of the park, you enter the forest. The trail initially stays east below the crest of the ridge, ascending north for 800 meters on a good

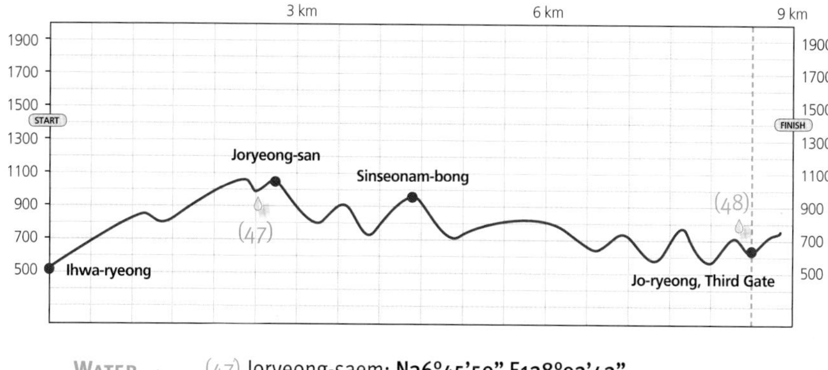

WATER STOPS
(47) Joryeong-saem: **N36°45'50" E128°02'42"**
(48) Gamro-su 감로수 (Jo-ryeong): **N36°48'24" E128°03'36"**

path through mature forest scattered with boulders. You climb 200 m in altitude before reaching the crest of the ridge. Once on the ridge, the trail turns northeast, and you climb gently for about 200 meters to a flat, cleared peak that houses a concrete helipad. Continuing northeast on a thin ridge, you have occasional views west over Yeonpung-myeon 연풍면 and east down the valley running up to Ihwa-ryeong. About 800 meters later, you meet a junction with one track heading northeast following the ridgeline and another heading northeast below the ridgeline. Both of these trails meet 500 meters later at Joryeong-saem 조령샘, a freshwater(47) spring built up with rocks where water flows through a steel pipe. Joryeong-saem is a reliable spring throughout the year, except in winter, when it is often frozen over. The trail ascends northeast past the spring, climbing steadily for about 400 meters before reaching the ridge. From there, the Baekdu-daegan turns northeast, ascending to a helipad set amongst a stand of Korean pines. From the helipad, you climb for another 200 meters to the summit of Joryeong-san (1,026m). Joryeong-san is named for the pass at the high point of the Great Yeongnam Road in Mungyeong Saejae Provincial Park (see p231) below. The peak is celebrated by a waist-high stele in the middle of a large clearing. Views are spectacular to the north and east over Mungyeong Saejae Provincial Park and its surrounding peaks. Looking north, you can view the razor thin ridge and rocky peaks that you will be crossing. On a clear day, you can see north to the rocky peaks of Worak-san National Park beyond the immediate ridgeline.

Joryeong-san 조령산 → Sinseonam-bong 신선암봉 E2

1.7km (1:00)

From Joryeong-san, the trail descends north along a razor thin ridge that becomes very rocky, with a fixed rope in place to aid your drop. About 700 meters later, you reach a steep drop-off, which will take you into a narrow saddle. From the saddle, the trail ascends north steeply for about 400 meters to an unnamed 887 m peak. From the peak, you head northeast briefly before turning northwest and descending gradually for 300 meters into a saddle below the steep face of Sinseonam-bong ("spirit immortal rock peak"). From the saddle, you walk across the edge of a large upturned boulder; a rope is in place across the boulder, which you should hold taut to keep your balance. Crossing this rock, you soon encounter another large boulder, which you have to walk across aided by another rope. One of these is named the Sinseon-bawi 신선바위 ("spirit immortal outstanding boulder"), from which the peak gets its name. These obstacles don't require technical climbing ability, but the long drops on both sides of the ridge demand caution, particularly in high winds, rain or icy conditions. Once across the last boulder, it's a short climb to the summit of Sinseonam-bong at 937m ABSL. The peak area is celebrated by a small stone stele on a west-slanting rock located the top of a steep cliff, scattered with craggy Korean pines and an awe-inspiring view northwest along the ridge and across the valley.

Third gate at Mungyeong Saejae

Sinseonam-bong 신선암봉 E2 → Jo-ryeong, Third Gate 조령 제3관문 C2

4.1km (2:00)

From Sinseon-bong, the trail descends northeast, dropping more than 100 m over a 500 meter section. The descent is aided by a series of fixed ropes that fall into a thin saddle. The trail continues northeast up the steep rock face, covering 120 m in altitude for the next 800 meters. It intensifies in steepness near the summit as you pull yourself up the rock face to an unnamed peak located at 928 m ABSL. There are more spectacular 360° views from here. This peak marks the start of another extremely rocky section of the ridge. Continuing northeast, you wobble over two sections of the trail over the next quarried 700 meters, which require the assistance of more fixed ropes. After the last set of ropes, the trail straightens to the north and becomes less precarious. The next kilometer provides you with some relief for your aching arms before the trail turns northwest and meets an impressive large boulder called Madae-bawi 마대바위 about 250 meters later. The boulder provides great views east across the valley to the rocky face of Bu-bong 부봉 (934m) and the ridge flanking it on both sides.

The trail continues northwest from Madae-bawi and climbs steeply but briefly up the southeastern face of Gitdae-bong. The trail then descends northeast to a track junction before climbing for about 100 meters up to a peak standing at about 730 m ABSL. From there, the trail turns north and descends steeply for the next 500 meters through stunning forest and out onto to the spectacular site of the Third Gate at Jo-ryeong.

Transport Info

Leaving the trail at Jo-ryeong, Third Gate: The western road continues to So-joryeong 소조령, where there is a "leports" (leisure and sports) park, and joins the extension of NH3 running 2 km northwest to the Saejae Hyugeso 새재 휴게소 and 1 km south to the Suokjeong Hyugeso 수옥정 휴게소.

Lodging

On the western side of the pass is a *jeongja* near some coffee machines, which is a good place to camp. Another 1 km west from the pass is the Joryeong-san Jayeon Hyuyangrim 조령산 자연휴양림, a Korea Forest Service cabin-style accommodation. A further 500 meters past the *hyuyangrim* is the Geumran Seowon 금란서원, a Confucian study center. The road forks a further 500 meters past the *seowon*, heading southwest and west, and on the corner of this junction is the Hotel San Green. The southwestern road passes by the Heungcheon-sa Temple 흥천사 and heads down a steep valley for about 3 km, passing the Suok Pokpo waterfall 수옥 폭포 before reaching Suokjeong Hyugeso on NH3. There are motels near the junction with NH3.

* Jo-ryeong 조령 and Saejae 새재 C2

Jo-ryeong (642m) is also known as Saejae. Both these names mean "bird pass" (bird is *jo* in Sino-Korean and *sae* in pure Korean), and the name comes from an old saying that the pass is so high that even birds can't cross it. Jo-ryeong is higher than the neighboring Haneul-jae and Ihwa-ryeong passes, which were popular road crossings before the Great Yeongnam Road was constructed during the Joseon Dynasty. Constructed in 1708, the third and final gate named Joryeong-gwan on the Great Yeongnam Road dominates the pass. Its fortress walls extend to the edge of the pass on both sides. Like all the gates on the road, it has a raised watchtower with a traditional tiled roof built above the gate. The Baekdu-daegan trail passes right through this grand gate. On the eastern side of the gate is a large grass field that acts as a popular resting spot for weary walkers arriving from the bottom of the pass. Although the field is inviting, camping here is not permitted. On the northern side of the field is a quaint little restaurant set on the fringes of the forest, serving fresh mountain vegetable meals, homemade *dongdong-ju,* coffee and canned drinks.

Roger & Andrew at the stele at Jo-ryeong

On the southern side of the field, near the trail, is a *sansin-gak*. This will be the first shrine to the Mountain Spirit you have come across on a mountain pass thus far on the trail. In times gone by, when mountain crossing was a much more dangerous affair, shrines like this one were common, as people prayed to the sansin for a safe crossing. Water(48) is available from a spring near the shrine. Former President Park Chung-hee's order to preserve the Yeongnam Road in its current unsealed state only stretched as far as the third gate, and the road on the western side of Jo-ryeong is paved. Beneath the gate on this side is an information board explaining the history of the pass. The board states that its original name was Cho-jeom, meaning "grassy pass." The name Saejae can also mean "space pass," as it is the space between Haneul-jae and Luri-jae (presumably meaning Ihwa-ryeong), or "new pass," as it became the primary crossing of the Baekdu-daegan with the construction of the Great Yeongnam Road. West from the Third Gate is a small park on the southern side of the road with a proud Baekdu-daegan stele standing at least 5 m tall from a grassy patch. The stele is inscribed with a map of the entire Korean peninsula, indicating the course of the ridge through the two Koreas and pointing out the location of Jo-ryeong.

Mungyeong Saejae Provincial Park 문경새재 도립공원

About 7km up the Chogok-cheon stream, in a tight valley between the impenetrable ridge that forms a "V" from Juheul-san in the east and Joryeong-san to the west, meeting acutely at Jo-ryeong ("bird pass"), stretches the renowned Mungyeong Saejae Provincial Park. This treasure of North Gyeongsang is only about 1 km wide, encompassing the only section of the Great Yeongnam Road that still looks as it did during the Joseon era, when it was built to connect the cities of Seoul, then known as Hanyang, and Busan. The old road runs to the pass through three large fortified gates and watch towers set 3 km apart. The park stretches wider at its southern end to include Hyeguk-sa Temple below Juheul-san. The areas around Mungyeong have always been important crossings of the Baekdu-daegan. As early as the 6th century, the Silla Kingdom was setting up various fortresses in the area, many of which are still visible along the ridge. By AD 553, they had control of the south Han River valley to the north and hence controlled most passes on the Baekdu-daegan. The lower pass of Haneul-jae, 9 km to the north, was the favored crossing for early carriage, and it wasn't until the Joseon period (1392-1910) that the Busan to Seoul road was built, crossing Jo-ryeong.

Following the Japanese Imjin invasion of 1592-1598, what is now known as the second gate, Jogok-gwan, was erected along with defensive walls in 1594. More than 100 years later, in 1708, during the reign of King Sukjong, the first gate (Juheul-gwan) and third gate (Joryeong-gwan) were erected as fortresses for national defense as well as to control traffic and protect travelers, traders, scholars heading to Seoul to take the national *gwageo* examination, and government officials heading into the provinces. In 1966, the three gates were designated together as Historical Relic No. 147. Ten years later, President Park Chung-hee (r. 1961-1979), a

Wonky ridge of Mungyeong Saejae © Liz Riggs

Mungyeong Saejae township with Juheul-san in the background

former teacher in the Mungyeong area and a man remembered for his sweeping modernization policies, ordered that the Great Yeongnam Road between the three gates never be paved and that the gates be restored to their former glory. The area was designated a provincial park the same year. Today, the only traffic passing over the Great Yeongnam Road is foot traffic, as most cars pass through tunnels running beneath Ihwa-ryeong, and the park has become one of Korea's great tourist destinations, where visitors can enjoy a leisurely stroll along the banks of the beautiful Chogok-cheon, read poems written by noted scholars of the time and carved on monuments lining the road, and stop in at the few restaurants set amongst the forest selling traditional Korean wines and delicious vegetable meals. The road is lined with many fine mature pine trees, many of which have scars cut in their trunks. The trees were marred in the early 1940s, toward the end of the Japanese occupation, when the war-starved Japanese army allegedly forced locals to extract resin from the pines for fuel. They are now known as the "wounded pines" and have become a bit of a symbol of Japanese occupation in the area. In 2000, the Korean Broadcasting Service (KBS) built an impressive film set between the first and second gates. The set is a scale model of a Joseon era Korean village made of plywood and fiberglass; it looks completely authentic and is said to be the largest of its kind in the world. The set is used predominantly for filming period dramas, which are very popular in Korea, and it is common to see filming in the park, with extras in full armor and fake beards often seen resting on the Great Yeongnam Road between scenes. Entrance to the film set is 2,000 won.

TRANSPORT INFO

The closest city to Mungyeong-eup 문경읍 is Jeomchon 점촌, which is also known as Mungyeong City. Buses run regularly throughout the day between Jeomchon and Mungyeong-eup. It appears the number is upwards of 30 a day. The ride takes 30 minutes and costs 2,500 won. Buses run to Jeomchon Bus Terminal 점촌 시외버스터미널 from Dong Seoul Terminal and Buk Daegu terminal. There are taxis running from Mungyeong-eup to Mungyeong Saejae (4.9 km) at a cost of around 4,000 won.

LODGING

Below the first gate is a vibrant tourist area with a number of very good restaurants, *minbak*, and vendors selling local products, souvenirs and various items. There is also a large ceramics museum near the entrance.

Mungyeong-eup is the gateway town to Mungyeong Saejae Provincial Park. A quiet town lying in the shadow of Juheul-san (1,106m), Mungyeong is famous for its *oncheon* 온천 (hot springs) and recently began to create an image for itself as a hotspot for outdoor activities in Korea, with a clay shooting range, paragliding operation, and a pedal-railcar experience on a disused railroad, all in the surrounding area.

DAY 2 From Jo-ryeong, Third Gate to Haneul-jae

- **Distance:** 9km
- **Time:** 4hr 15min

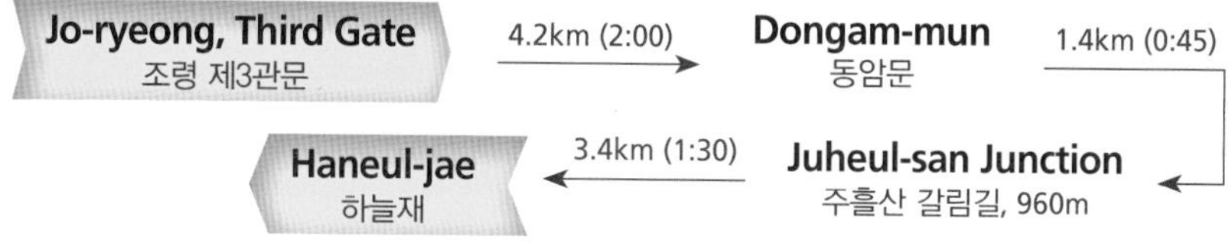

Leaving Jo-ryeong, you enter Worak-san National Park at Mapae-bong and traverse the eastern arm of the "V" that surrounds the Yeongnam Road. The trail passes the ruins of the ancient north and east gates to the valley and follows the ramparts of fortress walls between them. From the east gate, you climb the southern face of Bu-bong almost to the summit before turning away, though you may want to detour up and beyond the peak to look back on the peaks of Joryeong-san, Sinseon-bong and Gitdae-bong. The ridge leaves the Great Yeongnam Road's protective wall, avoiding mighty Juheul-san, and heads north past some spectacular boulders and vistas on the descent to Haneul-jae, another historic pass above the ruins of Mireuk-sa.

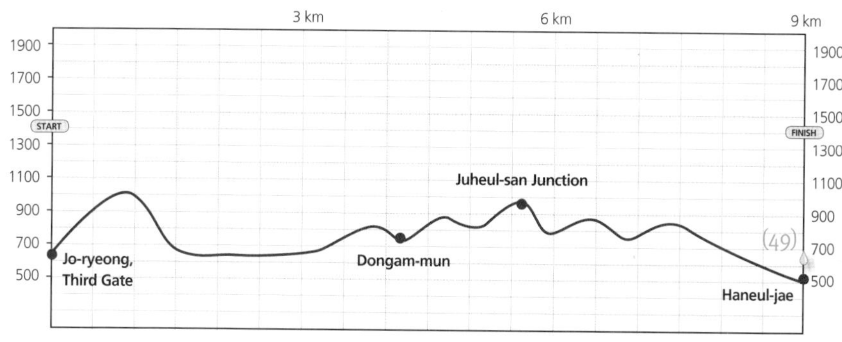

Water Stops (49) Haneul-saem 하늘샘: **N36°48'43" E128°06'43"**

Alternative Route

There is some confusion as into what initial parts of the Baekdu-daegan trail are closed within Worak-san National Park. At the time of print it would appear that the trail is open for the next 11 km from Jo-ryeong to Magol-chi (p255) but closed for the remaining 22.3 km in Worak-san to Beol-jae on NH59, some 2-3 days of walking later in section 9 of this book.

Option: About 300 meters before Magol-chi (Map p252) there is a track junction marked by a signpost with a 2.2 km trail that takes you northwest towards the summit of Mansu-bong 985 m ABSL. From there you can descend for about 2 km on a trail down to Mansu-gyo where there is a Hyugeso (restaurant) and park entrance. You might be able to locate a park map in this area. From there it's about a two-kilometer hike north on PR597 to another park entrance at Deokju-sa Temple and Worak-san mountain 1094 m. From Deokju-sa, you can hike east up to Worak-san summit and then walk north on a ridge over Chung-bong and Ha-bong peaks, down to the NH36. If you hitch east on this road it will take you to NH59 some 40 km later, passing the beautiful Chungju lake district on the way. At the NH59 its another 40 km hitch south to Beol-jae 벌재 (p263).

CLOSED SECTION Jo-ryeong, Third Gate 조령 C2 → Dongam-mun 동암문 C3

2hr (4.2km)

From Jo-ryeong, the trail heads into the forest at the edge of the northern extension of the third gate's fortress wall, passing a large boulder called Seon-bawi 선바위 on its way to the summit of Mapae-bong 마패봉 at 922 m ABSL.

Mapae-bong represents the southern border of Worak-san National Park 월악산 국립공원 (see p246), which forms for the remainder of this journey to Haneul-jae. Mapae-bong, also known as Mayeok-bong 마역봉, offers sweeping views north across Worak-san, including the distinctive sharp, triangular peak of Yeong-bong 영봉 at 1,097 m ABSL some 10 km to the northeast. The Baekdu-daegan trail turns east from Mapae-bong and drops almost 200 m in altitude over an 800 meter stretch into a saddle built up with fortress walls. This is known as Bugam-mun and is the ancient and forgotten northern gate into Mungyeong Saejae. The trail sporadically undulates for the next 2.5 km through rich, forgotten pastures of deciduous forest, bathed in gleaming light along the rims of the grey walls all the way to Dongam-mun ("east rock gate"). Throughout the passage, the fortress walls of Dongam-mun remain intact with memory.

CLOSED SECTION Dongam-mun 동암문 C3 → Juheul-san Junction 주흘산 갈림길 D3

1.4km (0:45)

From Dongam-mun, the trail continues south up the northern face of Bu-bong.

About 250 meters later, the trail passes a ruined rook that was once a watchtower of the east gate. A further 300 meters later, the trail arrives at a wooded junction where a track climbs west 500 meters toward Bu-bong 부봉, at 934 m ABSL. This peak has great views north and northwest over Worak-san National Park. From the junction, the trail undulates and pushes it way southeast up a wooded, rocky trail, passing over a 908 m peak. Then, 500 meters later, it arrives at a summit area located at 960 m ABSL and marked by a signpost. At this area, a track heads southeast 2.6 km to Juheul-san's highest peak, Ju-bong 주봉 (1,079m), with great views over Mungyeong-eup to the south...a recommended detour. The trail distinctively heads north from this junction, providing the hiker with views of the white face of Poam-san about 5 km to the northeast.

CLOSED SECTION Juheul-san Junction 주흘산갈림길 D3 → Haneul-jae 하늘재 C4

3.4km (1:30)

Descending from the junction, the trail drops about 150 m over a 580 meter stretch into Pyeongcheon-jae 평천재. Climbing north out of Pyeongcheon-jae, the trail reaches another junction, where it then turns northeast and starts a gentle climb for the next 700 meters to the summit of Tanhang-san 탄항산 located at 856 m ABSL. This is the last peak before Haneul-jae*, with good views over Worak-san National Park. The trail rolls southwest, some 400 meters later arriving at a rocky vista containing a curious rock called Gul-bawi 굴바위. The feature looks like it has fallen into a bacon slicer, and a pound of mince sits atop its two rashers. Also in this area is another impressive rock feature that looks like a giant upright thumb, severed at the knuckle, where the top portion has been precariously placed back onto its stump. The trail turns northeast from the rock parade, descending over a 766 m peak where it straightens to the north and continues on a steady downhill escape through a thickening forest of voice before coming out onto PR901 at Haneul-jae.

Roger near Gul-bawi

Haneul-jae

* Haneul-jae 하늘재 C4

The pass of Haneul-jae is located at about 550 m ABSL, on the northern side of a now unused road that is an extension of PR901 to the east. This old road is a historic passageway from days gone by and connects Gyeongsangbuk-do to the southeast with Chungcheongbuk-do to the northeast. The area surrounding the pass is forested in pine and native bush and does not see many a traveler or vehicle, as the western arm of the pass diminishes into a mountain road. However, two kilometers down this diminished mountain road hides the famous site of an ancient temple built in the 10th century period, called Mireuksaji. At the entrance to Haneul-jae is a large, impressive boulder with a plaque set into it, describing the meaningful and beautiful history of this pass. The pass appears to have been first put to use some 1,850 years ago. Summarized, the plaque translates as:

> With much graceful energy, the soft wind and the sweet fragrance of wild flowers spread quietly, a piece of cloud floats in the sky, a quiet stillness prevails through this pass of the Baekdu-daegan. After the beginning when God created the heaven and the earth, there were many travelers on this pass. This pass had a pivotal role connecting the Yeongnam (Gyeongsang-do area) and Giho (Seoul, Gyeonggi-do area) regions, and it has endured various hardships, joys and sorrows throughout its very long history. This is the pass of Gyerip-ryeong (Haneul-jae). It was opened in AD 156, during

the third year of King Adala's reign of the Silla dynasty as a route to attack the Goguryeo Kingdom to the north. Gyerip-ryeong was a big pass of the Silla period and is the lowest place between Juk-ryeong and Jo-ryeong. In the Three Kingdoms era, not only Silla but also Goguryeo and Baekje used this pass as a strategic measure for attacking the north or south. Silla established the Mungyeong area as its bridgehead and could advance into the reaches of the Han-gang River as a way of defending themselves against the attacks from Goguryeo and Baekje. It is said that General Ondal and Yeongaesomun of Goguryeo tried to regain the lost territory on this pass many times. It is also said that Wanggeon and General Charadae of the Mongols used this pass to attack the south. When King Gongmin took royal flight from his palace in the south to escape disaster from the trouble of Hongeonjeok, they also reportedly used this pass. There are many stories behind it. In the Goryeo era (918-1392), there were many Buddhist temples around Gyerip-ryeong, and the road became a pathway to sacred Buddhist grounds. Many of those places have now been destroyed by fire and the disturbances of war, from which now only the ruins of temples remain. We ruminate about the historical meaning of the Gyerip-ryeong pass, which has kept joys and sorrows mute and silent for a long, long, time; we erect this monument here to introduce the fragrance of past history to travelers and to pay a tribute to the memory of these meanings.

LODGING

Haneul-jae is nestled on a flat piece of hard ground elevated above the roadside. It consists of a shelter called Haneul-jae Sanjang 하늘재 산장, which is often locked up. To get access to it, call 054-571-2613 in advance. Failing that, it may be better to walk east from the pass, down the road for about 100 meters. On the southern side of the road there are a number of small homes, including an old derelict *minbak*. This area, if open, sometimes sells cold beer, *soju* and *ramyeon*. The best place to camp at this pass is on the flat, hard ground located outside the front of the shelter. The wild grass has been removed from the ground, and it is suitable for pitching a tent. There are about five large trees in this area, offering good shade during the day. Under the trees are numerous benches and elevated platforms that provide good areas for preparing food, or for splaying one's gear out to conduct maintenance checks. Between the outdoor area and the shelter, there is a spring(49) formed under a small circular concrete pad beneath a tap. There are no known toilet facilities at this pass. At night, there is a light switch located outside the shelter, on the top right-hand side of its front doors. The light source is sufficient to read a book at night. It is also possible to light a campfire at Haneul-jae, as long as only dead fall is used. There are three simple rules to the pass, displayed on one of the placards stuck to the outside of the shelter: (1) take your trash, (2) no parking of vehicles in this spot, and (3) do not make fires under the trees.

TRANSPORT INFO

Leaving the trail at Haneul-jae: Mireuk-ri 미륵리 is located 2 km northwest of Haneul-jae along the unsealed road that passes by the Mireuksaji temple ruins. Buses leave Chungju 충주시 to Suanbo 수안보 and on to Mireuk-ri 11 times a day from 5:40 am to 5:55 pm, and they return with the same frequency. About 1km southeast of Haneul-jae is the small village of Poham 포함. Buses leave Mungyeong-eup for Poham four times daily at 8:20 am, 12:05 pm, 3:35 pm and 7:35 pm, returning with the same frequency.

* Mireuksaji 미륵사지 C3

The temple site contains a 10 m tall but thin standing Buddha, carved from six blocks of stone. It is more than likely that Haneul-jae was the pass that Crown Prince Maui and Princess Deokju, the founders of this site according to legend, fled through whilst escaping from their defeated Silla-dynasty capital of Gyeongju. During their dash to seek religious refuge in the Geumgang-san ("Diamond Mountains"), which are now in North Korea, the brother and sister brace were persistently ordained in their dreams by a Buddhist saint who led them to the terraced site of what would become Mireuk-sa. While soothing their grief over the ruin of their country, they built the 10 m Buddha statue that still stands there today. The site flourished for the next 600 years before retreating into the surrounding bush. Mireuksaji was excavated as recently as 1977 by students from Chungju University. The 10 m Mireuk Buddha statue has a thin mortarboard balanced on a head that is unusually bright and polished compared to its tainted torso portion. Locals claim that the 10 m high head has never been known to be cleaned or polished, but remains clean by spiritual power.

The standing buddha at Mireuk-saji

THREE DAYS

32.2 km

SECTION 9

WORAK-SAN NATIONAL PARK

Haneul-jae → Jeosu-ryeong

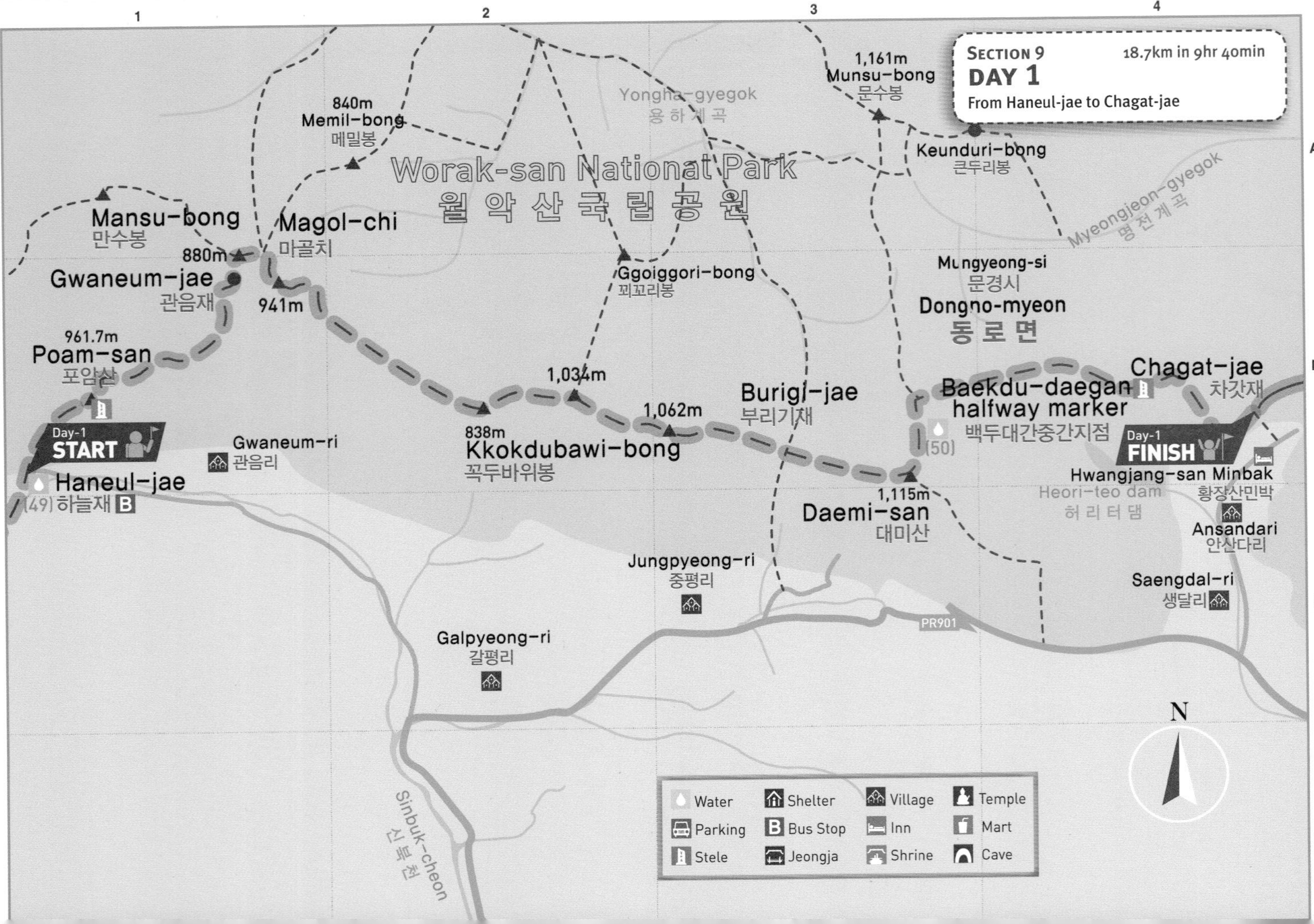
Section 9
18.7km in 9hr 40min
DAY 1
From Haneul-jae to Chagat-jae
1,161m
Munsu-bong
문수봉
840m
Memil-bong
메밀봉
Yongha-gyegok
용하계곡
Keunduri-bong
큰두리봉
Worak-san National Park
월악산국립공원
Myeongjeon-gyegok
명전계곡
Mansu-bong
만수봉
Magol-chi
마골치
880m
Gwaneum-jae
관음재
941m
Ggoiggori-bong
꾀꼬리봉
Mungyeong-si
문경시
Dongno-myeon
동로면
961.7m
Poam-san
포암산
1,034m
Chagat-jae
차갓재
Baekdu-daegan halfway marker
백두대간중간지점
Burigi-jae
부리기재
1,062m
838m
Kkokdubawi-bong
꼭두바위봉
Day-1 START
Gwaneum-ri
관음리
Haneul-jae
(49) 하늘재
(50)
Day-1 FINISH
Hwangjang-san Minbak
황장산민박
Heori-teo dam
허리터댐
1,115m
Daemi-san
대미산
Ansandari
안산다리
Jungpyeong-ri
중평리
Saengdal-ri
생달리
PR901
Galpyeong-ri
갈평리
Sinbuk-cheon
신북천
N
Water
Shelter
Village
Temple
Parking
Bus Stop
Inn
Mart
Stele
Jeongja
Shrine
Cave
1
2
3
4
A
B
C
D

DAY 1

From Haneul-jae to Chagat-jae

- **Distance:** 18.7km
- **Time:** 8hr 25min

This closed section forms a natural southern geographic boundary for Worak-san National Park as it moves through the Sobaek-sanmaek range toward the East Sea of Korea. The trail itself undulates nicely through tall, verdant deciduous forests that offer views to the north down into the very heart of beautiful Worak-san. Along this remarkable leg, the trail follows the remnants of the old fortress walls from the Silla Dynasty, possibly extensions of the Deokju-sanseong fortress walls.

Alternative Route

As mentioned in Section 8, the trail is closed from Magol-chi some 4.2 km into this leg. Please refer to option on p246 for leaving Magol-chi. However, if you choose to leave the trail at Haneul-jae you can take the mountain road and follow it northwest through the Park, going to the wonderful Mireuk-saji 미륵사지(p250). From there continue down the valley past the fortress gate, and visit Deokju-sa temple 덕주사. Refer to p246 for more information. Or from Haneul-jae you can take the sealed road 1 km southeast towards the small village of Poham, where you can catch a bus and connect with the PR901, and wait for a bus to Dong-no. Refer to p250 for more information on leaving Haneul-jae...of course only if you want to?

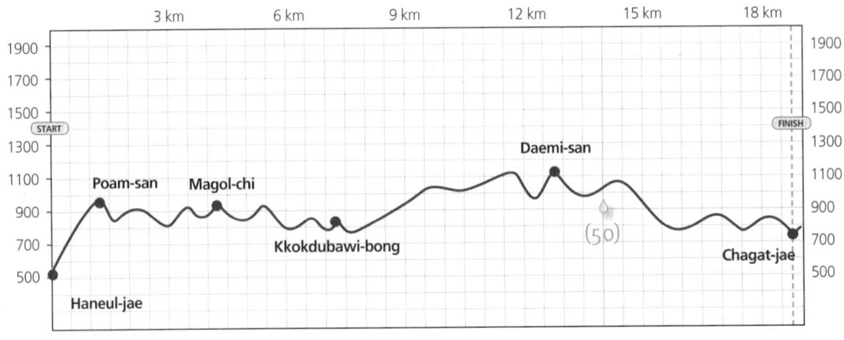

WATER STOPS (50) Nunmul-saem: **N36°49'00" E128°13'04"**

CLOSED SECTION Haneul-jae 하늘재 → Poam-san 포암산 B1 1.2km (0:50)

The trailhead north from Haneul-jae is 50 meters west of the Haneul-jae Sanjang 하늘재 산장, on the northern side of the road. As you head in a northerly direction, there is a small *doltap* located at a track junction 500 meters up the trail. To the west, there is a track descending for about 1.5 km toward Mireuksaji. From the *doltap*, the trail heads in a northeastern direction toward Poam-san, some 400 meters away. With the occasional assistance of fixed ropes, it takes hikers about 30 minutes to get to Poam-san, as they trudge through native stands of trees and bush before breaking out onto large mounds of white rock at its summit. The summit of Poam-san is marked by a cairn of rocks standing about 2 m in height, a small tablet

Looking from Poam-san

with Chinese script on it, and another small tree adorned with the hiking ribbons of the Baekdu-daegan. There are good views to be had from Poam-san. At about 200° south, some 5 km away, visitors can see the back of the dark, gnarly features of Juheul-san (1,079m), which presides over the quaint rural town of Mungyeong Saejae. Just over 2km to the north is the 983 m peak of Mansu-bong 만수봉, not to be mistaken with Worak-san's highest feature, Munsu-bong 문수봉 (1,161m), which is located deep inside the center of the park. Due east, some 10 km away, lies the saddle of Jageun-jae, which on a clear day can be seen stretching up from PR901 just beyond Daemi-san 대미산, the highest feature of today's walk on the Baekdu-daegan at 1,115 m ABSL.

The summit of Poam-san

CLOSED SECTION Poam-san 포암산 B1 → Magol-chi 마골치 A1 3km (1:20)

The trail from Poam-san to Magol-chi is well marked, with five signposts located on the 3 km trip to Magol-chi. The trail actually follows the route to Mansu-bong in a northeast direction, so it is important to recognize where the Baekdu-daegan veers east off this route some 3 km later. About 200 meters north of Poam-san, the trail makes a distinctive descent to the east at its first signpost. For the next 2.5 km, it undulates northeast toward the fifth signpost of this leg, located at 880 m ABSL. At that point, the Baekdu-daegan takes an easterly turn away from the track to Mansu-bong, which continues onward in a northwest direction. The trail from there keeps its height and heads due east for a short distance of 350 meters before arriving at a track junction known as Magol-chi. The Baekdu-daegan makes a distinctive turn to the south. About 250 meters later, the trail arrives at another unnamed peak located at 941 m ABSL. This peak offers good vistas to the northeast into Worak-san.

CLOSED SECTION Magol-chi 마골치 A1 → Kkokdubawi-bong 꼭두바위봉 B2 3km (1:20)

From 941 m, the trail takes a southeast direction for the next 3 km across the Sobaek-sanmaek (*sanmaek* means "range") stretching through Worak-san, Sobaek-san, and into the Taebaek-sanmaek on the east coast of South Korea. This section of ridge-walking is done through tall stands of deciduous forest on a distinctive earthen trail flanked by knee-high verdant bush at a consistent altitude of around 850 m ABSL. The trail will occasionally offer peeks at the white peaks of Worak-san National Park to the north. After 2 km, the trail meets a *doltap* at a track junction. There are numerous exits off the ridge along this route, most of them forking south. From there, the trail continues southeast, staying consistently high and meandering gently along the ridge, passing over numerous peaks before arriving at the peak of Kkokdubawi-bong, located at 838 m ABSL. The summit of this peak opens up to some views south toward the Sinbuk-cheon river, which runs south through Mungyeong Saejae some 10 km later.

CLOSED SECTION Kkokdubawi-bong 꼭두바위봉 B2 → Daemi-san 대미산 D3

5.5km (2:25)

From Kkokdubawi-bong, the trail begins its ascent into the 1,000 m zone. About 1 km later, the trail arrives at an unnamed peak located at 1,034 m ABSL. At this peak, there is a track heading north along a spur for about 2 km, taking the hiker deep into the bowels of central Worak-san National Park. From 1,034 m, the trail continues east, enjoying about 2 km of flattish ridge-walking to the next peak, which is located at 1,062 m ABSL. After that, the trail descends for about a kilometer, dropping 200 m in altitude along the way. The descent stops in a saddle at the track junction of Burigi-jae 부리기재, marked by a signpost. From there, the Baekdu-daegan continues east for about 1.5 km, climbing about 220 m in altitude until it reaches Daemi-san (1,115m), the highest feature of this leg, and one of the highest mountains in Worak-san. The peak of Daemi-san offers good all-around views, and it also has enough space on it to pitch a tent. At the summit, there is a track heading southeast for about 4 km toward PR901.

LODGING

The pass at Chagat-jae has enough space for a tent if need be, but it also offers the option of getting off the ridge and heading south for 1 km toward the small mountain farming village of Ansaengdal 안생달. In this area, a few of the modern houses operate as *minbak*, including Baro Minbak 바로민박 (T. 054-552-8447 / 011-522-8447), Baechang-gol Minbak 배창골민박 (T. 054-552-8445) and Hwangjang-san Minbak, a modern white home closest to the trailhead. There are no shops in Ansaengdal, but there is a small village located about 4 km further south at the junction with PR901, called Saengdal-ri 생달리.

CLOSED SECTION **Daemi-san** 대미산 D3 → **Chagat-jae** 차갓재 B4 6km (2:30)

From Daemi-san, the trail turns north and descends for about 400 meters into a saddle marked by a signpost. The signpost is actually a marker for water at Nunmul-saem 눈물샘(50), the only source hikers can find at this height on this leg. The spring can be found about 70 meters down the eastern side of the ridge on a small terrace. The water barely runs from this spring, so don't be surprised if it is dry at some stages of the year. From the saddle, the trail climbs 400 meters up to the next track junction, where it heads east and descends down what appears to be a spur, but is in fact a continuation of the ridge, as it skirts around the northern flanks of the Heori-teo dam 허리터댐. For the next 2 km, the trail roller-coasters over two unnamed peaks, where it meets a special object of the Baekdu-daegan.

TRANSPORT INFO

Leaving the trail at Chagat-jae: The small village of Saengdal-ri is located about 3 km south of Chagat-jae at the end of a mountain road that runs up to Ansandari 안산다리 below the pass. Buses leave Saengdal-ri and head east into Dongno-myeon five times a day from 8:20 am to 6:50 pm. From Dongno-myeon, buses head to Mungyeong-eup 15 times a day from 7 am to 6:30 pm.

* Halfway Mark of the Baekdu-daegan Trail 백두대간 중간지점 B4

Perched precariously in the middle of the trail at about 943 m ABSL, on a steep downhill incline, is a rather rudimentary monument celebrating and indicating the actual halfway mark of the Baekdu-daegan trail within South Korea. The monument was installed on September 14, 2007, after a previous marker was destroyed and removed. The monument proudly and boldly states that this spot is exactly 367.325 km between Cheonwang-bong to the south in Jirisan National Park and Jinbu-ryeong to the north at the very end of the Baekdu-daegan trail. This estimate means that the trail is 734.65 km long in South Korea...

Roger at the halfway marker of the BDDG

on foot!

After the halfway mark of the Baekdu-daegan trail monument, the trail continues its easterly descent to a saddle, passing through high stands of forest. About 300 meters later, the trail veers southeast for a kilometer before turning northeast as it descends to the pass of Chagat-jae, located in a saddle under a large mast.

WORAK-SAN NATIONAL PARK 월악산 국립공원

Worak-san 월악산 is located right in the middle of the Baekdu-daegan mountain range within South Korea, connecting Songni-san with Sobaek-san, and its rocky summit is named Yeong-bong 영봉, meaning "divine peak," or literally "spirit peak." The park has more than 22 small and large peaks. Its highest peak, at 1,161 m ABSL, is Munsu-bong, located on the eastern side of the park. The nearby towns of Suanbo 수안보 and Danyang 단양 are the main locations that accommodate visitors to Worak-san. Worak-san is famous for its steep, white, rocky peaks with jutting stands of native pine that weep and arc precariously from the thin, sharp ridges they jut from. During the Japanese and Mongol invasions of Korea, Worak-san was a haven for persons escaping the blight of their invaders. Overall, Worak-san is famous for its natural and cultural resources, and it is also a popular park to visit year round. Its stands of broadleaved trees turn a blood red during the fall, casting an invisible dye into the crystal clear freshwater mountain streams. It is said that when you cup your hands into the water of these streams, they turn red with the color of fall. It is also said that during the night, the moonlight reflects on the rocks and water and creates fluttering scenes of a fairyland with the moon shades in the groves.

DAY 2 From Chagat-jae to Beol-jae

- **Distance:** 7km
- **Time:** 4hr 10min

From this point, the ridge crest trail presents some rather challenging rock formations that force trekkers to pull themselves up steep ledges. Once on top of the ridge, hikers are faced with a daunting but spellbinding walk along a thin crest that has them balancing precariously over steep drop-offs whilst relying on fixed ropes. Following that, the ridge will widen a little, and hikers are then walking in an artist's landscape of fascinating displays of white rock rooted with small cloves of Pinus koreanus. This section of the trail is only 7 km long—and when it reopens, hikers are recommended to spend all day on it, taking their time to really "be in Korea."

CLOSED SECTION Chagat-jae 차갓재 → Jageun Chagat-jae 작은 차갓재 B1

1km (0:20)

From the village of Ansaengdal 안생달, there are two options for hikers to get back to the ridge. The first one is to return back to Chagat-jae by the same trail and hike east for almost a kilometer, over an unnamed peak located at 816 m ABSL, before arriving at the saddle of Jageun ("Little") Chagat-jae. The second option is to walk directly from the Hwangjang-san Minbak 황장산 민박 up the valley in a northeast direction, following a 4WD track until it reaches the

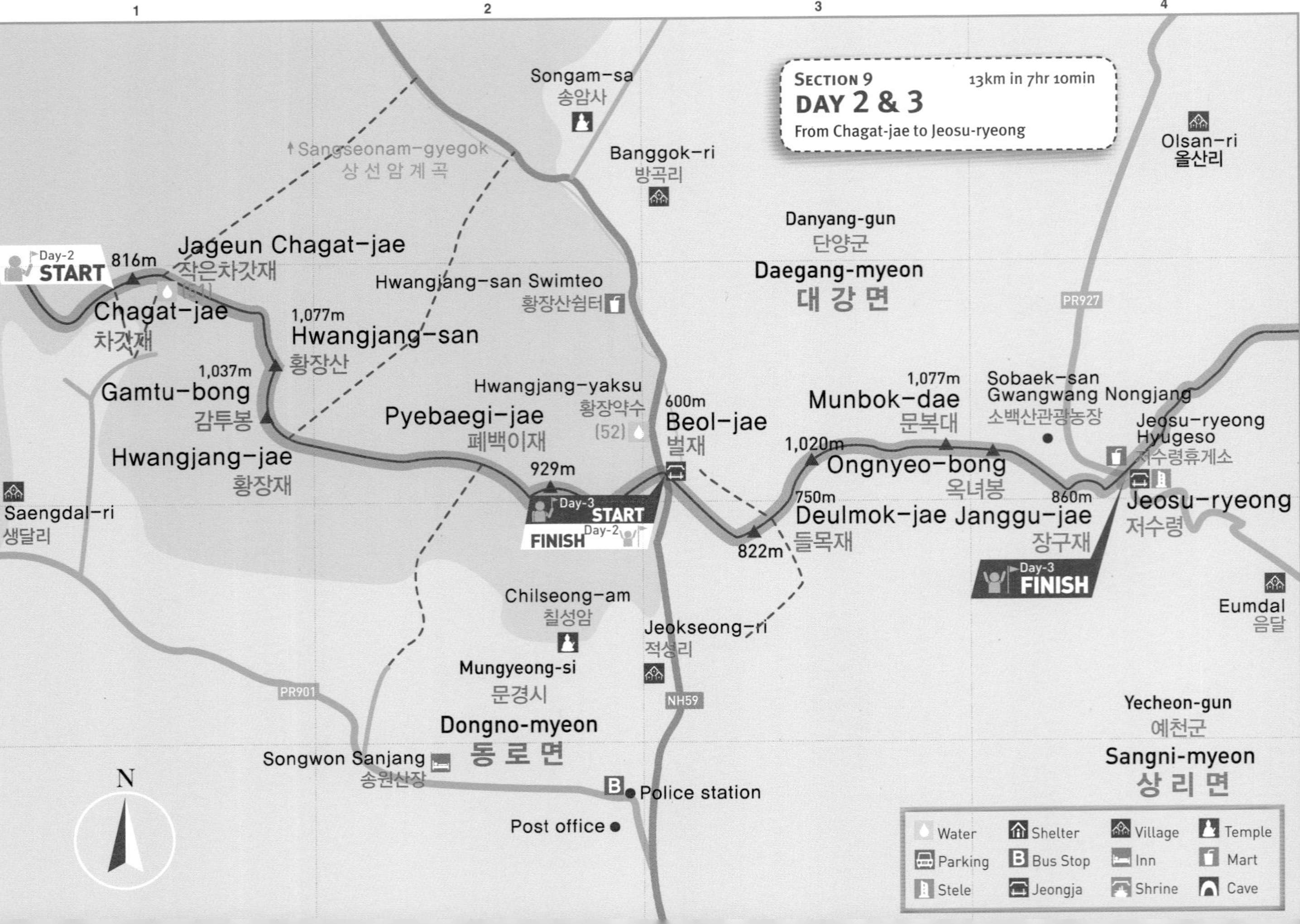

SECTION 9
DAY 2 & 3
13km in 7hr 10min
From Chagat-jae to Jeosu-ryeong
Day-2 START
816m
Jageun Chagat-jae
작은차갓재
Chagat-jae
차갓재
1,077m
Hwangjang-san
황장산
1,037m
Gamtu-bong
감투봉
Hwangjang-jae
황장재
Sangseonam-gyegok
상 선 암 계 곡
Songam-sa
송암사
Banggok-ri
방곡리
Hwangjang-san Swimteo
황장산쉼터
Hwangjang-yaksu
황장약수
(52)
Pyebaegi-jae
폐백이재
929m
Day-3 START
FINISH Day-2
600m
Beol-jae
벌재
822m
750m
Deulmok-jae
들목재
1,020m
Ongnyeo-bong
옥녀봉
1,077m
Munbok-dae
문복대
Sobaek-san Gwangwang Nongjang
소백산관광농장
860m
Janggu-jae
장구재
Day-3 FINISH
Jeosu-ryeong Hyugeso
저수령휴게소
Jeosu-ryeong
저수령
Danyang-gun
단양군
Daegang-myeon
대 강 면
PR927
Olsan-ri
올산리
Eumdal
음달
Saengdal-ri
생달리
Chilseong-am
칠성암
Jeokseong-ri
적성리
Mungyeong-si
문경시
Dongno-myeon
동 로 면
PR901
NH59
Songwon Sanjang
송원산장
Police station
Post office
Yecheon-gun
예천군
Sangni-myeon
상 리 면
N
Water
Shelter
Village
Temple
Parking
Bus Stop
Inn
Mart
Stele
Jeongja
Shrine
Cave

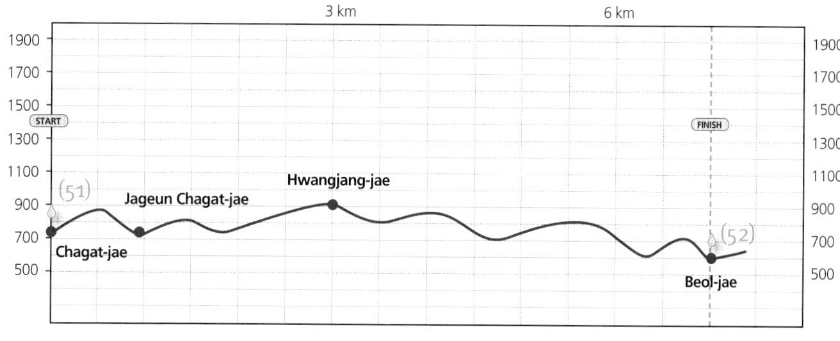

WATER STOPS

(51) Chagat-jae: **N36°48'55" E128°16'00"**
(52) Hwangjang-yaksu 황장약수 at Beol-jae: **N36°48'00" E128°19'09"**

trailhead at an abandoned quarry some 500 meters later. At this site, there is a large rock face housing a large set of steel doors. It would appear that they once acted as an entrance to the interior of the mountain, perhaps leading to a mine. The trail from there enters into the tree-line and meets the ridge some 300 meters later at Jageun Chagat-jae. Here, there is an abundance of water(51) gushing through the streams that run off the Baekdu-daegan. Likewise, there is more water on the northern side of Jageun Chagat-jae, which has a trail running northeast for 4 km toward NH59.

CLOSED SECTION Jageun Chagat-jae 작은 차갓재 → Hwangjang-jae 황장재 B1

2km (1:35)

At Jageun Chagat-jae, the trail climbs steeply in an east-to-southeast direction, arriving about 300 meters later at the base of a 10 m precipice with some ropes fixed at the top that descend down to its base. Using the ropes, hikers can straddle up the face of this obstacle and ascend to the top of a very impressive ridgeline. From here, the trail hugs and hangs its way along both the northern and southern side of a thin ridge, assisted in many places by fixed ropes. It is a spectacular and mentally provoking part of the trail, where hikers sometimes have to balance backwards over huge drop-offs, assisted only by a white rope of unknown history. This exciting saga continues for almost a kilometer until it ends at an unnamed peak, where the trail then turns south, arriving 500 meters later at Hwangjang-san 황장산, located at 1,077 m ABSL.

From Hwangjang-san, the trail becomes even better and offers trekkers the option of tightroping precariously along the "actual" spine of the ridge, which is made of hard-surfaced narrow rock. This tactic of trying to consistently remain on the lip of the highest features of the Baekdu-daegan is called "*jongju*," which means walking the actual crest of the Baekdu-daegan rather than the mountain system itself. There is popular debate in Korea over whether anyone has ever achieved this in its entirety. It would be a technical mountaineering achievement. About 300 meters later, the hiker arrives at Gamtu-bong 감투봉, located at 1,037 m ABSL. From this peak, there are more stunning viewing platforms looking west into the valley of Saengdal-ri 생달리, which has a striking cone-like peak jutting out of the landscape on the other side. From Gamtu-bong, the trail stays on the crest for 200 meters and heads southeast down some more fixed ropes to the pass of Hwangjang-jae.

CLOSED SECTION Hwangjang-jae 황장재 → Beol-jae 벌재 B3 4km (2:15)

From this track junction pass, the trail heads predominantly in an easterly direction along more fascinating rocky landscape. About 200 meters later, a natural helipad can be found, cultivated into the edge of the trail with leg-dangling views to the south. It is a great place to stop and take a rest. For the next 2 km, the trail is decorated by blemishes of large boulders that parade creative displays of *Pinus koreanus* protruding from the nooks and crannies of what is still a narrow crest. This area is a fine representation of the famous romantic visions of Northeast Asian landscapes depicted in traditional paintings. About 2 km after

Roger taking notes at a heli-pad just past Hwangjang-jae

the pass at Hwangjang-jae, hikers arrive at the pass of Pyebaegi-jae 페백이재. At this pass, there is a track running south for about 3 km toward PR901. From this pass, the trail continues east for about 800 meters, gaining about 100 m in altitude, to an unnamed peak standing at 929 m ABSL. From this peak, it is all downhill for the next 1.2 km, as the splendor and warmth of this leg comes to an end and the trail arrives at the pass of Beol-jae*.

* Beol-jae 벌재 B3

Located at 600 m ABSL, Beol-jae is connected by NH59 with the small junction township of Dongno-myeon, located 4 km to the south, and the small village of Banggok-ri 방곡리 2 km to the north. There are no amenities or immediate accommodations available at the quiet pass. However, water(52) can be located down the northern side of the pass in mountain runoffs.

Transport Info

Leaving the trail at Beol-jae: About 3 km north of Beol-jae on NH59 is the charming village of Banggok-ri 방곡리. From there, buses run to Danyang-gun five times a day from 7:50 am to 5:30 pm. About 5 km south of Beol-jae is the small town of Dongno-myeon 동로면. Buses don't run from Dongno to the pass, but taxis can be called from Dongno (Dongno Taxi T. 054-552-7891).

Lodging

On the eastern side of the road at Beol-jae, there is a *jeongja* with a sealed roof on it tucked away in the tree line. Unlike other *jeongja*, which have elevated floors, this one has particles of chipped wood spread out on the ground surface, allowing sleepers the benefit of some dry comfort. About 2 km north of Beol-jae on NH59 is Banggok-ri, a pottery village with a couple of very nice restaurants, including Hwangjang-san Swimteo 황장산 쉼터. NH59 turns northwest from Banggok-ri into Sangseonam-gyegok 상선암 계곡, flowing between Dorak-san 도락산 and Yongdu-san 용두산. A campground is located here 5 km from Banggok-ri, and there are also *minbak* in the area below Dorak-san near Sangseon-am temple, including Tongnamu-jip 통나무집 (T. 043-422-8620), Seonam Garden Minbak 선암가든민박 (T. 043-422-1447) and Dorak-san Garden 도락산가든 (T. 043-1577-2018). To the south, about 4 km from Beol-jae, is the town of Dongno-myeon, which has a bus terminal, shops and restaurants. There are no *minbak* in this town; however, about 2 km west out of town on PR901 is the excellent Songwon Sanjang 송원산장 (T. 054-553-0665 or 017-511-5668), a large modern building with huge park-like grounds. The proprietors will cook meals on request.

DAY 3

From Beol-jae to Jeosu-ryeong

- Distance: 6km
- Time: 3hr

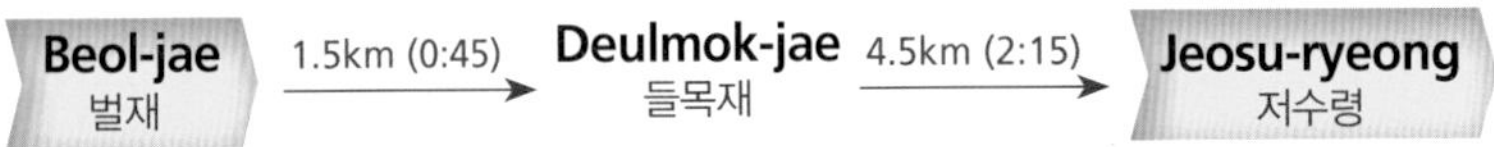

This leg is another short one, from Beol-jae to the western fringes of Sobaek-san National Park. The scenery, although remaining decent, does not offer the same uniqueness and majesty as the previous leg. From Beol-jae, the trail leaves the Worak-san National Park area and opens up into an area containing *Hydrangea macrophylla,* a deciduous shrub that usually grows up to 1-3 m tall. The leaves are of a simple ovoid-acute shape about 7-20 cm long, with a coarsely toothed margin. The flowers can be white or range from blue to purple to pink, depending on soil pH; in more acidic soils, the flowers will be blue, whereas alkaline soils yield a pinkish bloom. White-flowered varieties do not change color, regardless of the soil. Also known as big leaf hydrangea, the shrub is native to Japan, and the ones in this region were probably originally introduced to Korea during the occupation of the peninsula in the first half of the 20th century.

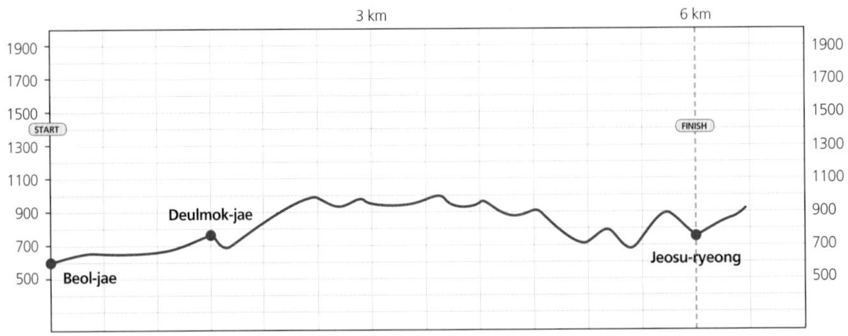

WATER STOPS No water stops for this course

Beol-jae 벌재 B3 → Deulmok-jae 들목재 C3 1.5km (0:45)

From Beol-jae, the trail reenters the deciduous bush line past a *jeongja* hidden under a tree canopy and ascends southeast straight up the ridge for about 1.2 km toward an unnamed peak located at 822 m ABSL. From there, the trail turns northeast and, after a short distance of 200 meters, drops down into the pass of Deulmok-jae, located at 750 m ABSL.

Deulmok-jae 들목재 C3 → Jeosu-ryeong 저수령 B4 4.5km (2:15)

From Deulmok-jae, it is a steady northeast climb for almost a kilometer up to an unnamed peak located at 1,020 m ABSL. From there, it is an easy and steady 1.2 km along the ridge in an easterly direction toward the highest point of this leg, Munbok-dae 문복대, located at 1,077 m ABSL. Munbok-dae is also called Unsu-bong 운수봉, and sometimes Ongnyeo-bong 옥녀봉, and should not be mistaken for another "Ongnyeo-bong" located less than 500 meters further along the trail. Munbok-dae offers great views to the south and west. From Munbok-dae, the trail stays at the same altitude and passes through more stands of deciduous forest containing more rocky outcrops. Some 500 meters later, you arrive at another high spot called Ongnyeo-bong. From here, the trail begins its descent down to Jeosu-ryeong. For the next kilometer, the trail descends from 1,000 m ABSL to about 900 m ABSL. Along this route, you can see the pass of Jeosu-ryeong some 2 km away in the east.

Just as the trail appears to reach the bottom of its descent, a small metal road intercepts the trail named Janggu-jae 장구재, located at 860 m ABSL. From there, the trail crosses straight over the metal road and back into the tree line, where it climbs back onto a small hill. On the other side of the hill, just before you reach the pass of Jeosu-ryeong*, there is a series of small marble tables that are used by the Cheonyong Mountain Association, probably a hiking club, to celebrate the rising of the sun during *sansin* ("mountain spirit") ceremonies.

* Jeosu-ryeong 저수령 B4

Jeosu-ryeong, located at about 800 m ABSL, is connected by PR927 with Yecheon 20 km to the south and Danyang 30 km to the north. Jeosu-ryeong lies almost exactly between the Worak-san and Sobaek-san National Parks. There are two tales about the origin of its name according to information found at the pass. The first tale describes how in the old days, the track up to the pass was so rough and steep that travelers walked with lowered heads on their way up, and so they named it that way (*jeo* means "low", and *su* means "head"). The second and spookier tale is that in the past,

Looking north from Jeosu-ryeong

during some of Korea's bloody battles, locals would take refuge at the pass to avoid attacks. All soldiers from invading nations who used this path were captured and killed by the locals and their heads cut off.

The current PR927 was completed in 1994, offering passage from Gyeongsang-do into Chungcheong-do and onward to the Seoul region and Gangwon-do. It now serves an important role in both tourism and the transport industry. Gone are the days of decapitations for all invading visitors. Despite its claims to play an important role for tourism, Jeosu-ryeong is not as well visited as other attractions in the Sobaek-san area due to its isolation and the emergence of the Juk-ryeong tunnel on NH55, about 20 km NNE of here, which cuts straight under Sobaek-san National Park. Juk-ryeong is also the endpoint for your next 20 km leg.

Transport Info

Leaving the trail at Jeosu-ryeong: About 800 meters northwest of Jeosu-ryeong is the Sobaek-san Gwangwang Nongjang 소백산 관광농장, a large beef farm with cabin accommodation. Buses leave here once a day for Danyang-gun at 7 am. A bus leaves Danyang Central Bus Terminal every morning at 6:10 am. Another 4 km north of the farm is the small village of Olsan-ri 올산리; buses leave here for Danyang-gun twice a day at 2:45 pm and 7:10 pm. The bus for Olsan-ri leaves Danyang Terminal at 1:30 pm and 6:45 pm. Also, 1.5 km down the southeastern side of the pass is a bus stop at Eumdal 음달. Buses from Yecheon-gun leave for Eumdal six times a day from 6:40 am to 7:40 pm and return to Yecheon-gun six times a day.

Lodging

At the pass, there is a large *hyugeso* that is now closed. Otherwise there is nowhere else at the pass to purchase food. About 800 meters on the northwest side of the pass is the Sobaek-san Gwangwang Nongjang (T. 043-422-9270) a farm-stay at the entrance to one of Korea's largest beef farms. It offers condo, *yeogwan*, and bungalow accommodation. Also at Jeosu-ryeong are some benches and a *jeongja* that has a sealed roof and is sleepable. There are some grassy areas that will allow a tent, although you might want to pitch it later in the day, once passers-by have left the area.

THREE DAYS

71.0km

SECTION 10

SOBAEK-SAN NATIONAL PARK

Jeosu-ryeong → Doraegi-jae

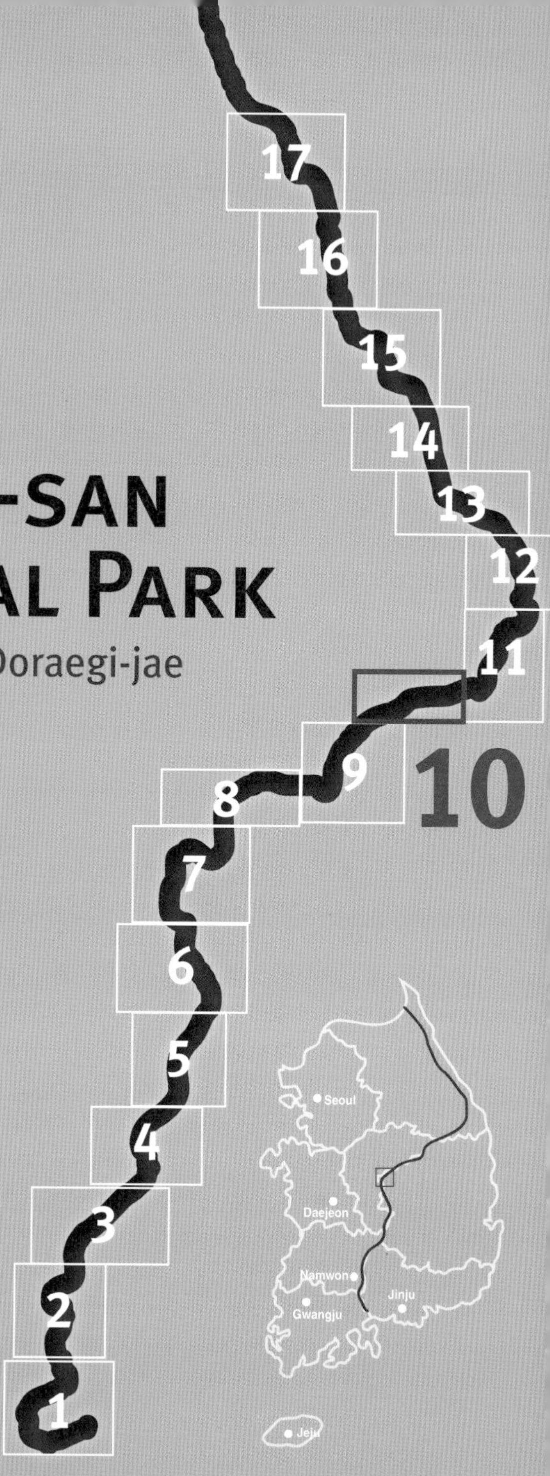

17
16
15
14
13
12
11
9
10
8
7
6
5
4
3
2
1

Seoul
Daejeon
Namwon
Jinju
Gwangju
Jeju

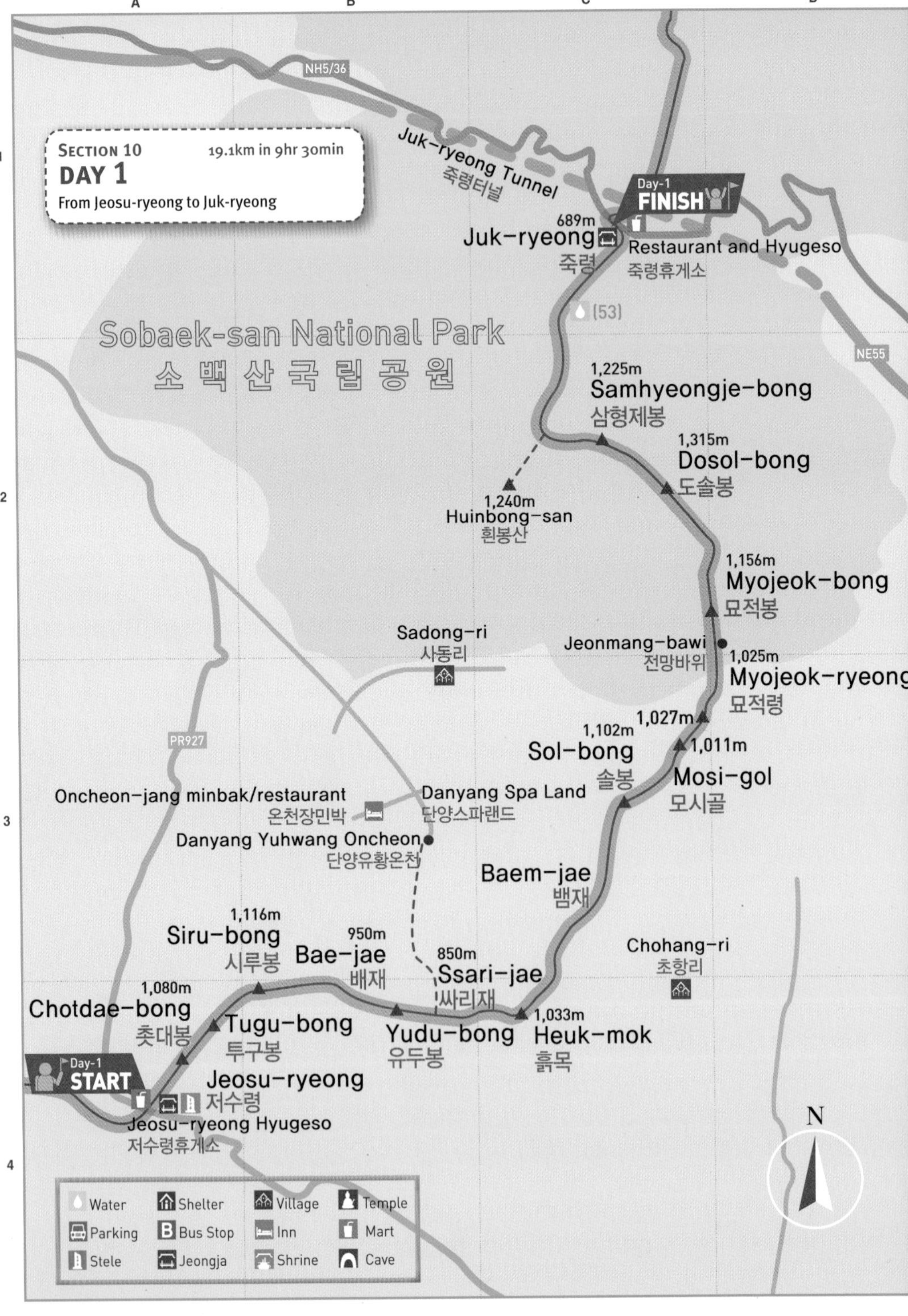

A
B
C
D
1
2
3
4
SECTION 10
19.1km in 9hr 30min
DAY 1
From Jeosu-ryeong to Juk-ryeong
NH5/36
Juk-ryeong Tunnel
죽령터널
Day-1
FINISH
689m
Juk-ryeong
죽령
Restaurant and Hyugeso
죽령휴게소
(53)
Sobaek-san National Park
소 백 산 국 립 공 원
NE55
1,225m
Samhyeongje-bong
삼형제봉
1,315m
Dosol-bong
도솔봉
1,240m
Huinbong-san
흰봉산
1,156m
Myojeok-bong
묘적봉
Sadong-ri
사동리
Jeonmang-bawi
전망바위
1,025m
Myojeok-ryeong
묘적령
1,027m
1,102m
1,011m
Sol-bong
솔봉
Mosi-gol
모시골
PR927
Oncheon-jang minbak/restaurant
온천장민박
Danyang Spa Land
단양스파랜드
Danyang Yuhwang Oncheon
단양유황온천
Baem-jae
뱀재
1,116m
Siru-bong
시루봉
950m
Bae-jae
배재
850m
Ssari-jae
싸리재
Chohang-ri
초항리
1,080m
Chotdae-bong
촛대봉
Tugu-bong
투구봉
Yudu-bong
유두봉
1,033m
Heuk-mok
흙목
Day-1
START
Jeosu-ryeong
저수령
Jeosu-ryeong Hyugeso
저수령휴게소
N
Water
Shelter
Village
Temple
Parking
Bus Stop
Inn
Mart
Stele
Jeongja
Shrine
Cave

DAY 1 From Jeosu-ryeong to Juk-ryeong

• **Distance:** 19.1km
• **Time:** 9hr 30min

From Jeosu-ryeong, climb quickly back up to the ridge and begin an undulating walk for 10 km to the southern frontier of Sobaek-san National Park (see p270). Notice instantly why it is a National Park, and study the big-grandeur rock formations ahead of you. Stop off at one of the many rocky outcrops you can clamber to and look southeast into Gyeongsangbuk-do and northwest into the rich valleys. At the end of your day, quench your thirst at the only mountain spring on this leg before heading down to the foot-tapping sounds of Korean trot music being pumped out at the pass of Juk-ryeong. Have a cold beer and stay in good accommodation above the hyugeso at the pass, or hitch down to the ginseng capital of Punggi and feel the vibes of old-school Korea.

Jeosu-ryeong 저수령 A4 → Heuk-mok 흙목 C4 6.5km (2:55)

From Jeosu-ryeong, there are about 11 main peaks to climb over. Seven of them are named. Starting at the ribbons located behind the major monument at the pass, you enter the tree line and walk up an elevation of about 300 m in just under 1 km until you get to the top of your first peak, Chotdae-bong 촛대봉, at 1,080 m. You are now effectively on the ridge. You remain at this altitude for another 1.8 km as you head northeast on the ridge, climbing over Tugu-bong 투구봉, with good views to the east,

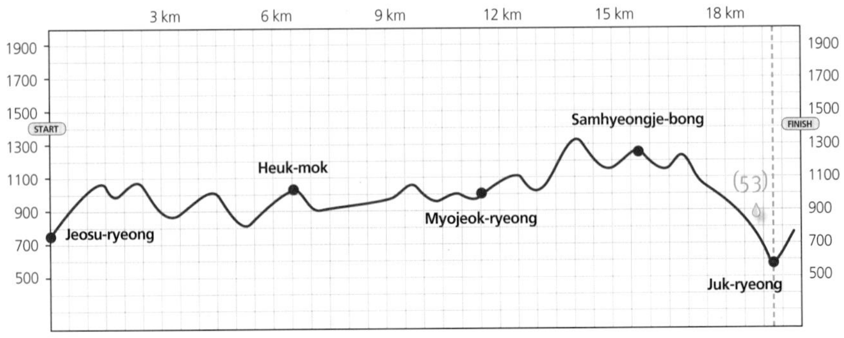

WATER STOPS (53) Almost at the end of this leg: **N36°53'14" E128°25'49"**

and Siru-bong 시루봉 at 1,116 m. From Siru-bong, you descend east into a saddle where, some 800 meters later, you climb back up toward an unnamed peak, passing a helipad just before the summit. From the unnamed peak, you descend east down the pine tree-flanked ridge, continuing for 1 km until you get to a signpost marking the saddle at the bottom of your descent as Bae-jae 배재, located at 950 m ABSL. From Bae-jae, you walk east, straight up to Yudu-bong 유두봉 at 1,059 m, and then descend 400 meters down to a signpost marking the pass of Ssari-jae 싸리재 at a track junction located at 850 m ABSL. The track heading north from the ridge goes to the Danyang *oncheon* (hot springs). From Ssari-jae, the going gets really good, and once you pass a rocky area, you walk for 400 meters at 1,000 m ABSL until you get to the peak of Heuk-mok at 1,033 m

The Danyang Yuhwang Oncheon 유황 온천 (T. 043-421-5725) is marked on the signpost at Ssari-jae and is located 2.7 km to the north. The thermal region is rich enough to support a second hot spring—Danyang Spa Land 단양 스파랜드 (T. 043-421-5757). There are a number of restaurants and accommodation options in the area, including the Oncheon-jang Minbak and Restaurant 온천장 민박식당 (T. 043-422-1291).

Heuk-mok 흙목 C4 → Myojeok-ryeong 묘적령 C3 5km (2:30)

From Heuk-mok, the trail starts to head in a northeast direction. For the next 5.5 km, you walk on some splendid ridge line with good sweeping views to the east, north and west. The terrain is favorable, and you can make up good time. After only

600 meters, you come across a *doltap*, followed shortly thereafter by a communications mast. About 400 meters later, you come to a signpost offering more great views to the southeast over Chohang-ri 초항리. Another kilometer later, you arrive at another signpost, marked by a helipad. This is the location of Baem-jae 뱀재. From Baem-jae, there is a gradual 1.5 km to the peak of Sol-bong 솔봉 at 1,102.8 m ABSL. A kilometer after Sol-bong, you drop down about 50 m in altitude to Mosi-gol 모시골, which is marked by a signpost and helipad. The ridge remains favorable and pleasant to walk on for the next 2 km, ascending over unnamed peaks located at 1,011 m and 1,027 m ABSL. About 500 meters after the last peak, you arrive at the pass of Myojeok-ryeong, located at 1,025 m ABSL. Myojeok-ryeong is also the start of the southern boundary of the Sobaek-san National Park. You are now just over the halfway point of this 19 km leg.

Myojeok-ryeong 묘적령 C3 → Samhyeongje-bong 삼형제봉 C2

4.1km (2:30)

About 300 meters after Myojeok-ryeong, there is a fantastic viewing point called Jeonmang-bawi 전망바위. The location should be obvious to you, as it features a plateau of flat bald rock that offers views west into the Sadong-ri 사동리 valley. For the next 700 meters, the Baekdu-daegan trail ascends 125 m in altitude over mainly open country before arriving at the summit of Myojeok-bong 묘적봉,

Views back along the trail from Jeonmang-bawi

The route to Dosol-bong

located at 1,156 m ABSL. Just before you get to the peak of Myojeok-bong, you will come across a small bronze plaque in the rock indicating the height of Myojeok-bong as 1,148 m. After Myojeok-bong (1,156m), you begin to venture into some bigger ground. The next 500 meters of the trail see you dropping about 70 m in altitude into a sharp saddle, followed by a 100 m steep climb up to a ledge that plateaus out about 130 m beneath Dosol-bong 도솔봉. There are some more great views from rocky outcrops in this area. From that ledge, the climb to Dosol-bong is made easier by some very steep wooden staircases that also support great views back to the south along the mighty Baekdu-daegan trail. Dosol-bong is the highest point you will reach on this leg at 1,315 m ABSL. It features a large open area, consisting of a helipad and *doltap*, that provides 360° views. Due north from the summit, you can see NH5/36 about 6 km away, as well as the saddle of Juk-ryeong. The trail for the next kilometer off Dosol-bong arcs in a northwest direction and drops about 160 m in altitude. At that stage, the trail arrives at the base of your next peak, called Samhyeongje-bong. The next 250 meters to its peak see you ascending about 150 m in altitude straight up some wooden staircases, covering steep terrain before arriving at the summit of Samhyeongje-bong at 1,225 m ABSL.

Samhyeongje-bong 삼형제봉 C2 → Juk-ryeong 죽령 C1

3.5km (1:35)

From there, the trail drops into another saddle through some more rocky terrain and climbs up to your next spot height at an area called Huinbong-san Damgol 흰봉산 담골, marked at 1,288 m ABSL, where the Baekdu-daegan trail takes a northerly bearing and begins its 3.5 km descent down to **Juk-ryeong***. The trail immediately drops into tree line, which will remain with you for most of the downhill leg. Some of the ground cover turns into low-lying shoots of bamboo. After almost 2 km, you walk directly over a concrete slab on the track. On it is a list of names that were scrawled into the concrete when it was still wet. They belong to the infantry soldiers of a logistics group of the 112th regiment of the 37th division of the South Korean Army. The division commander's name is Major General Yi Seung-nam, according to the translation. There is no known reason why it's there, apart from the fact that they probably did some digging and construction in the area at some stage...just another quirky moment in Korea. Shortly after crossing this, you come to a signpost marked by a helipad, where you will find some tombs that you walk past on your way to your first and only water stop(53) on this long leg. It is located at the bottom of a small depression on the eastern side of the trail and marked by a small plaque. The plaque is an obituary and literally reads as follows:

The stele of Juk-ryeong

> Here, Jong Cheol, our friend who liked mountains
> Returned to the bosom of the Baekdu-daegan.
> Rest in peace! Jong Cheol. 2001. 7.

Kim Geon-gi, Yi Jong-mok, Yi Chang-su, Heo Won-mu
Yecheon City, 54th Alumni Association, Mountain People

About 1.5 km later, you come to a well-worn path that is flat and firm. It takes you right out into a small parking lot at the Gyeongsangbuk-do or southern side of Juk-ryeong. At this stage, you'll be pretty happy to have completed 20 km of great ridge and excited by the activity and options that Juk-ryeong provides the hiker in way of accommodations, hot foods, shops, beverages, etc.

Congratulations! Juk-ryeong also represents about 400 km traveled on the Baekdu-daegan from Jiri-san Cheonhwang-bong.

* Juk-ryeong 죽령 C1

Juk-ryeong is located at 689 m ABSL and connected by NH5, which is also known as NH36. The small, vibrant country town of Punggi-eup 풍기읍 lies 10 km to its east, and the stunning town of Danyang-gun 20 km to its west. The Juk-ryeong tunnel on NE55 runs beneath the pass. Despite the fact that there is a 5 km long tunnel running underneath this pass, a large number of persons visit Juk-ryeong in their vehicles or on buses to hike Sobaek-san National Park. It is normally a busy, bustling place, and the air is full of the toe-tapping sounds of Korean *trot* music and the aromas of hot food accompanied by the merry banter of Koreans drinking *soju, dongdong-ju* or beer.

Geographically, Juk-ryeong is an old path that has been the main artery of the southeastern area of Korea for the last 2,000 years. Juk-ryeong is considered to be one of the three major gateways to the Yeongam Region in the Sobaek-sanmaek, along with Mungyeong Saejae and Chupung-ryeong, both of them located further back on the Baekdu-daegan trail. Given its age, location and height, Juk-ryeong is supposedly the most important among them. It is said that the road to Juk-ryeong has ninety-nine turns and that even the clouds stop to take a rest when crossing over the ridge. Juk-ryeong does have some stunning views and lookouts, and on a cool morning, one can stand at Juk-ryeong and look down onto the clouds as they rest beneath the pass.

Historically, according to the *Samguksagi*, Juk-ryeong was opened during the 5th year and 3rd month of the reign of Silla King Adala. Also, according to the *Donggukyeojiseungram*, during the 5th year of King Adala's reign, his subject Juk-juk died from exhaustion after his great efforts to establish Juk-ryeong. As a result of this, a shrine was built on it to pay homage to him. Information from the pass also states that during the Three Kingdoms period, the place was often locked in a bitter battle. Many generals campaigned for this pass: Goryeo King Jang-su in AD 470, Silla King Jin-heung 40 years later, and later the famous General Ondal, who stated, "I won't come back before I regain the area," showing how militarily critical it was to them.

Until 1910, during the Japanese colonial takeover, it was a common path for Gyeongsang-do region *seonbi* (Neo-Confucian scholars) who dreamt about passing the state examination to become high officials, and the place was always saturated with the joys and sorrows of many travelers and peddlers carrying their wares. On the Gyeongsangbuk-do side, there is a stele that was erected on December 6, 2006 by the Yeongju office of the Korea Forest Service. The translated information on the stele describes how, in the 5th year of Silla King Adala, a Buddhist monk who had attained spiritual enlightenment stuck his bamboo cane or walking stick into the earth and left it there. The stick transformed into a bamboo forest, and so the pass was aptly named *juk*, meaning "bamboo," and *ryeong*, meaning "pass." The upper waters of the Jukryeong-cheon stream now flow from that bamboo forest.

TRANSPORT INFO

Leaving the trail at Juk-ryeong: The majority of buses running between Danyang to the northwest and Yecheon to the southeast pass through the tunnels of the expressway below. However, three buses a day run over Juk-ryeong between the two centers. Danyang~Juk-ryeong~Punggi~Yecheon buses leave Danyang terminal at 7:50 am, 3 pm and 5 pm. Yecheon–Punggi–Juk-ryeong–Danyang buses leave Yecheon terminal at 9:40 am, 4:50 pm and 6 pm. You will obviously need to state your intention of going to Juk-ryeong, or else you will probably be ushered onto one of the frequently leaving Yecheon/Danyang buses heading through the tunnel.

LODGING

On both sides of the pass, there are restaurants that sell good quality *Hanguk eumshik* (general Korean meals). The Chungcheongbuk-do side on the northwestern end seems to be the busier, simply because it has the largest parking lot, allowing visitors to stop there. On this side, the most notable complex is the two-story building called the Chungbuk Restaurant and Hyugeso 충북 죽령휴게소 (T. 043-421-6240 or 017-522-6240), located nearest the crest of the pass. It is owned and operated by a friendly elderly couple and is open daily from 7 am to 10 pm. Inside, there is also a small superette with some basic food items that you can purchase to hike with. Above the store and restaurant are four new rooms that the owner has turned into accommodations. They are superb *ondol-bang* (room with underfloor heating) with cable TV, clean bathrooms and modern kitchenettes. They go between 20,000 and 30,000 won each. During the day, there are also a number of street vendors selling local curios. On the Gyeongsangbuk-do side of the pass, you can see a small grassy area that displays some *jangseung* (totem poles) and a small mountain spirit worship area at the base of a rock face. There is also a *jeongja* located near the stele, which will accommodate hikers if need be. To its southeast, some 10 km away on the Gyeongsangbuk-do side, lies the small town of Punggi-eup, which is famous for its ginseng products, a large hot baths complex, and one of Korea's greatest Neo-Confucian shrine academies, Sosu Seowon. It is also a cool little town to visit and rest in, as it offers some good accommodations. The more modern accommodations are located on the south side of the river, while the older and cheaper *minbak* are located in the old town center area. The Sobaek Motel 소백 모텔, located on a street corner directly opposite the police station, is worth a stayover, with friendly service and reasonably priced *ondol-bang* at about 25,000 to 30,000 won each.

Sobaek-san National Park 소백산 국립공원

Sobaek-san was designated a National Park in December 1987. The parklands consist of a total area of 322.383 km², crossing Danyang-gun in Chungcheongbuk-do, and Yeongju and Bonghwa-gun in Gyeongsangbuk-do. It is Korea's third largest national park and forms the basis of the Sobaek-sanmaek Range that extends from the Taebaek-sanmaek Range to the east, running from here all the way west and then south to Jiri-san. It is a key central part of the Baekdu-daegan. Most of Sobaek-san's major peaks stand between 1,200 m and 1,400 m ABSL, with the summit Biro-bong 비로봉 the highest at 1,439 m. Despite its diminutive name, there is nothing small about Sobaek-san, and it provides its hikers with long, sweeping ridges running from west to east, featuring unimpeded 360° views over wind-swept slopes and spurs. The ridge-top trail is often bald and flanked by wide fields of alpine grass and wild flowers, and the way it gently undulates allows trekkers relatively quick and untiring progress. Sobaek-san is sacred to Korean Buddhists, who have long venerated it as the spiritual residence of Biro-bul (Vairocana Buddha) and a teaching center of the Hwaeom ("flower garland") Buddhist Sect. Its slopes are rich in wild plants, consisting of edelweiss and royal azaleas that fully blossom in the spring to create lovely, graceful scenery, along with the largest community of yew trees in Korea, located beneath the Biro-bong summit at about 1,300m ABSL. It contains the magnificent Huibang-pokpo Waterfall 희방폭포. It is also extremely rich in Confucian and Buddhist sites, relics and contemporary culture, being home to the famous Buseok-sa 부석사, Biro-sa 비로사, Huibang-sa 희방사 and other temples, and also the Sosu Seowon 소수서원, Korea's first Neo-Confucian academy-shrine.

DAY 2 From Juk-ryeong to Gochi-ryeong

- Distance: 24km
- Time: 11hr 5min

This long 25 km leg stretches through Sobaek-san proper. Despite its distance, the trail's layout allows you to make up good ground in reasonable time. The trail heads predominantly northeast the entire time as it sweeps through an open landscape of alpine grass, yew trees, wildflowers, mountain springs and bald stands of rock that in the distance look like large ogres awaiting your passage. Near the halfway mark, you pass over Sobaek-san's highest feature, Biro-bong (1,439m), before entering the less-visited areas containing tall stands of trees. The long day sees you arriving at the isolated pass of Gochi-ryeong and its quaint *sansin-gak*. If you have enough food, camp at the pass, or walk 5 km south and get a room in the farmhouse of a family that makes their challenging living hunting for ginseng.

Juk-ryeong 죽령 D1 → 2nd Yeonhwa-bong 제2연화봉 C1

5km (1:30)

You will need to get an early start for this leg if you aim to get to the next vantage point on the ridge at Gochi-ryeong some 25 km later. There are no shelters within

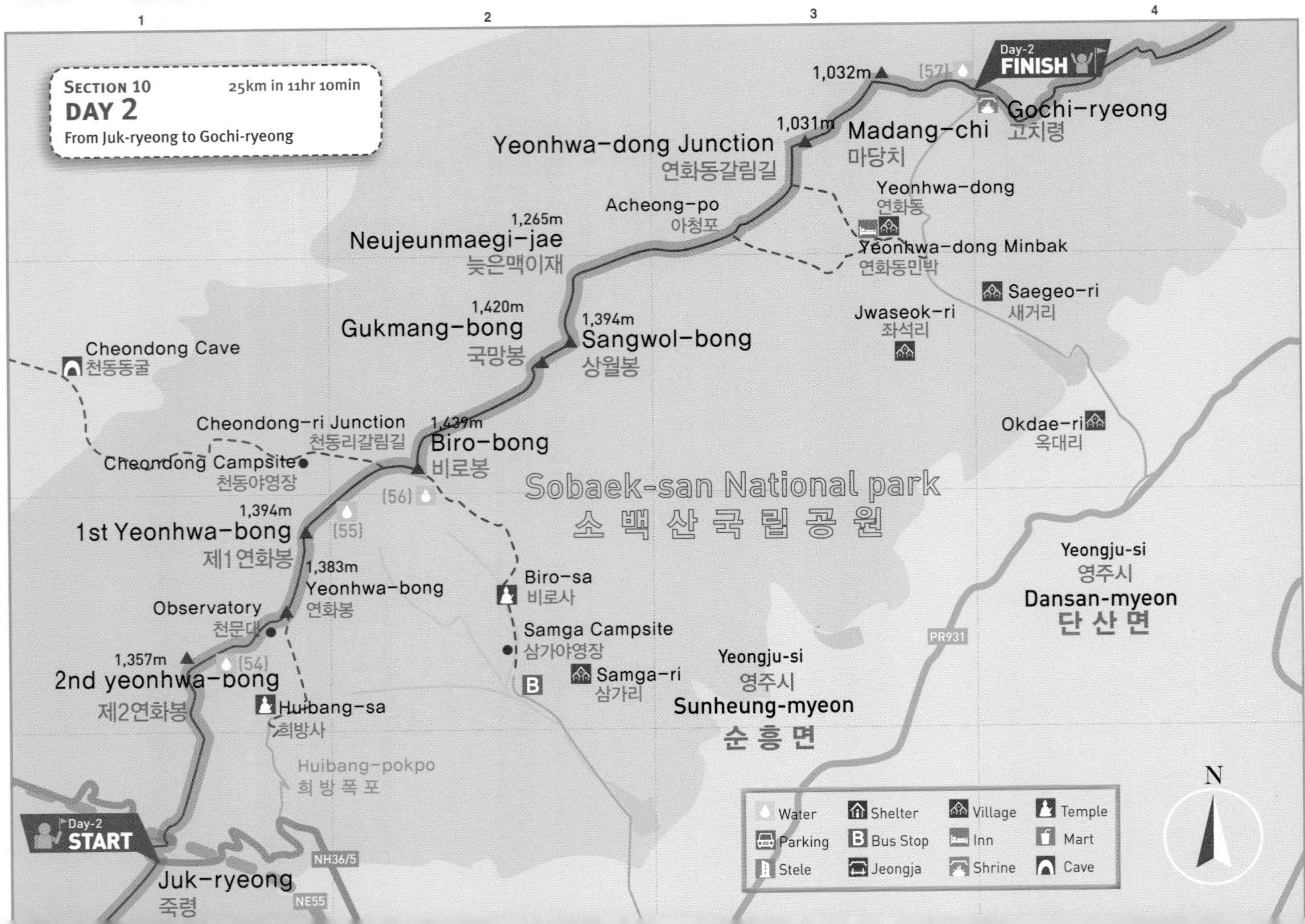

Section 10
DAY 2
25km in 11hr 10min
From Juk-ryeong to Gochi-ryeong
1
2
3
4
A
B
C
D
Day-2 FINISH
Day-2 START
1,032m
(57)
Gochi-ryeong
고치령
1,031m
Madang-chi
마당치
Yeonhwa-dong Junction
연화동갈림길
Yeonhwa-dong
연화동
Acheong-po
아청포
1,265m
Neujeunmaegi-jae
늦은맥이재
Yeonhwa-dong Minbak
연화동민박
Saegeo-ri
새거리
Jwaseok-ri
좌석리
1,420m
Gukmang-bong
국망봉
1,394m
Sangwol-bong
상월봉
Cheondong Cave
천동동굴
Cheondong-ri Junction
천동리갈림길
1,439m
Biro-bong
비로봉
Okdae-ri
옥대리
Cheondong Campsite
천동야영장
(56)
Sobaek-san National park
소 백 산 국 립 공 원
1,394m
1st Yeonhwa-bong
제1연화봉
(55)
1,383m
Yeonhwa-bong
연화봉
Biro-sa
비로사
Yeongju-si
영주시
Dansan-myeon
단 산 면
Observatory
천문대
Samga Campsite
삼가야영장
PR931
1,357m
(54)
2nd yeonhwa-bong
제2연화봉
Samga-ri
삼가리
Yeongju-si
영주시
Sunheung-myeon
순 흥 면
Huibang-sa
희방사
Huibang-pokpo
희 방 폭 포
NH36/5
Juk-ryeong
죽령
NE55
Water
Shelter
Village
Temple
Parking
Bus Stop
Inn
Mart
Stele
Jeongja
Shrine
Cave
N

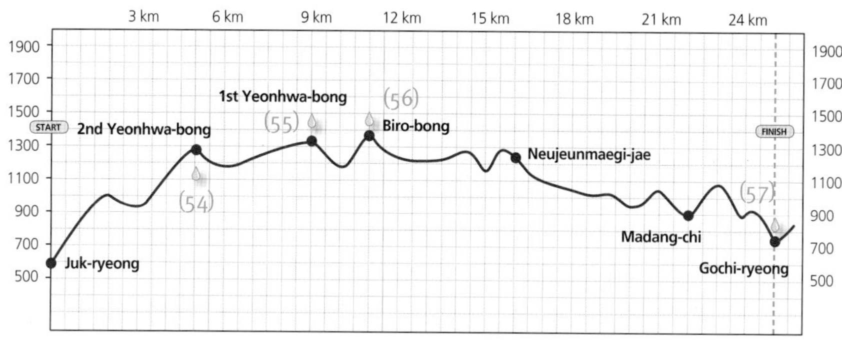

Water Stops

(54) 2nd Yeonhwa-bong: **N36°55'30" E128°26'55"**
(55) 1st Yeonhwa-bong: **N36°56'56" E128°28'22"**
(56) 300 meters down the southeastern side of Biro-bong: **N36°57'13" E128°29'14"**
(57) Gochi-ryeong: **N37°00'46" E128°35'25"**

Sobaek-san National Park.

The starting point to this leg is located on the Chungcheongbuk-do, or northwestern, side of the pass. There, you will see a paved road winding up through some trees behind a block of public toilets. A short distance up the road (100 meters) is a ranger's hut. Once through the ranger's gate, you walk on a sealed road for a good 7 km. The first 5 km see you ascending about 670 m in altitude from Juk-ryeong to 1,357 m ABSL at the first major peak of 2nd (Je-yi) Yeonhwa-bong. The walk up the road is windy and quite steep, but the fact that you can move fairly quickly over the flattish surface allows you to get a good start up to the ridge in good time. There are three peaks in this region all called Yeonhwa-bong. The first one is called 2nd Yeonhwa-bong, marking your return to the high ridge. There are several good spots along this road that provide you with great views east and west of the ridge. At 2nd Yeonhwa-bong, there is a large satellite dish that you will walk around.

2nd Yeonhwa-bong 제2연화봉 → 1st Yeonhwa-bong 제1연화봉 C1

4km (1:50)

From 2nd Yeonhwa-bong, your course changes direction northeast and you continue on a road that becomes unsealed. Just under a kilometer later, you come across a lookout platform on the right-hand side. There is also a signpost there

The Sobaeksan Optical Astronomy Observatory at 1st Yeonhwa-bong

indicating a spring(54) located 20 meters down the southeast side of the ridge. From this area, you can easily see the major peaks of Biro-bong and Gukmang-bong in the distance. The closest peak you can see from here is 2 km away, has an observatory on it and stands at 1,383 m ABSL, with the name of Yeonhwa-bong. At this peak, there are many viewing platforms from which to enjoy the scenery. Construction on the observatory began in June 1997 and was completed on May 13, 1999. It is owned and operated by the Sobaeksan Optical Astronomy Observatory and is open to the public by appointment. On the southern side of the summit, there is a track that glides along the top of a spur for 1.5 km before cutting sharply west down to the temple of Huibang-sa. After Yeonhwa-bong, the next peak is 1st Yeonhwa-bong at 1,394 m ABSL, some 1.5 km away. To get there, you descend into a slight depression and then walk up some steps. At the summit is a stone plaque with a poem on it titled "The Oath of Mountain Climbers." Translated, it says:

Mountain climbers search for the eternal world.
Until they reach their destination,
They get over their adversity with passion and cooperation.
There is never despair or abandonment.
Mountain climbers must assimilate with Mother Nature
And be without deception and decoration.
There is only a march to the true world of freedom, peace and love.

1st Yeonhwa-bong 제1연화봉 C1 → Biro-bong 비로봉 B2

2km (1:10)

The next leg from 1st Yeonhwa-bong to Biro-bong* is interesting because there is a lot of information on the trail (in Korean) about the local flora. One of those is a *yeonri-mok* 연리목, called the "tree of love" because of its intertwinement of two trees to form one. The area is rich in the Sobaek-san royal azalea called *cheoljjuk*, a Chinese word meaning "hesitate," or better translated as "bewitched," since travelers used to stop and marvel at the blossoms. The royal azalea is a poisonous plant and cannot be eaten, whereas the azalea can be eaten. Therefore, the Koreans also call the royal azalea the *gaekkot*, meaning "dog flower," and the azalea the *chamkkot*, meaning the "virtuous flower." The royal azalea begins to blossom in mid-May, and its bloom is affectionately known as the "pleasure of love." A kilometer after 1st Yeonhwa-bong is a signpost indicating a spring(55) located on the eastern side of the track. On your way to Biro-bong is a large stand of about 100 yew trees.

* Biro-bong 비로봉 B2

At the peak of Biro-bong, you have 360° views. On a good day, you can practically see the remaining 13 km of the ridge heading northeast. A stone plaque at the summit has a poem written on it, stating, "A great work (Sobaek-san) made by Heaven and

Biro-bong

Earth." More water is to be found 300 meters down a track, located on the southeastern side of the peak.

About 800 meters before Biro-bong, there is a track junction called Cheondong-ri Gallimgil. From there, a track descends west for 2 km to the Cheondong Campground 천동 야영장. A further 3 km down this trail is the Cheondong-ri park entrance and the Cheondong-donggul limestone cave system. This area has a number of *minbak* and restaurants and an additional campground.

Biro-bong 비로봉 → Neujeunmaegi-jae 늦은맥이재 B2

5km (2:30)

From Biro-bong, the trail veers grid-north for about 500 meters, descending some more staircases into the start of a large, undulating running saddle. The trail then turns northeast for 2 km, becoming open and vast, with large crops of rock jutting from the ridge. Arriving at a track junction marked by a signpost, the trail changes back to a northerly direction and ascends about 120 m in altitude for 300 meters,

Leaving Gukmang-bong

arriving at the bald, rocky summit of Gukmang-bong at 1,420 m ABSL. The trail leaves the subalpine zone and continues northeast, passing the summit of Sangwol-bong 상월봉 (1,394m) and then turning north for 1.5 km to Neujeunmaegi-jae, located at 1,265 m ABSL.

Gukmang-bong 국망봉 B2

This mountain was where, in the AD 100 period, Prince Maui, son of King Gyeongsun of the fledgling Silla kingdom, stood on his flight to Geumgang-san (now in North Korea) and shed tears of sorrow and regret as he looked back for one last time toward the kingdom he failed. Disappearing over the ridge, he later lived in Geumgang-san, clothed only in hemp (*maui* means hemp clothes).

TRANSPORT INFO

Leaving the trail at Biro-bong: If you decide to take more than one day crossing Sobaek-san, there is the option of dropping southeast off Biro-bong, the highest peak, and busing out from the road ends. Samga-ri 삼가리 is located about 5 km southeast of Biro-bong, below a campground and the Biro-sa temple 비로사. Buses run to Samga-ri six times a day from Yeongju 영주 at 6 am, 7:50 am, 9:50 am, 1:30 pm, 2:50 pm and 6:20 pm. There are often taxis waiting at the Biro-sa entrance, as the one-way walk from Juk-ryeong to Biro-sa is very popular. Alternatively, on the western side of the ridge at Cheondong-ri, buses run 15 times a day to Danyang from 7 am to 8:05 pm.

Neujeunmaegi-jae 늦은맥이재 B2 → Madang-chi 마당치 A3

6km (2:50)

From Neujeunmaegi-jae, the Baekdu-daegan trail turns east, remaining on a good, gentle downhill descent, passing one helipad 2 km later and arriving at a second another kilometer later. This helipad, marked by a signpost, is also a track junction known as Acheong-po 아청포. About 1.5 km later, you come across another track junction called Yeonhwa-dong Gallimgil. The trail continues northeast at 1,000 m ABSL through higher stands of trees, hosting occasional outcrops of rock that provide you with more good views of the valleys below. The remaining 3 km will also pass four signposts and one notable summit at 1,031 m ABSL before arriving at the pass of Madang-chi.

From Yeonhwa-dong Gallimgil 연화동 갈림길, located between Neujeunmaegi-jae and Madang-chi, the track on the right heading south runs about 2.5 km to Yeonhwa-dong, home to the Yeonhwa-dong Minbak 연화동 민박. The Yeonhwa-dong Minbak is a simple farmhouse with a spare room, which the friendly hosts will rent for 30,000 won. Hearty meals are prepared for 5,000 won a head.

Madang-chi 마당치 → Gochi-ryeong 고치령 A3 3km (1:15)

From Madang-chi, the trail continues in a northeast direction, ascending for the next 500 meters to a track junction located at 1,032 m ABSL. From there, you must follow the directions east to Gochi-ryeong* (written in English). The final 2 km of the walk to Gochi-ryeong sees you descending about 250 m in altitude and takes you through some stunning forest. Some of the trees stand at 20 and 30 m in height, making them some of the tallest ones you will see on the entire Baekdu-daegan. The area is not very well visited, and you will experience a great sensation of walking the Baekdu-daegan.

* Gochi-ryeong 고치령 A3

Gochi-ryeong is connected by a mountain road that links Okdae-ri 옥대리, in Gyeongsangbuk-do to the southeast, to the Danyang area in Chungcheongbuk-do to the north via PR935. There are no amenities at the pass apart from water(57), located off the road on the northern side. It is a seasonal spring and may not hold water in the drier months. Gochi-ryeong is an interesting pass that has *jangseung* and small hidden objects worth exploring floating around its site. To the right of the guardian tree and the important *sansin-gak* is a small trail. Also tucked away there is a small worship area marked by a makeshift rock platform with candles sometimes burning in it. Further to the back, on a small track behind the *sansin-gak*, you may stumble across a couple of small, rounded rocks lying on the ground amongst the deadfall. The rocks have some Korean and Chinese script (國仙王位) on them and are positioned in the manner of a seat or throne. Written in Korean are the words, "Hwarang will be a King." There is no direct meaning to this, except that during the Silla era, the *hwarang* were an elite cadre of youthful aristocratic Buddhist-inspired warriors—the best young men of the Silla Kingdom. These rocks are neither ancient nor historic; more than likely, they were put there very recently for some sort of private ritual and are just another one of those quirky finds you'll discover in Korea.

TRANSPORT INFO

Leaving the trail at Gochi-ryeong: Gochi-ryeong is a very quiet pass with little traffic. The closest bus stop to the south is over 4 km away at Saegeo-ri 새거리 in Jwaseok-ri 좌석리. Buses leave here for Dansan-myeon 단산면, and on to Yeongju, three times a day at 7:40 am, 12:40 pm and 6:30 pm. Buses for Saegeo-ri leave Yeongju at 7 am, 12:10 pm and 4:30 pm. Dansan-ri, located a further 7 km or so southeast of Saegeo-ri, has buses leaving for Punggi-eup 17 times a day.

LODGING

There is a heli-pad located just above Gochi-ryeong which also offers great camping options. There is a flat, grassy area behind the *sansin-gak* that can accommodate a tent. The Gochi-jae Minbak 고치재 민박 (T. 054-638-4544) is located 5 km south down the road from Gochi-ryeong, about 800 meters past the Saegeo-ri. The aforementioned Yeonhwa-dong Minbak 연화동 민박 (T.054-638-4535) is located in Yeonhwa-dong, 4 km to the south and then 1 km west from the Segeori Intersection. Yeonhwa-dong also has a modern pension 연화동 펜션 (T. 017-513-4488) with rooms starting at 60,000 won—visit www.yeonhwadong.com for bookings. There are no shops in Yeonhwa-dong; the nearest is still some 10 km away at Okdae-ri. If you have enough food, it may be better to camp at Gochi-ryeong, as it's a 6 km walk back to the ridge from the *minbak*...that's a 10 km diversion.

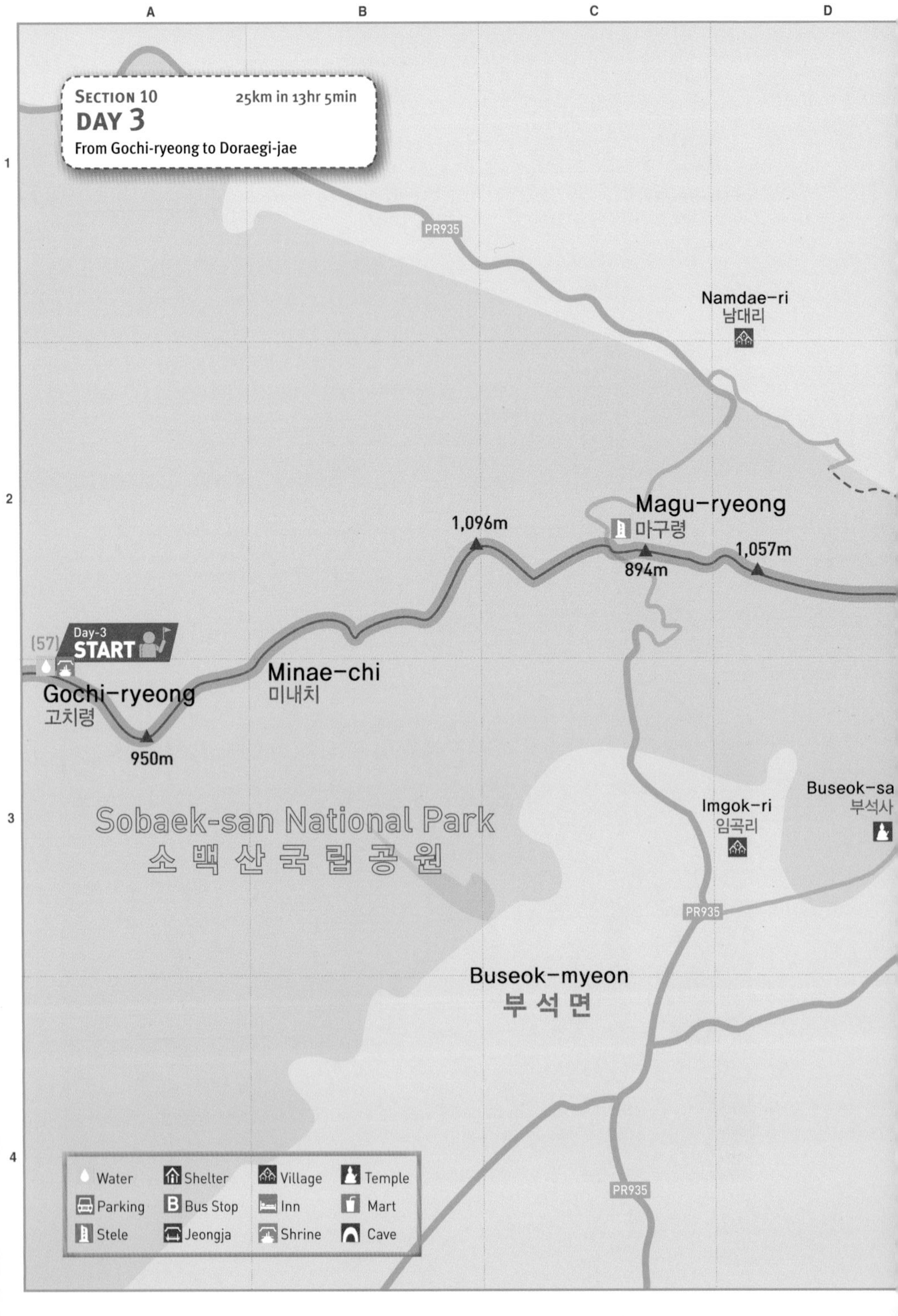

A
B
C
D
1
2
3
4
SECTION 10
25km in 13hr 5min
DAY 3
From Gochi-ryeong to Doraegi-jae
PR935
Namdae-ri
남대리
Magu-ryeong
마구령
1,096m
894m
1,057m
(57)
Day-3
START
Gochi-ryeong
고치령
950m
Minae-chi
미내치
Sobaek-san National Park
소 백 산 국 립 공 원
Imgok-ri
임곡리
Buseok-sa
부석사
PR935
Buseok-myeon
부 석 면
PR935
Water
Shelter
Village
Temple
Parking
Bus Stop
Inn
Mart
Stele
Jeongja
Shrine
Cave

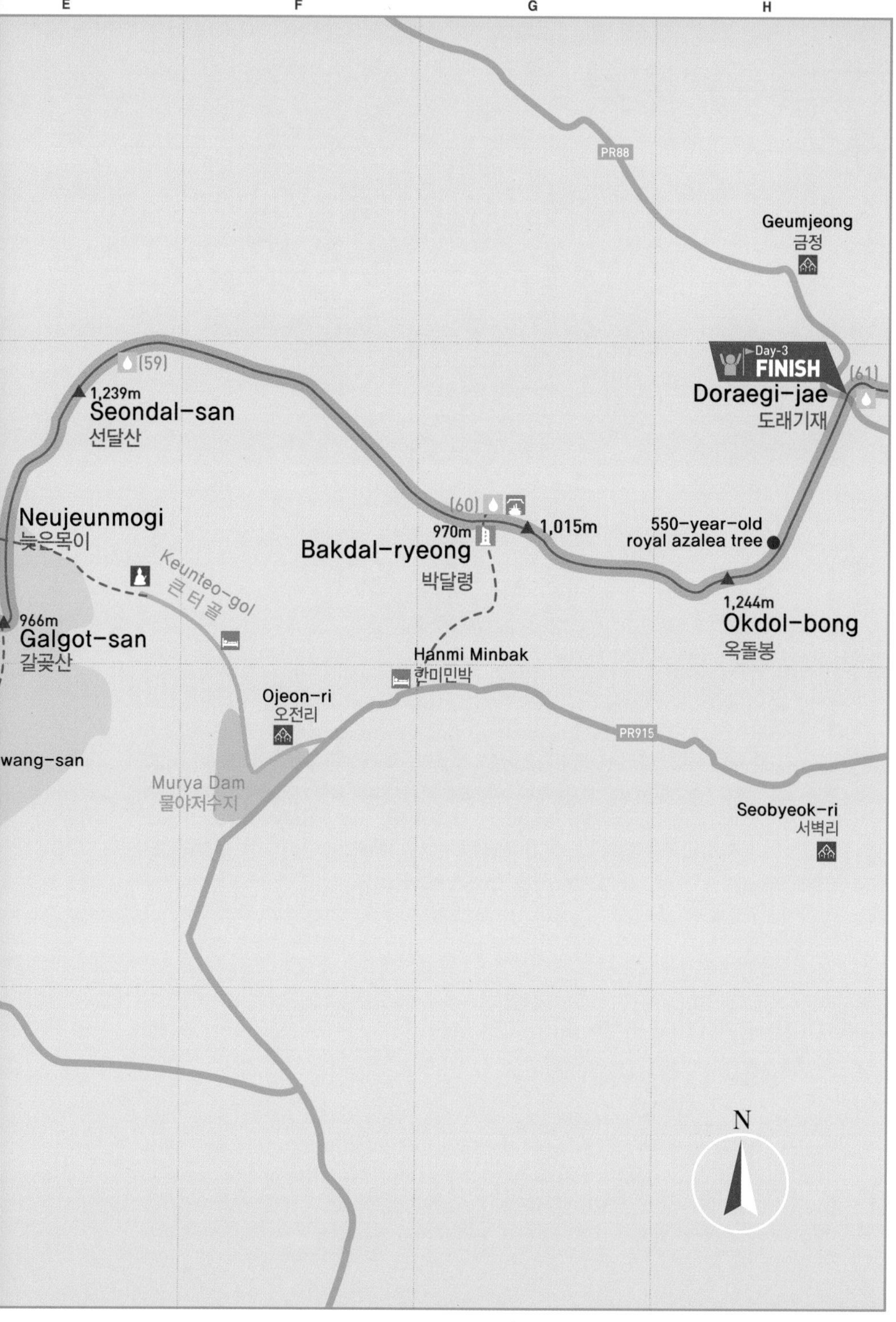

E
F
G
H
PR88
Geumjeong
금정
Day-3
FINISH
(61)
Doraegi-jae
도래기재
(59)
1,239m
Seondal-san
선달산
Neujeunmogi
늦은목이
(60)
970m
1,015m
Bakdal-ryeong
박달령
550-year-old
royal azalea tree
Keunteo-gol
큰 터 골
966m
Galgot-san
갈곶산
1,244m
Okdol-bong
옥돌봉
Hanmi Minbak
한미민박
Ojeon-ri
오전리
PR915
wang-san
Murya Dam
물야저수지
Seobyeok-ri
서벽리
N

DAY 3 From Gochi-ryeong to Doraegi-jae

• **Distance:** 25km
• **Time:** 13hr 5min

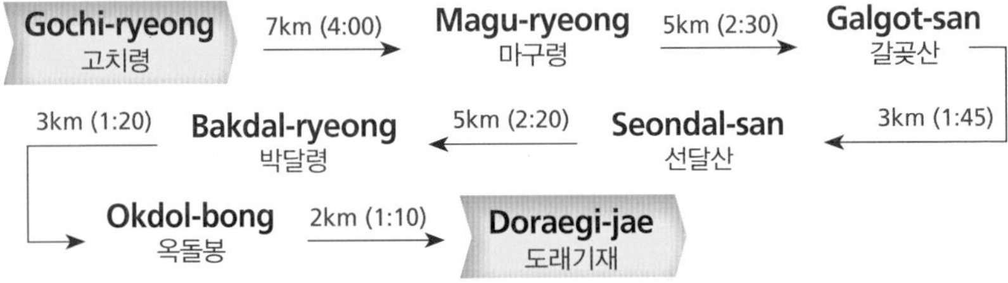

The next leg from Gochi-ryeong can be split into two days if you wish; otherwise, it's a good 24 km walk all the way to the next sealed road at Doraegi-jae on PR88. However, there are a couple of spots where you can get off the ridge if don't wish to camp on it. The most prominent one would probably be at Galgot-san, near the eastern boundary of Sobaek-san National Park, where there is a track leading down to the very impressive and historic temple of Buseok-sa. The majority of the trail travels east, passing through green, hilly sections of deciduous bush and slowly nudging its way toward Taebaek-san and the east coast of Korea.

Gochi-ryeong 고치령 A3 → Magu-ryeong 마구령 C2 — 7km (4:00)

The majority of this leg is marked every 500 meters with a signpost. The track remains heavily forested and ascends southeast for 500 meters to your first peak, at 950 m ABSL, after which it descends northeast for 2 km before arriving at an area called Minae-chi 미내치, which is marked by a signpost. From there, the trail continues in a northeast-to-easterly direction, passing two helipads and

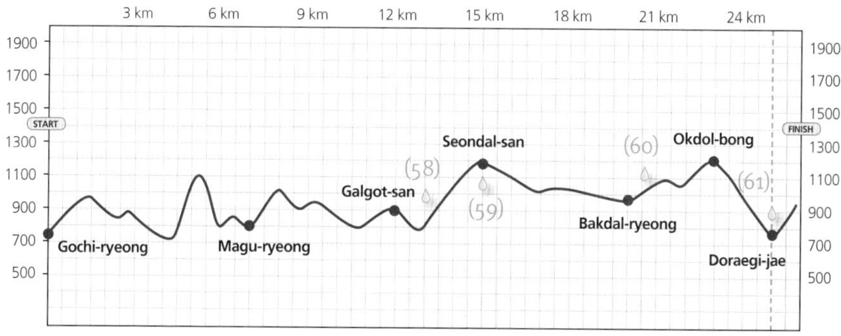

Water Stops

(58) Neujeunmogi: **N37°01'21" E128°42'09"**
(59) Seondal-san: **N37°02'19" E128°43'00"**
(60) Sansin-gak: **N37°01'32" E128°45'20"**
(61) Doraegi-jae: **N37°02'6" E128°48'06"**

maintaining its current altitude of about 850 m ABSL. At the second helipad, there will be a signpost, and the trail heads north, ascending 200 m for the next 800 meters to an unnamed peak, standing at 1,096 m ABSL and hosting good views to the north. From there, it's a 2 km descent through more splendid wooded forest to the pass of Magu-ryeong*, which is connected by an extension of PR935 running in a north-south direction.

* Magu-ryeong 마구령 C2

Some 10 km to your south is the village area of Imgok-ri 임곡리, and 4 km away to the north is the village area of Namdae-ri 남대리. At Magu-ryeong, you will see a fairly new two-meter high stele. It was actually erected there on October 16, 2007, the same day we stumbled out of the bush onto the pass to find a digger and dumptrucks working on it. There may well be some extra amenities in the area now; however, there is no water in this area unless you search down both sides of the road.

Casper stele of Magu-ryeong

Buseok-sa temple grounds

Magu-ryeong 마구령 C2 → Galgot-san 갈곶산 E2 5km (2:30)

From Magu-ryeong, you climb straight up a small brow and down into a saddle, then walk for the next kilometer, ascending 200 m in altitude before arriving at an unnamed peak marked by a helipad and located at 1,057 m ABSL. For the next three easterly kilometers, there is some beautiful, easygoing walking, meandering through an impressive forest region as the trail gradually descends to the peak of Galgot-san at 966 m ABSL. The wooded peak of Galgot-san is quite an important part of your walk because the easterly track you have been walking on suddenly arrives at a T-junction. If you look south or to your right, you may see ribbons gleaming in the shade of some trees. Past those ribbons, there is a track going down to the grand and famous temple of Buseok-sa*. It is only a 3.5 km walk down to the backyard of this picturesque and well-sited monastery steeped in remarkable history. If the monks see you stumbling out of the tree line from the sacred Baekdu-daegan...well, you may end up presenting them with a good impression.

* Buseok-sa 부석사 D3

Buseok-sa is a huge and majestic temple built in AD 676 by a monk known as Uisang, under the instruction of King Munmu of the Silla Dynasty, which

Mighty Buseok-sa

reigned from 57 BC to AD 935. One of the many legends kindled throughout the history of the temple's existence is related to the large, flat boulder that can be found on the temple's grounds. Ancient records say that Buseok-sa's founder, the great monk Uisang, was followed back to the Silla Kingdom from China by a dragon, which had transformed from a maiden who loved him and became his guardian.

When Uisang was commissioned by the monarch to build monasteries around the kingdom, he selected this site to build a great temple. However, he was met by a vehement crowd of local farmers who rejected the idea of the introduction of a foreign religion called Buddhism at this place on their holy mountain, where they had been worshipping since time immemorial. His dragon-girlfriend decided to intervene. She invisibly swept down from the sky and uplifted a huge boulder, levitating it above the heads of the mob, which in fear of Uisang's magical powers promptly acquiesced to his construction of a Buddhist temple at the site. In return, Uisang built a *sansin-gak* at the rear of the temple out of respect for the spirit of that mountain, which the locals had long venerated.

That boulder still lies just to the side of the famous Main Hall, the oldest remaining wooden building in Korea, and is named the *buseok*, or "floating rock"; the monastery is named after it. Buseok-sa is one of the best religious sites to visit in the nation, and we highly recommend that you stop by if at all possible.

It also has accommodations that may be available to you, and an occasional Temple Stay program, if you ask in a polite and genuine manner. If you stay over, you may be expected to attend some of the early morning prayer sessions in the ancient main temple, a haunting and moving experience. Some of the monks at these bigger venues speak English and will be keen to hear of your pursuit of the

TRANSPORT INFO

Leaving the trail at Buseok-sa: Buses run from Buseok-sa to Yeongju 15 times a day from 6:50 am to 8:30 pm, passing through Punggi-eup on the way. Buses run to Buseok-sa from Yeongju 15 times a day and from Punggi 20 times a day. Buseok Taxi is also available (T. 054-633-3103 or 054-636-1280).

spiritual energy of the Baekdu-daegan. Also in the area, at the entrance to the temple grounds, are many shops, curio-sellers, restaurants and *minbak*.

Galgot-san 갈곶산 → Seondal-san 선달산 E2 3km (1:45)

From Galgot-san, it is a 160 m descent for 1 km to the pass of Neujeunmogi 늦은목이. The pass is located in a large clearing under the forest canopy, which is big enough for a tent. This track junction marks roughly the halfway point of the 26 km leg to Doraegi-jae. There is also water(58) to be found at this junction on either side of the pass.

The walk from Neujeunmogi to the top of your first peak, Seondal-san (1,239m ABSL), sees you climbing in a northerly direction, ascending about 430 m in altitude over the next 2 km of distance. It's a strong, vigorous walk all the way to the top, with no false crests. At Seondal-san, there is a 1.5 m stele that appears recent. The top is open and flat, with good views to the east and south back down toward Murya Dam 물야 저수지 and Ojeon-ri 오전리. There is also a signboard about the Baekdu-daegan that was erected by the Yeongju Forest Service. Loosely translated, it states that the Baekdu-daegan is the roof of the Korean peninsula, running continuously with high and steep mountains, while its highest mountain, Baekdu-san in North Korea, is the national sacred mountain of all mountains and the main source of flowing energy emitted through the Baekdu-daegan.

Seondal-san 선달산 E2 → Bakdal-ryeong 박달령 G2 5km (2:20)

From Seondal-san, you are back on top of the ridge, and your walk will take you for the next 5 km in a northeast-to-east-to-southeast direction at altitudes ranging from 1,000 to 1,250 m ABSL. About 1 km after Seondal-san, you come to a signpost that marks the location of a spring(59) 150 meters down the south side of the ridge. Follow the trail down until you come to another signpost directing you left toward a small crop of rocks surrounded by mini-shoots of bamboo. Hidden in the cover will be the spring. Back on the ridge, you arrive about 500 meters later at a small rest area marked by a board with

Stele at Seondal-san

some information on it. From there, the trail extends in a gentle southeast direction for the next 3 km, passing though stands of deciduous forest until it arrives at a helipad. From the helipad, it is about 1 km to the pass of Bakdal-ryeong.

LODGING

Taking the trail heading southeast from this pass down the Keunteo-gol gorge 큰터골, you can find accommodation. A *minbak* is located in the small village along the banks of the stream; it is called the Seondal-san Minbak 선달산 민박 (T. 054-672-6587), and it's a great spot with large, reasonably priced rooms (30,000 won), a fully equipped kitchen and a nice outdoor area. About another 3 km down the road, past the dam where the road meets PR915, is the village of Ojeon-ri. Another kilometer to the northeast of that junction, you can find the Hanmi Minbak 한미 민박 (T. 054-672-2400).

Bakdal-ryeong G2 박달령 → Okdol-bong 옥돌봉 H2 3km (1:20)

From Bakdal-ryeong*, you ascend southeast for about 250 meters up to a spot height of 1,015 m ABSL. From there, you descend for 1 km into a depression located at 980 m ABSL, where you begin your ascent up to Okdol-bong. It is about a 1.5 km walk to Okdol-bong, ascending 260 m in altitude and passing some benches near its peak, which is located at 1,244 m ABSL. At its summit, there are some great views to the southeast.

* Bakdal-ryeong 박달령 G2

Bakdal-ryeong ("hardwood pass") is located 970 m ABSL on a mountain road traversing north-south over its saddle. It is an open pass, located in quite a remote area. However, there is a lot of information and attractions at this pass to stop and appreciate. When you walk out of the bush, you come onto a large cement helipad that is surrounded by a flat, open grassy area, giving you an opportunity to stretch out and facilitate a tent. To your left, on the same side of the pass as the helipad, there are some ablutions, with a spring(60) located crudely nearby. On the other side of the road, you will see a number of structures, notably a beautiful 2.5 m stele erected on October 18, 2006. It sits in the middle of a rock-fringed garden in front of a lovely wooden shelter. On the south side of the trail, you will see another large information board on the Baekdu-daegan next to a large wooden bench carved from a single piece of timber.

Behind those items, up on its own flat piece of land, you will see a small shrine. This is the *sansin-gak* of Bakdal-ryeong. Information found at this area states that Bakdal-ryeong is located between Seondal-san and Okdol-bong. In the past, it was frequented by peddlers and travelers moving between Gyeongsangbuk-do in the south and Gangwon-do in the north. The *sansin-gak* was remodeled in 1994, and religious services to the mountain spirit are performed here on the eighth day of every fourth moon (by the lunar calendar). You may also see some other large wooden tablets at this pass. The elongated one standing by itself, looking not dissimilar to a tombstone, has a poetic message on it stating:

> Let's take the lead in loving nature and protecting the environment.
> Keep the area clean always when in use.
> Here is a mountaineers' resting site.
> Bakdal-ryeong is an important point on the Baekdudaegan.

Aptly, the message is carved in wood. *Bakdal* is a kind of birch, and *ryeong* means "pass." There are also numerous other information boards from here on in toward Doraegi-jae, describing the rich diversity of the forest on the trail. We counted some 16 different species advertised on various boards, one of them being a more notable find that you will discover near the end of this leg. Once you've rested and refreshed yourself at this marvelous pass, you can now head off on the trail for the final 6 km to Doraegi-jae.

Okdol-bong 옥돌봉 → Doraegi-jae 도래기재 H2 2km (1:10)

From the summit, the trail turns northeast, where, 300 meters into your descent, you arrive at a helipad. From the pad, it is all downhill for the next 2.5 km through deciduous forest until you spill out at Doraegi-jae*. However, 600 meters after the helipad, located in the middle of nowhere, you come across an area with a boutique white picket fence and stools. For a moment, you may wonder if you have stumbled onto a European cemetery, a cottage, or the remnants of a cricket oval. However, inside the perimeter of the white picket fence is a royal azalea tree, or *cheoljjuk-namu*, determined in 2006 to be 550 years old. It is an impressive, wrangled, maddened-looking tree that stands there spreading its twisted branches outward in a "Hey, here I am" manner, lonesome on a forgotten trail. From this rare tree, it's only an hour's walk for the last 2 km to the road pass at Doraegi-jae. You'll be assisted by some steps closer to the bottom. Near the bottom, there are some signs indicating that you are walking on, or over, some old tunnels, but we couldn't locate any. At the pass, there is one old tunnel, located about 200 meters down the southern side of the road at Doraegi-jae, but it now appears to be locked up.

550-year-old royal azalea

* Doraegi-jae 도래기재 H2

Doraegi-jae straddles PR88 at about 770 m ABSL. At the pass, there is a tunnel with a nature bridge running over it, supporting the safe migration of animals over the road and, likewise, allowing traffic to pass through the pass without running wildlife over. The nearest place to find water(61) can be reached by turning left or north and walking about 200 meters down to an elbow in the road. There, on the left-hand side, you will find a clearing in the bush that has a stream with year-round water.

TRANSPORT INFO

Leaving the trail at Doraegi-jae: Although the pass appears to be quite isolated, it can be busy with vehicular traffic. Doraegi-jae is located between the small settlement of Geumjeong 금정, about 4 km to the northeast, and the larger village of Seobyeok-ri 서벽리 5 km to the southeast. Buses run from Geumjeong through to Seobyeok-ri and on to Chunyang-myeon 춘양면 two times a day at 8:10 am and 6 pm and return to Geumjeong twice a day. Chunyang-myeon is a decent-sized town located 12 km southeast of Seobyeok-ri on PR88, and buses can be taken from here to Bonghwa-gun and on to larger centers. Chunyang Taxi can be reached at 054-673-4123.

LODGING

Six kilometers south of Doraegi-jae is the road junction township of Seobyeok-ri on PR915, consisting of some accommodations. Located on the main road is the police station, on the left-hand side of which is a *minbak*. There is also a traditional-style home named the Songi-maeul Minbak 송이마을 민박 located about two blocks inside the village, next to the stream that runs through the heart of this township. This lovely place has a traditional-style porch and paper windows and will cost you about 30,000 won for a room, including use of the kitchen and bathroom. In the village on the main road, there are a couple of small shops where you can restock for the next leg. One of the shops is owned and operated by an old man who does his math on an abacus—so don't expect to be short-changed. The small village is a great place to stay over where you can chill out and have a beer or *soju* under the village guardian tree with the rest of the locals...the bliss that is rural Korea.

TWO DAYS

45.0km

SECTION 11

TAEBAEK-SAN PROVINCIAL PARK

Doraegi-jae → Pi-jae

17
16
15
14
13
12
10
9
11
8
7
6
5
4
3
2
1

Seoul
Daejeon
Namwon
Jinju
Gwangju
Jeju

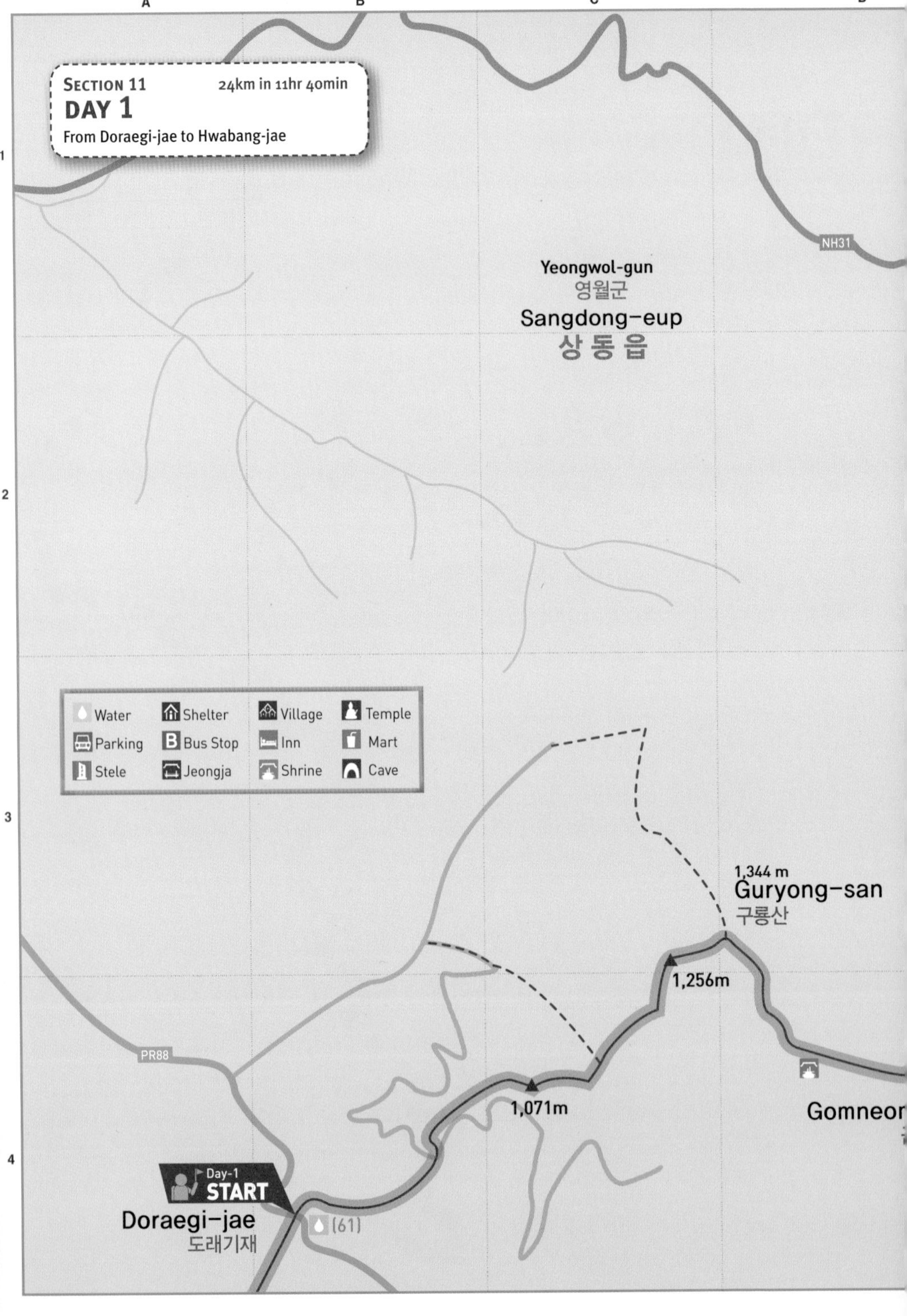
A
B
C
D
1
2
3
4
SECTION 11
24km in 11hr 40min
DAY 1
From Doraegi-jae to Hwabang-jae
NH31
Yeongwol-gun
영월군
Sangdong-eup
상동읍
Water
Shelter
Village
Temple
Parking
Bus Stop
Inn
Mart
Stele
Jeongja
Shrine
Cave
1,344 m
Guryong-san
구룡산
1,256m
PR88
1,071m
Gomneor
Day-1
START
Doraegi-jae
도래기재
(61)

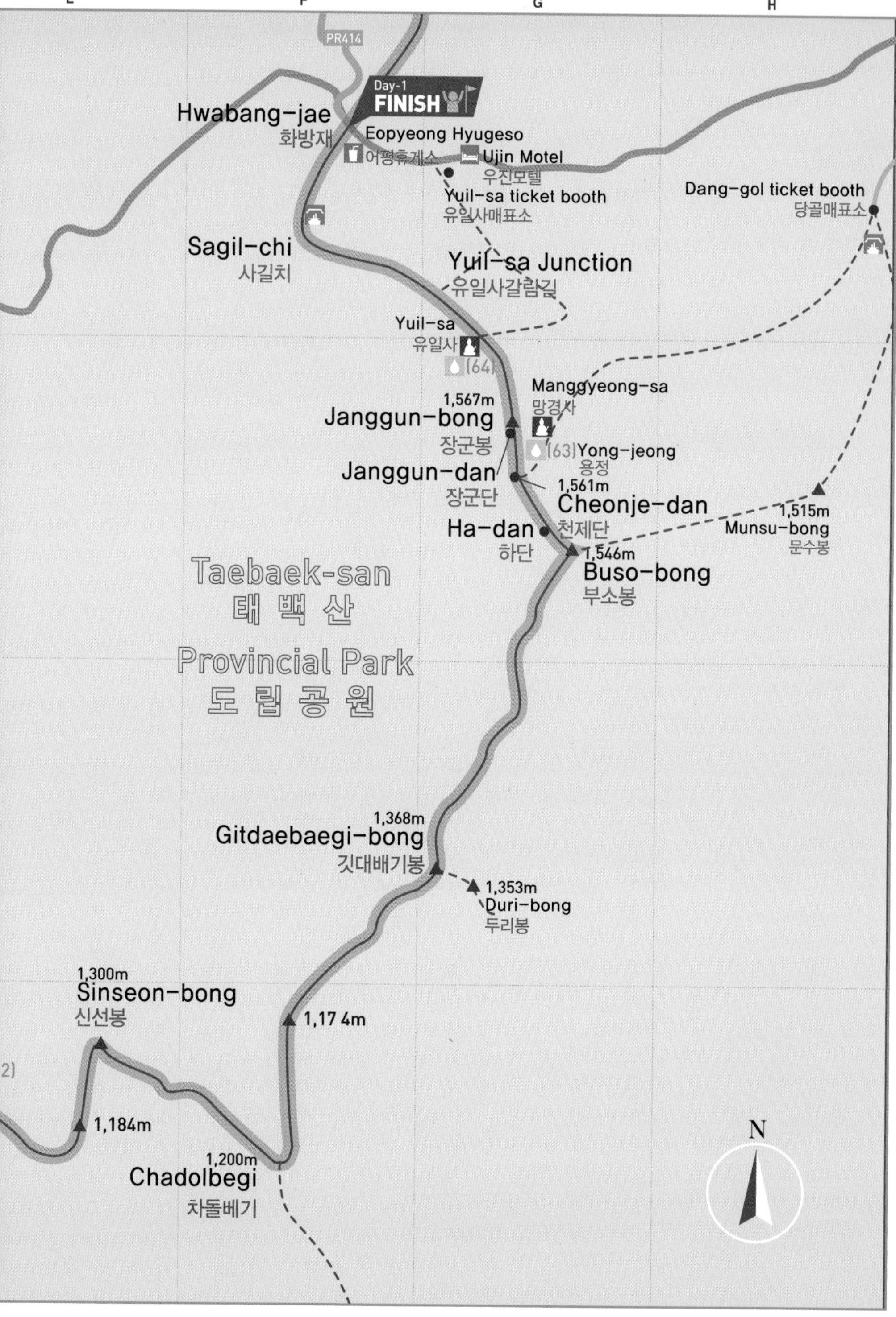

E
F
G
H
PR414
Day-1
FINISH
Hwabang-jae
화방재
Eopyeong Hyugeso
어평휴게소
Ujin Motel
우진모텔
Yuil-sa ticket booth
유일사매표소
Dang-gol ticket booth
당골매표소
Sagil-chi
사길치
Yuil-sa Junction
유일사갈림길
Yuil-sa
유일사
(64)
Manggyeong-sa
망경사
1,567m
Janggun-bong
장군봉
(63) Yong-jeong
용정
Janggun-dan
장군단
1,561m
Cheonje-dan
천제단
1,515m
Munsu-bong
문수봉
Ha-dan
하단
1,546m
Buso-bong
부소봉
Taebaek-san
태 백 산
Provincial Park
도 립 공 원
1,368m
Gitdaebaegi-bong
깃대배기봉
1,353m
Duri-bong
두리봉
1,300m
Sinseon-bong
신선봉
1,17 4m
62)
1,184m
1,200m
Chadolbegi
차돌베기
N

DAY 1

From Doraegi-jae to Hwabang-jae

- **Distance:** 24km
- **Time:** 11hr 40min

This leg from Doraegi-jae is the beginning of another geographical stage of the Baekdu-daegan. The ridge begins in a northeast manner, starting at Dragon Mountain, where a giant asp was once pulled from the heavens. The tombs on the ridge's summit whisper and guide you to the edges of the Taebaek-sanmaek range, the portal of the mountain gods. When you walk in the fall, the trail becomes an Eden of stunning forest that hallucinates its way through autumnal stands of vermillion fire. Breaking from the blazoned forest, the trail willows under the sacred peak of Taebaek-san as the magical loom of Cheonje-dan altar pulls you up its oil-stained shards of history, which jet you to the heavens like a sonic bolt of light.

Doraegi-jae 도래기재 B4 → Guryong-san 구룡산 D3 5.3km (2:40)

From Doraegi-jae, the Baekdu-daegan trail continues steeply northeast up a flight of steps, meeting a single tomb on a piece of flat ground some 250 meters later. A kilometer later, you come across a mountain road that traverses the ridge. From there, the trail continues ascending steadily, passing a helipad, and then arrives 500 meters later at another mountain road marked by a wooden shelter, allowing you to stop and rest. From there, it's a good 1.5 km northeast

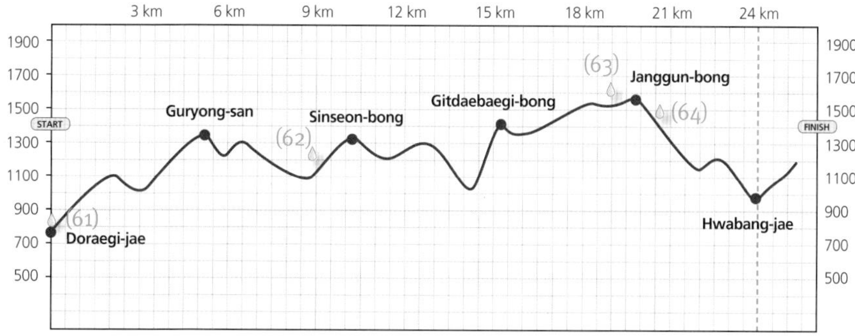

WATER STOPS

(62) Gomneomi-jae: **N37°02'46" E128°52'15"**
(63) Yongjeong spring: **N37°05'42" E128°55'14"**
(64) Yuil-sa: **N37°05'27" E128°55'13"**

climb up to Guryong-san (1,256m), ascending 350 m in altitude. The final meters to Guryong-san are quite steep, but you can be assured that you have broken the camel's back and reached the high ground of the Baekdu-daegan. Guryong-san is the highest mountain between Okdol-bong, back on the Soebaek-san leg, and the Taebaek-san range, which begins at the Gitdaebaegi area some 10 km further on. It also forms the middle between the Sobaek-sanmaek and the Taebaek-sanmaek and is one of the major water sources for the Nakdong-gang River in the south and the Namhan-gang River in the northwest, which flows into the Han-gang River in Seoul. The name Guryong-san ("nine dragons mountain") comes from a legend about a local woman carrying an urn of water back home from an alpine spring who saw nine dragons rising up toward the heavens. She managed to catch one of the dragons by its tail and pull it back down, and it turned into a snake upon landing on this ridge.

Guryong-san 구룡산 D3 → Sinseon-bong 신선봉 E4 5km (2:10)

From the summit of Guryong-san, the Baekdu-daegan trail makes a steep descent in a southeasterly direction and widens its girth, almost forming an old 4WD track. The trail will begin to cover more deciduous forest, containing species of *Celastraceae* and *Symplocaceae*. A kilometer on from Guryong-san, along a heavily wooded trail, you arrive at a set of benches next to a signpost. Down the southwestern side of this pass, you may be able to see a small wooden shack. This is in fact a *sansin-gak*. Inside it is a wooden tablet—it might be wrapped in white paper—mounted into a block of wood. The significance of a wooden tablet being used instead of a painting is that this is an old Confucian style or method of enshrining spirits. The use of Chinese characters is just part of the style; the characters usually make up the name of the person or, in this case, the spirit that is being enshrined. Using a painting also means enshrining the image of the spirit or figure that has been painted. Sometimes the shrine will have both a painting and a wooden tablet, thereby combining the two methods.

Sanshin-gak 1 km after Guryong-san

Back on the trail, the Baekdu-daegan continues in a southeasterly direction, where it soon turns into an old vehicle track continuing east for 2 km until it arrives at a mountain road that meets the ridge from the south. This junction is called Gomneomi-jae 곰넘이재 and is marked by a signpost. There is water(62) to be found on both sides of this pass. The closest source is only 50 meters down the mountain road on the south side of the ridge. It may be dry. If you bush-bash for about 300 meters down the north side of the ridge in a northeast direction, you will find a stream located at the bottom of a valley. It's a bit of an effort, but if you need water, then that's where it is. From Gomneomi-jae, the trail becomes an easterly 4WD track for 1 km, climbing 150 m in altitude before reaching an unnamed peak at 1,184 m ABSL. Here, the 4WD track comes to an end and the trail veers north, climbing up a series of new staircases toward Sinseon-bong at 1,300 m ABSL. On its summit is a tomb, offering more great views to the west. From Sinseon-bong, the trail makes a distinctive turn to the southeast, marking the beginning of a marvelous trail as it enters the Taebaek-sanmaek.

Sinseon-bong 신선봉 E4 → Gitdaebaegi-bong 깃대배기봉 G3

5km (2:50)

The trail from Shinseon-bong descends southeast, undulating its way through tall, beautiful deciduous forest. If you are fortunate enough to be doing this leg in the autumnal period, then you are in for a treat of vermilion sun-fire. As you walk along what is a windy and sometimes thin ridge, the bright hues of the autumn trail cast your face in an orange prism of color. The trail meanders for

Roger captured in a vermilion fire

another 2 km before it arrives at its last southern waypoint of the journey, called Chadolbegi 차돌베기 located at about 1,200 m ABSL. At Chadolbegi, there should be a signpost with some benches for you to sit down on and have a break. From this area, the Baekdu-daegan trail begins its journey north on a very good track that remains consistent in altitude for the next 3 km. After a kilometer, it swerves slightly northeast, beginning a 2 km climb up to Gitdaebaegi-bong at 1,368 m ABSL. At the summit of Gitdaebaegi-bong, continue walking north on the wooded summit for a short distance until you come across a small Baekdu-daegan stele in the ground identifying Gitdaebaegi-bong's height.

Gitdaebaegi-bong 깃대배기봉 G3 → Janggun-bong 장군봉 G2

4.5km (2:15)

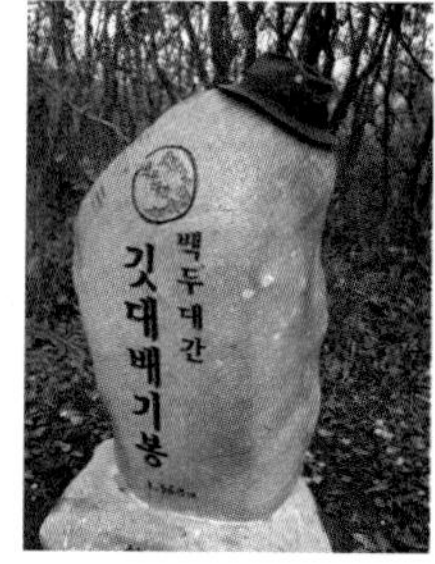

As you exit the wooded summit of Gitdaebaegi-bong, you see, far away to the north, the peak of Taebaek-san, with its prominent Cheonje-dan altar hunched like a black bear on its peak. The vegetation along the trail now becomes more barren as you begin to gain altitude on the leg to Taebaek-san, 4 km away. Distinctive yew trees return to the haunted ridge, standing there in their transfixed, gnarled manner. About 3 km later, you should arrive at the summit of Buso-bong 부소봉, where the trail heads in a northwest direction, dropping into a saddle where you will come across the first of three altars.

Korean Yew Tree

The yew tree actually holds spiritual significance internationally, as pointed out by David Mason in this paragraph: "These ancient evergreen survivors, found only on Korea's highest alpine ridges, are a famous feature of Taebaek-san's peak-areas. They are related to the yew trees common to northern Europe, held sacred by the Celts and other pagan peoples. Just like Koreans, they regarded them as symbols of immortality, markers of sacred spots and powerful charms against bad fortune and malign spirits. It is considered quite unlucky to damage one. Yew trees have remained symbolic to Christians as symbols of immortality and resurrection, and are highly respected by Buddhists. Korean shamans consider them to be enlightened ancestral beings."

The Three Altars G2

* Ha-dan 하단

The first, or lower, altar is known as Ha-dan and stands about 1.5 m high, assembled in an exposed square shape of loose bits of local rock like a stage. The age of this structure is estimated to be the same as the other two altars located on Cheonje-dan and Janggun-bong, which are known to be at least 1,000 years old. One popular belief is that Ha-dan was built for Hwanung, the son of the King of Heaven, Hwanin. Nowadays, it is hardly visited by local hikers, and shamans rarely hold any rituals at it; you will find it sitting in the saddle south of Cheonje-dan like a sulking younger sibling. The encounter with this altar may give you the first invigorating sense that you are now entering an area of deep sacred and spiritual significance to Korean shamanistic history. From Ha-dan, you can see the main altar of this area, which is called Cheonje-dan and located at 1,560 m ABSL on the summit area of Janggun-bong. When you walk out onto

The lonesome Ha-dan altar in Taebaek

the lower reaches of Janggun-bong, you enter onto a large plateau where, right in the middle, you instantly see the spectacular marvel of the middle altar known as Cheonje-dan.

* Cheonje-dan 천제단

Cheonje-dan, meaning "heaven ceremony shrine," is an oval, nine-tiered structure made of oil-stained shards of natural rock. Local legend claims that Cheonje-dan was built for the mythological founder of Korea, Dangun, who was the son of Hwanung, whom the lower altar may represent. It is by far the most visited and finest-looking structure of the three. On October 3 of every year, the National Foundation Holiday, large, colorful celebrations take place at Cheonje-dan, celebrating the mythical founding of the first Korean Kingdom in 2333 BC. Other ceremonies occur on the third day of the tenth moon (by the lunar calendar), and it is a rare occasion when no shamans can be found conducting rituals here, at any time of the year.

The myth associated with this site is famous and important in Korean culture. A long time ago, the King of Heaven, Hwanin, had a son called Hwanung who yearned to live on Earth. Hwanin studied earthly topography and decided that Taebaek-san was an appropriate site for the creation of a kingdom to benefit human beings. He sent his son, accompanied by the wind, rain, and clouds, down to the peak of Taebaek-san to start organizing human affairs. At about the same time, upon viewing the workings of Hwanung, a tiger and a bear yearned to become human beings as well and prayed for this to Hwanung. The heavenly lord assigned them both a test of worthiness, and while the tiger could not withstand the hardship, the bear could and was transformed into a woman named Ungnyeo (literally "bear woman"). However, as Ungnyeo had no partner to marry, she prayed to Hwanung for the blessing of a child. Hwanung sympathized with her, transformed into a man and mated with her. Ungnyeo later had a son and called him Dangun Wanggeom; he who later established a political and religious society

Cheonje-dan altar, Taebaek-san

Janggun-dan

known as the kingdom of Gojoseon ("Old Joseon") in 2333 BC, according to the myth. Represented by mandolin-shaped daggers and dolmens, the Gojoseon period is thought of as the origin of Korean civilization. At the end of his 1,900 year reign, Dangun retired as a mountain spirit, or *sansin*, in this area.

* Janggun-dan 장군단

About 250 meters further up the trail, you can see the third and last altar on this part of the ridge, Janggun-dan, meaning "guardian general altar." As it is the highest altar here, at 1,567 m ABSL, Janggun-dan is said to have been built for the King of Heaven, Hwanin. The Janggun-dan altar, perhaps due to its name and height, is well used by shamans and the like.

* Manggyeong-sa 망경사 G2

Beyond the tall stone tablet at Cheonje-dan, there is a trail going east down to one of the highest temples in South Korea, called Manggyeong-sa, which means "all-encompassing view temple." Manggyeong-sa is a fusion-style temple populated by *mudang* shamans and Buddhist monks, reclaiming local belief, so to speak. Persons who come to Manggyeong-sa are normally on a spiritual mission, seeking some form of severance from issues preventing them from progression in life. If these persons are serious about their plight, they are normally accompanied by a shaman. If you are granted permission to sleep here, you can be assured it will

Evening at Manggyeong-sa

be a busy night's rest. Throughout the night, you will sleep on one of those furiously heated Korean *ondol-bang* floors in a communal manner with every other visitor. Throughout the night, people will pass to and fro from the sleeping quarters whilst venturing to the pitch-black landscape of Cheonje-dan to perform their rituals. The night will only cost you 15,000 won per person, including a communal dinner and breakfast. Out the front of the building, there is also a small kiosk selling food items and soft drinks. Located next to the kiosk is a coffee machine. The mainly female staff is friendly to and curious about foreigners. Located at the same venue is the famous mountain spring(63) called Yong-jeong 용정, or "dragon well," which is claimed to be the highest spring in South Korea. The tablet at Yong-jeong translates as follows:

> Since ancient times, when they served a ritual for the worship of the heavenly gods, they used this mineral spring water from the highest spring of our country (1,470m). This water is the best among the famous 100 spring waters in Korea, because the sun rising from the East Sea shines on this spring before any other in the morning. Please feel the refreshing taste of this spring water, as it is incomparable with others, and be showered with the energy of Taebaek-san.

There is a legend saying that the carp, which symbolizes richness, fecundity, and prosperity, could be a dragon if it could pass up though the *Yong-mun,* or dragon gate (a set of fierce rapids in the middle of the Yellow River in China). The Korean version says that if a carp holding the same virtues can successfully pass up the Nakdong-gang River and through the fast-flowing waters of a swamp and cave to get to this spring, then it will also turn into a dragon.

Yong-jeong shrine at Manggyeong-sa

At the center of Manggyeong-sa is a *sansin-gak*. Inside this structure, there is a triad of deities featuring Dangun, a *sansin*, and Dokseong.

Janggun-bong 장군봉 G2 → Hwabang-jae 화방재 F1 4.2km (1:45)

The trail begins its descent to Hwabang-jae (900m) in a north-to-northwest direction as it passes through more stands of yew trees. About 1 km later, on the western side of the ridge, is a steep downhill track that goes to the temple of Yuil-sa 유일사. A nunnery, this temple was built in the middle of the 20th century and is tucked under the cold, hard, stony cliffs of the western ridge of the Baekdu-daegan. You can also find spring water(64) at this temple. Back on the ridge, the trail continues in a northwest direction, passing a *doltap* that marks a track junction called Yuil-sa Gallimgil 유일사 갈림길. From there, the trail veers west for 1 km, reaching an area called Sagil-chi* that contains a *sansin-gak*. Inside the *sansin-gak* is an impressive painting of the *sansin* for this pass.

* Sagil-chi 사길치 F1

When most people walked on foot or rode horses, Sagil-chi was the gateway to Gangwon-do. However, wild animals and bandit gangs were grave threats to the travelers, who thus established this *sansin-gak* and held rituals at it to beseech the Taebaek-san mountain spirit to ensure their safety. The rituals evolved into a local institution, recording 200 years of its major ceremonies, the longest such case in Korea and something the local community remains proud of. From Sagil-chi, it is only a 1 km walk down to the pass of Hwabang-jae, passing a small cabbage patch located in a lull during the last bound to the road pass.

* Hwabang-jae 화방재 F1

The road pass of Hwabang-jae is connected by NH31 with the mountain city of Taebaek, located 10 km to the east on NH35, and the riverside junction town of Sangdong-eup 상동읍 6 km to the west. Hwabang-jae is serviced by a large gas station and the Eopyeong Hyugeso 어평 휴게소, which serves hot food and cold beverages.

TRANSPORT INFO

Leaving the trail at Hwabang-jae: Buses run from Hwabang-jae into Taebaek five times a day from 9:10 am to 7:55 pm. Buses from Taebaek run to Hwabang-jae six times a day from 6 am to 7:55 pm.

LODGING

Minbak accommodation is available on the second floor of the Eopyeong Hyugeso, located at the pass. The nearest motel is the Ujin Motel 우진 모텔 (T. 033-553-6448) which is located about 800 meters east of the pass on NH31.

TAEBAEK-SAN PROVINCIAL PARK 태백산 도립공원

The Taebaek-san Provincial Park is a popular area for hikers. The major town of the area, aptly named Taebaek, is the hub of this region. More useful information on Taebaek can be found at the city's website: http://tour.taebaek.go.kr/site/en. Taebaek is a modern city and has all the facilities that travelers or hikers require for re-nourishing their tired bodies, including bars, hotels, *minbak*, Western takeaways, movie theaters, and shopping. Taebaek is understandably well serviced by a good public transportation system to and from the provincial park.

Taebaek-san Provincial Park was founded in 1989, and you may wonder why it is not yet a National Park. The Taebaek Mountains are part of the Taebaek-sanmaek mountain range, which runs down the east coast of Korea from Hwanryeong-san (1,268m) in North Korea, skirting along the East Sea before reaching Taebaek-san at Janggun-bong. It then continues south along the east coast of South Korea, forming the Nakdong-jeongmaek, before meeting the mouth of the river it creates, the Nakdong River, in Busan some 800 km later. This mountain range averages over 1,000 m in altitude and is also the source of South Korea's other prominent river, the Han-gang, which runs northwest through Seoul.

TRANSPORT INFO

Buses leave Taebaek Bus Terminal 태백 시외버스터미널 for the Dang-gol ticket booth 당골 매표소 park entrance 27 times a day from 7:38 am to 10:25 pm and for the Yuil-sa ticket booth 유일사 매표소 18 times a day from 6:30 am to 10:35 pm. Buses leave Dong Seoul Bus Terminal for Taebaek eight times a day from 6 am to 10 pm. Buses also regularly leave Taebaek for all the major cities of Gangwon-do (Chuncheon, Wonju, Donghae, Gangneung, etc.).

SECTION 11
21km in 9hr 35min
DAY 2
From Hwabang-jae to Pi-jae
1
2
3
4
A
B
C
1,281m
Bidan-bong
비단봉
Ssuabat-ryeong
쑤아발령
Day-2
FINISH
900m
Pi-jae
피재
NH35
1,418m
Geumdae-bong
금대봉
1,303m
Maebong-san
매봉산
Nakdong-jeongmaek
낙동정맥
NH38
Ssari-jae
싸리재
← Gohan-ri
고한리
1,442m
Eundae-bong
은대봉
Jajaknamu-saemteo
NH38

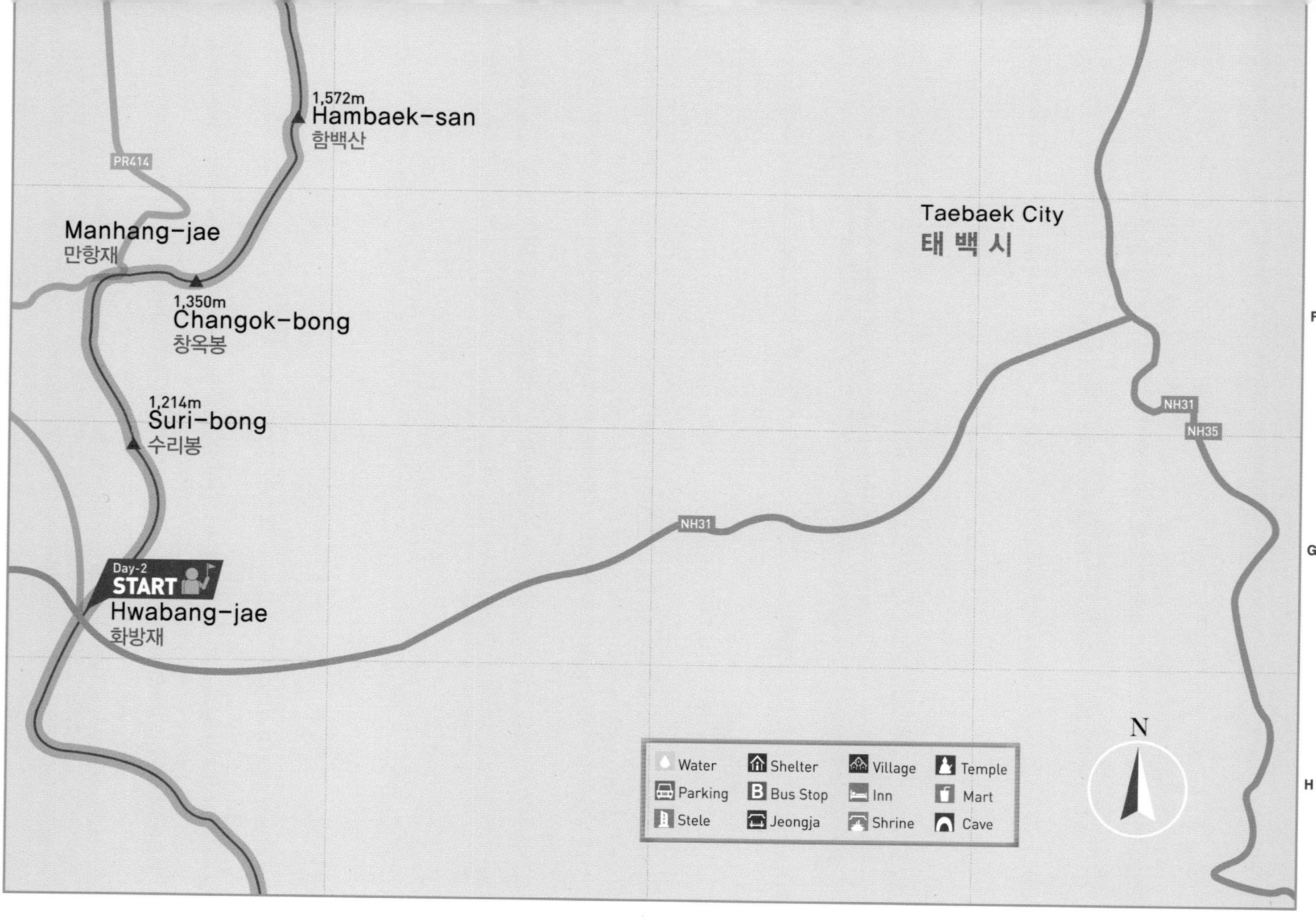
1,572m
Hambaek-san
함백산
PR414
Manhang-jae
만항재
1,350m
Changok-bong
창옥봉
1,214m
Suri-bong
수리봉
Day-2
START
Hwabang-jae
화방재
NH31
Taebaek City
태 백 시
NH31
NH35
Water
Shelter
Village
Temple
Parking
Bus Stop
Inn
Mart
Stele
Jeongja
Shrine
Cave
N
F
G
H

DAY 2 From Hwabang-jae to Pi-jae

• Distance: 21km
• Time: 9hr 35min

This long leg leaves the grandeur of the altars and temples of Taebaek-san and heads into the wooded ridge and fairly average zone north of the pass at Hwabang-jae. The first 7 km sees you arriving at your highest feature for today, Hambaek-san (1,572m). Fused at the summit, with its many cairns and small shrines, is a communications mast. Carrying on north, the trail sees you walk past your only water spring of the day and then over a vehicular tunnel drilled through the Baekdu-daegan at Dumundong-jae before sweeping east and arriving at the small wind turbine village near Maebong-san. A couple of kilometers later, you walk out onto the pass at Pi-jae, which is also the junction of another well-known long distance walk in Korea called the Nakdong-jeongmaek.

Hwabang-jae 화방재 G1 → Manhang-jae 만항재 F1 4km (1:45)

The Baekdu-daegan trail begins on the other side of the road, next to a mass of ribbons tied to a tree that is located between two homes, one of them quite dilapidated. Behind the homes stands a pine forest. Heading north, the trail ascends 300 m in altitude over the next 1.2 km to the summit of Suri-bong 수리봉, located at 1,214 m ABSL. Planted into the ground at the summit of Suri-bong is a

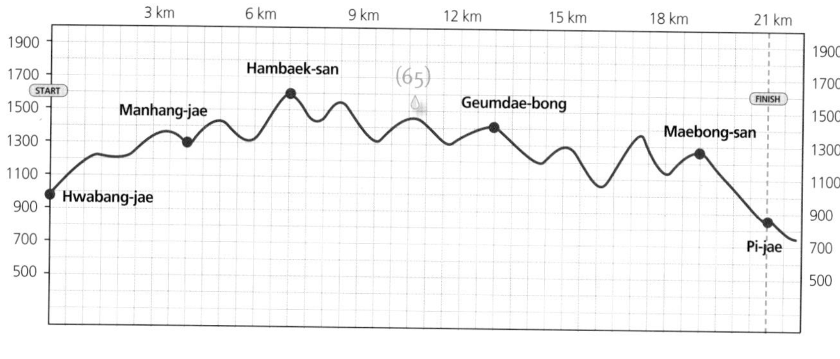

WATER STOPS (65) Jajaknamu-saemteo: **N37°10'33" E128°55'06"**

small stone stele. It was put there on September 1, 2007. Continuing northwest, the Baekdu-daegan meets a military facility, protected by a barbed wire fence, about 1.5 km later. Follow the trail past the facility until it comes onto a mountain road, which then takes you to a large, well-maintained helipad. From there, you can descend down the mountain road north for about 400 meters through pine forest to the pass of Manhang-jae, located on PR414.

Manhang-jae 만항재 F1 → Hambaek-san 함백산 E1 3km (1:20)

From Manhang-jae, you should turn right or east and walk down the sealed road for 150 meters to the first elbow in the road. From there, leave the road and continue walking in an easterly direction toward an information board and a set of public toilets located at the bottom of a 4WD track going up the ridge. From the base of the 4WD track, the trail ascends up the ridge, passing a mast before arriving some 600 meters later at your next high point of Changok-bong 창옥봉, located at 1,350 m ABSL. From there, the trail turns north, descending past another mast down to a sealed road. Walk about 30 meters south down to an elbow in the road, where you should then turn right and follow a sealed road for about 75 meters up a slight gradient until a signboard appears on your right, or the eastern side of the road. Beyond this signboard is a large, well-defined walking track, which is the trail that takes you up to Hambaek-san at 1,572 m ABSL. It's a good, steep 250 m ascent for the next 1.2 km of trail, assisted by stairs, until you reach the area of the sacred peak of Hambaek-san. The peak area

A giant yew tree on Hambaek-san

of Hambaek-san is quite large and shares its sacred land with a nearby KBS broadcasting facility with tower. On the actual summit of Hambaek-san is a distinctive rocky outcrop adorned with numerous cairns signifying its allegiance with the heavens. Atop this mass of rocky paraphernalia is a stele. From the summit, there are good 360° views, and to the east, you can see the city of Taebaek. On the northern side of the summit, you can see the continuation of the Baekdu-daegan ridge. To get there, walk down to a helipad and then follow an old barbed wire fence in a northern direction. A short distance later, you should be able to see an impressive old yew tree located behind the fence. The yew is recognized as part of a protection effort by the Taebaek National Forest Office. The big stainless steel sign standing in front of the yew states that this particular area has as many as 112 yew trees that have been treated by specialists to protect them from premature death.

Hambaek-san 함백산 E1 → Geumdae-bong 금대봉 D3 6km (2:50)

From here on in, you will be reentering a wooded forest aligned with numerous conservation efforts to preserve the area. Other species of yew can be seen in the vicinity, including the Japanese yew (*Taxus cuspidate*), which is widely grown in East Asia and North America. The specimens to be found in this region are known to be about 170 years old. In northeastern Russia, the same species of tree has been known to live for 1,000 years. The area is also wooded in birch as it

The summit of Hambaek-san

descends in a quite comfortable and undulating manner, frequently signposted by a small board with the words "APATHUPA Mountain" on it—a path up a mountain. Two kilometers after Hambaek-san, you come across a small signboard marked at a barely visible track junction. The small sign indicates the direction east to a spring(65) named Jajaknamu-saemteo 자작나무샘터. This spring is the only one on the Baekdu-daegan in the Hambaek-san area. It rises from the birch forest about 80 meters down the eastern track and forms one of the origins of the Nakdong-gang River further to the east.

If you follow the track east, it will pass north of a temple by the name of Eunjeok-am 은적암. About 1.2 km away, on the western side of the ridge, the spring allegedly sprouts out at the temple of Jeokjo-am 적조암 and forms the sources for the Joyang-gang, Dong-gang, and Han-gang Rivers, all of which eventually filter into the West, or Yellow, Sea. The actual spring itself is almost a non-event and consists of a small plastic pipe protruding from a rather shallow area of stone, deadfall, and earth. In the drier months it may be dormant. Continuing north, the Baekdu-daegan, trail descends into a saddle and then gains about 170 m in altitude as it ascends for 1 km up to its next peak of Eundae-bong 은대봉, located at 1,442 m ABSL. The summit is also a helipad and has a small stele on it, erected in September 2006. From there, the trail descends north to the next road pass, called Ssari-jae. It has now been replaced by two tunnels directing vehicular traffic traveling on NH38 under the ridge

* Ssari-jae 싸리재 G1

On the western side of the pass, you will be able to see a small restaurant and shop near an elbow in the road. It is called the Hambaek-san Swimteo 함백산 쉼터. It sells hot food and cold drinks and is a welcome stopover to recharge at. Just before the small shop, on the northern side of the road, are some public toilets located next to a large rocky area decorated with cairns and small mountain-venerating areas. Back at the pass, there is a large, gunmetal gray 4 m high stele that is made from a darker grain of rock. The Baekdu-daegan trail from here is clearly marked and located near a ticket office. It follows a 4WD track north for about 500 meters up toward a helipad, from which it continues for another 400 meters up to your next peak of Geumdae-bong (1,418m), marked by a small stele.

TRANSPORT INFO

Joining the trail at Ssari-jae: Buses don't run up to Ssari-jae. Taxis will run up to the pass from Taebaek to the southeast or Gohan-ri to the west. Gohan Boseong Taxi can be reached at 033-592-2552, and Taebaek Taxi at 080-581-6404.

Geumdae-bong 금대봉 D3 → Maebong-san 매봉산 B3

6km (2:50)

The trail from this peak continues northeast in a descending manner for 1.5 km before flattening out briefly and turning east, where it then arrives at a saddle called Ssuabat-ryeong 쑤아밭령, marked by a signpost. From there, the trail continues east and starts an ascent up to Bidan-bong 비단봉. The ascent offers great views to the south and southwest back to the Baekdu-daegan. At the summit of Bidan-bong (1,281m), there is another small stele where you can stand and look back along the impressive ridgeline that you have been walking along for most of the day. As you bound over the crest of Bidan-bong, you might be able to see some wind turbines in the distant southeast as you begin a shallow descent into a gully area containing farmland. Now, the trail from here might get a little confusing, but the trick is to understand that you are heading for where the wind turbines are, just over a kilometer away. Look for any of the Baekdu-daegan hiking ribbons ahead of you as trail blazers. If the conditions don't allow you visibility, the compass bearing from Bidan-bong to the wind turbines is 120° southeast at 1.5 km. Crossing the farmland and navigating your way to the ridge containing the wind turbines,

Looking south from Bidan-bong

you then walk directly under these large objects, which loom like modern-day guardians of the trail, until you get to the second to last wind turbine. There, you will see some ribbons on the right-hand side of it. Take the trail next to the ribbons back into the bush and walk the next 50 m to the top of the ridge. At the top, there is a short track heading south to the peak of Maebong-san at 1,303 m ABSL. The summit of Maebong-san is marked by a small stele and a large mast. To the southwest, the summit gives you good views back toward the Baekdu-daegan. After visiting Maebong-san, you can walk back to the track junction and begin your 2.5 km descent to Pi-jae.

Maebong-san 매봉산 B3 → Pi-jae 피재 B4 2km (0:50)

About 1 km after you leave Maebong-san, you come across another small stele located in a wooded forest in front of a stainless steel signpost. This marks the trailhead of South Korea's second longest long-distance hiking trail, the Nakdong-jeongmaek. The point you are standing at now is either the start or endpoint of what is a 430 km long trail stretching down the east coast of Korea before ending at the mouth of the Nakdong-gang River in Busan,

Wind turbines with Maebong-san in the background

Korea's second largest city. As you continue to walk down to Pi-jae, you pass the front gates to a pension called the Three Seas. The signboard for this complex is written in English. Not long after that, you walk out onto the road pass of Pi-jae*, located at 900 m ABSL.

* Pi-jae 피재 B4

Pi-jae is located on NH35 between Taebaek 6 km to the south and a long stretch of road heading north toward the Gwangdong-do Dam some 15 km away. In its garden area, on the eastern side of the road, are three triangular sculptures that protrude from the ground. The largest one represents the Nakdong-gang River, the second tallest represents the Han-gang River, and the smallest represents the nearby Oship-cheon stream 오십천. Pi-jae is the source of all three of these waterways. Strikingly enough, Pi-jae is also the 500 km mark for the Baekdu-daegan.

TRANSPORT INFO

Joining the trail at Pi-jae: Buses running along NH35 between Hajang-myeon 하장면 20 km to the northwest and Taebaek 6 km south cross Pi-jae. Buses leave Taebaek for Hajang-myeon every hour from 6:25 am to 6:25 pm. If you wish to get off at Pi-jae, you must state your intention to the driver. Since it is only 6 km north of Taebaek, taxis to Pi-jae are not expensive. Taebaek Taxi can be reached at 080-581-6404.

LODGING

Located in the same garden area is an old *jeongja* that overlooks an impressive valley to the east and the Nakdong-jeongmaek ridge to the southeast. The *jeongja* is most certainly a place you could sleep at once everyone has left the pass. The benefit of Pi-jae is that there is also a small restaurant there that makes hot meals and sells cold beer and other beverages. There is also a coffee machine out the front. At the top of the garden area, near where the Baekdu-daegan continues, is a block of public toilets.

Pi-jae rest area

THREE DAYS

52.7km

SECTION 12

THE SCENIC GORGE OF MUREUNG

Pi-jae → Baekbok-ryeong

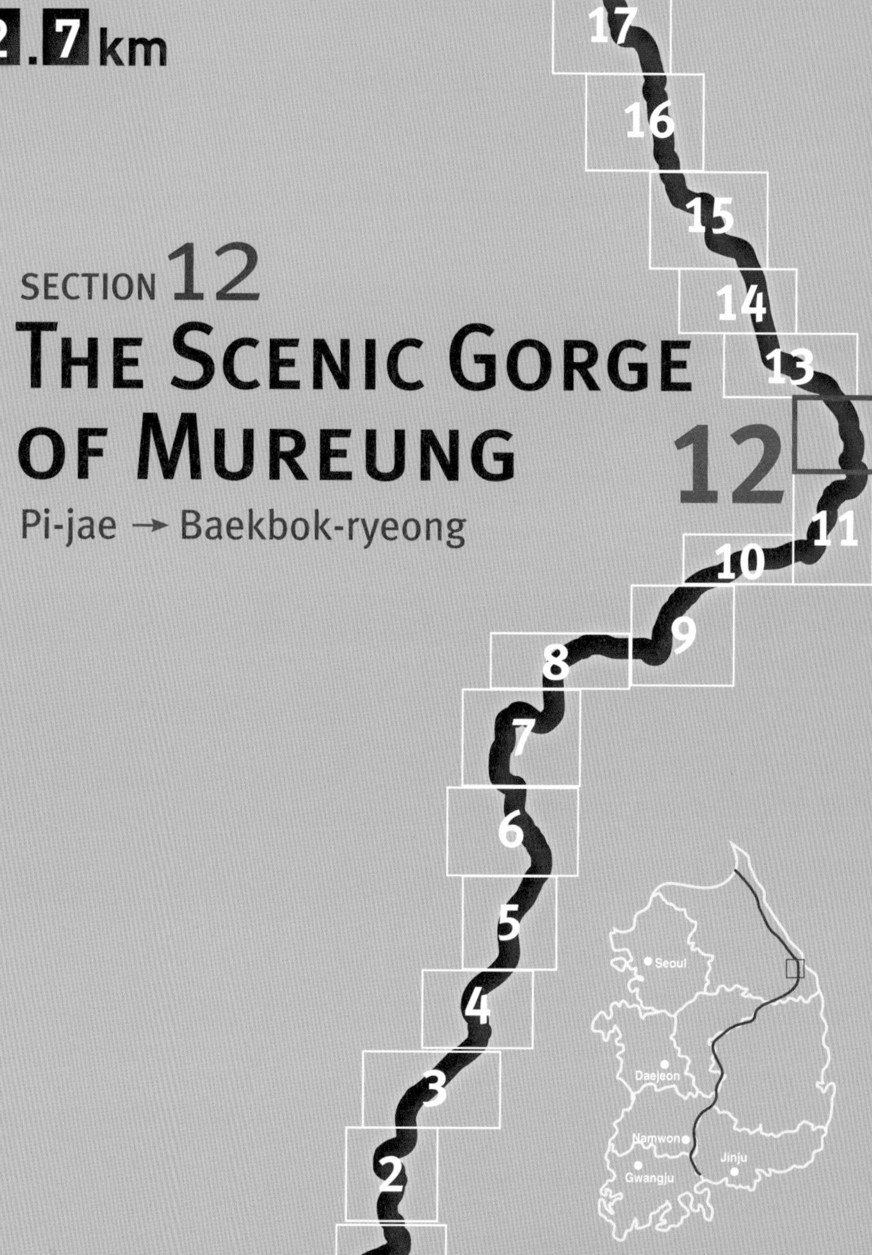

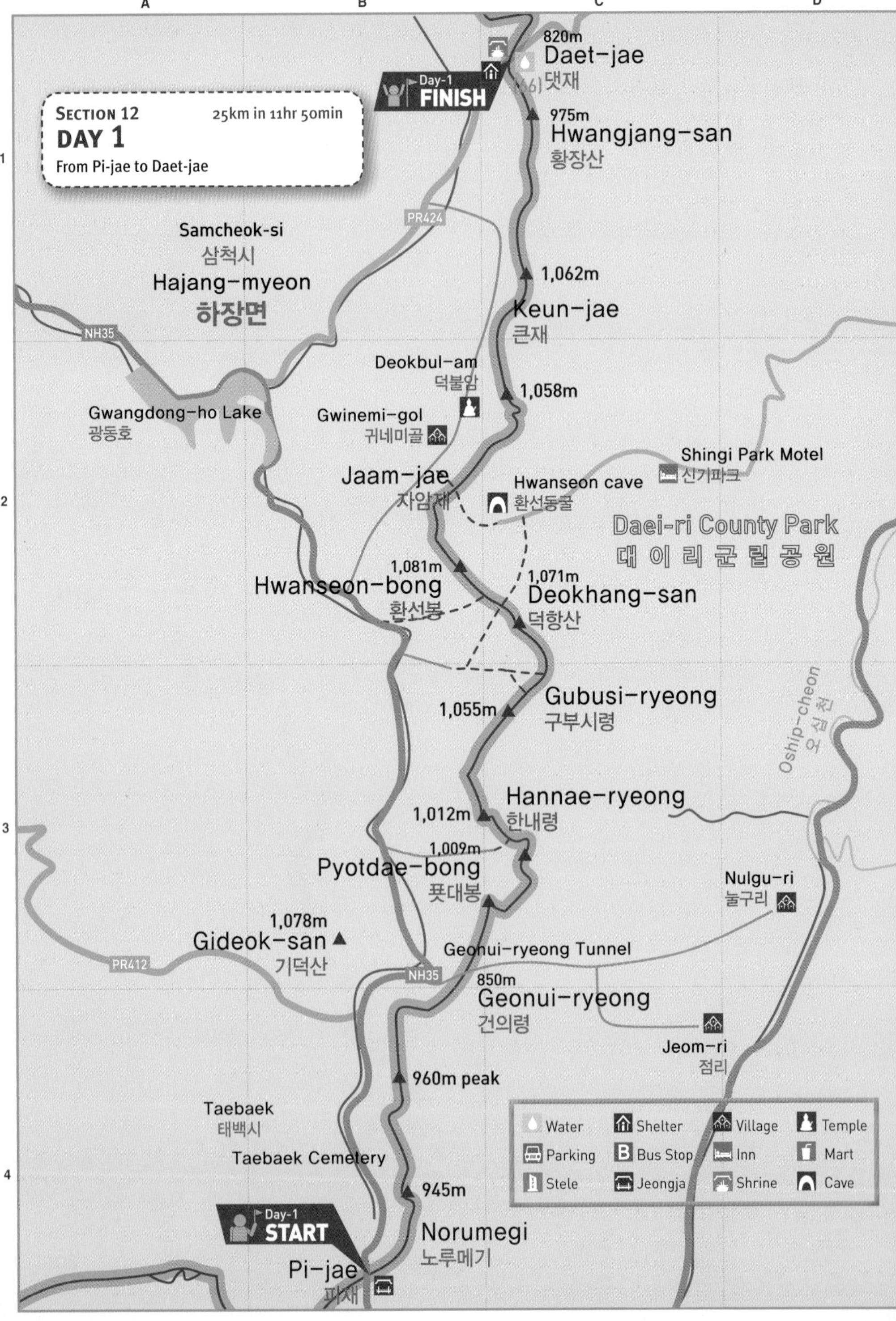

A
B
C
D
1
2
3
4
SECTION 12
25km in 11hr 50min
DAY 1
From Pi-jae to Daet-jae
Day-1 FINISH
820m
Daet-jae
댓재
975m
Hwangjang-san
황장산
PR424
Samcheok-si
삼척시
Hajang-myeon
하장면
1,062m
Keun-jae
큰재
NH35
Deokbul-am
덕불암
1,058m
Gwangdong-ho Lake
광동호
Gwinemi-gol
귀네미골
Shingi Park Motel
신기파크
Jaam-jae
자암재
Hwanseon cave
환선동굴
Daei-ri County Park
대 이 리 군 립 공 원
1,081m
Hwanseon-bong
환선봉
1,071m
Deokhang-san
덕항산
Gubusi-ryeong
구부시령
1,055m
Oship-cheon
오십천
Hannae-ryeong
한내령
1,012m
1,009m
Pyotdae-bong
푯대봉
Nulgu-ri
눌구리
1,078m
Gideok-san
기덕산
Geonui-ryeong Tunnel
PR412
NH35
850m
Geonui-ryeong
건의령
Jeom-ri
점리
960m peak
Taebaek
태백시
Taebaek Cemetery
945m
Day-1 START
Norumegi
노루메기
Pi-jae
피재
Water
Shelter
Village
Temple
Parking
Bus Stop
Inn
Mart
Stele
Jeongja
Shrine
Cave

DAY 1

From Pi-jae to Daet-jae

- **Distance:** 25km
- **Time:** 11hr 10min

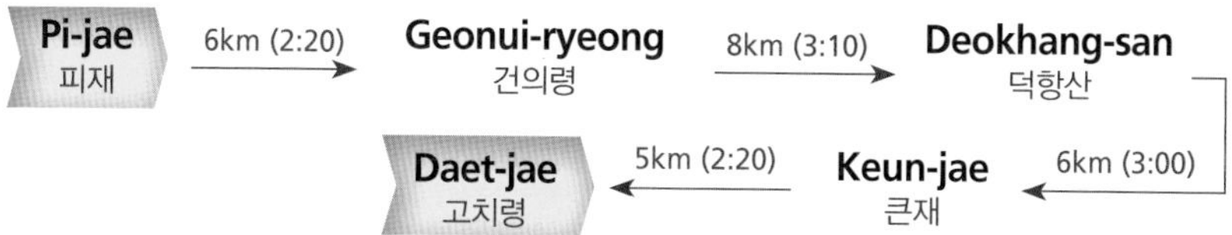

This 25 km leg of the Baekdu-daegan runs predominantly in a northern direction on the eastern side of NH35 before meeting PR424 at Daet-jae. The trail cranks onward, permeating the camouflaged hills like a Pacific swell. You can leave your hat on as you traverse Geonui-ryeong and wade back into the mountain current. As you approach the highest feature of this leg at Hwanseon-san, you can hear the hollow pounding of your boots echo over the caves of Hwanseon. Race for the pass as darkness approaches and enjoy the hospitality of the good folk of the Daet-jae Minbak.

Pi-jae 피재 B4 → Geonui-ryeong 건의령 B3 6km (2:20)

From Pi-jae, the trail begins at the top of the garden area, flanking a mountain road for 1 km before leaving it at a junction called Norumegi 노루메기. From there, the trail snakes north for 500 meters, making a distinctive sharp left to the west for 100 meters to the top of an unnamed peak at 945 m ABSL. From 945 m, the trail descends down to 850 m ABSL for 1 km and then swoops back up the ridge for 1.5 km to 950 m ABSL, after which it makes a distinctive easterly turn for 500 meters until it comes to a Korea Forest Service signboard titled, in English, *The Baekdudaegan Mountains*. The sign states that the last 7 km of trail from Maebong-san 매봉산 (on the other side of Pi-jae) to Geonui-

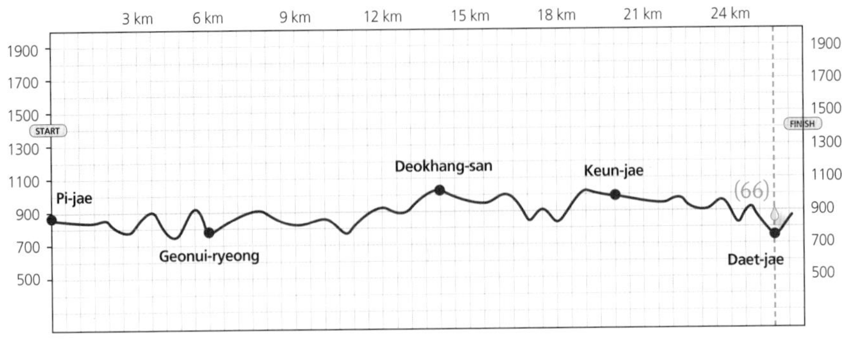

WATER STOPS (66) Daet-jae: **N37°22'56" E129°00'54"**

ryeong (500 meters further on) was restored in 2007. It quotes a source saying that the main mountain range of the Korean peninsula extends for a distance of 1,400 km. On your way to Geonui-ryeong, you may get some good views to the northwest, passing a tomb before arriving at a mountain road or forest track marking the pass of Geonui-ryeong. Information found at the pass states that at the end of the Goryeo kingdom, King Gongyang was sent into exile to Samcheok 삼척 and then killed at Geundeok Gungchon 근덕 궁촌. So as they crossed this pass, the faithful retainers of Goryeo hung their official hats and official uniforms on top of it and then crossed the pass, concealing themselves in Taebaek-san and saying that they would never enter government service again. *Geon* means "hat" and *ui* means "clothes"—hence, Geonui-ryeong. There is also a large map board here saying that an 18th century geographer called Sin Gyeong-jun classified the Baekdu-daegan as one *daegan* ("great ridge"), one *jeonggan*, and 13 *jeongmaek* ("subsidiary ridges") during the reign of the Joseon Dynasty's King Yeongjo:

> A *jeonggan* means a ridge that does not channel a river all the way to the sea within the Korean peninsula as a jeongmaek does. It instead channels the Duman-gang River (Tumen River) from the peaks of Baekdu-san in North Korea, where it later becomes the frontier of North Korea and China, and then in its last 15 km the frontier with Russia. Therefore, it has a different title from the 13 *jeongmaek*.

Geonui-ryeong 건의령 B3 → Deokhang-san 덕항산 C2

8km (3:10)

From Geonui-ryeong (850m), the trail cuts back into the pine forest in a northerly direction, steadily climbing for the next kilometer up to the peak of Pyotdae-bong 푯대봉 at 1,009 m ABSL. From there, it takes a sharp turn to the east, dropping off the summit for about 200 meters before turning in a northeast direction. The trail remains undulating at about this altitude for the next kilometer before it reaches an unnamed peak at 951 m ABSL. The trail from there continues for a short distance north before suddenly veering southwest and dropping quickly into a saddle called Hannae-ryeong 한내령. From there, it's a steep northwest climb for 500 meters to your next feature, located at 1,012 m ABSL. The trail stays within these altitudes for the next 2.5 km, nudging its way ahead in a predominantly northwest-to-northeast direction and passing through various cattle farms (some of them have poor fencing, allowing cattle to roam aimlessly amongst the trees on the protected ridge) to an unnamed peak at 1,055 m ABSL. From there, it drops sharply again for the next 500 meters before arriving at a *doltap* located in good wooded forest. This area is called Gubusi-ryeong 구부시령. There is ample space to pitch a tent at this pass.

At Gubusi-ryeong ("the pass that served nine husbands"), there is a signboard presenting the tale of a local woman from a nearby village. She was born under an unlucky star, and every man she married died—in the end, this totaled nine dead husbands—and the pass was thence named after this tragic passage in her life. It concludes that in Korea, a wife must serve her husband like a king until after his death. From this pass, the trail gradually ascends northwest for the next kilometer before reaching the summit of Deokhang-san.

Deokhang-san 덕항산 C2 → Keun-jae 큰재 C1

6km (3:00)

From there, the Baekdu-daegan starts to become more spectacular as you quite literally walk along a steep drop-off on the eastern side of the ridge. The trail is fringed with trees, and for the next 2 km you pass a wooden staircase to the east, which takes hikers down a steep spur for 2 km to the Hwanseon-donggul cave system. From the ridge, you should be able to see the tourist complex at Hwanseon. Continuing in a northwest direction, the trail continues to dish up many splendid views to the east, and about 1.5 km later, it arrives at a peak called Hwanseon-bong 환선봉, or Jigak-san 지각산, at 1,081 m ABSL. For the next kilometer, the trail descends quite steeply, traveling past a helipad to a saddle. There it rises over a small peak before dropping again and reaching the trail junction of Jaam-jae 자암재, which is marked by a signpost. On the eastern side of this pass is a 1 km route to the cave of Hwanseon Donggul.

At Jaam-jae, you should be able to notice the distinctive pasture and farming patches of the Gwinemi-gol 귀네미골 village surrounding Deokbul-am Temple 덕불암 on the western side of the ridge. The area appears to be mainly harvested for cabbage. The Baekdu-daegan trail hugs the fringes of these cabbage patches, sometimes taking you onto some of the mountain roads in this region—if in doubt, continue to look for the hiking ribbons as navigation tools. At the top of the hill north of your location, you should be able to see a round water tank. This is your endpoint for this region, located at 1,058 m ABSL. Upon reaching the water tank, look for some hiking ribbons located next to a fence line. The trail from there will head directly due north toward some pine trees. Follow it as it gradually descends downhill for the next kilometer before arriving at the pass of Keun-jae, located in a predominantly pine-forested area with a mountain road joining it from the western side of the ridge.

High alpine cabbage patches at Gwinemi-gol

* Deokhang-san 덕항산 C2

This peak shares its summit area with a small stone stele and a nearby fire tower. Deokhang-san (1,071m) got its name because it once acted as a natural fire barrier for people burning their crops after cultivation. The mountain is made from limestone, and beneath its summit is a network of caves. One of those cave networks is the source to one of Asia's most famous caves, Hwanseon-donggul, which is located only 2 km north from here. Translated, "Hwanseon-donggul" means "the cave of a fantastic Taoist hermit or mountain-wizard with supernatural powers."

* Hwanseon-donggul Cave 환선동굴 C2

The Hwanseon Donggul Cave claims to be the largest show cave in the East, meaning that it is accessible to recreational visitors. It is located in what people call Korea's Grand Canyon, in Gangwon-do's Samcheok. The height of the passages averages 15 meters, and the width 20 meters. The main chamber, 40 meters in diameter, features white sands and is big enough to hold thousands of people. The rivers inside the caves have formed ten pools and six waterfalls along the tour path. The cavern is loaded with a variety of stalagmites. Outstanding is a structure named after the Great Wall of China and an Okjwadae ("jade royal throne") in the main chamber. Numerous other caves of attraction adorn the area, including Gwaneum-gul, Sadari-bawi Baram-gul, Yangteo-mok Se-gul, Deokbat Se-gul, and Keun-jae Se-gul. This cave system is thought to have developed during the Sub-Paleozoic Era of the middle Cambrian Period some 550 million years ago.

The entrance to Daei-ri County Park 대이리 군립공원 and the Hwanseon Donggul Cave has a couple of *yeogwan*, including Hwanseon Yeogwan 환선 여관 (T. 033-541-9988) and, 2 km northeast of the park entrance, the Singi Park Motel 신기파크 모텔 (T. 033-541-5999).

Transport Info

Joining the trail at Hwanseon-donggul: Buses run to Hwanseon Donggul from Samcheok Bus Terminal 삼척 버스터미널 on the east coast. Buses from Samcheok to Hwanseon-donggul run six times a day, at 6:10 am, 8:20 am, 10:20 am, 2:20 pm, 5:20 pm and 6:50 pm. Buses from Hwanseon-donggul to Samcheok run eight times a day, at 6:50 am, 9 am, 11:20 am, 1:10 pm, 3:05 pm, 4:35 pm, 6 pm and 7:40 pm. The trip takes 40 minutes.

Keun-jae 큰재 → Daet-jae 댓재 C1

5km (2:20)

The next 5 km to Daet-jae sees you traveling through some fairly uninspiring terrain, with no major peaks to climb over; in fact, it is a gradual downhill stroll north to the pass of Daet-jae. The first 1 km sees you moving in a northeast direction, reaching a signpost located at 1,062 m ABSL. From there, the trail passes alongside some good forest region for the next kilometer before arriving at a trail junction marked by a signpost. It is a 3 km downhill run to Daet-jae from there. Continuing north on the Baekdu-daegan, the next 2.5 km sees you passing two signposts before climbing up to your last peak of the day, Hwangjang-san 황장산 (975m). The 600 meter descent to Daet-jae is through a thick, lush tree line spilling out onto Daet-jae. Just before you reach Daet-jae, you should notice a large blue water tank(66) that has water taps on the back of it.

* Daet-jae 댓재 C1

Daet-jae is located at approximately 820 m ABSL. It is traversed by PR424, which connects NH35, 9 km to the west, and NH38, 14 km to the east near Samcheok on the east coast of Korea. On the eastern side of this pass is a *sansin-gak* located in a small but quaint park area. Also located at the pass, in the form of architecture, is a large steel structure of meaning unknown to us.

Transport Info

Joining the trail at Daet-jae: Buses running between Samcheok and Hajang-myeon 하장면 cross Daet-jae and will stop for you to get on or off. They run three times a day, at 8:50 am, 2:40 pm and 6:40 pm. Buses for Hajang-myeon leave Samcheok three times a day, at 7:10 am, 1:30 pm and 4:30 pm. Samcheok is quite a large coastal city, from which buses head to large centers throughout the country.

Lodging

There is a *minbak* and store located here offering excellent service and food. The Daet-jae Hyugeso 댓재휴게소 and Minbak (T. 033-554-1123) has a great restaurant downstairs and rents clean rooms upstairs. Your hosts will be the friendly and hospitable Ryu family.

DAY 2

From Daet-jae to Sawonteo Junction

- **Distance:** 12.7km
- **Time:** 6hr 40min

The next leg of the Baekdu-daegan is effectively 29 to 30 km long. This will be a difficult and challenging achievement to meet if you are walking with heavy packs. The best option is to break it down into two days and enjoy the scenery of this beautiful leg. We would suggest that the hiker take the opportunity to visit one of Korea's most famous landscapes at Mureung Scenic Gorge or camp out on the ridge somewhere. There are many great unscheduled camping spots on the ridge where you could pitch a tent or sleep under the stars on a flat, rocky plateau overlooking Mureung Gorge. Otherwise, there are many more opportunities for you to detour off the ridge and walk down into Mureung, which is said to be the most beautiful valley in all of Korea. A diversion down into its craggy cliffs and multiple waterfalls is well worth it, but the climb back to the ridge is punishing—the price of beauty.

Daet-jae 댓재 H4 → Duta-san 두타산 F3 — 6.5km (3:00)

From Daet-jae, the trail starts directly opposite the *minbak* next to the *sansin-gak*, passing an old worship altar and ascending northeast for 1 km past some tall stands of pine. It then meets a signpost, signifying that you have reached the peak of Haetdaet-deung 햇댓등. From this vantage point, you have great views north of the ridge to Duta-san, about 5 km away. The trail from there turns sharply west for a kilometer, swooping down some steps into a shallow saddle area before

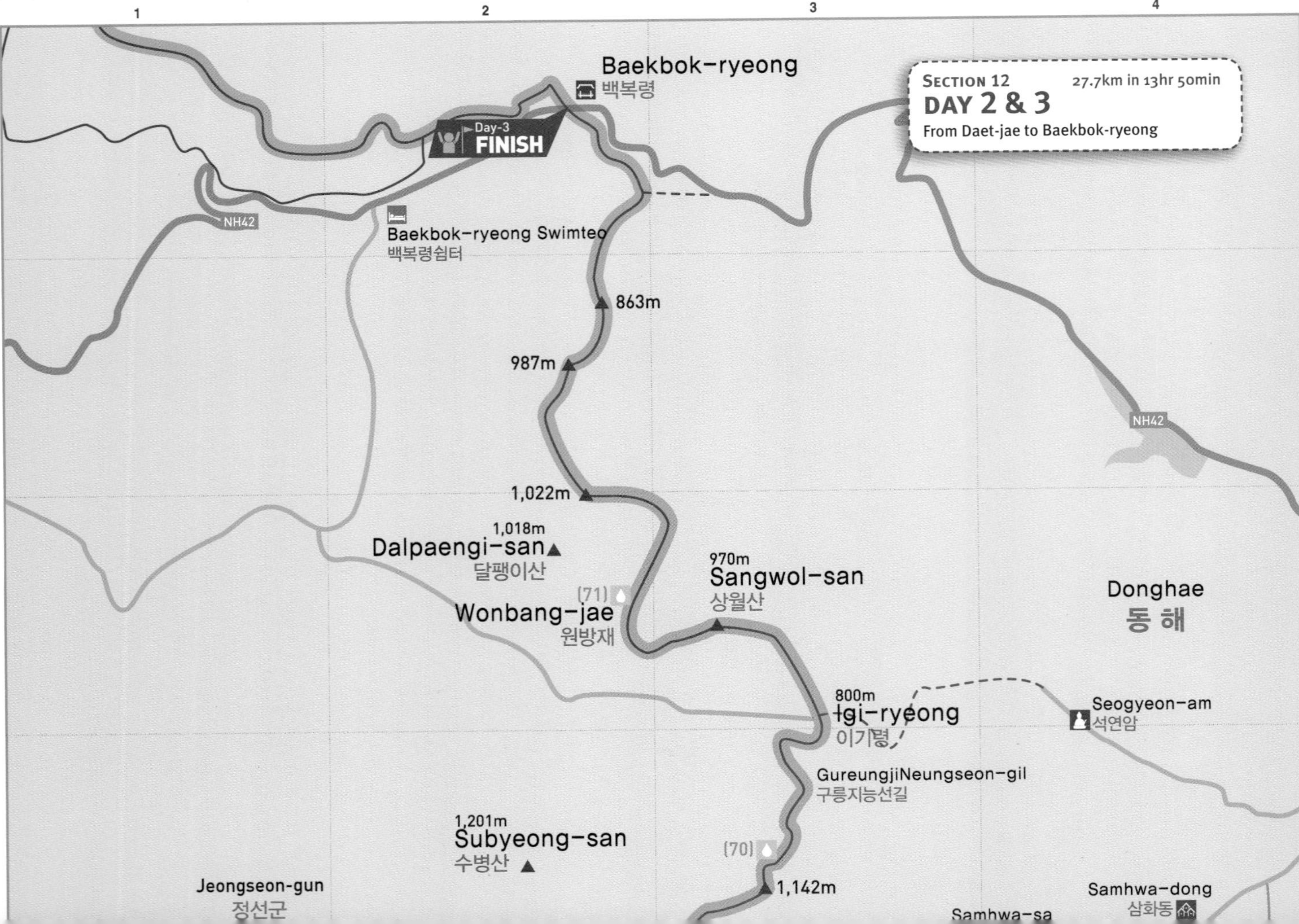
SECTION 12
27.7km in 13hr 50min
DAY 2 & 3
From Daet-jae to Baekbok-ryeong
1
2
3
4
A
B
C
D
Baekbok-ryeong
백복령
Day-3
FINISH
NH42
Baekbok-ryeong Swimteo
백복령쉼터
863m
987m
1,022m
1,018m
Dalpaengi-san
달팽이산
(71)
Wonbang-jae
원방재
970m
Sangwol-san
상월산
800m
Igi-ryeong
이기령
GureungjiNeungseon-gil
구릉지능선길
(70)
1,142m
1,201m
Subyeong-san
수병산
Jeongseon-gun
정선군
Donghae
동 해
NH42
Seogyeon-am
석연암
Samhwa-dong
삼화동
Samhwa-sa

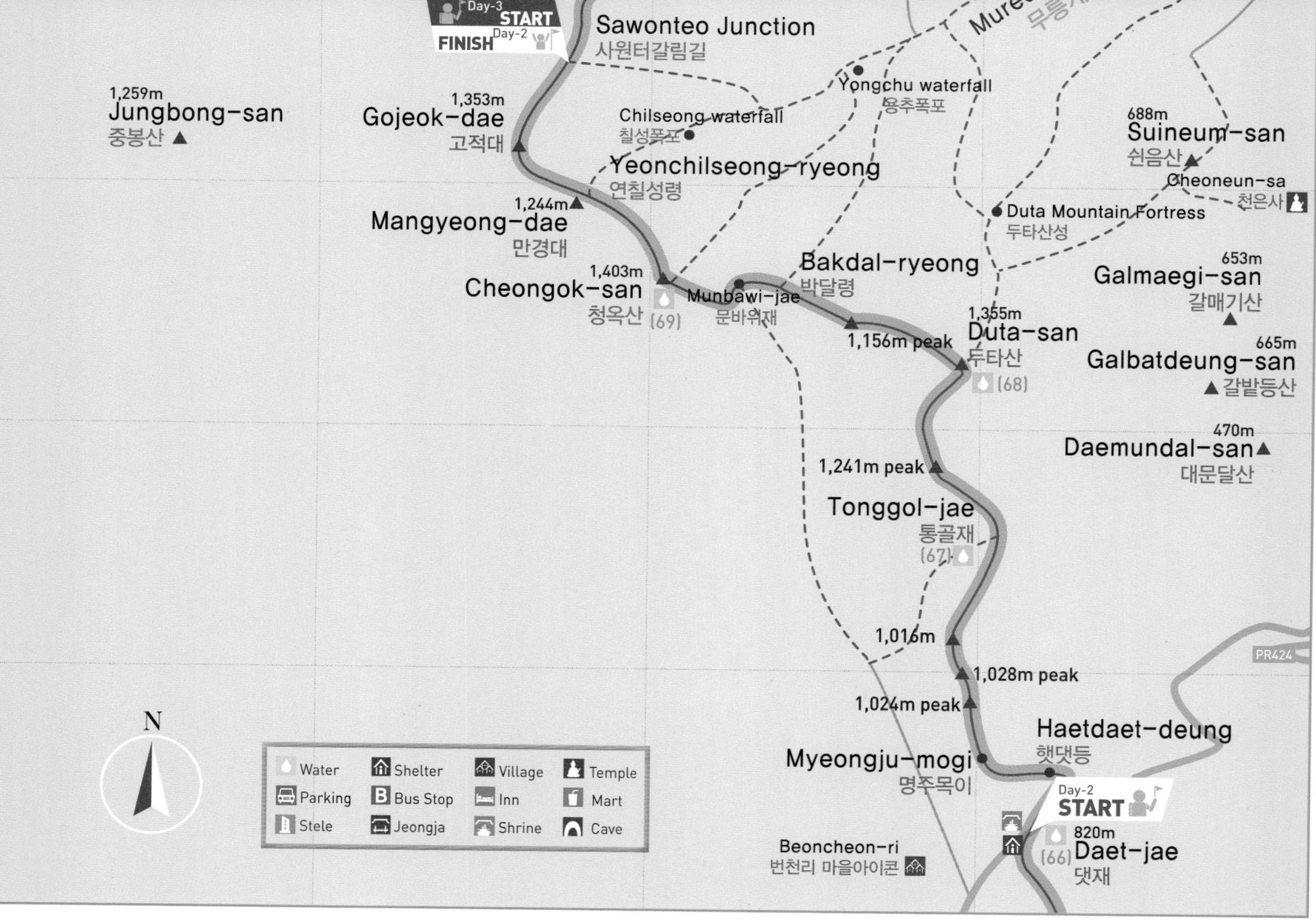
Day-3 START
Day-2 FINISH
Sawonteo Junction
사원터갈림길
1,259m
Jungbong-san
중봉산
1,353m
Gojeok-dae
고적대
Chilseong waterfall
칠성폭포
Yongchu waterfall
용추폭포
Yeonchilseong-ryeong
연칠성령
1,244m
Mangyeong-dae
만경대
1,403m
Cheongok-san
청옥산
(69)
Munbawi-jae
문바위재
Bakdal-ryeong
박달령
1,156m peak
1,355m
Duta-san
두타산
(68)
Duta Mountain Fortress
두타산성
688m
Suineum-san
쉰음산
Cheoneun-sa
천은사
653m
Galmaegi-san
갈매기산
665m
Galbatdeung-san
갈밭등산
470m
Daemundal-san
대문달산
1,241m peak
Tonggol-jae
통골재
(67)
1,016m
1,028m peak
1,024m peak
Myeongju-mogi
명주목이
Haetdaet-deung
햇댓등
Day-2 START
820m
Daet-jae
댓재
(66)
Beoncheon-ri
번천리 마을아이콘
PR424
N
Water
Parking
Stele
Shelter
Bus Stop
Jeongja
Village
Inn
Shrine
Temple
Mart
Cave
E
F
G
H

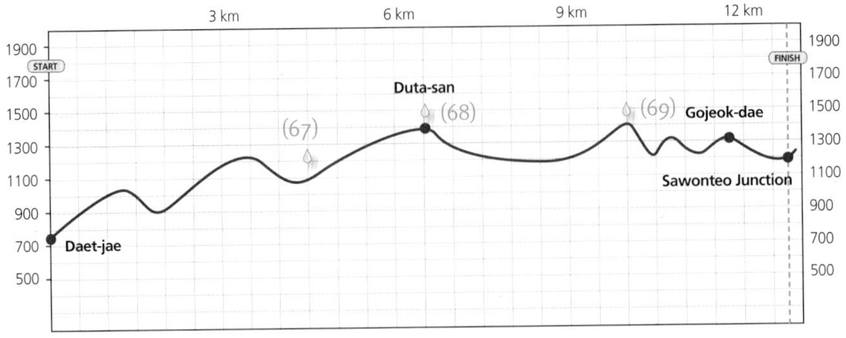

WATER STOPS

(67) Tonggol-jae: **N37°24'32" E129°00'30"**
(68) Duta-san: **N37°25'22" E129°00'25"**
(69) Cheongok-san: **N37°25'48" E128°58'30"**

arriving at an area known as Myeongju-mogi 명주목이. From there, the trail rises steadily north for the next 1.5 km before descending gradually for another 1 km down to a track junction located at 1,016 m ABSL. This area is known as Tonggol-jae 통골재. You can be confident of finding water(67) at this junction, located in a mountain stream, by following a westerly track down into the depression for 200 meters. From Tonggol-jae, the trail gets steep and begins its ascent to Duta-san, which is located at 1,355 m ABSL. The next 2 km gains about 350 m in altitude before arriving at the summit. There are many great views along this section of your climb.

* Duta-san 두타산 F3

Duta-san (1,355m) is a flat, open peak that holds a place of reverence amongst its locals. At the summit is a grassy tomb, with a mass of boulders located behind it providing resting spots. There is also water(68) to be found at this lofty height. If you approach the southeastern edge of the summit, you should be able to see a dusty track going down to what is a slow trickle of water coming out of a spring. This spring may be dry at certain times of the year. On the summit are a couple of tablets and plaques. The small stone tablet inserted into the ground, dated May 27, 2001, celebrates a regional effort involving 1,000 people who together planted 1,000 yew trees along 1,000 m high hilly sections of the Baekdu-daegan. They did so with all their hearts in an effort to pray for peace and the eternal development of their provinces. There is also a large platform with a huge rock placed on it. The inscription on the foundation beneath the huge rock notes that this is the first place to catch the sunrise in the morning as it honors the fallen heroes of this region. The word *duta* means to renounce worldly desires, avoid

Pinnacles north of Gojeok-dae

material gain, and instead practice the austerities and clear teachings of Buddha. Duta-san is the mother-mountain for the temples of Samhwa-sa 삼화사, Cheoneun-sa 천은사 and Gwaneum-am 관음암, all of which sit at the northern entrance to the mountain in Mureung Gorge. History states that as many as ten temples once existed in the gorge beneath the towering summits. Duta-san is also collectively known as Haedongsam-bong, meaning "sea east three peaks." The other two peaks that make up this trio are Cheongok-san and Gojeok-dae, located further north on the trail. The significance of that name is that at some stage on this leg, you will for the first time be able to see the East Sea stretching out beyond the beach resorts on South Korea's east coast. Duta-san is also known by its modern-day locals as Uigadeung 의가등—meaning "coat hanger-shaped peak." They say that to walk the ridge of these peaks realizes the praises of old poets.

Duta-san 두타산 F3 → Gojeok-dae 고적대 E2 5.2km (2:50)

The Baekdu-daegan descends down a crusty ridge in a northwest direction for 500 meters dropping 200 m in altitude. It then flattens out, passing two signposts before arriving at a *doltap* and a signpost 2 km later. This point is called Bakdal-ryeong 박달령 and has a three-kilometer easterly track running down into the depths of Mureung Gorge. At Bakdal-ryeong, you are standing at the base of the second part of the mountain trio, Cheongok-san 청옥산. The trail continues west for 300 meters, crossing and ascending over a distinctive rocky area before ascending south briefly and then turning back west again for the next 500 meters. It passes more impressive rock formations that jut in and out of the tree line before eventually arriving at a tomb site at the base of Cheongok-san (1,403m), the highest feature you will climb to on this leg of the Baekdu-daegan. The summit breaks out of the tree line and is represented by a solar-powered transmitter mast. There is also water(69) to be found at this peak, marked by a signpost that directs you to walk about 50 meters down the southwestern side of the peak. Once again, do not rely on finding water at these high-altitude stops. The signboard at the top of Cheongok-san says that it is one of the three mountains that represent

Roger climbing Gojeok-dae

the "sea east three peaks" (Haedongsam-bong 해동삼봉). Cheongok-san, meaning "sapphire mountain," has a reputation from ancient times as being a bit of a jewel, as it was once possible to find many different kinds of plants that grew naturally on this mountain for the purpose of making medicine. From Cheongok-san, the trail descends sharply northwest for 1 km until it hits a saddle at about 1,200 m ABSL, marked by a another *doltap*. This saddle is the pass of Yeonchilseong-ryeong 연칠성령, which features a signboard explaining that it was once called Nanchul-ryeong 난출령, meaning "precipitous and rugged," and that the peak to the northwest is called Mangyeong-dae 망경대 (1,244m), meaning "all-encompassing view platform." It is recorded that a famous Neo-Confucian scholar named Taekdang Yi Shik would come to the peak via this pass, stand there and look west toward Seoul, longing to return there. You can get to these views by looking out for little cuts on the side of the trail that take you out onto rocky platforms. Perhaps you too will be standing on one of those same platforms upon which the Neo-Confucian master once stood. The trail continues on a stony ridgeline fixed with ropes, offering great views back along the Baekdu-daegan for the last 200 meters to the peak of Gojeok-dae. At its 1,353 m summit, you can look back at the other two sections of the "sea east three peaks," Cheongok-san and Duta-san. The views from this area are quite brilliant, with vistas down into Mureung Gorge and more views of the remaining sections of the Baekdu-daegan to the northeast, revealing thin totems and pinnacles of hard rock jutting out along the flanks of the trail.

Gojeok-dae 고적대 → Sawonteo Junction 사원터 갈림길 E2

1km (0:50)

From Gojeok-dae, the ridge turns northeast and descends for a kilometer, arriving at your last option to leave the ridge and head into Mureung Gorge. This is an impressive kilometer as the trail runs alongside large plateaus of flat rock that look out down into Mureung Gorge. If you have come prepared and the night is warm, then there is no reason why you can't stop and sleep out on one of these flat rocky plateaus and enjoy the starry night as you look out at the sparkling lights of the squid boats hunting on the East Sea. The trail junction to Mureung Gorge is called Sawonteo-gallimgil. It is a fairly distinctive place located in a shallow saddle between two knolls.

Looking at the ridge to Sawonteo Junction

* Duta Mountain Fortress 두타산성 F4

Near Sawonteo Junction, there are some waterfalls about 500 meters southwest up the trail, along with some signage indicating directions to the remnants of stone walls from Duta Mountain Fortress. The signage states how, according to local folk legend, the fortress walls were first constructed during the legendary times of the second century in AD 102 by King Pasa, the fifth king of the Silla period. It was next reconstructed in 1414 by the mayor of Samcheok, and it stood 15 m in height, with a circumference of 2,500 meters. In 1592, during the Japanese invasion, a lot of people took refuge behind the walls and in the nearby fortress, raising an army at the same time. They set up fake soldiers in the gaps between the cliffs at the bottom of the walls' foundations, fooling the Japanese momentarily. Nevertheless, Japanese forces returned with force and, after three days of fierce fighting, took over the fortress. This area, as a result of the heroism displayed by the local inhabitants of the time, is imbued with patriotism and sublime spirit.

* Mureung Gorge 무릉계곡 E4

Mureung Gorge is a visit well worth your while. It hosts many beautiful and different waterfalls and abounds in famous rocks and boulders that are adorned with ancient scriptures, carved into their walls by old poets, monks, and scholars of days gone by. To get to Mureung Gorge proper, you must turn east from Sawonteo and walk the remaining 3 to 4 km to the temple of Samhwa-sa 삼화사, located at the mouth of the valley. It is a pleasant walk, consisting of a gentle descent over bridges alongside beautiful streams with fantastic verdant bush and flamboyant stands of colorful tree foliage. Near the end of the walk, you come out alongside the front gates of a large and stunning 1,000 year old temple called Samhwa-sa. According to old records, Great Master Jajang-yulsa founded this temple in AD 640, during the reign of Silla queen Seondeok. To help him build the temple, the great romancer Jajang seduced three wicked female spirits who had suffered great sorrow into helping him. The three spirits worked in such great harmony that they became awakened, and the temple was aptly named Samhwa-sa, meaning "three harmonies temple," while the village also came to be called Samhwa-dong 삼화동. Inside the temple is a three-story pagoda built between the end of the Silla period and the beginning of the Goryeo period. The temple also features an amenities store selling cold drinks and coffee.

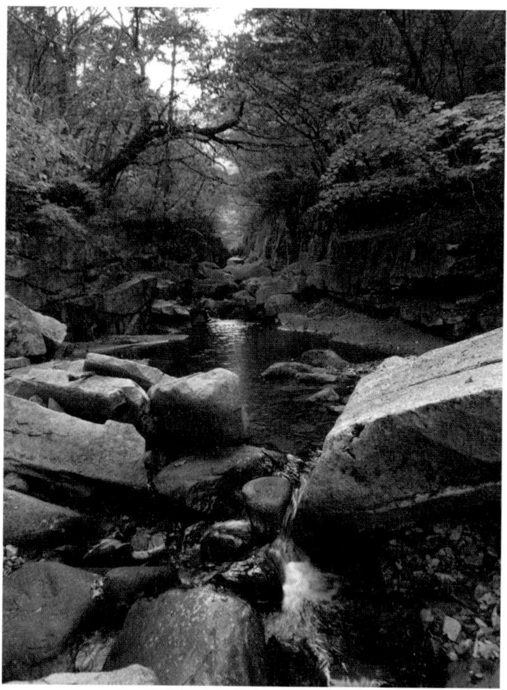

Mureung Gorge

LODGING

A short distance from the Samhwa-sa, you will reach the entrance to Mureung Gorge, which has an abundance of *minbak*, hotels, restaurants, and stores for you to stop, rest, shower, eat and drink in.

DAY 3 From Sawonteo Junction to Baekbok-ryeong

• **Distance:** 15km
• **Time:** 7hr 10min

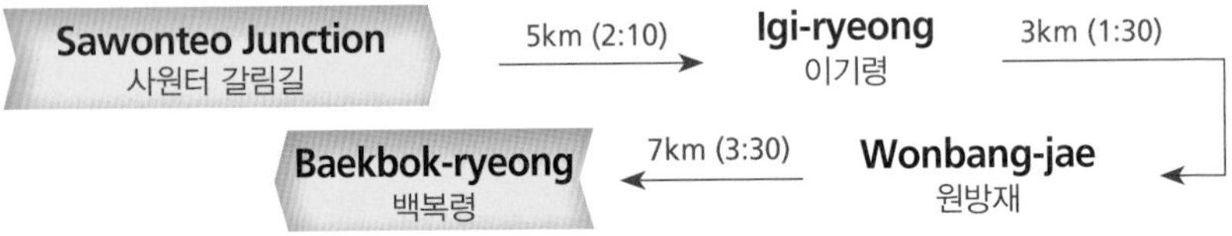

Sawonteo Junction 사원터 갈림길 → 5km (2:10) → **Igi-ryeong** 이기령 → 3km (1:30) → **Wonbang-jae** 원방재 → 7km (3:30) → **Baekbok-ryeong** 백복령

After a great rest in the scenic gorge of Mureung, you now pay the price of beauty. This time you climb back to the ridge with your head hanging wearily over the trail, with only your peripheral vision plucking the aura of colors that float in the air as the sun's rays refract through the leaves. As you return to the great ridge, doused in sweat, you turn and look back down the scenic gorge of Mureung, reminding yourself that it was worth it. You check your watch, turn north and alight to the hills, a meld of 10 km to make up to the pass. During your flight, the trail tends to fall away from the crest of the ridge and ends up clutching its western flank. However, the scenery remains good as you pass through deciduous forest. If you leave late or take your time, there will still be options for you to camp on some parts of the ridge near the two water stops you will find on this leg.

Sawonteo Junction 사원터 갈림길 E2 → Igi-ryeong 이기령 C3

5km (2:10)

The Baekdu-daegan trail continues in a northerly direction for 1 km, passing through more remarkable country before arriving at the summit of Galmi-bong 갈미봉, located at 1,260 m ABSL. After that, the trail, in effect, begins its downward journey to Baekbok-ryeong. From Galmi-bong, you descend down some steps and continue in a northeast direction for 1 km, finding more steps that take you in an easterly direction to a small saddle. From there, you ascend briefly to an unnamed peak marked by a helipad at 1,142 m ABSL. However, before that, you may have diverted along a contour around the western flank of the helipad, from which it arrives back on the ridge some 200 meters after. You now begin a long and gradual descent to Igi-ryeong, located 2 km away. Continuing downhill, you come out 1 km later onto a flat area located in a pine forest and known as Gureungji Neungseon-gil 구릉지 능선길. The area is marked by a set of benches and a signpost stating that you are 1.1 km from Igi-ryeong. Not far from these benches, in a westerly direction, is a mountain road. Walk out onto the road, turn left in a southerly direction, and continue for about 300 meters until you come to a right-hand elbow in the road. Here at this joint, you should be able to see water(70) gushing off the Baekdu-daegan. From Gureungji Neungseon-gil, the trail begins a snaky descent for the next kilometer before arriving at a deep saddle area containing a small path or road running east-west through it. This is Igi-ryeong. To the west of this pass is the same mountain road that you encountered before. If you go to this road, you will see directly on the other side of it an area that appears to

Rocky cliffs near Sawonteo Junction

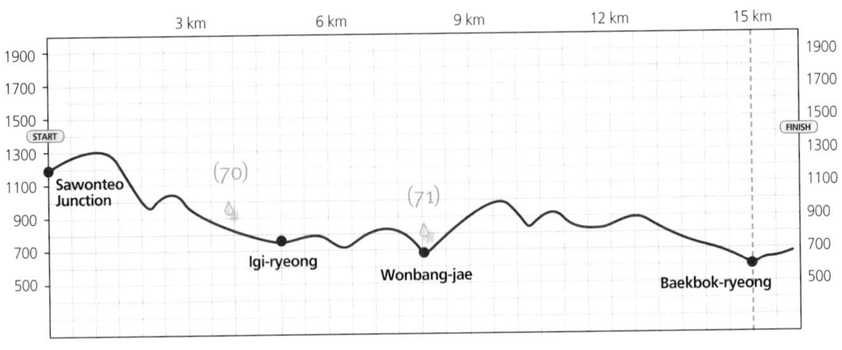

WATER STOPS

(70) Gureungji Neungseon-gil: **N37°25'30" E128°59'15"**
(71) Wonbang-jae: **N37°29'32" E128°58'20"**

be a camping site located amongst a stand of trees. There is also a spring at this site, but it may not be functional depending on the season.

Igi-ryeong 이기령 C3 → Wonbang-jae 원방재 C2 3km (1:30)

From Iri-ryeong (800m), the trail ascends northwest for 200 meters before arriving at a mast. From there, it continues its ascent, arriving at a helipad and then turning west and dropping into another saddle. From the saddle, the trail ascends for another 200 meters to the top of Sangwol-san 상월산 at 970 m ABSL. After that, it continues west for about another 300 meters, passing through some good forest. The last kilometer to Wonbang-jae sees you drop from about 900 m ABSL to about 730 m ABSL. At Wonbang-jae, more water(71) can be found if you walk west out onto the mountain road and then turn right in a northerly direction; at the bend in the road, you should be able to see a clear pool of water formed by a mountain stream.

Wonbang-jae 원방재 C2 → Baekbok-ryeong 백복령 A2 7km (3:30)

At Wonbang-jae, there is a signpost indicating that you are 7.09 km from Baekbok-ryeong. It is a good, hard 2 km climb from here to the top of your next unnamed peak at 1,022 m ABSL. Some of the spots along the way to this peak provide you with more good views to the east as the trail steers north for the first kilometer before arcing west for the last kilometer, meeting occasional staircases on its path. At the summit (1,022m) are a helipad and another signpost. Some more stairs assist you off this peak as you descend northwest for 1 km, passing through more impressive vegetation before arriving at an area that gives you good views to the west. From here, the trail makes a gradual change in direction to the northeast, where the next kilometer sees you climb over two peaks located at 987 m and 959 m ABSL. After 959 m, there is only one more peak to pass, located another 1.5 km away; it is the very end of the northeastern descent. From there, the trail turns northwest, and you should arrive 700 meters later at a viewing platform looking northeast. On a fine day, you will definitely be able to see the East Sea from here; this may also be the first time you have noticed the sea proper on your walk. If you have arrived in this area at dusk, you may see the phenomenon of squid boat lights casting disorienting specters. From this viewing platform, it is a sharp drop down to the isolated pass of Baekbok-ryeong some 300 meters later.

* Baekbok-ryeong 백복령 A2

The pass is connected by NH42, which runs east for 20 km to the coastal city of Donghae, a major port offering every urban amenity, and 20 km west to the next largest town of Imgye-myeon 임계면. It consists of some Baekdu-daegan signboards and a block of public toilets. There is no fresh water source at the pass.

Baekbok-ryeong

TRANSPORT INFO

Leaving the trail at Baekbok-ryeong: The town of Imgye-myeon is located 15 km southwest of Baekbok-ryeong. Buses run twice a day from Imgye-myeon over Baekbok-ryeong to Donghae on the east coast. Buses leave Imgye-myeon at 8:40 am and 7:04 pm. From Imgye-myeon, buses run to Taebaek three times a day at 10:10 am, 12:10 pm and 4:50 pm. Buses also leave Donghae for Imgye-myeon at 5:46 am and 4:30 pm.

LODGING

There is no paid accommodation to be found at the pass of Baekbok-ryeong. The nearest form of shelter is a *jeongja* built on a concrete pad, with a sealed roof and some benches nestled under it. On the eastern side of the pass is a rustic-style restaurant assembled from a tent. If it is open, it will sell hot foods and cold beverages. About 2.5 km southwest of the pass is the Baekbok-ryeong Swimteo 백복령 쉼터, identified by a strip of kiosks. At the end of this strip is a large restaurant offering modern, clean *minbak* accommodation. The town of Imgye-myeon, a further 15 km to the southwest along NH42, has a couple of good motels. Donghae is about 20 km southeast on NH42.

The rustic *hyugeso* at Baekbok-ryeong

THREE DAYS

43.0km

SECTION 13

THE RIDGE BY THE SEA

Baekbok-ryeong →
Daegwan-ryeong

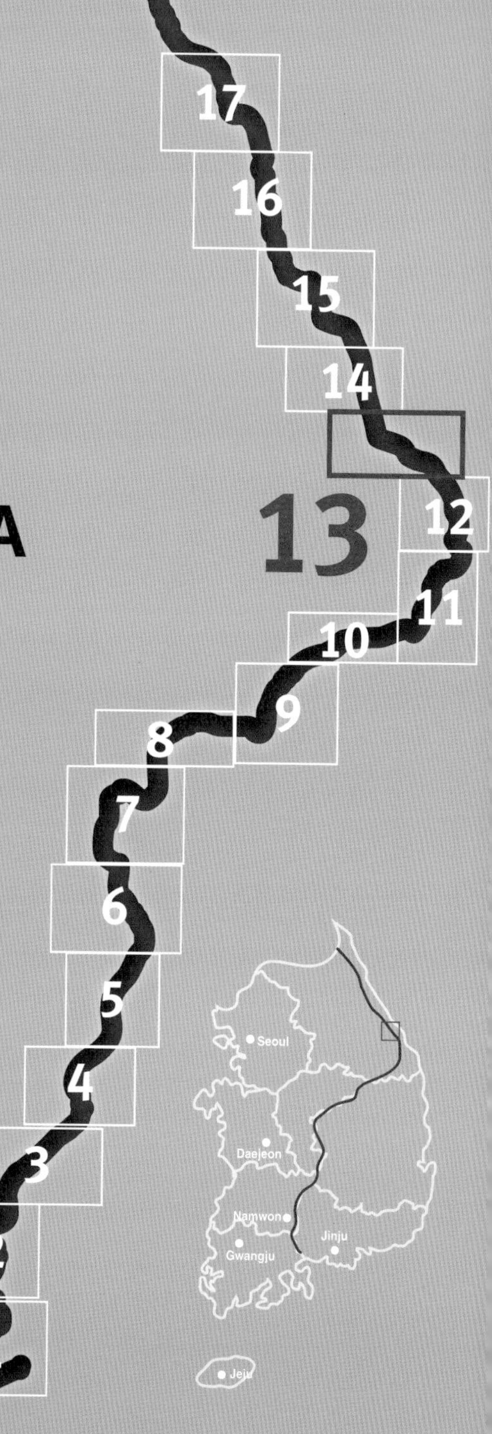

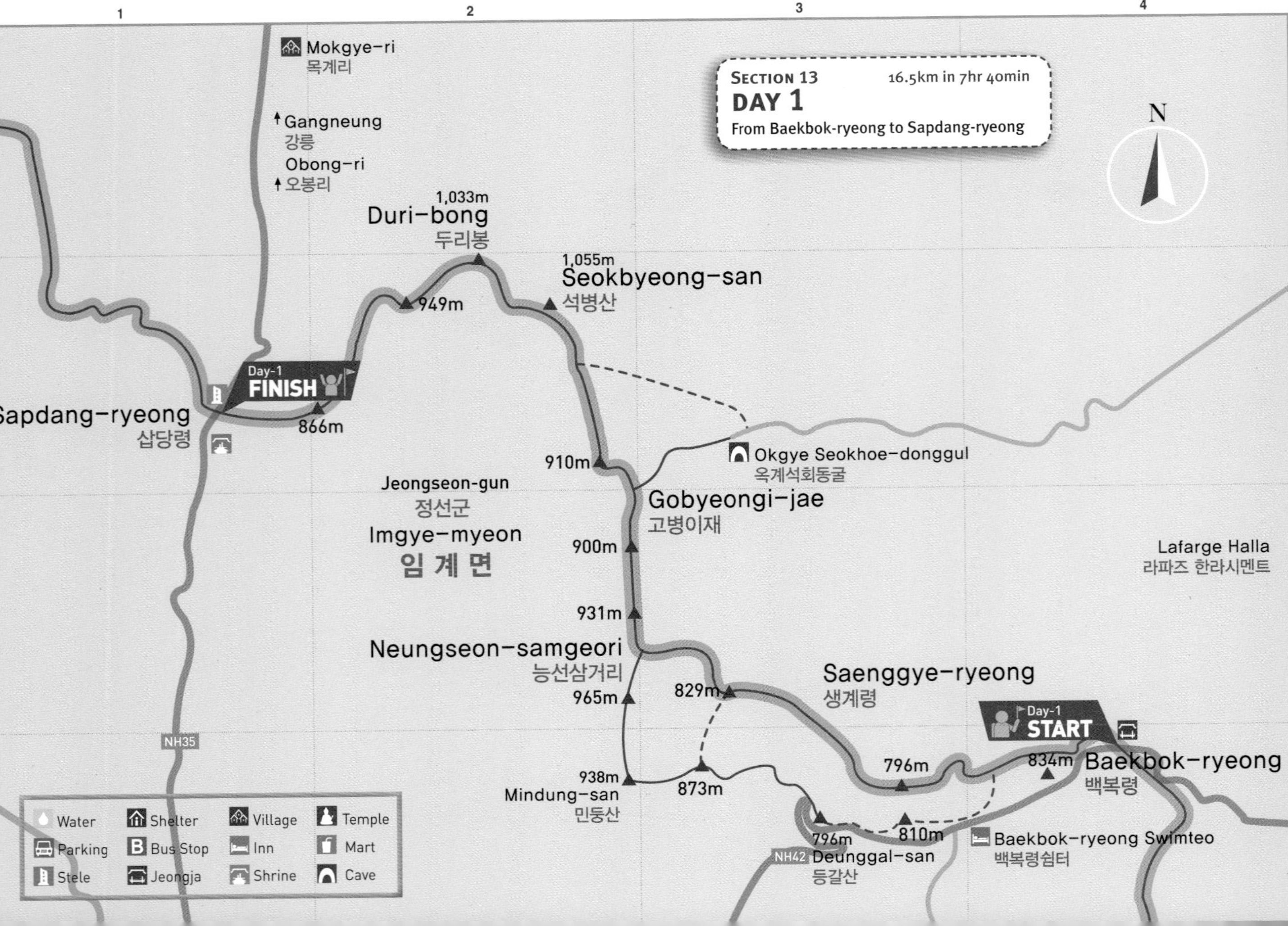
Section 13
16.5km in 7hr 40min
DAY 1
From Baekbok-ryeong to Sapdang-ryeong
N
1
2
3
4
A
B
C
D
Mokgye-ri
목계리
Gangneung
강릉
Obong-ri
오봉리
1,033m
Duri-bong
두리봉
1,055m
Seokbyeong-san
석병산
949m
Day-1
FINISH
Sapdang-ryeong
삽당령
866m
910m
Okgye Seokhoe-donggul
옥계석회동굴
Jeongseon-gun
정선군
Imgye-myeon
임 계 면
Gobyeongi-jae
고병이재
900m
931m
Lafarge Halla
라파즈 한라시멘트
Neungseon-samgeori
능선삼거리
965m
829m
Saenggye-ryeong
생계령
Day-1
START
NH35
938m
Mindung-san
민둥산
873m
796m
834m
Baekbok-ryeong
백복령
796m
810m
NH42
Deunggal-san
등갈산
Baekbok-ryeong Swimteo
백복령쉼터
Water
Parking
Stele
Shelter
Bus Stop
Jeongja
Village
Inn
Shrine
Temple
Mart
Cave

DAY 1 From Baekbok-ryeong to Sapdang-ryeong

• **Distance:** 16.5km
• **Time:** 7hr 40min

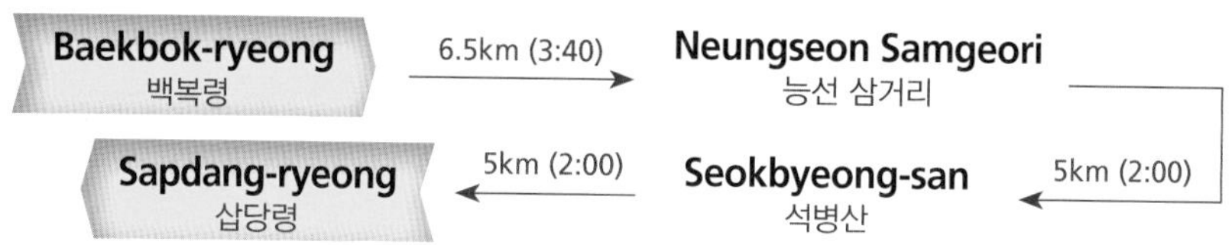

The next part of the trail sees you continue to walk on top of the large karst landforms of limestone formed around the Paleozoic Era, 480 million years ago. The area continues to produce cave formations that form under the very ridge on which you are walking, the result of millions of years of calcium carbonates forging underground rivers corroding their way through rock and stratum—a kind of chemical weathering.

Baekbok-ryeong 백복령 D4 → Neungseon Samgeori 능선 삼거리 C2

6.5km (3:40)

The Baekdu-daegan trail from Baekbok-ryeong begins on the other side of the road, behind the main signboard. This sign describes the Baekdu-daegan as the spine of Korea, stretching some 1,400 km in its entirety. It also states that during the late Joseon Dynasty (1392-1897), a utilitarian Confucian named Shin Gyeong-jun discovered all the ranges of Korea and assembled the main ones into one *daegan*, one *jeonggan*, and 13 *jeongmaek*, defining the main one as the one you are walking on, the Baekdu-daegan. The board then further describes the Baekdu-daegan as the symbol of the nation, with its branches reaching out and representing the spirit of the people. Whereas some signboards on the trail have iterated that the *jeongmaek* channel rivers within

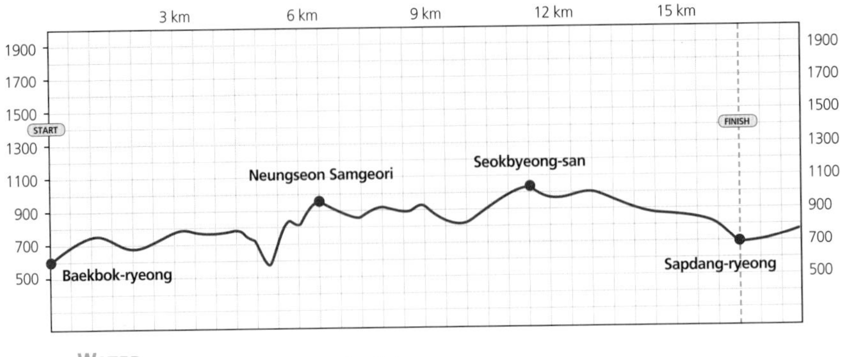

WATER STOPS No water stops for this course

Korea to the ocean, this board states that the *jeongmaek* have also formed holistic barriers between people, allowing them to diversify and form their own unique cultures.

From behind the signboard, the trail shoots straight into the tree line and up a steep incline, passing one mast and then summiting at a second mast, where it changes direction to the southwest. It's at this point that you can immediately see and "hear" the effects of a nearby mine that extracts raw materials from the earth for the production of cement, a vital commodity and ingredient that contributes to the amazing engineering feats of modern South Korea. The trail, as it heads west, appears to have been boned of its northern flank, as the mining operation encroaches with its metallic talons right up to the ridge. Following the trail southwest, it winds its way down the edges of the quarry before coming out at a small road pass connecting the quarry with NH42. The area to your right, on the northern side of the road, leads to the extracting area, and the whole scene is a muck of heavy vehicle tracks and dirty, polluted ponds of collection water. At this junction area is a signpost displaying the layout of the mine, including a plan for it to protect and cultivate six species of plant in this area. It looks newer than the second board, which was erected in April 2004 and states that the region is an ecological forest area under restoration from damage, and that there is a plan to monitor the area for the changing processes it experiences as a result of damage. It concludes that the site is an outdoor educational area for local schoolchildren. The ambition for these projects appears to have long disappeared, and the areas that they wish to reclaim are sadly empty and derelict. What is even more interesting is the supposed effort being made by the company responsible—Lafarge.

From the quarry entrance, the trail heads back into the tree line and contours around the northern front of an unnamed peak standing at 834 m ABSL. You pass a mast 200 meters later, continuing for another 400 meters until you reach what appears to be a fork in the trail. The right-hand, or north, fork is a continuation of the Baekdu-daegan, but if you miss it, don't worry, as the lower southern fork eventually joins the main trail about 6 km later at the pass of Neungseon Samgeori. The main trail passes a tomb 100 meters later as it continues west, joining a 4WD track momentarily before reaching an unnamed peak marked with a helipad about 400 meters later. The trail from there continues west for 400 meters and then begins a northwest direction, slowly descending for the next kilometer to the pass of Saenggye-ryeong 생계령, which is located at about 600 m ABSL. The trail climbs steadily back up the ridge from there for the next kilometer to an unnamed peak located at 829 m ABSL. Just before you reach the top of this peak, you will notice a large signboard standing next to the trail in a leafy hollow. It describes the makeup of a cave named Seodae-gul 서대굴. It explains that the Seodae-gul cave is derived from limestone and is 500 meters long, with a 300 meter main passage. It includes numerous small branches and contains vertical and horizontal

Views from the ridge of Baekbong-ryeong

passages, showing a stepped configuration overall. Speleothems such as stalactites, stalagmites, columns, flowstones, curtains and helectites actively grow inside the cave. Nineteen species of animal also live in the cave, including the ice bug and the clawed salamander. This is a rather fascinating signboard to stumble across in the middle of a leafy, tree-lined track with steep drop-offs to the north. However, the signboard doesn't describe where this cave is, as it is not open to the public and is a dangerous cave for curious minds to be wandering in.

From 829 m, the Baekdu-daegan trail stays on a north-to-northwest bearing for the next 400 meters before turning west. About 500 meters later, it reaches the top of another peak, marking the trail junction of Neungseon Samgeori. It offers great views north of the Baekdu-daegan. In the background (north), some 5 km away, you will be able to see Seokbyeong-san. There are also great views to the west and more views to the south back toward Mindung-san (938m) 2 km away, which is part of the alternative route for the Baekdu-daegan. The *samgeori* part of this pass's name means "three way junction," and *neungseon* means "ridge." Neungseon Samgeori is a good place to stop and recharge, taking in the majestic views of Korea's mountains.

Neungseon Samgeori 능선 삼거리 C2 → Seokbyeong-san 석병산 B2

5km (2:00)

From this junction, the Baekdu-daegan trail runs predominantly north for the next 2 km on good undulating ground, offering many great views to the east, north, and west of the ridge. From Neungseon Samgeori, the trail climbs steeply up to your next unnamed peak at 931 m ABSL. From there, it becomes a casual walk for the next kilometer to another unnamed peak standing at 900 m ABSL. At this peak, there should be another Korea Forest Service information board. Although these boards are always themed around the Baekdu-daegan, they do occasionally enlighten the hiker with further information on the great ridge, making it something of an educational journey as well. This board will remind the hiker that the Baekdu-daegan is the backbone of Korea, extending for 1,400 km and running through six provinces and 32 cities within South Korea. The ridge hosts as many as 1,326 species of plants and is a migration route for wildlife from the Asian continent to the peninsula. It is also the source of big rivers like the Han-gang, Geum-gang, Nakdong-gang, and Seomjin-gang. "Look after and protect the Baekdu-daegan for our descendants," it concludes.

About 500 meters after this peak, you should reach a trail junction located at an area known as Gobyeongi-jae 고병이재. It has a signpost indicating a track heading northeast off the ridge down to a cave known as Okgye Seokhoe-donggul 옥계석회동굴 500 meters away. Also at Gobyeongi-jae is a stainless steel signboard, this time describing the Baekdu-daegan as being "1,600 km long" and containing 13 *jeongmaek* (subsidiary ridges). It then goes on to introduce the most prominent peak of this leg, Seokbyeong-san, describing its meaning as a mountain that stretches away in a corrugated manner like a "stone folding-screen." From this pass, you climb up a small knob at 910 m ABSL, marked by a helipad and signpost. From there, you drop into a small saddle before making the last kilometer climb to the top of Seokbyeong-san at 1,055 m ABSL. The summit area is spectacular, with great views to the east, north and west. The actual summit is split into two pinnacles, with the northern one marked as the highest by a tablet naming the peak. In the hollow between the two peaks is a small shrine area where people pay their respects to the mountain spirit. Seokbyeong-san's other name is Irwol-mun 일월문, which means "gate of the sun and the moon." It can be presumed that the two pinnacles represent the sun and the moon. The gate is actually located on the northeast side of the peak, in the shape of a hole in a rock formation.

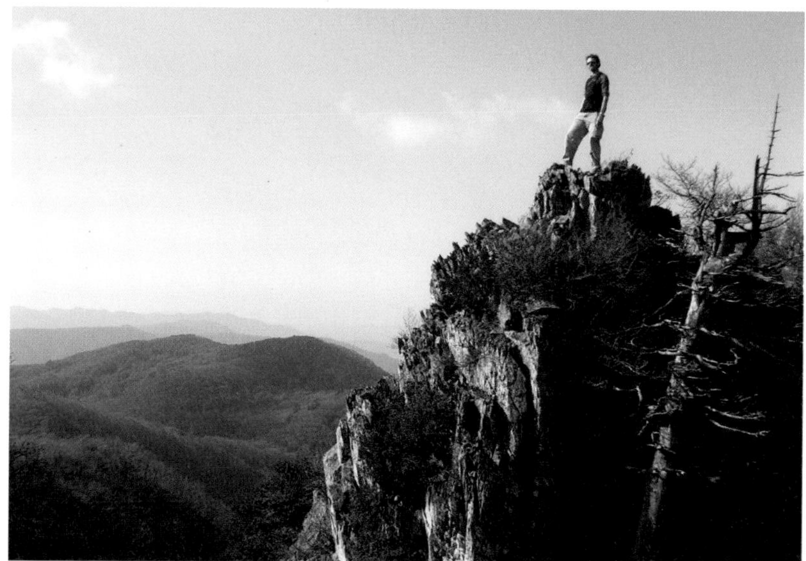

Roger in classic mountain pose on Seokbyeong-san

* Lafarge Halla 라파즈 한라시멘트 C4

Lafarge has recognized its obligation to the Baekdu-daegan under the Conservation of the Baekdu-daegan Act. In December 2003, it had to face up to this new law and duly set up a partnership with the Baekdu-daegan Conservation Society focusing on conservation of the Baekdu-daegan. The first project was the one launched on the very dilapidated signboard that you are standing and reading now (April 2004, p346). The main action of it was to launch a school offering ecological experiences for local elementary, middle, and high school students and future conservation activities, including the exploration of the Baekdu-daegan ridge in South Korea. Lafarge claims to have built a close relationship with environmental NGOs as a result of its contribution to the protection of the Baekdu-daegan, and to recognize the importance of the Baekdu-daegan to the minds of Korea people. If Lafarge is an environmentally friendly sustainer of the environment, then it has a unique opportunity to encourage the growth of the Baekdu-daegan as an ecological zone to be enjoyed by recreational users, rather than introducing poorly managed, forgotten education programs. On the trail, you will come across other attempts by Lafarge to introduce or grow wildflowers in the area for the next five kilometers, but none of them appears to have been maintained. Some of the small signboards you will come across indicate that

Lafarge Halla cement quarry near the Baekdu-daegan

species such as the dogtooth violet, the Adonis amurensis, and the rare *Leontice microrhyncha* all grow here.

Seokbyeong-san 석병산 B2 → Sapdang-ryeong 삽당령 B1

5km (2:00)

The trail from here turns northwest, passing through forest and knee-high stands of bamboo on good, easygoing ground. In places, it is also possible to see bomb craters left over from the Korean War; you may have picked up on this feature in other parts of the Baekdu-daegan, but in this area, as one gets closer to the DMZ, the bomb craters become more obvious.

For the next 1.3 km, the trail undulates gently, passing a helipad before arriving at Duri-bong 두리봉, which is located at 1,033 m ABSL. Duri-bong is a wooded peak with sets of tables and benches. It is a suitable area for camping if need be. From this point, the trail starts to arc in a southwest direction, passing through good forest canopy and pastures of bamboo. The area produces a species of lily native only to Japan, Korea and northeast China and known scientifically as *Erythronium japonicum*. The plant lives in deciduous forest areas and blooms with pink petals in April. Its leaves are edible, and it is a lily much admired for its beauty. After 1 km of southwest travel, you should reach an unnamed peak located at 949 m ABSL. After that, the trail steers northwest

The summit of Seokbyeong-san

for 300 meters before arcing back into a southerly direction. The trail then gradually drops in altitude, making your walking smooth and easy. Another 1.5 km onward and you reach a forested area with a spot height of 866 m ABSL. The last 500 meters continue to pass through tall stands of deciduous forest before the trail crosses a small road only 100 meters from your endpoint. It is quicker just to follow the trail over the road and head down the last slope to NH35.

The menhir at Sapdang-ryeong

* Sapdang-ryeong 삽당령 B1

This pass is connected by NH35. The nearest town south of Sapdang-ryeong is Imgye-myeon, some 12 km away, while north of the pass is a small lakeside village called Obong-ri 오봉리, located 20 km later on NH35 where it joins PR415. On the other side of the road is a *sansin-gak* alongside a large rock with "Sapdang-ryeong" written on it.

TRANSPORT INFO

Leaving the trail at Sapdang-ryeong: Buses running between Imgye-myeon 10 km to the south and Gangneung 강릉 on the east coast cross Sapdang-ryeong. They leave Imgye-myeon two times a day, at 6:20 am and 5:20 pm, and depart from Gangneung two times a day, at 5:40 am and 4:10 pm.

LODGING

There is no accommodation at Sapdang-ryeong. The only amenity is a small tented restaurant located on the southeastern side of the road. It serves hot meals but only has *dongdongju* and hot coffee as beverages. The Sapdang-ryeong Pension 삽당령 펜션 is located north of the pass in Mokgye-ri 목계리 and is the closest accommodation. This stylish chalet-style pension is very expensive, however, with rooms starting at 200,000 won!! Bookings can be made at www.sapdang.com (T. 033-648-2129 or 016-363-2123). North of the pass, the lakeside town of Obong-ri is 16 km further on along NH35 and has motel accommodation, supermarkets, and restaurants. The closest town to Sapdang-ryeong is Imgye-myeon, 9.5 km south along NH35. Imgye-myeon has a couple of good motels as well as restaurants, PC rooms, etc.

DAY 2

• **Distance:** 13.5km
• **Time:** 5hr 55min

From Sapdang-ryeong to Dangmok-ryeong

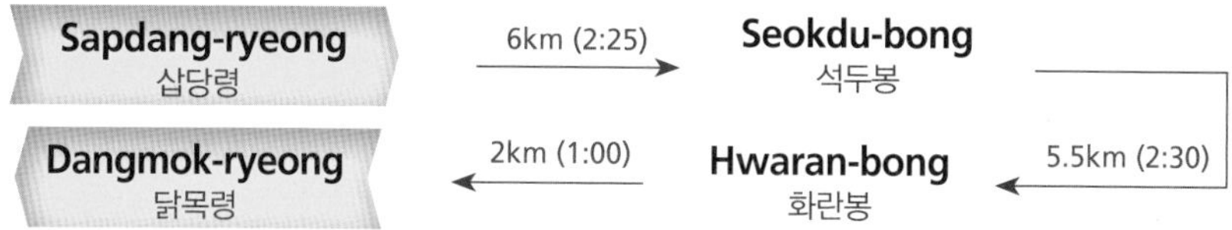

This section of the Baekdu-daegan is not a remarkable one. It is one of the easier sections in terms of time and distance and probably offers a good break after some previous days of long walks. However, its endpoint is at a road pass translated as "chicken neck pass," and the area is of a rural essence; it specializes in the production of wild honey, from which some of the locals have been known to squander their harvest into delicious cocktails as alms for those crazy balmy afternoons under the shady village guardian tree.

Sapdang-ryeong 삽당령 D4 → Seokdu-bong 석두봉 C3

6km (2:25)

The trail begins behind the large stone monument at Sapdang-ryeong and enters the pine forest, traveling east up a knoll for a short distance before turning north and continuing slowly uphill for the next kilometer until it hits a large, fenced-off mast. Just after the mast, the trail crosses a mountain road that's been flanking the ridge on your ascent. After crossing the road, the trail heads back into the tree line, winding its way up to the next peak at 862 m ABSL, where it then veers west and declines slightly in altitude for the next 800 meters before turning back into a northerly direction again. For the next 2 km, the trail keeps its northerly bearing and undulates nicely until it reaches a peak located at 978 m ABSL. From there, the trail swings to the west for a kilometer, dropping into a saddle before climbing back up to the next

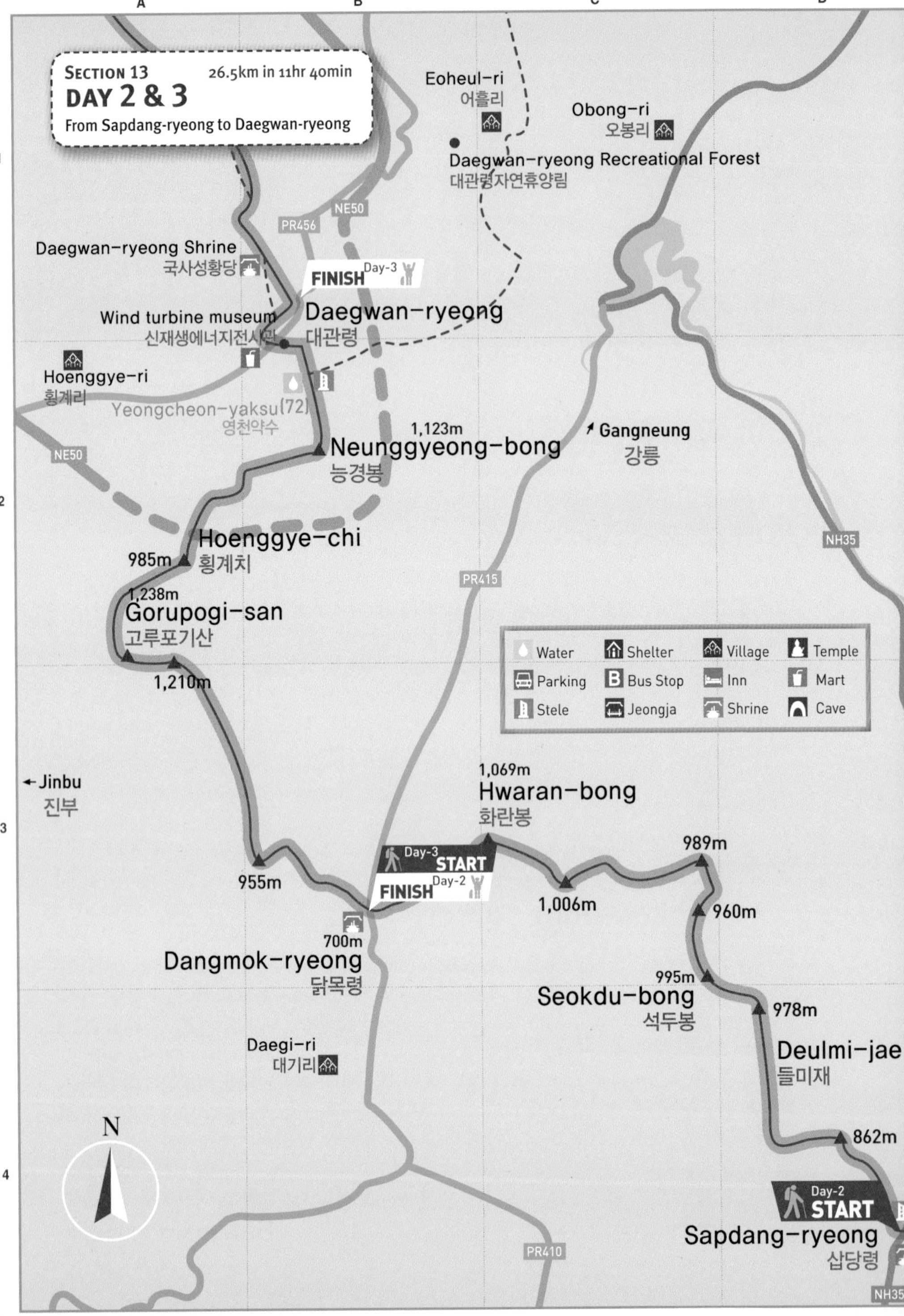
A
B
C
D
1
2
3
4
SECTION 13
26.5km in 11hr 40min
DAY 2 & 3
From Sapdang-ryeong to Daegwan-ryeong
Eoheul-ri
어흘리
Obong-ri
오봉리
Daegwan-ryeong Recreational Forest
대관령자연휴양림
NE50
PR456
Daegwan-ryeong Shrine
국사성황당
FINISH Day-3
Daegwan-ryeong
대관령
Wind turbine museum
신재생에너지전시관
Hoenggye-ri
횡계리
Yeongcheon-yaksu(72)
영천약수
1,123m
Neunggyeong-bong
능경봉
Gangneung
강릉
NE50
NH35
Hoenggye-chi
횡계치
985m
1,238m
Gorupogi-san
고루포기산
PR415
1,210m
Water
Shelter
Village
Temple
Parking
Bus Stop
Inn
Mart
Stele
Jeongja
Shrine
Cave
Jinbu
진부
1,069m
Hwaran-bong
화란봉
989m
955m
Day-3 START
FINISH Day-2
1,006m
960m
700m
Dangmok-ryeong
닭목령
995m
Seokdu-bong
석두봉
978m
Deulmi-jae
들미재
Daegi-ri
대기리
N
862m
Day-2 START
Sapdang-ryeong
삽당령
PR410
NH35

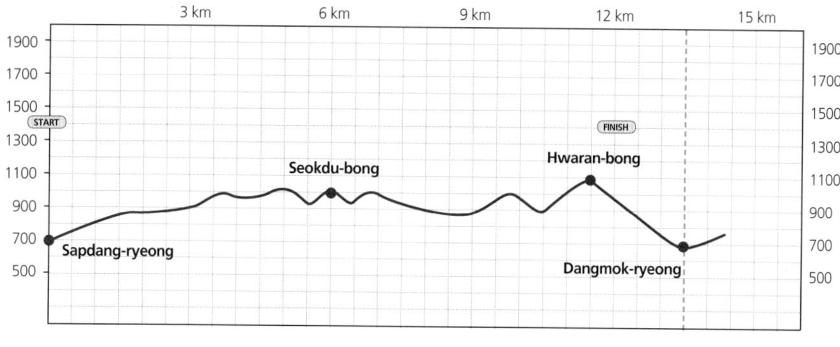

WATER STOPS

- None, but you should be able to locate some from villagers at Dangmok-ryeong

prominent feature of Seokdu-bong at 995 m ABSL. From this peak, you will finally be able to get some views, which have been hard to find in the heavy tree line.

Seokdu-bong 석두봉 → Hwaran-bong 화란봉 C3

5.5km (2:30)

From Seokdu-bong, the trail continues in a northerly direction for 2 km, passing through deciduous forest and knee-high bamboo shoots until it reaches an unnamed peak at 989 m ABSL. From there, it turns sharply west, passing through two saddles for the next 1.5 km before reaching an unnamed peak at 1,006 m ABSL. From there, you drop west into another saddle as the bamboo starts to wither out. You may also be able to see your next and largest feature of the day, Hwaran-bong (1,069m), a 600 meter walk away. There are more good views from this peak, but some of the better ones of the day are still to come.

Hwaran-bong 화란봉 C3 → Dangmok-ryeong 닭목령 B3

2km (1:00)

From there, the trail heads in a southwest direction for the final 2 km to your endpoint at Dangmok-ryeong. The trail enters an area of pine forest featuring large outcrops of white rock, where it drops suddenly in altitude. On the descent, you pass bald outcrops of rock shaded by crooked stands of native pine. From these shady recluses, you can see PR415 cutting through the "chicken neck" of Dangmok-ryeong. The trail continues its descent southwest before weaving its way out of the tree line and arriving, behind an old shed next to a farming area, onto Dangmok-ryeong.

The *sansin-gak* on the left at Dangmok-ryeong

* Dangmok-ryeong 닭목령 B3

Dangmok-ryeong, meaning "chicken neck pass," is located in a fairly isolated area at about 700 m ABSL. About 20 km to the north lies the small lakeside town of Obong-ri, as mentioned in the previous course. Five kilometers to the south exists a small settlement called Daegi-ri 대기리, famous for wild honey; it is located at the intersection of PR415 and PR410. There are no shops or amenities at the pass. On the western side of the road is a *sansin-gak* that may be locked up. It sits next to what appears to be a transport depot for farmers' wares, utilized from what may once have been an old ammunition depot during the war. There are some more signboards at the pass mapping out the local area as a hiking destination. One of those signs states that the region to the west, consisting of bee farms, is designated for the protection of native honey. On that note, it is not uncommon in this Gangwon-do area to find a local alcoholic beverage known as *Kkulsul* 꿀술 ("honey alcohol")—a delightful and compelling beverage made from a mixture of pure honey and *soju* (rice vodka).

Transport Info

Joining the trail at Dangmok-ryeong: Buses run to Dangmok-ryeong from Gangneung, leaving three times a day at 7:30 am, 1:30 pm and 6:20 pm. Buses leave Gangneung for Dangmok-ryeong at 6 am, noon and 5 pm.

Lodging

There is enough space at "chicken neck pass" to pitch a tent on a grassy area in front of the warehouse. Water can be found in local streams down the southern side of the pass on the eastern side of the road. Otherwise, if you're unsure about the water, approach a local at one of the nearby farms.

DAY 3

From Dangmok-ryeong to Daegwan-ryeong

- **Distance:** 13km
- **Time:** 5hr 45min

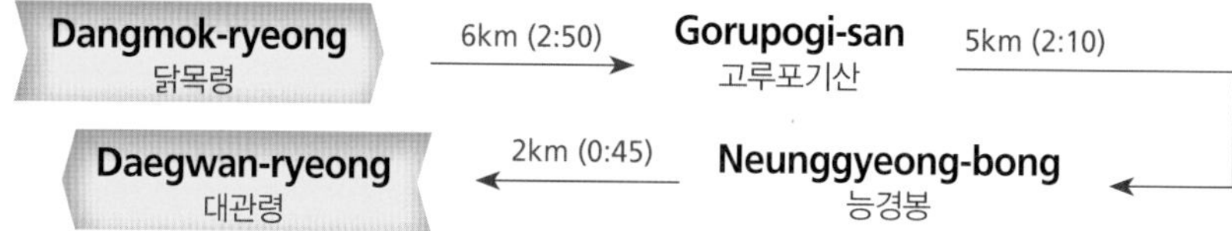

From Dangmok-ryeong, the trail begins alongside the signboards before cutting into the tree line. It then gradually ascends in a northwest direction for the next 7 km to its highest location at 1,240 m ABSL. From there, you can get views of the large city of Gangneung to the east, and you can also get your first glimpses of Odae-san National Park (see p376) to the north, with its path of wind turbines that beckon you into the park. From 1,240 m, the trail changes direction to the north and then to the northeast as it slowly descends down to Daegwan-ryeong, which is located at about 800 m ABSL.

Dangmok-ryeong 닭목령 B3 → Gorupogi-san 고루포기산 A2

6km (2:50)

The next 2 km sees you walking up your first distinctive peak, located at 955 m ABSL, before crossing a mountain road 1.5 km later. At 955 m, the trail undulates to the north for 1 km, passing a signpost and then making a short but steep 100 m climb. You should arrive 1.5 km later at another signpost, located at the foot of some more steep country. The next 700 meters see you ascending another 200 m in altitude, at the end of which you arrive at the top of an unnamed peak located at 1,210 m ABSL. From there, the trail heads west, where 900 meters later it reaches the summit of Gorupogi-san at 1,238 m ABSL. The summit itself has a small bald patch on it, a couple of signposts, a mast, and a small bench.

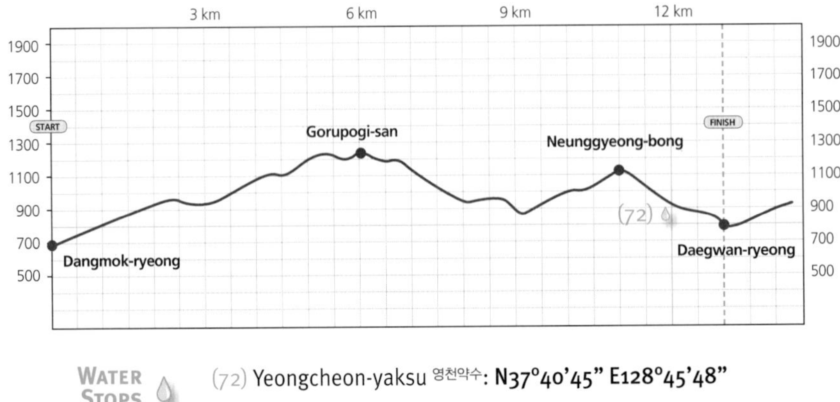

WATER STOPS (72) Yeongcheon-yaksu 영천약수: N37°40'45" E128°45'48"

Gorupogi-san 고루포기산 A2 → Neunggyeong-bong 능경봉 B2

5km (2:10)

From Gorupogi-san, the trail swings north, dropping into a saddle some 300 meters later, marked by a signpost and an old cairn. From there, the trail rises out of the saddle and flattens out at about 1,150 m ABSL. For the next kilometer, the trail descends northeast, losing 300 m in altitude before falling into a saddle. From there, it rises up to a spot height at 985 m ABSL, then drops again for 100 m into an area known as Hoenggye-chi 횡계치. You are now standing on the crest of the tunnel that penetrates the Baekdu-daegan, connecting NE50 from the east coast of Korea all the way to Seoul. Also from this region, if you haven't noticed already, you can see the wind turbines on the southern fringes of Odae-san National Park. At the right time of the year, this part of the trail produces some fine alpine wildflowers for the next 4 km to Neunggyeong-bong. At the open summit of Neunggyeong-bong is a small table indicating its name and height, providing you with good views to the east and north down to Gangneung, the biggest city on the northern half of Korea's east coast.

Neunggyeong-bong 능경봉 → Daegwan-ryeong 대관령 B2

2km (0:45)

The walk down to Daegwan-ryeong* is about 2 km long and heads mostly in a northerly direction. After 1 km, you come to your only water stop(72) of the day, which is unfortunately at the end of the trail. It is located just before the roadside area

The Stone Tower of Fortune

Just before the top of Neunggyeong-bong, you come across an impressive *doltap* located on the western side of the trail. It is called the "stone tower of fortune," and the signboard standing alongside it states, "Whenever our ancestors passed a steep mountain path, they picked up scattered stones on the road and heaped them one by one at a place on the roadside. Naturally roads were made, stones were piled (a stone heap of fortune), and they prayed for their good health and for safety on their journey at the stone heap, comforting their hearts. Like our ancestors' custom, we stand a stone tower (pagoda) of fortune here so that hikers who are walking the Baekdu-daegan and tracking its history can pray for their good health and safety. We wish everyone passing here to pile a stone at this stone tower with heart, to take with them the spirits and energy of Baekdu-daegan, and to be healthy and lucky forever."

that was once the main pass over the ridge. The water here comes from a spring and is superb in taste. As you walk your last stretches down to the ridge, you get good views of the wind turbines that are located here. You pass another rocky *doltap* and then turn west down to an impressively large monument of a turtle with a stele and cap on its back. This symbol is common throughout northeast Asia, signifying the basic oriental trinity of East Asian Confucian, Taoist and Buddhist thought comprising Heaven, Earth and Humanity. This theme is thousands of years old and known as Cheon-Ji-In 천지인 in Korea. The turtle represents the Earth, the standing black stone stele represents humanity and records what humans have done in their history, and the dragons on top represent Heaven's powers. These ones in particular are clutching the pearl of wisdom in the talons of their hind feet. This one at Daegwan-ryeong is one of the tallest you will see in Korea. Follow the steps down to the large parking area at Daegwan-ryeong, located right underneath the wind turbines.

Massive Cheon-Ji-In monument at Daegwan-ryeong

Wind turbines of Daegwan-ryeong

* Daegwan-ryeong 대관령 B2

The pass is connected by PR456 with the small village of Doam-myeon 도암면 5 km to the west and the village of Obong-ri 13 km off to the northeast, with the large seaside city Gangneung 8 km further on. There is no restaurant or store at Daegwan-ryeong, but there is a wind turbine museum. On the other side of the pass, there are some eateries, but their hours of operation are erratic and may only coincide with large bus tours that stop there to visit the nearby shrine located a further 700 meters up the ridge. There are some great views from the southeastern lip of the pass overlooking the East Sea.

Wind Turbine Museum 신재생에너지전시관 B2
• **Hour** 9 am to 6 pm (Closed on Mondays) • **Admission** 1,500 won

* Daegwan-ryeong Shrines 국사성황당 B1

About a kilometer up the other side of the pass lies the Daegwan-ryeong shrines, which contain the residence of the groundskeeper, a *seonghwang-sa* 성황사 ("tutelary spirit shrine"), a *sansin-gak* and some stone altars, some or all of which are often busy with a variety of shamanic practitioners. This shrine area is one of Korea's more famous blends of animistic faith and Confucian history. Historically, it has long been a sanctuary, with shrines devoted to the spirits who preside over or prevent drought, floods, storms, pestilence, harvests, and fishing in the nearby coastal area, and in particular Gangneung, at the eastern foot of the pass. Legend claims that the 9th

Wildflower Species

Jaburan, a hardy perennial that grows to heights of 15 to 100 cm and is, commonly known in other parts of the world as mondo grass, snake's-beard, and lilyturf, is found throughout the mountains in Korea and blooms from May to July with small blue or white flowers. *Hydrangea*, also known as *Hortsenia*, is a perennial native to Korea, Japan, the Himalayas, Indonesia, and North and South America. In Korea, it is distributed in the central and southern parts, with a flower that blooms in July and August. The Siberian *chrysanthemum*, found throughout the mountain ranges of Korea, is a perennial that grows to a height between 50 to 100 cm, with a flower that arrives between August and October. *Hosta longipes*, a perennial that grows in Jeju-do and the southern and central mountainous areas of Korea, grows between 30 and 50 cm in height, and its leaves and stems are edible once cooked. It produces a marvelous purple flower between July and August. The mountain *Hosta plantagenia*, which can be found next to mountain streams throughout the country, grows to 70cm in height and blooms between July and August.

century seon Buddhist master Beomil-guksa is now enshrined here as the *seonghwang* along with the *sanshin* of Daegwan-ryeong Pass. The larger one of the two structures (on the left) is the *seonghwang-sa*. However, the painting inside is more that of a warrior on horseback—another great debate of mystery in Korean history. The English information boards at the site state that some time after these two deities were enshrined here, they visited a 10th century army general, who then, as a result, won a local battle in this area against his rival, and so the painting may actually be of him. Ever since that time, the local residents have held ceremonies at these shrines on the morning of the fourth full moon of every lunar calendar year, which usually occurs

Daegwan-ryeong shrine

sometime in May. This event is the formal beginning of the annual Dano Festival, and it climaxes when the spirits possess the soul of a shaman and direct her to a young tree, which is decorated and cut down. This tree is then paraded down to the shrine of a female *sansin* at a city on the east coast and erected in front of it so that they can "mate" during the festival period, granting fertility and prosperity to the Gangneung area through good harvests from the sea and land. The Gangneung Dano-je Festival, one of Korea's best-known and most colorful traditional events, climaxes on the fifth day of the fifth moon, after which the sacred tree is burnt and the residents bid farewell to the spirits.

The stele at Daegwan-ryeong

Transport Info

Leaving the trail at Daegwan-ryeong: Apart from occasional coach tours, there is no bus service running to Daegwan-ryeong. The nearby town of Hoenggye-ri 횡계리 6 km to the west has a taxi service that will run to the pass; the number for Hoenggye Taxi is 033-335-5596. Otherwise, buses run from Hoenggye to Dong Seoul Terminal nine times daily from 7 am to 6:35 pm, and over to Gangneung every 15–20 minutes throughout the day. If you wish to leave the ridge, the nearest towns are Gangneung, 30 km to the east, and the small but pleasant town of Jinbu 30 km to the west. However, there will be many smaller towns and villages between these locations.

Lodging

It is possible to camp in the large park area around the huge turtle statue. The nearest town to Daegwan-ryeong is Doam-myeon 도암면, also known as Hoenggye-ri. This town is located about 5 km west on PR456 and has motel accommodation. To the northeast, Obong-ri is 13 km away on PR456, about 8 km west of Gangneung. This small village has a couple of motels and some good restaurants. The Korea Forest Service has cabins and campsites available at the Daegwan-ryeong Recreational Forest 대관령 자연휴양림 (T.033-641-9990 or 033-644-8327), located in Eoheul-ri 어흘리 up a mountain road that turns off PR456 9 km northeast of the pass. A trail runs down to Eoheul-ri from the Yeongcheon-yaksu spring 영천약수.

TWO DAYS

46.6 km

SECTION 14

ODAE-SAN NATIONAL PARK

Daegwan-ryeong → Guryong-ryeong

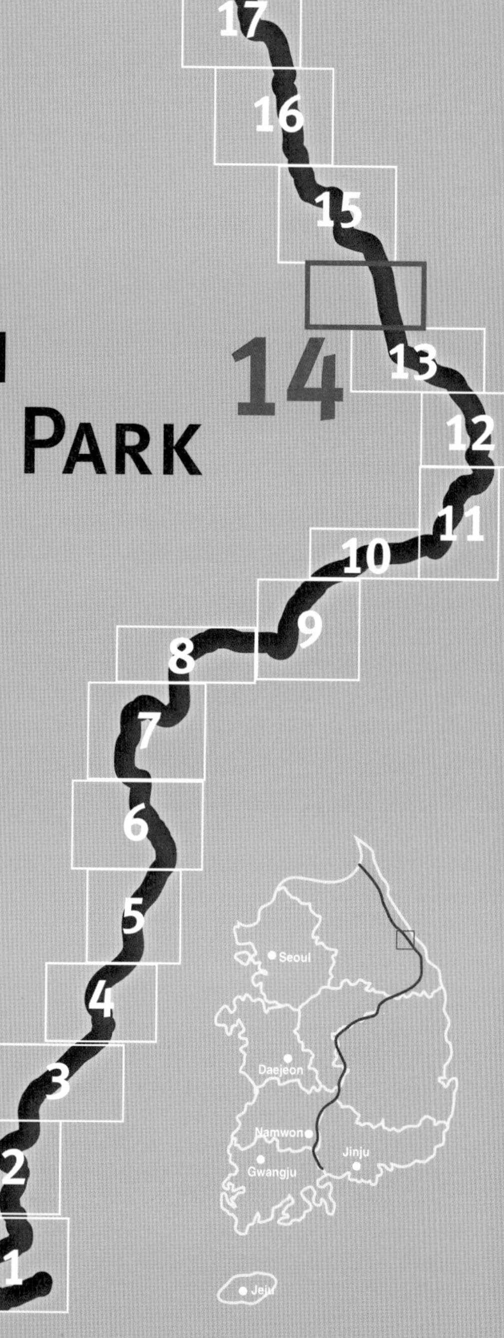

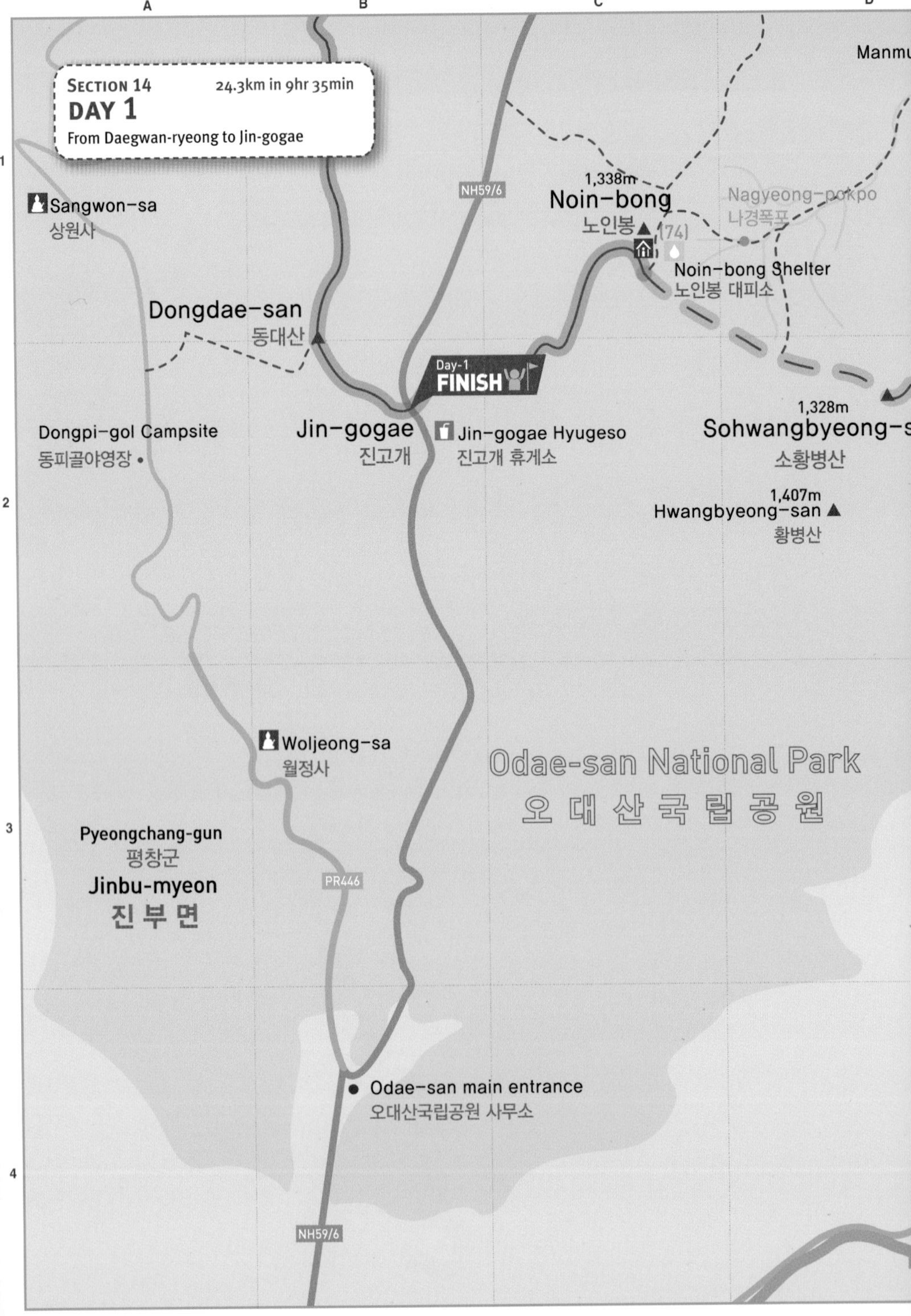

A
B
C
D
1
2
3
4
SECTION 14
24.3km in 9hr 35min
DAY 1
From Daegwan-ryeong to Jin-gogae
Manmu
Sangwon-sa
상원사
NH59/6
1,338m
Noin-bong
노인봉
(74)
Nagyeong-pokpo
나경폭포
Noin-bong Shelter
노인봉 대피소
Dongdae-san
동대산
Day-1
FINISH
1,328m
Sohwangbyeong-s
소황병산
Dongpi-gol Campsite
동피골야영장
Jin-gogae
진고개
Jin-gogae Hyugeso
진고개 휴게소
1,407m
Hwangbyeong-san
황병산
Woljeong-sa
월정사
Odae-san National Park
오 대 산 국 립 공 원
Pyeongchang-gun
평창군
Jinbu-myeon
진 부 면
PR446
Odae-san main entrance
오대산국립공원 사무소
NH59/6

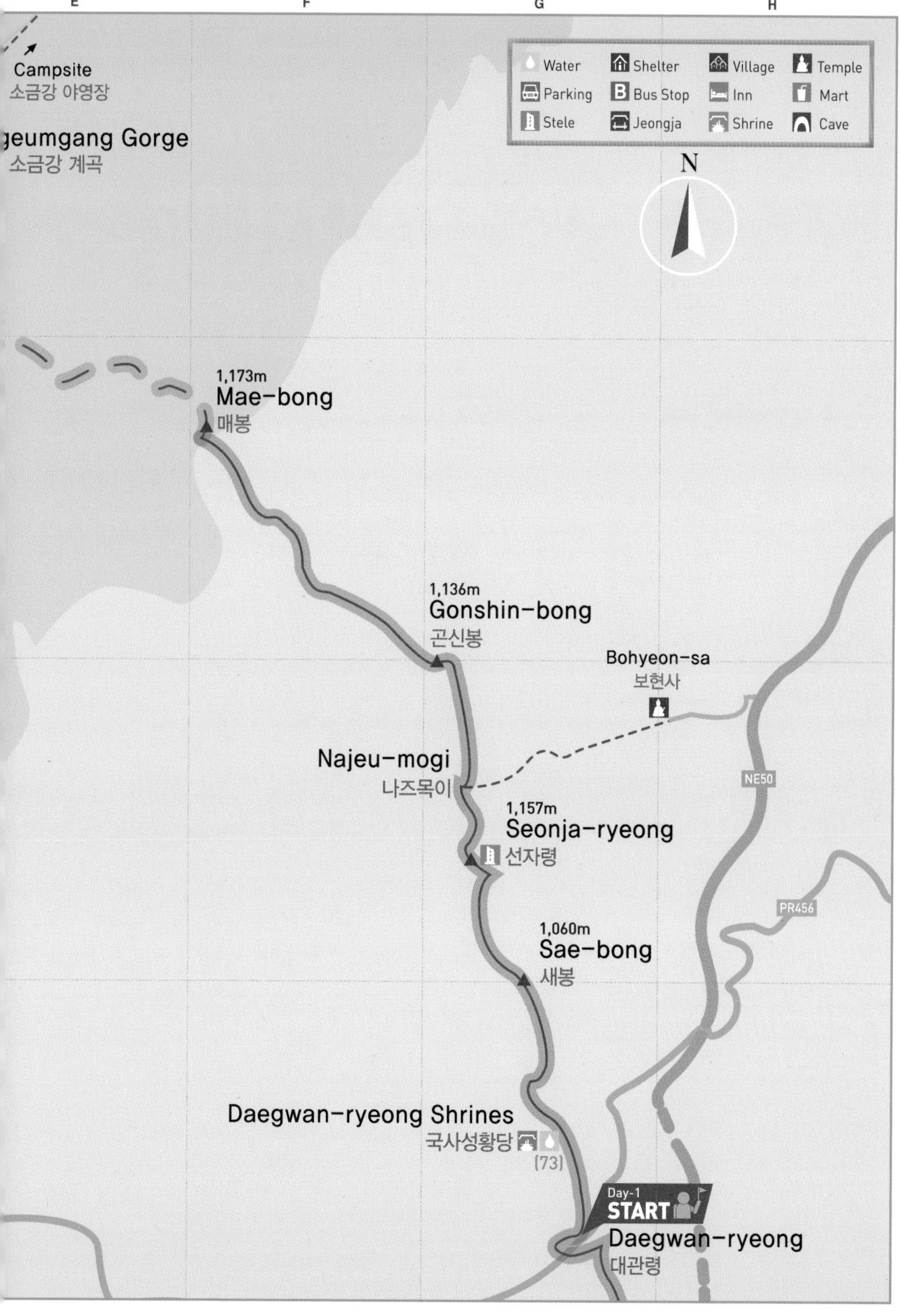
E
F
G
H
Campsite
소금강 야영장
geumgang Gorge
소금강 계곡
Water
Shelter
Village
Temple
Parking
Bus Stop
Inn
Mart
Stele
Jeongja
Shrine
Cave
N
1,173m
Mae-bong
매봉
1,136m
Gonshin-bong
곤신봉
Bohyeon-sa
보현사
Najeu-mogi
나즈목이
NE50
1,157m
Seonja-ryeong
선자령
PR456
1,060m
Sae-bong
새봉
Daegwan-ryeong Shrines
국사성황당
(73)
Day-1
START
Daegwan-ryeong
대관령

DAY 1 From Daegwan-ryeong to Jin-gogae

• **Distance:** 24.3km
• **Time:** 9hr 35min

Walk from the large stele turtle and the massive wind turbines at the top of the pass to the unique and historical shrines of Daegwan-ryeong. Study the history at the site, quench your thirst at the spring, and head back to the grassy ridgelines that will roll you up to the southern boundaries of the big, bald peaks of Odae-san. Bound over Sohwangbyeong-san and meticulously study the topography of the mountain of five platforms (Odae-san). Pick your ridgeline and walk to your highest peak of the day at Noin-bong. Stay in the shelter there and visit the sights of Sogeumgang Gorge, or carry on to make the pass at Jin-gogae, hitch a ride down to the south gate of Odae-san, and feel the magic at the temple of Woljeong-sa.

Daegwan-ryeong 대관령 G4 → Seonja-ryeong 선자령 G3

5km (2:05)

From Daegwan-ryeong, the Baekdu-daegan trail begins on the northern side of PR456. It cuts into the pine forest and then meanders casually east back up toward the crest of the pass again. It then joins a mountain road, passing some buildings and veering north as it approaches the ridge proper. After a kilometer, you arrive at a signpost directing you southwest, down into the valley toward the Daegwan-ryeong Shrines. There is water(73) available at this site. Refer to Section

13 for more information on the shrines.

The beauty of this section of the walk, and in fact one of the advantages of Odae-san 오대산, is that the landscape is predominantly open ground, allowing the hiker to have long vistas of the forthcoming terrain. For the next 1.5 km, the trail continues due north, slowly rising in elevation. Once at 1,050 m ABSL, the ridge stops gaining altitude and passes a peak called Sae-bong 새봉 at 1,060 m ABSL. About 1km later, it arrives at the summit area of Seonja-ryeong, marked by an impressive stele erected there on October 26, 2006, stating its height as 1,157 m ABSL. It was proudly put there as a celebration of the first year of the Baekdu-daegan as a protected area, and as a prayer for the reunification of Korea. On the back of the stele is some information about the feature from which it protrudes. It states that the peak has previously been called Daegwan-san 대관산, Bohyeon-san 보현산 and, most romantically of all, Manwol-san 만월산, meaning "full moon mountain." The story goes that it is called this because the peak area resembles the full moon rising above the temple of Bohyeon-sa 보현사, which is located 3 km northeast off the ridge from here.

Seonja-ryeong 선자령 → Gonsin-bong 곤신봉 G3 3km (1:00)

From Seonja-ryeong, the trail stays north, dropping into a saddle before rejoining the 4WD track 400 meters later. From there, you have the option of either following the 4WD track to the west or continuing along the ridgeline, following the ribbons as you do so. When you come to the bottom of the saddle, you should be met by a signpost. This area is called Najeu-mogi 나즈목이. For the next 2 km, the

Views from Seon-ja-ryeong

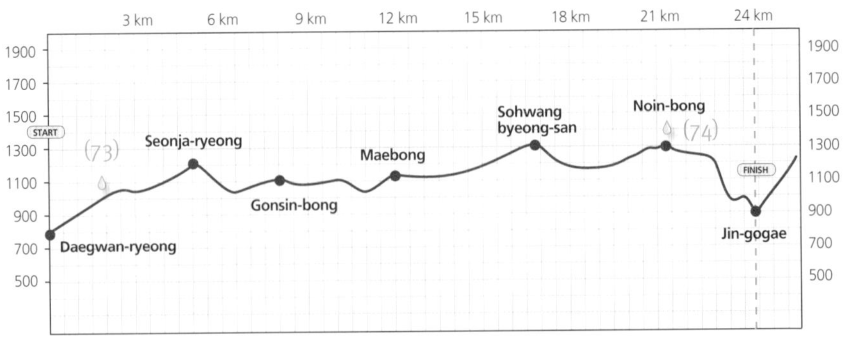

WATER STOPS

(73) Daegwan-ryeong Shrines: **N37°41'32" E128°45'25"**
(74) Noin-bong Daepiso 노인봉 대피소: **N37°45'32" E128°38'36"**

trail starts ascending again. About a kilometer later, it rejoins the 4WD track, and another 700 meters later, it turns sharply to the west as it begins its stretch up into Odae-san. Another 200 meters later, you arrive at the flat, indistinctive peak of Gonsin-bong at 1,136 m ABSL. From there, you should be able to see two distinctive features to your northwest. It is important to realize that the feature with the antenna and sphere at 280° is not your target. That is Hwangbyeong-san 황병산, which stands at 1,407 m ABSL and is the highest point you can see on this eastern side of Odae-san National Park, though not on the Baekdu-daegan crest line. Your target is about 1 km north of Hwangbyeong-san at 290°—not much of a difference.

Wind turbines at Seonja-ryeong

As there are also a number of roads in this area, it is quite simply easier to remember that there should be no roads to your right, or northeast of you; they should all be in the escarpment area to your left, or southwest of you.

Gonsin-bong 곤신봉 G3 → Mae-bong 매봉 F2 4km (1:40)

From Gonsin-bong, the trail remains in a northwest direction all the way to Mae-bong. It doesn't increase much in altitude, and the next 2 km are on easy, flattish ground, following a 4WD track. After those 2 km, you should arrive at a fork in the track. Take the right-hand, or north, arm of the fork and follow it for another 300 meters until you arrive at a small, round, depleted shelter. The trail from there starts swinging back into a northwest direction, leaving the 4WD track briefly before rejoining it again. It is from this region that you start a brief climb up to Mae-bong, which is also the National Park boundary for Odae-san.

Alternative Route

The 8.3 km section from Mae-bong to Noin-bong is CLOSED. The only alternative route is to walk up the Sogeumgang Valley 소금강 from the northeast entrance of Odae-san on NH6 to the peak of Noin-bong. Alternatively, you can take the bus up to the Jin-gogae ticket booth on NH6/59 and rejoin the Baekdu-daegan there.

CLOSED SECTION Mae-bong 매봉 F2 → Sohwangbyeong-san 소황병산 D2 4.8km (2:00)

The first 4 km of this closed section of the trail undulates at about the same altitude as Mae-bong (1,173m). The Baekdu-daegan arcs around in a westerly direction along the edge of an escarpment that descends to the south of the ridge. After 4 km, the trail begins its ascent for the final kilometer to Sohwangbyeong-san at 1,328 m ABSL. The trail itself doesn't necessarily go to the summit; it stays on the northern side of the large, round peak area, hugging the tree line. At about the western edge of the summit area, the Baekdu-daegan ridgeline can be seen running quite prominently 4 km northwest, forming a rolling saddle all the way to Noin-bong.

A lone tree near the summit of Sohwangbyeong-san

CLOSED SECTION Sohwangbyeong-san 소황병산 D2 → Noin-bong 노인봉 C1

3.5km (1:30)

From Sohwangbyeong-san, the trail drops about 150 m in altitude for the next 1.5 km before reaching the bottom of the saddle, where the trail meets another track heading in a northerly direction. This track descends to a waterfall area, known as Nagyeong-pokpo 낙경폭포, some 2 km later. That track actually joins the permitted northern route from Noin-bong through the beautiful Sogeumgang Gorge*. From the bottom of the saddle, the trail ascends northwest for the next 2 km to Noin-bong*, passing an exposed helipad located just above the shelter, tucked away on the northeastern lip of the peak.

* Sogeumgang Gorge 소금강 계곡 D1

This long, narrow stream-valley is supposed to be as beautiful as North Korea's Geumgang-san National Park—also on the Baekdu-daegan—and the prefix so means "small," thus suggesting a smaller version of one of Geumgang-san's gorges. It has also been called Cheonghak-dong 청학동 ("blue crane village") because people thought that it was shaped like a crane spreading its wings. It is the peaks above this valley that cause the endless array of waterfalls that pass through its clutches. Historically, Sogeumgang Gorge was once a place where great poets of Korea

The sunlit ridge from Sohwangbyeong-san to Noin-bong

resided during the 16th and 17th centuries. One of them, the famous Heo Gyun, supposedly wrote Korea's first novel, *Honggildong-jeon*, while living here. The story was written during the late Joseon period and told about a character called Hong Gil-dong who was famous for robbing the rich to feed the poor, much like the English folk hero Robin Hood. There are useful monuments and more information about this writer located at the entrance gates.

The upper area of the gorge through which the trail from the ridge passes is known as Manmulsang 만물상 and is a series of fantastic granite rocks and precipices that are like a natural mural depicting every form in creation. Each rock has its own legend according to its shape. One tower resembles an incense burner that exorcises evil spirits and thus is called Hyangno-bong 향로봉; this is a unique name in Korean mountain culture, as the last peak on the Baekdu-daegan in the restricted militarized zone is also called Hyangno-bong, and on its fortified summit sits a cast-iron incense burner. One of the other rock features resembles the sun and the moon playing hide-and-seek with each other. Still another feature here is called Tangeum-dae 탕음대, meaning "a hill for playing the *gayageum*," referring to the twelve-stringed Korean harp. Over a thousand years ago, a poetess once played here in praise of the elegance of a poetic life. Her tones can supposedly still be heard at night sweeping through the Manmulsang Gorge.

Picnicking at Sogeumgang Gorge

The valley is accessed from NH6 on the east coast of South Korea. There is a camping ground in the valley called Sogeumgang Campground, and it is located close to the bus stop. At the trail entrance to the Sogeumgang Gorge are a number of *minbak*, including the Mureung Sanjang 무릉산장 (T. 033-661-4132), Sanjang Minbak 산장민박 (T. 033-661-4309) and Seoul Minbak 서울민박 (T. 033-661-5636).

TRANSPORT INFO

Joining the trail at Sogeumgang: Buses leave Gangneung Terminal for Sogeumgang 13 times a day between 6:15 am and 9 pm. The 24 km trip costs 1,100 won.

* Noin-bong 노인봉 C1

At the summit of Noin-bong (1,338m) is a small stone plaque commemorating the height of the peak and its name. You also have fabulous views all the way back to the summit of Sohwangbyeong-san to the southeast.

The Noin-bong Shelter (T. 011-354-5579) sleeps about 30 people. As with all shelters, blankets are available for rent, and clean water is available. The Noin-bong Shelter is a great place to watch the sunrise over the East Sea and to see the lights of squid boats in the ocean at night. Noin-bong shelter is a first come, first served deal, but you can call the park office (T. 033-332-6417) if you wish. There is also water(74) at this shelter.

The summit of Noin-bong

Noin-bong 노인봉 C1 → Jin-gogae 진고개 B2 4km (1:20)

This section of the trail is open, allowing people to access Noin-bong from Jin-gogae. To get off Noin-bong, there is a trail from the western side of the summit, or another trail from the helipad near the shelter. Either way gets you down to the Jin-gogae Pass some 4 km later.

* Jin-gogae 진고개 B2

The pass is connected by NH6/59, with the main entrance to the park located 8.5 km south and the road junction of NH59 and NH6 some 15 km north. The area is supported by a large *hyugeso*. The store is well stocked with hot food, cold drinks, and other commodities useful for the trail. There are also toilets in the area, but there is no accommodation to speak of.

Transport Info

Joining the trail at Jin-gogae: Buses do not run to Jin-gogae. The nearest town, Jinbu-myeon 진부면, has a taxi service that will run to the pass; the number for Jinbu Taxi is 033-335-1050. Buses from Jinbu do run to Sangwon-sa Temple in Odae-san National Park eight times a day from 8:30 am to 4:40 pm, with a later bus running at 7:40 pm. Jinbu-myeon is a gateway town to Odae-san National Park and the surrounding ski area, and buses run regularly from Jinbu-myeon to Seoul, Wonju and other main centers.

Lodging

The *hyugeso* itself does not operate as a *minbak*. The Odae-san main entrance, located 8.5 km south of Jin-gogae at the junction of NH59 and PR446, has a lot of accommodation options, including *minbak*, motels and hotels. Odae-san National Park has a campground in the valley between the temples of Woljeong-sa 월정사 and Sangwon-sa 상원사. The Dongpi-gol Campsite 동피골 야영장 has 260 tent sites, and the fee depends on the size of your tent. Inquire at the main office in the park.

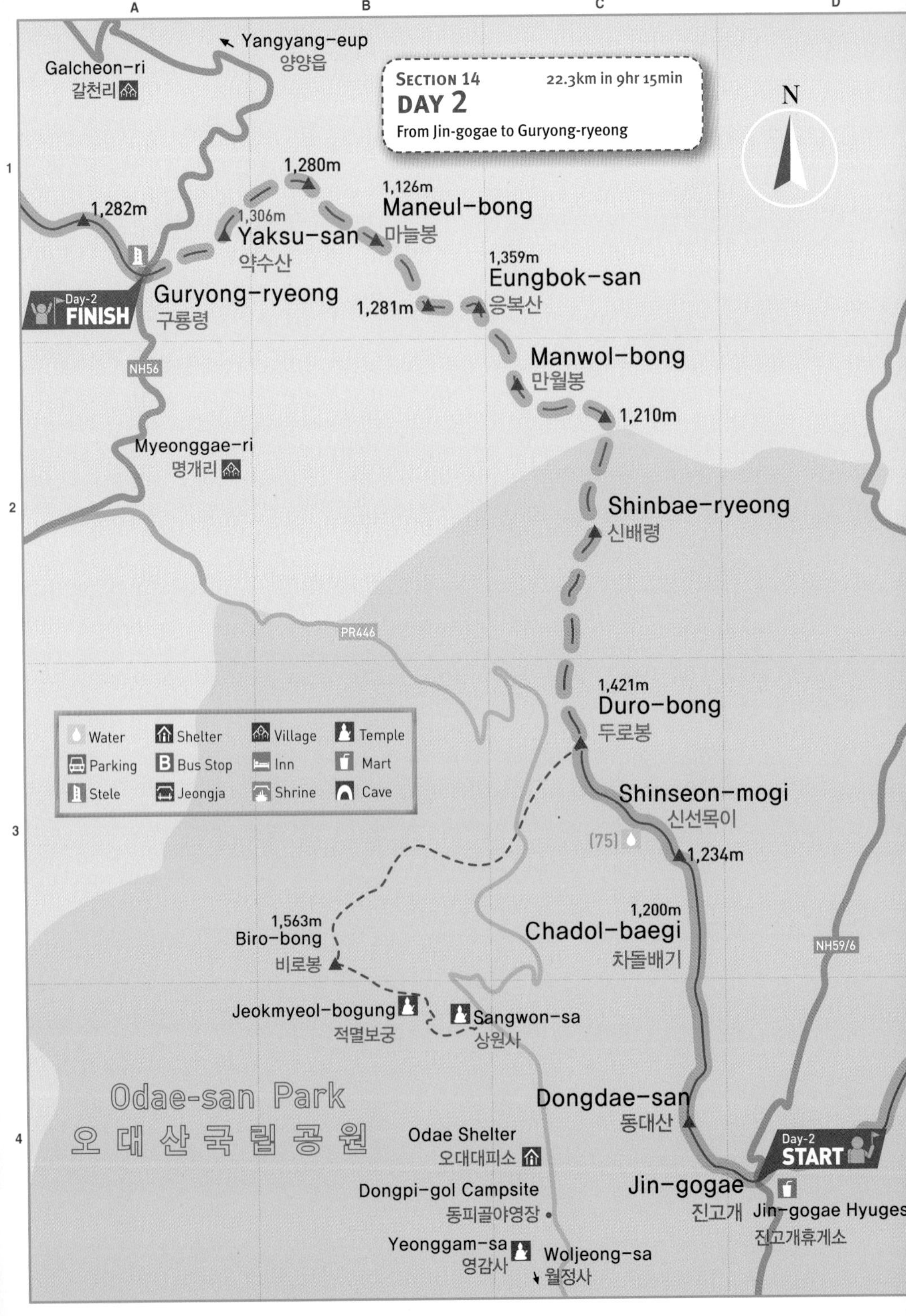

A
B
C
D
1
2
3
4
Yangyang-eup
양양읍
Galcheon-ri
갈천리
SECTION 14
22.3km in 9hr 15min
DAY 2
From Jin-gogae to Guryong-ryeong
N
1,280m
1,126m
Maneul-bong
마늘봉
1,282m
1,306m
Yaksu-san
약수산
1,359m
Eungbok-san
응복산
Day-2
FINISH
Guryong-ryeong
구룡령
1,281m
NH56
Manwol-bong
만월봉
1,210m
Myeonggae-ri
명개리
Shinbae-ryeong
신배령
PR446
1,421m
Duro-bong
두로봉
Water
Shelter
Village
Temple
Parking
Bus Stop
Inn
Mart
Stele
Jeongja
Shrine
Cave
Shinseon-mogi
신선목이
[75]
1,234m
1,200m
Chadol-baegi
차돌배기
1,563m
Biro-bong
비로봉
NH59/6
Jeokmyeol-bogung
적멸보궁
Sangwon-sa
상원사
Odae-san Park
오대산국립공원
Dongdae-san
동대산
Day-2
START
Odae Shelter
오대대피소
Dongpi-gol Campsite
동피골야영장
Jin-gogae
진고개
Jin-gogae Hyuges
진고개휴게소
Yeonggam-sa
영감사
Woljeong-sa
월정사

DAY 2 From Jingo-gae to Guryong-ryeong

• **Distance:** 22.3km
• **Time:** 9hr 15min

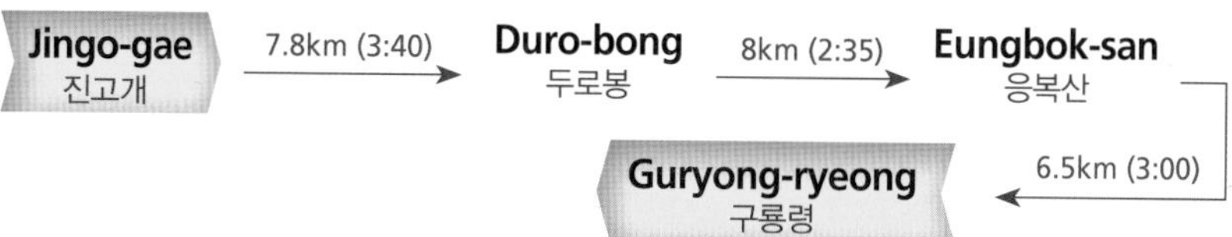

This is a stunning and resolute leg of the Baekdu-daegan that sees you walking onto some big ridges with large saddles. The terrain begins to take on a different air as it enters a more trans-Siberian landscape with barren, open country, supplying long, sweeping views north toward Seorak-san and Geumgang-san in North Korea. The walk also passes near the heart of Odae-san as the trail marches north along the eastern flanks of some very famous areas featuring great temples, one of them allegedly containing relics of Buddha himself. As the trail leaves the park in the north, it stretches out and arcs down to the high-altitude pass of Guryong-ryeong, the starting point of the Seorak-san region.

Jin-gogae 진고개 D4 → Duro-bong 두로봉 C3 7.8km (3:40)

From the pass at Jin-gogae, the trail starts at the bottom of an embankment on the western side of NH59/6. You will be able to see a flight of stairs going up to the bush line almost opposite the ranger's hut. It is a good 500 meter climb up a northwest spur that takes you to the summit of Dongdae-san 동대산. At the summit of Dongdae-san, there is a small stele and signboard displaying directions to the surrounding mountains. There is supposedly a group of Mongolian oak trees in the vicinity as well. From the summit, the Baekdu-daegan trail heads north, descending in altitude as it takes you for 2.5 km down into a saddle. The saddle area you are now in is known as Chadol-baegi 차돌배기. The trail from there hovers

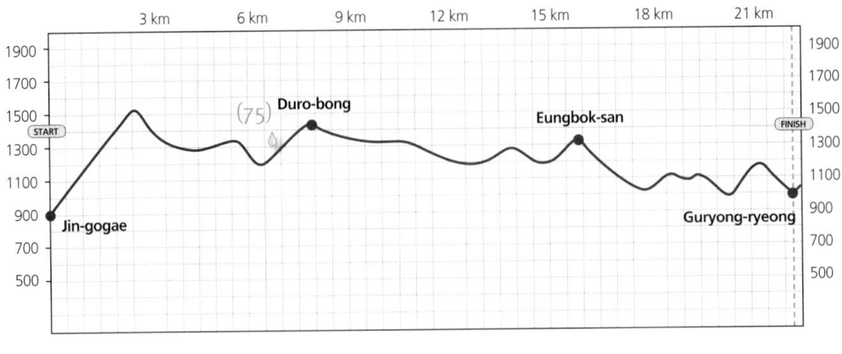

WATER STOPS (75) Sinseon-mogi: **N37°48'25" E128°35'39"**

at its current altitude of 1,200 m ABSL and undulates north for another kilometer before you reach a signpost on the trail. Another 700 meter stretch of trail sees you dropping into another saddle before arriving at another peak at 1,234 m ABSL. From there, the trail drops for the next 400 meters toward another saddle, named Sinseon-mogi 신선목이. You might be able to see a track from here running west off the ridge into a deep valley about a kilometer away. If you follow this track downhill for about 100 meters, you will find water(75). Back on the ridge, the trail climbs northwest on its route to Duro-bong for the next kilometer, after which the trail descends for 300 meters into a shallow saddle, meeting a signpost at the bottom. From there, the trail continues up the ridge for another 400 meters before panning out onto the summit of Duro-bong at 1,421 m ABSL, marking the end of the open section. At the summit, there is a flat open area acting as a helipad, with a small stele celebrating the peak located around its edge. Duro-bong offers the hiker many more great opportunities to take in the 360° views.

Alternative Route

At Duro-bong, there is a track from the summit going southwest, joining another ridgeline all the way to Biro-bong some 7 km away and forming a great circular route. If you follow the same track for 2 km, you will discover that it meets a mountain road to the right of the crest of a pass. This alternative gives you the option of turning north and walking a twisted 15 km all the way down to where it joins NH56, about 6 km south of Guryong-ryeong, the end point of this leg of the walk. From there, you will have to hitch or arrange a taxi up to Guryong-ryeong. There is only one bus that runs over the pass, doing so once a day.

CLOSED SECTION Duro-bong 두로봉 C3 → Eungbok-san 응복산 B1 8km (2:35)

From Duro-bong, the trail enters the tree line and drops steeply off the summit, passing in and out of tree cover. In the right spot, the hiker can see the conical shape of Daecheong-bong 대청봉 in Seorak-san some 50 km away. The trail then gently cascades down a smooth and easygoing ridgeline for the next 2 km before reaching a pass known as Sinbae-ryeong 신배령. From this pass, the trail continues to descend for 2 km into the region forming the northern boundary of Odae-san National Park, marked by a small fence. The last point of the park is an unnamed peak at 1,210m ABSL, which offers great views to the north. After leaving the park, the trail starts to ascend and arc to the northwest for the next 2 km before it gets to the peak of Manwol-bong 만월봉. At its summit area are more good views of the chain of peaks connected by the Baekdu-daegan, doing a semi-circular northwestern route. From Manwol-bong, the trail drops into another saddle and arrives 500 meters later at the peak of Eungbok-san, at 1,359 m ABSL. From Duro-bong, the trail enters the tree line and drops steeply off the summit, passing in and out of tree cover. In the right spot, the hiker can see the conical shape of Daecheong-bong in Seorak-san some 50 km away. The trail then gently cascades down a smooth and easygoing ridgeline for the next 2 km before reaching a pass known as Sinbae-ryeong. From this pass, the trail continues to descend for 2 km into the region forming the northern boundary

Eungbok-san with Daecheong-bong in the background

of Odae-san National Park, marked by a small fence. The last point of the park is an unnamed peak at 1,210 m ABSL, which offers great views to the north. After leaving the park, the trail starts to ascend and arc to the northwest for the next 2 km before it gets to the peak of Manwol-bong. At its summit area are more good views of the chain of peaks connected by the Baekdu-daegan, doing a semi-circular northwestern route. From Manwol-bong, the trail drops into another saddle and arrives 500 meters later at the peak of Eungbok-san, at 1,359 m ABSL.

CLOSED SECTION Eungbok-san 응복산 B1 → Guryong-ryeong 구룡령 A1

6.5km (3:00)

For the next 500 meters, the trail from Eungbok-san drops west onto another peak at 1,281 m ABSL. From there, it drops steeply in a northwest direction for 600 meters before arriving at a saddle. From the saddle, the trail ascends steeply, rising about 150 m in altitude northwest to the summit of Maneul-bong 마늘봉 ("garlic peak") at 1,126 m ABSL. From there, the trail undulates northwest for another 1.2 km, providing good views to the north. At an unnamed peak located at 1,280 m ABSL, the trail turns dramatically off its summit in a southwest direction and quickly loses altitude, dropping about 100 m before it hits another saddle on the ridgeline. From this region, the hiker may be able to get more views of the peaks of Geumgang-san in North Korea, past Seorak-san. After that, the trail rises again and starts to veer south, where about 1km later it comes out onto the summit of Yaksu-san 약수산 at 1,306 m ABSL. This peak, which has clusters of rock on it, should provide you with majestic views west into the mountains of Gangwon-do near the DMZ. The hiker should also be able to see the steep drop down into Guryong-ryeong about 1 km away to the west.

* Guryong-ryeong 구룡령 A1

The isolated pass at Guryong-ryeong ("nine dragon pass") is located at 1,031 m ABSL on NH56, which runs north for 20 km to NH44, near Osaek Valley, and south for 40 km to Jinbu-myeon, near Odae-san National Park. There is also a nature bridge with a dual carriageway tunnel running beneath it, but the trail doesn't pass over the bridge. Guryong-ryeong does appear to be celebrated and has a number of features representing the Baekdu-daegan. The first and most notable item is the gargantuan stele erected on October 18, 2006. It was supposedly the tallest monument on the trail as of the end of 2008, with the one at Hwa-ryeong a close second. On the back of the tower is an inscription explaining that the next 48

The stele at Guryong-ryeong

km of ridgeline represents the twisted and concertinaed features of nine dragons entangled in a death roll. The area also is proclaimed to have tens of thousands of valleys and one thousand peaks.

TRANSPORT INFO

Joining the trail at Guryong-ryeong: Buses running between Yangyang-eup on the east coast and Hongcheon-eup to the southwest cross Guryong-ryeong once a day. The bus leaves Hongcheon Terminal at 7:10 am and reaches Guryong-ryeong two hours later. The bus from Yangyang-eup leaves at 8:10 am and reaches Guryong-ryeong one hour later.

LODGING

The *hyugeso* at Guryong-ryeong appears closed, but the area outside is suitable for camping. About 6 km to the south along NH56 is the junction with PR446, the turnoff to the Nae-myeon Odae-san park entrance in Myeonggae-ri 명개리. Up this road is the Seunghui Hwangto Minbak 승희 황토 민박 (T. 011-9654-8461), a peaceful little place set amongst the mature forest of remote northern Odae-san. North of the pass in Galcheon-ri 갈천리, 10 km away down the steep, winding NH56, is the more upmarket Guryeong-ryeong Hwangto-bang Pension구룡령 황토방 펜션 (T. 033-914-5300). Call the number or visit www.9dragonhill.com for bookings. Rooms at the pension start at 110,000 won.

ODAE-SAN NATIONAL PARK 오대산 국립공원

Odae-san, meaning "five platforms mountain," is home to 860 species of plant life; 26 known species of mammal, including wild boar, goral and deer; 85 species of birds, including five colored woodpeckers; 1,124 species of insects; and 31 species of freshwater fishes. It attracts about one million visitors to its peaks and valleys every year. Odae-san is known as one of the greatest mountains in Korea and has a bevy of cultural and historical assets. The main entrance to Odae-san is at the south end of the park at Woljeong Ticket Booth 월정 매표소. Near the entrance of the park are two camping grounds and two shelters. The park's roundish shape generates good one-day hiking trails. Odae-san's peaks and ridges are mainly covered with soil and vegetation, unlike most other mountains in Gangwon-do, which mostly feature exposed rock on their crests. Odae-san National Park is an area worth investigating further, and as some of the Baekdu-daegan sections within it are closed, it offers, in turn, a nice alternative to get off the trail and do some exploring of the many other sites, waterfalls, hermitage-temples, peaks and gorges that are open to the public. The highest peak of this mountain cluster is actually outside the park boundaries to the southwest: the mighty Gyebang-san, at 1,577 m ABSL. Its slopes, most often approached from the high pass on NH31, and the surrounding regions to the north, west and south are some of Korea's remotest, least-trammeled forestlands.

Historical Temples

Upon returning from China, the important Silla Dynasty master monk Jajang-yulsa named this area "Odae-san" due to its topographical and religious similarity with a famous sacred mountain complex in China called Wutai-shan. Not too far from the front gates is Woljeong-sa Monastery. This famous Buddhist temple, this region's headquarters for the national Jogye Order, was built by Jajang in AD 645. At the center of the temple grounds is the octagonal, nine-storied pagoda he built to enshrine relics, standing 15.5 m in height but leaning 15° to the southeast. It is also possible to visit the location where the National Royal Archives of the Joseon Dynasty were once stored, due to this valley's remoteness from invading armies and favorable geomantic features. Halfway between Woljeong-sa and Sangwon-sa, on a noticeable bend in the road, is a turnoff to Yeonggam-sa 영감사, located about 500 meters up an old

Woljeong-sa

vehicle track on the western side of the road. The library buildings were built here in 1606, and there were three other such sites around the nation where copies of official records were kept to avoid theft and destruction. Unfortunately, the surviving documents at this site were confiscated by the Japanese colonial authorities in the early 1900s, and most of them subsequently burned up at Tokyo Imperial University during the 1923 Kanto Earthquake.

Another famous temple on the grounds, called Sangwon-sa, sits a further 10 km up the road entrance to Odae-san at the base of the mountains. It was also built by the famous master Jajang, and it is the route toward Odae-san's highest mountain peak, called Biro-bong 비로봉 standing at 1,563 m ABSL. Inside the temple grounds exists a bronze bell called the Sangwonsa-dongjong 상원사동종. It is the oldest existing bell in Korea, constructed in AD 725. It stands 1.68 m high, has a diameter of 91 cm, and weighs 3,300 lbs. The bell has stood there for 1,200 years and has seen the full history of Korea. Its chime is said to make varying noises according to the time of the year, and it can be heard through every valley in the region. Odae-san was declared by Jajang to be the Korean residence of Munsu-bosal ("the Bodhisattva of Wisdom"), said to sometimes appear in various guises to test people's faith and ethics. There is a well-known tale recounting how mid-Joseon King Sejo once encountered this deity in the form of a small boy while bathing in the nearby stream, and the mysterious meeting cured the monarch's skin disease. Sejo ordered the carving of a larger than life-sized statue of Munsu-bosal as the boy from lovely wood, and it is still enshrined here at Sangwon-sa; a famous National Treasure, it is visited and venerated by many. Two kilometers after the temple of Sangwon-sa, on the way up to Biro-bong, you can visit the very famous and sacred site of Jeokmyeol-bogung 적멸보궁, containing the *sarira* relics of Buddha carried by Jajang from China. They are buried beneath a flat, grassy hump behind the shrine building, where you should be able to watch numerous people bowing, praying or contemplating before the relic site.

Transport Info

Joining the trail at Odae-san National Park: Buses leave Jinbu terminal for Odae-san National Park 12 times daily, at 6:20 am, 7:40 am, 8:30 am, 9:30 am, 10:40 am, 11:40 am, 12:40 pm, 2:10 pm, 3:30 pm, 4:30 pm, 6:20 pm and 7:40 pm. All these buses head to Woljeong-sa Temple. The 8:30-4:30 buses continue on past Woljeong-sa to Sangwon-sa Temple deeper in the park. Buses leave the park for Jinbu-myeon at 6:40 am, 8 am, 9:20 am, 10:30 am, 11:30 am, 12:40 pm, 1:50 pm, 3:10 pm, 4:20 pm, 5:20 pm, 6:40 pm and 8 pm. The first and last two buses leave from Woljeong-sa. The 9:20-5:20 buses leave from Sangwon-sa and pass Woljeong-sa 15 minutes later.

Lodging

The main Woljeong entrance has the Dongpi-gol Campsite 동피골 야영장 located close to the Odae shelter 오대 대피소. This campsite can hold about 260 medium-sized tents, and camping fees vary depending on the size of your tent. The Odae Shelter has a capacity of about 45 people: 30 for the shelter, and 15 for the lodge, at about 30,000 won per family. A kitchen is available at the shelter. It is also possible to stay at this temple for a fee of around 40,000 won as part of the temple-stay program. Visit http://eng.templestay.com or www.woljeongsa.org to make a reservation. Alternatively, you can call the temple at 033-332-6664.

40
주정차금지
불법주차단속

TWO DAYS

43.5km

SECTION 15
NINE DRAGONS PASS

Guryong-ryeong →
Hangye-ryeong

17
16
15
14
13
12
11
10
9
8
7
6
5
4
3
2
1

Seoul
Daejeon
Namwon
Gwangju
Jinju
Jeju

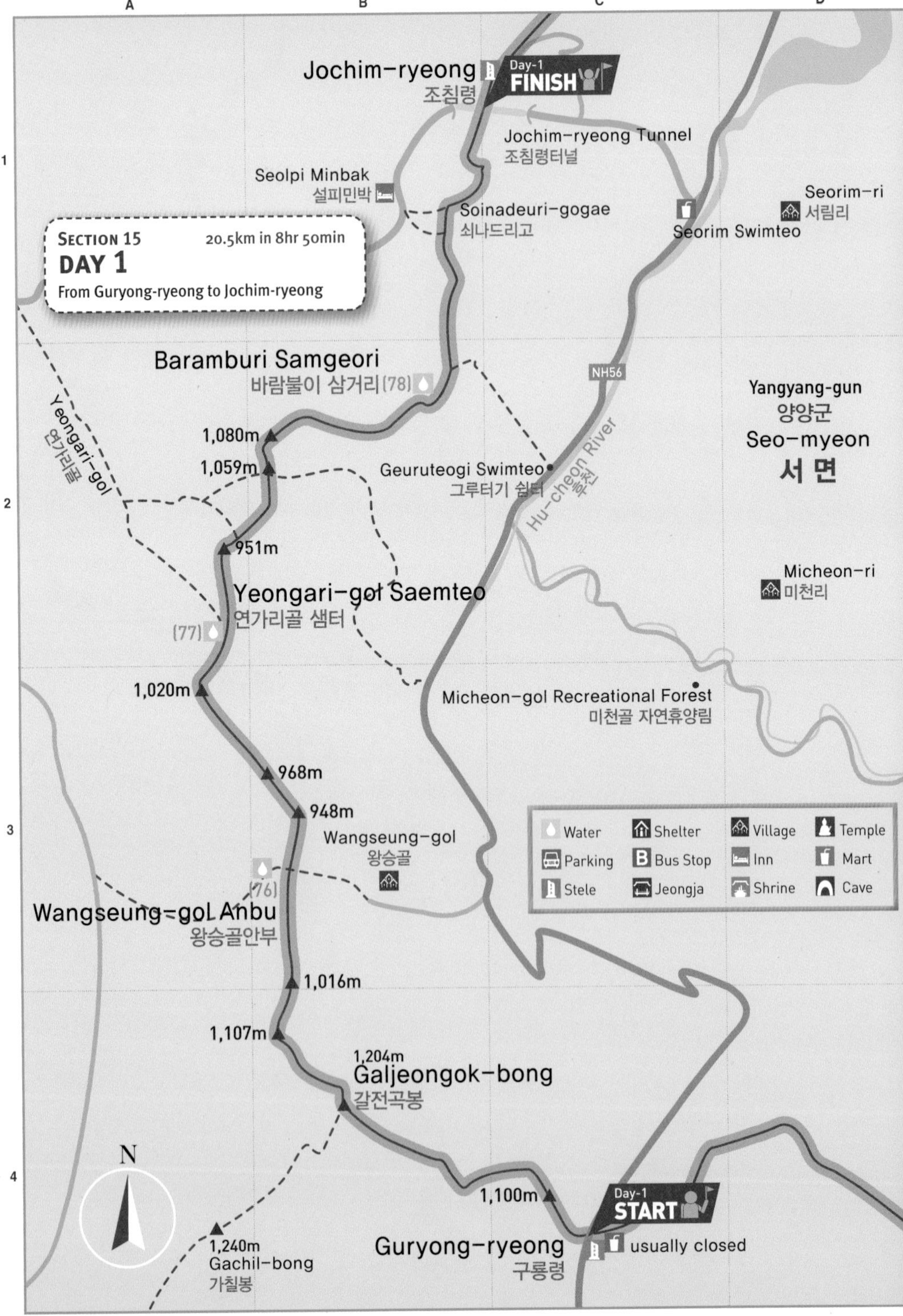

A
B
C
D
1
2
3
4
Jochim-ryeong
조침령
Day-1
FINISH
Jochim-ryeong Tunnel
조침령터널
Seolpi Minbak
설피민박
Soinadeuri-gogae
쇠나드리고개
Seorim-ri
서림리
Seorim Swimteo
SECTION 15
20.5km in 8hr 50min
DAY 1
From Guryong-ryeong to Jochim-ryeong
Baramburi Samgeori
바람불이 삼거리
(78)
NH56
Yangyang-gun
양양군
Seo-myeon
서면
Yeongari-gol
연가리골
1,080m
1,059m
Geuruteogi Swimteo
그루터기 쉼터
Hu-cheon River
후천
951m
Micheon-ri
미천리
Yeongari-gol Saemteo
연가리골 샘터
(77)
1,020m
Micheon-gol Recreational Forest
미천골 자연휴양림
968m
948m
Wangseung-gol
왕승골
Water
Shelter
Village
Temple
Parking
Bus Stop
Inn
Mart
Stele
Jeongja
Shrine
Cave
(76)
Wangseung-gol Anbu
왕승골안부
1,016m
1,107m
1,204m
Galjeongok-bong
갈전곡봉
N
1,100m
Day-1
START
Guryong-ryeong
구룡령
usually closed
1,240m
Gachil-bong
가칠봉

DAY 1 From Guryong-ryeong to Jochim-ryeong

- **Distance:** 20.5km
- **Time:** 8hr 50min

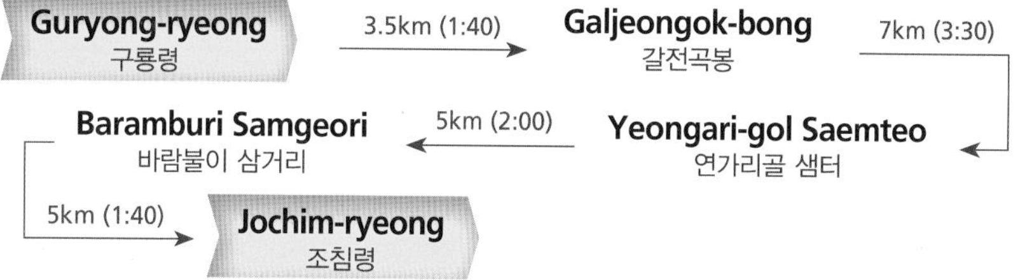

From Guryong-ryeong, you continue to walk on an undulating ridge averaging about 1,000 m ABSL all the way to Jochim-ryeong. During the day, you take in the tumultuous grandeur of the mountains in this area. The ridge starts in a northwest direction for 5 km before turning north all the way to Jochim-ryeong for the remaining 17 km. The ridge is steady and easy to walk on, well marked and well worn as it filters through a reforestation of needle- and broad-leaved trees put there to intensify resistance against the weather and to enhance the beauty and scenery. It is probably a stunner to walk in the warm verdant months of Korea between May and mid-October, and it is well resourced with water on its western flank. As per the legend of the area, it feels like you are combing your way along the narrow, winding back of a dragon, arriving eventually at the dusty, isolated pass of Jochim-ryeong, which supports a megalithic stele.

Guryong-ryeong 구룡령 C4 → Galjeongok-bong 갈전곡봉 B4

3.5km (1:40)

The next leg of the walk starts on the western side of the road at the base of a set of wooden stairs. Follow the steps up to the crest of the ridge and begin your

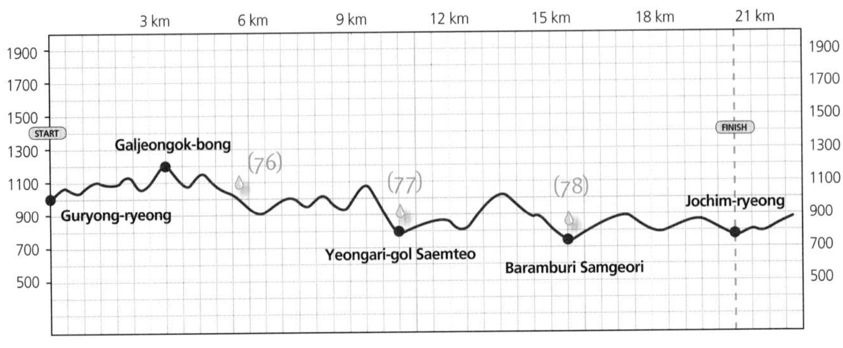

WATER STOPS

(76) Wangseung-gol Anbu: **N37°54'51" E128°28'32"**
(77) Yeongari-gol Saemteo: **N37°55'51" E128°28'13"**
(78) Baramburi Samgeori: **N37°57'38" E128°29'45"**

march 500 meters in a northwest direction to an unnamed peak at 1,100 m ABSL. From there, the trail undulates west for 500 meters before changing its path back to a northwest direction and arriving 2 km later at the peak of Galjeongok-bong (1,204m), marked by your first signpost.

Galjeongok-bong 갈전곡봉 B4 → Yeongari-gol Saemteo 연가리골샘터 A2

7km (3:30)

From this peak, the trail descends sharply in a northerly direction for about 500 meters, dropping 150 m in altitude before flattening out a little and then ascending up to your next unnamed peak located at 1,107 m ABSL. For the next 2 km, the trail remains in a northerly direction, dropping from 1,107m ABSL to about 820 m ABSL. It passes through a series of six saddles and ever shorter peaks before spilling out onto a pass known as Wangseung-gol Anbu 왕승골 안부. The pass is easily recognized, as it is signposted and has a corral of small tree stumps and benches in the middle of it. Water(76) can be found at this pass about 100 meters down the western track. There is a sign at the Wangseung-gol Anbu pass stating that the Baekdu-daegan is peculiar to Korea's geography. It quotes its length throughout the peninsula as 1,494 km, otherwise describing its geography like others previously reported. The sign continues on to say, rather patriotically, that the Baekdu-daegan begins at the sacred mountain of Baekdu-san (2,744m), which sits right on the Chinese border within Korea, guarded to the east and west by the natural barriers of the Duman-gang (Tumen River) and Amnok-gang (Yalu River), which is the birthplace of the mythological father of Korea, Dangun Wanggeom. It also states that the great 15th century king Sejong militarily secured Korea's sides of those great rivers so that the entire sacred Baekdu-san could truly belong to Korea. From Wangseung-gol Anbu, the trail continues north for 500 meters, ascending up the ridge and reaching a beautiful tomb located on the eastern side of the trail. The next 2.5 km sees the trail pull northwest through some good wooded countryside, climbing up to another unnamed peak located at 1,020 m ABSL and marked by a helipad. From there, the trail turns northeast, dropping about 250 m in altitude for the next kilometer to the pass of Yeongari-gol Saemteo.

Yeongari-gol Saemteo 연가리골 샘터 A2 → Baramburi Samgeori 바람불이 삼거리 B2

5km (2:00)

At the pass of Yeongari-gol Saemteo (spring), there is another cleared area with some stumps and benches providing the opportunity to rest and cook up a meal. The pass has two signs explaining that the needle- and broad-leaved trees in this area make the air fresh and help absorb dust. The sign further states that one hectare of needle-leaf trees filters about 30 to 40 tons of dust a year, and that broad-leaved trees filter out about 68 tons of dust per year via their pores, or stomata. The sign continues on to mention how in an urban environment, trees also act as noise buffers, and how a 50 meter wide forest will reduce 10-15 decibels of noise. It concludes by saying that a forest can block out the hot sunbeams and reduce air temperatures by 3 to 4°C. Now to support that: the other sign under it is titled "The Forest Is a Green Dam." In the rather quirky mannerisms characteristic of the Korean language when directly translated, it says that a forest is called a "green dam" because it holds rainwater within it and streams that water slowly downhill. A forest, in turn, will help control the flow of that rainwater, reducing waste and purifying the water. The images show how when it rains, the forest controls floods, and when it doesn't rain, it still regulates water. The same sign concludes that the forest is cultivated by the sunlight that shines into the bottom of the forest, allowing small trees to grow and stimulating the

Yeongari-gol Saemteo

decay of fallen leaves, thus creating fertile soil in the hydrated soil of the green dam.

There are also some good water sources(77) in this area about 50 meters down the western track in a mountain stream. From there, the trail ascends for the next kilometer in a northerly direction before turning northeast, passing through stands of knee-high bamboo forest for the next kilometer and ending up at an unnamed peak located at 1,059 m ABSL. From there, the trail ascends for 300 meters to 1,080 m, with great views to the east toward Micheon-ri 미천리. From this point, the trail starts to bend its way to the east and begin a 2 km descent down to Baramburi Samgeori. Marked by a signpost, Baramburi Samgeori offers enough space for camping, and water(78) can be found on the northwestern side of the ridge again.

Baramburi Samgeori 바람불이 삼거리 B2 → Jochim-ryeong 조침령 C1 — 5km (1:40)

The trail from there rises out of the saddle, ascending 100 m in altitude before it begins its northerly descent to Jochim-ryeong. About 1 km later on a fairly open ridgeline, you should come across a signpost and prominent track junction area. At this point, you are only 1.5 km from Jochim-ryeong, which is just a couple of low peaks away. Just before the pass, you will end up on some elevated wooden pathways. These platforms take you onto a dirt road at Jochim-ryeong. Continue north on the dirt road and observe the old stele on the eastern side of the road.

The fallen meteor of Jochim-ryeong

Then look north and see the megalith-shaped monument of Jochim-ryeong, jammed into the earth like a fallen meteor.

* Jochim-ryeong 조침령 C1

Jochim-ryeong sits on an old dirt road at 770 m ABSL and is actually the halfway point of the entire Baekdu-daegan in Korea. Down on the roadside, PR418 runs 4 km east to the village of Seorim-ri 서림리 at the intersection with NH56. To the west, PR418 meanders for a good 20 km to the roadside village junction of Hyeon-ri, where it meets NH31. There is now a flash tunnel located under the ridge that is part of PR418. The only way off the pass is via the old dirt road, which snakes its way down both sides of the pass. The spectacular rotunda monument at Jochim-ryeong sits like a frozen, curled-up mammoth and was "somehow" put there on October 25, 2007 by the good workers of the Korea Forest Service. Jochim-ryeong was so named because it is said that the pass is so high that even birds cannot fly over it within a day. There is another signboard at the pass with a map of the area explaining the important spiritual significance of the Baekdu-daegan. It goes on to explain some of the vegetation that can be located 16 km north of here in the Jeombong-san 점봉산 area inside Seorak-san National Park. It states that the area is a compendium of the genetic resources of virgin primeval forest, with 854 species of plants growing wildly there, including Mongolian oak and linden trees. As many as 36 species endemic to Korea, like the thistle of Jeombong-san, are preserved in this area.

The windy PR418 east from Jochim-ryeong

TRANSPORT INFO

Leaving the trail at Jochim-ryeong: Buses do not run to the high pass of Jochim-ryeong. To the east, PR418 meets NH 56 at Seorim-ri, where buses head into Yangyang 양양 five times a day between 7:05 am and 5 pm.

LODGING

About 1 km west of the pass, south along PR418, are *minbak* such as Seolpi Minbak 설피 민박. Four kilometers east of the pass, at the junction with NH56 at Seorim-ri, are *minbak* and camping grounds located next to the Hu-cheon River 후천강.

DAY 2 From Jochim-ryeong to Hangye-ryeong

• Distance: 23km
• Time: 10hr 35min

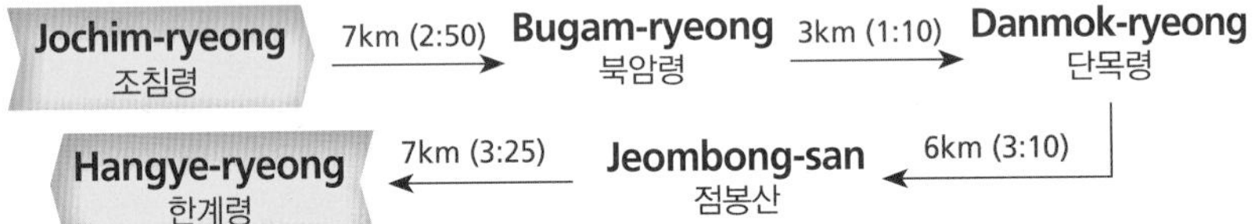

This section sees you enter the southern regions of Seorak-san National Park. The trail increases in altitude up to about 1,400 m ABSL. The nearest water source is 7 km into your journey, followed by another 3 km later. Ten kilometers into the walk, the trail becomes closed, but there are routes off it from there. The closed section is 15 km long from Danmok-ryeong to Hangye-ryeong at the end of the trail. This section passes high and mighty above the famously beautiful Osaek Gorge. At the end of its passage, it stumbles out onto the highway pass of Hangye-ryeong, which features a large restaurant, snack-sellers and rest areas. At the bottom of this road, on the western side, is the beautiful Osaek Gorge, which is worth a stayover and rest before you begin your final approach to the end of the Baekdu-daegan in South Korea.

Jochim-ryeong 조침령 F4 → Bugam-ryeong 북암령 F3

7km (2:50)

The trail starts next to the monument via an elevated wooden pathway skirting up the ridge in a northerly direction. The first 2 km of the trail is a steady ascent in a northerly direction to a height of about 943 m ABSL. From there, you have good views to the east back down the valley of NH56. The trail then turns west, where it drops into a small saddle before ascending for about 500 meters to a height of 1,018 m ABSL. From there, it turns northwest, dropping gradually for a kilometer to a signpost located in a small saddle at 962 m ABSL. In this area, you

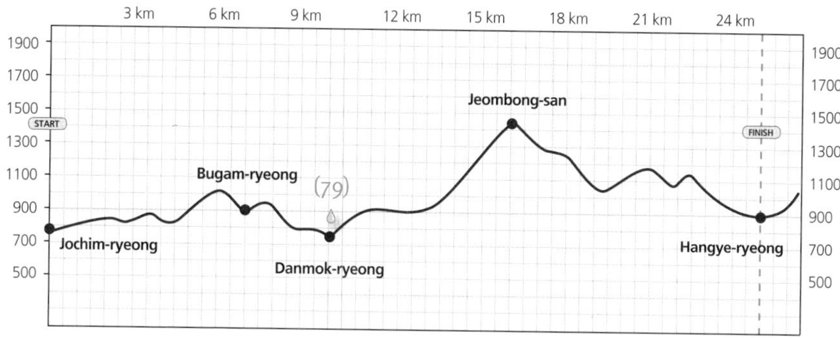

WATER STOPS (79) Bangtae-cheon at Danmok-ryeong: **N38°01'42" E128°28'44"**

should be able to see a large dam to the west, with a wind turbine standing on its southwestern edge. It is called the Sangbu Dam 상부댐 and may act as a last-ditch water source for you if need be. From this point, the trail elevates itself for the next 700 meters up the ridge to about 1,100 m ABSL. It stays at about this altitude for the next 2 km, passing through distinctive rocky areas before reaching a height of 1,136 m ABSL. From that altitude, the ridge offers great views to the northeast. From there, it drops into another saddle area where, about 500 meters later, you arrive at a pass known as Bugam-ryeong.

Bugam-ryeong 북암령 F3 → Danmok-ryeong 단목령 E2

3km (1:10)

From Bugam-ryeong, the trail bounds over one more peak before descending for the next kilometer in a northwest direction toward the dotted lines of the southern boundary of Seorak-san National Park (see p410). About a kilometer later, you arrive at a distinctive saddle called **Danmok-ryeong***, which marks the park's boundary.

At Danmok-ryeong, there are *jangseung* (guardian spirit poles), signboards, benches, and a small stele. Danmok-ryeong is a trail junction, with tracks running north and south from the trail.

* Danmok-ryeong 단목령 E2

The pass at Danmok-ryeong clearly states that the Baekdu-daegan trail is closed from here on in. The signboards say it is closed out of a wish to preserve the last

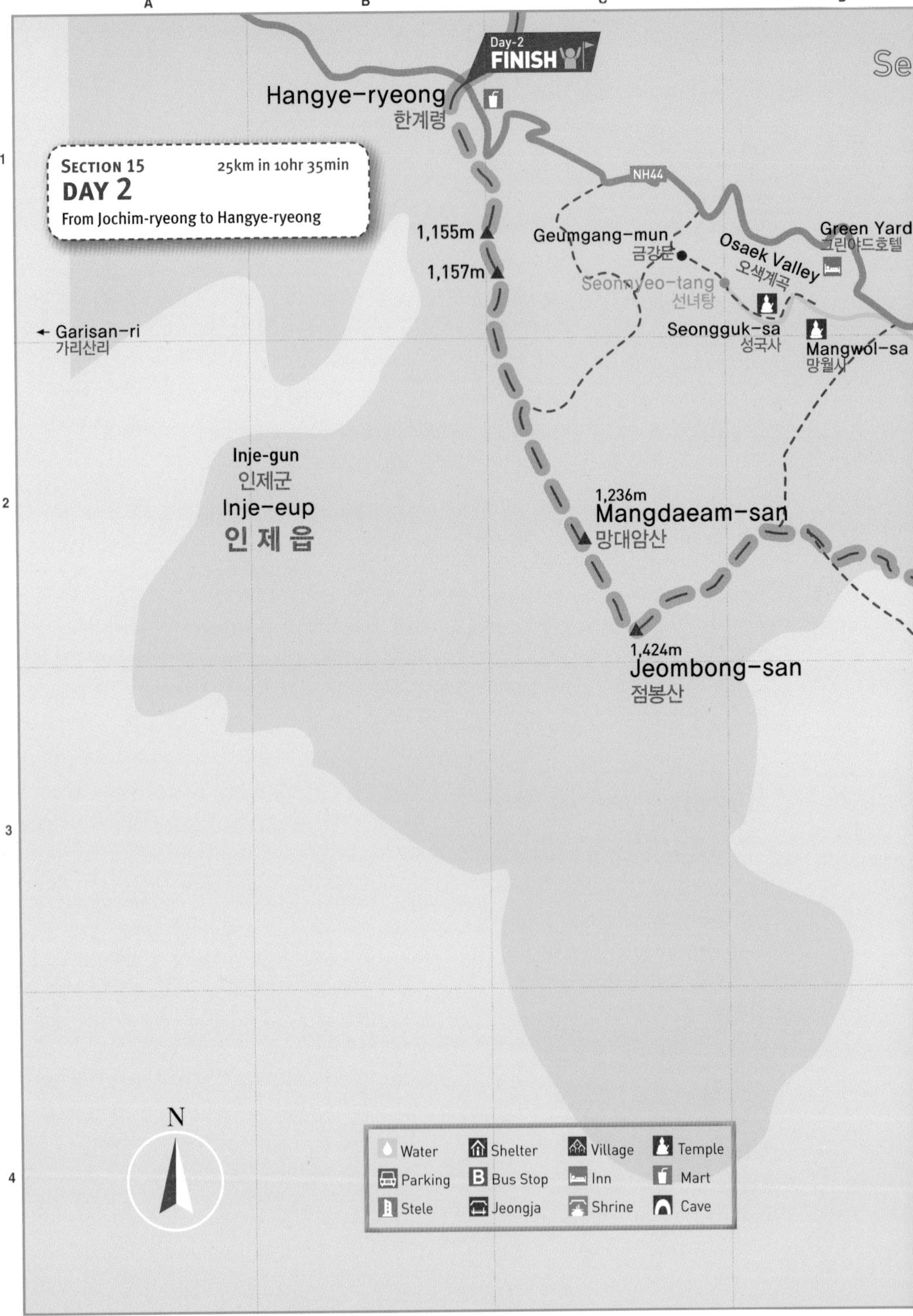
A
B
C
D
1
2
3
4
Day-2
FINISH
Hangye-ryeong
한계령
SECTION 15
25km in 10hr 35min
DAY 2
From Jochim-ryeong to Hangye-ryeong
NH44
1,155m
1,157m
Geumgang-mun
금강문
Seonnyeo-tang
선녀탕
Osaek Valley
오색계곡
Green Yard
그린야드호텔
Seongguk-sa
성국사
Mangwol-sa
망월사
Garisan-ri
가리산리
Inje-gun
인제군
Inje-eup
인 제 읍
1,236m
Mangdaeam-san
망대암산
1,424m
Jeombong-san
점봉산
N
Water
Shelter
Village
Temple
Parking
Bus Stop
Inn
Mart
Stele
Jeongja
Shrine
Cave

E
F
G
H
san National Park
산 국 립 공 원
Masan-ri
마산리
-cheon Stream
오 색 천
Yangyang
양양
882m
1,020m
Danmok-ryeong
(79) 단목령
Bugam-ryeong
북암령
Samgeo-ri
삼거리
Ggotnimine-jip
꽃님이네집
Banqtae-cheon Stream
1,136m
1,138m
1,000m
Sangbu Dam
상 부 댐
943m
NH56
900m
830m
Day-2
START
Jochim-ryeong
조침령
Jochim-ryeong Tunnel
조침령터널
PR418

shelters for wildlife and plants in Korea, in particular species such as the Korean wildcat (*Felis silvestris*) and the brown hawk owl, a nocturnal bird of about 32 cm in height. You might also notice a wooden tablet hanging from a wooden post and carved with rather odd script. It is apparently written in an old, primitive Chinese script and simply says "sandalwood ridge"—perhaps an older name for this area. On the stone stele, which was erected in December 2005, is a message from the manager of the Inje National Forest. It states that this section of the Baekdu-daegan between Jochim-ryeong and Jeombong-san (the next distinctive peak, located west of here) has been maintained by the names of the people placed on the opposite side of the stele. The area is now being conserved due to the rare plant species and virgin broadleaf forests that exist here. Further along the ridge, there are some examples of the deciduous *Fraxinus rhynchophylla*, or Korean ash tree, which grow to 25 m in height. The tree is well known for its medicinal effects and is used in the treatment of liver diseases, diarrhea and dysentery, eye diseases such as cataracts, coughs and asthma. The bark contains *aesculin*, which has analgesic, anticoagulant, and anti-inflammatory characteristics. The bark also contains an agent called *fraxetin*, which has an inhibitory effect on the central nervous system and is a stronger and safer anodyne than aspirin. The plant extract from this tree is also known to act as a strong barrier protecting against ultraviolet rays, while the wood is used for making cabinets. The common Korean name for this tree is *mulpure-namu*, meaning "water blue tree," as it is said that when you dip its branches into the water, the water turns blue. The wood of the tree is tough and strong and is used in the manufacture of musical instruments, farming implements, and sporting goods (bats, racquets, etc.).

Jangseung at Danmok-ryeong

LODGING

In Samgeo-ri 삼거리, there are two *minbak*. The northern one is the Kkotnimine-jip 꽃님이네집, and the southern one is Seolpi Sanjang 설피 산장. There are some private homes at the end of this track that may be able to help out with advice or transportation if need be. From Samgeo-ri, the mountain road continues south for another 8 km, reaching PR418 on the western side of Jochim-ryeong.

Alternative Route

The northern track is the shortest route to civilization, but it is also a closed trail. It meanders down a valley due north for 4 km before ending up at the Osaek-cheon Stream 오색천 (which has the potential to turn into a large, raging river at certain times of the year) alongside NH44. From there you should turn left and hitch a ride west up to Hangye-ryeong some 15 km later where the trail opens again, or refer to transportation section on p394.

The shorter (1.5 km), southern track heads to a mountain road, passing the mountain stream(79) of Bangtae-cheon Stream 방태천. The village at the end of the track is called Samgeo-ri. However, from this village, it is still a good 8 km back to the western side of Jochim-ryeong on PR418. To get to Hangye-ryeong you would have to hitch east from Jochim-ryeong to NH56, then north (left) for 15 km to NH44, then west (left) for 25 km to Hangye-ryeong.

CLOSED SECTION Danmok-ryeong 단목령 E2 → Jeombong-san 점봉산 C2

6km (3:10)

The trail turns southwest and climbs almost 500 m in altitude for 2 km before summiting at the peak of Jeombong-san. The summit of Jeombong-san consists of an open area that accommodates a roundish boulder acting as a monument for the summit. On the boulder, it states that Jeombong-san (1,424m) was voted the most beautiful mountain in Korea during a 21st century contest. On a good day, the peak offers splendid views to the north and south.

The snowy summit of Jeombong-san

CLOSED SECTION Jeombong-san 점봉산 C2 → Hangye-ryeong 한계령 B1

7km (3:25)

The trail from Jeombong-san immediately descends off the peak in a northwest direction, passing first through head-high bush before tucking into a deciduous tree line. After 1.8 km, it reaches the rocky outcrop of Mangdaeam-san 망대암산, located at 1,236 m ABSL. It continues descending in the same direction for the next 2 km until it reaches a saddle at the bottom of the ridge located some 900 m ABSL. From this saddle, the trail ascends northwest, rising over the next kilometer to about 1,150 m ABSL. This area offers some great views east down into the Osaek Gorge area.

Another kilometer later, the trail becomes narrower as it develops into a thin, rocky edge. It then descends sharply down one side of a rocky precipice, dropping into a small saddle. This is the critical part of the trail. It is a very rocky area—a compass bearing north at 345°—will make it easier for the hiker to continue through this section. After the last 600 meters of the trail, you come out onto the intersection of NH44 and a mountain road, currently under construction, that runs southwest 15 km down a valley toward the Garisan-ri 가리산리 area. From there, there are two options for the hiker. The easier is simply to get to NH44 and walk 1 km up the sealed road to the Hangye-ryeong rest area on top of the pass. The other option is to find the trailhead from the road and head back into the mountain ridge for a 20 minute walk until it comes out at the pass at Hangye-ryeong.

* Hangye-ryeong 한계령 B1

Connected by NH44, Hangye-ryeong sits at about 900 m ABSL. About 10 km to the east lies the Osaek-gyegok Village—Osaek-ri 오색리, while the small town of Wontong-ri 원통리 is located 20 km to the west. At the pass is a large *hyugeso*, allowing you to purchase a hot dinner and cold beer. There is no accommodation at Hyangye-ryeong.

* Osaek Gorge 오색 계곡 D1

Osaek-gyegok ("five colors gorge") is located in the southern section of Seorak-san along NH44, between Yangyang in the east and Inje 인제 in the west. One story holds that it was so named because a tree with five different-hued flowers

TRANSPORT INFO

Joining the trail at Hangye-ryeong: Passenger buses do not cross Hangye-ryeong. Being a very scenic drive, it is a fairly easy place to get a lift from, but taxis will make the trip if needed. Contact Wontong Taxi (T. 033-461-3369) or Yangyang Call Taxi (T. 022-671-2300).

on it once grew in this valley, while another posits that the famous mineral-rich spring water at its mouth sparkles in the sunlight with five brilliant colors.

Osaek Gorge is surrounded by the mountains of Seorak-san (Daecheon-bong) and Jeombong-san. A beautiful mountain stream of pure water gushes through a steep-walled ravine, with very old-growth pine groves, and the gorge is also renowned for its rare birds, tall pines and colorful trees. It is a spectacular area to visit in any season of the year. From Osaek-ri, there is a 5 km walk up the valley for visitors. The walk passes through the temples of Mangwol-sa 망월사 and Seongguk-sa 성국사. At the start of the walk, you will notice a line of people gathering spring water from two holes in the broad streamside rocks below the grounds of Seongguk-sa (across the bridge). It is said that the naturally carbonated water from this source is of such high quality that it can help to cure diabetes, stomach problems, high and low blood pressure, and constipation.

A footbridge in beautiful Osaek Gorge

On your walk up the valley, you will come across many information boards, none of them translated into English. One of them depicts a cave called Jujeon-donggul 주전동굴. It is said that during the Joseon period, a group of bandits disguised as Buddhist monks stayed in this cave while minting illegal coins. Back then, the cave was hidden away by large rocks and trees. People passing inadvertently down the valley could hear the affectionate sound of the coins being dropped to the ground from above. This story remained a mystery to modern-day Koreans until a flood in 2006 revealed the cave, thereby proving at least the basis of the folktale. Further up the trail, you come across a pond called Seonnyeo-tang 선녀탕. There is a myth about this pond saying that since long ago, groups of heavenly angels (fairy girls, a.k.a. *seonnyeo* or "immortal women") would descend to this pond and bathe in it. They would remove their clothes on a nearby flat piece of rock and flutter into the water. Korean folktales have long said that if a man who witnessed this could steal the robe of one of these beauties, she would not be able to fly back up to the sky, and he could take her as his wife. To cap

Osaek Gorge

that story, it is said that on a clear moonlit night, it is possible to see the *seon-nyeo* returning to the pond and removing their clothes before cascading into the water and immersing themselves in enjoyment.

There are numerous waterfalls located up the gorge, one of them having been formed by two 1,000-year-old snakes that once swam in a pool together, people say. Often they would try and soar to the sky in an attempt to become dragons. The female of the pair never made it and eventually became the waterfall above the pond. Also, you will see a distinctive rock feature up the trail allowing people space to pass under. This rock is called Geumgang-mun 금강문 and represents the center of Osaek Gorge. It is said that passing through it provides you with protection against evil spirits. Its name translates to "diamond gate," saying that once you have passed through it, you are entering the beautiful area of the Jujeon, Deungseon and Yongso Waterfalls in different ravines above it.

TRANSPORT INFO

Joining the trail at Osaek Gorge : The closed trail heading north from Danmok-ryeong runs for 4 km to Masan-ri 마산리, which is located 3 km east of Osaek Gorge. Buses run from Yangyang to Osaek hourly throughout the day from 6:20 am to 7:30 pm. Osaek Gorge is a very popular entrance to Seorak-san National Park, and buses run directly here from Dong Seoul Terminal, leaving seven times a day between 6:30 am to 6:05 pm.

LODGING

As you return to the tourist village at the mouth of Osaek Gorge, there are many different accommodation options, including the Green Yard Hotel, which features excellent Korean-style hot spring spas in which to rest your weary body. There are also some smaller "motels." Some restaurants in the tourist village above offer meals, including rice cooked with this water in stone pots, along with wild mountain vegetable meals, a unique and relatively affordable health-giving experience.

FOUR DAYS

39.0km

SECTION 16

SEORAK-SAN NATIONAL PARK

Hangye-ryeong → Jinbu-ryeong

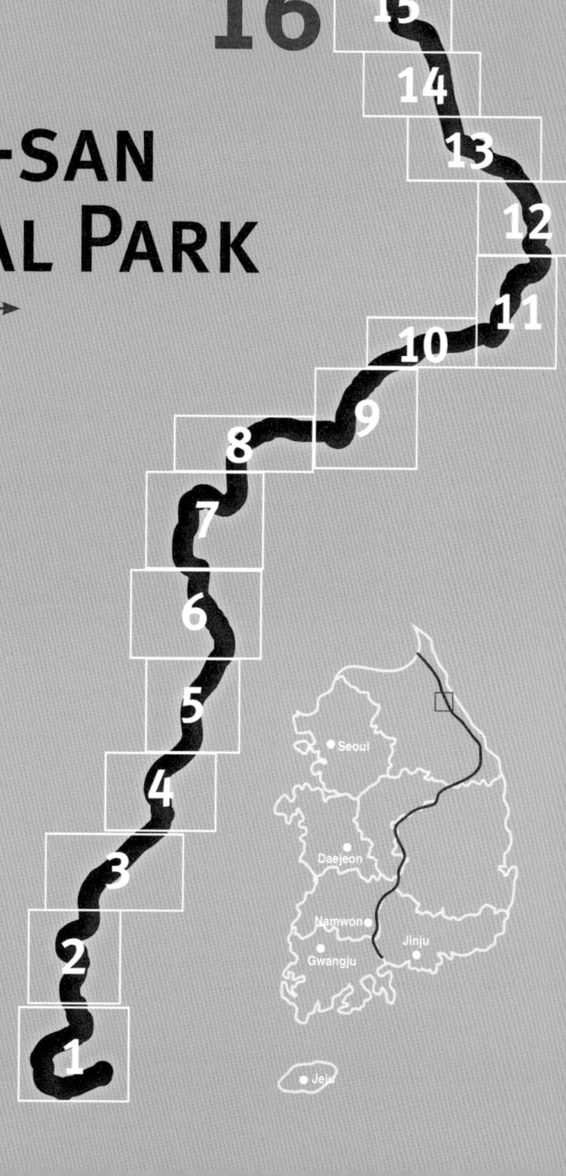

SECTION 16
14.8km in 9hr 35min
DAY 1 & 2
From Hangye-ryeong to Madeung-ryeong
1,080m
1,318m
1,381m
Hwangcheol-bong
황철봉
Jeohang-ryeong
저항령
Jeohang-ryeong Gorge
저항령고개
Sokcho →
속초
Ulsan-bawi
울산바위
Gyejo-am
계조암
Heundeul-bawi
흔들바위
Naewon-am
내원암
Seorak-dong
설 악 동
Oeseorak
외 설 악
Anyang-am
안양암
Seorak-san Hotel
설악산 관광호텔
Sinheung-sa
신흥사
Kensington Hotel
켄싱턴 호텔
Geumgang-gul Cave
금강굴
Annak-sa
안락사
Biseon-dae Hyugeso
비선대 휴게소
Biseon-dae
비선대
Day-2
FINISH
Madeung-ryeong
마등령
Madeung-ryeong Samgeori
마등령 삼거리
Naeseorak
내 설 악
1,298m
Nahan-bong
나한봉
Ose-am
오세암
Yeongsi-am
영시암
Dinosaur spine
공룡능선
1,328m
Hwachae-bong
화채봉
1
2
3
4
A
B
C
D

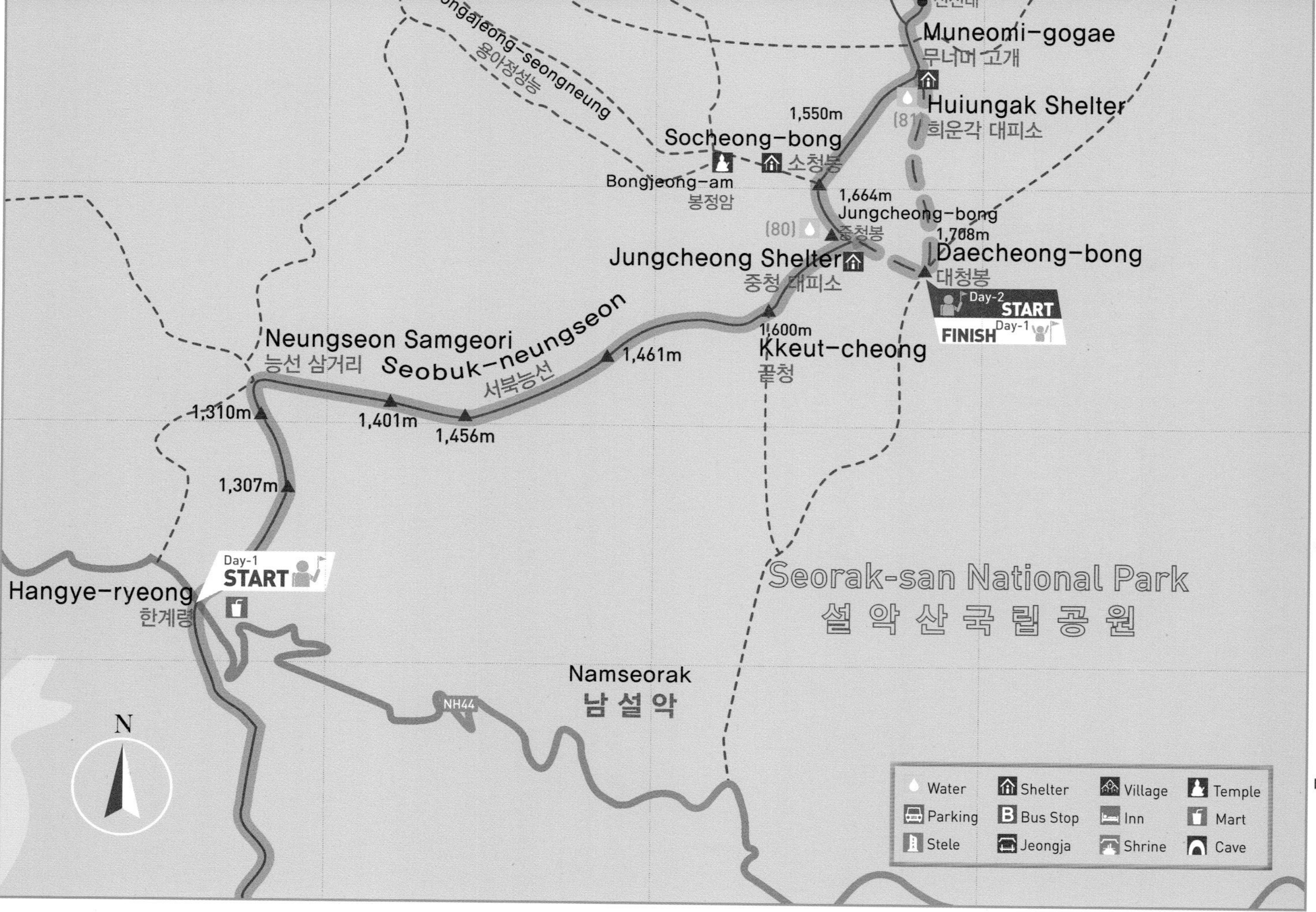
Muneomi-gogae
무너미 고개
Huiungak Shelter
희운각 대피소
1,550m
Socheong-bong
소청봉
Bongjeong-am
봉정암
1,664m
Jungcheong-bong
중청봉
(80)
(81)
1,708m
Daecheong-bong
대청봉
Jungcheong Shelter
중청 대피소
Day-2 START
Day-1 FINISH
1,600m
Kkeut-cheong
끝청
Neungseon Samgeori
능선 삼거리
Seobuk-neungseon
서북능선
1,461m
1,310m
1,401m
1,456m
1,307m
Day-1 START
Hangye-ryeong
한계령
Seorak-san National Park
설악산국립공원
Namseorak
남설악
NH44
N
Water
Shelter
Village
Temple
Parking
Bus Stop
Inn
Mart
Stele
Jeongja
Shrine
Cave
E
F
G
H

DAY 1 From Hangye-ryeong to Daecheong-bong

• **Distance:** 8.5km
• **Time:** 4hr 20min

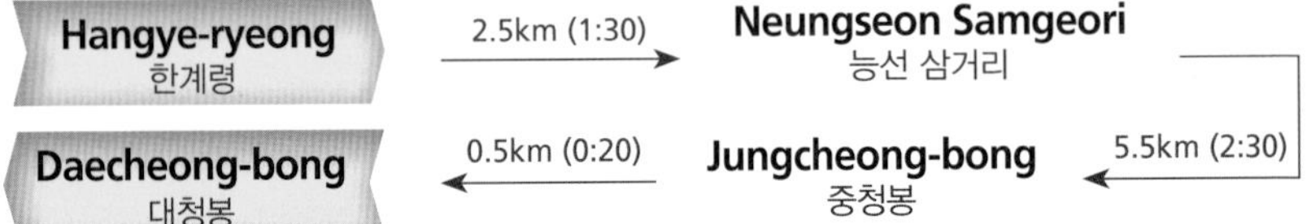

This section of inner Seorak-san is wondrous in its appearance, and its beauty is almost beyond description. The size of Seorak-san provides the hiker with many hiking trails, and apart from the Baekdu-daegan itself, there is probably a good extra month's hiking and exploration to be done in this craggy terrain. Because significant sections of the Baekdu-daegan trail are currently closed for nature conservation purposes, you will indeed get a chance to explore some of these other trails, as they lead from the closed sections down into the interesting and culturally rich valleys of this fascinating region of Korea. This leg to Daecheong-bong sees you walking predominantly north for 2 km before turning east for the remaining 6 km. It is quite remarkable how during the South Korean stretch of the Baekdu-daegan, the two most notable features of the walk appear at the beginning, with Cheonwang-bong (1,915m) the mainland's highest summit), and near the end, with Daecheong-bong (1,707m) the second highest), where you can sleep in the National Park Shelter. Get up early in the morning and watch the sun rise over the East Sea, view its early morning rays as they light up the peninsula, and catch a glimpse of North Korea.

Hangye-ryeong 한계령 G1 → Neungseon Samgeori 능선 삼거리 F1

2.5km (1:30)

The trailhead to Daecheong-bong starts on the northern side of the pass, next to the public toilets. It is indicated by a flight of concrete steps going straight up the side of the mountain. The staircase from Hangye-ryeong sees you climb about 350 m in altitude for the first kilometer as you reach your first spot height, located at 1,307 m ABSL. From there, the trail descends slightly into a gnarly saddle located 500 meters away before arriving at the track junction of Neungseon Samgeori. The Baekdu-daegan trail is the eastern arm of this track junction, and the signpost at this location clearly states the routes to Jungcheong-bong and Daecheong-bong

Neungseon Samgeori 능선 삼거리 F1 → Jungcheong-bong 중청봉 F3

5.5km (2:30)

Turning east from Neungseon Samgeori, the trail drops slightly in altitude and follows a rocky, craggy path along some spectacular terrain. For the next kilometer, you should be gifted with many good views north into the inner confines of inner Seorak-san National Park before reaching an unnamed peak at 1,401 m ABSL. The Baekdu-daegan continues traveling eastward for another 700 meters over more large, rocky outcrops before ascending to the next signpost, located at about 1,456 m ABSL. The next kilometer sees you swooping into a gentle saddle before ascending to 1,461 m ABSL, a peak marked by another signpost. After that, the next 1.5 km sees you cover some good ground on a relatively flat ridge until the last section of it, which sees you hitting the face of Kkeut-cheong 끝청, climbing a good 150 m in altitude before reaching its summit at 1,600 m ABSL. From there, the trail changes its

From Jungcheong-bong

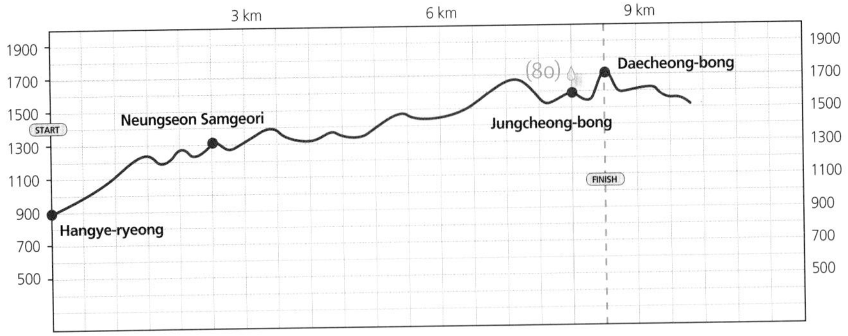

WATER STOPS (80) Jungcheong Shelter: **N38°07'06" E128°27'44"**

direction slightly to the northeast as it begins its craggy ascent to Jungcheong-bong. About 1 km later, you should come out at the roundish summit of Jungcheong-bong, located at 1,664 m ABSL. The most distinctive features to be seen at Jungcheong-bong are two round communications dishes on its summit. At its summit area are a signpost and another track running north from the ridge. The northern track is actually part of the Baekdu-daegan trail, as the main route from the summit of Daecheong-bong, which you can now easily see, is closed. The Jungcheong Shelter 중청봉대피소 sleeps about 150 people, and in its busy season, you should try to make advance reservations at http://english.knps.or.kr.

Jungcheong Shelter

Its facilities include a kitchen and a main administration office, which sells more basic amenities for hikers, including rice and instant noodles. However, you are better off coming prepared with your own food, as the variety of food items at these stores can be disappointing and expensive. Costs should be about 7,000-8,000 won for a space on a wooden floor. It will cost you an extra 1,000 won for a woolly blanket, which makes a good sleeping mat—allowing you to discard your sleeping bag—as these shelters are incredibly well heated at night.

Jungcheong-bong 중청봉 → Daecheong-bong 대청봉 F3

0.5km (0:20)

There is no need for directions to the mighty Daecheong-bong summit from here, as it looms above you to the east like a dormant volcano. The climb to its top is done predominantly over barren earth and rock. At its rocky summit is a menhir simply saying "Daecheong-bong," in *hangeul*, with "1,708 m" carved into the face above the name. Nearby is another menhir with a brief poem inscribed on it, saying *yosan yosu*, or "love nature." From Daecheong-bong, there are fantastic 360° views. To the north and west, you can look at the endless mountain tops that make up Seorak-san National Park. To the south, you should easily be able to pick out Jeombong-san and the southern section of the Baekdu-daegan in Seorak-san, and to the east, you can easily view the East Sea and Sokcho. It is worth getting to the summit in time for sunrise in the hope that the weather will produce a magnificent vista for you. In the evening, the sunsets are also understandably terrific. However, if you're not in the mood to get to the summit for a sunset, there is an easier option from the Jungcheong Shelter. If you take the trail east from there, it will contour around the northern face of Jungcheong-bong. Once you can see west, you are still high enough to get great shots of the sunsets over western Seorak-san.

Sunset from Jungcheong-bong

DAY 2

From Daecheong-bong to Madeung-ryeong

- **Distance:** 7.5km
- **Time:** 4hr 45min

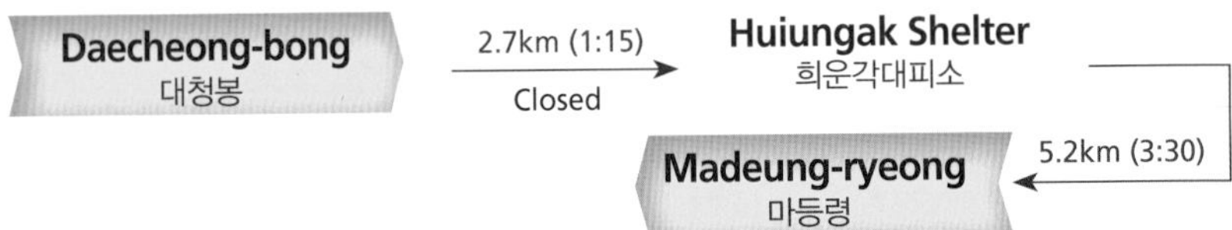

Day two of the Seorak-san Mountains sees you walking through the very torso of this spectacular region. You walk along, through, beside, and over endless ruptures of unexplainable rock formations that fill your mind with wonder and imagination. The landscape could almost be from another planet; indeed, you begin to understand the invocations of the old local folk stories of this region. Leaving Daecheong-bong, you walk down into the pit of the dinosaur and edge your way up its spine, scouting in and out of its horns of rock, stopping at the great vistas that halt your movement, panoramic distractions. Reaching the end of the spine and taking the detour from the closed section down through the picturesque track to Biseon-dae. Getting up the next morning, shedding the heavy pack, and conducting day explorations of outer Seorak-san as your path on the Buddhist trails enchant you with a world of mountain spirits, tigers, and legends.

CLOSED SECTION Daecheong-bong 대청봉 F3 → Huiungak Shelter 희운각 대피소 E3 — 2.7km (1:15)

As the Baekdu-daegan trail is strictly closed from the summit of Daecheong-bong, the alternative route starts a fraction west of the Jungcheong Shelter on the northern face of Jungcheong-bong. It is well marked and indicated by signpost directing a downward northern route toward Socheong-bong 소청봉, which is your next prominent peak at 1,550 m ABSL some 500 meters from the track junction. Most of that descent is assisted by wooden staircases. From there, the Baekdu-daegan trail begins a steep descent in a northeastern direction down a gnarly spur line to the next National Park shelter of Huiungak. In the 1.2 km it takes you to get there, you drop about 400 m in altitude. The walk, however, is very spectacular, and you should be able to see quite clearly to your north the famous "dinosaur spine" of Seorak-san only a couple of kilometers in the distance.

At the bowel of your leg from Socheong-bong, you will have arrived at the quaint little shelter of Huiungak, which like Socheong Shelter is small in stature, accommodating about 80 people. There were renovations going on in 2007, and it may well accommodate more people now. There is a freshwater source(81) to be found at the shelter in the form of a mountain stream, along with toilet facilities and basic hiking commodities.

Huiungak Shelter 희운각 대피소 E3 → Madeung-ryeong 마등령 C2

5.2km (3:30)

From Huiungak Shelter, the next leg sees you maintaining your current altitude of around 1,200 and 1,300 m ABSL. The walk is, however, quite tough in places as it contours the horns of the dinosaur spine, known in Korean as the Gongryong-neungseon 공룡능선. The dinosaur spine connects your end point of Madeungryeong Samgeori with Daecheong-bong. It is also part of the Baekdu-

Looking east from the ridge

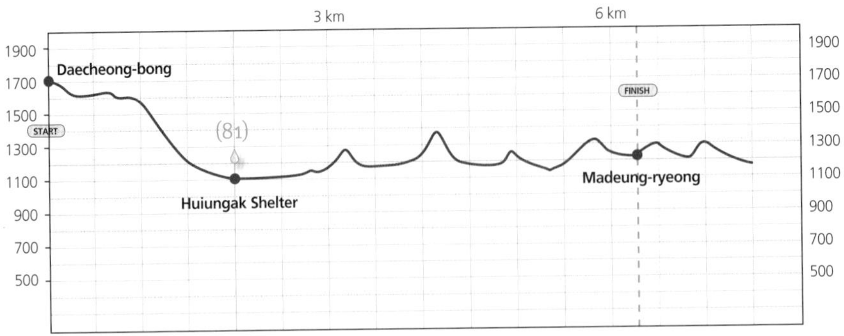

WATER STOPS (81) Huiungak Shelter: **N38°07'45" E128°28'00"**

daegan. Its scenery, consisting of a soaring line of sharp peaks, has overwhelmed onlookers for millennia. Understandably, you are not able to walk along the actual crest of the dinosaur spine, as in places it would be completely impossible without climbing equipment. It is also more than likely prohibited. However, for the bolder sorts, it may be worth it in places to drop your pack and free-climb the crests of this magnificent ridgeline, as it has some remarkable and out-of-this-world viewing points on top of some of its vertebrae. Be prepared for a mind-blowing experience on this leg to Madeung-ryeong.

Leaving the shelter in a northerly direction, the Baekdu-daegan trail meets up 250 meters later with a track junction known as Muneomi-gogae 무너미고개.

Dinosaur spine

Madeung-ryeong Samgeori

The Baekdu-daegan continues northwards, shortly thereafter forking into two tracks. The left fork contours down the side of the dinosaur's spine and meets up with the Baekdu-daegan again some 500 meters later. The proper option is the right-hand fork, which steers you in a northeastern direction up the spine of the dinosaur to a small but magnificent plateau named Sinseon-dae 신선대. The name means a lookout and spiritual practice platform for the Taoist "spirit immortals," many of which have long been rumored to linger in Seorak-san. From Sinseon-dae, the next 4 km stretch takes you in a northwestern direction as you slowly snake and concertina your way along the dinosaur's spine to the prominent saddle and junction of Madeungryeong Samgeori, which cuts through the dinosaur's back like an axe mark. It is almost impossible to explain the next 4 km in detail, as the terrain is so full of passable obstacles. But bear in mind that this is not a difficult leg—persons of all ages complete it. The views are incredible, and it's worth taking your time and embracing the moment.

About another 300 meters north of Madeungryeong Samgeori, you should come to a signpost and a signboard. The signpost will indicate to you that you are at the Madeung-ryeong pass. The signboard, tucked away in the bush just north of the trail, indicates to the hiker that the trail from here on in is closed. The signboard has a picture of a chamois-type mountain goat or antelope that is probably a Manchurian goral. It appears to have been mauled by a mountain cat of some nature. The signboard translates to say "This area is the last place for wild animals and plants to take refuge. Antelopes and *sansomdari* (a rare and remote plant), which are at the risk of extinction, inhabit this region. Let's yield this place to nature." Beyond the signboard, the trail should be roped off, preventing further access on the mighty ridge all the way to Daegan-ryeong 대간령 in northern Seorak-san National Park some 16 km later. For the sake of the continuation of the Baekdu-daegan, information on the remaining sections of the Baekdu-daegan in Seorak-san will be explained in days three and four of this Section, just in case the track is one day open again. Otherwise, the only legal option that remains for you as the hiker is to get off the ridge. This obstacle does not, however, detract from the advantages of visiting other regions of Seorak-san. From this point on your journey, it is best to get off the trail east at Madeung-ryeong and walk down the scenic leg toward the rocks of Biseon-dae.

You immediately descend a flight of stairs onto the rocky ledges of this area. About a kilometer later, you will come across a signpost near a notably rocky part of this walk. Another two kilometers later, you pass beneath the cave of Geumgang-gul 금강굴. You may hear the hollow taps of a moktak being chimed through the ravines of the valley as a Buddhist monk meditates in the cave.

* Biseon-dae 비선대 C3

After you pass beneath the lower face of the cave, there are some more natural rocky steps that take you down to Biseon-dae rock. Legend states that this waterfall is a place where some were so overcome by its beauty that they ascended to the heavens. You should soon notice the small ranger's hut and foot bridge that takes you over the Tomak-gol 토막골 stream, where you exit into the Biseon-dae Hyugeso 비선대 휴게소. The Biseon-dae Hyugeso is a great place to stop, rest and take in a large feed of well-cooked local cuisine. The facility sells cold beer and soft drinks and has public toilets. It overlooks the Biseon-dae rock, upon which many local tourists/hikers will be basking, lapping up its divine presence. The major trail running south from here would take you up the spectacularly beautiful Cheonbuldong-gyegok 천불동계곡 ("thousand Buddha gorge") leading up to Daecheong-bong.

* Tongil Daebul 통일대불

About 2.5 km later, you come out at the large and popular eastern gate entrance area. The most notable feature there is the grand 14.6 m high gilt bronze Buddha sitting near the entrance of the temple of Sinheung-sa 신흥사. The statue is known as the "*Tongil Daebul*," meaning the "great unification Buddha statue." It sits on a 4.3 meter high pedestal made of the same metallic substance, and it weighs 108 tons. The giant structure represents one important wish of Korean people—the reunification of a country divided for over half a century.

* Temples of Outer Seorak-san

The temple of Sinheung-sa is located by signpost just slightly north or behind the Tongil Daebul statue. The temple was built by Jajang-yulsa in AD 652 during the reign of Queen Jindeok of the Silla dynasty. The temple has 40 branch temples in the northern part of Gangwon-do. Inside its confines is the 120.3 m^2 Geungnak-bojeon building, whose name means "precious building to enshrine Amitabha, the Buddha of infinite light." It was built in 1647, during the Joseon Dynasty, and was repaired in 1750 and 1821, maintaining the architectural style of the late Joseon period.

Other temples of interest are also located on the track up to the famous Ulsan-bawi rock. A temple of shabby appearance known as Anyang-am 안양암 is the first, located only 500 meters up the northern track behind Sinheung-sa. The next temple on this track is Naewon-am 내원암 some 1.5 km later.

Another kilometer after that is the very famous temple of Gyejo-am 계조암. At this temple site is a large boulder sitting precariously on a flat plateau of rock, with the name of Heundeul-bawi 흔들바위. If you approach this large chunk of monolithic rock from the right point, you can rock it backwards and forwards with the push of one arm. The hermitage of Gyejo-am is nestled under the face of Ulsan-bawi and is formally represented by a cave in which the famous Buddhist monk Jajang-yulsa dwelled in AD 652. The cave was originally the place where the three founders of the Buddhist sects Jajang, Dongsan, and Bongjeong met and practiced asceticism. Later on in time, other famous monks like Wonyho and Uisang practiced meditation there as well. The cave is located at the foot of a large rock called *Moktak*, which resembles the hollow wooden instrument used by monks during recitation of sutras, mantras, or other Buddhist scrolls. On the cave walls is the engraving *Gyejo-am Geungnakjeon*, meaning "hall of paradise." Geojo-am is the place of the continuation of spiritual discipline.

* Ulsan-bawi 울산바위 A3

Above Gyejo-am is the infamous rocky ridgeline formation of Ulsan-bawi. It stands out like a knife's edge from either the high slopes of the Baekdu-daegan or the neon-lit streets of nearby Sokcho. It is only a 500 meter walk from Gyejo-am, and it is definitely worth a day's hike along its sometimes difficult and thin crest. The views from its spiky top are, obviously, outstandingly great. Even more intriguing is one of the ancient legends of Ulsan-bawi, whose origins are unknown. It goes like this:

There is a very beautiful, big rock in Seorak-san. It stands alone and looks like a small mountain range. There are no trees on its steep slopes and sharp peaks. It is called "Ulsan-bawi." According to legend, Ulsan-bawi has an interesting history. Long ago, Korea's chief mountain spirit decided to build a new mountain in Gangwon-do. He wanted to make it the most splendid mountain in the whole world, but he needed help. So he called the other mountain spirits together and told them about his plan. The chief mountain spirit asked, "Do you have any good ideas?" After a while, one mountain spirit said, "Let's each bring the most beautiful piece of our own mountains to Gangwon-do." "That sounds good! We can put all the pieces together to make a new mountain," said the chief. All the mountain spirits went back to their lovely mountains to select beautiful pieces of rock. Carefully pulling

Ulsan-bawi

them off, they took them to Gangwon-do. However, the mountain-spirit from Ulsan, being proud and haughty, wanted his rock to be the biggest and best. So he chose a piece of rock ten times bigger than any other. It took a long time to dig it up. As he walked north carrying the huge rock, he often stopped to rest, so it was not easy for him to get to Gangwon-do on time. Meanwhile, the other mountain spirits had all brought their pieces of mountain to Gangwon-do. Working together, they at last finished building a beautiful mountain. They decided to call it Geumgang-san. The chief spirit sent word to the Ulsan mountain spirit, telling him that Geumgang-san was finished. He told him to take his piece of mountain back home. When he heard that, the Ulsan spirit was furious. In a rage, he threw his piece of rock to the ground and went back to Ulsan. Even today you can see that piece of mountain where he threw it. It still stands there lonely and proud, just like its creator.

SEORAK-SAN NATIONAL PARK 설악산 국립공원

Seorak-san National Park is one of South Korea's more famous national parks, renowned for its high, craggy mountains and beautiful seasonal displays of kaleidoscopic colors. The 400,000 km^2 park is divided into three parts: the very popular Oeseorak 외설악, or "outer Seorak-san," to the east near the coast and Sokcho, and the peacefully remote Naeseorak 내설악, or "inner Seorak-san," to the west in Inje-gun (both of these regions are divided by the Baekdu-daegan). The third sector is Namseorak 남설악, or "south Seorak-san," referring to all that is south of NH44, including Gari-san, Jeombong-san and the Osaek area, which the Baekdu-daegan passes through to get to Hangye-ryeong and beyond. The densely touristed area called Seorak-dong 설악동, the entranceway to Outer Seorak from Sokcho, is considered the "main" area of the park and offers many famous attractions.

There is no best time to visit Seorak-san, but the most popular times are spring and autumn, as the valleys and ridges become ablaze with mountain flora. In spring, there is a royal azalea flower festival, together with blossoming trees and gradual warming on the heights. However, the hot, humid months of summer hold a special place in the hearts of others as the mountains become enshrouded in low white clouds, causing magical scenery around the nooks and crannies of its many high crags. Autumn warrants great acclaim from what seems like a million visitors as the gorges and slopes become inflamed in fierce hues of red, orange and yellow from the many deciduous trees, contrasting so well with the green pines and gray cliffs. It is said that being in the mountains at night in the deep winter, when the peaks and valleys become whitened in "snow flowers" and ice glazes, causes magical optical illusions to the eye and mind under the soft beams of a full moon.

Seorak-san reportedly has 1,400 species of animals within its boundaries, including antelope, musk deer, and otter. More recently, there have been confirmed sightings of mountain lynx cats that feast on species of mountain goats or antelope—part of the reason the northern section of the walk in Seorak-san is currently closed. Over the years, there have also been numerous rumors of sightings of leopards, Bandal bears, and even the Korean tiger, which is believed to be extinct. As this is so close to the dangerous DMZ zone, there are very occasional alerts about reported sightings of North Korean commandoes making reconnaissance incursions.

Transport Info

Leaving the trail at Seorak-san National Park: There are numerous buses and taxis running from the Park's gate to the nearby city of Sokcho, which has regular service running from most major cities throughout South Korea.

Lodging

There are numerous *minbak* and hotels located outside the eastern gate entrance to Seorak-san National Park. Two grand hotels are the Seorak-san Gwangwang Hotel 설악산 관광호텔 and the Kensington Hotel 켄싱턴 호텔, which drives its guests to the entrance of the park in a bright red double-decker bus. Nearby Sokcho is a pleasant place to visit, a touristy port town. There are many eateries and cheaper *minbak* to sleep in along the portside in the older section of Sokcho. It is also the appropriate urban area to base yourself in when you are not staying inside the National Park.

Looking east to Sokcho from the ridge

DAY 3 From Madeung-ryeong to Misi-ryeong

• Distance: 9km
• Time: 4hr 45min

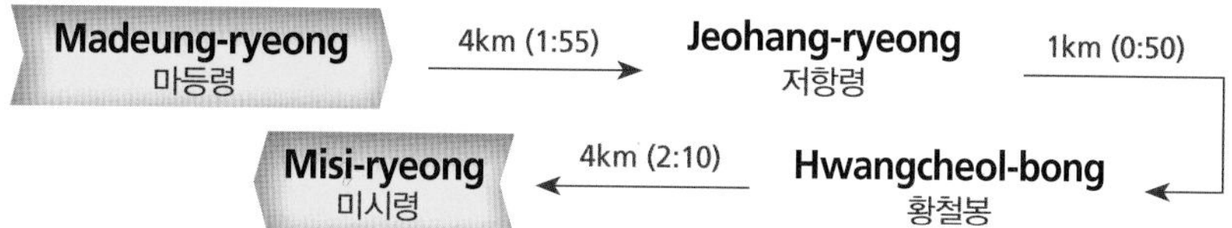

The closed section from Madeung-ryeong to Misi-ryeong is an impressive, isolated mountain ridge that shunts its way northeast, northwest, and then north down to the pass at Misi-ryeong 9 km later. On its tumultuous crest, you look west into an infinite landscape of spurs and valleys. In other parts, the terrain looks like a mighty mountain spirit has knocked the tops off some of the peaks with his staff, causing square slabs of rock to shrapnel in a conical manner around the broken summits. You can also clearly see the continuation of the Baekdu-daegan through northern Seorak-san as it stretches and arcs its way north and the west toward the DMZ. Because the trail is closed, the aura and presence of this area are quite mystifying, and you may be visited by the wings of large raptor birds that hone and drill the area for the jittery mountain goral. At the end of your day, walk down to Misi-ryeong and enjoy hot roasted potatoes and a cold beer. No accommodations here, so hitch down to the city of Sokcho and soak the body at a *jjimjilbang* or sauna, or at the Seorak Hot Springs Resort.

CLOSED SECTION Madeung-ryeong 마등령 G3 → Jeohang-ryeong 저항령 F3

4km (1:55)

The summit of Madeung-ryeong is located at 1,326 m ABSL, about 500 meters north of the Madeungryeong Samgeori track junction back on the ridge of the

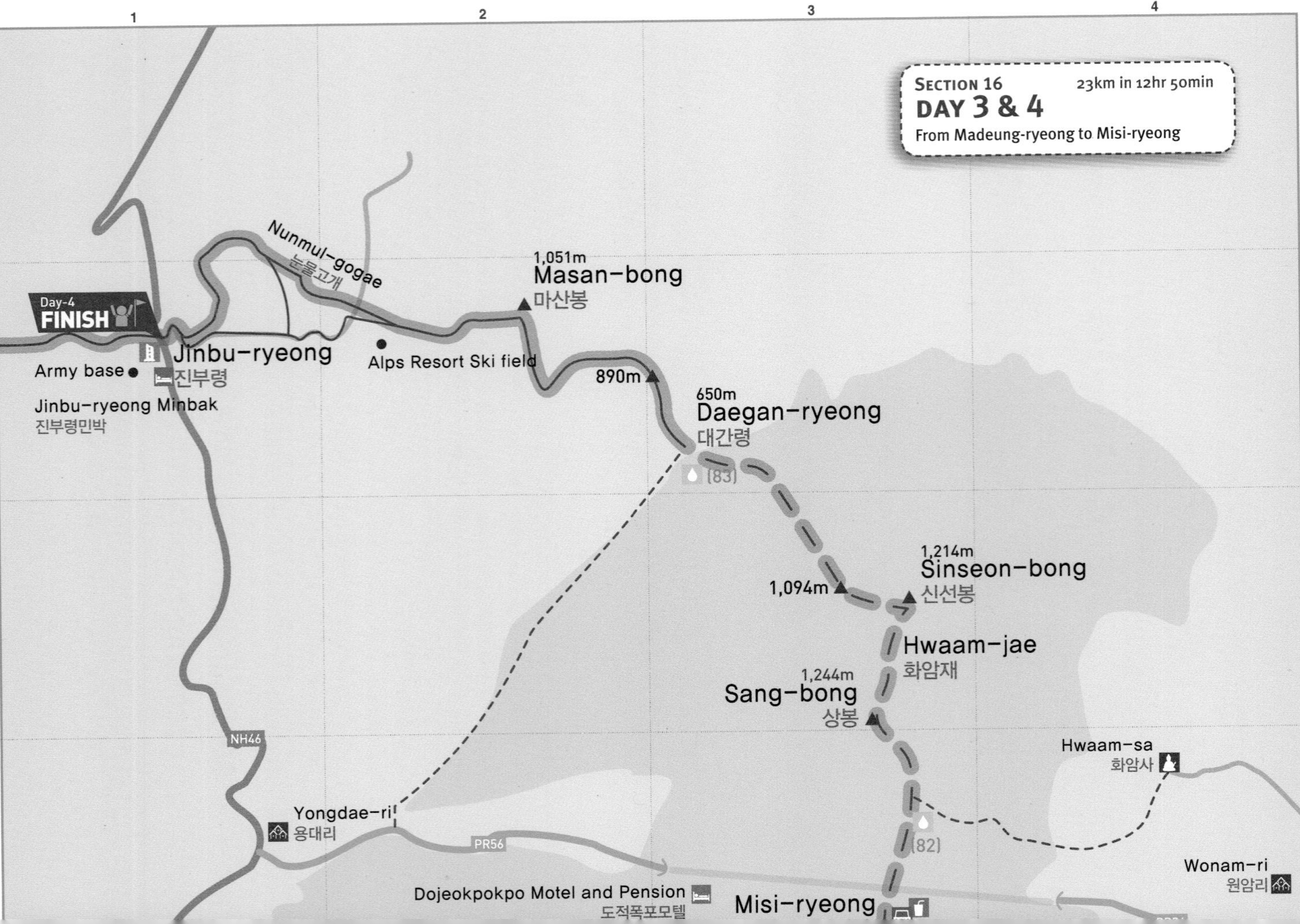

SECTION 16
23km in 12hr 50min
DAY 3 & 4
From Madeung-ryeong to Misi-ryeong
1
2
3
4
A
B
C
D
Day-4
FINISH
Jinbu-ryeong
진부령
Army base
Jinbu-ryeong Minbak
진부령민박
Nunmul-gogae
눈물고개
Alps Resort Ski field
1,051m
Masan-bong
마산봉
890m
650m
Daegan-ryeong
대간령
(83)
1,094m
1,214m
Sinseon-bong
신선봉
Hwaam-jae
화암재
1,244m
Sang-bong
상봉
Hwaam-sa
화암사
(82)
NH46
Yongdae-ri
용대리
PR56
Dojeokpokpo Motel and Pension
도적폭포모텔
Misi-ryeong
Wonam-ri
원암리

1,080m
Ulsan-bawi
울산바위
Gyejo-am
계조암
1,381m
Hwangcheol-bong
황철봉
1,318m
Obong-san
오봉산
Naewon-am
내원암
Jeohang-ryeong
저항령
Sinheung-sa
신흥사
Jeohang-ryeong Gorge
저항령계곡
1,249m
Seorak-san National Park
설 악 산 국 립 공 원
1,178m
Day-3
START
1,326m
Madeung-ryeong
마등령
Baekdam-sa
백담사
Baekdam Shelter
백담대피소
E
F
G
H
N
Water
Shelter
Village
Temple
Parking
Bus Stop
Inn
Mart
Stele
Jeongja
Shrine
Cave

WATER STOPS No water stops for this course

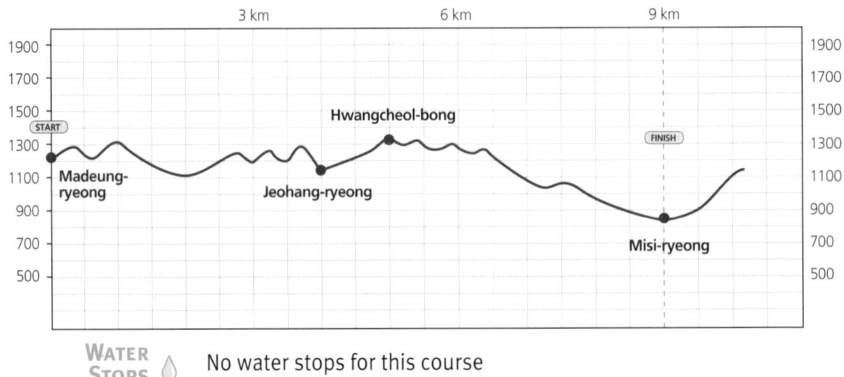

Baekdu-daegan above Cheonbul-dong Valley 천불동 계곡, which lies to the east. From there, the trail instantly descends through wooded forest in a northwestern direction before exiting the woodland and entering a ridgeline covered in thin, brackish wood. After loping through that area, the trail undulates again, and after 500 meters, it approaches more rocky outcrops that continue onward for 200 more meters before the trail descends out of the area. From about this altitude, the trail starts to elevate again. Ahead lies the spiky, rocky feature of a distinctive ridgeline that resembles the dinosaur spine. The trail rises to meet this feature.

The valley to Sinheung-sa from Jeohang-ryeong

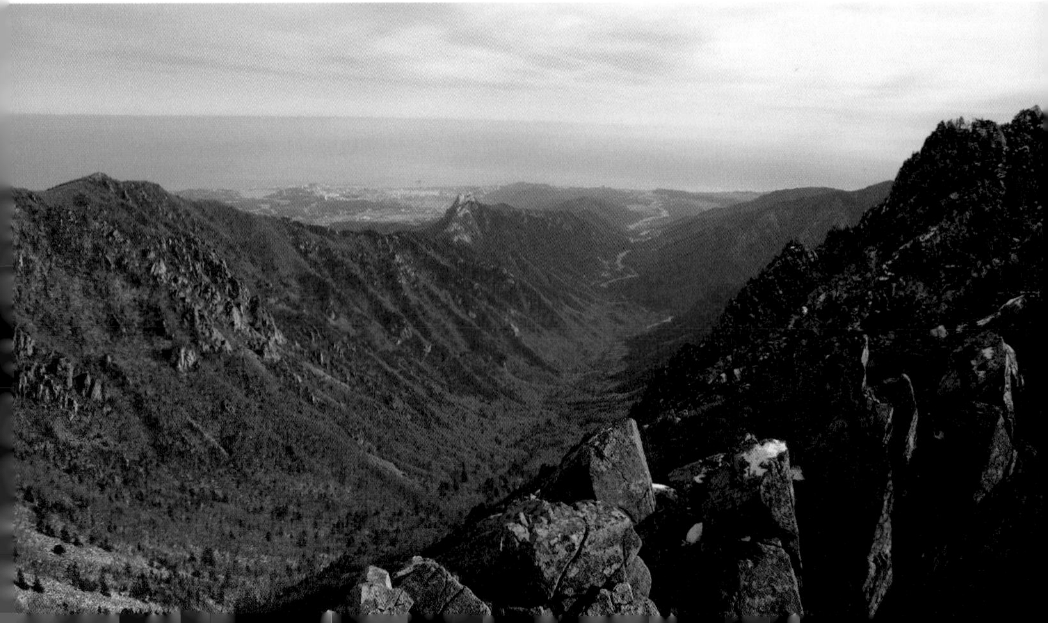

Once the trail starts to veer northward, it begins a descent down to the pass of Jeohang-ryeong some 400 meters away. The descent is still rocky and cumbersome but not overly steep. Jeohang-ryeong is located at about 1,125 m ABSL in the saddle of what once was a track junction. Just before the junction, the hiker can get impressive views of Jeohang-ryeong Gorge 저항령 계곡, which stretches east for about 5km all the way to the backyard of the temple of Sinheung-sa.

CLOSED SECTION Jeohang-ryeong 저항령 F3 → Hwangcheol-bong 황철봉 E3

1km (0:50)

The walk is basically a one kilometer grind ascending about 250m in altitude. However, it is a "cool" walk that brings the hiker onto a large exposed summit area supporting the odd stand of *Pinus koreanus*. The majority of the views are northeast, straight along the path of the Baekdu-daegan as it continues its rocky bound toward the next feature, which stands at about 1,381m ABSL 1.2km in the distance.

CLOSED SECTION Hwangcheol-bong 황철봉 E3 → Misi-ryeong 미시령 D3

2:10 (4km)

The next kilometer of the trail heads in a northeast direction, maintaining its current altitude of around 1,300 m ABSL over undulating rocky terrain before reaching a distinctive summit that stands at 1,318 m ABSL. From there, the trail heads north on a downward rocky pursuit resembling the remains of a giant hailstorm with one-meter-square chunks of granite rock strewn over the path. The bottom of this rocky descent is indicated by the final peak of this leg at an unnamed height of 1,080 m ABSL. From there, the walk down to the pass at Misi-ryeong should take around 40 minutes to complete, covering about 1.5 km in distance and dropping around 250 m in altitude to approximately 800 m ABSL.

* Misi-ryeong 미시령 D3

At Misi-ryeong, the Baekdu-daegan is connected by PR56 with the city of Sokcho about 10 km to the east and the small town of Yongdae-ri 용대리 7 km to the west. A *hyugeso* and large parking facility can be found at Misi-ryeong. The *hyugeso* does not have accommodations, and as both the north and south sides of the ridge are now closed for hiking, it is unknown how long this large wooden-style store will survive. Inside its walls, it has a well-stocked restaurant serving hot dishes and cold beer. There is also a well-maintained store there that sells hiking snack foods, hot coffee, and roasted whole potatoes. The *hyugeso* also has public toilets and a ranger's hut.

TRANSPORT INFO

Leaving the trail at Misi-ryeong: The only way to get off Misi-ryeong is by hitching a lift. Since the construction of the new tunnel passing below Misi-ryeong, buses no longer cross the pass, and you will need to take a taxi from Sokcho: Sokcho Taxi (T. 033-633-3222).

LODGING

About 2.5km west of Misi-ryeong on PR56 is the Dojeokpokpo Motel and Pension 도적폭포 모텔 (T. 033-462-3356 or 011-9787-6016), whose motel rooms go for about 30,000 won and pension rooms for 60,000-70,000 won. Another 5 km west of there is the road junction of NH46 and PR56, located at the small tourist and restaurant village of Yongdae-ri, which has a number of *minbak* such as the Naeseorak Teuksanmul Minbak 내설악 특산물 민박 (T. 033-462-9393). About 6 km to the east on the way to Sokcho is the Wonam-ri Hot Springs area 원암리 온천지구, which has a number of resorts and hotels. The seaside city of Sokcho has the full range of accommodations.

Looking north from Hwangcheol-bong to Misi-ryeong with Sang-bong in the background

DAY 4

From Misi-ryeong to Jinbu-ryeong

- **Distance:** 14km
- **Time:** 7hr 55min

Return to the ridge and walk up into the ghostly points of northern Seorak-san. Arrive at the spiritual peak of Sinseon-bong; say a prayer, bid farewell to the ocean and head west away from the coast toward your last point. Descend down to Daegan-ryeong, the exit of Seorak-san, and see if you still have four hours left in your day to alight to Jinbu-ryeong. If not, you have to walk off the ridge again. From the wind-swept, isolated pass of Daegan-ryeong, climb back up the ridge, clambering over the remnants of an ancient rock storm. Reach your last high point of this mammoth journey at Masan-bong and take a look at the road pass beneath you. Walk down toward the road, passing through an enormous ski resort that is now closed down. An old clock tower stands there—still in time. Walk through the small town that once supported this ski lodge; stop and feel its abandonment. Continue walking down a sealed road and march out to Jinbu-ryeong Pass, stopping short at the DMZ and kissing the obelisk that stands there. Rejoice with other hikers who may have finished that day as well. Turn around, look back at the way you came, and thank the great white ridge and the people of Korea for allowing you to safely walk the 735 km mountain system in Korea!

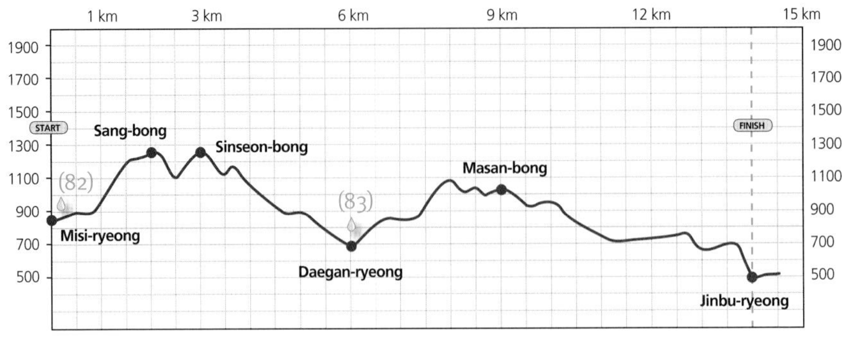

Water Stops

(82) 1 km north of Misi-ryeong: **N38°13'16" E128°26'36"**
(83) Daegan-ryeong: **N38°15'01" E128°25'08"**

Misi-ryeong 미시령 D3 → Sang-bong 상봉 C3 2km (1:30)

From Misi-ryeong, the Baekdu-daegan trail begins behind the public toilets located on the eastern side of the *hyugeso*. The entrance is understandably fenced off. The trail goes straight up the face of the ridge for the next 2 km, rising from 800 m ABSL to 1,244 m ABSL. However, after the first kilometer, the trail arrives at a lull in the wooded area where an old, barely used mountain spring(82) exists. At this point, there is a track that travels down the eastern side of the ridge for 3 km, exiting out behind the *sansin-gak* at Hwaam-sa Temple. Another 500 meters after this junction, the trail begins to ascend out onto the top of the ridge, where for the next 300 meters it stays at about 1,200 m ABSL before arriving at the crude, egg-shaped *doltap* located at the summit of Sang-bong. Located at the base of this odd feature is an old stone tablet with the word "Sang-bong" etched into its face. At the summit, there are great views to the east and west.

* Hwaam-sa 화암사 D4

Hwaam-sa was originally built in AD 769. It was destroyed in 1623 and rebuilt in 1625. Since that period, it has been rebuilt many times. In 1912, it was given its current name of Hwaam-sa, and it was rebuilt again in 1915. During the Korean War, it was cindered to the ground and remained unrestored until 1991, when it was rebuilt as part of the 17th World Jamboree held that August in Korea. At the front gates to the temple is a garden containing 15 sarira towers from the Joseon dynasty.

Sang-bong 상봉 → Sinseon-bong 신선봉 C3 1km (0:50)

From Sang-bong, the Baekdu-daegan trail dips sharply for about 500 meters down a rocky ridge to a saddle located at about 1,080 m ABSL. The descent down to the saddle still provides some excellent views to the east. At the base of the saddle, the trail begins its ascent up to the mystical peak of Sinseon-bong. The trail stays on its due course northwards before reaching the wooded southwestern face of Sinseon-bong. To get to the rocky outcrop of Sinseon-bong located at 1,214 m ABSL, there is a track to the right that takes the hiker north the remaining 30 meters or so to the summit. At the top of this majestic and incredible feature, one may feel the same gust of ghostliness that the peak is aptly named for. The name "Sinseon-bong" refers to a place of departure for spirits. It is a unique name for what is the last northern direction of the Baekdu-daegan in South Korea outside the DMZ. The summit overlooks the East Sea. The peak is strangely similar to other sacred places in the world that revere the departure of their dead through points on the earth that represent emissions of energy.

The cairn of Sang-bong

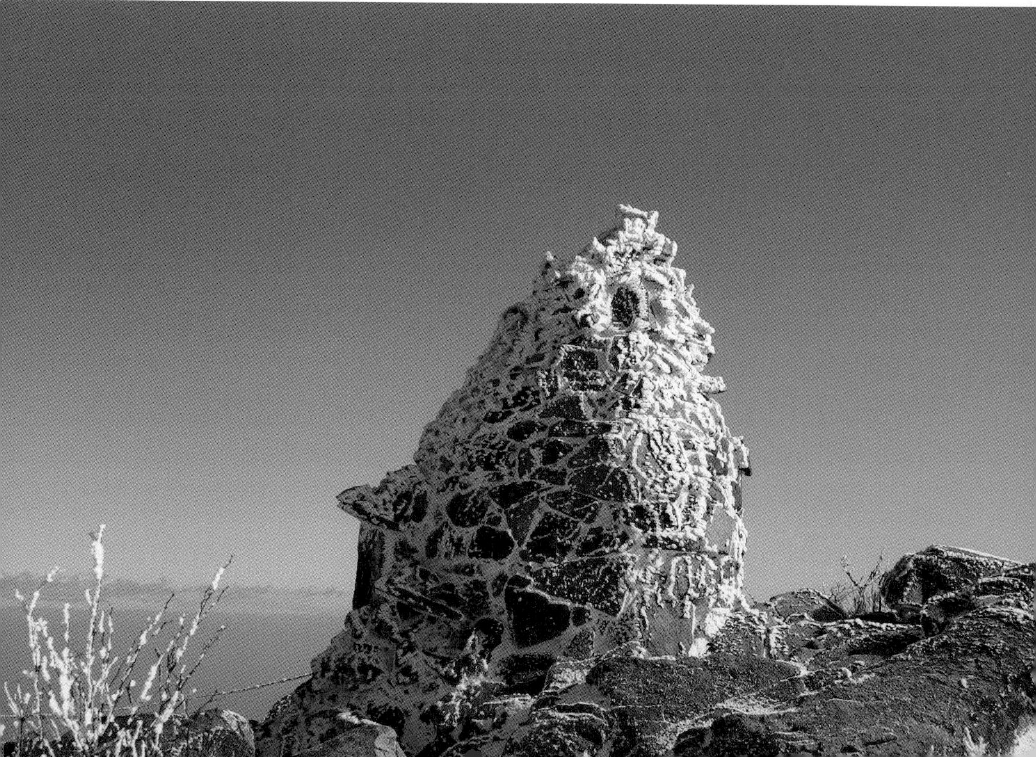

Sinseon-bong 신선봉 C3 → Daegan-ryeong 대간령 B3

3km (1:20)

The majority of the walk down to this pass is through wooded forest. The first 500 meter stretch continues to see it clambering through open expanses of broken rock toward the knob of an unnamed height located at 1,094 m ABSL. This area also offers good views back toward Sinseon-bong. From there, it is basically a continuous drop all the way down to Daegan-ryeong, which is located about 650 m ABSL. About a kilometer from the 1,094 m feature, you come across a helipad. From there, the trail clambers over one more patch of rock before turning into a westward direction and spilling out onto the pass at Daegan-ryeong.

Daegan-ryeong is a saddle that is north-south facing. It doesn't get much sun, and it is hidden in the shadows of the steep ridges that flank its western and eastern sides. At Daegan-ryeong, there is an old wooden signpost identifying the pass by its name, as well as a sign on it pointing the direction to Masan-bong, your next peak. On some nearby trees are homemade boards that members of other hiking trails have used to sign their names on previous passages. The bowels of the pass itself appear to be mainly loose rock, some of which has been used to form a wind block on the southern side of the pass. Water(83) can be found down the southern side of the pass in a mountain stream.

On the way to Daegan-ryeong

Daegan-ryeong 대간령 B3 → Masan-bong 마산봉 B2

3km (1:55)

From the windy, isolated pass of Daegan-ryeong, which literally means "ridge pass," the trail heads northwest straight up the wooded slope to the top of your first feature, located at 890 m ABSL. The first few hundred meters see you passing through a wooded forest and then up to the open clearing as you reach the foot of a feature located at 890 m ABSL. The terrain becomes quite interesting, with large chunks of strewn boulders cast out all over the side of the hill. At the 890 m peak, you have some more great views to the northeast. This area is quite exposed to the harsh trans-Siberian winds of winter and the steely, coarse sea winds of the East Sea. The trees in this area are all permanently arced westward. You may also notice in this area numerous manmade bunkers or sentry posts, constructed by soldiers who appear to occasionally train in this area. After the 890 m peak, the trail continues in a northwest direction, maintaining its current altitude for the next 300 meters before beginning its slow, twisting ascent toward Masan-bong. The trail now takes on a more easterly direction for the next kilometer before arcing slightly south and reaching another rocky outcrop. At this stage, the trail turns sharply right and continues with its ascent north toward Masan-bong. All the while, it ducks in and out of the tree line onto rocky formations. After turning north, you should arrive 500 meters later at the peak of Masan-bong at 1,051 m ABSL. Masan-bong is the last peak on the recreational part of the Baekdu-daegan in South Korea; the actual last peak, Hyangno-bong 향로봉, lies inside the restricted zone of the DMZ.

Masan-bong 마산봉 B2 → Jinbu-ryeong 진부령 B1

5km (2:20)

You should easily be able to see the downward leg toward Nunmul-gogae 눈물고개 from Masan-bong. You may also be able to see the large clock tower that stands at the back of the abandoned ski resort—*are the hands on the clock stuck at 11:14 am or pm?* There is not much else to explain for the downward leg, except that from Masan-bong, it travels east through more wooded forest. It eventually comes out behind the ski lifts at the top of the ski field. You may also notice that the makers of the ski field cut precariously close to the crest of the Baekdu-daegan in order to get more run to the top of the ski slopes. They have practically chiseled out the south-facing slope of the Baekdu-daegan to achieve this! There is a hole in the fence that you can go through to explore the now defunct ski field and its rusting abandoned chair lifts. From this location, you can either walk down the ski slope or go back behind the fence and follow the trail alongside it. Near the bottom of the ski slope, about where the clock tower is, the trail goes right through a large stand of pine trees alongside the northern perimeter of the alpine ski resort. Follow this track through the pine forest; the trail will dump you out onto the parking lot next to the huge buildings of empty accommodations. You walk around the ghostly features of the empty ski resort and continue northeast across a large parking lot until you see a 4WD track or a set of ribbons marking the spot for your return back into the bush. Keep following this track until it basically hits the road again a short distance later. This is your opportunity to stop and investigate the struggling little village that once made its living from skiers. There are some small stores located in the center that sell hot food and amenities. In the hub of the village are the council buildings, while on the lawn outside the front of the buildings is a stainless steel signboard with three margined notices on it explaining the virtues of some of its previous citizens. The first story, on the left-hand side of the board, states how in 1931, a man by the name of Ham Dong-seok responded to a natural disaster that occurred in this region, afflicting all farmers with starvation. He, in turn, went around collecting contributions in grain from the public, and he subsequently gave the offerings to the suffering farmers, enabling them to survive their disaster. The second and middle story is about a district chief who, in a similar but augmented manner compared to Ham Dong-seok, dedicated his leadership to saving his people from starvation. The third and last person to be commemorated is schoolteacher Ra Byeong-gyu, who in 1935, after the food shortage, began teaching the young and old people of this village diligent study habits and literacy.

Trail down to the ski resort

There are two options from here to get to Jinbu-ryeong. The first is simply to follow the road east out of Nunmul-gogae and down to Jinbu-ryeong some 2 km later on NH46. The other and more purist option is to go back to the last place from which you entered the township. Otherwise, the trail is in a northeast direction from the village; you walk along a sealed road for a moment before ducking up alongside the edges of some small farmlets. Just look for the hiking ribbons and follow them if you see them. The remaining section of the Baekdu-daegan in Nunmul-gogae arcs around a mountain road along the northern side of the basin that comprises Nunmul-gogae. Once the trail starts to loop south, you are heading toward the final downhill section of the walk. Passing under a mast, the trail cuts back into a tree line and rather clumsily makes its way down to the sealed road, which slithers its way down to NH46. On the trail just above this road, you may see some more military bunkers set up to respond to any national emergencies. Coming out onto the road, you see a small grassy area on the downward southern section. In this area, there are numerous plaques and tablets devoted to those wealthier members of Korean society who found it necessary to make their own commemorations to hiking the Baekdu-daegan. From this area, you can basically see the large stele standing at Jinbu-ryeong. Reentering the tree line, the trail cuts straight down the slope, meeting the road again. Cross the road back into the tree line, and walk your final 100 meters through the bush and out onto the pass at Jinbu-ryeong behind the celebration area.

* Jinbu-ryeong 진부령 B1

The final road pass of the Baekdu-daegan in South Korea is connected by NH46, which intersects with PR56 8 km to the south at Yongdae-dong 용대동. North of Jinbu-ryeong, PR46 travels about 20 km northeast to the seaside town of Goseong 고성. At Jinbu-ryeong, there is a large stone monument erected in September 2006. On its back, it says that the Baekdu-daegan is the backbone of Korea, connecting its southern and northern ecosystems. It goes on to add that some parts of the Baekdu-daegan have been destroyed by indiscriminate development, and that even now there are more problems with the conservation and utilization of the trail.

There are various other monuments on both sides of the road at Jinbu-ryeong, but the main one is clearly the large stele. On the southern side of Jinbu-ryeong is the main shopping area, consisting of some small stores that sell hot food, cold beer, and other amenities. On the opposite side of the road is the military base that patrols the remaining area west and north of here as part of the demilitarized zone. There is no public access to the Baekdu-daegan beyond that point, at least not without the permission of the military. More information on this leg can be found in the brief Section on Hyangno-bong. And 735 km later, that's about it... in South Korea, that is.

TRANSPORT INFO

Leaving the trail at Jinbu-ryeong: From the end of the trail, buses run into Sokcho eight times a day from 8:35 am to 7:10 pm. Buses also leave Jinbu-ryeong for Seoul nine times daily from 6:55 am to 5:45 pm. Six of these buses are destined for Sangbong Terminal, and three for Dong Seoul terminal. Buses for Jinbu-ryeong leave Seoul from Sangbong Terminal six times a day from 7:10 am to 5:15 pm. These buses are headed for Sokcho, so you will have to state your desire to stop at Jinbu-ryeong.

백두대간
진부
기 백두대간
006년 3월12일~2007년11월10일
주최:이우학교

18.0 km

SECTION 17

INTO THE DANGER ZONE

Jinbu-ryeong → Hyangno-bong near the DMZ

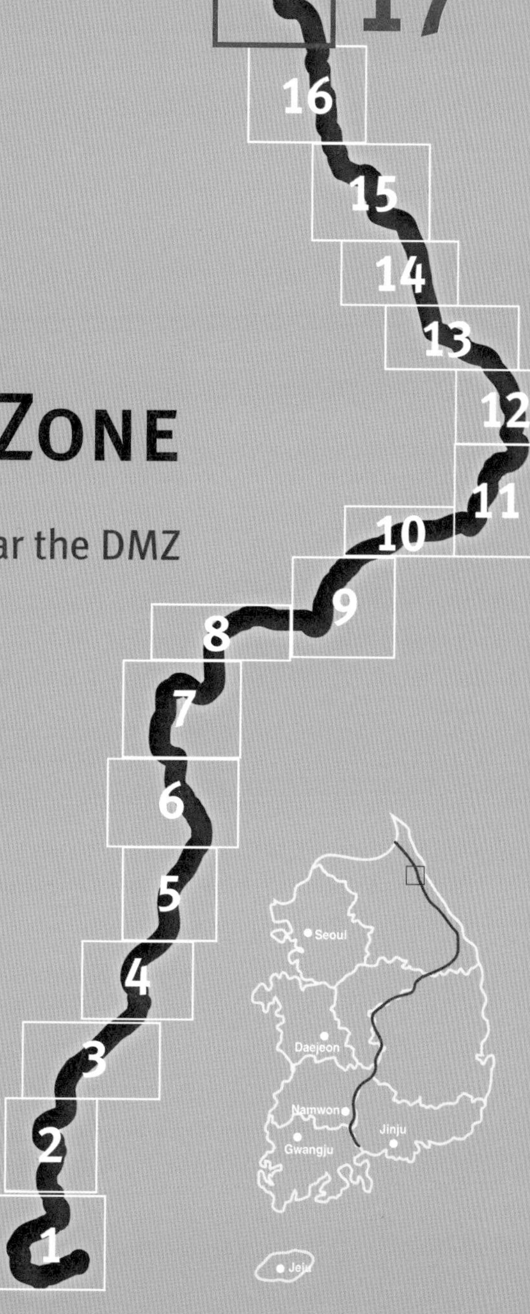

The Last Part of the Baekdu-daegan Trek

Jinbu-ryeong → Hyangno-bong near the DMZ

It is unlikely that you will get permission to walk into the civilian-regulated military zone to Hyangno-bong ("incense burner peak"), but the best way to find out would be to approach and ask the guard at the gates to the Jinbu-ryeong army camp opposite the pass's menhir monument. If your inquiry results in your being granted permission, you will then be escorted past the barrier arm and onto a vehicle track located next to the front gates of the camp. Depending on the time the soldiers have available, you may be asked to do this leg in the back of their jeep. Photography in the area is strictly controlled—ask your escorts what's appropriate. Once you are at Hyangno-bong, looking into North Korea, you will not be allowed to take any photographs north of that or of anything located within sight of the North Koreans—like the observation post you are standing in. For the sake of the journey, we were allowed to walk on this vehicle track for the 18 km it takes to get to Hyangno-bong, tailed by a patient army captain in his jeep. Anyway, we were not allowed to leave the road, which hugs the highest contour of the Baekdu-daegan ridge. There is nothing that exciting about the scenery in this region. There are no stands of high trees or waves of peaks and saddles; it is just a 4WD army track making its most pragmatic and natural way up to one of South Korea's proud "tripwire" frontline units. But the sheer fact that you are walking in a restricted area that is barely visited by outsiders is exciting enough in itself, and a reflective and alternative way to end a long journey of freedom.

The icy road up to Hyangno-bong beyond the end point at Jinbu-ryeong

Andrew and Roger standing at the peak of Hyangno-bong

The area is known as the Hyangno-bong Zone. The summit of Hyangno-bong stands at 1,296 m ABSL about 2 km south of the 4 km wide DMZ (demilitarized zone) between North and South Korea. In accordance with its name, there is a large, beautiful cast iron incense-burning pot located at the top of the peak amidst all the military paraphernalia. There are only two geographical features in the Hyangno-bong Zone that are worth mentioning: the peak of Chiljeol-bong 칠절봉 and a valley named Gojin-dong 고진동, which runs east-west between the two Koreas.

Designated a natural monument in 1973, the Hyangno-bong Zone is inhabited by a variety of flora and fauna. There are reportedly no fewer than 648 species of flora to be found in this zone, 27 of them endemic to Korea. Of its 739 known species of insects, at least 40 new species were found in this zone during a 1972 survey that led to its subsequent designation as a national monument. There are also over 40 different species of Mammalia in this zone, including wild boars, deer, elk and possibly Bandal ("half moon") bears. The Gojin-dong valley to the north is known to have thick stands of lush virgin forest consisting of Mongolian oak and acicular pine and fir trees growing amongst deciduous species within the actual wired-off DMZ.

Jinbu-ryeong 진부령 → Hyangno-bong 향로봉 approx. 18km

From the barrier gate, you simply walk west up the vehicle track for about 4 km as it winds its way up to Chiljeol-bong, which is located at 1,172 m ABSL. From there, the road turns north toward Hyangno-bong. You will probably be able to see the buildings occupied by the military on top of the peak. This road is actually visible from the Seorak-san leg between Madeung-ryeong and Misi-ryeong in Seorak-san National Park. About 7 km short of Hyangno-bong, you come to a rest area, which, surprisingly enough, has a number of Baekdu-daegan ribbons hanging in the branches of the trees. They must have been placed there by dogged Baekdu-daeganers who snuck up to the ridge, addicted to its spirit. On the west side of the road at this pass is an enclave of constructed rock providing a rest area for visitors. On the eastern side of the road is a boulder mounted on a stand made from cement and local rock. The inscription on the boulder simply says "Hyangno-bong." Next to the menhir is a plaque commemorating the life of a soldier who served in this region. The plaque has a picture of Lt. Col. Kim Chil-seop, who, on November 19, 2004, became a paragon of sacrifice while trying to save the life of a subordinate who had been struck by electricity. His sincere military spirit will always be in the hearts of the men he served with. Also, on the back of the monument, there is a list of other soldiers who appear to have died while serving in this region. One of those soldiers died two days after Lt. Col. Kim, and I wonder if it was the subordinate he so fatally tried to save.

The zone is definitely off-limits to the public as you approach what is the first of a series of military checkpoints. After passing through these checkpoints, you eventually arrive at the military station at Hyangno-bong. Numerous facilities are located in this area, including the mess, barracks, a church, and an observation post. From the observation post, you can clearly see into North Korea and, further on in the distance, the large humping back of Geumgang-san National Park. Beneath the observation tower, the peak celebrates its name with the previously mentioned cast iron incense burner. Also by that cauldron are a larger stone replica of an incense-burning pot and two round *doltap* cairns. In the middle of all these objects is a slab of granite upon which visitors can place urns. Also located in the area are

other plaques and monuments paying homage to the peak. One of them talks about how Hyangno-bong is one of 12,000 peaks that inhabit the Geumgang-san sub-range. The peak's name originated from observations made by locals, who said that the summit resembled the shape of an incense burner when it was shrouded in white clouds. In one area, there are three roundish boulders mounted next to each other on stands of red brick. They are odes commissioned by three different major generals. As you face them, the one on the left, from a Major General Oh, reads:

"*Ah, Hyangno-bong!*
The Namgang always looks the same;
But my comrades who fell here in the fierce war are invisible"

The one in the middle is written by a Major General Bak and reads:

"*Ah, Hyangno-bong!*
Hyangno-bong soars high into the sky here!
Wishing for the reunification of Korea,
The Gwanmang-dae (observation tower) has been set up here"

And the remaining poem, written by a Major General Park, reads;

"*To welcome the new millennium,*
all of the soldiers of Ulji Army
pledge to guard their homeland
here at Seolro-bong ("snow stove peak")"

Conclusion

Overall, if you are able to visit the peak of Hyangno-bong, then it is a worthy and weird experience for what has been a long and remarkable journey. As you stand on the Gwanmang-dae 관망대 looking north, having walked 750 remarkable mountain kilometers to get here, your head is full of wonder and ambition about this mysterious peninsula. And you yearn to walk further north along the Baekdu-daegan as she broods her way up the peninsula to the mythological birthplace of the people of the *Hanbando*—at the sacred peak of Baekdu-san, the great white mountain of the great white ridge.

Kia Kaha.

Appendix

Essential Korean

Essential Korean

Outside of the main centers, there is little English spoken in Korea, and along the Baekdu-daegan, you will encounter very few locals who can communicate freely with you. Learning a little Korean before setting off will serve you well along the trail and in towns and will no doubt add to your experience. If you can't speak any Korean, it's not the end of the world, as rural Koreans are a patient lot, and you will soon become a master of friendly body language, which should never be underestimated. It is highly recommended, however, that you take some time and learn to read the Korean alphabet, *hangeul*, as well as a few basic pleasantries before heading off. *Hangeul* is very easy to learn and can be picked up by most people after a couple of days of study. It is very helpful along the trail, as signposts, advertisements for accommodation, menus and bus schedules are for the most part written entirely in Korean.

Korean Language in the Guide

Throughout the guide, we have maintained the Korean names for most features along the trail. These are frequently repeated, and translating them into English will only confuse Korean hikers when you try to describe them, and yourself when you are seeking directions. It won't be very far down the trail before you are freely using and understanding words like *bong*, *ryeong*, *gyegok* and *bawi*. We have intentionally added hyphens between the proper nouns and terms such as *ryeong* or *gyegok* in order to let you get a grip on the language better and more easily.

Features along the Trail		
a mountain	~san	산
a prominent rock	~bawi	바위
a peak	~bong	봉
a valley/gorge	~gyegok	계곡
a pass	~ryeong	령
a gorge	~gol	골

a pass	~jae	재
a stream	~cheon	천
a pass	~gogae	고개
a river	~gang	강
a pass	~chi	치
a fresh water spring	~saem	샘
a saddle	~anbu	안부
a mineral water spring	~yaksu	약수
a cairn	~doltap	돌탑
mountain spirit shrine	Sansin-gak	산신각
a pavilion for resting	Jeongja	정자
a rest area (often with a restaurant and convenience store)	Hyugeso	휴게소

Places and Areas

a city area	~si	시
a town area	~eup	읍
a county	~gun	군
a sub-county	~myeon	면
a village area	~ri	리
a village	~maeul	마을
a village area/ neighborhood/district	~dong	동

Temples

Temple	jeol	절

Jeol is the non-specific term for a temple; for example, Daewon Temple is not called Daewon-jeol.

Major temples are usually followed by the suffix *-sa* (사), with supporting temples or hermitages called *-am* (암), but they are also sometimes given other names such as -dae (대, "platform"), *-jeongsa* (정사, "retreat temple"), and *-seonwon* (선원, "meditation center").

Useful Language

The following language guide is specific to the trail and will help you with general greetings as well as obtaining supplies, seeking accommodation, asking directions, and dealing with transport and food. To help you further, it is always a good idea to carry a lightweight Korean phrase book or English–Korean dictionary, both of which are available at bookstores in all major centers.

Greetings

Hello.	Annyeong hasimnikka / Annyeong haseyo. 안녕하십니까? / 안녕하세요.
Goodbye.	Annyeonghi gaseyo (if the listener is leaving) / Annyeonghi gyeseyo (if the listener is staying). 안녕히 가세요 / 안녕히 계세요.
What's your name?	Ireumi moeyo? 이름이 뭐에요?
My name is...	Je ireumeun ...imnida. 제 이름은 ... 입니다.
Where are you from?	Eodieseo osheosseumnikka? 어디에서 오셨습니까?

I'm from...	Jeoneun _____-eseo wasseoyo. 저는 ____에서 왔어요.
Nice to meet you.	Mannaseo bangap seumnida. 만나서 반갑습니다.

Basic Terms

Yes.	Ne/Ye.	네/예.
No.	Ahniyo.	아니요.
Please... (always attached to the end of a request)	...Haejuseyo.	...해주세요.
Thank you.	Gamsa hamnida.	감사합니다.
You're welcome.	Cheonmaneyo.	천만에요.
Excuse me.	Sillye hamnida.	실례합니다.
Sorry.	Jwoesong hamnida.	죄송합니다.

How to Ask for Directions

I am walking to ~	Jeoneun ~ ro gago isseoyo.	저는 ~로 가고 있어요.
Where is...?	...eodie isseoyo?	...어디에 있어요?
I'm looking for a...	...reul/eul chatgo isseoyo.	...를/을 찾고있어요.
I'm lost.	Gireul ireosseoyo.	길을 잃었어요.
Let's go together.	Gachi-gayo.	같이 가요.

Questions Words

How much is this?	Igeo eolma eyo? 이거 얼마에요?
Please give me one.	Hana juseyo. 하나주세요.
Do you speak English?	Yeongeo haseyo? 영어 하세요?
Where are you going?	Eodiro gaseyo? 어디로 가세요
I am walking to ~	Jeoneun ~ ro gago isseoyo. 저는 ~로 가고 있어요.
Where does this trail go?	Igoseun eodiro ganeun deungsanro imnikka? 이곳은 어디로 가는 등산로입니까?
Can you help me?	Dowa jusil su isseoyo? 도와 주실 수 있어요?
Do you have any water?	Mul isseoyo? 물 있어요?
Can I camp here?	Yeogiseo yayeonghaedo doemnikka? 여기서 야영해도 됩니까?

Accommodations

I'm looking for a ....

... chatgo isseoyo. ... 찾고 있어요.

- Accommodation / suk-bak-si-seol 숙박시설
- Homestay guesthouse / min-bak-jip 민박집
- campground / ya-yeong-jang 야영장

Do you have any rooms available?

jigeum bang isseoyo? 지금 방 있어요?

Do you have a room with a bed?

Chimdae bang isseoyo? 침대 방 있어요?

Do you have hot water?

Tteugeoun mul isseoyo? 뜨거운 물 있어요?

Can I leave some things here?

Jim-eul nwadul su isseoyo? 짐을 놔둘 수 있어요?

How much is it...?

... eolmayeyo? ... 얼마예요?

- per night / harut bam 하룻밤
- per person / han saram 한 사람

Days of the Week

- Sunday iryoil 일요일
- Tuesday hwayoil 화요일
- Thursday mogyoil 목요일
- Saturday toyoil 토요일
- Monday weoryoil 월요일
- Wednesday suyoil 수요일
- Friday geumyoil 금요일

Directions

• North	bukjjok	북쪽	• South	namjjok	남쪽
• East	dongjjok	동쪽	• West	seojjok	서쪽
• Left	woenjjok	왼쪽	• Right	oreunjjok	오른쪽

Go straight.
Jikjin haseyo.
직진 하세요.

Turn left.
Oenjjokeuro gaseyo.
왼쪽으로 가세요.

Turn right.
Oreunjjokeuro gaseyo.
오른쪽으로 가세요.

Go up.
Wijjokeuro gaseyo.
위쪽으로 가세요.

Go down.
Araejjokeuro gaseyo.
아래쪽으로 가세요.

Transportation

Please take me to...
... gajuseyo. ... 가주세요.

How can I get to...?
...e eotteoge gayo? ...에 어떻게 가요?

What time does the ... leave/arrive?
... eonjae tteonayo/dochakhaeyo? ... 언제 떠나요/도착해요?

• bus	beoseu	버스
• train	gicha	기차

Where is the nearest bus stop?

Gajang gakkaun beoseu jeongryujang-eun eodi-imnikka?

가장 가까운 버스 정류장은 어디입니까?

A ticket to ~ , please.

~ euro ganeun pyo-reul juseyo.

~으로 가는 표를 주세요.

Can you take me to ~ ?

Jeo-reul ~ ro deryeoda jusil su isseoyo?

저를 ~로 데려다 주실 수 있어요?

Can you pick me up from ~ ?

~ ro jeo-reul taeureo osil su isseoyo?

~로 저를 태우러 오실 수 있어요?

Food

- breakfast achim 아침
- dinner jeonyeok 저녁
- eat meogeoyo 먹어요
- lunch jeomsim 점심
- snack gansik 간식
- drink masyeoyo 마셔요

I would like ___, please.

___ juseyo. ___ 주세요.

Please give me more water.

Mul deo juseyo. 물 더 주세요.

Please ring up the bill.

Gyesan hae juseyo. 계산 해주세요.

Food

Not too spicy, please.
Neomu maepji anke hae juseyo.
너무 맵지 않게 해 주세요.

I'm full. Baebulleoyo. 배불러요.

It was delicious. Masisseosseo-yo. 맛있었어요.

Sun-du-bu	soft tofu with kimchi and vegetables	순두부
Do-to-ri-muk	acorn jelly	도토리묵
Pa-jeon	a flat omelet with a variety of toppings	파전
Kim-chi-jeon	a kimchi omelet	김치전
Gam-ja-jeon	potato omelet	감자전
Hae-mul-pa-jeon	seafood and vegetable omelet	해물파전
Doen-jang-jji-gae	thick soybean paste soup with side dishes	된장찌개
Kim-chi-jji-gae	thick kimchi soup with side dishes	김치찌개
Mae-un-tang	spicy fish soup	매운탕
Dak-baek-suk	whole chicken, rice and ginseng stew	닭백숙
Sam-gye-tang	chicken, ginseng and rice broth	삼계탕
Deo-deok-gu-i	spicy grilled *deodeok* root (*Codonopsis lanceolata*) with side dishes	더덕구이
Dak-do-ri-tang	spicy chicken stew	닭도리탕
Beo-seot-jeon-gol	mushroom and beef broth	버섯전골
Dong-dong-ju	unfiltered rice wine	동동주
Mak-geol-li	filtered rice wine	막걸리
So-ju	a spirit traditionally distilled from rice and widely popular across Korea	소주
Maek-ju	beer	맥주
Baek-se-ju	a spirit distilled from glutinous rice and flavoured with various herbs	백세주
Bok-bun-ja	mountain berry wine	복분자
Deo-deok-ju	a spirit made from the root of a species of bonnet bellflower (*Codonopsis lanceolata*)	더덕주
Kol-la	cola	콜라
Sa-i-da	cider, Sprite, 7Up (lemonade)	사이다
Ju-seu	juice	주스
Mul	water	물

Emergencies

Help!	Dowa juseyo!	도와주세요!
Call...!	...bulleo juseyo!	...불러 주세요!

- a doctor / uisa 의사
- the police / gyeongchal 경찰
- an ambulance / gugeupcha 구급차

I'm sick.	Apa-yo.	아파요.
It hurts here.	Yeogi-reul dacheosseoyo.	여기를 다쳤어요.
My ~ hurts.	~ reul dacheosseoyo.	~를 다쳤어요.
I have a ~ .	~i isseoyo.	~이 있어요.

Trail Vocabulary

Backpack	배낭 bae-nang	Bandage	붕대 bung-dae
Band Aid	밴드에이드 Ban-changgo	Batteries	배터리 bae-teo-ri
Bedroll	담요 dam-yo	Boots	등산화 deung-san-hwa
Camping stove	휴대용 가스버너 hyu-dae-yong ga-seu-beo-neo	Compass	나침반 Na-chim-ban
Crampons	아이젠 a-i-jen	First aid kit	비상약품 bi-sang yak-pum
Flashlight	회중전등 hoe-jung-jeon-deung	Gas bottles	부탄가스 bu-tan-ga-seu
Headlamp	전조등 jeon-jo-deung	Insect repellent	해충약 hae-chung-yak
Jacket	자켓 ja-ket	Lighter	라이터 la-i-teo
Map	지도 ji-do	Matches	성냥 seong-nyang
Pocket knife	휴대용 칼 hyu-dae-yong kal	Rope	로프 ro-peu
Scissors	가위 ga-wi	Shoelaces	신발끈 sin-bal-kkeun
Sleeping bag	침낭 chim-nang	Socks	양말 yang-mal
Sun block	썬 크림 sseon keu-rim	Tape	스카치 테이프 seu-ka-chi te-i-peu
Tent	텐트 ten-teu	Toilet paper	휴지 *hyu-ji*
Toothbrush	칫솔 chit-sol	Toothpaste	치약 chi-yak
Trekking poles	등산 폴 deung-san pol	Bus station	버스 정류장 beo-seu jeong-ryu-jang
Bank	은행 *eun-haeng*	Hiking store	등산 용품 가게 deung-san yong-pum ga-ge

(*hyphens are placed between syllables)

Trail Vocabulary

Convenience store	편의점 pyeon-ui-jeom	Library	도서관 do-seo-gwan
Hospital	병원 byeong-won	Museum	박물관 bak-mul-gwan
Market	시장 si-jang	Pharmacy	약국 yak-guk
PC room / Internet café	PC방 PC-bang	Post office	우체국 u-che-guk
Police station	경찰서 gyeong-chal-seo	Supermarket	슈퍼마켓 syu-peo-ma-ket
Restaurant	식당 sik-dang	Headache	두통 du-tong
Train station	기차역 gi-cha-yeok	Diarrhea	설사 seol-sa
Fever	열 yeol	Stomachache	복통 bok-tong
Cold	감기 gam-gi	Foot	발 bal
Food poisoning	식중독 sik-jung-dok	Shin	정강이 jeong-gang-i
Toothache	치통 chi-tong	Hamstring	슬건seul-geon
Toe	발가락 bal-ga-rakl	Leg	다리 da-ri
Ankle	발목 bal-mok	Hip	엉덩이 eong-deong-i
Knee	무릎 mu-reup	Stomach	배 bae
Thigh	허벅지 heo-beok-ji	Chest	가슴 ga-seum
Groin	사타구니 sa-ta-gu-ni	Finger	손가락 son-ga-rak
Buttocks	엉덩이, 둔부 eong-deong-i, dun-bu	Elbow	팔꿈치 pal-kkum-chi
Ribs	갈빗대 gal-bit-dae	Back	등 deung
Arm	팔 pal	Mouth	입 ip
Hand	손 son	Ear	귀 gwi
Shoulder	어깨 eo-kkae	Nose	코 ko
Neck	목 mok	Closed	폐쇄된 pye-swae-doen
Tooth	이, 치아 i, chi-a	Slippery	미끄러운 mi-kkeu-reo-un
Eye	눈 nun	Crowded	혼잡한 hon-jap-han
Head	머리 meo-ri	It's rainy.	비가 와요. Biga wayo.
Hiking Trail	등산로 deung-san-rol	It's snowy.	눈이 와요. Nuni wayo.
Wet	젖은 jeo-jeun	It's cold.	추워요. Chuwoyo.
Dangerous	위험한 wi-heom-han	It's stormy.	폭풍우가 쳐요. Pokpunguga chyeoyo.
Caution	조심 jo-sim	Clear skies	맑은 하늘 malgeun haneul
It's sunny.	화창해요. Hwachanghaeyo.	It's foggy.	안개 낀 날 angae kkin nal
It's windy.	바람이 불어요. Barami bureoyo.	Fine weather	날씨가 좋아요. Nalssiga joayo.
It's hot.	더워요. Deowoyo.		

(*hyphens are placed between syllables)

백두대간

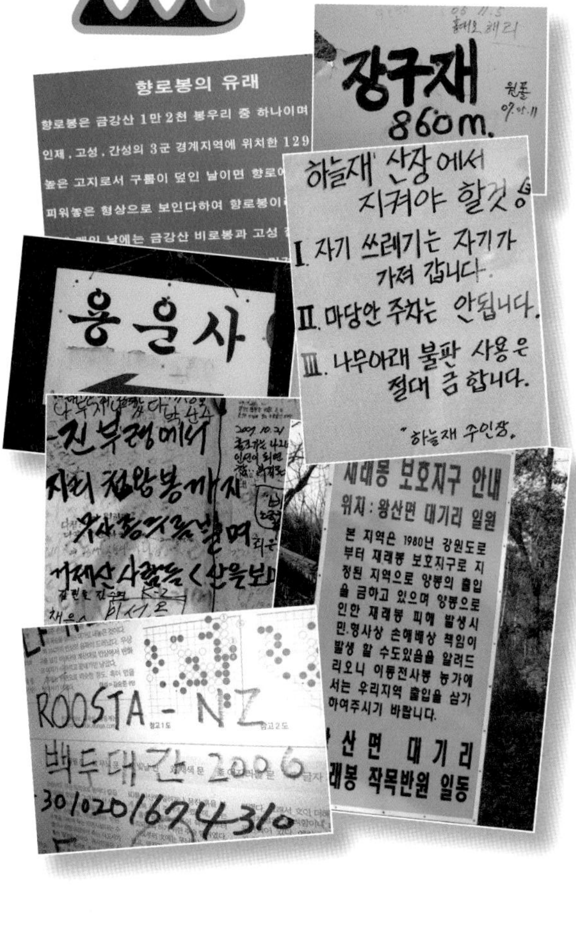
향로봉의 유래
향로봉은 금강산 1만 2천 봉우리 중 하나이며
인제, 고성, 간성의 3군 경계지역에 위치한 129
높은 고지로서 구름이 덮인 날이면 향로
피워놓은 형상으로 보인다하여 향로봉이
날에는 금강산 비로봉과 고성
장구재
860m.
하늘재 산장에서
지켜야 할것들
I. 자기 쓰레기는 자기가
가져 갑니다.
II. 마당안 주차는 안됩니다.
III. 나무아래 불판 사용은
절대 금 합니다.
"하늘재 주인장.
웅은사
진부령에서
지리 천왕봉까지
무사종주를 빌며
ROOSTA - NZ
백두대간 2006
301020167 4310
재래봉 보호지구 안내
위치 : 왕산면 대기리 일원
본 지역은 1980년 강원도로
부터 재래봉 보호지구로 지
정된 지역으로 양봉의 출입
을 금하고 있으며 양봉으로
인한 재래봉 피해 발생시
민.형사상 손해배상 책임이
발생 할 수도있음을 알려드
리오니 이동전사봉 농가에
서는 우리지역 출입을 삼가
하여주시기 바랍니다.
산면 대기리
래봉 작목반원 일동

About the Authors

Roger Shepherd

rasnzwlg@hotmail.com | www.hikekorea.com

Roger Shepherd was born in Porirua, New Zealand. At a young age he traveled overseas to Africa, where he ended up living for the next nine years. Working in the wildlife industry in South Africa, Mozambique, and Zambia as a game handler, ranger, and safari guide, Roger learned his craft for outdoor exploration on foot through the management of National Parks security and tourism. He returned to New Zealand in 1998 and first traveled to Korea in 2000. In 2001, he returned to New Zealand, where he joined the NZ Police and NZ Territorial Army. In 2006, with a stack of holiday leave to use, Roger returned to Korea for some hiking and, through friend Andrew Douch, was informed of the presence of the Baekdu-daegan. He subsequently set out on foot to explore the Baekdu-daegan, and soon realized the potential for an English-language guide book. Organizing a team, he asked his Korean based hiking buddy Andrew Douch to assist, and through his planning and research found a new friend in mountain culture expert Professor David A. Mason, who agreed to support the expedition from an academic perspective. With that, Roger returned to Korea in September 2007, and together with Andrew Douch, both walked the 735 km length of the Baekdu-daegan. The empirical journey of research was completed in 70 days, and they both spent the next two years writing the guide book, with David A. Mason proofreading and advising.

Roger is now an appointed Honorary Ambassador of Tourism to South Korea and continues to hike, write, and photograph Korean mountain culture.

Andrew Douch

trekkorea@gmail.com

Andrew was raised on the slopes of a volcano on the North Island of New Zealand. In 1998, he attained a Bachelor of Social Sciences from the University of Waikato, and he has since lived in Wellington and the Korean cities of Daegu, Andong, Pohang and Yangsan.

Over almost a decade in Korea, Andrew has dedicated much of his time to exploring its mountainous regions and has become a familiar face in many a remote mountain village. His explorations led him to discover the Baekdu-daegan Trail, and a dream was born to walk the great ridge. In 2007, he joined his old mate Roger Shepherd for the expedition that resulted in this book.

Andrew is now based near the famous Tongdo-sa temple complex in the province of Gyeongsangnam-do, where he teaches high school English and continues to roam Korea's highlands.

David A. Mason

mntnwolf@yahoo.com

David A. Mason is a Professor of Korean Tourism at Kyung Hee University and researcher on the religious character of Korea's mountains. Prior to assuming this post, he worked for the Ministry of Culture and Tourism for 5 years, and served 14 years as a professor of English out in the Korean countryside. A citizen of the United States and native of Michigan, he has been living in South Korea since the early 1980s. He earned a master's degree in the history of Korean religions from Yonsei University and has been an avid mountain-hiker. He has authored six books on Korean culture and tourism, including *Spirit of the Mountains*, about Korea's traditions of spiritual mountain worship. His popular websites on sacred Korean mountains, Buddhism, folk culture and mountain spirits can be found at www.san-shin.org, www.baekdu-daegan.com and www.zozayong.com.

Acknowledgements

This Guide Book is dedicated to all the good people of the Baekdu-daegan Mountain System that we met on our journey.

Special Thanks

A special thanks must go to Jeong Kyoo-hwan and Sung Byung-oh for producing the countless translations for this book in a speedy manner. Special thanks also to Prof. David Mason for his support, friendship, and the countless hours he spent proofreading the manuscript.

Acknowledgment List

The following people are also recognized for their support in this project.

Shawn Morrissey
Mike Allbee
David Sargeant
Chris Meder and Liz Riggs
NZ Paramedic Nigel White
NZ Army Surgeon Major Graham Wesley
Dr. Yang Jong-sung of the National Folklore Museum
Kim Hyeon-hui
Park Eun-gyeong

The following Kyung-hee University students for their assistance in translations.

"Dando" Han Dong-geun
"Grace" Han Song-i
"Shane" Kim Kyu-min
"Dorothy" Im E-rang
"MJ" Hong Min-jung
"Jennifer" Kim Su-jung

Korean Embassy of the Republic of Korea in New Zealand

Jung Sang-chun
Hong Jin-wook
Monica Kang

And thanks must also go to the team at Seoul Selection for their patience in publishing this book.

Credits

Written by Roger Shepherd & Andrew Douch with David A. Mason
Photographed by Roger Shepherd & Andrew Douch

Publisher Kim Hyung-geun

Editor Lee Jin-hyuk
Assisting Editor Park Hae-reen
Copy Editor Colin A. Mouat
Proofreader Chung Kyung-a

Designer Jung Hyun-young
Assisting Designer Kim Young-ju
Cartographer Lee Bok-hyun